USING

SIMPLY ACCOUNTING® FOR WINDOWS®

Version 8.0

USING

SIMPLY ACCOUNTING® FOR WINDOWS®

Version 8.0

Peter H. Fuhrman

André N. Choquette

Prentice Hall

Toronto

Canadian Cataloguing in Publication Data

Fuhrman, Peter H. (Peter Harry), 1942–
    Using Simply Accounting for Windows, version 8.0

Includes index.
ISBN 0-13-029391-1 (college)   0-13-093072-5 (trade)

1. Simply Accounting for Windows (Computer file). 2. Accounting – Computer programs.
I. Choquette, André, 1968–   . II. Title.

HF5679.F876 2001   657'.0285'5369   C00-933130-1

0-13-029391-1 (college)
0-13-093072-5 (trade)

Vice President, Editorial Director: Michael Young
Senior Acquisitions Editor: Samantha Scully
Marketing Manager: James Buchanan
Associate Editor: Susanne Marshall
Production Editor: Marisa D'Andrea
Copy Editor: Karen Hunter
Production Coordinator: Patricia Ciardullo
Page Layout: Paula Gray/Artplus Ltd.
Cover Design: Anthony Leung
Cover Image: PhotoDisc

1 2 3 4 5   05 04 03 02 01

Printed and bound in Canada.

Bound to stay open

CONTENTS

CHAPTER 1
COMPUTERIZED ACCOUNTING

CHAPTER 2
INSTALLING AND CUSTOMIZING SIMPLY ACCOUNTING FOR WINDOWS

PART II COMPREHENSIVE PRACTICE CASE — OVERNIGHT DELIVERY COMPANY

CHAPTER 3
CREATING DATA FILES AND CUSTOMIZING THE SIMPLY ACCOUNTING SYSTEM

CHAPTER 4
SETTING UP THE GENERAL LEDGER FOR
OVERNIGHT DELIVERY COMPANY

CHAPTER 5
THE GENERAL LEDGER—ENTERING OPENING BALANCES AND JOURNAL ENTRIES

CHAPTER 6
ACCOUNTS RECEIVABLE

CHAPTER 7
ACCOUNTS PAYABLE

CHAPTER 8
INVENTORY

CHAPTER 9
PAYROLL

CHAPTER 10
PROJECT COSTING

CHAPTER 11
REPORTING AND GRAPHING

CHAPTER 12
BANK RECONCILIATION AND MONTH-END ADJUSTMENT ENTRIES

CHAPTER 13
CLOSING THE BOOKS AND OTHER MATTERS

PART III COMPREHENSIVE PRACTICE CASE — NATIONAL SUPPLY COMPANY

CHAPTER 14
COMPREHENSIVE PRACTICE CASE—
NATIONAL SUPPLY COMPANY

PART IV COMPREHENSIVE PRACTICE CASE — CANADIANA DECORATING SALES & SERVICE INC.

CHAPTER 15
COMPREHENSIVE PRACTICE CASE —
CANADIANA SALES & SERVICE INC.

PREFACE

HOW TO USE THIS BOOK

Welcome to *Using Simply Accounting for Windows, Version 8.0*. If you are new to Simply Accounting for Windows, then you should work through this book beginning with Chapter 1. If you are somewhat familiar with the program, then you can start at any chapter depending on what part of Simply Accounting you want to review. You might start by reviewing the new features of Version 8.0 and then work through the corresponding chapter in Part II, Overnight Delivery Company. For this purpose, we have made the book modular by supplying the data files for particular points in the main exercise for Overnight Delivery Company.

At the back of this book is a CD-ROM which contains the data files for Overnight Delivery Company, as mentioned above. Please note that you will require the Simply Accounting for Windows Version 8.0 program to utilize the data sets on this disk.

Keep in mind that when Computer Associates updates tax tables, it adds a letter to the version number of the program. For example, you may have a version 8.0B, which means that the program's tax tables have been updated. Therefore, if payroll or sales taxes have changed for a particular province or if you are using a version with updated tax tables, it may cause some discrepancies between some of the screen shots and printouts in this book and what you might get using the updated version.

As you work through particular chapters, you will notice hints and tips as follows:

 provides you with a time-saving hint with relation to a particular function or operation of Simply Accounting for Windows.

 provides you with informative small business accounting hints that can benefit your particular business.

To get an overview of the Simply Accounting System for Windows, read Chapter 1 first. If the Simply Accounting program is not installed, then you must start with Chapter 2. Beginning with Chapter 3, you work with the Overnight Delivery Company case as you convert its manual accounting system to Simply Accounting for Windows.

Two comprehensive practice cases—the National Supply Company and Canadiana Decorating Sales and Service Inc.—allow you to test yourself on how well you know Simply Accounting.

The **National Supply Company** in Chapter 14 is a practice case that parallels the chapters in Part II. As you complete each chapter in Part II, you can turn to Chapter 14 and work through instructions similar to Overnight Delivery Company, except that no help is provided when setting up the company or when making entries. The National Supply Company exercise can be completed after you have completed each of the chapters for the Overnight Delivery Company, or, if you prefer, work though the entire case after finishing Chapter 13.

The **Canadiana Decorating Sales and Service Inc.** in Chapter 15 provides a realistic business situation. This practice case allows you to take the role of the accounting staff for a small business and work through the setup, day-by-day, and periodic operations of Simply Accounting for Windows. The Canadiana case in Chapter 14 is best completed after you have worked through the two cases: Overnight Delivery Company and National Supply Company. You start with setting up the company and creating the chart of accounts. Then you make entries into the general ledger, which include adjustment entries, transaction entries for purchases and sales, and payroll entries. As you bring in each new ledger, the amount of time spent to make the entries is reduced dramatically. At the same time, information required to make intelligent business decisions increases as the program compiles the entries.

WEB SITES

Two Web sites support this text. They are:

- **www.pearsoned.ca/fuhrmanchoquette8**, the Pearson Education Canada course-specific Web site which supports the text. This site provides a password-protected Instructor's Resource Manual with Solutions and Test Item File for the text, as well as the Journal Entries for Overnight Delivery Company. It also contains backup points for Chapter 14 (National Supply Company) and Chapter 15 (Canadiana Decorating Sales and Service Inc.).
- **www.UsingSimply.com**, the authors' own support site for this book (and past/future releases). From within this Web site you can access the following: book updates, free Simply Accounting Version 8.0 trial software, a discussion board, an additional practice case, live chat with fellow users and the authors, and more.

The following is a short overview of each of this book's chapters, as well as its appendix.

Introduction

This book teaches you the basic operation of the Simply Accounting system for Windows. The following provides a brief outline of each chapter.

Chapter 1

This chapter explains what computerized accounting is, who should computerize, and the features of the Simply Accounting system for Windows as well as the new features added to Version 8.0. You will get a brief overview of the various ledgers that make up the Simply Accounting system. In addition, some idea of the limitations as well as the ease of use of this system are discussed. Finally, you will learn about the hardware required to run the Simply Accounting system for Windows.

Chapter 2

In Chapter 2, you will learn how to install the Simply Accounting system for Windows on your computer. You will also learn how the various keyboard keys are used in the program and how to navigate through the Simply Accounting environment.

Chapter 3

In Chapter 3, you will learn how to create your company data files and how to customize Simply Accounting for your business. You will also get an overview of the various accounting ledgers. Finally, you will learn how to save your data files, exit the program, and create a backup procedure for backing up your data files as you work through this book.

Chapter 4

In Chapter 4, you will learn about the chart of accounts—the types of accounts used in the Simply Accounting program. Then you will enter the accounts from a previous manual accounting system into Simply Accounting for Windows. You will also learn how to modify and delete accounts and display the chart of accounts on the screen or print it out on paper. Finally, you will make journal entries and create and recall some recurring monthly stored entries.

Chapter 5

In Chapter 5, you will enter the opening balances from a trial balance from the previous manual accounting system, and display and print the financial statements. You will then set up the bank reconciliation feature, learn about online banking, and make some journal entries.

Chapter 6

In Chapter 6, you will be introduced to the first subledger—accounts receivable—and shown how a subledger can benefit the accounting function. In converting from a manual accounts receivable system to a computerized one, you have to prepare a customer list, gather the outstanding receivable balances for the various customers, and prepare the system to record the GST. Then you will add the customers to the accounts receivable module, enter the opening balances, and display and print a variety of reports. You will then be ready to enter some accounts receivable entries, including credit card sales and recurring sales entries. You will also learn how to adjust an invoice, enter customer payments, handle GST and HST, and enter and handle sales quotes. Thereafter you will print out an audit trail as the final exercise in this chapter.

Chapter 7

In Chapter 7, you will learn about the accounts payable ledger, and how to convert from a manual accounts payable system to the computerized Simply Accounting system for Windows. You will enter vendor accounts and the historical balances for each vendor. You will also learn how to delete vendor accounts, as well as how to modify vendor information. You will then display various reports on the monitor screen, and enter a number of transactions to record invoices and payments.

Chapter 8

In Chapter 8, you will first get an overview of the nature of inventory: types of inventory, how to handle purchase adjustments, how to record sales and adjustments for returns, the various inventory methods, and the various methods of costing inventory. Then you will go through the steps of converting a manual inventory system to the Simply Accounting for Windows system. You will examine the various ways of displaying data entered and how to print various inventory reports. After changing the inventory ledger to the READY mode, you will enter some current transactions: purchases, sales of goods, and transfers of inventory. Printing of invoices, generating an audit trail, and exporting the files complete the chapter.

Chapter 9

In Chapter 9, you will get an overview of the complexities of payroll accounting and how to calculate the various employee deductions. Then you will convert the manual payroll system to the Simply Accounting system. You will enter information for some employees into the ledger and then enter payroll data to prepare their pay. In the last part of the chapter, you will learn how to correct payroll information that was inadvertently entered incorrectly.

Chapter 10

In Chapter 10, you will acquire a basic understanding of the purpose of the project ledger of the Simply Accounting system for Windows. You will learn how to organize this module, add and delete cost centres, and modify information about a cost centre. Then you will make entries into project accounts through the various subledgers. Finally, you will display and print the various reports available, as well as export a file for manipulation in a spreadsheet.

Chapter 11

In Chapter 11, you will use the graphing features of Simply Accounting first introduced in Version 4.0 and expanded in Version 5.0. You will prepare a variety of graphs and enhance them with titles and legends. You will also become more familiar with the various reports available from within Simply Accounting, and learn about printing out forms and using the custom report option.

Chapter 12

In Chapter 12, you will prepare a bank reconciliation using Simply Accounting's bank reconciliation feature. After completing it, you will make some month-end adjusting entries.

Chapter 13

In Chapter 13, you will look at the accounting cycle and examine the procedures that you must follow at different times of the year. You will also prepare the various reports for GST, PST, and other withholding taxes, and prepare adjusting entries to the appropriate accounts. Finally, you will print out the financial statements. In addition, you will learn about keeping backups, the storage limits of the Simply Accounting system for Windows and why it is necessary to purge data, auditing considerations, and the setting of passwords.

Chapter 14

In Chapter 14, you are given the instructions for a practice case called National Supply Company. Each section in Chapter 14 corresponds to one of the Overnight Delivery Company Chapters 3 to 13. After completing each chapter from Chapter 3 on, you can apply the knowledge gained to a brand new situation. You can complete each section in this chapter as you work through the Overnight Delivery Company chapters, or leave the exercise for later.

Chapter 15

In Chapter 15, you are introduced to the second practice case, Canadiana Decorating Sales and Service Inc. You will not get any tutorial information for this practice exercise, but only general instructions as to what you must do. It is comprehensive with a variety of entries for each of the modules covered in the previous chapters. Upon finishing this practice set, you should have a good understanding of how Simply Accounting can be used in a business.

Appendix A

This appendix briefly lists the contents of the CD-ROM and provides a short description of the installation process for the backup points.

DEDICATION

This book is dedicated to Pierre Joseph Choquette. He was my father, my mentor, and my friend; he will be missed, but not forgotten. Not only was I proud to say he was my father, but also my teacher, who taught me that even when you are an adult, your father can still provide valuable wisdom and lessons in life. I hope to honour him by offering the same guidance and wisdom to his granddaughter. Dad, we all miss you.

– André N. Choquette

ACKNOWLEDGEMENTS

We are indebted to many individuals who have been actively involved in the preparation of this text. Much appreciation goes to the reviewers of this book who provided valuable insight: Alice Beddoe, Fanshawe College; Robert Dearden, Red River Community College; Liz Evans, Nova Scotia Community College; and Larry Gillis, Concordia University/Dawson College.

We would also like to thank Pearson Education Canada; in particular, thanks to Samantha Scully, Susanne Marshall, Marisa D'Andrea, Karen Hunter, and Patricia Ciardullo for their help in getting this project off the ground and through the various publishing stages.

Particular thanks go to Mary Watson from ACCPAC International Inc., who provided us with the latest information and latest versions of Simply Accounting for Windows, and helped us in numerous other ways.

Last, but not least, we must again thank our families for their patience, understanding, encouragement, and support while we were preparing the manuscript.

Peter H. Fuhrman
André N. Choquette

ABOUT THE AUTHORS

Peter H. Fuhrman has an M.B.A. degree from the University of Alberta. He is the author of *Business in the Canadian Environment*, now in its seventh edition. He is also the co-author of *Microcomputers for Management Decision Making, Using Simply Accounting for DOS, Using Simply Accounting for Windows, Using ACCPAC Plus 6.1 for DOS*, and *Using ACCPAC for Windows*, some published in Canadian and U.S. versions. He taught in the faculty of business at Fraser Valley College (now known as the University College of the Fraser Valley) in British Columbia for 15 years, and has also been a faculty member of the Open Learning Agency in British Columbia since 1979, engaged in teaching and developing course materials and televisions programs for both the college and university divisions. He also consults with private clients.

André N. Choquette is the principal partner of Choquette & Company Accounting Group, an accounting firm in British Columbia that consults and assists in the development of private businesses and personal financial planning. His speciality is taxation. He is the co-author of *Using ACCPAC Plus 6.1 for DOS, ACCPAC for Windows*, and *Simply Accounting for Windows* in various versions. In addition to his accounting practice, he also teaches computerized accounting courses in British Columbia.

Part I

THE SIMPLY ACCOUNTING SYSTEM

In Part I you will be introduced to the Simply Accounting system. In Chapter 1, you will get a general idea of how Simply Accounting operates, the ledgers available, the computer hardware requirements needed to run the program, and the features of the program. In Chapter 2 you will learn how to install the Simply Accounting for Windows program.

CHAPTER 1

COMPUTERIZED ACCOUNTING

CHAPTER 1

COMPUTERIZED ACCOUNTING

OBJECTIVES

After reading this chapter you will be able to

1. Understand the basic features of the Simply Accounting for Windows system and the various modules that make up the total system.
2. Understand the computer hardware required to run the Simply Accounting for Windows system.
3. Understand the general program features of the Simply Accounting for Windows system and the new features of Version 8.0.

TO COMPUTERIZE OR NOT TO COMPUTERIZE

There was a time when the question of computerizing could be debated because computer equipment was expensive to purchase and accounting packages were difficult to use. Today these are no longer valid considerations even for very small businesses. With easy-to-use computer accounting packages such as Simply Accounting for Windows, a time-consuming, sometimes boring chore is made more efficient and interesting. Above all, information for management decision making can be kept current.

THE SIMPLY ACCOUNTING FOR WINDOWS SYSTEM

Every new version of Simply Accounting for Windows caters more to the small and home-based business. The Business Assistant is designed to keep you organized by providing To-Do lists and checklists that help you stay on track in meeting your business and personal goals. Business Advice provides tips on various aspects of running a business, and the new Business Guide steps you through the process of starting a new business in your province. In addition to the Business Assistant, Version 8.0 of Simply Accounting for Windows has many new features that make it easier to use the accounting program in your business.

Simply Accounting for Windows is a full-featured, integrated accounting package which includes General Ledger, Accounts Receivable, Accounts Payable, Inventory, Payroll, and Job Costing. An integrated accounting system means that you have to enter particular business transaction data only once. For example, if you record a sale through Accounts Receivable, the Inventory will be adjusted automatically to reflect the sale, and both accounts in the General Ledger will also be updated to reflect the sale. Even though the Simply Accounting for Windows package is integrated, you can also use each of the modules independently.

GENERAL LEDGER

As in any accounting system, the General Ledger module is the focal point of the system. All financial reporting statements, as well as the detail of the ledger accounts, originate from this module. A balance sheet and/or an income statement can be printed as soon as the last entry has been recorded into the General Ledger.

ACCOUNTS RECEIVABLE

The Accounts Receivable module is designed to produce invoices for sales of merchandise or on billing of services. These invoices are then tracked by customer and date. An aged trial balance of each amount owing can be produced. Monthly statements can be produced for each customer, helping to improve cash flow.

ACCOUNTS PAYABLE

The Accounts Payable module is similar to the Accounts Receivable module. Good control over accounts payable is important to ensure that all bills are paid on time, maintaining a good credit rating and avoiding service charges by suppliers. Good control also allows the user to take advantage of discounts offered by suppliers. The Accounts Payable module also provides cash flow reports to help determine the cash needs of the business in the near future.

PAYROLL

The Payroll function is probably one of the most time-consuming accounting functions. Simply Accounting for Windows significantly reduces the time required to process payroll. It will handle many different kinds of pay structures and calculate tax payable based on built-in tax tables. This feature eliminates the need for the user to input the relevant tax tables.

INVENTORY

The Inventory module is used to track inventory and maintain adequate inventory levels, as well as transfer the cost of goods sold to expense accounts. The revenue generated by sales is entered through the Accounts Receivable module, which automatically transfers the appropriate amount to cost of sales and reduces inventory accordingly. Existing inventory levels are always available and are as current as the last entry.

PROJECT COSTING

The Project module allows a company to track revenues and expenses by project or department. Many companies want to know the specific costs associated with a particular job or department. For example, a contractor may be building three houses at the same time. The contractor would be interested in knowing the costs of building as well as the profit made from each house. The Project module will allow him or her to assign an invoice or payment to each job, or even part of an invoice or payment to a job. A report can then be produced comparing the income and expenses for that particular project.

SYSTEM REQUIREMENTS

Simply Accounting for Windows requires a Pentium PC, 32 MB of RAM, 60-100 MB of disk space, although a Pentium II, 233mhz or higher, 64 MB of RAM and 100 MB of hard disk is recommended for better performance. It also requires a minimum 256 colour VGA monitor. Windows 95 or higher must be used as the operating system. You should also use one of the office suites, Microsoft Office or Word Perfect Office, as well as a MAPI compliant e-mail program, such as Outlook or Outlook Express, so that the extra features built into Simply Accounting for Windows can be used.

You will need a printer to print out the various reports and maintain a hardcopy audit trail. Any narrow carriage printer supported by Windows is acceptable. A wide carriage printer is ideal for accounting purposes as you can print reports in regular 10 or 12 character pitch, making them easier to read.

Simply Accounting for Windows is designed for use with a mouse although, some accounting operations are easier to perform with the keyboard.

PROGRAM CAPACITY

The Simply Accounting for Windows program is fast and easy to use. It is unlikely that a small business would ever exceed its capacity for ledger accounts, number of vendors, number of employees and so on. The Simply Accounting for Windows system has all the attributes of a larger and more expensive package at a significantly lower price, and will be more than adequate for a small business's accounting needs.

GENERAL FEATURES OF SIMPLY ACCOUNTING FOR WINDOWS

If you have ever purchased a computer software package, you know that sooner or later it will be upgraded adding new features to meet new user requirements. While some software upgrades only include minor changes usually to correct problems, Simply Accounting Version 8.0 contains important features that improve the previous versions of the program. The following discusses some of the major program features of Simply Accounting for Windows, followed by a discussion of the new features of Version 8.0.

HOME-BASED COMPANY TO BIG-BIZ INC.

If you started your business operating out of your home with yourself as the manager/employee, you may be ready to add new employees. Simply Accounting can handle this expansion easily. For example, you wouldn't need payroll if you were the only person in the business, but as you hire new employees you can begin using the Payroll module.

UNLIMITED PROGRAM CAPABILITIES

Simply Accounting for Windows Version 8.0 allows you to run a company of virtually any size. You can maintain up to 5,000 general ledger accounts and up to 32,000 entries for each of the five ledgers (General Ledger, Accounts Payable, Accounts Receivable, Payroll, and Project). For each of these entries and for report totals, the maximum numerical value is $999,999,999.99, in other words, a billion dollars.

Keep in mind that if your business grows past a certain point in terms of employees or sales you will need to use a more sophisticated accounting package such as ACCPAC for Windows. However, for the typical small business, Simply Accounting Version 8.0 is more than adequate.

CASH OR ACCRUAL ACCOUNTING

Simply Accounting allows you to choose between either cash or accrual-based accounting. Accrual-based accounting is the most common method. It recognizes revenue and expenses as they are incurred (i.e., when you receive the phone bill it becomes an expense). On the other hand, the cash-based method recognizes revenue and expenses only after the cash has been disbursed or received. In the example of the phone bill, it would not be recognized as an expense until it is actually paid. Whichever format you choose, it is important that you consider the advantages and disadvantages of each method.

MULTI-CURRENCY

Simply Accounting for Windows Version 8.0 now supports multi-currency accounting. This will allow your business to transact operations in both Canadian and foreign currency. The most common configuration would be a company that operates in both Canadian and American currencies. With Simply Accounting for Windows Version 8.0, you will be able to operate both currencies within the same data configuration, with functions to value and convert your U.S. dollars to Canadian equivalents.

CONFIGURATION WITH ON-LINE BANKING

Simply Accounting for Windows Version 8.0 allows you access the Internet in order to perform various tasks, such as downloading your bank statements from your bank. This will make it easier and faster to complete your bank reconciliation.

ELECTRONIC MAIL FOR YOUR VENDORS AND CUSTOMERS

Simply Accounting Version 8.0 provides you with the option of sending purchase orders and invoices to your vendors and customers via e-mail. This will speed up processing time and if your customer is also using Simply Accounting for Windows, they will be able to import the invoice into their payables and avoid having to manually re-enter the information.

BUDGET REVENUE AND EXPENSES

In today's competitive business environment, it is important to budget and plan for your business's future success. A feature of Simply Accounting allows you to enter budget figures for revenue and expense accounts and to show these figures in income statement reports that display actual to budget performance.

AUTOMATIC OR MANUAL PAYROLL DEDUCTIONS

If you have ever performed a manual payroll, you will know how time-consuming and frustrating searching through Revenue Canada payroll tax tables can be. These tables are included in the Payroll module which allows you to let the computer make payroll calculations automatically. Even so, Simply Accounting for Windows allows you to easily override these automatic payroll calculations with manual entries.

ONE PAYMENT FOR MANY INVOICES

This feature allows you to select the applicable invoices that you wish to pay and the amount of payment for each and then prepare one cheque for payment. This feature is also available within the Accounts Receivable module and allows you to spread one payment over several individual accounts receivable invoices.

FLEXIBLE AGING PERIODS

In both the Accounts Payable and the Accounts Receivable module you can select the aging period that you wish to use for reporting purposes. This is very important for cash flow analysis. You can easily determine your cash inflow from your Accounts Receivable by time period and match this inflow with your expected outflow from Accounts Payable. Of course, it also makes it easy to keep track of how your customers are paying their bills and what invoices are overdue. Similarly, the Accounts Payable aging allows you to effectively disburse your payments, using your available payment terms and taking advantage of discounts whenever possible.

FLEXIBLE INVENTORY REPORTING OPTIONS

Simply Accounting allows you flexibility in reporting inventory items on the gross margin and/or markup basis. Furthermore, you can select the sorting order by either item number or item description.

CLEAR PAID INVOICES FOR SOME OR ALL OF YOUR CUSTOMERS AND/OR VENDORS

Keeping a detailed payment history may have it's benefits, however, too much of this information can also hinder the performance and speed of printing your receivable and payable reports. You have the option to clear all paid invoices, selected by date or selected by customers/vendors.

IMPORT GENERAL JOURNAL ENTRIES

Simply Accounting for Windows allows you to import general journal entries from a software package such as Lotus 1-2-3 or Excel.

EXPORT ANY REPORT TO ALMOST ANYWHERE

To make reporting as flexible as possible, Simply Accounting for Windows allows you to export any report that you can print within Simply Accounting for Windows. The format that you can export ranges from a text file to a formatted Lotus 1-2-3 or Excel file. You can then use the report date within third-party packages for graphical reporting and/or analysis.

FLEXIBLE INVOICE, CHEQUE, AND STATEMENTS PRINTING

You can use preprinted forms such as invoices and cheques with Simply Accounting, choose the font type and size, and print them on any laser, dot-matrix or ink-jet printer.

USE SIMPLY ACCOUNTING ON A NETWORK

Even though only one user can access Simply Accounting for Windows at any given time, the program can be installed on a network to allow accessibility by all computer work stations.

CASH PURCHASES AND SALES IN ONE EASY TRANSACTION

Simply Accounting for Windows allows you to easily enter cash purchases or make cash payments by choosing this feature under the respective Receivables or Payables module.

PROJECT/JOB COSTING

The Project or Job Costing module allows you to track the revenue and expenses for individual projects without compromising the structure of your accounting records.

For example, consider a real estate developer who is building three separate homes to sell. By using the Project module, the developer will be able to track the revenue and expenses for each of the three homes as well as the profit and loss for all three homes together. The developer may find that he has made sufficient profit on two of the three homes but has lost substantial profits on the third house due to the costs incurred. Using this detailed form of tracking revenue and expenses, the developer will realize that should he build the same style of home again, he will either have to reduce his costs or increase his selling price (revenue) to ensure profitability.

Project or job costing accounting can be used for any type of business, from a hair salon which wants to track the revenue and expenses by each stylist's chair, to a retail outlet wanting to track profitability by designer, to a manufacturer wanting to track revenue and expenses by location. This powerful feature is covered in detail in Chapter 11.

EXCHANGE INFORMATION WITH OTHER WINDOWS PROGRAMS VIA DDE

When most of us hear of "DDE" within the Windows environment, we cringe in fear of a highly technical function. However, DDE (Dynamic Data Exchange) for Simply Accounting for Windows is very easy to use, from creating a form letter for customers within Word Perfect to designing a spreadsheet within Lotus 1-2-3 or Excel. Contained on your Simply Accounting for Windows CD-ROM are several Microsoft Office Ready documents that allow you to exchange information from Simply Accounting for Windows and the Microsoft Office Suite.

GST/HST (GOODS AND SERVICES TAX/HARMONIZED SALES TAX) MADE EASY

To make tracking GST/HST as easy as possible, Simply Accounting for Windows allows you to enter the tax on screens that resemble either customer invoices or vendor purchases. When you print the GST/HST report, it provides you with all of the detail that is required to complete your GST/HST return.

CALCULATE AND TRACK THE QST (QUEBEC SALES TAX)

Simply Accounting for Windows allows easy tracking of QST for reporting purposes.

BANK RECONCILIATION

No longer will you have to complete your bank reconciliation by hand. Simply Accounting for Windows Version 8.0 has integrated a complete bank reconciliation feature. You can easily clear your cashed cheques and deposits from the listing, and enter adjustments such as bank service charges and bank interest.

CUSTOMIZABLE REPORTS

Even with the wide range of internal reports, from financial statements (balance sheet and income statements) to Payroll, Receivables, and Payables reporting, you have the ultimate flexibility to create or modify custom reports through the powerful CA-RET (pronounced carrot) report writer.

FLEXIBLE PAYROLL INCOME/DEDUCTION MAINTENANCE

To take care of differences in your company's income sources and employee deductions, Simply Accounting for Windows allows you to define up to two extra income types (seven in total) as well as five user-defined deduction fields (nine in total).

GENERATING T4S — ONE EASY STEP

Simply Accounting for Windows allows you to print your employee T4 slips at the end of the calendar year in one easy step, (select employees and print). This function ensures that your T4s contain accurate information.

CUSTOMERS AND CREDIT LIMITS

Managing receivables is often critical, especially in a small business. Simply Accounting for Windows takes care of this task by informing you, when you enter a customer invoice, if your customer is over their established credit limit.

COMPLETE DATA PROTECTION

Simply Accounting for Windows allows you to quickly check that your data have not been corrupted due to computer failure and that your books are balanced.

PASSWORD PROTECTION — UP TO FOUR LEVELS

To ensure that only authorized people can access your accounting data, you can set up four levels of security through passwords.

ACCOUNTING TIPS

Simply Accounting for Windows has included accounting tips throughout the program to assist you in the operation of the accounting package. However, should you not wish to view these hints and tips, you can disable this option.

ACCOUNTING ADVICE

By clicking on the Advice icon, you can receive advice with regard to your business decisions and plans. Examples would be advice on handling overdue accounts in Accounts Receivable or about managing cash flow.

STORE MORE THAN ONE YEAR'S DATA

Simply Accounting for Windows 8.0 allows you to store two full years of accounting information—the current year and the previous year. This allows you to compare the current year's financial statement to the previous year's. You can also post year-end adjusting entries to the previous year, and you can print the previous year's T4 slips for your employees without having to maintain two sets of company data.

MAINTAIN TWO YEARS OF PAYROLL DATA

Simply Accounting for Windows allows you to keep a two full years of payroll data, allowing you to use this information for your payroll reporting requirements.

GRAPHING CAPABILITIES

In addition to viewing financial information in a standard report, Version 8.0 allows you to display and print this information using several graphs. This visual tool is available for such reports as:

Payables by Aging Period

Receivables by Aging Period

Expense and Net Profit as Percentage of Revenue

Sales versus Receivables

Sales versus Budget

Expense versus Budget

Current Revenue versus Last Year's Revenue

Four pie charts showing breakdown of total revenue, breakdown of total expenses, payables by vendor, and receivables by customer. A bar graph showing current receivables versus current payables.

COMPARATIVE REPORTING

Simply Accounting for Windows 8.0 provides comparative reporting for both the balance sheet and the income statement. This reporting feature allows you to compare periods within the current year as well as periods in the previous year.

INVENTORY TURNOVER TRACKING

You can keep a record of details related to the turnover of your inventory. This allows you to determine which inventory items are selling and which are not, and enables you to determine profit margins based on inventory turnovers.

LOOK UP POSTED INVOICES

You can look up invoice information and even reprint posted invoices in the event one of your customers requests a second copy or a replacement for a lost invoice.

STORE AND RECALL RECURRING ENTRIES

If you have charges that must be re-entered periodically—rent payments, customer monthly fees, insurance payments—you can input this information as a recurring entry, saving you considerable time and work.

CALCULATE GST/HST AND PST ON PURCHASES AUTOMATICALLY

With Simply Accounting for Windows, GST/HST and PST is automatically calculated on purchases. You have the ability to accept the calculated default amount or enter a different amount.

INFORMATIVE STATUS BAR

Simply Accounting for Windows includes a status bar—a line of text at the bottom of most Simply Accounting Windows. This status bar displays important information concerning the functions or options that are available.

PREPARE, STORE AND PRINT PURCHASE ORDERS

When you generate a purchase order, Simply Accounting automatically updates the quantity on order. If only a partial shipment is received, the program keeps track of the items and quantities back-ordered. You can also print out a purchase order, which can be customized using CA-RET forms.

NEGATIVE INVENTORY

If you record a sale before you have purchased the inventory, Simply Accounting will allow your inventory levels to dip below zero, if you choose this option.

AUTOMATIC ADJUSTMENT OF JOURNAL ENTRIES

To correct an invoice, select the incorrect one and enter the correct information. The program calculates any differences and makes all the reversing and adjusting entries for you. Even if you have cleared an entry you can still reverse it manually.

EASY BACKUPS

Simply Accounting has a Backup and Restore command that makes it simple to perform these operations from within the program. It even reminds you when it is time to backup your data based on the chosen time period.

DISCOUNTS AND PAYMENT TERMS

Simply Accounting lets you enter payment terms for each vendor and customer. This includes the percentage discount allowed for a specified number of days, as well as the number of days before full payment is due. It also reminds you when discounts are about to expire and when invoices are coming due. When you update your previous version of the program, the terms are blank. You can enter the terms for each vendor or customer or enter the same terms for all customers.

DRILL DOWN FROM REPORTS TO SEE DETAILS AND RELATED INFORMATION

When you double-click on a part of a financial statement or report, the program displays details or related information.

TO-DO LISTS

Simply Accounting reminds you when outstanding invoices or recurring entries are coming due. This includes sales and payments so that you avoid interest charges or take advantage of discounts. You will also be reminded when customer accounts become overdue and the remaining balance amount.

CALCULATE TAXES IN THE PURCHASES JOURNAL

Simply Accounting calculates the GST and PST for each item on a purchase invoice, using the tax rates specified.

CASCADING REPORTS MENUS

To shorten the Reports menu and make it easier to find the report you need, many commands have been moved to cascading submenus.

WIZARDS HELP YOU WITH COMPLEX TASKS

A wizard is a program helper that outlines a series of steps that you must take when attempting a complicated procedure. A wizard appears automatically when you chose New from the setup menu, when you start Simply Accounting with a new data file, or when you chose the Setup Wizard from the Setup menu. Similarly, a Restore Wizard helps you restore data backups quickly and easily when you chose Restore from the File menu.

NEW FEATURES OF SIMPLY ACCOUNTING FOR WINDOWS VERSION 8.0

Some of the new features of Simply Accounting for Windows Version 8.0 are designed for easier setup of your particular business.

EASIER SETUP

The business guide helps you set up a company quickly by listing the tasks that must be completed. It describes each task, such as obtaining licenses or registering business names, in simple language and tells you where to find more information.

LINKING TO OTHER PROGRAMS

You can now share your Simply Accounting data with the Microsoft Office Suite simply by using the enclosed office forms. If you can't find a report that satisfies your needs within Simply Accounting, you can export the required information to the Microsoft Office suite.

You can also download bank statements from your financial institution and import the data into Simply Accounting. This speeds up reconciliation and reduces the possibility of errors.

EASIER SETUP OF ACCOUNTS

It is now easier to move accounts to different parts of your account list by using the drag and drop capability. By using Tab and Shift Tab you can demote or promote an account or account group.

REMOVAL OF "SET READY"

You can now enter transactions more quickly than in previous versions, as historical transactions no longer have to be entered before the General Ledger can be set to Ready. You can enter historical transactions during the entire first fiscal year.

NEW E-MAIL FEATURES

You, your vendors or your customers can now communicate by e-mail and send and import invoices, sales quotas, and purchase orders with e-mail programs. This can save considerable time and reduce errors because information does not have to be entered twice.

Simply Accounting can also automatically send confirmation of receipt of an invoice or purchase order.

MORE FLEXIBILITY

You can now process transactions with dates anywhere in the current fiscal year including dates in the future. You are no longer tied to the session date.

You can use two linked bank accounts for each of the purchases and sales transactions, and store a ship-to address for customers.

The following are enhancements on a ledger-by-ledger basis have been added to Version 8.

GENERAL LEDGER ENHANCEMENT

Multi-currency accounting allows you to maintain more than one currency within the data files

Open Financial Exchange (OFX) support for downloading bank and credit card statements and automatic reconciliation

Account reconciliation for liability and equity accounts

Filters transactions in account reconciliation by date

Improved account reconciliation reports

Use any date in the current year for transaction entry. "Session Date" restriction removed

Enter transactions concurrently with history. "Set Ready" restriction removed

New Type view eases the process of creating and maintaining the list of accounts

Easier entry of budget amounts

Displays transaction entry number as transactions are entered

New Excel "side-by-side" balance sheet

New Excel "side-by-side" income statement

PURCHASES AND PAYMENTS ENHANCEMENTS

Imports invoices and quotes e-mailed from vendors

E-mails acknowledgment of receipt of purchase invoices and purchase quotes

Handles credit card purchases

Two linked bank accounts

E-mail a vendor directly from the vendor's record

Retains display of vendor when preparing two or more invoices

Stores vendor's tax ID number

"Purchase on account" and "Purchase with payment" combined into "Invoice." "Pay Later" added as a payment option

SALES AND RECEIPTS ENHANCEMENTS

Imports orders e-mailed from customers

Two linked bank accounts

E-mail a customer directly from the customer's record

Retains display of customer when preparing two or more invoices

Stores a ship-to address for customers

"Sale on account" and "Sale with payment" combined into "Invoice"

Displays subtotals before taxes on customizable invoices

PROJECT COSTING ENHANCEMENTS

Set up project budgets

Allocate any account to a project

New project budget report

New project allocation report

PAYROLL ENHANCEMENTS

Three additional income fields (plus a second overtime rate) and five additional deduction fields

Payroll cheque runs

Set default payroll deductions as percentages

Flags whether payroll income categories are taxable or not

Default hours added to employee record

Default benefits added to employee record

Separate Wages-Expense-linked account provided for each income field

Active/Inactive employee status flag

Automatically checks validity of employee SIN (Social Insurance Number)

Excel two-week employee worksheet

NEW SYSTEM-WIDE FEATURES

Checklists added to the Business Assistant

New Business Guide informs you on how to set up a company in your province

Home window, icon window, and forms entry screens customizable with new textured bitmaps. (Requires Windows Display Properties set to "High Colour-16 bit" or greater)

Multi-key search capability in all selection boxes

Optional prenumbered forms

"Printed on" date on reports

Exports reports in Excel 97 format

Copies data from a network to a local drive during a session and copies it back when finished

Restores a backup from the Select Company window

Uses common Windows dialogs in the Conversion utility

Toolbar button brings the Home window to the front

Automatically deletes old details at year-end if needed

Permits on-line registration during installation

Links to the Simply Accounting Certified Consultants web page

Refreshes Excel spreadsheet data when a file is opened

Includes Mailmerge macros for Word documents. (Requires Office 97)

Simply Accounting for Windows is now an ideal package for business people with no previous experience in accounting. It is an easy program with which to create financial statements. The graphs and reports allow you to easily see how you are performing compared to the budgeted amounts.

In this book we assume that the fictional company has been using a manual accounting system and is now changing over to a computerized accounting system using Simply Accounting Version 8.0.

CHAPTER 2

INSTALLING AND CUSTOMIZING SIMPLY ACCOUNTING FOR WINDOWS

CHAPTER 2

INSTALLING AND CUSTOMIZING SIMPLY ACCOUNTING FOR WINDOWS

OBJECTIVES

After working through this chapter you will be able to

1. Install the Simply Accounting for Windows program onto your hard disk using both the Express and Custom methods.

2. Know when it is best to convert from a manual to a computerized accounting system.

In this chapter you will learn how to install Simply Accounting for Windows Version 8.0 on your computer. If the program has already been installed on your computer but you would like to know how to complete this procedure, use a different directory from the default directory indicated in this book to avoid copying over your previous installation. You can remove these directories again later.

HOW COMMANDS ARE INDICATED

You will be guided through the procedures for each module in the Simply Accounting system with the following graphic symbols. They indicate what you should do.

⬆️, ⬇️, ➡️ and ⬅️	indicate that you should use the arrow keys to scroll through various directory boxes or scroll through reports and various lists
Tab	to get to the next field
Enter	to complete a command
Backspace	to delete a character to the left of the cursor using the backspace key
D X	these are examples of letters that you have to press to activate various menu commands in Windows and Simply Accounting
space bar	sometimes you have to press the space bar to open a field
Alt + F4	represents a combination command that closes menus

We will use the mouse in most instances. However, Simply Accounting for Windows allows you to use certain keys on your keyboard to perform particular operations. In some instances, pressing the Tab key, for example, is much quicker than taking your hand off the keyboard and using your mouse. In those instances we will show those keystrokes.

Important note: Using the right and left mouse buttons

With Windows 95/98 you have the ability to use the **left** or **right** mouse button to activate various commands. If we indicate that you should click your mouse we mean that you should use the usual left mouse button. We will specifically indicate when you should use the right mouse button.

HINTS AND TIPS

As you work through particular chapters, you will notice hints and tips as to program operation or accounting procedures. These are identified with the following symbols.

 Program Hint

provides you with a time-saving hint related to a particular function or operation of Simply Accounting for Windows

 Accounting Hint

provides you with informative small business accounting hints that can benefit your particular business

STARTING AND USING MICROSOFT WINDOWS

The Microsoft Windows 95/98 operating system starts automatically when you turn on your computer. Once booted up, it leaves you at the so-called desktop. From there, you can start the various programs.

Throughout this book we will assume that you know how to start Windows.

INSTALLING SIMPLY ACCOUNTING FOR WINDOWS VERSION 8.0

When you purchase Simply Accounting for Windows you will get several manuals along with the program CD-ROM.

There are several ways to install a new program in Windows 95/98. Insert the CD-ROM into your CD-ROM drive. This action usually starts the installation process. If your system does not recognize the CD in the CD-ROM drive then use the following procedure:

Start from the Windows desktop.

Click on the **Start** icon on the task bar.

Select the **Run...** command from the **Start** menu.

You may have to type in the name and path as shown.

If you are installing using a CD-ROM:

X:\Launch.exe

where **X** represents your CD-ROM drive.

Figure 2.1
Run window
(with entry)

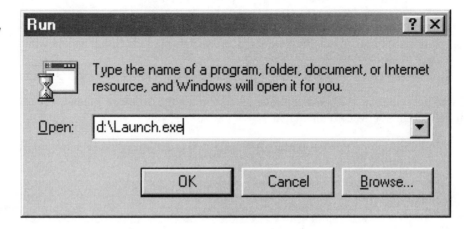

Your Run window should now resemble Figure 2.1. D: refers to the CD-ROM drive from where the program is to be installed. You may have to change this depending on the drive letter your CD-ROM represents. Continue by

Clicking on the **OK** button.

Simply Accounting will now continue to load the installation program.

During the installation loading process, the Simply Accounting for Windows installation program will create a Setup Wizard to guide you through the installation process.

Figure 2.2
Welcome
window

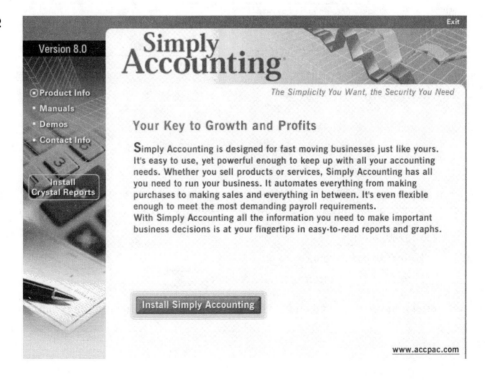

Once the Setup Wizard has been created, Simply Accounting for Windows will display the opening Welcome window (Figure 2.2). From within this window you can continue with the installation of Simply Accounting for Windows, view product information and on-line manuals, receive contact information, and install Crystal Reports for Windows, a powerful reporting module that we will discuss later. Continue by

Clicking on the **Install Simply Accounting** button.

The installation program will take several moments preparing for the installation. After a couple of moments, Simply Accounting for Windows will display the Install Shield window. Continue by

Clicking on the **N**ext button. Alternately, you can also press (Alt) + (D).

Simply Accounting will now continue by displaying the Software License Agreement. Once you have read this screen, continue by

Clicking on the **Y**es button. Alternately, you can press either **Y** or (Enter) because the **Y**es button is highlighted.

Figure 2.3
User
Information
window

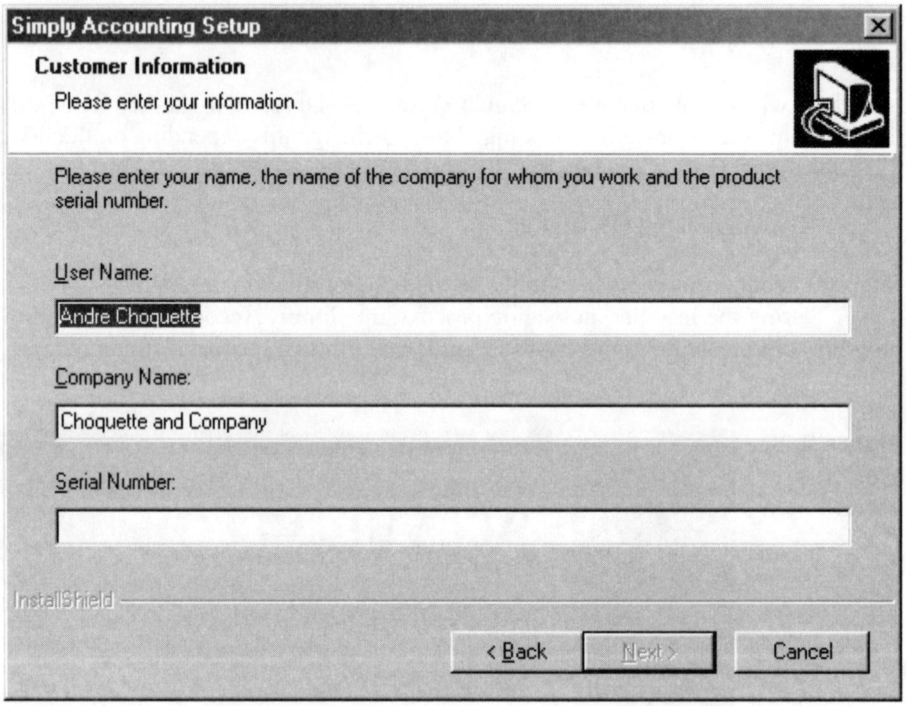

The Simply Accounting for Windows setup program now asks you to provide the User information for your copy of Simply Accounting for Windows (Figure 2.3). Continue by entering

Your Name (Tab)
Your Company Name (Tab)
Your Simply Accounting Serial Number (Tab)

Your serial number is located on the bottom of the Simply Accounting Software box.

Once you have entered the previous information, a registration confirmation window appears. You can now check the information you entered. If you want to make corrections, click on the **No** button. If everything is correct, continue by

Clicking on the **Yes** button. Alternately, you can press either **Y** or Enter.

Figure 2.4
Choose
Destination
Location
window

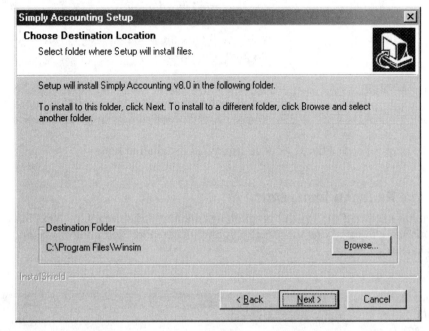

Simply Accounting will now display the Choose Destination window, (Figure 2.4). The default location is **C:\Program Files\Winsim** and we recommend you use the suggested path. Continue by

Clicking on the **Next** button. Alternately, you can press either N or Enter. (If you wish to return to the previous window, you can also select the **Back** button.)

If the program destination directory does not already exist on your hard drive, Simply Accounting for Windows will prompt you to confirm the creation of this directory. Continue by

Clicking on the **Yes** button. Alternately, you can press **Y** or Enter.

Figure 2.5
Setup Type
window

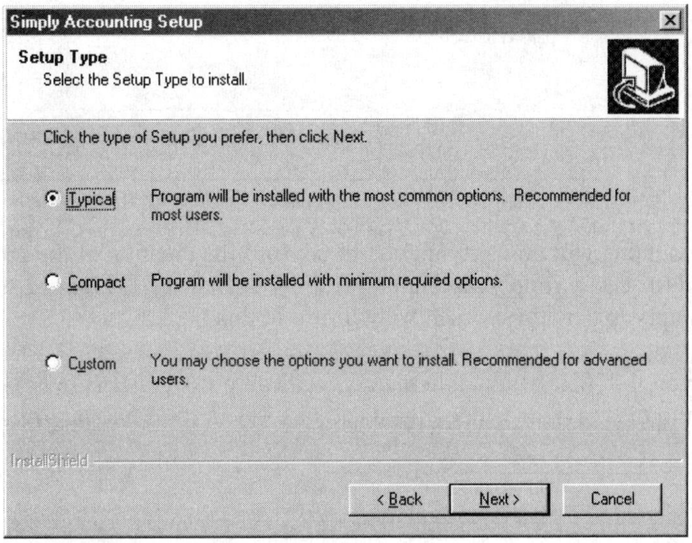

Simply Accounting for Windows will now prompt you to select the type of installation (Figure 2.5). The available options include:

Typical   will install Simply Accounting for Window program files, report files, sample files, and company template files. *This is the suggested installation*

Compact   will install only the essential Simply Accounting for Windows program and report files

Custom   will allow you the option of installing the specific program, report, and template files. *This option is suggested only for persons experienced with software installation*

For the purpose of this book, we will display all installation types.

TYPICAL PROGRAM INSTALLATION

If you have selected the **Typical** program installation (and selected the **Next** button), Simply Accounting will install the suggested program files, report files, company template files, and sample files.

Figure 2.6
Select
Program
Folder
window

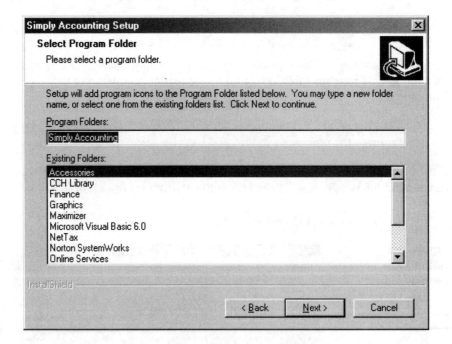

Simply Accounting will now prompt you to confirm the creation of the program folder which will be used to access Simply Accounting from your Start List (Figure 2.6). The default program folder is Simply Accounting, which we will use in this book. Continue by

Clicking on the **Next** button. Alternately, you can press either **N** or Enter. (If you should wish to return to the previous window, you can also select the **Back** button.)

Figure 2.7
Start Copying
Files (Typical)
window

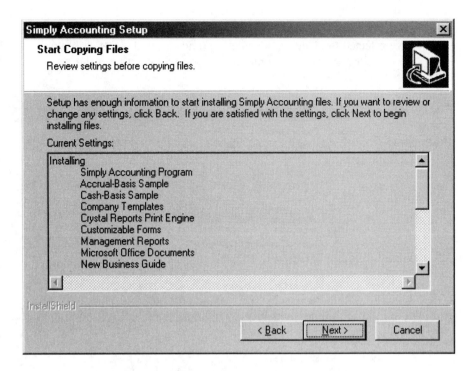

Simply Accounting for Windows will then ask you to confirm the typical installation options (Figure 2.7). Continue by

> Clicking on the **Next** button. Alternately, you can press either or **N** or ⌷Enter⌷ (If you should wish to return to the previous window, you can also select the **Back** button.)

Simply Accounting will then continue with the installation of the typical installation for Simply Accounting for Windows. You can now go to the **Installation Progress** section below.

COMPACT PROGRAM INSTALLATION

If you have selected the **Compact** program installation (and selected the **Next** button), Simply Accounting will install the minimum program files, report files, company template files, and sample files.

Simply Accounting will now prompt you to confirm the creation of the program folder which will be used to access Simply Accounting from your Start List (Figure 2.6). The default program folder is *Simply Accounting,* which we will use in this book. Continue by

> Clicking on the **Next** button. Alternately, you can press either **N** or ⌷Enter⌷. (If you should wish to return to the previous window, you can also select the **Back** button.)

Simply Accounting for Windows will then ask you to confirm the compact installation options. Continue by

> Clicking on the **Next** button or press either **N** or ⌷Enter⌷.

Simply Accounting will then continue with the installation of the compact installation for Simply Accounting for Windows. You can now go to the **Installation Progress** section below.

CUSTOM PROGRAM INSTALLATION

If you have selected the **Custom** installation (and selected the **Next** button), Simply Accounting allows you to select the program options that you will want to install.

Figure 2.8
Select
Components
window

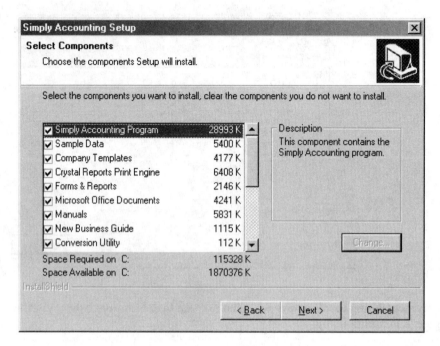

Simply Accounting for Windows now asks you to confirm which components you want to install (Figure 2.8). By default, all of the components will be installed which include the following:

Simply Accounting Program	This component is required to run Simply Accounting for Windows. This selection will include all of the program files including the help files.
Sample Data	This component includes sample files so you can practice using Simply Accounting for Windows.
Company Templates	Company Template files include shell files for specific industries. You can choose which business type is closest to yours and use that particular chart of accounts. It is easier to delete or modify a few accounts than to create an entirely new chart of accounts.
Crystal Reports Print Engine	This component is required if you wish to print custom report files.

Forms & Reports   This component includes sample Crystal Report files that can be used with your company's data files to print custom documents.

Microsoft Office Documents   This component includes various Microsoft Office documents for use within both Microsoft Word and Excel programs. Using these documents will allow you to extract Simply Accounting information.

Manuals   This component will install the Simply Accounting manuals (printed copies included within the Simply Accounting package). The electronic versions of these manuals are in Adobe PDF format.

New Business Guide   This component will install the informative New Business Guide program. This program will assist those new to establishing their businesses with information of available government registration and similar services.

Conversion Utility   If you want to convert Simply Accounting for DOS files to Simply Accounting for Windows Version 8.0, you must install this component.

Demos   This option will install several program demos which will demonstrate several program operations. You will need to have a sound card installed to use any of these demos.

From within the Select Components window (Figure 2.8) you can choose the applicable components to install by selecting (or unselecting if not required). You will now be asked to select the Program folder (Figure 2.6) followed by confirmation of the Start Copying Files window (Figure 2.7).

Practice Exercise 2.1

INSTALLING SIMPLY ACCOUNTING
Continue with selecting the Typical Installation along with the default Simply Accounting Program group.
When Simply Accounting displays the Start Copying Files window, (note Figure 2.7), continue by selecting the **Next** button.

INSTALLATION PROGRESS

During the installation process, Simply Accounting for Windows displays its progress through several status bars to show you how long it will take to install the program.

Once the installation has been completed, you will be asked to register your version of Simply Accounting on-line. You may continue with this process or decide to register either by mail or facsimile instead.

For the purpose of this book continue by selecting the **No** button from within the Register Simply Accounting window.

Once the setup process has been completed, Simply Accounting will prompt you to restart your computer. Continue by

Clicking on the **Finish** button.

CONVERTING YOUR ACCOUNTING SYSTEM

Before installing the Simply Accounting program you may have been using another accounting program or a manual accounting system. In either case, you must convert your records to the Simply Accounting program.

TIME OF CONVERSION

The timing of a conversion requires some planning. The most convenient time to convert is at year-end. This is the time when all balances in the accounts are correct and reconcilable. You can therefore ensure that the information that you are starting with is accurate.

While year-end is the most convenient time, you may choose to convert anytime. If you purchase your computer and/or the Simply Accounting program in the middle of the year, it makes sense to computerize your accounting system immediately. However the conversion process will require careful planning for a smooth transition.

SIMPLY ACCOUNTING FOR WINDOWS FORMS

The Simply Accounting for Windows system uses standard forms for payroll cheques, accounts receivable statements, and invoices.

These forms have been created specifically for use with the Simply Accounting for Windows system and can be obtained from most stationery stores. Although you do not have to use these forms, they will simplify your procedures and ensure that your business correspondence looks professional.

Part II

COMPREHENSIVE PRACTICE CASE

Overnight Delivery Company

This section will systematically introduce you to all of the accounting modules in the Simply Accounting for Windows system. Assume that you are converting from a manual accounting system to the Simply Accounting for Windows system.

In Chapter 3 you will create the company data files and customize the program for your needs. In Chapter 4 you will set up the General Ledger chart of accounts. In Chapter 5 you will enter the opening balances and set up the integration accounts for Overnight Delivery Company. In Chapter 6 you will enter some adjusting journal entries. In succeeding chapters you will learn about Accounts Receivable, Accounts Payable, Inventory, Payroll, and Project costing. You will also learn how to use the new graphing feature of Simply Accounting. Finally you will prepare closing entries for the year.

CHAPTER 3

CREATING DATA FILES AND CUSTOMIZING THE SIMPLY ACCOUNTING SYSTEM

CHAPTER 3

CREATING AND CUSTOMIZING THE SIMPLY ACCOUNTING DATA FILES

OBJECTIVES

After working through this chapter you will be able to

1. Create a new company data file.
2. Customize Simply Accounting for Windows to suit your needs.
3. Setup some key requirements for government and employees.
4. Change settings in the ledgers and in the Simply Accounting program.
5. Close a session and backup your data.

CREATING THE COMPANY DATA FILES

In the previous chapter you installed the Simply Accounting for Windows program files on your hard drive so you could use the program. However, currently no data files exist for your company.

Simply Accounting for Windows allows you to have several sets of data files in the same subdirectory. This is handy, for example, if you are an accountant who keeps the books for a number of companies; you can keep the data files for all companies in the same directory. On the other hand, if you have several companies or locations for which you keep separate books, you can again store them in one subdirectory.

With Simply Accounting it is easy to create data files for a business. However, before you computerize any business it is important to plan how to go through the conversion process to eliminate any future problems.

STARTING THE SIMPLY ACCOUNTING FOR WINDOWS PROGRAM

We will assume that Simply Accounting for Windows has been installed. To load the program under Windows 95 or Windows 98, start from the desktop by

Clicking once with the left button of your mouse on the **Start** button.

Figure 3.1
Start
Button

Move the mouse cursor to the **Programs** menu option to open the **Program** menu.

Locate and click on the **Simply Accounting** menu option.

Figure 3.2
Simply
Accounting
program
group

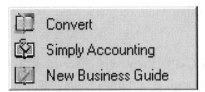

From the Simply Accounting program group (Figure 3.2), continue by

Clicking on the Simply Accounting program icon.

Note: Simply Accounting allows you to use both the left and right mouse button for various commands. When we say "click" we refer to clicking once with your left mouse button. If you have to carry out a command with the right mouse button, we will indicate that by saying "right click."

The Simply Accounting program will now load and then show the Simply Accounting Select Company window (Figure 3.3).

Figure 3.3
Simply Accounting
open file window

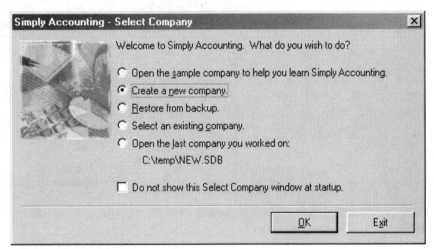

CREATING NEW COMPANY DATA FILES

The Select Company window, shown in Figure 3.3 is displayed each time you load Simply Accounting for Windows, (providing that you do not disable it by putting a check mark into the "Do not show" option). You can now select from the following options:

Open a sample company to help you learn Simply Accounting

allows you to open one of the Simply Accounting for Windows sample files provided as part of the program. These sample programs can assist you in learning the Simply Accounting program.

Create a new company

allows you to create a new company data file.

Restore from backup

allows you to restore previously backed up copies of your company data files. The Simply Accounting backup option is located in the Simply Accounting for Windows program and will be reviewed later in this chapter.

Select an existing company

allows you to locate and open a previously created company data file.

Do not show this Select Company window at startup

will prevent the Select Company window (Figure 3.3) from being displayed. Instead the Open File window will be displayed when you start the Simply Accounting for Windows program.

Continue from within the Select Company window (Figure 3.3) by

Selecting the **Create a new company** option.

Clicking on the **OK** button.

Figure 3.4
Setup Wizard
window

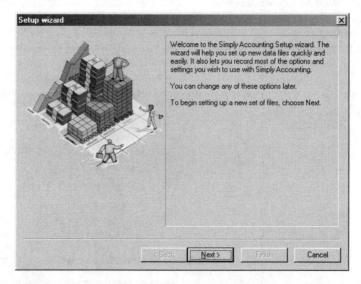

Simply Accounting will now guide you through the creation of your new company data files (Figure 3.4). Continue by either

Clicking on the **Next** button or by pressing [Alt] + [N] or [Enter].

Figure 3.5
Use a Template
for Your List of
Accounts? window

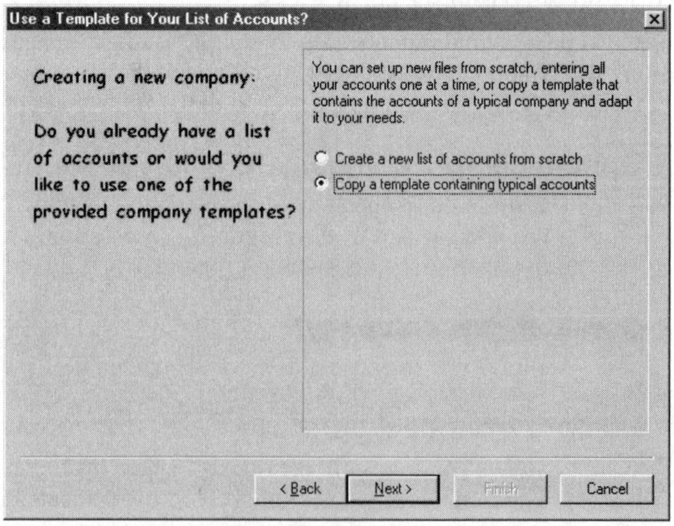

Simply Accounting will now prompt you to either set up a new data file or copy a template containing typical accounts (supplied by Simply Accounting) (Figure 3.5). These template files contain a suggested chart of accounts for use in a particular type of business. For the purpose of this book, however, we will create a new list of accounts from scratch.

Since you want to start a new file, continue from the Use a Template for Your List of Accounts window (Figure 3.5) by

> Clicking the **Create a new list of accounts from scratch** option (note that a dot is in the box next to **Copy a Template field**).

> Click on the **Next** button.

Figure 3.6
Enter a File
Name window

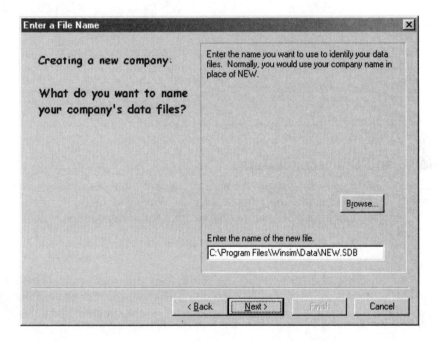

Simply Accounting will then ask you to confirm the file name for your company data file (Figure 3.6). The default file name should read **C:\Program Files\Winsim\data\new.sdb.**
Continue from the Enter a File name window (Figure 3.6) by

> Changing the new file name to **C:\Program Files\Winsim\data\odc.sdb**

HINT: We suggest that you use the above file name as this book will refer to this file name throughout the following chapters.

*You will notice that the Enter a File Name window, (Figure 3.6) also contains a **Browse** button. This allows you to change the default directory by browsing the directory structure on your hard drive. For the purpose of the book, we will use the default Simply Accounting for Windows data directory.*

Once you have change the file name, continue by

> Clicking on the **Next** button.

Figure 3.7
Dates window

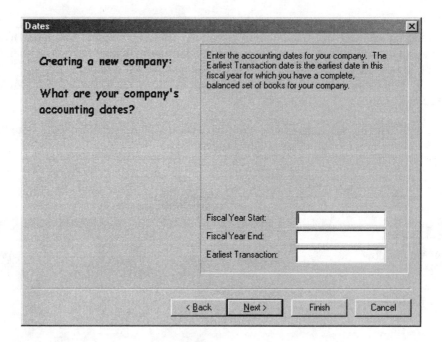

Fiscal and Conversion Dates

The next step depends on whether you are starting a new business or converting your data from a manual set of records to Simply Accounting for Windows.

As shown in Figure 3.7, Simply Accounting for Windows asks you to provide the following three dates:

Fiscal Start   is the first day that your company's current fiscal year begins. This may be different from the date shown above depending on when you are using the program.

Fiscal End   represents the last day of your company's current fiscal year. Again this date may differ from the one above.

Earliest Transaction   is the date that your company converts its old accounting records over to Simply Accounting for Windows. This date will also differ from the one above.

> **HINT:** *Before you continue, let's look at the meaning of the fiscal year and why planning must occur for a business just starting out. The **Fiscal Start** can be any day from January 1st to December 31st. The **Fiscal End** date must be no more than 365 days after the **Fiscal Start**. So you have a choice as to your company's fiscal year-end.*
>
> *There are two major reasons to select a fiscal year-end other than December 31st: to save on taxes or to allow your business to have a year-end in a slow time of the year. Typically, retail stores have fiscal year-ends after Christmas, usually in February during their slow season.*

If your company is just starting out and you expect to earn a taxable income within the next 365 days, you will want to defer this tax payable for as long as possible. Or, if you expect that your company will experience a loss for the first three months, followed by a profit for the next year afterwards, you may want to have your fiscal year-end within the next three months so that your company will not experience taxes payable for up to 15 months (three months plus the fiscal year of 12 months).

Perhaps the most important advice is that you take the time in deciding your fiscal year-end. Ask a professional accountant if you have any questions or concerns to ensure that you are not in conflict with the rules and regulations of Revenue Canada.

Entering Fiscal and Earliest Transaction Dates

Perhaps the most confusing date is the **Earliest Transaction** date (Figure 3.8). If your business is just starting out, the **Earliest Transaction** date will be the same as the **Fiscal Start** date. Since you are just starting out, there is no need to convert from previous accounting records.

For existing businesses that are converting their accounting records, selecting the **Earliest Transaction** date must again involve some planning and preparation.

The proper steps when you are converting your accounting records to any new accounting system are as follows:

1. First, you must close off your manual set of records. Although this does not have to occur at the end of a fiscal year, it should occur at the end of one of your monthly reporting periods. By closing your set of records you will enter all transactions up to the closing date in the old accounting system. For example, if you chose to close your old accounting system on July 31, 2001, you would enter transactions up to and including July 31, 2001. Any transactions for August 1, 2001 and thereafter would be entered into Simply Accounting for Windows — your new accounting system.

2. Balance and reconcile your old (and now closed) set of accounting records. Make any adjusting entries under the closing date in the old accounting system. The end result will be a fully balanced and reconciled accounting system that has been closed off.

3. Enter the opening balances and outstanding invoices — receivable, payable, opening payroll, and inventory information — into Simply Accounting for Windows. The date for these entries can be the closing date for the old system (the **Earliest Transaction** date), which is July 31, 2001 in our example.

4. Ensure that the new accounting system's opening amounts have been balanced to the old accounting system. Once everything has been balanced, you are ready to use Simply Accounting for Windows. At this point you would enter any transactions after the July 31, 2001 closing or **Earliest Transaction** date.

It is very important that you follow these steps. If you try to convert from your old system using any other method, you might encounter many errors.

Now enter the Company Dates as follows. At the **Fiscal Start** enter

010101 ⌷Tab   to enter the **Fiscal Start** date. This is the date on which your company's current fiscal year begins.

123101 ⌷Tab   to enter the **Fiscal End** date. This is the date on which your company's current fiscal year ends.

073101 ⌈Tab⌉   to enter the Earliest Transaction. As this date differs from the **Fiscal Start** date, it is assumed that this company will be converting from another set of accounting records over to Simply Accounting for Windows.

HINT: ENTERING DATES IN SIMPLY ACCOUNTING

Within Simply Accounting for Windows, you can enter program and transactional dates by entering the six-digit date (mmddyy format), no hyphens, spaces or dashes required.

The format used for the purpose of this book is the mmddyy format. In order to change to this date format, please select the Regional Settings option from within the Windows Control Panel.

Figure 3.8
Dates window
(Dates entered)

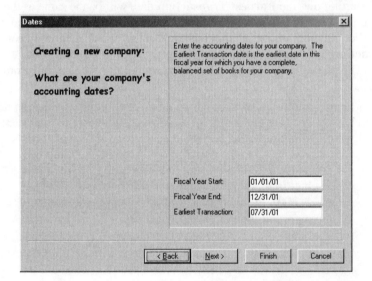

If your company Dates window matches the one shown in Figure 3.8 above, continue by

Clicking on the **Next** button.

Figure 3.9
Business
Activities
window

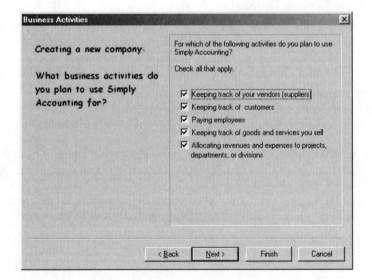

Business Activities Window

Simply Accounting for Windows will now prompt you to confirm the business activities your company plans to use within Simply Accounting for Windows (Figure 3.9).

If you were to unselect any of the displayed options, the associated ledgers and journals would not be displayed for use in the program. You can however, select to use the undisplayed ledgers and journals or activities from within the **Settings** option of the Simply Accounting for Windows program.

For the purpose of this book, we will be using and accessing all program activities. Continue from the Business Activities window (Figure 3.9) by

Clicking on the **Next** button.

Figure 3.10
Company Name
and Address
window

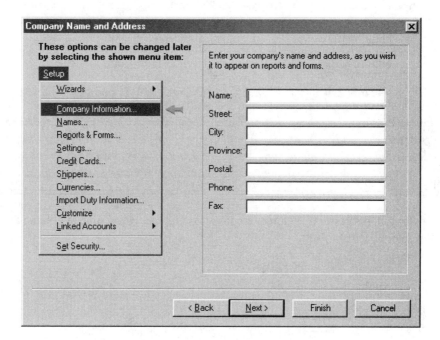

Company Information

Simply Accounting will now prompt you to enter your company's name and address (Figure 3.10). This information is used when you print reports, invoices, and similar documents.

> **HINT:** *You can also change your company's name and address information by selecting the **Company Information** option from within the **Setup** menu. You can access this menu from within the main Simply Accounting window.*

Continue by entering the following:

Overnight Delivery Company ⌈ Tab ⌉ to enter the **Name** for your company.

> **HINT:** *If you are working through this exercise in a classroom environment where other individuals will use the same company name you may want to change it slightly so that you can easily identify it on subsequent startups. Otherwise you will have to copy your data files to a diskette. Your instructor will probably indicate what you should do.*

300-3665 Kingsway [Tab]   to enter the **Street** address for your company.

Vancouver [Tab]   to enter the **City**.

British Columbia [Tab]   to enter the **Province**.

> *HINT: Simply Accounting will default all future cities and provinces for your vendors, customers, and employees to your city and province. This default value can, however, be changed.*

Continue by entering the postal exactly as shown.

v5r5w2 [Tab]   to enter the **Postal** code.

6044638202 [Tab]   to enter the **Phone** number.

6044638210 [Tab]   to enter the **Fax** number.

> *HINT: Simply Accounting will automatically format all postal codes along with telephone and facsimile numbers by inserting the appropriate spaces, brackets, and hyphens. Simply Accounting will also capitalize the letters in your postal code.*

If everything is correctly entered, continue from within the Company Name and Address window (Figure 3.11) by either

Clicking on the **Next** button.

or pressing

[Alt] + [N]   to select the **Next** button.

Terminology within Simply Accounting for Windows

Figure 3.11
Terminology
window

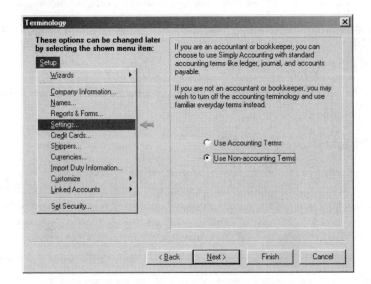

Simply Accounting for Windows allows you to select the menu and command terminology option within the program (see Figure 3.11). This option allows you to use either standard accounting terms or non-accounting terms, based on your experience in accounting and bookkeeping.

For the purpose of this book, the standard accounting terms will be used.
Continue from within the Terminology window (Figure 3.11) by

> Selecting the **Use Accounting Terms** option.

Once you have changed the Terminology option to the Use Accounting Terms option, continue by

> Clicking on the **Next** button.

The Business Number

Figure 3.12
Business
Number
window

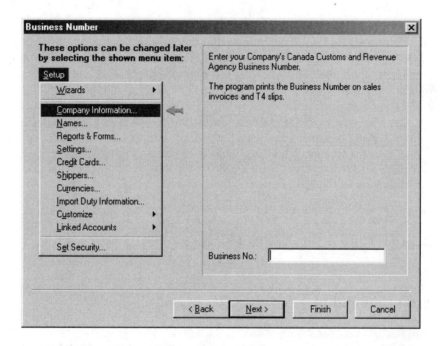

As of January 01, 1997, Revenue Canada Taxation replaced the old GST, Payroll, and Corporate Tax Numbers with the new Business Number. This is a single number that will identify these accounts (Figure 3.12).

If you don't have a business number, you can skip this option. However, if your business collects GST or remits payroll deductions, you will require a business number from Revenue Canada Taxation. Continue from within the Business Number window (Figure 3.12) by entering

> **100145405** ⌷Tab⌷   to enter the **Business No.** for the *Overnight Delivery Company.*

Continue by either

> Clicking on the **Next** button.

or pressing

> ⌷Alt⌷ + ⌷N⌷   to select the **Next** button.

Figure 3.13
Quebec Sales
Tax window

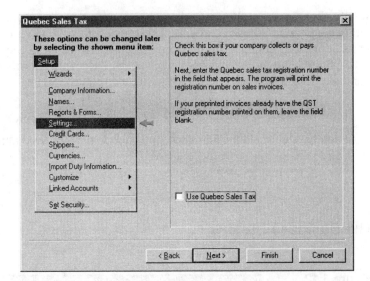

If your business is located or operates within the Province of Quebec, you may collect and remit QST (Quebec Sales Tax) (Figure 3.13). Simply Accounting will now prompt you to select this option (if applicable). By selecting this option, Simply Accounting will activate the QST options as well as prompting you to enter the QST account number that will be included on your sales invoices.

Since the *Overnight Delivery Company* (the company used in this section of the book) is located in British Columbia and does not collect or remit QST, you should not select this option. Continue from the Quebec Sales Tax window (Figure 3.13) by either

Clicking on the **Next** button.

or pressing

[Alt] + [N]   to select the **Next** button.

Payroll Definitions

Figure 3.14
Payroll Definitions
- Incomes window

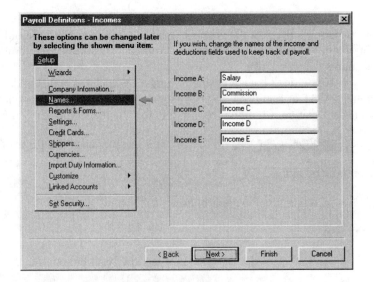

Simply Accounting will now prompt you to accept, or edit and accept, the payroll income names that will be used within your Payroll module (Figure 3.14).

Simply Accounting allows you to record up to five payroll types (along with hourly wages). As each business will be unique with the number and types of income, you can customize these options for your company's payroll structure.

These income types can be for both taxable and non-taxable income sources. Continue from the Payroll Definition - Incomes window (Figure 3.14) by entering

Tab	to accept **Income A** as the default *Salary.*
Tab	to accept **Income B** as the default *Commission.*
Bonus Tab	to enter the description for **Income C.**
Exp Reimb Tab	to enter the description for **Income D.**
not used Tab	to enter the description for **Income E.**

Figure 3.15
Payroll
Definitions
- Incomes
window
(entered)

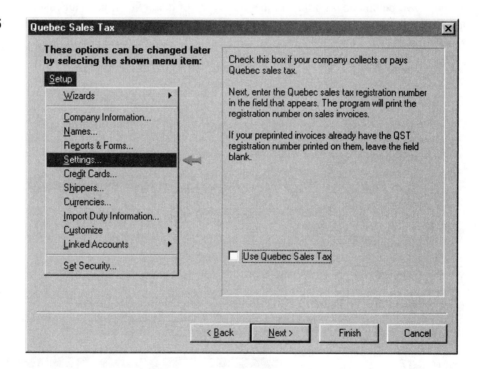

If your Payroll Definitions - Incomes window resembles Figure 3.15, continue by either

Clicking on the **Next** button.

or pressing

Alt + N   to select the **Next** button.

Figure 3.16
Payroll Definitions -
Deductions window

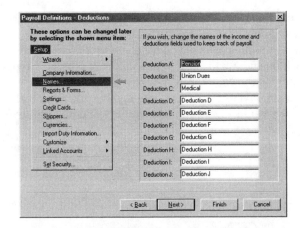

Simply Accounting will now prompt you to accept, or edit and accept, the payroll deductions names that will be used within your Payroll module (Figure 3.16).

Simply Accounting allows the recording of up to ten payroll deduction types. As each business will be unique with the number and types of deductions, you can customize these options for your company's payroll structure. Continue from the Payroll Definition - Deductions window (Figure 3.16) by entering

Dental ⌈Tab⌉   to enter the description for **Deduction A**.

CSB ⌈Tab⌉   to enter the description for **Deduction B**.

Medical ⌈Tab⌉   to enter the description for **Deduction C**.

Donations ⌈Tab⌉   to enter the description for **Deduction D**.

Stock Plan ⌈Tab⌉   to enter the description for **Deduction E**.

not used ⌈Tab⌉   to enter the description for **Deduction F**.

not used ⌈Tab⌉   to enter the description for **Deduction G**.

not used ⌈Tab⌉   to enter the description for **Deduction H**.

not used ⌈Tab⌉   to enter the description for **Deduction I**.

not used ⌈Tab⌉   to enter the description for **Deduction J**.

Figure 3.17
Payroll Definitions -
Deductions window
(entered)

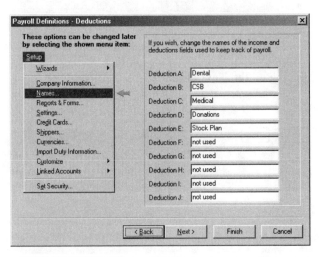

If your Payroll Definitions window looks like Figure 3.17, continue by either

> Clicking on the **Next** button.

or pressing

> [Alt] + [N]   to select the **Next** button.

Tax and Projects

Figure 3.18
Tax and Project
Names window

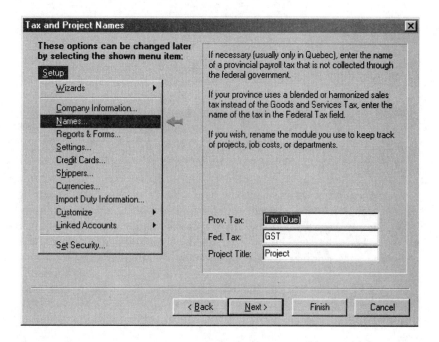

You can now confirm or edit the Tax and Project Names (Figure 3.18). These definitions include the name for the Provincial Payroll Tax that is not collected federally (usually only Quebec), the name for the federal tax (GST) as well as the Project title. Project's are used within Simply Accounting to allow you to track revenue and expenses by user-defined jobs or projects. This feature will be explained in detail in Chapter 11.

As the default definitions shown in Figure 3.18 are suitable for *Overnight Delivery Company,* continue by either

> Clicking on the **Next** button.

or pressing

> [Alt] + [N]   to select the **Next** button.

Printer Settings

Figure 3.19
Printer
Settings
window

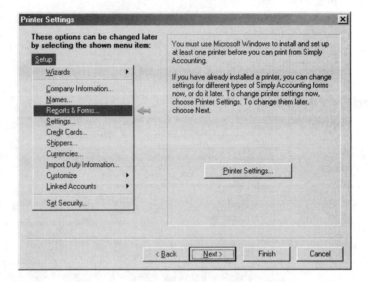

Simply Accounting will now provide you with the option of either setting up or changing your current default Windows printer settings for use with Simply Accounting for Windows (Figure 3.19). Simply Accounting for Windows allows you to set up different printers for use within the program. For example, you could have a dot-matrix printer to print invoices that are in multiple parts, and a laser printer to print your reports. Continue by either

Clicking on the **Printer Settings**... button.

or pressing

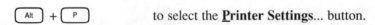 to select the **Printer Settings**... button.

Figure 3.20
Printers
window

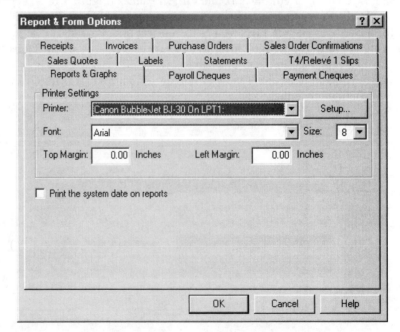

As shown in Figure 3.20, you can select a suitable printer and/or change the font type/size and margins for each type of paper output.

In this book we assume that you have a Windows 95/98 compatible printer already installed, so the printer options can remain as shown in the default window for each type of output.

Continue from the Printer window by

Clicking on the **OK** button.

Once you have returned to the Printer Settings window (Figure 3.19), continue by either

Clicking on the **Next** button.

or pressing

Alt + N   to select the **Next** button.

Inventory Turnover

Figure 3.21
Track
Inventory
Turnover
window

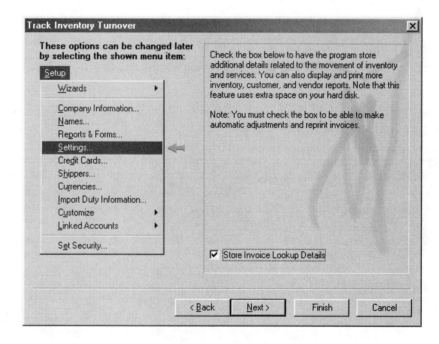

Simply Accounting for Windows supports both the tracking of inventory turnover and storing of posted invoice details for later reference. Although both of these options require hard disk space for storage of data, the space required is minimal compared to the added benefit of being able to track your inventory turnover and look up previously posted purchase and sales invoices.

For the exercises in this book you must have both the **Track Inventory Turnover** and **Store Invoice Lookup Details** options selected. We suggest that if you use Simply Accounting for your company that you do the same.

Continue from the Track Inventory Turnover window (Figure 3.21) by either

Clicking on the **Next** button.

or pressing

Alt + N   to select the **Next** button.

Cash versus Accrual Accounting

Figure 3.22
Cash-Basis
Accounting
window

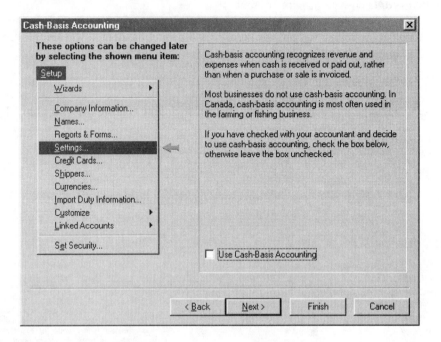

As shown in Figure 3.22, Simply Accounting for Windows will now ask you whether your company or organization uses the cash basis for accounting.

HINT: Cash-based accounting is an accounting method where you realize revenue and expenses when funds are received or disbursed, compared to the accrual method of accounting which realizes revenue when it is earned and when expenses are incurred. Although the standard practice in business today is to use the accrual method of accounting, you may still choose to use the cash-based method of accounting.

An example of the difference between the cash and accrual basis for accounting is as follows:

John Doe Company receives a phone bill for $50.00 plus $3.50 GST on January 10, 2001 with a billing date of January 1, 2001. This bill is not paid until the due date which is February 10, 2001.

Under the accrual method of accounting the above phone bill would be realized as an expense on January 1, 2001, which is the date that the expense was incurred by the company — billing date.

Under the cash basis of accounting, the bill would not be realized as an expense until February 10, 2001 which is the date that the bill is paid.

Which ever method you select, you should take the time to consult an experienced accountant regarding this matter.

The exercise in Appendix B leads you through cash-based and accrual-based accounting methods.

In this book, we will use accrual-based accounting. Be sure that the **Use Cash-Basis Accounting** option is *not selected*.

Continue from the Cash-Basis Accounting window by either

Clicking on the **Next** button.

or pressing

   to select the **Next** button.

Budgeting

Figure 3.23
Budgeting
window

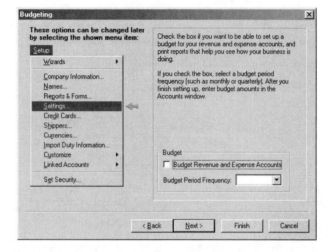

An important feature of Simply Accounting for Windows is the ability to track your company's performance against a predefined budget. Budgeting for your business is strongly recommended to ensure that you can track your company's growth and performance.

Continue from the Budgeting window (Figure 3.23) by

Clicking on the **Budget Revenue and Expense Accounts** options. *This will select this option.*

Click on the little black down arrow next to **Budget Period Frequency.** A drop down list will appear.

Choose the *Monthly* frequency by putting your mouse pointer on it to highlight and then clicking once.

Figure 3.24
Budgeting
window
(changed)

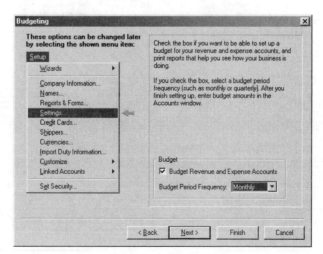

Check to ensure that your Budgeting window resembles Figure 3.24. Then continue by either

Clicking on the **Next** button.

or pressing

⌈ Alt ⌋ + ⌈ N ⌋   to select the **Next** button.

Figure 3.25
Budgeting
(Project)
window

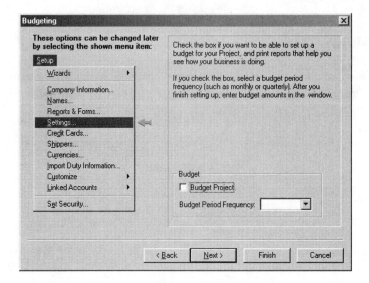

Simply Accounting for Windows also allows you to budget your projects. This ensures that your projects (area specific revenue and expenses) meet the budget determined by management.
Continue from the Budgeting window (Figure 3.25) by

Clicking on the **Budget Project** option. *This will select this option.*

Click on the little black down arrow next to **Budget Period Frequency.** A drop down list will appear. Choose the *Monthly* frequency by putting your mouse pointer on it to highlight and then clicking once.

Figure 3.26
Use Cheque
No. as the
Source Code
window

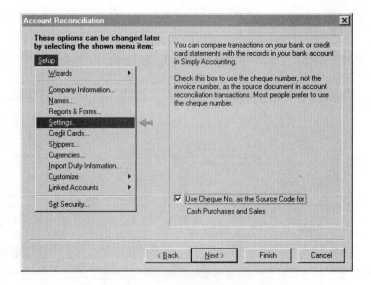

For cash purchases and sales, the cheque number will be used as the source (document) number. Check to ensure that your Account Reconciliation window resembles Figure 3.26. Then continue by either

Clicking on the **Next** button.

or pressing

[Alt] + [N]   to select the **Next** button.

Federal Sales Tax — GST and HST

Figure 3.27
Federal Sales
Taxes window

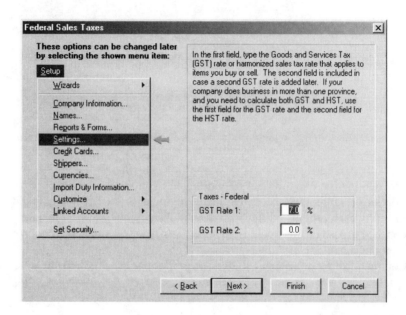

As shown in Figure 3.27, you are now prompted to enter the applicable GST/HST rates of tax. Although there are two rate fields, at the present time one GST rate of 7.0% and one HST rate of 15.0% is levied.

> **HINT: GST/HST ISSUES**
> *Currently in Canada, both GST (Goods and Services Tax) and HST (Harmonized Sales Tax) are applicable. For the purpose of this book, transactions will be examined for both tax types.*

Continue from the Federal Sales Tax window (Figure 3.29) by pressing

[Tab]   to accept 7.0% as the **GST Rate 1.**

15.0 [Tab]   to enter the **GST Rate 2.**

Continue by either

Clicking on the **Next** button.

or pressing

[Alt] + [N]   to select the **Next** button.

Provincial Sales Tax

Figure 3.28
Provincial Sales
Taxes window

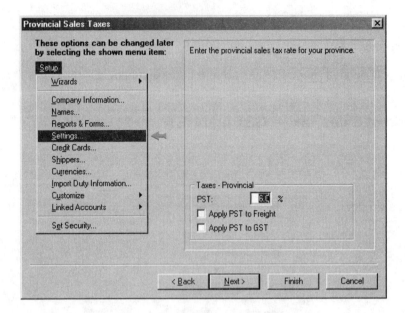

Simply Accounting for Windows has now prompted you for the applicable Provincial Sales Tax rate and options (Figure 3.28). Since both the Provincial Sales Tax rate charged and the exemptions allowed in each province differ, you should check with your provincial government.

For the purpose of this book, *Overnight Delivery Company* collects Provincial Sales Tax on some products at a rate of 7.0%.

Continue from the Provincial Sales Taxes window (Figure 3.28) by entering

7.0 [Tab]   to enter the applicable **PST** rate.

[Tab]   to skip (unselected) **Apply PST to Freight** option. As the *Overnight Delivery Company* is based in British Columbia, at the time of printing, the collection of Provincial Sales Tax on freight revenue is not applicable.

[Tab]   to skip (unselected) **Apply PST to GST** option. At the time of printing, within British Columbia PST is not levied on chargeable GST, however this method is used in other provinces within Canada.

HINT: *You should contact your provincial government to determine if you should be collecting PST on your freight revenues and if you should be charging PST on the GST tax charged on sales.*

Continue from the Provincial Sales Taxes window by either

Clicking on the **Next** button.

or pressing

[Alt] + [N]   to select the **Next** button.

Payroll - Taxable Income

Figure 3.29
Payroll - Taxable
Income window

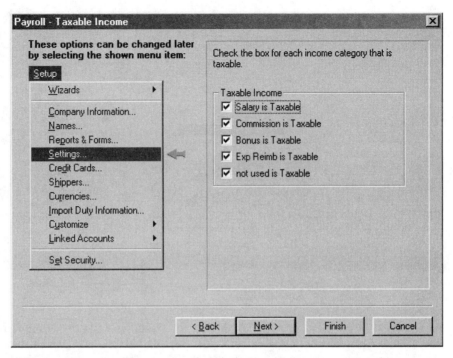

Simply Accounting for Windows will now prompt you to specify which of the previously specified payroll income types are taxable (for payroll remittances and taxes) (Figure 3.29).

Continue from the Payroll-Taxable Income window (Figure 3.29) by pressing

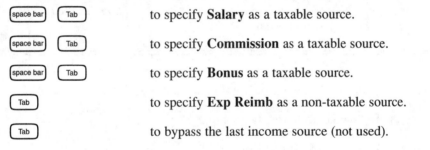

space bar Tab	to specify **Salary** as a taxable source.
space bar Tab	to specify **Commission** as a taxable source.
space bar Tab	to specify **Bonus** as a taxable source.
Tab	to specify **Exp Reimb** as a non-taxable source.
Tab	to bypass the last income source (not used).

Continue from within the Payroll - Taxable Income window (Figure 3.29) by either

Clicking on the **Next** button.

or pressing

Alt + N   to select the **Next** button.

Payroll Deductions

Figure 3.30
Payroll - Deductions
window

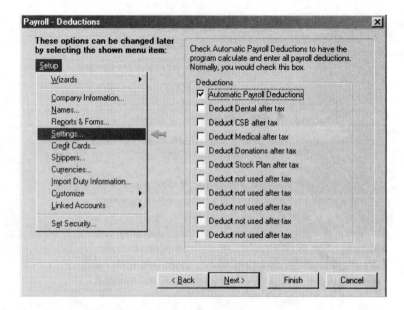

As shown in Figure 3.30, Simply Accounting for Windows will now prompt you to select if you want Simply Accounting to calculate the payroll deductions (CPP, EI, Income Tax, and QPP [if applicable]). You must also inform Simply Accounting as to which of your employee deductions are deducted before income tax is deducted (non-selected) or after income tax is deducted (selected).

> **HINT:** *You will notice that the deductions listed are those deductions entered within the Payroll Definitions window (Figure 3.16).*

Continue from the Payroll - Deductions window (Figure 3.30) by

> Clicking the **Deduct Dental after tax** option.
>
> Clicking the **Deduct CSB after tax** option.
>
> Clicking the **Deduct Medical after tax** option.
>
> Clicking the **Deduct Donations after tax** option.
>
> Clicking the **Deduct Stock Plan after tax** option.

Continue from within the Payroll-Deductions window (Figure 3.30) by either

> Clicking on the **Next** button.

or pressing

> (Alt) + (N)   to select the **Next** button.

Figure 3.31
Payroll - Deductions
(Deduction rate)
window

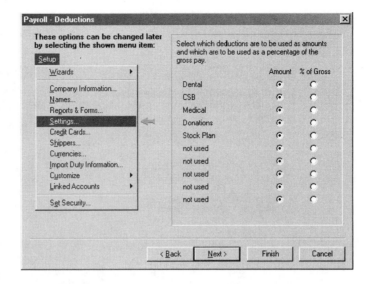

Simply Accounting for Windows will now allow you to specify how the defined deductions will be calculated (Figure 3.31). Continue by

Clicking the *Percent* column for the **Stock Plan** deduction.

Figure 3.32
Payroll - Deductions
 (Deduction rate -
changed) window

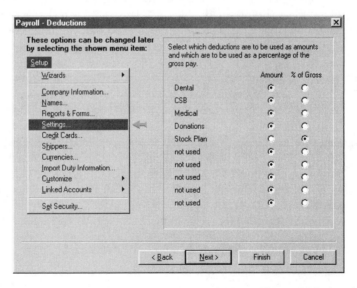

Continue from within the Payroll - Deductions (Deduction rate) window (Figure 3.32) by either

Clicking on the **Next** button.

or pressing

(Alt) + (N)   to select the Next button.

Employment Insurance and Employer Health Tax

Figure 3.33
EI and EHT
Factors window

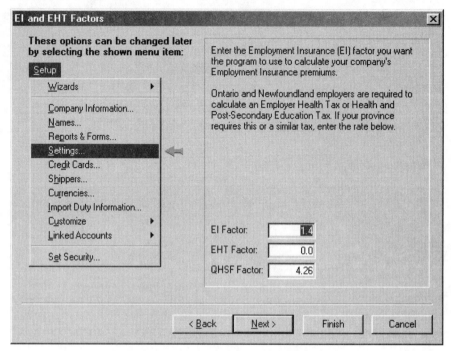

Simply Accounting for Windows requires you to enter the factors for both the EI (Employment Insurance) and EHT (Employer Health Tax). This is the percentage or factor that you as an employer must pay. For EI this factor is the amount that you must contribute for each dollar that your employee has deducted for EI. The EHT factor is a predefined factor.

> **HINT:** *For those companies within the Province of Newfoundland, you can use the EHT field for the factor rate for the Newfoundland Health and Post-Secondary Education Tax.*

For the purpose of this book, we will accept the default EI factor of 1.4 and 0.0 for EHT as this is not currently levied within the Province of British Columbia, where *Overnight Delivery Company* is based.
Continue from the Payroll - Factors window (Figure 3.33) by either

Clicking on the **Next** button.

or pressing

   to select the **Next** button.

Simply Accounting Forms

Figure 3.34
Forms window

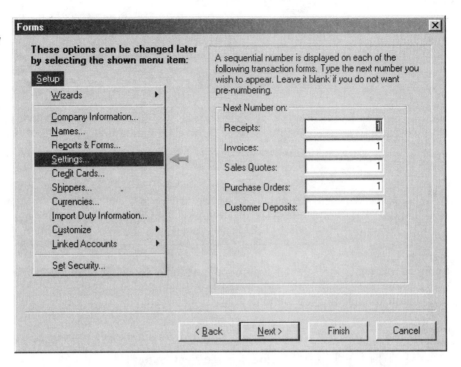

As Simply Accounting for Windows will track your used and next invoice and cheque numbers (for payables and payroll), you are now asked to provide the next invoice number along with the next payables and payroll cheque number, (Figure 3.34).

> *HINT: When entering the next invoice number, it will be the first invoice that you will enter in Simply Accounting after your conversion to Simply Accounting. For example, if you have already issued invoice 506 in your manual records, the next invoice number that you would provide would be 507. The same procedure is used when entering the next payable and payroll cheque number.*
>
> *If you use one bank account for issuing cheques for both accounts payable and payroll, then enter the same cheque number in both fields as shown for Overnight Delivery Company below.*

Continue from within the Forms window, (Figure 3.34) by entering

104 ⌷Tab⌷   as the next number for your cash **Receipts**.

4551 ⌷Tab⌷   as the next number for your sales **Invoices**.

301 ⌷Tab⌷   as the next number for your **Sales Quotes**.

⌷Tab⌷   to accept 1 as the next number for your **Purchase Orders**.

104 ⌷Tab⌷   to enter the next number for the Customer Deposits.

Figure 3.35
Forms window
(entered)

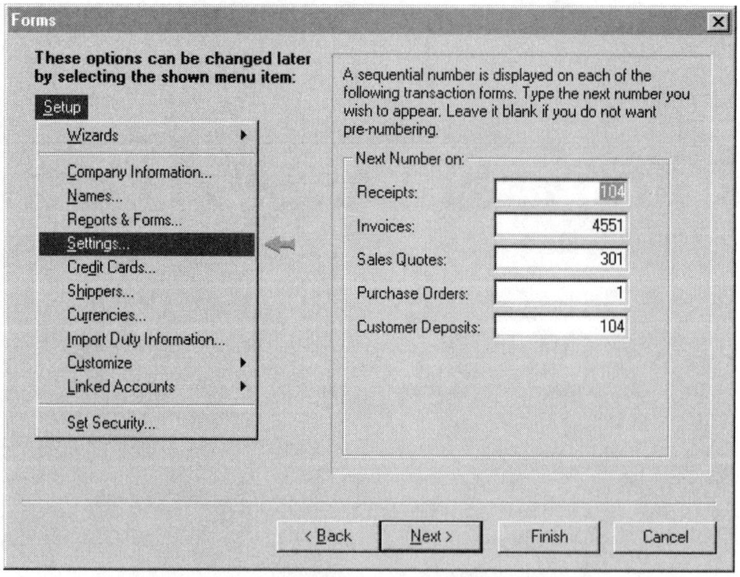

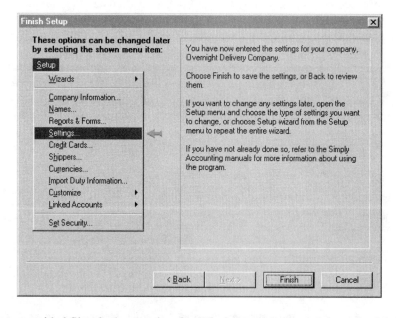

If your Forms window resembles Figure 3.35, continue by either

Clicking on the **Next** button.

or pressing

Alt + N   to select the **Next** button.

Figure 3.36
Finish Creating
a New
Company
window

That's it. You have now provided Simply Accounting for Windows with all of the required information to create your company data files (Figure 3.36).

Remember, you can change any of your options with the **Back** button to scroll back through the previous option windows.

> **HINT**: *You can also select the **Cancel** button to abort the data creation process—you will then return to the Select file name window (see Figure 3.3). You can also select the **Help** button for help on each option window.*

If you have entered the options as directed above, continue from the Finish Creating a New Company window (Figure 3.36) by

Clicking on the **Finish** button.

Simply Accounting will then continue with the creation of the company data files.

Figure 3.37
Simply Accounting
main window

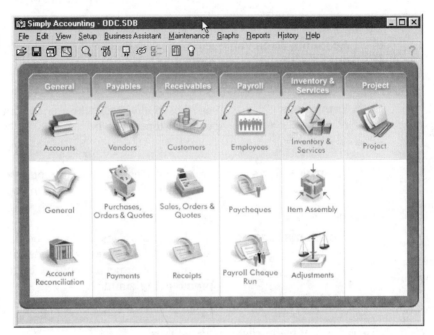

Once Simply Accounting has created the data files for your company, the Simply Accounting main window will be displayed (Figure 3.37). This window is the starting point for all operations within Simply Accounting for Windows.

A QUICK LOOK AT THE SIMPLY ACCOUNTING LEDGERS

As shown in Figure 3.37, this window displays several icons divided into three sections. The first section of icons are ledger icons.

Figure 3.38
Ledger icons

These icons (Figure 3.38) allow you to access the ledgers into which you would enter various information. From left to right in Figure 3.38 you would enter the following information:

General Ledger accounts and budget information   an example of a General Ledger account is your bank, sales revenue or telephone expense account.

Accounts Payable vendors   your Accounts Payable vendors are those individuals and businesses to whom you owe money for business purchases. Examples would be your telephone company, Revenue Canada Taxation and others.

Accounts Receivable customers   customers are those to whom you sell products or services.

Employees   are those individuals who are paid hourly, salaried, or commissioned income.

Inventory items   are for entry and maintenance of inventory and service items that are sold or provided to your customers.

Project management   this ledger provides you with the flexibility of tracking revenue and expenses on user-defined projects. Examples of projects would be by region, department, promotion or similar.

We will discuss each of these ledgers in detail later.

In the second section (Figure 3.39), you will find the group of journal icons.

HINT: You will notice that all of the journal icons have a red (no-entry) circle on each icon. This informs you that you can not enter this journal until you have set the associated ledger to ready, (see Chapter 4).

Figure 3.39
Journal icons

These icons allow you to access each of the journals within Simply Accounting for Windows. The purpose of these journals is as follows:

General — for entering general journal entries such as monthly depreciation of your fixed assets or allocation of a pre-paid expense.

Account Reconciliation — allows you to use the bank reconciliation feature.

Purchase Orders and Quotes — for entering accounts payable and cash purchases such as your monthly business phone bill or office supplies purchases as well as inventory purchases.

Payment Cheques — for issuing accounts payable cheques for payment against accounts payable purchases.

Sales, Orders and Quotes — for entering accounts receivable as well as cash sales.

Receipts — for entering payment from your customers for accounts receivable sales on account.

Paycheques — for entering your company's payroll transactions.

Automatic Payroll Run — for generating a payroll for your employees based on predefined information.

Item Assembly — for recording transfers of inventory from one inventory account to another.

Adjustments — for entering adjustments against your inventory such as the markdown of your inventory due to shrinkage, theft and/or spoilage.

The last set of icons (Figure 3.40) are for general use.

Figure 3.40
General icons

These icons (from left to right) allow you to do the following:

Open a highlighted ledger or journal.

Save the data files to your hard disk.

HINT: *We recommend that you save your data files to your hard disk on a regular basis. This will prevent data loss if your computer should hang up or if there is a power failure. To simplify this operation, you can press* [Ctrl]+[S] *to save your data.*

Backup your data files to a diskette (note example later in this chapter).

Export data to Microsoft Access (for external use).

Find a topic based on a highlighted ledger icon (for example, to find an account if the account icon is highlighted).

Access the setup functions for your company.

Advance the Using Date as explained in Chapter 5 and later chapters.

Display the To-Do list which provides you with information regarding recurring entries and similar information.

Display the checklist option which will track entered checklist tasks.

Display a report based on a highlighted ledger or journal icon, such as a list of vendors on file if the vendors icon is highlighted.

Display the Simply Accounting Advice window. The Advice within Simply Accounting will provide you with general accounting and management advice for your business.

Open the Simply Accounting Help system. This window opens to the help topic specific to the highlighted ledger, journal or function that you are currently working within. You can also browse a list of topics or search for specific help topics.

CHANGING YOUR COMPANY SETTINGS

You have now created the data files and entered the fiscal dates and conversion date along with the opening settings. You can change any of these settings by accessing the specific settings option.

Continue from within the Simply Accounting-ODC window (Figure 3.37) by either

Clicking on the **Setup** menu (Figure 3.41).

or pressing

[Alt] + [S]   to invoke the **Setup** menu (Figure 3.41).

Figure 3.41
Setup Menu

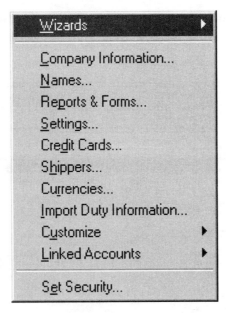

The **Setup** menu (Figure 3.41) allows you to change any of the information that you previously entered. You can access each section directly by clicking on it and editing the information. Or you can invoke the provided Simply Wizards to help you. Simply Accounting also provides Wizards for Settings, linked accounts (integrating modules to the General Ledger) and modified accounts.

Figure 3.42
Setup Wizard
Menu

> Settings...
> Linked Accounts...
> Modify Accounts...

Each of the Simply Wizards "walks" you through each of the processes (similar to the way you walked through the Company Setup Wizard earlier in this chapter). If you make a mistake, you can easily return to the previous screen by selecting the **Back** button, or click **Next** to move on to the next screen within the Wizard.

Instead of using the Wizards to "walk you" through various company settings, linked accounts or modified accounts options, you can access individual options through the **Setup** menu (Figure 3.41).

Figure 3.43
Company
Information
window

Company Information	
Name: Overnight Delivery Company	Fiscal Start: 1/1/01
Street: 300-3665 Kingsway	Fiscal End: 12/31/01
City: Vancouver	Earliest Transaction: 7/31/01
Province: British Columbia	Session: 7/31/01
Postal: V5R 5W2	Latest Transaction: 7/31/01
Phone: (604) 463-8202	
Fax: (604) 463-8210	
Business No.: 100145405	
	OK Cancel

Selecting the **Company Information** option displays the Company Information window (Figure 3.43) from where you can change your company's name, address, business number, and company fiscal dates.

HINT: *You can only change the Fiscal and Conversion dates prior to the setting of the General Ledger module to the Ready mode, (see Chapter 5).*

Figure 3.44
Names
window

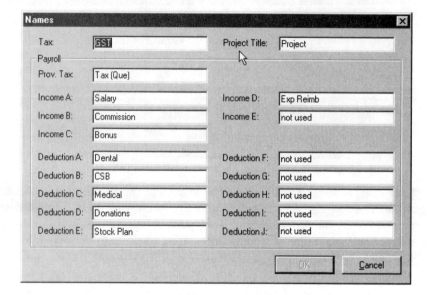

Selecting the **Names** option will display the Names window (Figure 3.44). This window allows you to customize named areas and fields within Simply Accounting for Windows.

Figure 3.45
Report & Forms
Options window

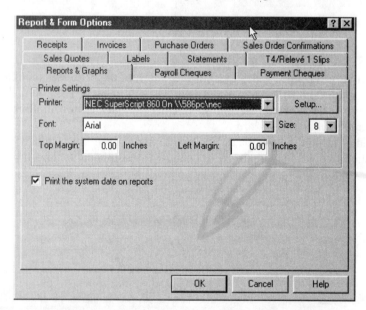

The **Reports & Forms** option will in turn display the Reports & Forms (Figure 3.45) allowing you the option of defining which printer will print your reports, statements, invoices, and cheques (accounts payable/payroll). This window is a multi-tabbed window where you can select the applicable document type to specify the printer options. Within this window you can also select custom report formats for each available report option.

CUSTOMIZING SIMPLY ACCOUNTING FOR WINDOWS

Simply Accounting for Windows allows you to customize several settings such as interest charged on overdue invoices or the dates for calculating aging periods, among others.

Figure 3.46
Settings
(Display)
window

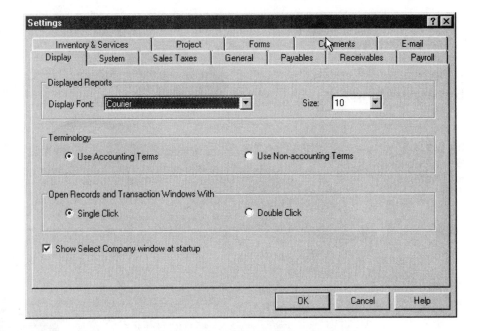

The **Settings** menu option will display the Settings multi-tabbed window which allows you to specify the default selections for all of the ledgers and journals. Each of the tabbed windows are displayed as follows:

Display

In Figure 3.46 you can see the settings for what Simply Accounting shows on your monitor and how it is displayed. These settings include the following:

Display Reports

Display Font   is the font that will be used to display icon text as well as all text within screens and on-screen reports.

Size   specifies the font size.

Terminology   allows you the option of selecting to display either accounting or non-accounting terms within menu and screens. *For the purpose of this book, you should have previously selected to* **Use Accounting Terms**.

Open Records and Transaction Windows With	provides you with the option of selecting either a single or double click to open the associated ledgers and journals within Simply Accounting.
Show Select Company Window at Startup	will in turn display the opening window, (Figure 3.3) which will allow you to easily select from several file options.

System Settings

Figure 3.47
Settings window
for Systems

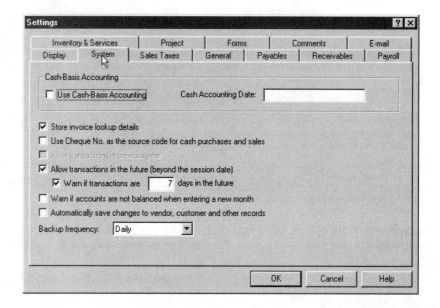

From the **Settings** window for System (Figure 3.47) you can change or select the following options:

Cash-Basis Accounting

Use Cash-Basis Accounting	allows you to select the cash-based method of accounting.
Cash Accounting Date	the date on which you began cash accounting. This will allow Simply Accounting for Windows to display the information within the ledgers accordingly.
Store invoice lookup details	will provide you with access to previously posted invoices for reprinting or editing.

Use Cheque No. as the source code for cash purchases and sales   allows you to specify that Simply Accounting insert the cheque number (from your company for cash purchases and from your customer for cash sales).

Allow transactions in previous year   will allow you to enter transactions into the previous year. Selection of this option should be done with extreme care.

Allow transactions in the future (beyond the session date)   will allow you to enter future transactions (such as post-dated cheques or invoices). Care should also be taken with the selection of this option.

Warn if transactions are xx days in the future   will provide you with a warning based on the specified number of days into the future you make an entry.

Warn if accounts are not balanced when entering a new month   will provide you with a warning if you attempt to enter a new month without first balancing the trial balance (opening balances).

Backup frequency   allows you to have Simply Accounting remind you when you should backup your data files to a diskette. You can select from the listed frequencies or enter a custom frequency (number of days).

Figure 3.48
Settings window for Sales Tax

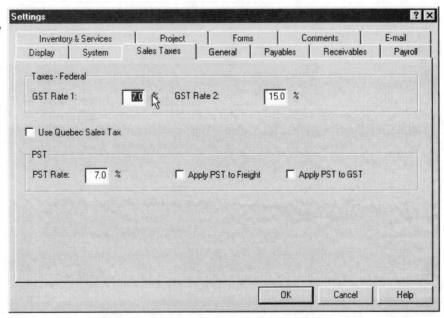

From within the **Settings** window for Sales Tax you can specify the GST, PST, as well as QST (Quebec Sales Tax) options and rates. These options include whether to apply PST to both freight or GST.

General Settings

The General Settings options include activation of the bank reconciliation feature and budgeting feature as well as setting specific options for the other ledgers.

Figure 3.49
Settings window
for General
options

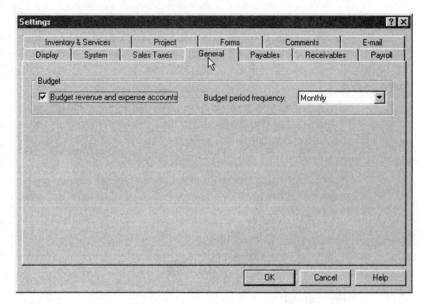

The General options in the **Settings** window include:

Budget Revenue and Expense Accounts	allows your business to budget revenue and expenses against forecasted amounts.

Payables Settings

Figure 3.50
Settings window
for Payables

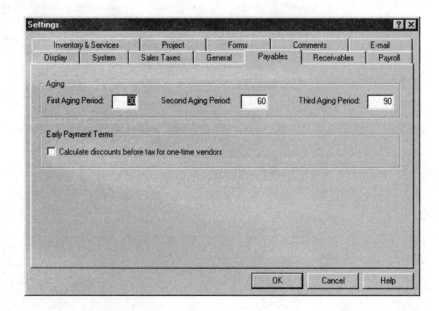

As shown in Figure 3.50, the **Settings** window for payables displays the following options:

Aging	allows you to specify the aging periods for your accounts payable.
Early Payment Terms	will let you select the option to **Calculate discounts before tax for one-time vendors**. One-time vendors are those vendors from whom you will make cash purchases (payment at the time of purchase) and whom you will not want to add to your database.

Receivable Settings

Figure 3.51
Settings window for Receivables

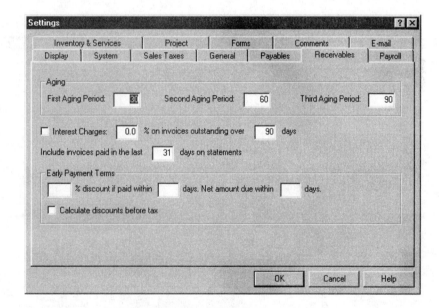

As shown in Figure 3.51, the options for the **Settings** window for Receivables include

Aging	allows you to specify the aging periods for your accounts receivable.
Interest Charges	allows you to select whether interest charges will be applied against overdue customer invoices. You can then select the percentage amount of interest to be charged on the invoice at a selected number of days overdue.

> **HINT:** *Interest charged by Simply Accounting for Windows appears on your customer's statement but is not automatically added to your customer's account balance. You will have to make these entries manually.*

**Include Invoices
Paid in the Last xx
Days on Statement**

this allows you to specify the number of days of paid sales invoices that are to be included in the customer's statement.

**Early Payment
Terms**

allows you to specify the default terms for your company. You do, however, have the flexibility of assigning specific terms for each customer and overriding these terms for each invoice is desired. These terms can include a discount and Simply Accounting will account for these discounts accordingly. You also have the option of whether to calculate the applicable discount before or after taxes.

Payroll Settings

Figure 3.52
Settings window
for Payroll

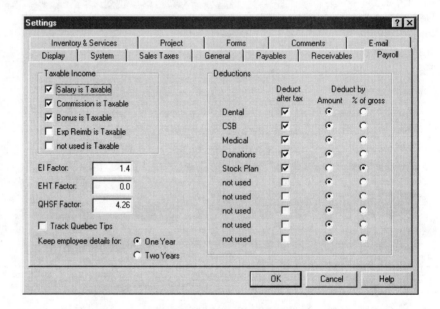

As shown in Figure 3.52, the **Settings** window for Payroll includes the following options:

Taxable Income

will allow you the option of specifying which income types will be subject to payroll taxes.

EI Factor

is the employer portion of employment insurance premiums that are paid in respect to the employee's portion (currently 1.4 times the employees' contributions).

EHT Factor

specifies the employer's Extended Health Tax factor rate that is paid for Ontario employees.

QHSF Factor   specifies the Quebec Health Savings factor rate.

Track Quebec Tips   specifies that Quebec employee tip income will be
                         tracked by Simply Accounting for Windows.

Keep Employee   allows you to specify what period of time employee
Details for   payroll detail is to be retained by Simply Accounting for
                         Windows, (for reference purposes).

Deductions   allows you the options of specifying whether deduction
                         types are to be deducted before or after tax and whether
                         the deduction will be a flat amount of percentage of
                         gross payroll income.

Inventory and Services

Figure 3.53
Settings window
for Inventory
and Services

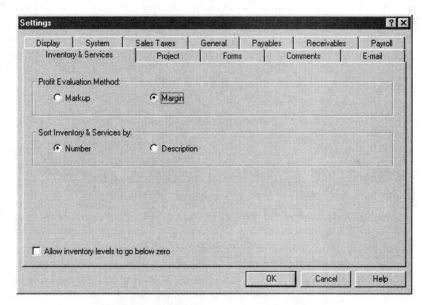

As shown in Figure 3.53, the Settings window for Inventory and Services includes:

Profit Evaluation   allows you to specify whether Simply Accounting for
Method   Windows displays the potential profit from your inven-
                         tory on a *Markup* or *Margin* basis.

> *HINT*: The decision to use either the *Markup* or *Margin* basis will depend on your
> reporting requirements. The formulas are calculated as follows:
>
> *Markup = [(Selling price - Cost) / Cost] x 100*
>
> *Margin = [(Selling price - Cost) / Selling Price] x 100*

Sort Inventory Ledger by	allows you to specify whether your Inventory ledger will be sorted and displayed or printed in the order of *inventory number* or *inventory item description*.
Allow Inventory Levels to go Below Zero	allows your inventory to drop below zero. This is normal with businesses the provide mail order or similar services using on-demand inventory.

Project Settings

Figure 3.54
Settings window
for Project

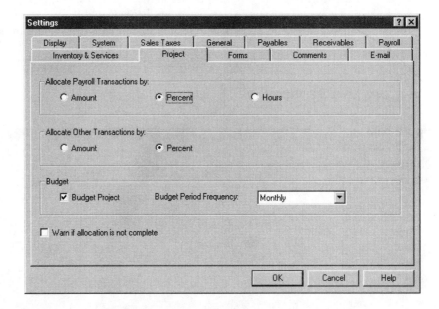

From the **Settings** window for Project (Figure 3.54), you can select from the following options:

Distribute Payroll Journal by	allows you to select how to distribute your payroll journal entries to your projects. You can select to distribute by Amount of payroll dollars, Percentage of payroll dollars per project, or Hours of payroll per project.
Distribute Other Journals by	allows you to distribute all other journals (sales and purchases) by either Amount in dollars or Percentage for each project.
Budget	will allow you to specify the option of budgeting for your projects and the associated budgeting frequency.
Warn if Distribution is Not Complete	provides a warning if you haven't allocated project amounts during a journal entry.

Forms Settings

Figure 3.55
Settings window
for Forms

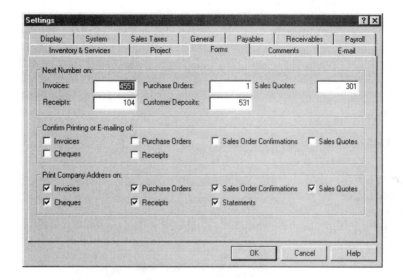

The Settings window for Forms displays the following options:

Next Number on: allows you to specify the next Invoices, Purchase Orders, Sales Quotes, Bank 1 & 2 Cheques, Payroll Cheques, and Receipts.

Confirm Printing for: allows you to have Simply Accounting warn you if you attempt to post an Invoice, Purchase Order, or Cheque without printing the document first.

Print Company Address on: allows you to deselect having your company's address printed on each type of computer forms.

Comments

Figure 3.56
Settings window
for Comments

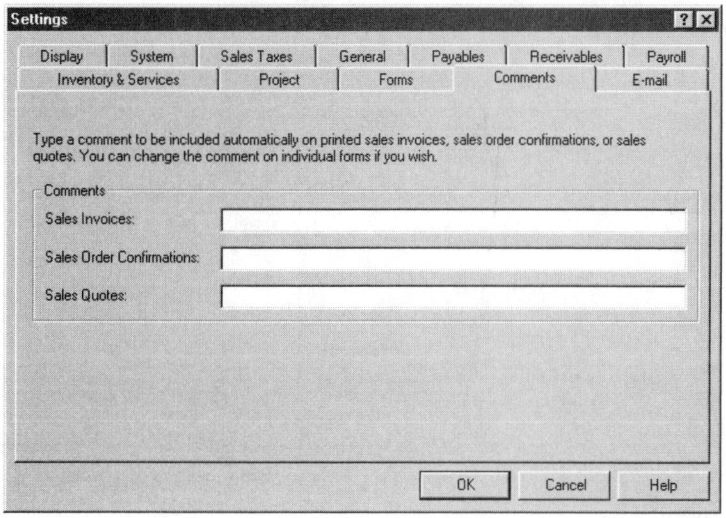

As shown in Figure 3.56, the **Settings** window for Comments, the options are:

Comments   provides you with the flexibility of specifying the default
                          comments that will be printed on the bottom of your Sales
                          Invoices, Sales Order Confirmations, and Sales Quotes.
                          These comments are defaulted and can be customized for
                          each applicable document at the time of entry.

E-mail

Figure 3.57
Settings window
for E-mail

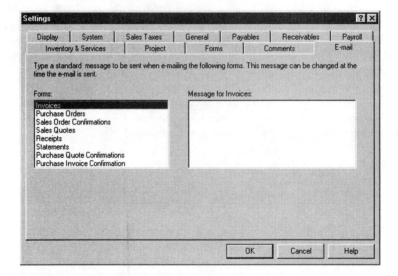

Within Figure 3.57, the **Settings** windows for E-mail allows you to specify the default e-mail
message for each applicable documents that can be sent by e-mail to your customers or vendors.

Other Setup Options

Figure 3.58
Credit Card
Information
window

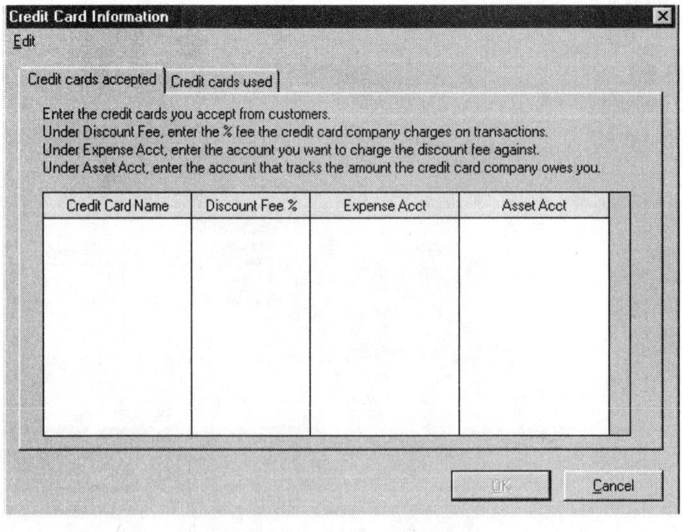

Credit Cards   allows your company to set up the credits cards (Figure 3.58) that are available for use by your customers as well as those credit cards that you use within your business (for purchases). *This feature will be described in detail within the Accounts Receivable and Accounts Payable chapters.*

Figure 3.59
Shipping
Information
window

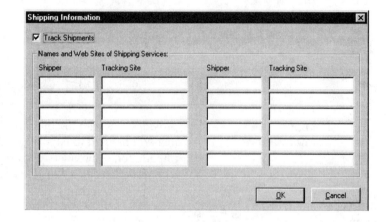

Shippers   provides your business with the option of tracking courier shipments by entering the courier company along with the applicable web site for tracking purposes, (note Figure 3.59). *This feature will be described within the Accounts Receivable chapters.*

Figure 3.60
Currency
Information
window (sample
entered)

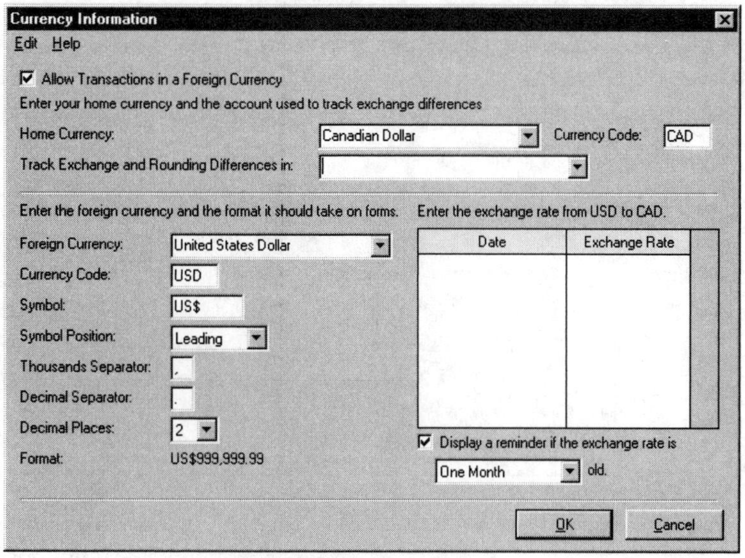

Currencies   allows you to set up the currencies that your company handles. Simply Accounting for Windows will handle the valuation of each of the currencies based on the exchange rates provided. *This option will be discussed in detail in Chapter 4.*

Figure 3.61
Import Duty
Information
window

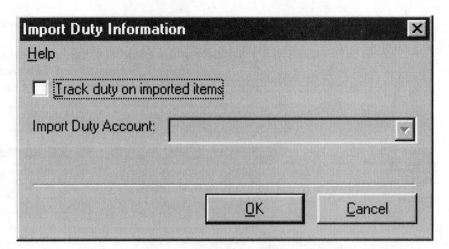

| **Import Duty Information** | provides you with the option of assigning the account that will be used to expense import duties incurred from importation of products. *This options will be discussed within the Accounts Payable chapter.* |

Figure 3.62
Customize
menu

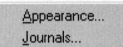

Customize   Will allow you to customize the appearance and features of Simply Accounting such as:

Figure 3.63
Appearance
window

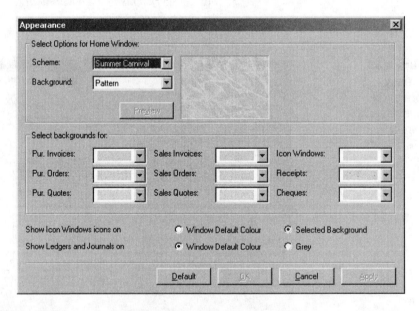

Appearance   provides you the flexibility of selecting the backgrounds, colours, and fonts for use within Simply Accounting windows.

Figure 3.64
Customize
Journals window

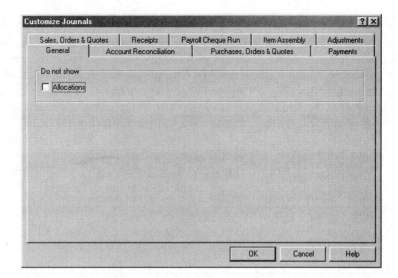

Journals	allows you to customize which options and fields will be displayed within the various Simply Accounting journals.
Linked Accounts	is a required option that will allow you to integrate each of the Simply Accounting for Windows modules. This option must be completed before you can begin to make current transactions into each applicable module. *This option will be reviewed within each applicable module chapter.*
Set Security	allows you to specify up to three levels of security for your accounting data. This can prevent access to information or can restrict access as read-only.

Practice Exercise 3.1

PRACTICE EXERCISE 3.1 CUSTOMIZING SIMPLY ACCOUNTING

Using the above discussion for reference, change the following settings:

In the **Receivable Settings** window (Figure 3.51) select to charge interest on overdue invoices at a rate of 2.5% on invoices outstanding over 30 days.

In the **Receivable Settings** window (Figure 3.51) set the default invoice terms as 2.0% discount within 10 days with net payment within 30 days. This discount should be calculated before tax. Select **Y**es to updating all customers' terms.

In the **Payroll Settings** window (Figure 3.52) select to keep Employee Details for two years.

In the **Inventory & Services Settings** window (Figure 3.53) select to Allow inventory levels to go below zero.

In the **Forms Settings** window (Figure 3.55) change the next Purchase Order number to 105.

In the **Comments Settings** window (Figure 3.57) enter the Default invoice comment as *Thank you for your business*. Also change the Sales Order Confirmations comments to *Please review and confirm your sales order* and the Sales Quotes comments to *Thank you for your interest in our products and services*.

When you have completed this exercise, return to the Simply Accounting - ODC window as shown in Figure 3.37.

SAVING YOUR DATA

When you enter information or business transactions in Simply Accounting for Windows, the information is stored in Random Access Memory (RAM) only and not saved permanently on disk. Although this speeds up working with the data, it has some disadvantages. If for some reason your computer were to "hang"— not respond to any commands — or if there was a power failure you would lose all of the data that you had entered up to that point in the new session. There is also the possibility of accidentally shutting down the computer, which would also lose your data.

Simply Accounting automatically saves your data when you exit the program in the normal manner. Nevertheless, you should save your data to disk regularly while you are working.

Regardless of where you are in the Simply Accounting for Windows program, you can easily save your data to disk using either the keyboard or the mouse.

Press ⌷Ctrl⌷ + ⌷S⌷   to **S**ave your data.

or

At the Simply Accounting - ODC window Figure 3.37, press ⌷Alt⌷ + ⌷F⌷. This command will invoke the **File** menu, which is located on the top menu bar.

If you wish to save your data to the existing data set (ODC.ASC), press ⌷S⌷, which will activate the **Save** menu option.

If you wish to save your data to a new data set, press ⌷A⌷ to active the **Save As** menu option. A window will then appear, asking you to enter the name of the new data set.

or

Click on the ⌷Save⌷ **S**ave icon.

BACKING UP YOUR DATA

Simply Accounting has an automatic backup utility that easily allows you to backup your data.

Continue from the Simply Accounting-ODC window (Figure 3.37) by

Clicking the ⌷Backup⌷ **Backup** icon.

or pressing

⌷Alt⌷ + ⌷F⌷   to select the **File** menu (from within the Simply Accounting - ODC window).

⌷B⌷   to select the **Backup**... menu option.

Figure 3.65
Simply Backup
window

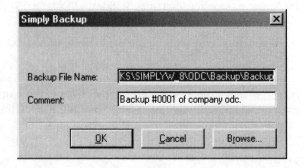

Continue by

Inserting a blank formatted diskette into your disk drive A.

Continue from the Simply Backup window (Figure 3.60) by entering

A:\odc3\odc ⌊ Tab ⌋   to enter the **Backup File Name**.

Using Simply 8 - Chapter 3 ⌊ Tab ⌋   to enter the **Comment**.

The **OK** button is now highlighted. You can now either click on it or press the ⌊ Enter ⌋ key to create your backup.

Figure 3.66
Simply Backup
window
(changed)

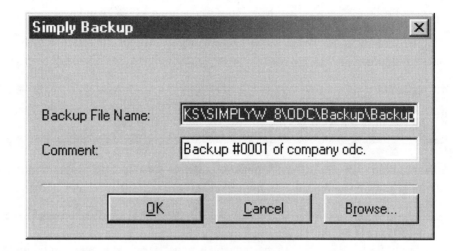

If your Simply Backup window resembles Figure 3.66, continue by

Clicking on the **OK** button.

Simply Accounting for Windows will then back up your data to the A: drive. Once this has been completed, Simply Accounting will provide a Backup complete window (Figure 3.67). Instead of backing up your data files to a diskette you can use any drive on your computer. In some instances, you may have a high capacity ZIP drive or some other removable media. You can also backup your data files to the hard drive as an additional copy in case the main data files are corrupted in some manner.

Figure 3.67
Simply Accounting
Backup complete
window

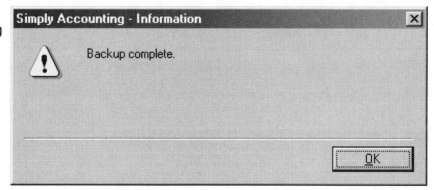

FINISHING THE SESSION

Whenever you are finished working with Simply Accounting you must save your data and you should create a back up as well. Then return to your Windows Desktop or your Windows Program Manager. When you are finished using Simply Accounting for Windows, you can exit the program in three ways.

Make sure you are at the Simply Accounting - ODC window. Then

Press [Alt] + [F] followed by [X] to activate the **E<u>x</u>it** option from the **<u>F</u>ile** menu item.

Use your mouse to click on the **<u>F</u>ile** menu item. Then click on the **E<u>x</u>it** menu option, or double-click on the Control menu box.

Press [Alt] + [F4] at the Simply Accounting - ODC window.

Simply Accounting for Windows will automatically save all entered information to the appropriate data set.

Pressing [Alt] + [F4] to close Simply Accounting will ensure that Simply Accounting for Windows first saves your data before exiting.

It is important that you exit the Simply Accounting for Windows program in this manner to ensure that all accounting information has been saved to disk.

FURTHER PRACTICE

To get further practice with the concepts you have learned in this chapter go to Chapter 14 and work through Section 3 of the National Supply Company.

CHAPTER 4

SETTING UP THE GENERAL LEDGER FOR OVERNIGHT DELIVERY COMPANY

CHAPTER 4

SETTING UP THE GENERAL LEDGER FOR OVERNIGHT DELIVERY COMPANY

OBJECTIVES

After working through this chapter you will be able to

1. Know the purpose of the General Ledger.
2. Develop the chart of accounts.
3. Know the purpose of integration accounts.
4. Enter the chart of accounts into the Simply Accounting program.
5. Resolve problems with accounts as well as edit, modify, and delete accounts.
6. Display and print the chart of accounts.
7. Make journal entries using the General Ledger.
8. Create and recall recurring entries.

PURPOSE OF THE GENERAL LEDGER

The **General Ledger** is the heart of any accounting system. It contains all of the major accounts from which information is compiled to generate the financial statements. You can update these accounts through regular journal entries that represent the business transactions that have taken place over time. By using the double-entry accounting system of debits and credits, you can check to ensure that the accounts balance. This means that the total dollar amount of assets must equal the total dollar amount in the liabilities section and in the equity section. Balancing accounts is done through a trial balance to which adjusting entries can be made before printing the financial statements. Because the General Ledger is the most important part of an accounting system and often the only module that a business needs to computerize, it is necessary to have a good understanding of what that module does.

Look at the cash account in the General Ledger. In this account you keep track of all deposits made to the bank account (debits) and all the cheques, charges, and withdrawals (credits). In addition, you keep track of the date that each transaction took place, the nature of the transaction, and how it originated. The dollar value of each transaction is either added or subtracted from the previous balance. The cash balance at the end of the year represents the amount of money left in the company.

If the company started with a balance of $250.00 on December 1, deposited $500.00 from sales during the day, and wrote a cheque to the telephone company with cheque no. 44 for $142.50, the General Ledger account for cash would resemble the following:

CASH		DR.	CR.	BALANCE
Opening balance				250.00
Dec. 1	Sales Dec. 1.	500.00		750.00
Dec. 1	Cheque #44 Telephone Co.		142.50	607.50

The General Ledger keeps track of all accounts that belong to one of the major categories shown on the balance sheet and income statement — assets, liabilities, owner's equity, revenues, and expenses. At fiscal year-end, the balance in each account will be the amount shown in the appropriate place on the balance sheet and on the income statement.

In converting a manual accounting system to the Simply Accounting for Windows system, we must start with the chart of accounts. The chart of accounts lists each business account along with its assigned number. This chart of accounts must contain every account in the business to which transactions will be posted during the year. Although we can add accounts as needed, it is more cumbersome to add accounts during the data input stage than it is to do so at the beginning.

With a computerized accounting system such as Simply Accounting, you can access 5,000 accounts, which means that expenses can be distributed over more accounts without making the system unmanageable.

By keeping accounts separate, management will have more specific information about the operation of the business. Separate accounts also quickly tell us which costs are too high. It may turn out, for example, that the computer data line in the above example is the culprit responsible for high telephone charges.

Therefore, before we begin the conversion process, we must consider how detailed we want our accounting system to be. The first step is to design a complete chart of accounts before we enter any transactions into the Simply Accounting program. The design of the chart of accounts must comply with the parameters established by the Simply Accounting for Windows system.

DEVELOPING THE CHART OF ACCOUNTS

When setting up your chart of accounts under the Simply Accounting for Windows system, you must consider a number of things.

SECTION HEADINGS AND SECTION TOTALS

A balance sheet consists of three major sections — ASSETS, LIABILITIES and EQUITY. The income statement consists of two major sections — REVENUES and EXPENSES.

The Simply Accounting for Windows system calls these *section headings*. For each section, the program provides a range of accounts which you can use for your business. These account ranges are as follows:

ASSET accounts	1000	to	1999
LIABILITY accounts	2000	to	2999
EQUITY accounts	3000	to	3999
REVENUE accounts	4000	to	4999
EXPENSE accounts	5000	to	5999

Accounts are printed in numerical order within their sections on the financial statements. Each of the five section headings have corresponding section totals. These are:

TOTAL ASSETS

TOTAL LIABILITIES

TOTAL EQUITY

TOTAL REVENUE

TOTAL EXPENSE

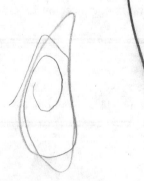

The section headings and section totals are assigned and printed automatically and cannot be changed. You do not have to define or assign account numbers to them.

The Simply Accounting for Windows program arranges these sections in a particular way on the printed financial statements. Accounts in the assets section are shown on the left side of the balance sheet and accounts in the liabilities and equity section are shown on the right. Similarly, accounts under the revenue section are shown on the left and accounts under the expense section are shown on the right.

BLOCK HEADINGS AND BLOCK TOTALS

Under each of these section headings you may have several block headings to allow you to customize these statements for your particular business. Each block heading must have a corresponding block total. For example, you may have CURRENT ASSETS and FIXED ASSETS. The corresponding block totals would be TOTAL CURRENT ASSETS and TOTAL FIXED ASSETS.

Within a particular block you can place accounts on the right or left side. Accounts that do not need subtotals can be placed on the right side. If you place accounts on the left side they must be followed by a subtotal.

In this case, the accounts for "Petty Cash" and "Bank - Royal" are left-side accounts because they are shown on the left side of the asset column. Their total value is shown by the subtotal, Total Cash, a right-side account because it is placed on the right side of the asset section.

Similarly, under the block heading FIXED ASSETS, a number of fixed asset accounts and depreciation accounts are left-side accounts because they are on the left side of the assets section. The Subtotal for these accounts is a right account because it is in the right side of the asset section as is the account for Land.

You must take care when developing the chart of accounts to ensure that you have included proper subtotals and block totals. The program will not print out the reports until this has been corrected. It will, however, provide error messages if you have made mistakes and will not let you go to another phase of the program until the error has been corrected.

Types of Accounts

There are six definable types of accounts in the Simply Accounting for Windows system, each indicated by a letter as follows:

H ~ ~~1000 - 1999~~ This indicates a **Group Heading.** This account is printed in boldface. It is not a postable account, meaning that no dollar amounts can be assigned to it. It is simply a subheading in a section of accounts. Examples are CURRENT ASSETS and CURRENT LIABILITIES shown in Figure 4.20.

A This is also a postable account that will be printed as a **Subgroup Account** within a particular block section. Examples are Cash, Bank - Royal, and Building.

S   This is a **Subgroup Total** account and is used to provide a subgroup total of a group of subgroup accounts immediately above it. The subgroup total is calculated and automatically printed on the right side within the block section. Examples are Total Cash, GST Refund (Owing).

G   This is a postable account, which means that it can have an opening balance and have journal entries posted to it. This account is entered as a **Group Account.** Examples are Cash and Accounts Payable.

X   The **X** account signifies the account that will be used to summarize the current revenues and expenses or the current earnings of the business. Each time a journal entry that affects a revenue or expense account is made, the value of current earnings changes. It is not a postable account and there can be only one of these types of accounts in the chart of accounts. It is automatically placed on the right side within the equity section.

T   This represents a **Group Total**. It represents the total balance of all right-side accounts and all subtotal accounts above it or since the last block total. It is not a postable account so you cannot assign opening balances to it or enter journal entries into it. The program automatically calculates the total and prints the balance on the right side of the block section. Examples are TOTAL ASSETS and TOTAL CURRENT LIABILITIES.

Postable and Non-Postable Accounts

As is probably evident by now, Simply Accounting for Windows identifies all block headings, subtotal accounts, right- and left-side accounts, and block totals as accounts. However, not all of these so-called accounts are postable accounts. **Postable** accounts can have opening balances and can have journal entries debited or credited to them. **Non-postable** accounts are block headings, block totals, and subtotal accounts.

Properties of Accounts

As mentioned, Simply Accounting for Windows allows you to use a four-digit numbering system. Accounts may have a positive or negative value up to $999,999,999.99. The total of any account may not exceed this amount.

An account in the General Ledger can have a negative balance. Normally asset accounts have debit balances. However, if you were overdrawn in your bank account, then you would have a credit balance in this account that would be shown as a negative amount. Accumulated depreciation and other accounts that may have credit balances but that are normally shown under the assets section are also shown with negative signs.

Integration Accounts

Simply Accounting for Windows is a fully integrated accounting system. Some accounts in the General Ledger will therefore be automatically updated when a journal entry is made in any other module. For example, when you make a payment in the Purchases Journal, you are prompted for the name of the supplier and the invoices that you wish to pay. The associated journal entry credits the cash account and debits the accounts payable account in the General Ledger automatically. To do that, the program must know which accounts are to be associated in this manner.

Integration accounts are shown in boldface. Other accounts are set up to help you create a basic chart of accounts. These extra accounts as well as some of the integration accounts can be changed or deleted if necessary.

SETTING UP THE CHART OF ACCOUNTS

The easiest way to create a chart of accounts for the Simply Accounting for Windows system is to take a set of your detailed financial statements that were prepared previously and, using the numbering parameters above, assign an account number to each account and identify what type of account it is. This will ensure that you will not leave out any accounts and that all the accounts are in the correct order.

Figures 4.1A and 4.1B show the financial statements for Overnight Delivery Company at July 31, 2001. Since the previous accounting system was a manual system, these financial statements are laid out differently from the layout provided by the Simply Accounting for Windows system — liabilities follow assets and equity follows liabilities. Similarly, in the income statement, expenses follow revenues.

Overnight Delivery Company
Balance Sheet
July 31, 2001

ASSETS
CURRENT ASSETS

Petty Cash	200.00	
Bank - Royal	18,525.35	
Bank - Bank of Montreal	100.00	
Total Cash		18,825.35
Accounts Receivable		10,312.06
Inventory - Truck Parts		7,905.00
Office Supplies		55.67
Prepaid Insurance		435.00
TOTAL CURRENT ASSETS		37,533.08

FIXED ASSETS

Building	31,000.00	
Accm Depn - Building	(5,000.00)	
Equipment	1,700.00	
Accm Depn - Equipment	(500.00)	
Automotive	35,224.00	
Accm Depn - Automotive	(5,500.00)	
Leasehold Improvements	12,150.00	
Accm Amort - Leaseholds	(3,400.00)	
Subtotal		65,674.00
Land		18,000.00
TOTAL FIXED ASSETS		83,674.00
TOTAL ASSETS		121,207.08

LIABILITIES
CURRENT LIABILITIES

Accounts Payable	20,730.21
GST Charged on Sales	0.00
GST Paid on Purchases	0.00
GST Owing (Refund)	0.00
PST Payable	0.00
Interest Payable	0.00
Wages Payable	0.00
TOTAL CURRENT LIABILITIES	20,730.21

LONG-TERM DEBT

Mortgage Payable	42,797.00
Note Payable - L. Cronkin	2,000.00
TOTAL LONG-TERM DEBT	44,797.00
TOTAL LIABILITIES	65,527.21

EQUITY
CAPITAL

Capital Account - J. Demers	24,274.87
Current Earnings	31,406.00
TOTAL EQUITY	55,680.87
TOTAL LIABILITIES AND EQUITY	121,207.08

Figure 4.1A Balance Sheet for Overnight Delivery Company as at July 31, 2001, prior to conversion

Overnight Delivery Company
Statement of Income
For the year ended July 31, 2001

SALES
Sales - Truck Parts	16,666.55
TOTAL SALES REVENUE	16,666.55

SERVICE
Regular Freight	59,615.00
Overnight Freight	23,519.00
Air Freight	8,615.00
TOTAL SERVICE REVENUE	91,749.00

MISC REVENUE
Bank Interest	0.00
TOTAL MSC REVENUE	0.00

TOTAL REVENUE	108,415.55

COST OF SALES
Cost of Sales - Truck Parts	10,358.00
TOTAL COST OF SALES	10,358.00

OPERATING EXPENSES
Supplies	985.00
Fuel and Oil	14,519.00
Repairs and Maintenance	3,615.00
Insurance	1,415.00
TOTAL OPERATING EXPENSES	20,534.00

ADMINISTRATIVE EXPENSES
Rent	3,900.00
Telephone and Pager	2,453.85
Utilities	1,615.87
Office Stationery	456.78
Coffee Supplies	316.55
Janitorial	1,457.22
Salaries and Benefits	23,659.55
Accounting and Legal	3,456.00
Advertising and Promotion	2,456.00
Licences	1,555.00
Insurance and Taxes	122.00
Bank Charges and Interest	2,357.73
Other Freight	12.00
Depreciation and Amortization	2,300.00
TOTAL ADMINISTRATIVE EXPENSES	46,118.55

TOTAL EXPENSES	77,010.55

NET INCOME	31,405.00

Figure 4.1B Income Statement for Overnight Delivery Company as at July 31, 2001, prior to conversion

Assigning Account Numbers

When assigning account numbers, remember one of the rules of good coding: leave room between the numbers so that you can add other accounts later if necessary. For example, if you used the following account numbers at the beginning, you may have problems later if you want to add additional accounts.

1000	Current Assets
1001	Petty Cash
1002	Bank
1003	Accounts Receivable
1004	Total Current Assets

With this number system, you couldn't add a second bank account because you couldn't fit it in. Therefore you should leave room between the numbers to fit in future accounts as needed. Ensure that your chart of accounts is properly designed from the start as it is more difficult to change it later.

Practice Exercise 4.1

Assign account numbers and account types to each item in the set of financial statements for Overnight Delivery Company shown in Figure 4.2A and Figure 4.2B. Remember the parameters of the Simply Accounting program for grouping accounts. Use pencil so you can change the numbers if required.

NOTE: Account numbers and types are shown for the first few accounts as an example. The asterisks represent accounts that are already present in the chart of accounts that was provided on the disk in this book. Do not remove them. Be sure to position your new accounts between the existing ones, remembering the numbering system outlined above. The account headings with broken lines beside them must remain.

IMPORTANT NOTE: You should work through this exercise yourself on a separate piece of paper so that you understand how to set up the chart of accounts. You should then compare your account codes to the printout of the chart of accounts in Figure 4.13. If your account codes differ from those shown you should change them to conform to the coding in this book because the discussion and exercises in the rest of this book will refer to our account coding. If you want to keep your own account coding you will have to adjust your account entries when you enter transactions later.

Overnight Delivery Company
Balance Sheet
July 31, 2001

Account Type	Description	Amount		Number
	ASSETS			
H	CURRENT ASSETS			
A	Petty Cash	200.00		1030
A	Bank - Royal	18,525.35		1040
A	Bank - Bank of Montreal	100.00		1050
S	Total Cash	18,825.35		1100
G	Accounts Receivable	10,312.06		1150
G	Inventory - Truck Parts	7,905.00		1200
G	Office Supplies	55.67		1250
G	Prepaid Insurance	435.00		1300
T	TOTAL CURRENT ASSETS	37,533.08		1400
	FIXED ASSETS			
	Building	31,000.00		
	Accm Depn - Building		(5,000.00)	
	Equipment	1,700.00		
	Accm Depn - Equipment		(500.00)	
	Automotive	35,224.00		
	Accm Depn - Automotive		(5,500.00)	
	Leasehold Improvements	12,150.00		
	Accm Amort - Leaseholds		(3,400.00)	
	Subtotal	65,674.00		
	Land	18,000.00		
	TOTAL FIXED ASSETS	83,674.00		
	TOTAL ASSETS	121,207.08		

Account Type	Description	Amount	Number
	LIABILITIES		
H	CURRENT LIABILITIES		2000
G	Accounts Payable	20,730.21	2050*
	GST Charged on Sales	0.00	
	GST Paid on Purchases	0.00	
	GST Owing (Refund)	0.00	
	PST Payable	0.00	
	Interest Payable	0.00	
	Wages Payable	0.00	
T *	TOTAL CURRENT LIABILITIES	20,730.21	2600
	LONG - TERM DEBT		
	Mortgage Payable	42,797.00	
	Note Payable - L. Cronkin	2,000.00	
	TOTAL LONG - TERM DEBT	44,797.00	
	TOTAL LIABILITIES	65,527.21	
	EQUITY		
H	CAPITAL		3500*
G	Capital - J. Demers	24,274.87	3550*
G	Current Earnings	31,406.00	3600*
T	TOTAL EQUITY	55,680.87	3700*
	TOTAL LIABILITIES AND EQUITY	121,207.08	

Figure 4.2A Balance Sheet for Overnight Delivery Company

Overnight Delivery Company
Statement of Income
For the year ended July 31, 2001

Account Number		Amount	Account Type
	REVENUE		
*			
	SALES		
	Sales - Truck Parts	16,666.55	
	TOTAL SALES REVENUE	16,666.55	
	SERVICE		
	Regular Freight	59,615.00	
	Overnight Freight	23,519.00	
	Air Freight	8,615.00	
	TOTAL SERVICE REVENUE	91,749.00	
	MISC REVENUE		
	Bank Interest	0.00	
	TOTAL MISC REVENUE	0.00	
	TOTAL REVENUE	108,415.55	
	EXPENSE		
	COST OF SALES		
	Cost of Sales - Truck Parts	10,358.00	
	TOTAL COST OF SALES	10,358.00	
	OPERATING EXPENSES		
	Supplies	985.00	
	Fuel and Oil	14,519.00	
	Repairs and Maintenance	3,615.00	
	Insurance	1,415.00	
	TOTAL OPERATING EXPENSES	20,534.00	
	ADMINISTRATIVE EXPENSES		
	Rent	3,900.00	
	Telephone and Pager	2,453.85	
	Utilities	1,615.87	
	Office Stationery	456.78	
	Coffee Supplies	316.55	
	Janitorial	1,457.22	
	Salaries and Benefits	23,659.55	
	Accounting and Legal	3,456.00	
	Advertising and Promotion	2,456.00	
	Licences	1,555.00	
	Insurance and Taxes	122.00	
	Bank Charges and Interest	2,357.73	
	Other Freight	12.00	
	Depreciation	2,300.00	
	TOTAL ADMINISTRATIVE EXPENSES	46,118.55	
	TOTAL EXPENSE	77,010.55	*
	NET INCOME	31,406.00	*

Figure 4.2B Income Statement for Overnight Delivery Company

ENTERING THE CHART OF ACCOUNTS
INTO THE SIMPLY ACCOUNTING PROGRAM

We will assume that you have loaded Windows and that you are at the Windows desktop.

Important Note: Before you continue, copy the starter files from the included CD-ROM. The source directory should be X:\sw0803. We would suggest that you use the enclosed installation program (X:\Setup) to install these files. Remember that X: represents the drive that contains your CD-ROM.

These files contain the majority of the above accounts, thus preventing you from repetitive data entry.

Click the start button in the lower left-hand corner of your screen. From the program list pick the Simply Accounting program. Then click on the Simply Accounting program icon to start the program.

Figure 4.3
Simply Accounting
Program Icon

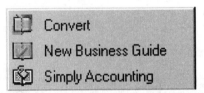

In a few moments, the opening screen that contains your name and registration number will appear. When this screen disappears you will see the Simply Accounting - Select Company window as shown in Figure 4.4.

Figure 4.4
Simply
Accounting -
Select Company
window

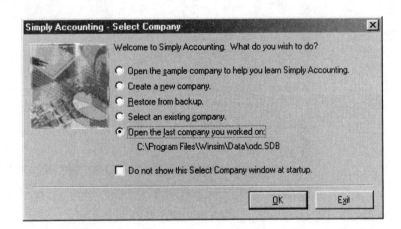

In the Simply Accounting - Select Company window, you can select a previously opened file, select another company file, create a new file, or open the sample file provided by Simply Accounting for Windows. Continue by

Selecting *Open the last company you worked on,* which should be
C:\PROGRAM FILES\WINSIM\DATA\ODC.ASC.

If the above file and path are not displayed with the above option, choose *Select an existing company* option and locate the appropriate data file for use within this book.

Click on the **OK** button.

Figure 4.5
Simply Accounting -
Session Date

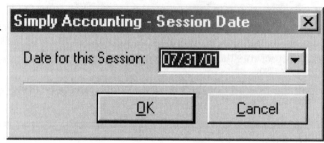

Simply Accounting for Windows will now prompt you to select the appropriate Session Date (Figure 4.5). This date will provide you with a data entry window. However because you have not entered any General Ledger accounts, you will be unable to enter journal entries at this point.
Continue by

Clicking on the **OK** button.

Figure 4.6
Simply Accounting -
ODC window

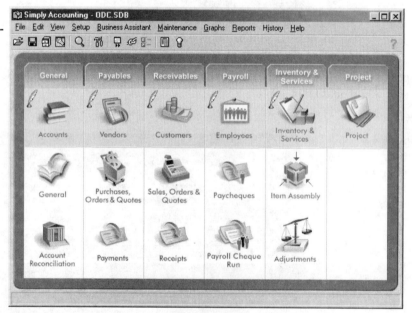

OPENING THE GENERAL LEDGER

From the Simply Accounting - ODC window (Figure 4.6) you must now invoke the General Ledger. Continue by

Double-clicking on the **Accounts** icon.

Figure 4.7
Accounts window

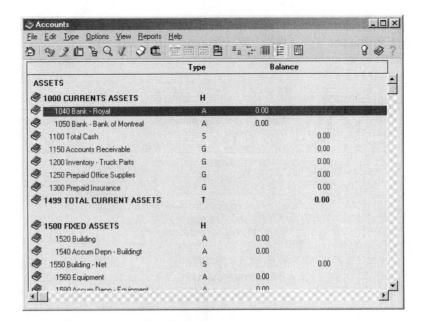

The General Ledger **Accounts** window will now be displayed (Figure 4.7). You want to display the chart of accounts report. Continue from the Accounts window, (Figure 4.7) by

Moving your mouse cursor to the **Reports** menu option that appears at the top of the Accounts window (see Figure 4.7).

Clicking your mouse button to activate the **Reports** option.

Figure 4.8
Reports menu

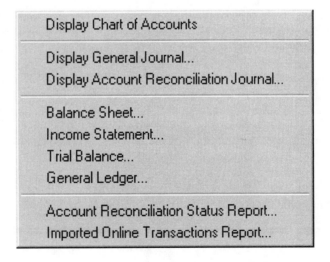

Click on the **Display Chart of Accounts** option from within the **Reports** menu (Figure 4.8).

Figure 4.9
Chart of Accounts
window

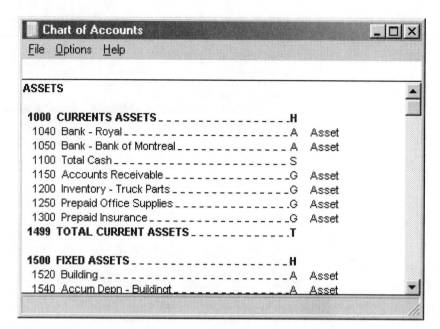

As shown in Figure 4.9, your Chart of Accounts only contains one account that is the program's default account for Current Earnings. If there were more accounts you could view them by pressing or by clicking your mouse cursor on ⬇ in the scroll box on the right side of the window (this scroll bar will automatically appear should there be more account icons then can be displayed within the window).

Continue from within the Chart of Accounts window by either

Clicking the close icon (the box with the x) located in the top-right corner of the Chart of Accounts window (Figure 4.9). This will close the Chart of Accounts window. You will return to the Accounts window (Figure 4.7).

or pressing

Alt + F4   to close the Chart of Accounts window. You will return to the Accounts window (see Figure 4.7).

Adding Accounts to the Existing Chart of Accounts for ODC

You can now add the account names and numbers to the Simply Accounting for Windows system.

Important Note: Be sure to use the account numbers shown in Figure 4.2A and 4.2B rather than the ones you entered as a practice exercise to ensure compatibility with the rest of the book.

Continue from the Accounts window (Figure 4.7) by either

> Clicking the **Create** icon.

or pressing

> [Alt] + [E]   to display the **Edit** menu
>
> [C]   to select the **Create** menu option. You can also click on Create with your mouse cursor.

Figure 4.10
General Ledger
window

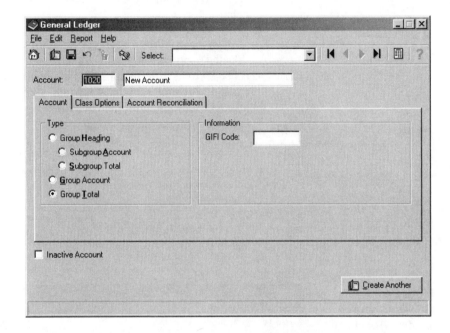

As displayed in the General Ledger window (Figure 4.10), the cursor is now blinking in the Account field.

> We will continue with the entry of the first account. Continue by entering

> **1030** [Tab]   to add the new **Account** under number 1030.

Once you press the [Tab] key to move to the next field, the Simply Accounting for Windows program highlights the words "New Account" in the account name field. You can overwrite these words by typing a new account name, or you can edit any name that appears by using the [←] or [→]. In this case type

> **Petty Cash** [Tab]   to enter the account name.

> [Alt] + [A]   to change the **Account Type** to a **Subgroup Account**. Simply Accounting for Windows defaults to a **Group Account** because this is the most common type of account used. We want a subgroup of all cash accounts, so this account must be a **Subgroup Account**. You can also select the **Subgroup Account** by placing your mouse cursor on the button next to it.

Tab	to move to the GIFI Code.

Tab	to bypass the **GIFI Code** field. This option will allow you to enter the specific GIFI code as defined by Revenue Canada. This reporting will allow integration with your business's taxation reporting.

Tab	to bypass <u>O</u>**mit from Financial Statements if Balance is Zero.** If you were to check this box, Simply Accounting would not print the account if it had a zero balance. For this practice case, we want all accounts printed regardless of the account balance.

Tab	to bypass the **A<u>l</u>low Project Allocations.** This option (if selected) will permit you to allocate amounts (from this account) to user-defined projects. While project costing is normally for income statement accounts only, Simply Accounting also provides you with the flexibility of project costing your balance sheet accounts as well.

Tab	normally you would now enter the opening **balance** for the Petty Cash account. However, in this tutorial we will enter the chart of accounts first. You will enter the opening balances in Chapter 5.

Tab	to bypass the **Inactive Account** option. This option can be selected.

Figure 4.11
General Ledger
window (Petty
Cash entered)

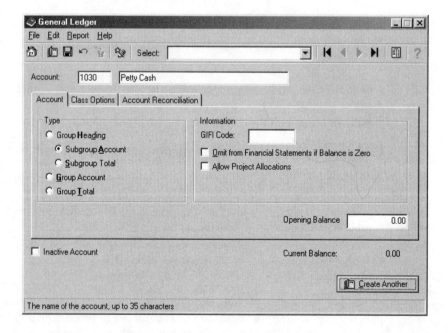

Once you have compared your General Ledger window to Figure 4.11 for accuracy, continue by either

> Clicking on the **Create Another** button.

or pressing

> [Alt] + [C]   to **Create** the Petty Cash account and save it to memory. Once Simply Accounting has saved the entry, a blank new account General Ledger window will be displayed (Figure 4.10).

Before we enter any more accounts, let's display the existing chart of accounts.

If you have not retrieved the template for ODC from your CD-ROM and want to instead enter all of the accounts, review Figure 4.20 and enter the appropriate account.

Displaying the Chart of Accounts

As you enter new accounts, you may want to display the chart of accounts periodically to check it. With your mouse

> Click on the **Reports** menu option in the General Ledger window.

> Click on the **Display Chart of Accounts** submenu option.

or press

> [Alt] + [R]   to invoke the **Report** menu option

> [D]   to invoke the **Display Chart of Accounts** submenu option

Figure 4.12
Chart of Accounts window

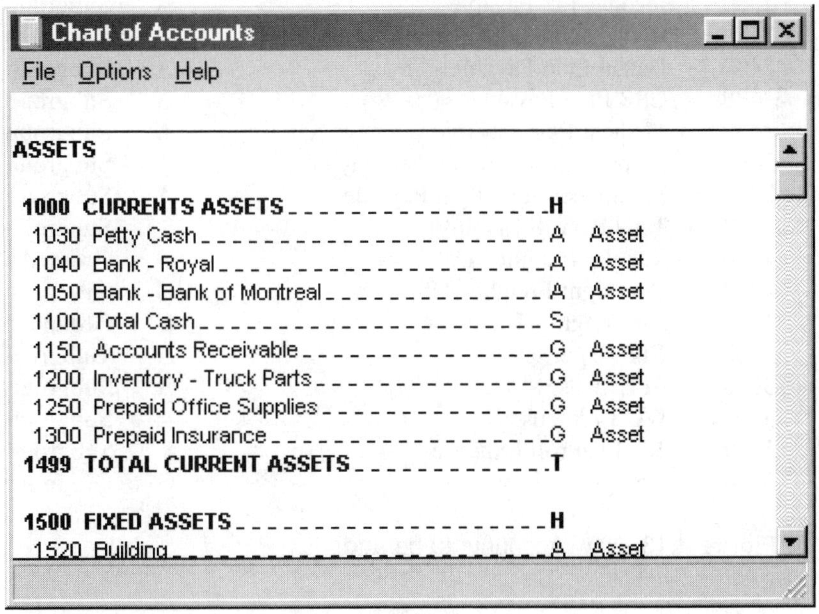

Within the Chart of Accounts window (Figure 4.12), you can move down through the chart by clicking on the [↓] in the scroll box. Alternately, you can move around the Chart of Accounts window by pressing the [↑], [↓], [←] or [→] arrow keys.

You can maximize the window to fill the screen by clicking on the maximize icon located in the top-right corner of the Chart of Accounts window.

Continue from the Chart of Accounts window by either

Clicking the close icon located in the top-right corner of the Chart of Accounts window (Figure 4.12). This will in turn close the Chart of Accounts window. You will return to the General Ledger window (Figure 4.11).

Or press

[Alt] + [F4]   to close the Chart of Accounts window. You will return to the General Ledger window (Figure 4.11).

Practice Exercise 4.2

Repeat the steps outlined above to add the remainder of the accounts shown in Figure 4.13. This exercise would apply if you have retrieved the ODC template from the enclosed CD-ROM

1060	Bank - Seafirst US Dollar	A	Subgroup Account
1600	Automotive	A	Subgroup Account
1620	Accum Amort - Automotive	A	Subgroup Account
1630	Automotive - Net	S	Subgroup Total
2320	CPP Payable	A	Subgroup Account
2340	EI Payable	A	Subgroup Account
2360	Income Tax Payable	A	Subgroup Account
2380	WCB Payable	A	Subgroup Account
2400	Dental Plan Payable	A	Subgroup Account
2420	CSB Plan Payable	A	Subgroup Account
2440	Medical Plan Payable	A	Subgroup Account
2460	Employee Donations Plan Payable	A	Subgroup Account
2470	Employee Stock Plan Payable	A	Subgroup Account
2499	Total Payroll Liability	S	Subgroup Total
4320	Regular Freight - US	G	Group Account
4340	Overnight Freight - US	G	Group Account
4360	Air Freight - US	G	Group Account
5660	CPP Expense	A	Subgroup Account
5680	EI Expense	A	Subgroup Account
5700	WCB Expense	A	Subgroup Account
5799	Total Payroll Expense	S	Subgroup Total
5950	Foreign exchange	G	Group Account

Figure 4.13 New Accounts to be added

Modifying Accounts

To modify an account — change the name, define reconciliation and on-line banking status, enter an opening balance — start from the **General Ledger** window shown in Figure 4.12.

There are two arrows to the right of the window. To scroll through the accounts, place your mouse cursor on the (↓) and click on it. Each time you click, you move to the next account. If you hold down the left mouse button, you will move through the accounts quickly.

As you scroll through the accounts, you will notice that a small flashing box moves down the scroll bar. The location of this box in relation to the top and bottom of the scroll bar gives you an approximate idea of where you are in the chart of accounts. If you place your mouse cursor on this box and press the left mouse button and hold it down, you can then drag this box up or down. As soon as you release the mouse button, the program will display the account that resides at that location in the chart of accounts. The closer you are to the bottom of the scroll bar, the closer you are to the end of your chart of accounts. With practice you can use this method to quickly jump to the approximate place in your chart of accounts and then slowly scroll backwards or forwards to the exact account you want.

You can also get to the appropriate account by selecting it from the pull down **Select** field (top middle of General Ledger window).

Another method to get to an account quickly is to use the Find submenu option, which is located on the **Edit** menu.

Click on it or use your keyboard to open the Find Account window (Alt) + (E), (F). If you know the approximate number of the account you can type in the first number and the cursor highlight jumps to the first account beginning with that number. You can then click on the up or down arrows to move the highlight over the account that you want in that number group. You can also use the arrow keys on your keyboard.

When you have the proper account highlighted, click on the **Find** button or press (Tab) followed by (Enter). You will then return to the General Ledger window showing the proper account.

To modify any of the information, press (Tab) to move to the desired field. This highlights the existing information which is removed as soon as you start typing in the new account name, for example. If you just want to edit a character, then click on that character which removes the highlight. Then type in the change and remove any excess letters with the Backspace key or the Delete key.

To save the changes made, either close the General Ledger window or retrieve a different account. You will be prompted to either confirm each change or have Simply Accounting save the changes automatically.

Practice Exercise 4.3

MODIFICATION OF ACCOUNTS
Continue with the retrieval and modification of the following accounts:

Account 2300 (Wages Payable) to change the account type from Group Account to Subgroup Account.

Account 5640 (Salaries and Benefits) to change the account type from Group Account to Subgroup Account.

Once you have completed this exercise, return to the Simply Accounting - ODC Window.

PROBLEMS WITH ACCOUNTS

Once you have entered all of the accounts, you will want to display the balance sheet. To do so, return to the Simply Accounting - ODC window. (Figure 4.6).Continue by either

> Clicking on the **Reports** menu.

or pressing

 to select the **Reports** menu.

Figure 4.14
Reports menu

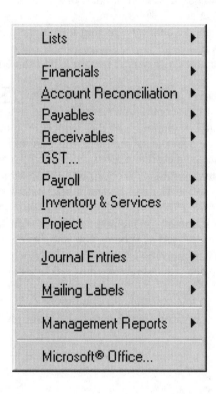

From the Reports menu (Figure 4.14), continue by either

> Clicking on the **Financials** menu option.

or pressing

F to select the **Financials** menu option.

Figure 4.15
Reports (Financials
option) window

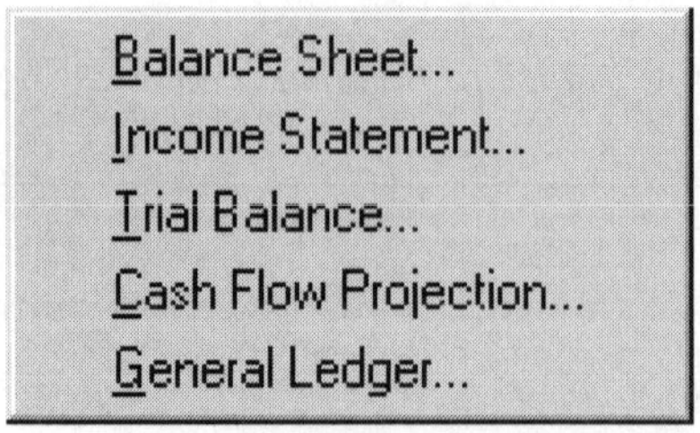

Continue from the Reports - Financials menu (Figure 4.15) by either

Clicking on the **B**alance Sheet menu command.

or pressing

B
to select the **B**alance Sheet menu command.

If there is an error in your chart of accounts, this error will be displayed with an error message similar to Figure 4.16.

Figure 4.16
Chart of Accounts
Error window

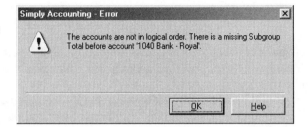

To correct this error, you would return to the Accounts window, by selecting the Accounts icon from the Simply Accounting - ODC window. From the Accounts window, you would locate and edit the account causing the error message. You would then return to the Simply Accounting - ODC window to re-display the Balance Sheet report window (see above example). If you receive an error message you can correct the problem by displaying the Chart of Accounts and comparing them to Figure 4.20. However, if you were setting up your chart of accounts for your business you would display it on the screen or print it out. Two common problems are caused by improper account types and missing block headings and totals. Check for the following:

Make sure that all accounts are numbered according to the Simply Accounting for Windows system parameters. Also make sure they are of the proper type. For example, if you have a series of left accounts you must have a subtotal account.

Make sure that you have a block heading and a corresponding block total account.

You will continue to get an error message until you resolve all problems of this nature.
If there are no errors, you will be prompted for the selection of the type of balance sheet (comparative or normal) along with the reporting date. Continue by

Clicking the **OK** button to confirm the default **As at** date of 07/31/01.

Figure 4.17
Balance
Sheet window

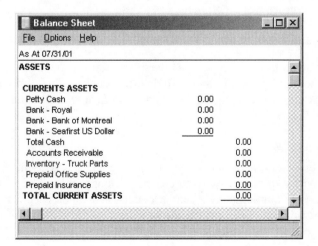

Simply Accounting will now display the Balance Sheet window displayed as shown in Figure 4.17. Continue from the Balance Sheet window (Figure 4.17) by either

Clicking on the close icon. You will then return to the Simply Accounting - ODC window (Figure 4.6)

or pressing

| Alt | + | F4 | to close the Balance Sheet window and return to the Simply Accounting - ODC window (Figure 4.6).

DELETING ACCOUNTS

Because the Simply Accounting for Windows system allows you to add new accounts as your business grows, you will not have to be concerned about running out of account number space. Nevertheless, you should only keep the accounts that are necessary. Unused accounts take up memory and may make your system more difficult to manage. However, do not delete any integration accounts which are required for the program to update the General Ledger accounts automatically. You also cannot delete an account that has had transactions posted to it. If you attempt to delete one of these accounts, the program will print a message on the screen, indicating that the account cannot be deleted.

To delete an existing unused account, start from the **General Ledger** window.

Find the account that you want to delete by either scrolling through the **General Ledger** window or by using the **Find** menu option located on the **Edit** menu.

To delete the account, press

| Alt | + | F | to invoke the **File** menu option

| R | to invoke the **Remove** submenu option

| Y | to confirm the deletion of the displayed accounts. If you decide not to delete the account, you would press | N | to invoke the **No** button.

You can also use your mouse to complete the above set of commands.

Click on the **Edit** menu option.

Click on the **Remove** menu option.

Click on the **Yes** button to delete the account.

You can also remove an account by clicking on the appropriate account icon in the Accounts window (Figure 4.9) to highlight the account. To delete it, click on the third icon in the menu bar which resembles a waste basket. You are then asked to confirm your decision.

WORKING WITH CLASSES

Simply Accounting for Windows allows you to group your chart of accounts by type. This feature allows you to report your company's figures by selecting groups of accounts. An example would be the reporting of your company's bank accounts. Instead of selecting the various accounts, you can instead select to report the *Banks* class.

Figure 4.18
General Ledger -
Class Options window

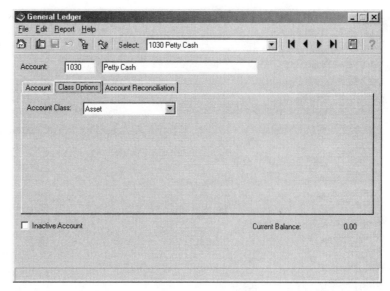

As shown in Figure 4.18, the class option can be modified within the General Ledger window.

Practice Exercise 4.4

PRACTICE EXERCISE 4.4
Continue with the modification of the class option for the accounts shown in
Figure 4.19.
Once you have completed this exercise, return to the Simply Accounting - ODC window
(Figure 4.6).

Account		**Class**
1030	Petty Cash	Cash
1040	Bank - Royal	Bank (leave options blank)
1050	Bank - Bank of Montreal	Bank (leave options blank)
1060	Bank - Seafirst US Dollar	Bank (leave options blank)
1150	Accounts Receivable	Accounts Receivable
1200	Inventory - Truck Parts	Inventory
1250	Prepaid Office Supplies	Current Asset
1300	Prepaid Insurance	Current Asset
1520	Building	Capital Asset
1540	Accum Depn - Building	Capital Asset
1560	Equipment	Capital Asset
1580	Accum Depn - Equipment	Capital Asset
1600	Automotive	Capital Asset
1620	Accum Depn - Automotive	Capital Asset
1640	Leasehold Improvements	Capital Asset
1660	Accum Amort - Leaseholds	Capital Asset
1800	Land	Capital Asset
2050	Accounts Payable	Accounts Payable
2100	GST Charged on Sales	Accounts Payable

2110	GST Paid on Purchases	Accounts Payable
2150	PST Payable	Accounts Payable
2200	Interest Payable	Debt
2300	Wages Payable	Current Liability
2320	CPP Payable	Current Liability
2340	EI Payable	Current Liability
2360	Income Tax Payable	Current Liability
2380	WCB Payable	Current Liability
2400	Dental Plan Payable	Current Liability
2420	CSB Plan Payable	Current Liability
2440	Medical Plan Payable	Current Liability
2460	Employee Donations Plan Payable	Current Liability
2470	Employee Stock Plan Payable	Current Liability
2750	Mortgage Payable	Debt
2770	Note Payable - L. Cronkin	Debt
3550	Capital - J. Demers	Owner/Partner Contributions
4050	Sales - Truck Parts	Revenue
4220	Regular Freight	Revenue
4240	Overnight Freight	Revenue
4260	Air Freight	Revenue
4320	Regular Freight - US	Revenue
4340	Overnight Freight - US	Revenue
4360	Air Freight - US	Revenue
4410	Bank Interest	Other Revenue
4430	Purchase Discounts	Other Revenue
5050	Cost of Sales - Truck Parts	Cost of Sales
5220	Supplies	Expense
5240	Fuel and Oil	Expense
5260	Repairs and Maintenance	Expense
5280	Insurance	Expense
5300	Sales Discounts	Expense
5520	Rent	General & Admin Expense
5540	Telephone and Long Distance	General & Admin Expense
5560	Utilities	General & Admin Expense
5580	Office Stationery	General & Admin Expense
5600	Coffee Supplies	General & Admin Expense
5620	Janitorial	General & Admin Expense
5640	Salaries and Benefits	Payroll Expense
5660	CPP Expense	Payroll Expense
5680	EI Expense	Payroll Expense
5700	WCB Expense	Payroll Expense
5800	Accounting and Legal	General & Admin Expense
5820	Advertising and Promotion	General & Admin Expense
5840	Licenses and Permits	General & Admin Expense
5860	Insurance and Taxes	General & Admin Expense
5880	Bank Charges and Interest	General & Admin Expense
5900	Other Freight	General & Admin Expense
5920	Depreciation	Expense
5950	Foreign exchange	Expense

Figure 4.19 Chart of Accounts (Class Option)

PRINTING THE CHART OF ACCOUNTS

Be sure that your computer is properly connected to the printer and that the printer is on-line. Continue from the Simply Accounting - ODC window (Figure 4.6) by

Clicking on the **Report** menu option (Figure 4.14).

Clicking on the **Lists** menu option.

Clicking on **Chart of Accounts** menu option.

Once your screen displays the chart of accounts window, click on the **File** menu option.

Click on the **Print** menu option.

Your chart of accounts should resemble Figure 4.20, except that liabilities are printed after assets, and expenses are printed after revenues.

Figure 4.20 Chart of Accounts report

Overnight Delivery Company
Chart of Accounts

ASSETS

1000	CURRENTS ASSETS	H	
1030	Petty Cash	A	Cash
1040	Bank - Royal	A	Bank
1050	Bank - Bank of Montreal	A	Bank
1060	Bank - Seafirst US Dollar	A	Bank
1100	Total Cash	S	
1150	Accounts Receivable	G	Accounts Receivable
1200	Inventory - Truck Parts	G	Inventory
1250	Prepaid Office Supplies	G	Current Asset
1300	Prepaid Insurance	G	Current Asset
1499	TOTAL CURRENT ASSETS	T	
1500	FIXED ASSETS	H	
1520	Building	A	Capital Asset
1540	Accum Depn - Building	A	Capital Asset
1550	Building - Net	S	
1560	Equipment	A	Capital Asset
1580	Accum Depn - Equipment	A	Capital Asset
1590	Equipment - Net	S	
1600	Automotive	A	Capital Asset
1620	Accum Amort - Automotive	A	Capital Asset
1630	Automotive - Net	S	
1640	Leasehold Improvements	A	Capital Asset
1660	Accum Amort - Leaseholds	A	Capital Asset
1670	Leasehold Improvements - Net	S	
1800	Land	G	Capital Asset
1899	TOTAL FIXED ASSETS	T	

LIABILITIES

2000	CURRENT LIABILITIES	H	
2050	Accounts Payable	G	Accounts Payable
2100	GST Charged on Sales	A	Accounts Payable
2110	GST Paid on Purchase	A	Accounts Payable
2120	GST Owing (Refund)	S	
2150	PST Payable	G	Accounts Payable
2200	Interest Payable	G	Debt
2300	Wages Payable	A	Current Liability
2320	CPP Payable	A	Current Liability
2340	EI Payable	A	Current Liability
2360	Income Tax Payable	A	Current Liability
2380	WCB Payable	A	Current Liability
2400	Dental Plan Payable	A	Current Liability
2420	CSB Plan Payable	A	Current Liability
2440	Medical Plan Payable	A	Current Liability
2460	Employee Donations Plan Payable	A	Current Liability
2470	Employee Stock Plan Payable	A	Current Liability
2499	Total Payroll Liability	S	
2699	TOTAL CURRENT LIABILITIES	T	
2700	LONG-TERM LIABILITIES	H	
2750	Mortgage Payable	G	Debt
2770	Note Payable - L. Cronkin	G	Debt
2899	TOTAL LONG-TERM LIABILITIES	T	

EQUITY

3000	CAPITAL	H	
3550	Capital - J. Demers	G	Owner/Partner Contributions
3600	Current Earnings	X	Current Earnings
3799	TOTAL CAPITAL	T	

REVENUE

4000	SALES	H	
4050	Sales - Truck Parts	G	Revenue
4199	TOTAL SALES REVENUE	T	
4200	SERVICE	H	
4220	Regular Freight	G	Revenue
4240	Overnight Freight	G	Revenue
4260	Air Freight	G	Revenue
4320	Regular Freight - U.S.	G	Revenue
4340	Overnight Freight - U.S.	G	Revenue
4360	Air Freight - U.S.	G	Revenue
4399	TOTAL SERVICE REVENUE	T	
4400	MISC REVENUE	H	
4410	Bank Interest	G	Other Revenue
4430	Purchase Discounts	G	Other Revenue
4499	TOTAL MISC REVENUE	T	

EXPENSE

5000	COST OF SALES	H	
5050	Cost of Sales - Truck Parts	G	Cost of Sales
5199	TOTAL COST OF SALES	T	
5200	OPERATING EXPENSES	H	
5220	Supplies	G	Expense
5240	Fuel & Oil	G	Expense
5260	Repairs and Maintenance	G	Expense
5280	Insurance	G	Expense
5300	Sales Discounts	G	Expense
5499	TOTAL OPERATING EXPENSES	T	
5500	ADMINISTRATIVE EXPENSES	H	
5520	Rent	G	General & Admin. Expense
5540	Telephone and Long Distance	G	General & Admin. Expense
5560	Utilities	G	General & Admin. Expense
5580	Office Stationery	G	General & Admin. Expense
5600	Office Supplies	G	General & Admin. Expense
5620	Janitorial	G	General & Admin. Expense
5640	Salaries and Benefits	A	Payroll Expense
5660	CPP Expense	A	Payroll Expense
5680	EI Expense	A	Payroll Expense
5700	WCB Expense	A	Payroll Expense
5799	Total Payroll Expense	S	
5800	Accounting and Legal	G	General & Admin. Expense
5820	Advertising and Promotion	G	General & Admin. Expense
5840	Licenses and Permits	G	General & Admin. Expense
5860	Insurance and Taxes	G	General & Admin. Expense
5880	Bank Charges and Interest	G	General & Admin. Expense
5900	Other Freight	G	General & Admin. Expense
5920	Depreciation	G	Expense
5950	Foreign exchange	G	Expense
5999	TOTAL ADMINISTRATIVE EXPENSES	T	

Generated On: 7/24/01

BACKING UP YOUR DATA FILES

Continue at this point with the backup of your Simply Accounting data files, (refer to Chapter 3 for instructions).

Backup File Name: A:\odc4a\odc

Comment: Using Simply 8 - Chapter 4a

MAKING JOURNAL ENTRIES

Even through we have not provided Simply Accounting for Windows with our opening balances, we can begin with the entry of current journal entries.

CHANGING THE SESSIONS DATE

Before we continue, we must first advance our session date from the current July 31, 2001. Continue from the Simply Accounting - ODC window (Figure 4.8) by

> Selecting the **Maintenance** menu.

> Selecting the **Change Session Date** option.

Figure 4.21
Change Session
Date window

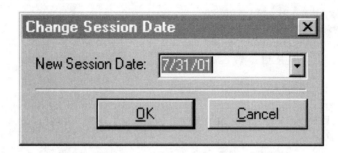

Continue from within the Change Session Date window (Figure 4.21) by entering

081501 ⌷Enter⌷   as the **New Session Date**.

⌷Alt⌷ + ⌷o⌷   to accept the new session date as more than one week from the previous session date.

Figure 4.22
Checklists window

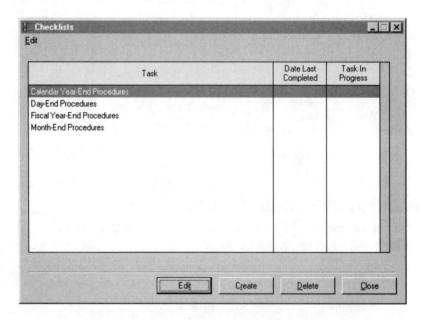

Simply Accounting for Windows will display the Checklists window (Figure 4.22). This window can be used to enter and organize accounting and administrative items that are not related to specific Simply Accounting for Windows entries. Examples might include scheduling a task to telephone Mr. Jones for a sales confirmation.

As you have not entered any entries, continue by

Clicking on the close button or option. In Windows 95/98, this is the small X button displayed in the top-right corner of the window or by

pressing [Alt] + [F4] to close this window.

Figure 4.23
To-Do Lists
window

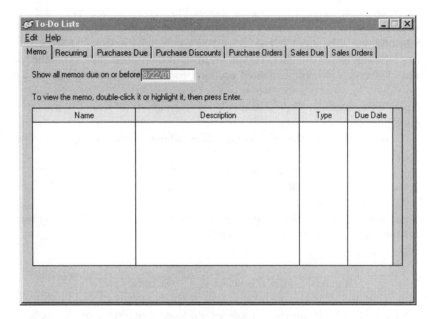

Simply Accounting for Windows will also display the To-Do Lists window (Figure 4.23). This window will normally display any entries that are outstanding in Simply Accounting for Windows. Examples include memo entries, purchases where payments are due, and pending sales orders.

As you have not entered any applicable entries, the To-Do Lists window will remain empty. Continue by

Clicking on the close button or option. Within Windows 95/98, this is the small X button displayed in the top-right corner of the window. Windows 3.1 requires you to select the options button (top-left corner) and then select the close option. You can also press [Alt] + [F4] to close this window.

A REVIEW OF DEBITS AND CREDITS

It might be helpful to briefly review the concept of debits and credits. Because we are using the double-entry accounting system, a debit to one set of accounts must be offset by a credit to another set of accounts. Therefore, every transaction requires two entries so that the accounts are always in balance. This balancing of the accounts within each entry is a control feature.

Think of the balance sheet with assets on the left side of the ledger and liabilities and equities on the right side. Similarly, you can view the income statement with expense accounts on the left side of the ledger and revenue accounts on the right side.

An increase in left-side accounts (assets and expenses) always means that you debit those accounts. In turn, that debit must be offset by a credit to an account on the right side of the balance sheet or income statement (liabilities, equities and revenue), otherwise the accounts would no longer be in balance. For example, if you increase assets, you must register a corresponding increase in one or more accounts on the right side of the ledger (liabilities or equities) or the two sides will not be in balance. However, since the increase on the asset side was a debit, the increase on the liabilities or equities side must be a credit. Similarly, a decrease in an asset account is a credit. This means that the right side of the ledger (liabilities or equities) must also be decreased. But a decrease on this side must be a debit.

Let's look at how this works on the income statement. When you make a sale to a customer on credit, you increase (debit) accounts receivable — an asset account that is on the left side of the ledger. Our second entry for this transaction must also increase an account but on the right side of the ledger to keep the two sides in balance. However, this entry must be a credit entry since the other one was a debit entry. The account that we must increase would be sales revenue.

When the customer eventually makes that payment, we get a cheque that goes into the bank. Since this increases an asset account, the bank balance, it must be a debit. To offset this increase in an asset account we must decrease (credit) accounts receivable, which, however, is also an asset account. Therefore this latter transaction affects only the left side of the ledger but everything remains in balance.

The following entries may clarify the above transactions.

> Dr. Accounts Receivable   (increase)
>   Cr. Sales Revenue   (increase)

These entries are made into opposite sides in the ledger; therefore they increase both accounts, which means that everything is in balance.

> Dr. Bank   (increase)
>   Cr. Accounts Receivable   (decrease)

These entries operate on the left side of the ledger; therefore one must be an increase and the other must be a decrease to keep everything in balance.

Remember the following rules when working with debits and credits.
Asset and expense accounts can be considered to be on the left side of the ledger. For these accounts, a debit is a positive entry and a credit is a negative entry.

Liabilities, equities, and revenues can be considered to be on the right side of the ledger. For these accounts, a credit is a positive entry while a debit is a negative entry.

Contra-asset accounts, such as accumulated depreciation, and contra-revenue accounts, such as sales discounts, are treated in reverse fashion. An increase in these accounts requires a negative entry and a decrease requires a positive entry.

USING THE GENERAL JOURNAL

While you are able to make virtually any type of entry within the General Journal, it is recommended that this journal be used only for those entries that can not be entered within the remaining Purchases, Payments, Sales, Receipts, Inventory, or Payroll journals.

However, the following example will display how to enter various journal entries (all types) using the General Journal.

> **HINT:** *TRACKING GST AND SIMPLY ACCOUNTING*
>
> *Within Simply Accounting for Windows, you can track the amount of GST collected and paid as long as you restrict the entry of GST applicable entries within the General Journal (use the Sales and Purchase Journals instead). However, this book will show you how to determine your required GST remittance, including entries made within the General Journal.*

Continue from within the Simply Accounting-ODC window (Figure 4.6) by

Opening the **General Journal** (Click on icon).

Figure 4.24
General Journal window

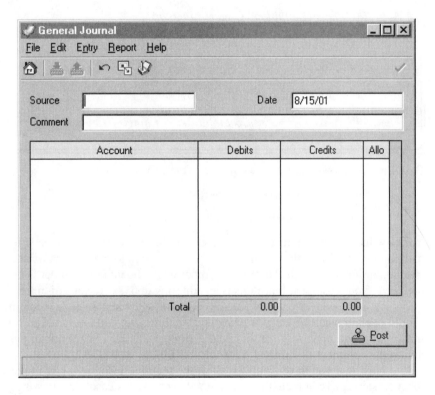

Let's look at the first journal entry that you will be making.

With the current mortgage payable balance of $42,797.00, we need to make an entry for the interest charged on this mortgage. The mortgage interest rate is 8.5% with the last interest entry made on July 31, 2001. We must therefore make an entry for the interest from August 01 to August 15, 2001.

To take care of this interest expense, we need to make an accrual expense entry for the interest from August 01, 2001 until August 31, 2001. This interest is calculated as follows:

([Principal × interest rate%] / 365) × number-of-days = expense

([$42,797.00 × 8.5%] / 365) × 15 = $149.50

The next step is to determine which accounts will be affected by this journal entry. Based on our chart of account, the following two accounts will be affected:

5880 Bank Charges and Interest

2750 Mortgage Payable

Now you must determine which account will be debited and which account will be credited.

> **HINT:** *To remember which accounts should be debited or credited, use the following chart:*
>
> *Acct 1000-1999 (Assets) Debit = increase*
>
> *Acct 2000-2999 (Liabilities) Credit = increase*
>
> *Acct 3000-3999 (Equity) Credit = increase*
>
> *Acct 4000-4999 (Revenue) Credit = increase*
>
> *Acct 5000-5999 (Expense) Debit = increase*
>
> *Therefore, Assets + Expense = Liabilities + Equity + Revenue.*

Based on the above chart, you would make the following entry.

5880	Bank Charges and Interest	Dr. 149.50	
2750	Mortgage Payable		Cr. 149.50

You now have to determine the source code for this entry. The source code for an entry is the document number that will allow you to trace the entry back to the source document. In the case of a cheque, the source code is the cheque number while the invoice number is the source code for an invoice to your customer. Since this is an adjusting entry, you can assign the source code **ADJ01.**

When making the actual journal entry you must also include a comment. This comment should explain what the entry is when you print the General Ledger report in the future. You must remember, however, that this field is limited in size. For the above journal entry, you can assign the comment as **Interest Accrual 08/01/01 to 08/15/01.**

Now that you have compiled all of the required information to make your journal entry, the next step is to complete the source document (in this case the adjusting journal entry form). This is required to maintain a correct paper trail or audit trail. Note how the following journal entry form has been completed.

Source	ADJ01		Date	08/15/01
Comment	Interest Accrual 08/01/01 to 08/15/01			
Account	Account Name		Debit	Credit
5880	Bank Charge...		149.50	
2750	Mortgage Pay			149.50
	Total		149.50	149.50

Now you can make the journal entry. Continue from the General Journal window (Figure 4.24) by entering

ADJ01 ⌈ Tab ⌉   to enter the **Source.**

⌈ Tab ⌉   to accept 08/15/01 as the **Date** for this journal entry.

Interest Accrual 08/01 to 08/15/01 ⌈ Tab ⌉

to enter the **Comment.**

Simply Accounting for Windows now requests that you enter the first account number.

> **HINT:** *If you don't know the appropriate account number, you can press enter to retrieve a listing of the account numbers. You can then press the first digit of the account number (1 for Assets, 2 for Liabilities, 3 for Equity, 4 for Revenue, and 5 for Expenses) to jump to that section of the chart of accounts.*

Continue by entering

5880 ⌈ Tab ⌉   to enter the first **Account** number.

Simply Accounting assumes that the first entry will be a debit entry. (If you want the first entry to be a credit entry, press the ⌈ Tab ⌉ key to jump to the credit field). Type

149.50 ⌈ Tab ⌉   to enter the **Debit** value.

2750 ⌈ Tab ⌉   to enter the second **Account** number.

⌈ Tab ⌉   to accept 149.50 as the **Credit** for this account.

> **HINT:** *MOVING BACK TO THE DEBIT COLUMN*
>
> *By default, Simply Accounting will attempt to balance the entry, (in the above example a default credit). If you want to return to the debit column instead, simply delete the default credit, followed by pressing* ⌈ Shift ⌉ + ⌈ Tab ⌉ *to move backwards to the debit column.*

Figure 4.25
General Journal
(Entered) window

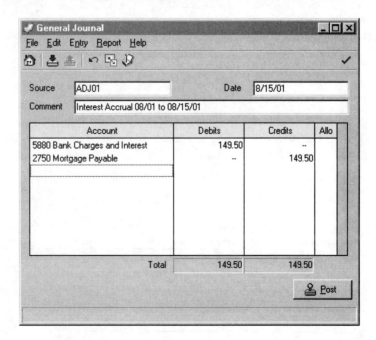

Your General Journal window should now resemble Figure 4.25. At this point, you can continue with the **Posting** of the entry. This process will then update the General Ledger and financial statements with your entry. Continue by

Clicking on the **Post** button (top-right corner).

or pressing

(Alt) + (P)   to **Post** this entry.

CREATING RECURRING GENERAL JOURNAL ENTRIES

Simply Accounting for Windows also provides you with a powerful feature that allows you to store repetitive entries for future use. This will save you valuable data-entry time.

The example entry will be for the weekly expensing of the prepaid insurance that has been used. Instead of entering this repetitive entry once per week, you will only have to create this entry once and then recall this entry for posting in future weeks.

Continue from the General Journal window (Figure 4.24) by entering

ADJ02 (Tab)   to enter the Source.

080301 (Tab)   to enter the Date.

Expense prepaid insurance (Tab)

to enter the Comment.

5860 (Tab)   to enter the Account.

15.00 (Tab)   to enter the Debit amount.

1300 (Tab)   to enter the next Account.

(Tab)   to accept the default Credit amount.

Figure 4.26
General Journal
window (Entered)

At this point you have entered the insurance expense entry (Figure 4.26). Prior to posting, you will want to create a recurring entry so that this entry can be re-used at a later point.

Continue from the General Journal window (Figure 4.26) by

Clicking on the **Store** button or press ⌈ Ctrl ⌋ + ⌈ T ⌋.

From within the Store Recurring Transaction window by pressing

⌈ Tab ⌋ to accept the **Recurring Transaction Name.**

W ⌈ Tab ⌋ to select **Weekly** as the Frequency.

Figure 4.27
Store Recurring
Transaction window

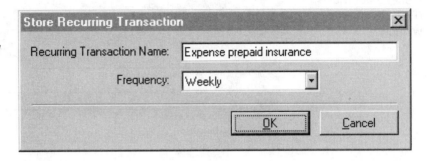

Continue from the Store Recurring Transaction window (Figure 4.27) by

Selecting the **OK** button, or pressing ⌈ Enter ⌋

As you return to the General Journal window (Figure 4.26) you will notice that the **Recall** recurring button is now also available for selection. However, continue by

Posting your entry, use your mouse or press ⌈ Alt ⌋ + ⌈ P ⌋.

RECALLING STORED ENTRIES

We will now want to continue with the posting of the above entry for the second week within August, 2001. We could re-enter the journal entry or simply recall the previously stored entry.

Continue from within the General Journal window (Figure 4.24) by

Selecting the **Recall** button or press ⌈ Ctrl ⌋ + ⌈ R ⌋.

Figure 4.28
Recall Recurring
Transaction window

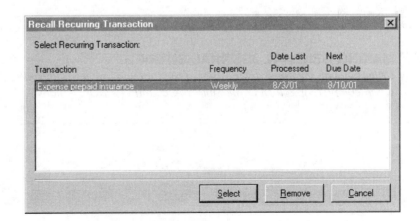

From within the Recall Recurring Transaction window (Figure 4.28) you will notice that not only has Simply Accounting for Windows created this recurring entry, but it also knows that the next posting is required for August 10, 2001. Continue by

Clicking the **Select** button to retrieve the prepaid insurance entry.

Once the recurring entry has been retrieved continue by entering

ADJ03 ⌨Tab⌨   to enter the Source.

Figure 4.29
General Journal
(Recalled entry)
window

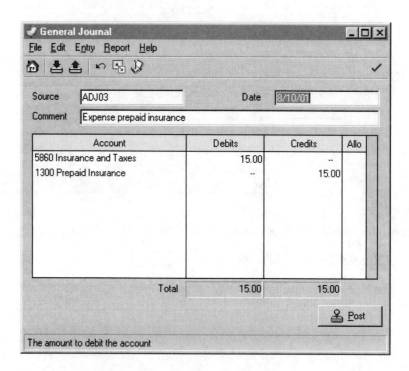

You will notice from the General Journal window (Figure 4.29) that Simply Accounting has created the latest prepaid insurance entry with the correct date. Continue by

Posting this prepaid insurance entry.

Practice Exercise 4.5

MAKING GENERAL JOURNAL ENTRIES
Continue with the entry and posting of the following general journal entries.
Upon completing, return to the Simply Accounting - ODC window.

August 02, 2001 a sales invoice number 503 was issued to R.T. Leob for Regular Freight services of $600 plus $42 GST.

Description	Sale to R.T. Loeb				
Source	Date	Account Name	Account	Debit	Credit
Inv503	08/02/01	Accounts Receivable	1150	642.00	
		Regular Freight	4220		600.00
		GST Charged on Sales	2100		42.00
			Total	642.00	642.00

You received the phone bill (dated August 04, 2001) from Bell Telephone (Source Aug/01) in the amount of $50.00 plus $3.50 GST. This bill will be paid at a later time.

Description					
Source	Date	Account Name	Account	Debit	Credit
Aug/01		Expense		50	
		A/Payable			53
		GST Paid	3.50	3.50	3.50

On August 05, 2001 you issued cheque #108 to JM Holdings for the rent for the month of August, $1,000.00 (paid from the Royal Bank account).

Description					
Source	Date	Account Name	Account	Debit	Credit
Chq108		Rent Expense 5520		1000	
		Bank			1000

On August 10, 2001 you issued cheque #109 to pay the phone bill to Bell Telephone in the amount of $53.50 (paid from the Royal Bank account).

Description					
Source	Date	Account Name	Account	Debit	Credit
Chq109		A/Payable			
		Roay Bank			

On August 15, 2001 you received a payment from R.T Loeb for the outstanding invoice from August 02, 2001 (Inv 503). The customers cheque number was cheque #617 deposited to the Royal Bank account.

Description						
Source	Date	Account Name	Account	Debit	Credit
Chq617		Cash			
		Accounts receivable	- -		

BACKING UP YOUR DATA FILES

Continue at this point with the backup of your Simply Accounting data files (refer to Chapter 3 for instructions).

Backup File Name: *A:\odc4b\odc*

Comment: *Using Simply 8 - Chapter 4b*

FINISHING THE SESSION

Now that you have completed this chapter you must save the data and return to the Windows desktop.

Make sure you are at the Simply Accounting - ODC window as shown in Figure 4.6. Then press

| Alt | + | F4 |

to close the data set as well as the Simply Accounting for Windows program.

FURTHER PRACTICE

To get further practice with the concepts you have learned in this chapter go to Chapter 14 and work through Section 4 of the National Supply Company.

CHAPTER 5

THE GENERAL LEDGER—ENTERING OPENING BALANCES AND JOURNAL ENTRIES

CHAPTER 5

THE GENERAL LEDGER — ENTERING OPENING BALANCES AND JOURNAL ENTRIES

OBJECTIVES

After working through this chapter you will be able to

1. Enter the opening balances from the trial balance into the accounts.
2. Display the trial balance and the financial statements.
3. Set the integration accounts.
4. Change the General Ledger to READY mode.
5. Set up the Bank Reconciliation feature.
6. Use Simply Accounting On-Line Banking feature.
7. Make General Ledger entries.

SETTING UP FOREIGN EXCHANGE

Before we continue with the entry of the opening balances, you will need to set up Simply Accounting to handle foreign exchange currencies. Continue by

    Starting Simply Accounting for Windows.

    Select to open the ODC (Overnight Delivery Company) data set.

    Accept the default Session date of 08/15/01.

Figure 5.1
Simply Accounting - ODC window

To use the Foreign Exchange features within Simply Accounting, the first step is to set up the foreign exchange option.

Continue from within the Simply Accounting - ODC window (Figure 5.1) by trying exercise 5.1.

Practice Exercise 5.1

Create a General Ledger Account with the following:

Account	5350
Desc	Import Duties
Type	Group Account
Class	Expense

Once you have created the above account, return to the Simply Accounting - ODC window (Figure 5.1).

IMPORT DUTY CONFIGURATION

Normally when you are purchasing products from outside the country, you will encounter government duties on the importation of the products. Simply Accounting can effectively handle the importing duties associated.

Continue by selecting the **Setup** menu.

From within the **Setup** menu select the **Import Duty Information** option.

Figure 5.2
Import Duty
Information
window

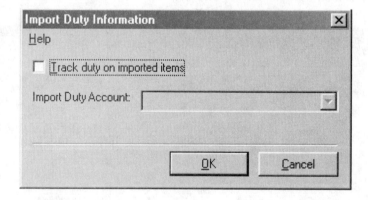

Continue from the Import Duty Information window with the following

Select the **Track duty on imported items** option.

Select **5350 Import Duties** as the **Import Duty Account**.

Simply Accounting will now post the Import Duties to the above account. Continue by

Clicking the **OK** button.

SETTING UP CURRENCIES IN SIMPLY ACCOUNTING

The next step is to inform Simply Accounting which currencies you will be handling in your business for purchases and sales.

Continue from within the Simply Accounting - ODC window (Figure 5.1) by

Selecting the **Setup** menu.

Selecting the **Currencies** option.

Figure 5.3
Currency
Information
window

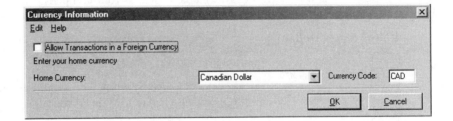

Continue from within the Currency Information window by

Selecting the **Allow Transaction in a Foreign Currency** option.

Figure 5.4
Currency
Information
(selected)
window

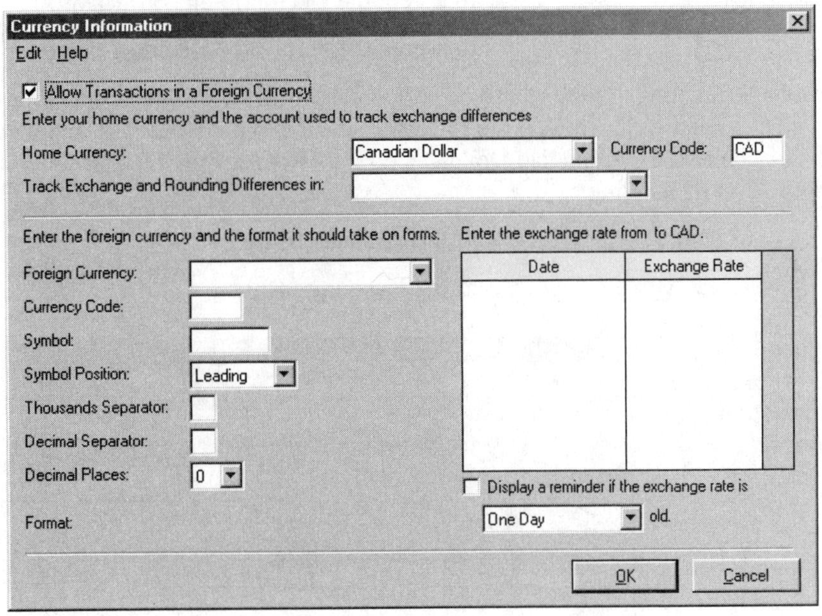

Continue from within the Currency Information window by pressing

[Tab]   to move to the **Home Currency** option.

[Tab]   to accept *Canadian Dollar* as the **Home Currency**. The Home
                 Currency is the base currency for your company. If your com-
                 pany was operating in the United States, the Home Currency
                 would be *U.S. Dollar*.

[Tab]	to accept *CAD* as the **Currency Code**. The currency code is based on the currency codes established within Windows. The selection of the code establishes how currency figures are displayed in screens and reports by Simply Accounting.
5950 [Tab]	to enter the account set up to **Track Exchange and Rounding Differences**. This is the account into which exchange and rounding figures will be posted during the valuation of the foreign currency accounts.

The next step is to establish the foreign exchange in which your company will be negotiating transactions. Continue from within the Currency Information window, (Figure 5.4) by entering

United States Dollar [Tab]	to select the **Foreign Currency**.
[Tab]	to accept *USD* as the **Currency Code**.
[Tab]	to accept *US$* as the **Symbol**. The symbol is the currency symbol that will be display for this currency.
[Tab]	to accept the **Symbol Position** as *Leading*. This will define the above currency symbol to be displayed before the actual figure.
[Tab]	to accept the **Thousands Separator** as ,. While this is the normal **Thousands Separator,** for other foreign currencies, thousands separator may differ.
[Tab]	to accept the **Decimal Separator** as ".".
[Tab]	to accept the number of **Decimal Places** as *2*.

Simply Accounting requires that you periodically provide exchange rates for the foreign currency so that it can convert the foreign exchange to the Home Currency, in this case U.S. Dollars converted to Canadian Dollars. Continue from within the Currency Information window (Figure 5.4) by entering

081501 [Tab]	as the exchange **Date**.
1.5125 [Tab]	as the **Exchange Rate**.

Figure 5.5
Currency
Information
window
(Exchange
entered)

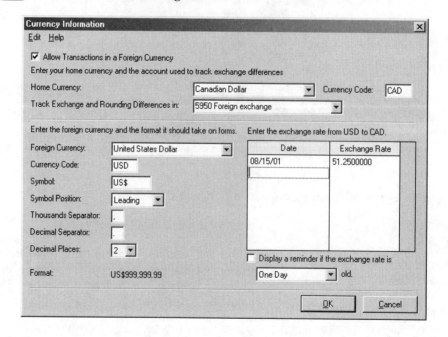

Your Currency Information window should now resemble Figure 5.5. Continue by

Selecting the **Display a reminder if the exchange rate option.** This allows Simply Accounting to display a reminder if you have not provided an updated exchange rate on a daily basis. You can change the updating to weekly or monthly, however for the purpose of this exercise in this book we will leave this frequency as *One Day*.

You have now completed the Currency Information options, continue by

Selecting the <u>O</u>K button which will close the Currency Information window. You will then return to the Simply Accounting - ODC window (Figure 5.1).

Practice Exercise 5.2

Continue with the modification of the following General Ledger accounts. You will be required to change the **Currency** option to *USD* as noted within Figure 5.6:

Account	Description
1060	Bank - Seafirst US Dollar

Once you have completed this exercise, return to the Simply Accounting - ODC window (Figure 5.1).

ENTERING THE OPENING BALANCES

After setting up the chart of accounts for Overnight Delivery Company in the previous chapter, you must now enter the account balances that exist at the time of conversion. The Simply Accounting for Windows system refers to this as historical data. In accounting terms, it is known as the **opening trial balance**.

The only accounts that require historical balances are those accounts to which we can post journal entries. These are the accounts marked with an L (left) or an R (right). The subtotals and totals for these accounts are calculated automatically by the program based on the transactions entered. The heading accounts, of course, have no dollar balances.

THE OPENING TRIAL BALANCE OF THE MANUAL ACCOUNTING SYSTEM

The opening trial balance for Overnight Delivery Company is shown in Figure 5.6. Make sure that you do not miss entering any of these amounts or the system will not balance. Please note that the accounts may not be listed in account number order.

Overnight Delivery Company
Trial Balance
July 31, 2001

	DR.	CR.
Petty Cash	300.00	
Bank - Royal	18,525.35	
Accounts Receivable	10,312.06	
Inventory - Truck Parts	7,905.00	
Office Supplies	55.67	
Prepaid Insurance	435.00	
Building	31,000.00	
Equipment	1,700.00	
Automotive	35,224.00	
Leasehold Improvements	12,150.00	
Land	18,000.00	
Accm Depn - Building		5,000.00
Accm Depn - Equipment		500.00
Accm Depn - Automotive		5,500.00
Accm Amortization - Leaseholds		3,400.00
Accounts Payable		20,730.21
Mortgage Payable		42,797.00
Note Payable - L. Cronkin		2,000.00
Capital - J. Demers		24,274.87
Sales - Truck Parts		16,666.55
Regular Freight		59,615.00
Overnight Freight		23,519.00
Air Freight		8,615.00
Cost of Sales - Truck Parts	10,358.00	
Supplies	985.00	
Fuel and Oil	14,519.00	
Repairs and Maintenance	3,615.00	
Insurance	1,415.00	
Rent	3,900.00	
Telephone and Long Distance	2,453.85	
Utilities	1,615.87	
Office Stationery	456.78	
Coffee Supplies	316.55	
Janitorial	1,457.22	
Salaries & Benefits	23,659.55	
CPP Expense	864.35	
EI Expense	1246.05	
WCB Expense	757.10	
Accounting and Legal	2,209.95	
Advertising and Promotion	834.55	
Licenses and Permits	1,555.00	
Insurance and Taxes	122.00	
Bank Charges and Interest	2,357.73	
Other Freight	12.00	
Amortization	2,300.00	
	212,617.63	212,617.63

Figure 5.6 Opening Trial Balance, Overnight Delivery Company.

Notice that the **total debits** and **total credits** for our opening trial balance are equal. This must always be the case as we are using the **double-entry accounting** system.

ENTERING THE OPENING BALANCES

The next step in the process of making the General Ledger ready for the *Overnight Delivery Company* is to enter the opening balances for each of the General Ledger accounts. We have simplified this process by including data files contained on the CD-ROM that include the majority of the opening balances.

Important Note: Before you continue, exit Simply Accounting and copy the starter files from the included CD-ROM. These files contain the majority of the above accounts with opening balances, thus preventing you from repetitive data entry.

The source directory should be X:\sw0805 where x: represents the drive letter for your CD-ROM drive. Use the enclosed installation program (X:\Setup) to install these files.

Continue from the Simply Accounting main window (Figure 5.7). Accept the default Session Date *(08/15/01)*.

Figure 5.7
Simply
Accounting-ODC
main window

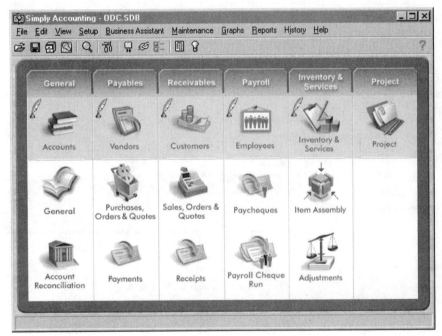

Starting from the Simply Accounting - ODC window (see Figure 5.7), continue by

Double-clicking on the **Accounts** icon.

Figure 5.8
Accounts
window

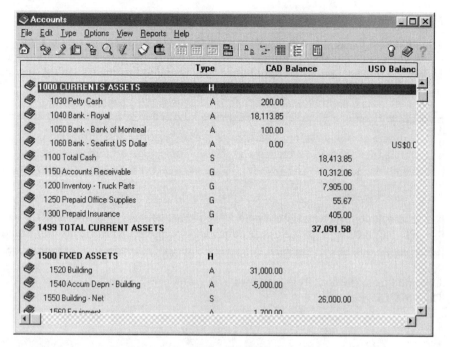

Continue from within the **Accounts** window (see Figure 5.8) by either

Clicking on the **Find** icon, located within the **Accounts** window.

or pressing

Alt + E   to display the **Edit** menu.

F   to select the **Find** option, (from within the **Edit** menu).

Figure 5.9
Find window
(Accounts)

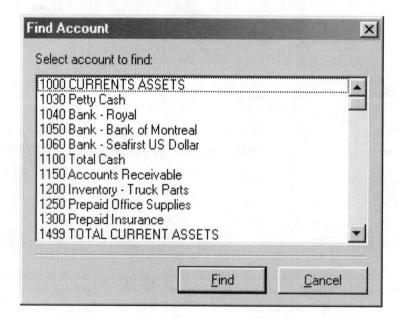

Continue from the Find Account window (Figure 5.9) by pressing

⬚ 5	to jump to the expense section of the chart of accounts.
⬚ ↓ (several times)	until you have located *5600 Coffee Supplies* account.
⬚ Enter	to retrieve account *5600 Coffee Supplies*.

HINT: *HOW TO ENTER OPENING BALANCES QUICKLY*

You can also press either ⬚ Pg Up *or* ⬚ Pg Dn *to locate the desired account. Since the trial balance is grouped by category (assets, liabilities, equity, income, and expenses) you can also press the first number of the account type to jump to that section of accounts. For example, press* ⬚ 2 *to jump to the 2000-2999 range which is for liabilities or* ⬚ 2 *to get to the beginning of the 5000-5999 range which is expenses.*

Another method of entering opening balances or changing amounts is to click on the first account icon (or any account for which you want to make changes) with your mouse to open it. Put your mouse cursor to the left of the zero in the balance field and click once. Then hold the mouse button down as you drag the cursor over the zeros (or the amount) in the balance field. This will highlight the zeros. You can now type in the opening balance amount. When you are finished, click on the down arrow on the right side of the scroll bar at the bottom of the General Ledger window. The next account in the account order will be displayed. If it is a heading or total account, click on the arrow again until you get an account which requires an opening balance.

Figure 5.10
General Ledger window (Coffee Supplies)

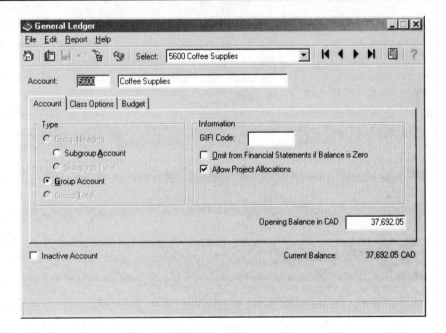

In the General Ledger window, you will notice three tabbed buttons titled:

Account	where you can modify the account type, selection of omission from financial statements, (if balance is zero), project allocation, GIFI code, and opening balance.

Class   where you can define the class type for each account.

Budget   where you will be able to enter and maintain the budgeting for this account.

Simply Accounting will then retrieve this account (Figure 5.10). Continue by

Clicking on the **Opening Balance in CAD**.

HINT: You will notice that Simply Accounting will ask you to enter the Home Currency in the Opening Balance (Canadian Dollars for the purpose of this book). If your chart of accounts contains foreign balances, you will need to convert these balances to the Home Currency (Canadian) prior to entry within Simply Accounting for Windows (as Opening Balances).

You will notice that the Opening Balance is $37,692.05. This figure was required in order to allow the open data set to be balanced (for the purpose of this book). Continue by entering

316.55 ⎡ Tab ⎤   to enter the **Opening Balance**.

HINT: REPLACING OR CORRECTING OPENING BALANCES

In the above example, you have replaced the previous opening balance for the Coffee Supplies account. This can be repeated until you have successfully entered the opening balances for every account.

Important Note: When entering account balances, Simply Accounting automatically puts the amount into either the debit or credit column based on the type of entry. For example, the Cash account is an asset account and therefore usually a debit entry. If you enter a positive cash balance, the account will be debited. If your opening cash balance is negative, meaning that the account is overdrawn, you would enter the amount with a minus sign preceding it.

The reverse is true for liability accounts. For example, Accounts Payable is a liability account and therefore usually a credit entry. If you want to increase the balance in this account, you would add a positive number. If you want to decrease the balance in this account, you would add a negative number.

Continue from the General Ledger (History) window by

Clicking on the **Forward** button (located within the toolbar).

> *HINT: FORWARD, BACKWARDS, TOP, AND BOTTOM BUTTONS*
>
> *This Forward button will allow you to advance the account display by one account. Alternatively, you can press the Backward button to display the previous account or either the Top or Bottom button to jump to the first or last account within the chart of account.*

Practice Exercise 5.3

ENTERING OPENING BALANCES

Enter the remaining amounts (Janitorial to Amortization expense) from the trial balance shown in Figure 5.7, (balances have already been entered for all accounts from the Petty Cash to the Coffee Supplies).

VIEWING THE SIMPLY ACCOUNTING TRIAL BALANCE

When you have entered all of the opening balances, you **must** look at the trial balance and make sure that the total debits equals the total credits. If they do not, you have made a mistake somewhere. You should then compare each amount in the trial balance with the opening balance amount shown on paper. To view the trial balance, you can use either the mouse or the keyboard.

To display the Trial Balance, Continue from the General Ledger window (Figure 5.10) by either

Clicking on the **Close** icon within the **General Ledger** window.

or pressing

[Alt] + [F4]   to close the **General Ledger** window.

From within the Accounts window, continue by

Clicking on the **Report** menu.

Clicking on the **Trial Balance** menu option.

Figure 5.11
Trial Balance
Options window

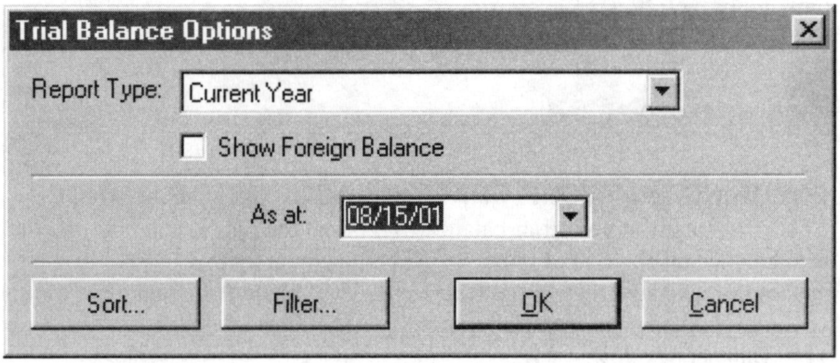

From within the Trial Balance Options window (Figure 5.11) you can select from the following options:

Comparative Trial Balance	allows you to display and print a side-by-side trial balance report, using two selectable report dates.
As at Date	is the date at which the trial balance will be displayed. Since the trial balance amounts can change from day to day, instead of reporting for a period of time, you are reporting at a set point in time.
Show Foreign Balance	includes foreign balances in foreign and home currencies.

Continue from within the Trial Balance Options window (Figure 5.11) by

Selecting the **Historical Opening Balances** option (Report type).

HINT: *CHOOSING REPORTING DATES*

In Simply Accounting, you can select report dates in two ways. First, you can enter the date manually. Second, if the date is either the start of the year, the current session date or the conversion date, you can use the pull down option to display these dates for selection.

From with the Trial Balance report window, continue by

Clicking on the down scroll button, (located in the bottom right of the Trial Balance window) until you reach the end of the report.

HINT: *When you open the trial balance initially, you can only view the accounts that appear inside the window. To expand the window to the full screen, press* [Alt] + [space bar] *to invoke the control icon. Then press* [X] *to invoke the* **Maximize** *menu option. To return to the windowed trial balance, press* [Alt] + [space bar] *followed by* [R] *to invoke the* **Restore** *menu option.*

Continue with the following exercise

Practice Exercise 5.4

ENSURING THAT YOUR CHART OF ACCOUNTS BALANCES

Check the totals on your trial balance to see that they are equal and that they match the trial balance displayed in Figure 5.6. If you have an incorrect amount then review your entries to make sure they agree with Figure 5.6. Make the changes in the same way that you entered the balances earlier. Once your trial balance balances, remain within the Trial Balance window.

Once you have completed the above exercise, continue by either

Clicking on the **Close** icon within the Trial Balance report window.

Important Note: If the trial balance does not balance (debits equal credits), you will be asked to place the difference in an applicable account. Select an applicable account which will be adjusted by the difference. You will then have to compare the printed trial balance to Figure 5.6 and adjust the applicable accounts.

DISPLAYING THE FINANCIAL STATEMENTS

In Simply Accounting for Windows, the financial statements are defined for you based on the chart of accounts that you set up earlier.

A firm's financial statements consist of two main statements: a **balance sheet,** which is a representation of the company's financial position at a particular time, and the **income statement,** which is a listing of revenues and expenses over a specific period. To display both of these statements, proceed from the Accounts window.

To display the balance sheet continue by

905-426-2017

Selecting the **Report** menu.

Selecting the **Balance Sheet** menu option within the **Report** menu.

To display the income statement

Select the **Report** menu.

Select the **Income Statement** menu option.

ENTERING BUDGET INFORMATION

Budgeting is an optional but recommended step. Simply Accounting has a budget feature that allows you to compare your actual figures for revenue and expense accounts against budget amounts that you determine based on your business outlook. By comparing budget to actual figures you can get some idea of how your business is actually performing against your plan.

Simply Accounting allows you the option of budgeting for only those income and expense accounts that you select.

Continue from the Accounts window by either

Clicking on the **Find** icon.

or pressing

| Alt | + | E | to select the **Edit** menu.

| F | to select the **Find** menu option.

Once the **Find Account** window is displayed (Figure 5.4), continue by

Selecting (and retrieving) account *4050 Sales - Truck Parts*.

From within the General Ledger window

Select the **Budget** tabbed button.

Click on the **Budget this Account** option.

Figure 5.12
General Ledger
(Budget) window

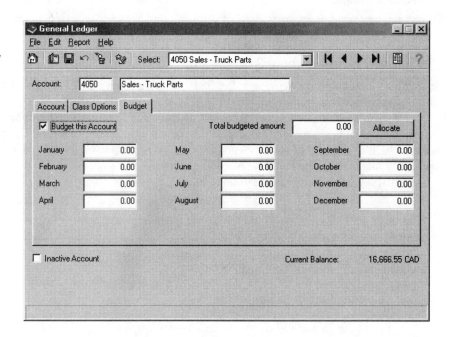

The General Ledger window will now change to display the budget entry fields (Figure 5.12). Continue by pressing

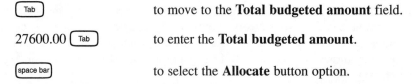

Tab	to move to the **Total budgeted amount** field.
27600.00 Tab	to enter the **Total budgeted amount**.
space bar	to select the **Allocate** button option.

You will notice that the annual budget of *$27,600* has been evenly allocated throughout the twelve budgeting periods. You could however change individual period budget amounts if you expect your revenues or expenses to fluctuate during the fiscal year.

Practice Exercise 5.5

Continue with the entry of the following Total budgeted amounts for the following revenue and expense account. These budget amounts can be evenly allocated through out the fiscal periods:

Sales - Truck Parts	27,600.00
	(done)
Regular Freight	100,800.00
Overnight Freight	42,000.00
Air Freight	18,000.00
Regular Freight - US	8,000.00
Overnight Freight - US	21,000.00
Air Freight - US	10,000.00
Bank Interest	120.00
Cost of Sales - Truck Parts	18,000.00
Supplies	21,600.00
Fuel and Oil	24,000.00
Repairs and Maintenance	6,000.00
Insurance	1404.00
Rent	6,600.00
Telephone and Long Distance	2,400.00
Utilities	2,640.00
Office Stationery	900.00
Coffee Supplies	540.00
Janitorial	2,400.00
Salaries & Benefits	42,000.00
CPP Expense	4,200.00
EI Expense	6,000.00
WCB Expense	1,344.00
Accounting and Legal	6,000.00
Advertising and Promotion	2,350.00
Licenses	225.00
Insurance and Taxes	620.00
Bank Charges and Interest	540.00
Other Freight	600.00
Depreciation	3,960.00

Once you have completed this exercise, close the General Ledger window along with the Accounts window, you will then return to the Simply Accounting - ODC window (Figure 5.7).

BACKING UP YOUR DATA FILES

You want to create a backup of your data now. Select either the **Backup** icon or select the **Backup** menu option from within the **File** menu to backup your Simply Accounting data files.

When backing up your files, use the following selections:

Backup filename: *A:\ODC\odc5A\odc*

Comment: *Using Simply 8 - Chapter 5 part a*

For further information on how to use the backup feature, please refer to Chapter 3.

COMPLETING THE CONVERSION PROCESS

You have entered your opening balances, so the conversion process is almost complete. You will now need to continue with the establishment of the required integration accounts.

THE SIMPLY ACCOUNTING INTEGRATION ACCOUNTS

Simply Accounting for Windows is a totally integrated accounting system. Integration means that when an entry is made in one of the subledgers (e.g., Accounts Payable, Accounts Receivable, etc.), the General Ledger is updated automatically. There is no need to make another entry into the General Ledger or to make a transfer of an entry from the other modules manually. Similarly, the current earnings account automatically records the difference between the total year-to-date revenues and the total year-to-date expenses. The current earnings balance is then automatically added to the retained earnings account when a new accounting year starts. In order for the Simply Accounting system to be able to make these entries, it must know which accounts the entries are to be posted.

As we work through each chapter, we will provide the integration accounts for each module. For the General Ledger, we will provide the retained earnings account. This will be the account that will be used to post the fiscal year-end profit or loss, when you move to the new fiscal year.

Continue from the Simply Accounting - ODC window (Figure 5.7) by

Clicking the **Setup** menu.

Clicking the **Linked Accts** menu option within the **Setup** menu.

Clicking the **General** menu option from within the **Linked Accts** submenu.

Figure 5.13
General Linked
Accounts window

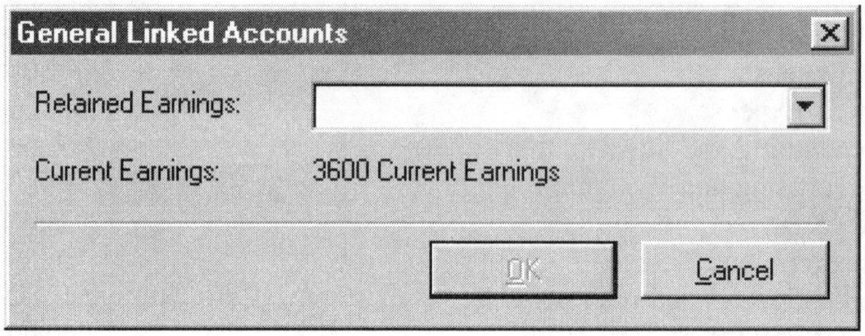

From within the General Linked Accounts window (Figure 5.13), continue by

Selecting account *3550 Capital - J. Demers* as the **Retained Earnings** account.

Clicking the **OK** button.

Clicking **YES** to confirm that account 3550 Capital J. Demers account class will be changed to Retained Earnings.

HINT: CURRENT EARNINGS ACCOUNT

Within the General Linked Accounts window (Figure 5.13), Simply Accounting has already selected account 3600 Current Earnings as the account. This account was established when we first created our data files and will be used to display the current earnings on the balance sheet report.

COMPLETING THE HISTORICAL CONVERSION (GENERAL LEDGER)

Now that you have completed the historical conversion, you can enter current transactions in Simply Accounting's General Ledger. To change from the historical mode to the current mode, which will prevent further modification of historical balances, you will need to first convert all other selected modules (Payables, Receivables, Payroll, and Inventory). Once you have converted all of these modules, you will be able to change out of the conversion mode.

Figure 5.14
Simply
Accounting -
ODC main
window

Continue from within the Simply Accounting - ODC window (Figure 5.14) by completing the following exercise.

Practice Exercise 5.6

From within the **Account** window, continue with finding and retrieving the following account:

Account no. *1040 Bank - Royal*

Figure 5.15
General Ledger
(Bank - Royal)
window

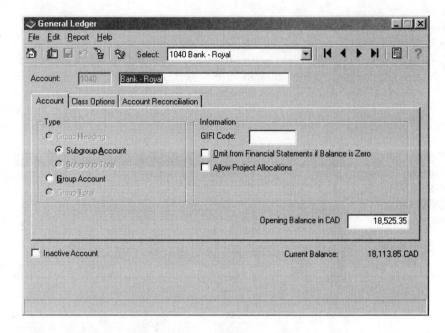

SETTING UP THE BANK RECONCILIATION FEATURE

As the account that you have just retrieved is the company's bank account, you will want to ensure that this account makes use of the powerful Bank Reconciliation feature. Continue by

> Clicking the **Account Reconciliation** tab.

Within the **Account Reconciliation tab,** continue by

> Clicking on the **Save Transactions for Account Reconciliation**.

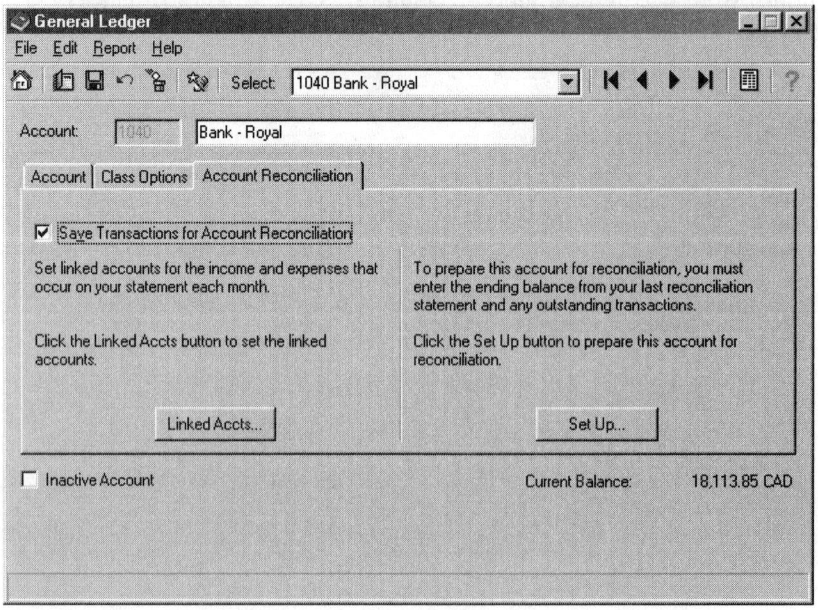

Figure 5.16
General Ledger
(Account
Reconciliation)
window

Simply Accounting will now require you to complete the following functions to have your Bank Reconciliation feature ready for use (Figure 5.16). These two functions include:

Linked Accts   will allow you to establish defined bank revenue and bank service charge linked accounts. This will in turn save you time when reconciling your bank account.

Set Up   is required in order to inform Simply Accounting of any outstanding cheque and deposits that have not cleared the bank statement, and are thus unreconciled.

Continue from within the General Ledger (Account Reconciliation) window (Figure 5.16) by

Clicking on the **Linked Accts** button.

Figure 5.17
Bank
Reconciliation
Linked Accounts
window

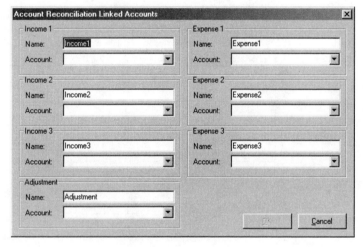

As shown in Figure 5.17, the Bank Reconciliation Linked Accounts window allows you to specify default income and expense accounts that will be used when you reconcile this bank account. An example of an income account would be for the receipt of bank interest while a very common expense category would be for bank service charges. Continue by entering

Bank Int ⎡Tab⎤   to enter the **Name** for *Income #1*.

4410 ⎡Tab⎤   to enter the **Account** for *Income #1*.

Practice Exercise 5.7

Continue by inserting the following <u>expense</u> integration account:

Name   *SCharge*
Account   *5880*

Once you have completed this exercise, you should have clicked the OK button to return the General Ledger (Account Reconciliation) window (Figure 5.16).

The next step is to inform Simply Accounting of any outstanding cheques and deposits (that have not been cleared from the bank statement). You will also be asked for the last reconciled balance as per the bank statement. Continue by

> Clicking on the **Setup** button.

Simply Accounting will now prompt you to select transactions from other journals or enter them one at a time if you choose. If you have already entered bank entries in Simply Accounting, you may be able to select the outstanding items from the previously entered items. However, since both transactions that have been entered in Simply Accounting and in the manual ledger (previous to July 31, 2001) are still outstanding (note Chapter 4) continue by

> Clicking the **No** button to specify that you do not want to select entries from previously entered transactions, thus entering outstanding items one at a time.

Figure 5.18
Set Up Account
Reconciliation
window

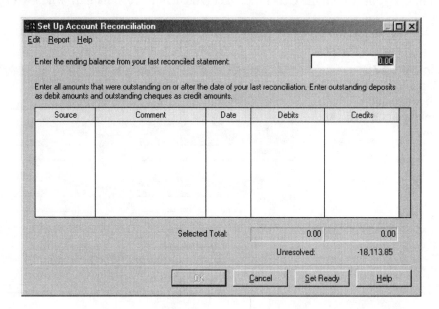

Simply Accounting will require you to enter all of the transactions that have not cleared the last bank statement, and are therefore outstanding. You will also be required to enter the last Reconciled Ending Balance. Notice that the current window (Figure 5.18) displays an unresolved amount of (**18,113.85**). This amount must be zero before this account is ready for the next reconciliation (note below). Continue by first entering

> **20178.85** ⌈ Tab ⌉   to enter the ending balance from your last reconciled statement. This is the closing bank statement or reconciled ending balance from that last reconciliation completed.

Simply Accounting will now require you to enter the outstanding transactions. Continue by pressing

> **105** ⌈ Tab ⌉   to enter the **Source** for this outstanding transaction.

> **Cheque** ⌈ Tab ⌉   to enter the **Comment**.

> **07/28/01** ⌈ Tab ⌉   to enter the **Date** for this transaction.

Tab

to skip past the **Debit** field. You would use the **Debit** field if you have an outstanding transaction that would result in the last ending balance increasing. An example would be an outstanding deposit.

1200.00 Tab

to enter the **Credit** for this outstanding transaction.

Practice Exercise 5.8

Continue to enter the following outstanding bank reconciliation transactions:

Source	106
Comment	Cheque
Date	07/29/01
Debit	—
Credit	400.00
Source	107
Comment	Cheque
Date	07/31/01
Debit	—
Credit	53.50
Source	108
Comment	Cheque
Date	08/05/01
Debit	—
Credit	1000.00
Source	109
Comment	Cheque
Date	08/10/01
Debit	—
Credit	53.50
Source	617
Comment	Deposit
Date	08/15/01
Debit	642.00
Credit	—

Figure 5.19
Set Up Account
Reconciliation
window (entered)

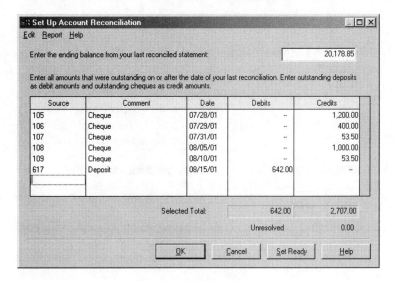

Once you have completed the above exercise, your unresolved balance should be zero (Figure 5.19). If this is the case, continue by

> Clicking on the **Set Ready** button. This will signal to Simply Accounting that you have successfully entered the outstanding transactions from your last reconciled bank statement until now.

> Clicking on the **OK** button within the Simply Accounting Bank Set Ready warning window. This will confirm that once you have set the bank reconciliation to ready, it can not be reversed.

ON-LINE BANKING

Simply Accounting for Windows also provides for access to on-line banking through your preferred bank. Continue from within the General Ledger (Account Reconciliation) window (Figure 5.13) by

> Clicking on the **Class Option** tab.

Figure 5.20
General Ledger
(Class Options)
window

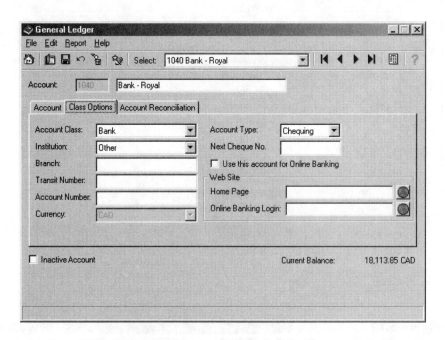

Within the Class Option tab (Figure 5.20) continue by pressing

Tab (3 times)		to move to the **Institution** field.
Tab		to accept the **Institution** as *Other*. This field is used for the selection of the bank accounts directly supported through Simply Accounting for Windows.
0095 Tab		to enter the **Branch** number.
04730 Tab		to enter the **Bank Transit Number**.
4475-304 Tab		to enter the **Bank Account Number**.

Tab   to accept *Chequing* as the **Bank Account Type**. You could also select from the other account types which include Savings, Money Market, and Line of Credit.

110 Tab   as the **Next Cheque Number.**

space bar   to select to **Use this Account for On-line Banking**.

www.royalbank.com Tab   to enter the Home Page web site address.

ww1.royalbank/english/ib/sgne.html Tab
to enter the **On-line Banking Login** web site address.

As you have now provided the on-line banking information, continue by

Closing the General Ledger window.

Practice Exercise 5.9

Enter the **Accounts** window and **Find** and retrieve account **#1050 Bank - Bank of Montreal.** Continue by clicking on the **Account Reconciliation** tabbed button, followed by clicking the **Save Transactions for Account Reconciliation** option.

Within the General Ledger (Account Reconciliation) window, continue with the creation of the following **Linked Accts:**

    Type Income *Income 1*
    Name   *Bank Int*
    Account   *4410*

    Type Expense *Income 1*
    Name   *SCharge*
    Account   *5880*

Continue from within the General Ledger (Account Reconciliation) window by selecting the **Set Up** button. Answer **No** to Selecting outstanding amounts from previous journal entries.

From within the Set Up Account Reconciliation window, continue by

Leaving the **ending balance from your last reconciled statement** as 0.00.

Click the **Set Ready** button and confirm this action.

Practice Exercise 5.10

Enter the **Accounts** window and **Find** and retrieve account **#1060 Bank - Seafirst US Dollar.** Continue with changing the currency (within the Class Option tab) to **USD (US Dollar).** Then continue by clicking on the **Account Reconciliation** tabbed button, followed by clicking the **Save Transactions for Account Reconciliation** option.

Within the General Ledger (Account Reconciliation) window, continue with the creation of the following **Linked Accts:**

Type Income *Income 1*
Name   *Bank Int*
Account   *4410*

Type Expense *Income 1*
Name   *SCharge*
Account   *5880*

Continue from within the General Ledger (Account Reconciliation) window by selecting the **Set Up** button. Answer **No** to Selecting outstanding amounts from previous journal entries.

From within the Set Up Account Reconciliation window, continue by

Leaving the **ending balance from your last reconciled statement** as 0.00.

Click the **Set Ready** button and confirm this action.

Once you have completed this exercise, return to the Simply Accounting - ODC window (Figure 5.14).

MAKING GENERAL LEDGER ENTRIES

Practice Exercise 5.11

Continue from the Simply Accounting - ODC window by changing the session date (option available through the **Maintenance** menu) to **08/31/01.**

Practice Exercise 5.12

Enter the following foreign exchange rates (**Currencies** option from within the **Setup** menu):

Date	Exchange Rate
08/21/01	1.5244
08/28/01	1.5199

Change the exchange rate reminder frequency from *One Day* to *One Week.*

Once you have completed this exercise, return to the Simply Accounting - ODC window (Figure 5.14).

Continue from the Simply Accounting - ODC window (Figure 5.14) with

Opening the **General Journal.**

MAKING FOREIGN CURRENCY GENERAL JOURNAL ENTRIES

As you have already made General Journal entries, extending this exercise for foreign General Journal entries is quite easy.

Figure 5.21
General
Journal
window

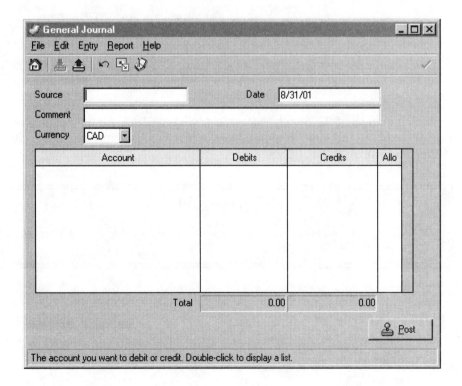

Continue from the General Journal window (Figure 5.21) by entering

Chq102 Tab   as the **Source**.

081601 Tab   as the **Date**.

Deposit from J. Demers Tab   as the **Comment**.

U Tab   to select *USD* as the **Currency**.

Figure 5.22
General Journal
window (Foreign
Exchange rate)

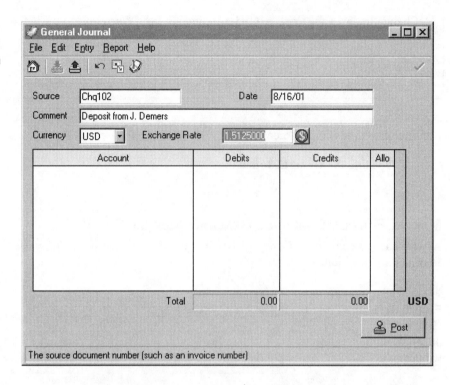

As shown in Figure 5.22, Simply Accounting will now display the closest Exchange Rate to the date of the entry. This rate is retrieved from the Foreign Exchange rate table (**Currencies** option within the **Setup** menu).

HINT: SELECTING THE APPROPRIATE RATE

You can select the appropriate rate by selecting the Dollar sign icon beside the Exchange Rate field.

Continue from within the General Journal window (Figure 5.22) by pressing

Tab

Tab   to move to the Account field.

1060 Tab   to enter the **Account**.

10000.00 (Tab)   to enter the **Debit** amount.

3550 (Tab)   to enter the **Account**.

(Tab)   to accept the default **Credit** amount (*10,000*).

Figure 5.23
General
Journal
(Done)

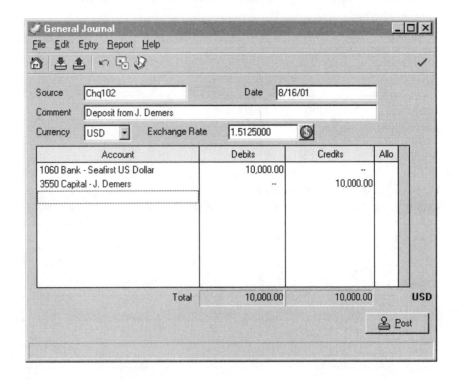

Your General Journal window should resemble Figure 5.23. Once this entry is posted, Simply Accounting will revalue this entry to Canadian currency using the applicable exchange rate.

Continue from within the General Journal window (Figure 5.23) by

Posting your General Journal entry.

Practice Exercise 5.13

GENERAL JOURNAL ENTRIES
Continue with the entry of the following journal entries within the General Journal module. Review Chapter 4 for instructions, if required.

Once you have completed this exercise, return to the Simply Accounting - ODC window (Figure 5.14).

On August 17, 2001, you retrieved the prepaid insurance (recurring entry) and posted this entry using Source Code ADJ104.

On August 18, 2001 you issued Cheque no.110, (Royal Bank Account) to purchase coffee supplies from the Java Hut. The amount of the purchase was $60.00 plus $4.20 GST.

Description:					
Source	Date	Account Name	Account	Debit	Credit
Chq110					

August 21, 2001 a sales invoice number 504 was issued to Vancouver New & Used Books for Regular Freight services of $500 plus $35 GST. The customer will pay later.

Description:					
Source	Date	Account Name	Account	Debit	Credit
Inv504					

You received the Hydro Bill (dated August 22, 2001) from B.C. Hydro (Source Aug/01) in the amount of $150 plus $10.50 GST. You will pay this bill later.

Description:					
Source	Date	Account Name	Account	Debit	Credit
Aug/01					

On August 24, 2001, you retrieved the prepaid insurance (recurring entry) and posted this entry using Source Code ADJ105.

On August 31, 2001 you received a payment from Vancouver New & Used Books for the outstanding invoice from August 21, 2001 (Inv 504). The customers cheque number was Cheque no. 985 deposited to the Royal Bank account.

Description:					
Source	Date	Account Name	Account	Debit	Credit
Chq985					

On August 31, 2001 you issued Cheque no.111 from the Royal Bank to pay the outstanding B.C. Hydro bill (see above entry).

Description:					
Source	Date	Account Name	Account	Debit	Credit
Chq111					

On August 31, 2001 you recorded bank service charges in the amount of $5.25 USD for the Seafirst Account. Use ADJ106 as the source and make sure that this entry is recorded in USD currency with the default currency rate.

Description:					
Source	Date	Account Name	Account	Debit	Credit
ADJ106					

Practice Exercise 5.14

PRINTING FINANCIAL STATEMENTS

Continue with the entry of the following exchange rate:

Date	Exchange rate
08/31/01	1.5101

Continue with the printing of the Balance Sheet (as at 08/31/01) and the Income Statement (period from 08/01/01 to 08/31/01). Be sure to select to revalue your foreign accounts option (accepting the default foreign exchange rate of 1.5101) when printing the Balance Sheet report. Review the previous instructions within this chapter, if required.

HINT: *REVALUATION OF FOREIGN ACCOUNTS*

Revaluation of your foreign accounts within Simply Accounting is a process in which Simply Accounting updates all foreign accounts from the original values to updated values based on the latest foreign exchange rates.

BACKING UP YOUR DATA FILES

Continue with selecting either the **Backup** icon or select the **Backup** menu option from within the **File** menu to backup your Simply Accounting data files.

When backing up your files, use the following selections:

Backup filename: *A:\odc\ODC5B*

Comment: *Using Simply 8 - Chapter 5 Part b*

For further information on how to use the backup feature, please refer to Chapter 3.

FINISHING THE SESSION

Now that you have completed this chapter you must save the data.

To end this session, make sure you are at the Simply Accounting - ODC window. Continue by closing the program (closing the Simply Accounting - ODC window).

Further Practice

To get further practice with the concepts you have learned in this chapter go to Chapter 14 and work through Section 5 of the National Supply Company.

CHAPTER 6

ACCOUNTS RECEIVABLE

CHAPTER 6

ACCOUNTS RECEIVABLE

OBJECTIVES

After working through this chapter you will be able to

1. Explain the importance of an accounting subledger.
2. Prepare for the changeover from a manual accounts receivable system to a computerized system.
3. Add customers to the Simply Accounting for Windows Accounts Receivable. subledger, and later modify customer information or delete customers.
4. Enter opening balances of existing customer accounts.
5. Display and print summary and detail listings.
6. Enter current credit and cash sales using the Sales journal.
7. Enter current accounts receivable payments using the Receipts journal.
8 Reconcile the accounts receivable entries with the General Ledger.
9. Know why it is important to have an audit trail and how to prepare one.

THE PURPOSE OF SUBLEDGERS

The General Ledger is the main ledger in any accounting system. It establishes the trial balance and provides the information for both the balance sheet and the income statement. Why then do we have to be concerned with subledgers?

You can operate an accounting system using only the General Ledger. However, you then have to manually reconcile both the accounts payable and accounts receivable. This may not be a problem if you have only a few customers or vendors. However, if you had hundreds of customers or vendors it would be a difficult if not impossible task. Subledgers provide the following two major benefits:

1. They help to speed up the process of data entry into the accounting system, thus making the accounting task much simpler.
2. They provide detailed information that is readily available.

INCREASED SPEED OF DATA ENTRY

As you know, all journal entries are made up of a series of debits and credits that, in total, equal each other (double-entry bookkeeping). These entries are then posted individually into the General Ledger. This method of data entry for similar entries can be cumbersome and slow.

By using subledgers you can speed up data entry substantially because certain types of entries are similar. For example, let us look at two journal entries for cash disbursements (payments by cheque).

To pay the telephone bill for $150.00 with a cheque from the bank account, you make the entry

Dr. Telephone Expense	$150.00	
Cr. Bank		$150.00

To pay a salary to one of your employees, you make the entry

> Dr. Salary Expense $600.00
>   Cr. Bank $600.00

As you can see, each cash disbursement entry has a corresponding credit entry to the Bank account, because you are paying by cheque. Since all credits are to the Bank, why not enter them as one total? This allows you to use the Payment journal to enter all cheque payments as debits. At the end of each entry, the total amount debited can be credited to the Bank account which is the common credit entry. Entries in other subledgers—Payable, Receivable, Payroll, and Inventory—are treated in a similar manner.

PROVIDES USEFUL INFORMATION

The second advantage of a subledger is that it can provide useful, detailed information about certain aspects of a business. For example, if you use the General Ledger to analyze the Accounts Receivable balance, you will find that the General Ledger will only tell us how much money our credit customers owe us, but nothing else.

For proper management of Accounts Receivable, however, we need more detailed information. We would want to know such things as

- who owes us the money
- what phone number to call to enquire about payment of overdue accounts
- whom to contact
- when to expect receipt of the money
- how long it has been since the charge was made
- whom should you provide with credit
- how much has a customer purchased on credit

We can get this additional information by using an Accounts Receivable subledger that allows us to keep track of such information.

Subledger Listing

To ensure that the subledger agrees with the appropriate control account in the balance sheet, we usually make a listing of the components on a regular basis—each month or each week. This listing can provide us with important information. For example, if we had a balance in accounts receivable of $3,150.00, the control account in the General Ledger—Accounts Receivable— would tell us the total amount that we will collect, but it wouldn't tell us (without a bit of investigation on our part) who owes us the various payments. An Accounts Receivable subledger, however, provides us with all the following important information:

Acme Delivery	$ 145.00
Falcon's Hardware	116.00
Hallmark Cards	66.00
Jello Desserts	214.00
Land Grow Carriers	1,455.00
Rancho Communications	919.00
Western Freight Carriers	235.00
Total	$ 3,150.00

The total of the subledger listing must agree with the control account—Accounts Receivable, in the General Ledger. Without this listing you could not be sure if your accounts receivable were in fact paid or who paid it.

Each of the Simply Accounting system subledgers provides the above information. As you work through each chapter that describes one of the subledgers you should become very familiar with what each subledger does, what kinds of entries are included in each subledger, what the various subledger listings are, and what the associated control account in the General Ledger is.

PURPOSE OF THE ACCOUNTS RECEIVABLE SUBLEDGERS

The Accounts Receivable subledger is used for tracking the credit sales of a business organization and recording customer payments. These transactions are entered through the Sales and Receipt journals, respectively. The subledger allows you to prepare a report called an Aged Accounts Receivable Listing. This listing indicates the customers that owe the company money, how much each customer owes, and the time that has elapsed since the sale was made. This provides the credit manager with some idea when payment from the customer can be expected and also identifies slow payers.

The Accounts Receivable subledger also provides a listing of each customer with their address and telephone number. This listing can be used by the credit manager to contact customers who are delinquent with their payments or who have exceeded their credit limit. As well, this listing can be used for mailing of promotional material to enhance your sales.

SOURCE DOCUMENTS

In Accounts Receivable, we use the source documents that track our customers' purchases and subsequent payments for those purchases.

First, the Accounts Receivable subledger allows us to record sales information using the Sales journal. The information that we require would come from the sales invoice. A journal entry to record sales is as follows:

Dr. Account Receivable	xxx
Cr. [Various sales accounts]	xxx
Cr. Goods & Services Tax (if applicable)	xxx
Cr. Provincial Sales Tax (if applicable)	xxx

The Sales journal will also take care of the cost of goods sold, if we were selling an inventory item. This is covered in greater detail in Chapter 9 describing the Inventory subledger.

The debit entry is always to Accounts Receivable. The credit entry could be distributed to one or more sales accounts and applicable provincial and federal sales tax payable accounts.

Second, the Accounts Receivable subledger with the Receipts journal allows us to record customer payments — the amount, the invoice against which a payment is being made, and the name of the customer. The journal entry for cash receipts is

Dr. Cash	xxx
Cr. Accounts Receivable	xxx

The credit entry is always to Accounts Receivable.

OPEN ITEM ACCOUNTING

The Simply Accounting for Windows system uses the open item method of accounting for accounts receivable as opposed to the balance forward method. The open item method keeps track of all individual invoices as well as the payment made on behalf of each invoice. This method allows you to identify how much is owing from a specific customer, and which invoices are unpaid. In comparison, the balance forward method simply subtracts the payment from the balance owing and shows the new balance. It does not identify specifically which invoices the customer has paid.

The ability to identify specific invoices is the key to good internal control. For this reason, the open item method is superior to the balance forward method as it only accounts for the total owing and not for specific invoices. The open item method would be difficult to implement under a manual accounting system, but a computerized accounting system such as Simply Accounting makes it possible.

Once the invoices are fully paid, you have the option of retaining this information in the system or clearing it out. If you clear it out of the system, or Purge it, the information is lost forever except for the printed copy that you retained. In most instances, that is what you will do after a certain amount of time has elapsed.

The open item method of accounting for invoices provides you with the following kinds of information.

Interest on Late Payments

The open item method allows you to calculate interest charges on overdue accounts receivable because the outstanding invoice amounts and the time that they have been outstanding are clearly indicated.

If you charge interest on a customer's overdue balance, it would be entered into the system as an invoice and the customer would pay it with the regular payment. You would record the interest charge with a credit to interest income.

Bad Debts

The open item method also identifies outstanding invoices so that you can make a judgment as to whether or not you think they will be collectible. To record such an invoice, you would put through a negative invoice with the debit going to Bad Debt Expense.

Prepayments

There are times when your customer wants to make a prepayment for goods or services that will be received at some future date. To record this transaction, you would enter it as a negative invoice, using the cheque number as the invoice number.

GOODS AND SERVICES TAX ACCOUNTING

Simply Accounting for Windows has included the necessary structure to handle accounting for the Goods and Services Tax (GST). GST is charged on all services and goods that qualify (consult Revenue Canada for details). Periodically an amount of GST will be remitted to the Receiver General. This amount is the difference between the amount of GST received from sales minus the amount of GST paid on purchases for the business. If the balance is positive, then GST is remitted to the Received General. If the balance is negative, then the business can file for a refund. The remittance must be filled out displaying the amount of GST collected and paid, along with a total of all goods purchased and a value for sales completed. In order to make this filing easy to complete, Simply Accounting for Windows will produce the necessary Goods and Service Tax report for you (note the GST menu option under the Report option).

COMPUTERIZING ACCOUNTS RECEIVABLE

Before you can begin to convert your manual accounts receivable system to the Simply Accounting system, you must organize your existing data. Let's look at what is involved in organizing data.

ORGANIZE CUSTOMER RECORDS

There are three steps to organizing your customer records.

1. Prepare a customer listing.

2. List the outstanding invoices and enter them.

3. Agree the total outstanding invoices to the control account, Accounts Receivable, in the General Ledger to ensure that they balance.

PREPARE A CUSTOMER LISTING

If you have your company's customer information ready for entry, you can prepare a complete listing of customers who can purchase goods from you on credit, as shown in Figure 6.1. You need their name, street address, city, province, postal code, telephone, and fax number as well as a contact name. The Simply Accounting program will then sort the customers into an alphabetical listing for easy access. The list in Figure 6.1 has been compiled for Overnight Delivery Company.

Name	Address
Cassar Homes Inc. (Entered)	Contact: Sharon Watson 1258 15th Ave. N.E. Vancouver, B.C. V2S 8R7 Phone: 604-456-8585 Fax: 604-456-8597 Terms: 2/10 Net 30 days Currency:CAD Credit Limit $5,000
City Software (Entered)	Contact: Nick Parry 15858 98th Ave. Burnaby, B.C. V6C 3Y7 Phone: 604-544-8632 Fax: 604-544-8633 Terms: 2/5 Net 30 days Currency:CAD Credit Limit $4,500
McMillan Mills Inc. (Entered)	Contact: Phillip Smith 23 Industrial Way Vancouver, B.C. V4N 8Y4 Phone: 604-458-6521 Fax: 604-458-5566 Terms: 2/10 Net 30 days Currency:CAD Credit Limit $5,000

Modern Computer Services (Entered)	Contact: Donald Cormier #32 - South Gate Plaza Vancouver, B.C. V9C 7U8 Phone: 604-455-7878 Fax: 604-455-5839 Terms: Net 30 days (Discount percent and days field left blank). Currency:CAD Credit Limit $2,500
Quality Custom Furniture	Contact: Peter Moore 5555 Royal Ave. Richmond, B.C. V3Z 4V4 Phone: 604-458-7777 Fax: 604-458-7778 Currency: CAD Terms: 2/10 Net 30 days Credit Limit $5,000
Ricco Logistics	Contact: Desiree Lee 540 Irvine Way Seattle, WA 92050 Phone: 260-432-4321 Fax: 260-432-4022 Terms: Net 30 days (Discount percent and days field left blank). Currency: USD Credit Limit $5,000 USD
Solar Heat Control Products	Contact: R.M. Russell 45865 Stewardson Way Burnaby, B.C. V3C 7J7 Phone: 604-455-4545 Fax: 604-455-4483 Terms: Net 30 days Currency: CAD Credit Limit $5,000
TFM International Inc.	Contact: Roxanne Dunwoody Suite 401-1320 Pike Ave Seattle, WA 90034 Phone: 206-736-0272 Fax: 206-736-0274 Terms: Net 30 days Currency: USD Credit Limit: $5,000 USD
Vancouver New & Used Books	Contact: Marie Smith 466 Bay St. Vancouver, B.C. V8N 9N9 Phone: 604-556-8545 Fax: 604-556-8546 Terms: 2/10 Net 30 days Currency: CAD Credit Limit $5,000

Figure 6.1   Customer listing for Overnight Delivery Company

List Outstanding Invoices

Make a list of all unpaid invoices for each customer, inclusive of any GST, up to the time of conversion. The listing should include the date of the invoice, the invoice number, and the amount owing. Any partial payments made by customers against these invoices must also be listed. The unpaid invoices at the end of July 2001 for Overnight Delivery Company are listed in Figure 6.17.

Reconcile to Control Account

Reconcile the total of all outstanding receivables to the balance in the Accounts Receivable account in the existing General Ledger or your trial balance. You must ensure that these two totals agree or you will have problems when you want to change your Simply Accounting Accounts Receivable subledger to READY mode. If you compare the total of Figure 6.17 to the balance in account #1150 in the opening trial balance, you will see that they are the same, $10,312.06. Therefore the balance agrees to the control account.

BACKING UP YOUR DATA FILES

This is a lengthy chapter that requires a large amount of data entry and the chance of making errors exists. If you make an error in a subsequent procedure and your data files are out of balance, you can copy the data files from your backup over the data files on your hard disk and re-enter the data from that backup point on. You will not have to go back to the beginning of the chapter and re-enter a great quantity of data.

Practice is another reason for creating backups periodically as you proceed through the chapter. For example, you may want to practice editing data, or repeat a particular procedure to learn it more thoroughly. With periodic backups you can do that easily.

In this chapter there are four points where it is wise to create a backup. You can number these backups

ODC6A	after entering customer information
ODC6B	after entering customer opening balances
ODC6C	after entering the sales invoices
ODC6D	final backup after completing Chapter 7

You can create these backups on the diskette that you have used up until now for backing up data files from previous chapters. Alternatively, you can create subdirectories on your hard drive and copy the data files from the ODC subdirectory in the appropriate backup subdirectory.

If you are not sure about the backup procedure, refer to Chapter 3.

ENTERING CUSTOMERS

Before you can continue with the entry of sales invoices and receipt payments, you must first create your customer list.

To speed up the data entry time, we have entered several of the customers that appear in Figure 6.1.

Before you continue, copy the starter files from the included CD-ROM. The source directory should be X:\sw0806. We would suggest that you use the enclosed installation program (X:\Setup) to install these files.

Once you have copied the above data files, continue by

Starting Simply Accounting for Windows.

Selecting the ODC (Overnight Delivery Company) data file.

Confirming the Session Date as *08/31/01*.

Closing the To-Do Lists window.

Closing the Checklists window.

Figure 6.2
Simply
Accounting -
ODC window

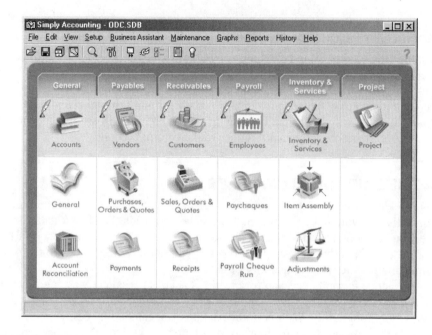

Continue from within the Simply Accounting - ODC window (Figure 6.2) by

Double-clicking on the **Customers** icon.

Figure 6.3
Customers
window

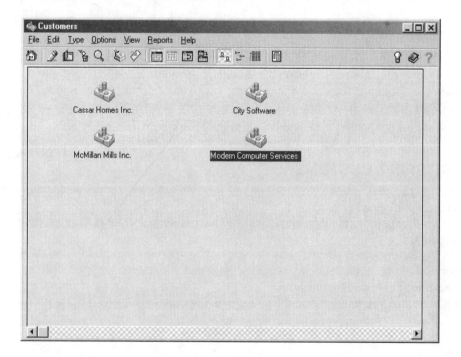

Within the Customers window (Figure 6.3) you will notice that four customer's icons already exist. These have already been created for you and demonstrate how the Customers window can be used to locate a desired customer record.

Within the Customers window, you have similar icons as to those that appear within the Accounts window, (note Chapter4). These include:

Edit (Pencil icon)   **Edit** menu, **Edit** command
allows you to edit the current highlighted customer icon.

Create (Ledger book)   **Edit** menu, **Create** command
allows you to open the Accounts Receivable Ledger for entry of a new customer.

Remove (Trash can)   **Edit** menu, **Remove** command
allows you to delete (upon successful confirmation) the highlighted customer record.

Find (Magnifying Glass)   **Edit** menu, **Find** command
allows you to open the Find window so that you can locate a desired customer record.

Continue from within the Customers window (Figure 6.3) by

Selecting the **Create** icon or selecting the **Create** command from within the **File** menu.

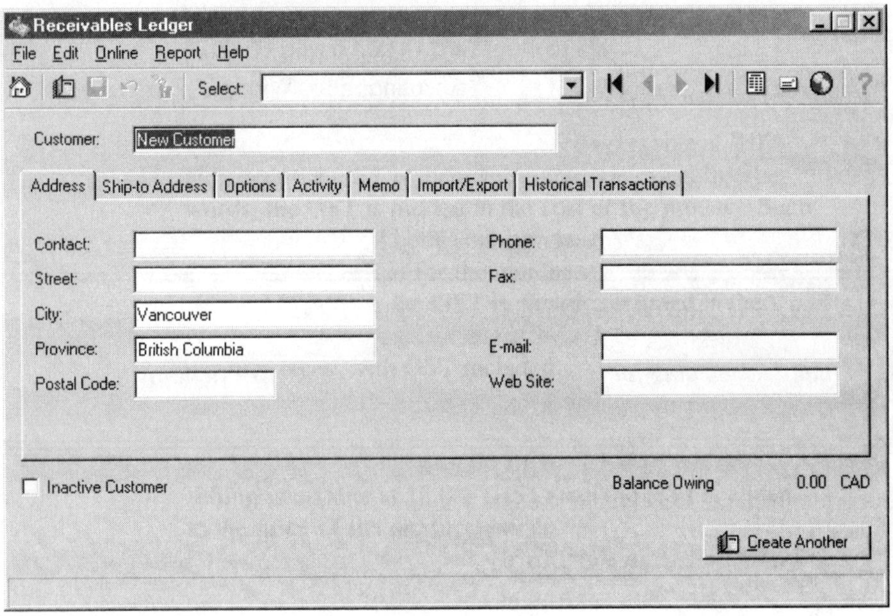

Figure 6.4
Receivables
Ledger
window

Within the Receivable Ledger window (Figure 6.4), you will notice that a tabbed display exists within the display. These include the following areas:

Address	is where you enter the customer's address, phone, facsimile, and Internet information.
Ship-to Address	is the default address if your customer should request a separate shipping address.
Options	allows you to specify discounts and payment terms along with printing and GST options.
Activity	prompts you to enter the year-to-date sales along with last year's sales and credit limit for your customer.
Memo	allows you to enter a memo concerning a particular customer. You can also select to have the memo displayed within the To-Do Lists window at a specific date.
Import/Export	allows your customer to import and process invoices from your company providing they use Simply Accounting for Windows Version 8.0.
History	prompts you to enter the historical invoices and payments prior to converting to Simply Accounting.

> *HINT: ENTERING HISTORICAL TRANSACTIONS*
>
> *Simply Accounting for Windows allows you to enter historical invoices and payments, but only after you have created the customer record.*

Continue from the Receivables Ledger window (Figure 6.4) by entering:

Quality Custom Furniture    to enter the **Customer's Name**.

> *HINT: ENTERING CUSTOMER NAMES*
>
> *Keep in mind that the Name field is used to sort the customer list. Therefore, when you enter customer names, be sure to enter them with the last name first, followed by a comma and then the first name.*

Peter Moore (Tab)   to enter the **Contact**.

5555 Royal Ave. (Tab)   to enter the **Street** address.

Richmond (Tab)   to replace the default **City**.

(Tab)   to accept the default **Province**.

HINT: *DEFAULT CITY AND PROVINCE*

Simply Accounting has copied the city and province fields from your own company profile. As demonstrated above, you can over write the default text or accept.

---

v3z4v4 (Tab)   to enter the **Postal Code**.

6044587777 (Tab)   to enter the **Phone** number.

6044587778 (Tab)   to enter the **Fax** number.

HINT: *ENTERING POSTAL CODE, PHONE, AND FAX NUMBERS*

In Simply Accounting for Windows, postal codes can be entered without capitalization, spaces, or hyphens. Simply Accounting will format them appropriately.

Similarly, you can enter the telephone and facsimile 10-digit number (area code + number) without entering brackets, spaces, or hyphens. Simply Accounting for Windows will format them using brackets and hyphens as required.

Continue from the Receivables Ledger window (Figure 6.4) by

Clicking the **Options** tabbed button.

Figure 6.5
Receivable
Ledger (Options)
window

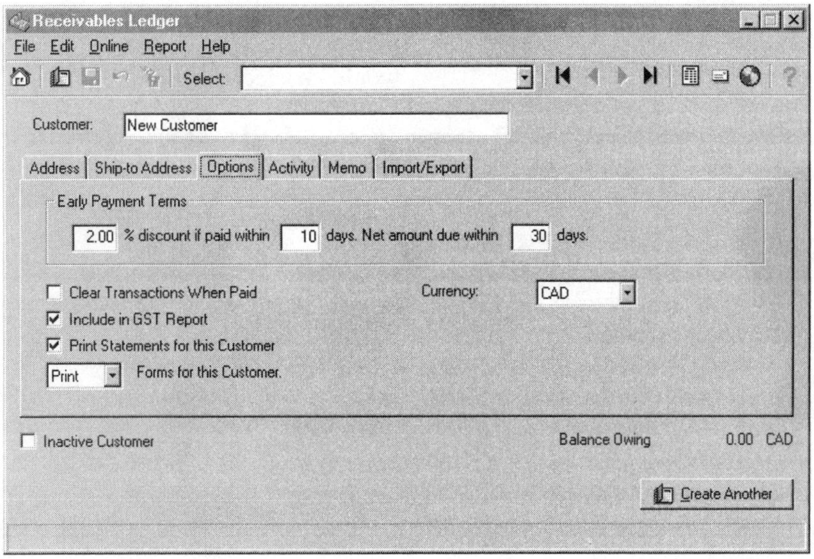

From within the Receivables Ledger (Options) window (Figure 6.5) you can select from the following options:

Early Payment Terms   allows you to specify payment terms for your customer. For example, you can specify a discount if the customer pays within a specific number of days, or simply specify that the net payment is due after a specified number of days. The default terms allow for a 2.0% discount to be given, provided that the customer pays within 10 days. If not paid within 10 days, then the customer owes the complete bill within 30 days, (to maintain current billing status).

Clear Invoices When Paid   allows you to specify whether Simply Accounting will automatically remove invoices and associated payments from within the Receivables module once the invoice has been paid in full. This option, while ensuring that your Accounts Receivables aging reports displays only outstanding transactions, also sacrifices the availability of a customer history for inquiry purposes.

HINT: *CLEAR INVOICE WHEN PAID OPTION*

You should not select this option for each customer so that you can retain the most complete customer transaction history for inquiry purposes. You can however remove date specific transactions (fully paid) for specific customers from within the **Maintenance** *menu, (Simply Accounting - ODC) window.*

Include in GST Report   provides you with the option of specifying whether this customer is to be included in the GST report. Normally, you would select this option if your customer is registered for collection of GST or HST. However, for customers that are not registered for GST or HST, you would unselect this option.

HINT: *GST REPORTING WITHIN SIMPLY ACCOUNTING*

From Simply Accounting, you will be able to display and print a single page report that includes all GST collected and paid for your business. To use this feature, however, requires you to enter all sales in the Sales Journal and all purchases in the Purchase Journal.

If you only use the General Ledger then any entries you make for GST are not included in the GST report. You can however generate a General Ledger report that includes the GST applicable accounts. Recall that we have already made entries in the General Journal that included GST.

Print Statements for this Customer allows you to specify the option of whether this customer will receive a statement of their invoices. The printing of the statements is a reporting option and must be used if you plan to charge interest on overdue accounts.

HINT: *PRINTING STATEMENTS FOR CUSTOMERS*

While Simply Accounting provides a powerful Statement printing option, you should only use this reporting option if you currently issue an invoice. While issuing a statement reminds customers of the payments due, it may end up slowing down your receivables as some customers will become accustomed to paying the statement amount instead of the previously issued invoice.

As mentioned above, if you are planning to have Simply Accounting calculate overdue interest on invoices, you must print statements for those customers. While Simply Accounting will make this calculation, it will not make the entry in the Receivable module. Therefore you must create individual invoices for interest charges that are then shown on each customer's statement.

Print/Email Forms for this Customer allows you to specify whether customer invoices, quotes, and statements are to be printed or sent by electronic mail (e-mail) to the customer.

Currency allows you to specify the currency in which transactions will be processed. By default the currency is CAD (Canadian dollars) based on the Currencies options within the Setup menu.

As the default terms are correct for this customer, continue by:

Clicking on the **Activity** tabbed button.

Figure 6.6
Receivable
Ledger (Activity)
window

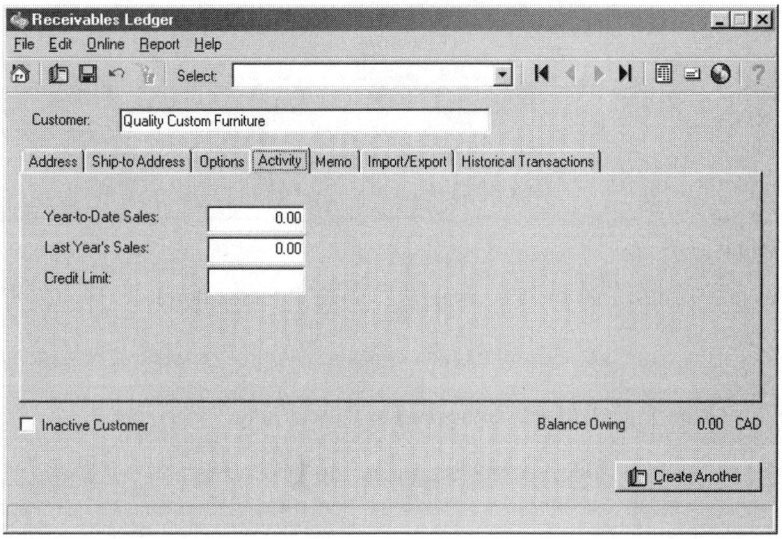

Continue from within the Receivables Ledger (Activity) window by pressing:

| Tab | to move to the **Year-to-Date Sales** field. |

| Tab | Tab | Tab | to move to the **Credit Limit**. |

While the entry of statistical information relating to Year-to-Date and Last Year's Sales is important, for simplicity purposes we have skipped this data entry.

5000.00 | Tab | to enter the **Credit Limit** for this customer.

HINT: DETERMINING AN APPROPRIATE CREDIT LIMIT

While extending credit to your customers is risky, it also translates into increased sales and cash flow. If you are a small business owner, you take a gamble with each new customer when you extend credit to them. You should therefore request a credit application so you can check the customer's credit standing. You may also want to have a personal creditor liability for the directors or any customer who is incorporated. You should generally start your new customers with a low credit limit and slowly increase it according to the customer's current payment activity.

Continue from within the Receivables Ledger (Activity) window by

Clicking the **Memo** tabbed button.

Figure 6.7
Receivables
Ledger (Memo)
window

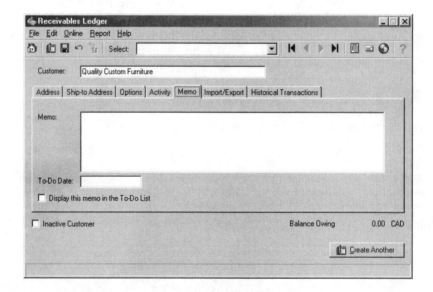

Continue from within the Receivables Ledger (Memo) window (Figure 6.7) by

Entering the **Memo** text as *Contact customer regarding re-order request.*

Entering **09-15-01** as the **To-Do Date**.

Select the **Display this memo in the To-Do List**.

Simply Accounting will now display and remind you to contact this customer regarding the re-order request.

Continue from within the Receivables Ledger (Memo) window (Figure 6.7) by

Clicking on the **Import/Export** tabbed button.

Figure 6.8
Receivables
Ledger
(Import/Export)
window

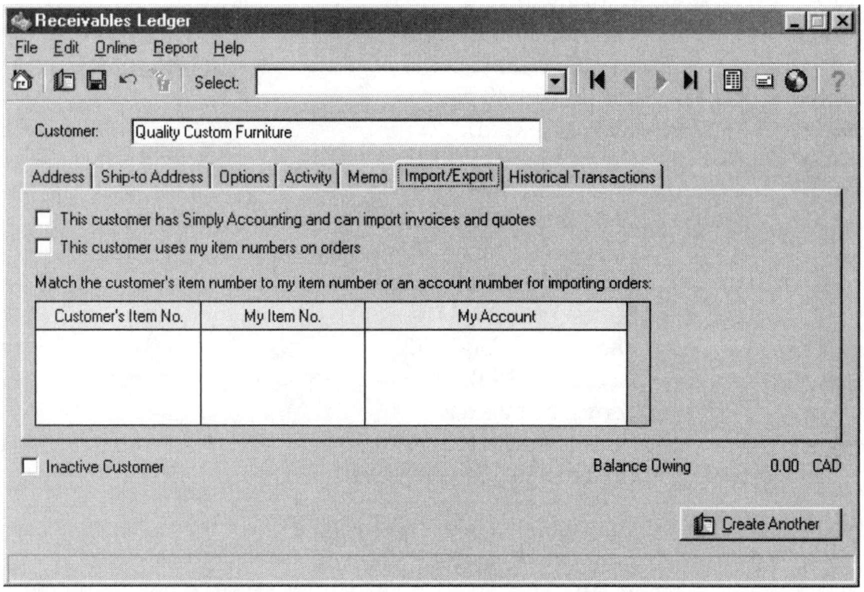

Within the Receivables Ledger (Import/Export) window (Figure 6.8) you can specify if this customer uses Simply Accounting and can import your invoices. If this is option is available, you can then enter your customer's inventory code and the corresponding inventory code for your company. This will then allow your customer to receive and import sales invoices as purchases, with automatic allocation to the applicable inventory items for your customer.

The last tabbed area is for the entry of the **Historical Transactions**. This will be reviewed later in the chapter.

As you have entered all relevant information for this customer, continue by

Clicking on the **Create Another** button.

Practice Exercise 6.1

ENTERING CUSTOMERS

Continue with the entry of the following customers:

Ricco Logistics
Contact: Desiree Lee
540 Irvine Way
Seattle, WA 92050
Phone: 260-432-4321
Fax: 260-432-4022
Terms: Net 30 days (Discount percent and days field left blank).
Currency: USD
Credit Limit $5,000 USD

Practice Exercise 6.1 continued

Solar Heat Control Products
Contact: R.M. Russell
45865 Stewardson Way
Burnaby, B.C. V3C 7J7
Phone: 604-455-4545
Fax: 604-455-4483
Terms: Net 30 days
Currency: CAD
Credit Limit $5,000

TFM International Inc.
Contact: Roxanne Dunwoody
Suite 401-1320 Pike Ave
Seattle, WA 90034
Phone: 206-736-0272
Fax: 206-736-0274
Terms: Net 30 days
Currency: USD
Credit Limit: $5,000 USD

Vancouver New & Used Books
Contact: Marie Smith
466 Bay St.
Vancouver, B.C. V8N 9N9
Phone: 604-556-8545
Fax: 604-556-8546
Terms: 2.5/10 Net 30 days
Currency: CAD
Credit Limit $5,000

Once you have completed this exercise, close both the Receivables Ledger and Accounts window. You will then return to the Simply Accounting - ODC window (Figure 6.2).

Then continue with the following:

Continue with the selection of the **Calculate Discount before tax** option within the Settings/Receivables window.

Then return to the Simply Accounting - ODC window.

BACK UP YOUR DATA FILES

Continue by backing up your data files. Call this backup:

Backup Filename:	A:\odc\ODC6A
Comment:	Receivables Part a

If you are unsure of how to complete the backup procedure, please refer to Chapter 3 for complete instructions.

MODIFYING CUSTOMER INFORMATION

There are times when you have to change customer information, such as address or billing terms.

To modify a customer's record, continue from the Simply Accounting - ODC window (Figure 6.2) by

Opening the **Customers** window and selecting the **Customer's** icon.

Figure 6.9
Customers
window

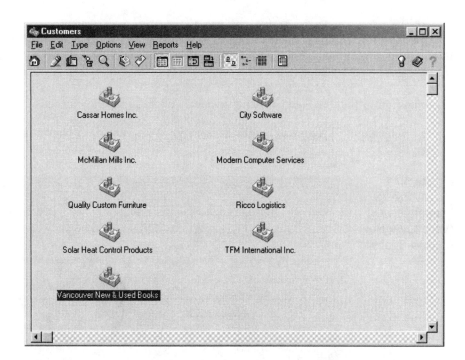

Select the **Find** icon (magnified glass icon) from within the **Customers** window (Figure 6.9) or press ⬚ Alt ⬚ + ⬚ E ⬚ to access the **Edit** menu followed by selecting the **Find** menu option.

Figure 6.10
Find Customer
window

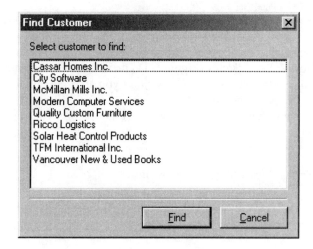

Within the Find Customer window (Figure 6.10), Simply Accounting displays a list of your customers in alphabetical order.

You can select the appropriate customer by either using your keyboard (⬆ or ⬇ and Enter to select) or your mouse.

HINT: *SCROLLING THROUGH CUSTOMER LISTS*

When you want to locate a desired customer through the Find Customer window (Figure 6.10), you can press the first letter of the customer's name to jump to that area of the customer list, Example: Press the letter S *to jump to Solar Heat Control Products.*

Continue from within the Find Customer window (Figure 6.10) by

Selecting (and retrieving) the customer record for Vancouver New & Used Books.

Figure 6.11
Receivables
Ledger window
(Vancouver New
& Used Books)

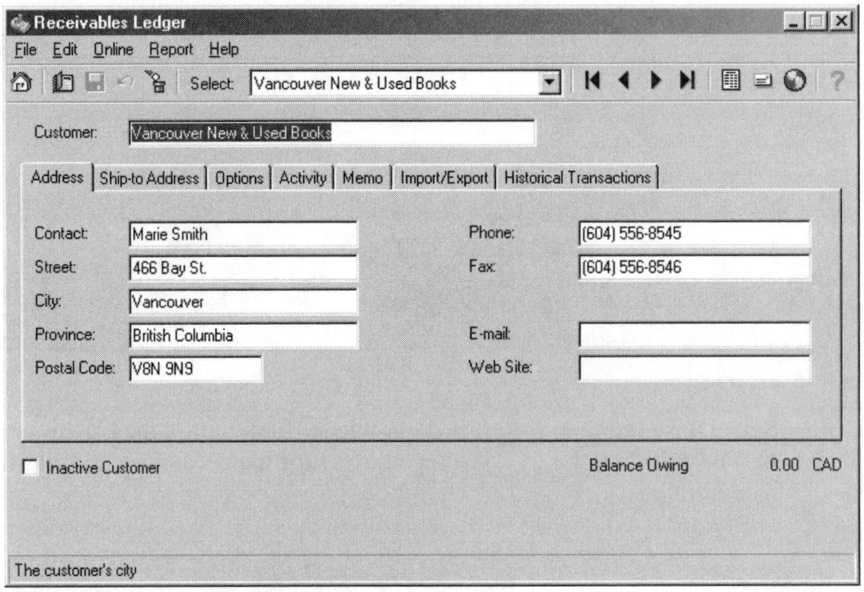

You will notice that when Simply Accounting displays the Receivables Ledger window for Vancouver New & Used Books (Figure 6.11) there is no Create button as when you added a new customer earlier in the chapter. This is because you are in the modification (or deletion) function of Simply Accounting for Windows.

To save any changes made to your customer record, you can do any of the following:

Select and display another customer's record.

Close the Receivables Ledger window.

Select the **Create** button to signal to Simply Accounting for Windows that you want to create a new customer.

NAVIGATING THROUGH THE CUSTOMER LIST

As mentioned above, you can locate customer records by selecting the **Find** option from within the **Edit** menu. This also applies to the Receivables Ledger window (Figure 6.11). However, you can also scroll through the customer list by

Clicking the **Play (Forward)** button located within the toolbar - Receivables Ledger window to move forward one customer record.

Clicking the **Play (Reverse) button** to move back one customer record.

Clicking the **Fast Forward** button to jump to the last customer within the list.

Clicking the **Rewind** button to jump to the first customer within the list.

ENTERING THE HISTORICAL INVOICES

As the Overnight Delivery Company is converting its accounting system to Simply Accounting, we will now need to provide Simply Accounting with a list of the customer invoices and partial payments that make up the Accounts Receivables balance of $10,312.06, as per the trial balance.

Continue from within the Receivables Ledger window (Figure 6.11) by

Clicking on the **Historical Transactions** tabbed button.

> **HINT:** *ENTERING CUSTOMER HISTORICAL TRANSACTIONS*
>
> *To be able to enter your customers' historical (outstanding) invoices and partial payments, you must first create the customers' records and then retrieve the created record.*

Figure 6.12
Receivables Ledger (Historical Transactions) window

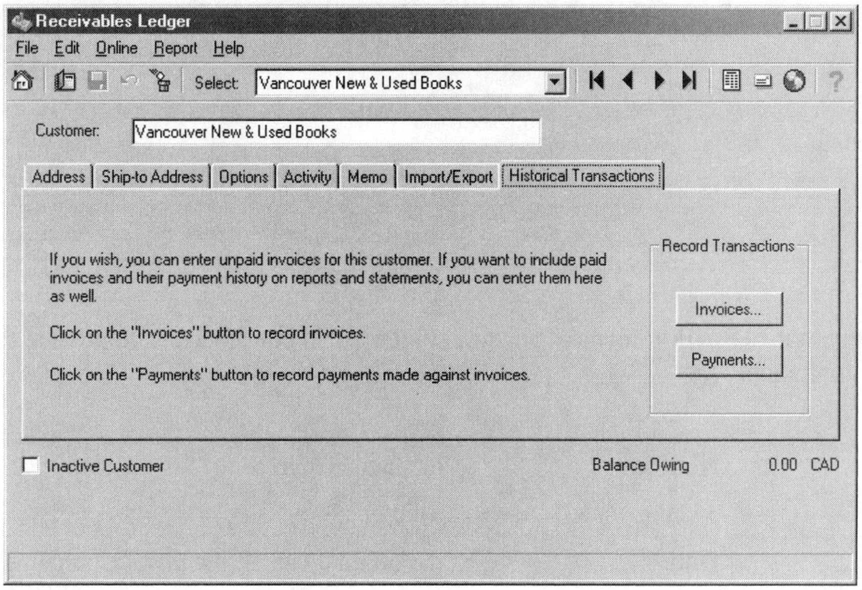

In the Receivables Ledger (History) window (Figure 6.12) you can select from the following:

Invoices   where you enter historical (outstanding) invoices at the time of converting to Simply Accounting.

Payments   where you enter partial payments that were made against the above historical invoices.

An example of how to handle historical invoices and partial payments would be an original invoice for $100.00 to which the customer made a partial payment of $25.00, thus the net owing for this invoice would be $75.00. You would enter the original invoice of $100.00, followed by a partial payment of $25.00. This will provide the Receivables Ledger with the level of detail that will allow you to track the original invoice along with the partial payment.

Continue from within the Receivables Ledger (Historical Transactions) window (Figure 6.12) by

Selecting the **Invoices** button.

Figure 6.13
Historical
Invoices
window

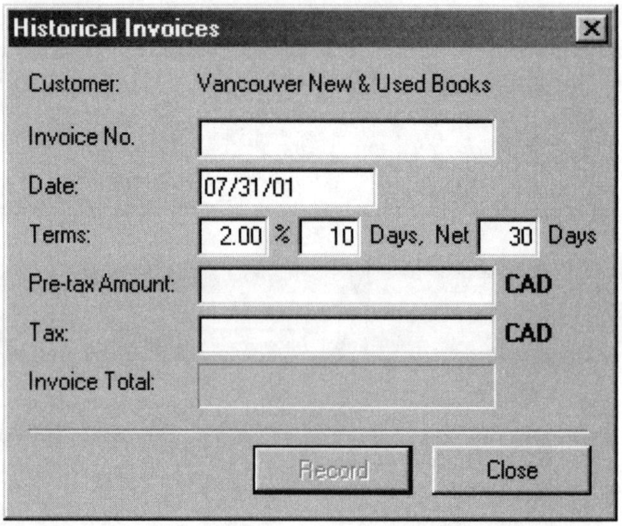

Within the Historical Invoices window (Figure 6.13) you are asked to provide the following information:

Number   the invoice number.

Date   the original date of the invoice (when issued).

Terms   payment terms for this invoice, (displays default for customer record but can be modified).

Pre-tax Amount   the amount owing (net of taxes). This is displayed because we have selected to calculate discounts net of taxes, thus Simply Accounting will require the invoice amount (net of taxes).

Tax   the amount of tax owing on the invoice.

Continue from within the Historical Invoices window (Figure 6.13) by entering

4440 [Tab]   to enter the **Invoice Number**.

07/12/01 [Tab]   to enter the **Invoice Date**.

[Tab] [Tab] [Tab]   to accept the default **Payment Terms**.

86.66 [Tab]   to enter the **Pre-tax Amount**.

6.07 [Tab]   too enter the **Tax**.

Figure 6.14
Historical
Invoices
(Entered)
window

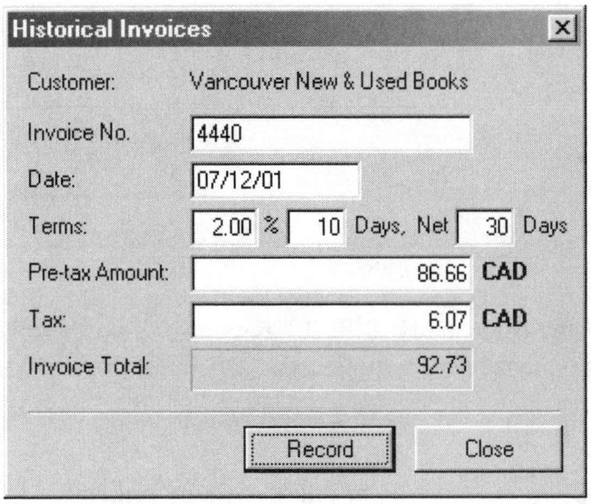

If your Historical Invoices window resembles Figure 6.14 (Invoice total of $92.73), continue by

Clicking the **Record** button.

As we are currently done with the Historical Invoices for Vancouver New & Used Books, continue by

Clicking the **Close** button.

HINT: RECORDING HISTORICAL INVOICES

*It is important that you click the **Record** button to save your historical invoice. You will only select the **Close** button when you are finished with the entry of the historical invoices for this customer, thus returning to the Receivables Ledger window (Figure 6.12).*

ENTERING HISTORICAL PAYMENTS

In some instances, you may have received a partial payment for an invoice, with the remaining amount still outstanding. In this instance, you must enter the original invoice as well as the partial payment that has been made against this invoice. This will provide both you and the customer with the detail pertaining to the original invoice as well as the partial payment.

Continue from the Receivables Ledger (History) window with Vancouver New & Used Books retrieved (Figure 6.12) by

Clicking on the **Payments** button.

Figure 6.15
Historical
Payments
window

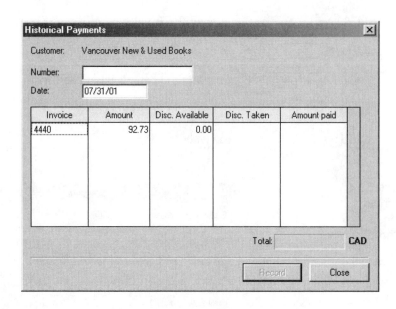

As shown in Figure 6.15, the Historical Payments window displays the historical invoices against which payments can be applied for Vancouver New & Used Books. Continue by entering

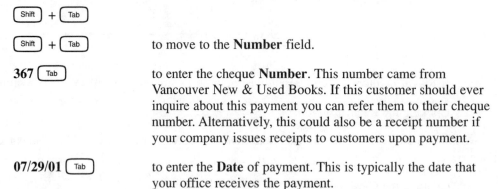

Shift + Tab	
Shift + Tab	to move to the **Number** field.
367 Tab	to enter the cheque **Number**. This number came from Vancouver New & Used Books. If this customer should ever inquire about this payment you can refer them to their cheque number. Alternatively, this could also be a receipt number if your company issues receipts to customers upon payment.
07/29/01 Tab	to enter the **Date** of payment. This is typically the date that your office receives the payment.

Simply Accounting will then allow you to enter the Amount paid for each outstanding invoice for Vancouver New & Used Books. Continue by pressing

| Tab | to move to the Discount Taken for invoice 4440. |
| Tab | accept the default discount taken (**0.00**). |

Simply Accounting now assumes that the default payment will be the total amount for invoice 4440. As this is not the case, continue by entering

50.00 ⌈ Tab ⌉   to override the default Amount paid for invoice 4440.

Figure 6.16
Historical
Payments
window
(entered)

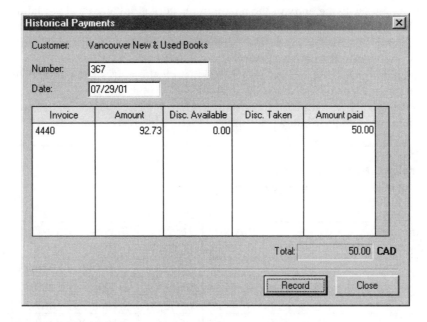

Your Historical Payment window for Vancouver New & Used Books should now resemble Figure 6.16. Should this be case, continue by

Clicking the **Record** button. This will record the above partial payment entry.

As we now want to return to the Receivables Ledger window (Figure 6.12), continue by

Clicking the **Close** button.

HINT: HISTORICAL OR CURRENT ENTRIES?

As with the General Ledger module, Simply Accounting for Windows Version 8.0 allows you to enter current invoices and payments prior to entering the historical invoices and partial payments. This example was demonstrated within the General Journal in Chapter 5.

You should, however, first enter the historical invoices and partial payments. This will ensure that you have the appropriate historical information, especially if one of your customers decides to remit a current payment for a historical invoice.

Practice Exercise 6.2

ENTERING HISTORICAL INVOICES AND
PARTIAL HISTORICAL PAYMENTS

Continue with the entry of the remaining historical invoices and partial historical payments as shown in Figure 6.17.

Enter the historical invoices first, followed by the entry of the historical partial payments. Remember to **Record** each entry.

Remember that you previously entered historical invoices and partial historical payments for Vancouver New & Used Books, (do not re-enter).

Once you have completed this exercise, close the Receivables Ledger window. You will then return to the Simply Accounting - ODC window (Figure 6.2).

Overnight Delivery Company
Listing of Accounts Receivable
July 31, 2001

Customer	Inv #	Date	Terms	Pre-Tax	Tax	Amount
Cassar Homes Inc.	4434	07/01/01	2/10net30	1,923.13	194.62	2,067.75
	4448	07/12/01	2/10net30	1,336.25	93.54	1,429.79
	4430	06/18/01	2/10net30	280.37	19.63	300.00
	4419	06/12/01	2/10net30	467.29	32.71	500.00
	4418	06/11/01	2/10net30	460.35	32.22	492.57
City Software	4446	07/15/01	2/5net30	92.99	6.51	99.50
McMillan Mills Inc.	4429	07/12/01	2/10net30	771.51	54.01	825.52
	4438	07/21/01	2/10net30	201.27	14.09	215.36
	4299	06/02/01	2/10net30	305.34	21.37	326.71
	4442	07/09/01	2/10net30	1,612.89	112.90	1,725.79
	4439	07/10/01	2/10net30	282.36	19.76	302.12
	4433	07/05/01	2/10net30	771.50	54.00	825.50
Modern Computer Services	4431	07/12/01	net30	53.74	3.76	57.50
	4450	07/15/01	net30	27.96	1.96	29.92
Quality Custom Furniture	4437	07/19/01	2/10net30	630.21	44.12	674.33
	4449	07/29/01	2/10net30	124.72	8.73	133.45
Solar Heat Control Product	4428	07/12/01	net30	1,549.69	108.48	1,658.17
Vancouver New & Used Books	Entered	07/12/01	2/10net30	86.66	6.07	92.73
	4447	07/21/01	2/10net30	154.53	10.82	165.35

Partial Payments						
Name	Chq No.	Payment		Inv. No.	Discount	Amount
Cassar Homes Inc.	1189	07/30/01		4448	0.00	1,000.00
McMillan Mills Inc.	289	07/29/01		4429	0.00	500.00
Modern Computer Services	816	07/31/01		4450	0.00	10.00
Vancouver New & Used Books	Entered	07/29/01		4440	0.00	50.00
	369	07/30/01		4447	0.00	50.00
Total						10,312.06

Figure 6.17 Listing of outstanding receivables and partial payments for Overnight Delivery Company

Practice Exercise 6.3

ENTERING GENERAL LEDGER ACCOUNTS

Continue with the entry (creation) of the following General Ledger Accounts (review Chapter 4 for instructions):

For the fields for which no information is given, accept the default values.

Account Number:	2105
Description:	HST Collected on Sales
Type:	Subgroup Account
Account Class:	Current Liability

Account Number:	2115
Description:	HST Paid on Purchases
Type:	Subgroup Account
Account Class:	Current Liability

Account Number:	4020
Description:	Other Freight
Type:	Group Account
Account Class:	Revenue

Account Number:	1155
Description:	Credit Card Receivables
Type:	Subgroup Account
Account Class:	Accounts Receivable

Account Number:	1159
Description:	Total Accounts Receivable
Type:	Subgroup Total

Account Number:	5885
Description:	Credit Card Merchant charges
Type:	Group Account
Account Class:	Expense

Continue with the modification of the following account:

Account Number:	1150 (Accounts Receivable)
New Type:	Subgroup Account
Account Number:	2120 (GST Owing (Refund))
New Description:	GST/HST Owing (Refund)

Once you have completed this exercise, return to the Simply Accounting - ODC window.

LINKING TO THE GENERAL LEDGER

Before you are able to enter current transactions in the Sales and Receipts journals, and set the Receivables module to current status (READY mode), you have to first specify the required integration accounts.

Continue from within the Simply Accounting - ODC window (Figure 6.2) by

Selecting the **Setup** menu.

Selecting the **Linked Accounts** menu command within the **Setup** menu.

Selecting the **Receivables** menu command within the **Linked Accounts** submenu.

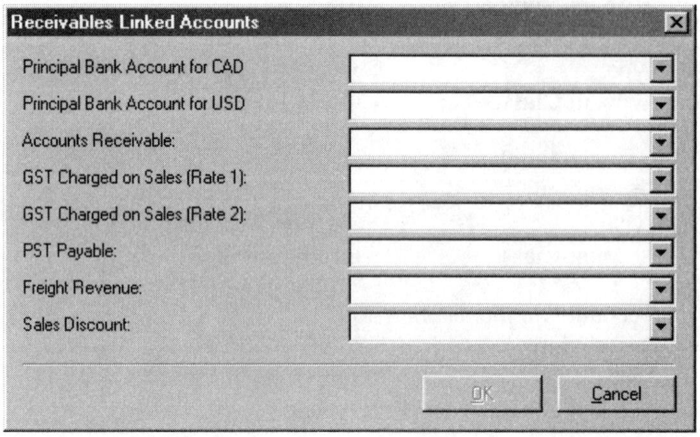

Figure 6.18
Receivables
Linked
Accounts

Within the Receivables Linked Accounts window (Figure 6.18), you are asked to provide the following General Ledger accounts:

(1) Principal Bank Account for CAD
(2) Principal Bank Account for USD

are the bank accounts which you can select to deposit customers' payments (receipts).

Accounts Receivable

is the account that will be used as the Accounts Receivable control account for all Accounts Receivable transactions.

GST Charged on Sales (Rate 1)
GST Charged on Sales (Rate 2)

are the two GST/HST accounts for the collection of GST (Goods and Services Tax) and/or HST (Harmonized Sales Tax).

PST Payable

is the account used for the collection of PST (Provincial Sales Tax).

Freight Revenue

is the account that will be used for the posting of the freight revenue (if applicable). This field is required as the Sales Journal window includes a separate designated Freight Revenue field.

Sales Discount

is the account that will be used for any sales discounts that have been provided to your customers.

Practice Exercise 6.4

ENTERING RECEIVABLE LINKED ACCOUNTS

Continue with the entry of the required Receivables Linked Accounts using the pull down arrow for each account field.

Once you have entered all of the required Receivables Linked Accounts, compare your entries to Figure 6.19 to ensure accuracy.

If your selected Receivables Linked Accounts match those displayed in Figure 6.19, Click OK to return to the Simply Accounting - ODC window (Figure 6.2).

Figure 6.19
Receivables
Linked Accounts
window (entered)

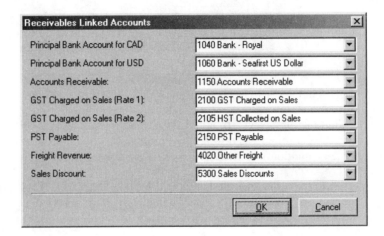

BALANCING TO THE GENERAL LEDGER

At this point, you have entered both your customers and historical balances. You will now want to ensure that the total historical invoices (less partial payments) match the Accounts Receivable balance in the trial balance (as of July 31, 2001— Conversion date). If you are not in balance, make any necessary changes. You have to be in balance prior to setting the Accounts Receivable module to current entry status (READY mode). Once you set the module to current status (READY mode), you will not be able to modify the opening balances.

DISPLAYING THE CUSTOMER AGED REPORT

Continue from within the Simply Accounting - ODC (Figure 6.2) by

Selecting the **Report** menu.

Selecting the **Receivables** menu option.

Selecting the **Customer Aged Report** option.

HINT: ACCESSING RECEIVABLE REPORTS

*While the **Reports** menu in the Simply Accounting - ODC screen provides access to all related receivables reports, you can also display and print all receivables reports through the **Reports** menu within the Customers window (Figure 6.9).*

Figure 6.20
Customer
Aged Report
Options window

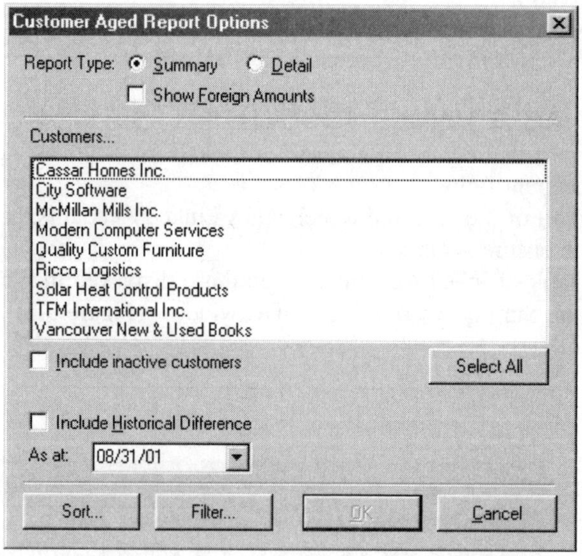

Continue within the Customer Aged Report options window (Figure 6.20) by

Clicking the **Select All** button. This action will select all customers to be included within the Customer Aged Report. Alternatively, you could select individual customers (single or multiple) by clicking on each customer in the displayed list.

Clicking on the **Include Historical Difference** option. This action will automatically check the Receivables total net balance owing to the General Ledger receivables account (specified in the above Linked Accounts exercise) and display any difference.

Change the **As at** date to *07/31/01*. This will resemble the balances at the conversion date for this company.

Ensure that the **Summary/Detail** option is set to **Summary**. This will suppress all transaction detail and display customer balances (aged). If you select Detail it will include all invoice details along with payment detail. You should do this only if you don't balance to the General Ledger.

Click the **OK** button.

Figure 6.21
Customer
Aged
Summary
window

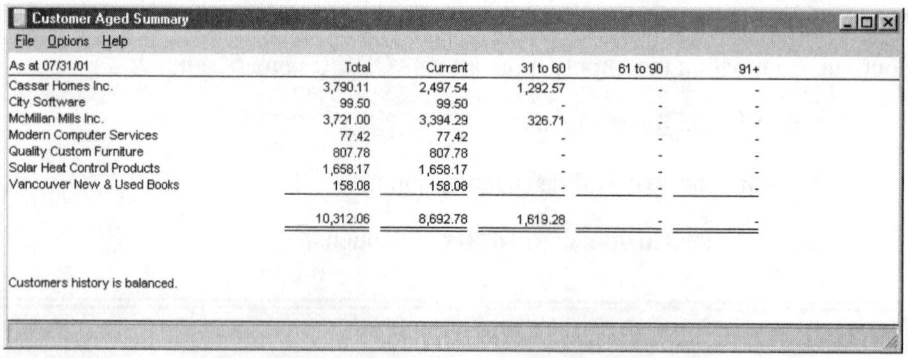

As at 07/31/01	Total	Current	31 to 60	61 to 90	91+
Cassar Homes Inc.	3,790.11	2,497.54	1,292.57	-	-
City Software	99.50	99.50	-	-	-
McMillan Mills Inc.	3,721.00	3,394.29	326.71	-	-
Modern Computer Services	77.42	77.42	-	-	-
Quality Custom Furniture	807.78	807.78	-	-	-
Solar Heat Control Products	1,658.17	1,658.17	-	-	-
Vancouver New & Used Books	158.08	158.08	-	-	-
	10,312.06	8,692.78	1,619.28	-	-

Customers history is balanced.

Continue by comparing your Customer Aged Summary window to Figure 6.21. The results displayed on your screen should match that shown in Figure 6.21 for each customer, as to total and also as to aged totals. If not, display the Customer Aged Report in detail and match your entries to those in Figure 6.17.

> **HINT:** *USING THE REPORT DRILL-DOWN FEATURE*
>
> *Simply Accounting for Windows provides a reporting drill-down feature. Place your mouse over a financial amount, where the mouse cursor changes to display a magnifying glass. Then click your left mouse button and Simply Accounting will display the detail pertaining to that financial amount (drilling down to the detail).*
>
> *For example, you can use this feature if you are having a problem balancing to the amounts displayed in Figure 6.21.*

If your figures check and you balance to the General Ledger, thencontinue by

closing the Customer Aged Summary window, (and any other report window — if you used the report drill-down feature). You will then return to the Simply Accounting - ODC window (Figure 6.2).

If, however, you <u>do not</u> balance to the General Ledger, you can still correct the historical invoices and partial payments.

"Drill down" in your report on any customer balances that do not balance. In the detail report take note of the customer, invoice, or receipt number and difference.

While it would be quite easy to enter an adjustment to a historical invoice or adjustment receipt payment to balance to the General Ledger, this will create confusion later when you attempt to apply a payment from your customer or generate a statement for your customer, because your customer may not recognize the adjustment entry. Instead do the following:

Apply an adjustment payment to the invoice that is in error. You should also do this if you have errors in the partial payment amount. The amount of the payment should be the remaining amount to bring the historical invoice balance to zero. Simply Accounting will provide the default payment amount.

The next step is to overcome an integrity issue with Simply Accounting that will prevent you from using the same invoice number twice (for the same) customer. You can do this as follows:

From the Simply Accounting - ODC window, select the **Maintenance** menu.

From the **Maintenance** menu, select the **Clear Paid Transactions** menu option.

Select the **Clear paid Customer Invoices** submenu option from within the **Clear Paid Transactions** menu.

Figure 6.22
Clear Paid
Customer
Transactions

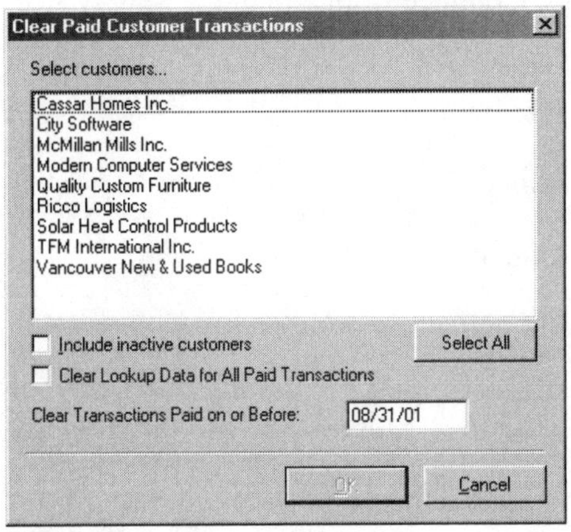

Continue from the Clear Paid Customer Invoices window (Figure 6.22) by

> Selecting the customer that is in error (click on the customer within the list).

> Change to **Clear Invoices Paid on or Before** date to the conversion date of 07/31/01.

The **Clear Invoice Lookup Data for all Paid Invoices** option will not have an effect as this will only remove lookup detail pertaining to current (non-historical invoices).

> Click the **OK** button.

Simply Accounting will ask you to confirm this option. You should **Backup** your data first. This option is available from the confirmation window.

Once you remove the Paid Customer Invoices for the customer in error, you can then continue with the re-entry of the invoice in error (and any applicable historical receipt payments). Then continue with displaying the Customer Aged Report to ensure balancing to the General Ledger.

BACKING UP YOUR DATA FILES

At this point, return to the Simply Accounting - ODC window (Figure 6.2) and continue with the backup function.

> Call this backup:

Backup Filename:	A:\odc\ODC6B
Comment:	Receivables Part b

Once you have completed the backup process, return to the Simply Accounting - ODC window (Figure 6.2).

COMPLETING THE CONVERSION

Having entered the opening balances, the conversion process from a manual to a computerized accounts receivable system is virtually completed. There are three things left to do.

1. Review Accounts Receivable Settings.
2. Set the integration accounts.
3. Change from Historical mode.

REVIEWING ACCOUNT RECEIVABLE SETTINGS

Prior to continuing with the entry of current invoice and receipts payments, it is recommended that you review the Receivables settings. Continue from within the Simply Accounting - ODC window by

> Selecting the **Setup** menu.

> Selecting the **Settings** menu option.

From within the **Settings** window, continue by

> Selecting the **Receivables** tabbed button.

Figure 6.23
Settings
(Receivables)
window

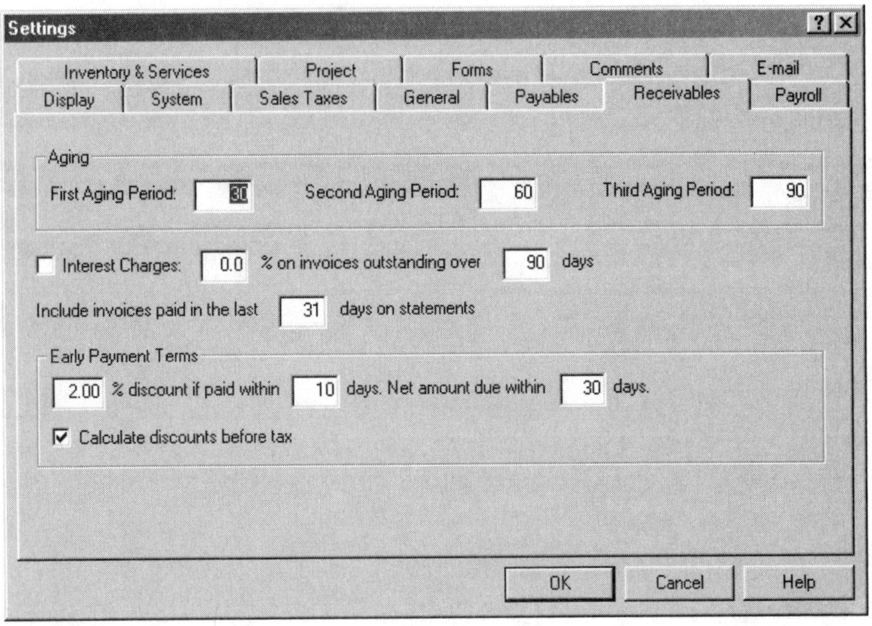

As displayed in Figure 6.23, the Settings (Receivables) window will be displayed. The fields that are shown in Figure 6.23 are the following:

Aging	When you printed both the Customer Aged Summary and Customer Aged Detail reports, you would have noticed that the report separates the outstanding balances by 30, 60, and 90 days. This is called aging. It allows you to determine the number of days that an invoice has been outstanding for each customer. However, for some businesses 30, 60, 90 days is not helpful if they offer terms such as Net 7 days, for example. In this case, the appropriate aging periods would be 7, 14, and 21 days.
Interest Charges	Some companies charge interest on outstanding invoices. Simply Accounting for Windows will generate the appropriate interest charges and report these amounts whenever statements are printed. You must tell Simply Accounting the rate of interest to be charged and how many days an invoice must be overdue before interest is charged. However, you will have to enter these interest charges as invoices.
Include invoices	This option allows you to decide which invoices will be printed on the statements that are sent to customers. For example, a company may only wish to include invoice history for the past 10 days.
Early Payment Terms	Specify the default terms for new customers. This includes an option to select whether or not to calculate the discount before of after tax.

Continue by

Clicking on the **Sales Taxes** tabbed button within the Settings window (Figure 6.23)

Figure 6.24
Settings
(Sales Taxes)
window

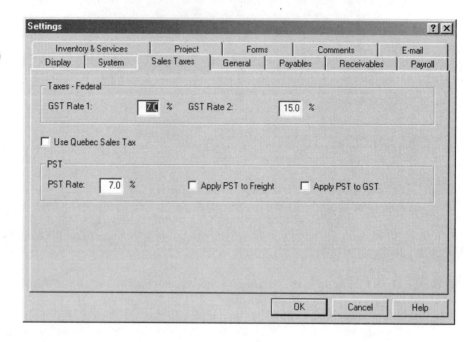

The Settings (Sales Taxes) window as shown in Figure 6.24, contains the following options:

GST Rate 1 and 2	The Goods and Services Tax will probably apply to your business. You have to insert the rate that is to be charged. Simply Accounting for Windows allows you to use two GST rates in the Receivables ledger. We will cover this in the book later with the inclusion of both GST (Goods and Services Tax) and HST (Harmonized Sales Tax).
Use Quebec Sales Tax	The Quebec Sales Tax is applicable for those companies conducting sales within the Province of Quebec.
PST	Most provinces impose a provincial sales tax on selected or all goods and services. If your province collects PST, you will have to enter the appropriate percentage to be charged on sales. If you are in a province that collects the HST (Harmonized Sales Tax) instead, your own company data files would not include a PST rate. However, for the purpose of this book, we will assume a 7.0% PST rate.
PST on Freight	In some provinces, freight revenue is subject to PST. If this is the case in your province, you will have to set this option.
PST on GST	In some provinces, the PST is calculated on the total price of the goods and/or services after the GST has been added.

Practice Exercise 6.5

For this chapter, ensure that the following options are set for the Receivables Ledger and for Sales taxes.

Aging	30, 60, 90
Interest Charges	2.5% on invoices 30 days overdue
Include invoice...	31 days on statements
Terms	2% 10, Net 30 days
Calculate discounts...	Yes (Checked)
GST rate 1	7.0%
GST rate 2	15.0%
Quebec Sales Tax?	(box not checked)
PST rate	7.0%
PST on Freight?	No (box not checked)
PST on GST?	No (box not checked)

The defaults shown can be changed with either the mouse or the keyboard. Click on the fields that you wish to change or press [Tab] to scroll through the fields. Notice that once you change any of the fields, the OK button becomes active. Once you have made the necessary changes, click on the OK button. You will then return to the Simply Accounting - ODC window.

If asked, be sure to select No to the updating of the customer items to match the new terms. This feature will update your customers, should you have a company wide change in payment terms.

TRACKING THE PROVINCIAL SALES TAX

New Sales

As long as you have defined a PST rate, you will have the option to charge provincial sales tax on each item that you enter into the Sales journal. Once you save the invoice, Simply Accounting for Windows will automatically post the correct amount of PST to the PST Payable account that has been assigned during the integration process, which we will discuss in a moment. Periodically you will have to remit this amount to your provincial government office. We will discuss this fully in Chapter 13.

TRACKING THE GOODS AND SERVICES OR HARMONIZED SALES TAX

New sales

If you have defined at least one GST rate, you have the option to assign GST to all goods or service entered into the Sales journal.

When you enter invoices into the Sales journal, Simply Accounting will calculate the correct amount of GST and post this amount to the GST Charged on Sales account, which has been defined through the Accounts Receivables integration process.

New purchases

When you make a purchase, the amount of GST charged to you by the vendor appears on the invoice that you receive. Simply Accounting will track this tax automatically and will post this amount to the GST paid on purchases account.

Remember that the GST on purchases is not an expense, nor is it to be considered as part of inventory or any other asset. It is a CONTRA-LIABILITY account. The amount of qualifying input tax credits paid during a reporting period will be deducted from the GST charged on invoices to your customers when you next report to Revenue Canada.

Clearing GST Accounts

At the end of each reporting period, you must calculate the amount due to the government or the amount due to you as a refund. This is done by listing the accounts up to the end of the due date and subtracting one from the other. We will discuss this fully in Chapter 13.

CHANGING TO CURRENT ENTRY MODE

> *HINT: WHEN CAN YOU ENTER CURRENT ENTRIES?*
>
> *Within Simply Accounting for Windows 8.0, you can begin your entry of current accounts receivable entries after you have set up your customers and linked the Receivables module to the General Ledger. You do not have to switch to the current entry mode; just start with making current entries. However, as suggested earlier in this chapter, you should enter all outstanding invoices in case one of your current receivable entries includes a payment for one of those invoices.*

The final step in our conversion process is to change the ledger from the "Historical mode" to the "Current Entry" mode. Remember, once you have changed the ledger to the Current Entry mode, you cannot return to the Historical transaction mode. Therefore you must be absolutely sure that the historical balances you entered are correct since you will not be able to change them.

As a safety precaution the Simply Accounting system will not allow you to change a ledger to the current entry mode until two conditions are met:

1. The General Ledger is in Current Entry mode.
2. The ledger is in balance with the control account—Accounts Receivable—in the General Ledger.

If the General Ledger is not in Current Entry mode, a message will tell you so. You will have to go into the General Ledger and make it "current entry ready" first.

If an out-of-balance window is displayed, it means that the Receivables Ledger is not in balance with the control account. If you get an error message it probably means that you forgot to enter one or more outstanding invoices or payments into the Receivables Ledger. Print a Customer Aging Report and check the amounts that you entered. Then make the necessary changes.

COMPLETING THE CONVERSION PROCESS

You have entered your opening balances, so the conversion process is almost complete. You will now need to continue with the establishment of the required integration accounts.

ENTERING ACCOUNTS RECEIVABLE JOURNAL ENTRIES

All accounts receivable transactions are entered through a series of journal entries in the Sales and Receipt journals. These type of transactions are:

1. Sales journal : Invoiced Sale   Dr. Accounts Receivable or Cash
           Cr. Sales Revenue
           Cr. GST Charged on Sales
           Cr. HST Charged on Sales
           Cr. PST Payable

2. Sales journal : Cash Sale   Dr. Cash
           Cr. Sales Revenue
           Cr. GST Charged on Sales
           Cr. HST Charged on Sales
           Cr. PST Payable

3. Receipts journal : Payments   Dr. Cash
           Cr. Accounts Receivable

Note: In this book we are not charging PST for services since this is not required in British Columbia and may not be true for your province. In most provinces, PST only applies to goods sold. However, we will include invoices that include HST (Harmonized Sales Tax).

The following entry is an example.

August 1, 2001	Dr. Accounts Receivable	77.65	
	Cr. GST Charged on Sales		5.08
	Cr. Regular Freight		72.57

(to record sale to McMillan Mills Inc., #4551)

As mentioned before, subledgers have common accounts to which debits or credits can be posted as one total. For Accounts Receivable, each customer entry will have a credit to a revenue account such as sales or general revenue and a debit to Accounts Receivable. Because the debit entry is always to Accounts Receivable (except in the case of a cash sale which will be discussed later in this chapter), the program can keep track of debits and enter the total automatically at the end of our session.

ACCEPTING CREDIT CARDS FOR SALES

Simply Accounting allows you to maintain several types of credit cards for payments from your customers.
       Continue from the Simply Accounting - ODC window (Figure 6.2) by

Selecting the **Setup** menu from within the Simply Accounting - ODC window.

Selecting the **Credit Cards** menu option.

Figure 6.25
Credit Card
Information
window

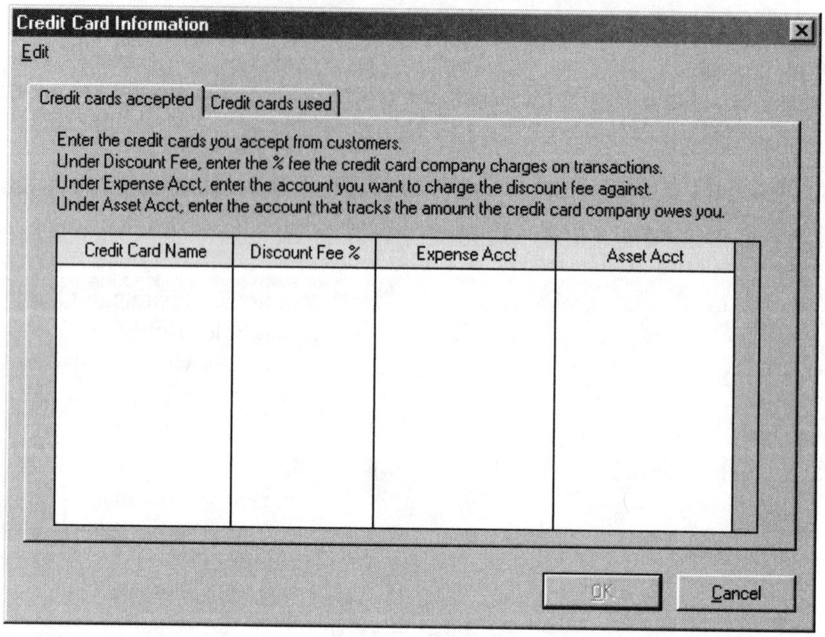

Continue from within the Credit Card Information window (Figure 6.26) by entering

VISA [Tab]   as the first Credit Card Name.

2.5 [Tab]   to enter the **Discount Fee %** that is charged by the credit card
company as a merchant transaction fee on each sale received
on this credit card.

5885 [Tab]   to enter the Expense Account. This account is used to expense
the credit card merchant account.

1155 [Tab]   to enter the Asset Account. This account is used to track the
amount owed to you from your credit card company.

Practice Exercise 6.6

ENTRY OF RECEIVABLES CREDIT CARD INFORMATION

Continue with the entry of the following merchant credit card information:

Credit Card Name:	MasterCard
Discount Fee:	2.0
Expense Acct:	5885
Asset Acct:	1155

Credit Card Name:	AMEX
Discount Fee:	3.5
Expense Acct:	5885
Asset Acct:	1155

Once you have completed this exercise, compare your Credit Card Information window
to Figure 6.26.

Figure 6.26
Credit Card
Information
window
(entered)

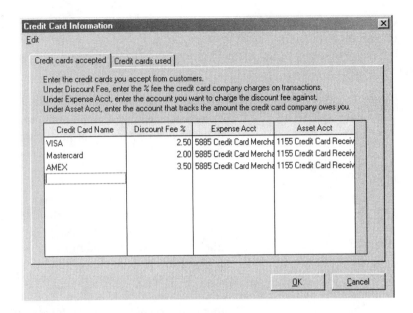

If your Credit Card Information window resembles Figure 6.26, continue by

Clicking the **OK** button to close the Credit Card Information window. Select **Yes** to have Simply Accounting modify the account class for credit card for the accounts used. You will then return to the Simply Accounting - ODC window (Figure 6.2).

HINT: CREDIT CARDS USED?

For the Credit Cards Used tabbed button, we will enter that credit card information in Chapter 7 — Accounts Payable module.

ENTERING SALES

To enter the sale listed above to McMillan Mills Inc., start from the Simply Accounting - ODC window (Figure 6.2).

Click (to open) the Sales Orders & Quotes icon.

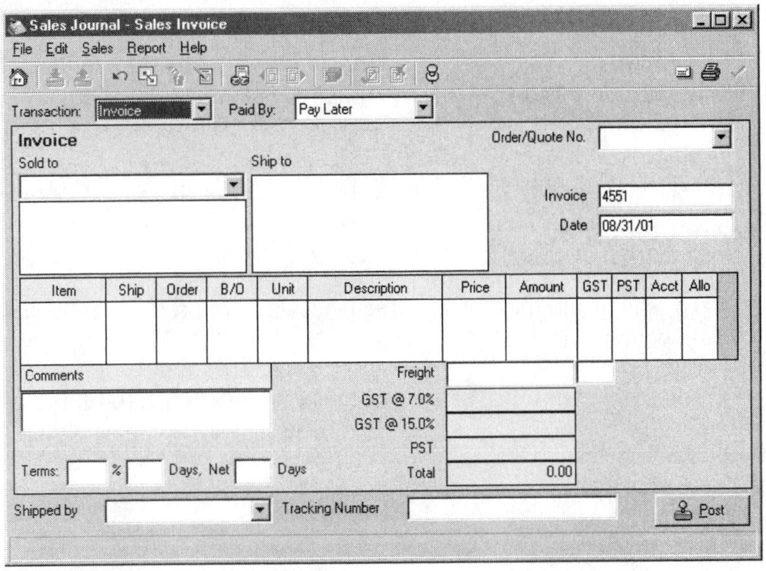

Figure 6.27
Sales Journal
window

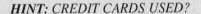

Simply Accounting will now display the Sales Journal window shown in Figure 6.27. Before continuing, you must determine which type of transaction you are completing. You have three choices as displayed along the top-left side of the Sales Journal entry window. These transaction types include:

Invoice	is used when you are completing a regular sale where the customer is billed for the products or services. The mode of payment is handled in the next choice box.
Sales Order	will maintain and track a sales order that has been received from your customer. This sales order ensures that the corresponding purchase order that was issued by your customer will be entered and filled upon receipt of the inventory.
Quote	allows you to enter and print out a sales quote (inventory, service or both). If the customer should accept the sales quote, Simply Accounting for Windows can then convert the sales quote to a regular invoice.

The default selection is an invoice which we will use for this sale.

The next field at the top of the Sales Journal entry window pertains to the mode of payment. Several selections are available:

Pay Later	the sale is billed to the client and put on account. The client will pay later.
Cash **Cheque**	the sale is paid for by cash or cheque. This will be covered in a later section.
Visa **Mastercard** **Amex**	the sale is paid at the time of billing (point of sale). These type of transactions are covered later in this chapter.

The default selection is **Pay Later** which we will use for this sale. Continue by pressing

[Tab] twice   to move to the **Sold To** field.

The next step is to locate the customer for whom we are producing this invoice.

Using your mouse

Click on the pull down arrow located beside the **Sold To** field.

Using your keyboard

[Alt] + [↓]   to invoke the pull down list.

You will notice that a pull down list has appeared. The names (with one exception) are customers that you have entered earlier in this chapter. The exception is the customer titled <One time customer>. This option is used to enter a cash sale. We will describe this type of sale later in this chapter.

HINT: *USING YOUR MOUSE WHEN ENTERING INVOICE INFORMATION*

Entering information into this form involves entering both characters and numbers. Use your Tab *key to move from field to field as you enter information so you don't have to take your hands off the keyboard. However, if you have to skip a number of fields, it may be easier to place your mouse pointer in that field and then enter the data. You will develop your own method of handling the mouse and the keyboard keys depending on what you are doing.*

Let's enter an invoice.

↑ or ↓   to move the highlighted cursor bar. Place this bar over the customer titled McMillan Mills Inc.

Tab   to select McMillan Mills Inc. as the **Sold To** customer.

The cursor now highlights the first character in the **Ship to** field. Simply Accounting has retrieved the address for the customer you specified (McMillan Mills Inc.). However you have the option of entering a different shipping address.

Continue by pressing

Tab (5 times)   to move the cursor to the **Order/Quote No.** field

The **Order/Quote** field is used to retrieve an existing Sales Order or Quote. Both of these features will be covered later in this chapter.

Continue by pressing

Tab   to move to the **Invoice** field.

Simply Accounting for Windows will keep track of your sales invoice numbering system. Previously you established (through either the Settings or Settings Wizard functions) the next invoice form number.

The next Invoice should read 4551. If so, continue by pressing

Tab   to move to the **Date** field.

08/01/01 Tab   to change the default date from 08/31/01 to 08/01/01

The cursor is now in the **Item** field. This field is used when you sell coded inventory or services. We will discuss these transactions in Chapter 8.

HINT: *USING THE ITEM FIELD*

As mentioned above, normally Simply Accounting uses the Item field for the inventory code, however you can use this field to enter a non-inventory code for reference by your customer.

As we are not using any of the inventory related fields, press

[Tab]   (3 times)   to move the cursor to the Description field

---

HINT: *USING THE SHIP AND UNIT FIELDS*

*Even though you have not selected an inventory item, you could use the **Ship To** to enter a quantity such as number of items or hours spent, along with a unit of measure such as "each" or "hours." If you use the **Ship** field, you should also use the **Price** column to enter the per unit selling price. Simply Accounting will then calculate the **Amount** (Ship to times Price).*

Monthly Freight Charge [Tab] to provide the necessary **Description** for this invoice.

As mentioned above, the **Price** field is used in relation to the **Ship** field. If you were to enter a **Ship** value along with a **Price** value, Simply Accounting will calculate the **Amount** field based on the Ship figures times the Price Value.

Continue from within the Price field by pressing

[Tab]   to move to the **Amount** field.

72.57 [Tab]   to enter the amount of the Regular Freight sale.

Your cursor will now be positioned in the GST field. To view the options available for this field, press

to invoke the Select GST window.

Figure 6.28
Select GST
window

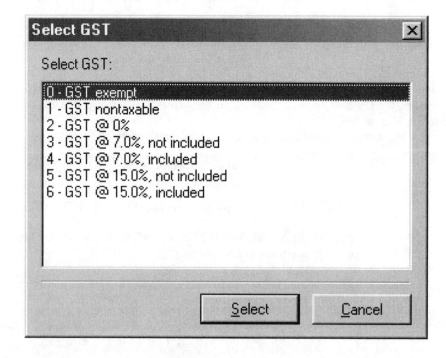

You will notice that the Select GST window (Figure 6.28) displays six possible options:

0 – GST Exempt   use this option if the good or service that you are selling is exempt from GST.

1 – GST nontaxable   use this option if the particular item is not taxable for GST. If you are unsure of whether a certain good or service is nontaxable, Revenue Canada Customs and Excise department can provide you with a listing of such goods and services.

2 – GST @ 0%   use this option if you are telling Simply Accounting that this good or service is taxable but at a zero rate. In other words, it is taxable, but @ 0%. Please contact Revenue Canada Customs and Excise in order to determine which items are subject to this classification.

3 – GST @ 7.0% not incl.   use this option if the product or service that you are selling is taxable at 7.0% and the GST is added to the price of the product. For example, if you purchased a $100.00 item the total amount including GST would be $100.00 plus $7.00 (7.0%) for the GST.

4 – GST @ 7.0% incl.   use this option if the good or service is taxable at 7.0%. However the GST is included in the sale price. In other words, the GST is hidden in the cost of the product. Such an example would be if your purchased $10.00 of gasoline. When you paid for this purchase, you would only be charged $10.00 as the GST is already included in the purchase of gasoline in Canada, which is charged on a per liter basis, with GST included.

5 – GST @ 15.0% not incl.   use this option if the product or service that you are selling is taxable at 15.0% (HST) and the HST is added to the price of the product/service.

6 – GST @ 15.0% incl.   use this option if the good or service is taxable at 15.0% (HST). However the HST is included in the sale price.

For this invoice, enter

3 (Enter)   to select 3 - GST @ 7.0% not included. This is the default GST selection that will be used in all invoice entries throughout this book (unless otherwise specified).

The cursor is now positioned in the PST field. If you were selling an item from inventory, the correct PST would appear in the form of a percentage. As well, you could modify this rate or enter a new rate even if you are not selling an inventory item. Simply Accounting allows entry of a percentage rate up to a four digits. As you are selling a PST-exempt service, press:

| Tab | to move to the **Account** field. |

As you are now in the **Account** field, you must specify the correct Revenue account to which this item applies. To find this account, press

| Enter | to invoke a window titled Select Account. From here you can locate the desired account using the up or down arrow keys and the first number of each account group, (1 for Assets, 2 for Liabilities, 3 for Equity, 4 for Revenue, or 5 for Expenses). For this line, select account number 4220 – Regular Freight and press |

HINT: *SELECTING ACCOUNTS*

Press 4 to jump to the Revenue accounts 4000 – 4999 section. This will save you the time of scrolling through the complete chart of accounts list.

| 4 | to jump to the Revenue section of accounts. |

| ↓ several times | to highlight 4220 – Regular Freight. |

| Enter | to accept 4220 – Regular Freight as the account. |

Now that you have entered the details for this invoice, you can either

Click you mouse within the **Comments** field.

Your comments should read "Thank you for your business." Continue by pressing

| Tab | to move to the **Freight amount** field. |

If you were selling a product that involved a freight charge to be billed to the customer, you would have to indicate both the amount of freight to be charged and the applicable GST/HST code for the freight amount charged (Figure 6.29). As you are not charging freight on this invoice, press

| Tab | Tab | to move to the **Terms discount**. The displayed discount information has been retrieved from your customer's record, however you have the option of changing these terms. For this example continue by pressing |

| Tab | Tab | Tab | to accept the default **Terms** as 2.0% discount within 10 days, net payment within 30 days. |

The remaining **Shipped by** and **Tracking Number** fields are used when you ship products and wish to have these shipments tracked. Refer to Chapter 8 for more information on this feature.

Figure 6.29
Sales Journal window with invoice data entered prior to posting

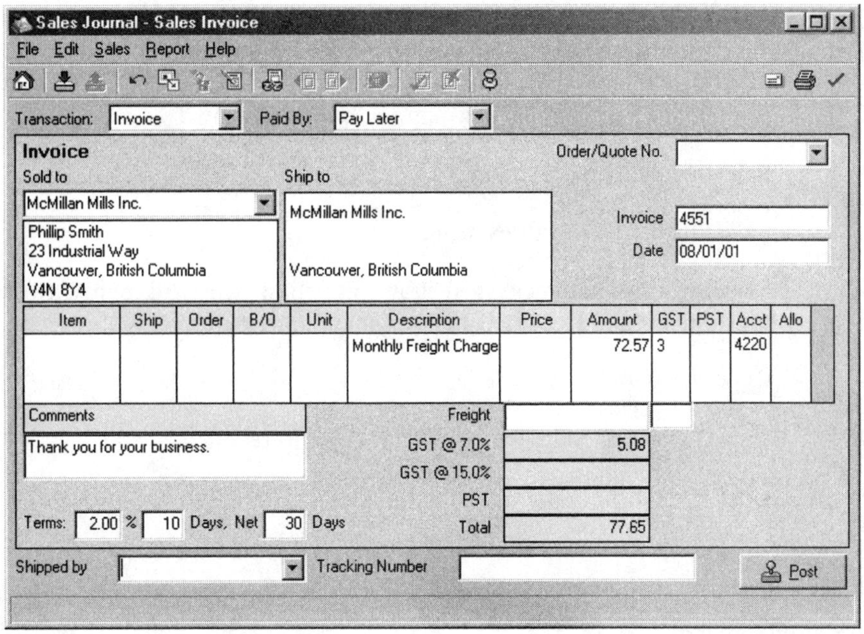

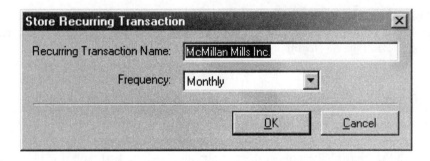

RECURRING ENTRIES

As with General Journal entries, you can also Store and Recall Sales invoices. In the above entry, the invoice is for a monthly freight charge, so this invoice will be recurring on a monthly basis. Continue by pressing

Ctrl + T

to select to **Store this invoice**. You could also select the **Store** button.

Figure 6.30
Store Recurring Entry window

Since the default information within the Store Recurring Entry window (Figure 6.30), Monthly Frequency, is correct, continue by pressing

Enter

to create this recurring invoice. You will then return to the Sales Journal window. You could however change either the **Recurring Transaction Name** or the **Frequency**.

At this point, you could print this invoice by selecting the **Print** option from the **File** menu. However, for this example continue by pressing

Alt + P

to post the entry.

Alt + F4

to close the Sales Journal window.

Now that you have posted the above entry for McMillan Mills Inc., you can view this invoice through the **Customer Aged** option, located on the **Reports** menu. You can access this menu option by using either your mouse or keyboard.

Continue from the Simply Accounting - ODC window by

Selecting the **Reports** menu.

Selecting the **Receivables** menu option.

Selecting the **Customer Aged** submenu option. This will invoke a window titled **Customer Aged Report Options**, (note Figure 6.20).

Click the **Detail** report option.

Click McMillan Mills Inc. as the customer to report.

Click the **OK** button.

Figure 6.31
Customer Aged
Detail report

Customer Aged Detail							
File Options Help							
As at 08/31/01			Total	Current	31 to 60	61 to 90	91+
McMillan Mills Inc.							
4299	06/02/01	Invoice	326.71	-	-	326.71	-
4433	07/05/01	Invoice	825.50	-	825.50	-	-
4442	07/09/01	Invoice	1,725.79	-	1,725.79	-	-
4439	07/10/01	Invoice	302.12	-	302.12	-	-
4429	07/12/01	Invoice	825.52	-	825.52	-	-
289	07/29/01	Payment	-500.00	-	-500.00	-	-
4438	07/21/01	Invoice	215.36	-	215.36	-	-
4551	08/01/01	Invoice	77.65	77.65	-	-	-
			3,798.65	77.65	3,394.29	326.71	-

The window titled Customer Aged Detail as shown in Figure 6.31, will now appear. You will notice that the last invoice (the one that was just entered) is displayed as a current invoice.

Continue by closing the Customer Aged Detail window.

Practice Exercise 6.7

Enter the remainder of the service revenue transactions for the month of August as listed in Figure 6.32. Remember that we just recorded the first entry for McMillan Mills Inc. DO NOT record it again. As well, select GST Code 3 and no PST. If you get a message that a customer has exceeded the credit limit, click on Yes to accept it. All invoices are to be billed (customer to pay later).

At the bottom of the invoice listing are U.S. customer invoices. Follow the instructions carefully.

The Invoice for Modern Computer Services is a monthly freight invoice and should be saved as a recurring entry with a monthly frequency.

Accept the default terms for all invoices.

> *HINT: VIEWING THE JOURNAL ENTRY*
>
> *After you record all freight charges and the GST, check your entry before you post it. If you wish to display the General Ledger accounts that the invoice will effect, press* ⌐Alt⌐ + ⌐R⌐ *followed by* ⌐D⌐. *This will display the Sales Journal Entry window. Once you have finished viewing this window, close the Sales Journal Entry window and return to the Sales Journal window.*
>
> *Also, when you are selecting your customers' names, you can speed up this process by typing part of the customer's name within the Sold to field. For example, type Cassar to recall Cassar Homes Inc.*
>
> *Remember also that you can select the appropriate Revenue account by pressing the first digit of the account range that you wish to jump to:* ⌐4⌐ *for the Revenue accounts.*

Overnight Delivery Company
Service Revenue Journal
August 2001

Inv.#	Date	Customer		Type	Amount	
4551	Aug 1	McMillan Mills Inc.		Regular	72.57	Entered
				GST	5.08	Entered
			Total invoice.......:		77.65	
4552	Aug 1	Cassar Homes Inc.		Regular	497.50	
				Airfreight	25.00	
				GST	36.58	
			Total invoice.......:		559.08	
4553	Aug 4	Modern Computer Services		Overnight	2,520.75	
				Regular	220.29	
				Airfreight	21.00	
***RECURRING INVOICE -				GST	193.34	
MONTHLY FREQUENCY***			Total invoice.......		2,955.38	
4554	Aug 5	Quality Custom Furniture		Regular	1,150.82	
				Airfreight	13.95	
				GST	81.53	
			Total invoice.......:		1,246.30	
4555	Aug 7	Solar Heat Control Products		Airfreight	275.59	
				GST	19.29	
			Total invoice.......:		294.88	
4556	Aug 7	City Software		Overnight	519.50	
				GST	36.37	
			Total invoice.......:		555.87	

4557	Aug 12 Solar Heat Control Products	Overnight	997.35
		GST	69.81
	Total invoice.......:		1,067.16

4558	Aug 15 Cassar Homes	Regular	219.57
		Overnight	310.45
		Airfreight	27.50
		GST	39.03
	Total invoice.......:		596.55

4559	Aug 15 Modern Computer	Airfreight	1,313.22
		GST	91.93
	Total invoice.......		1,405.15

4560	Aug 15 Solar Heat Control Products	Airfreight	3,345.70
		Regular	517.30
		GST	270.41
	Total invoice.......:		4,133.41

The following invoices are for U.S. Currency customers. When entering the following invoices ensure the following three conditions are met:

1. Accept the default Exchange Rate for each invoice.
2. Leave both the GST and PST fields blank.
3. Select the appropriate U.S. revenue accounts (separate from Canadian).

| 4561 Aug 15 | Ricco Logistics | Airfreight | 1,650.00 |
| | Total invoice.......: | | 1,650.00 USD |

| 4562 Aug 15 | TFM International | Regular freight | 250.00 |
| | Total invoice.......: | | 250.00 USD |

Figure 6.32   Overnight Delivery Company—Service Revenue Journal

BACKING UP YOUR DATA FILES

You must now return to the Simply Accounting - ODC window and backup your data. If you are unsure of this process, please refer to Chapter 3.

Please use the following when backing up your data files:

Backup filename: A:\odc6c\odc
Comment: Receivables Part c

RECALLING CUSTOMER INVOICES

Simply Accounting for Windows allows you to view, as well as re-print, posted sales invoices. If your customer requests a duplicate invoice you can print one. If you are reviewing the posted invoices within a particular period of time you can easily access those posted invoices.

Continue from the Simply Accounting - ODC window (Figure 6.2) by

Opening the **Sales** journal icon.

Within the Sales Journal (Figure 6.27),

Press ⌨ Ctrl + ⌨ L to select the **Look up** icon. Alternatively, you can select this icon with your mouse.

Figure 6.33
Invoice Lookup
options window

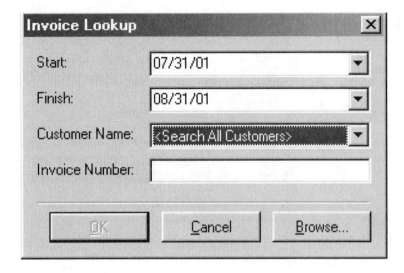

Simply Accounting allows you to either specify the exact invoice that you wish to view/re-print or you can select to **Browse** based on selected criteria (Figure 6.33).

Because the OK button is dimmed, it means that it is not available for use. To be able to use it you have to first select an exact invoice to display. Continue by

Clicking the **Browse** button to view all invoices within the selected criteria (from 07/31/01 to 08/31/01).

Figure 6.34
Select an
Invoice window

Date	Invoice	Journal Entry#	Original Amt
8/15/01	4562	29	250.00
8/15/01	4561	28	1,650.00
8/15/01	4560	27	4,133.41
8/15/01	4559	26	1,405.15
8/15/01	4558	25	596.55
8/12/01	4557	24	1,067.16
8/7/01	4556	23	555.87
8/7/01	4555	22	294.88
8/5/01	4554	21	1,246.30

Select An Invoice

Select invoice to display...

Simply Accounting for Windows will now display all of the invoices that fall within the selected criteria (Figure 6.34). Continue by pressing

[Pg Dn] [Enter]   to select invoice 4551 on 08/01/01.

Figure 6.35
Sales Journal–
Invoice Lookup
window

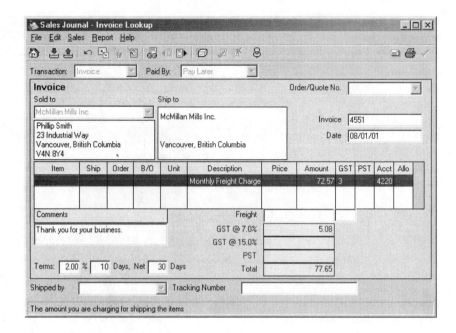

Simply Accounting for Windows now displays this posted invoice (Figure 6.35).

You will notice that the **Post** button is not available for use as this invoice has been previously posted.

You can print any of these invoices by selecting the Print option from the **File** menu or by pressing

[Ctrl] + [P]   to select the **Print** icon.

ADJUSTING AN INVOICE

Simply Accounting for Windows supports the ability to adjust a previously posted invoice. This feature is very useful if you have to make an adjustment to the invoice.

Continue from the Sale Journal window (Figure 6.35) by pressing

[Ctrl] + [A]   to select the **Adjust Invoice** icon.

Figure 6.36
Sales Journal
(Adjust Invoice)
window

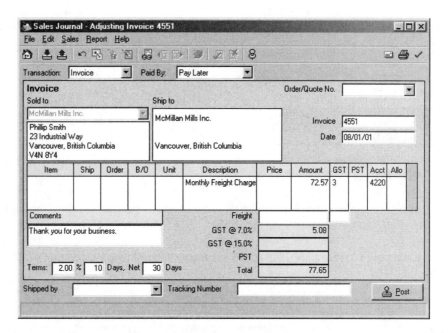

As shown in Figure 6.36, Simply Accounting for Windows now allows you to adjust the existing posted invoice. However, any changes made to the invoice will be treated as a separate invoice. For example, if you wanted to increase this invoice by $5.00, you would enter $77.57 as being the amount for account 4220 (as displayed). This will in turn allow Simply Accounting to create a new invoice for $5.00 plus GST. Continue by

> Clicking your mouse in the existing amount for the monthly freight charge of 72.57. This will in turn highlight this figure.

Continue by entering

> 77.57 to enter the new (adjusted) amount.

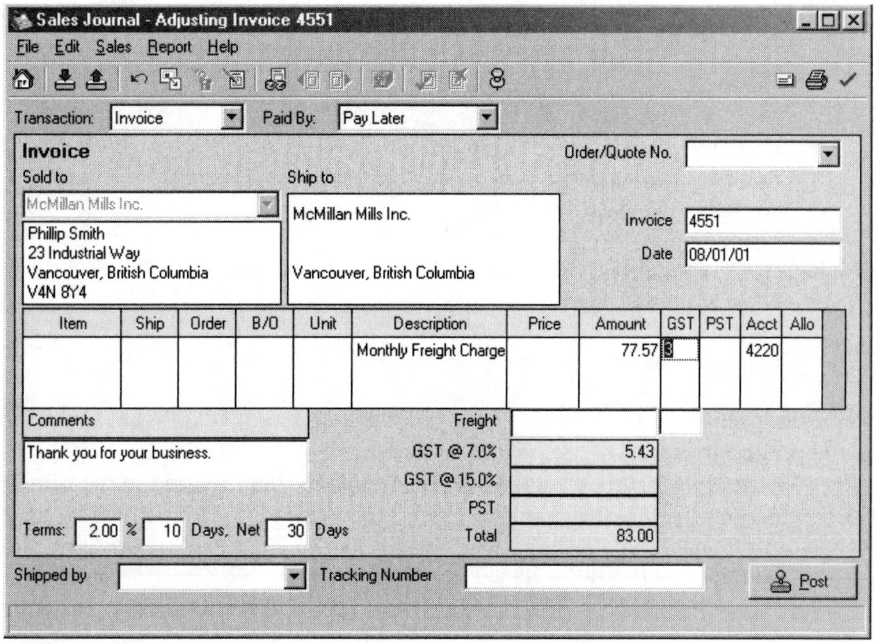

Figure 6.37
Sales Journal
(Adjusting
Invoice)
window

Your Sales Journal window should now resemble Figure 6.37. If so, continue by pressing

Alt + P   to **Post** this adjustment invoice.

Alt + F4   to close the Sales Journal window.

Practice Exercise 6.8

PRINTING CUSTOMER DETAIL

Continue with the displaying and printing of the Customer Aged Report for McMillan Mills Inc. on a detailed basis. Compare this report with the window shown in Figure 6.38. You will notice that invoice 4551 is now 83.00 in total instead of the original 77.65.

Once you have completed this exercise, return to the Simply Accounting - ODC window.

Figure 6.38
Customer Aged
Detail for McMillan
Mills Inc.

Customer Aged Detail							
File Options Help							
As at 08/31/01			Total	Current	31 to 60	61 to 90	91+
McMillan Mills Inc.							
4299	06/02/01	Invoice	326.71	-	-	326.71	-
4433	07/05/01	Invoice	825.50	-	825.50	-	-
4442	07/09/01	Invoice	1,725.79	-	1,725.79	-	-
4439	07/10/01	Invoice	302.12	-	302.12	-	-
4429	07/12/01	Invoice	825.52	-	825.52	-	-
289	07/29/01	Payment	-500.00	-	-500.00	-	-
4438	07/21/01	Invoice	215.36	-	215.36	-	-
4551	08/01/01	Invoice	83.00	83.00	-	-	-
			3,804.00	83.00	3,394.29	326.71	-

Double-click to display Invoice details

ENTERING CUSTOMER RECEIPTS (PAYMENTS)

The second type of transaction that occurs in the Receivables Ledger is the receipt of payments from customers. These transactions are entered in the Receipts journal.

Now let's record the following payment:

Customer	Solar Heat Control Products
Date of Payment	August 3, 2001
Customer Cheque#	356
Payment Amount	$1,658.17
Applied against invoice# 4428	

The necessary journal entry is as follows:

Dr. Cash   1,658.17
Cr. Accounts Receivable   1,658.17

Remember, this is a standard accounts receivable entry so we only have to allocate the payment to the proper invoice.

To enter the payment, activate the Receipts journal, located in the Simply Accounting - ODC window. Continue by

Clicking on the Receipts icon.

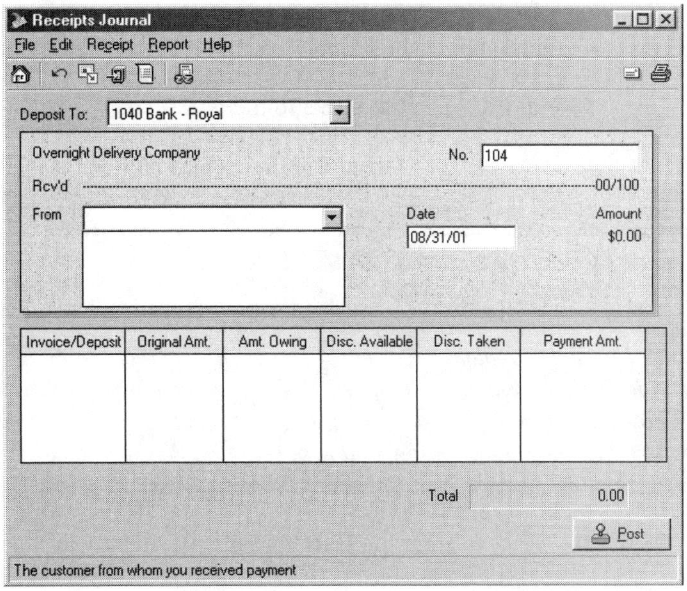

Figure 6.39
Receipts Journal
window

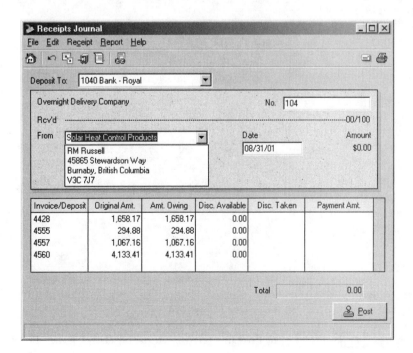

Simply Accounting will now display the Receipts Journal window shown in Figure 6.39. Continue to record the above payment received from Solar Heat Control Products. You will find that the easiest way to record payments is by using your keyboard. However, you do have the option of using your mouse.

Even though within the Receipts Journal you are being asked for the customer's name, you have the option of selecting the bank account to which this payment will be deposited. Continue by accepting the default 1040 Bank - Royal as the bank account in which the deposit will be debited.

Continue by

Selecting Solar Heat Control Products as the customer that issued the receipt payment.

Figure 6.40
Receipts Journal
window with
customer name
entered

Your Receipts Journal window should now resemble Figure 6.40. Continue by pressing

| Tab | (several times) | to move to the **No.** field.

| Tab | to accept the receipt number associated with this payment.

HINT: *RECEIPTS FOR PAYMENTS RECEIVED*

Simply Accounting for Windows assumes that your company will be issuing a receipt for each payment received. If this is not correct, you can instead enter the customer's cheque number associated with the payment. Simply Accounting for Windows will however prompt you to confirm that the receipts number is not in sequence. Confirm this message window and proceed.

08/03/01 | Tab | to enter the **Date** that this payment was received.

You will notice that in the lower half of the Receipts Journal window, Simply Accounting has displayed the outstanding invoices that are associated with this customer. In this case, Solar Heat Control Products has several invoices outstanding, all of which Simply Accounting for Windows will display. If any of these invoices should have discounts available, Simply Accounting will automatically display the available invoices. You can now allocate payments to specific invoices. Press

| Tab | to move to the **Disc. Taken** column for invoice 4428.

0 | Tab | to enter the **Discount taken**.

| Tab | to accept the default payment of 1,658.17 for invoice no. 4428.

Figure 6.41
Receipts Journal
with payment
entered

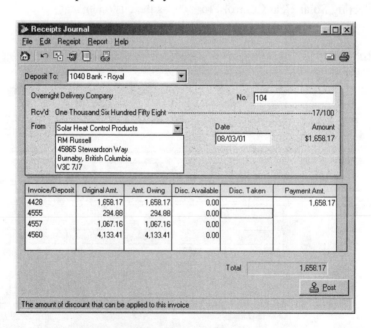

If your Receipts Journal resembles Figure 6.41, press

| Alt | + | P | to **Post** this payment to Solar Heat Control Product's invoice no. 4428.

Practice Exercise 6.9

Enter the remaining payments of the cash receipts journal in Figure 6.42 into the Receipts journal. Remember the first entry has already been made.

Remember that you must enter 0 in any highlighted payment amount if you are not applying a payment against that particular invoice.

Deposit all cheques (unless specified) to the Royal Bank account.

For U.S. customers, accept the Seafirst bank account and accept the default exchange rate.

When you have made all of the entries, press ⸤ Alt ⸥+⸤ F4 ⸥ to close the Receipts Journal window.

Overnight Delivery Company
Cash Receipts Journal
August 2001

Date	Recvd from	Rect#	Inv #	Discount	Amount	Notes
Aug 3	Solar Heat	104	4428		$1,658.17	Recorded
Aug 4	McMillan Mills Inc.	105	4299		326.71	
			4429		325.52	
			4438		215.36	
					867.59	Deposit to Royal Bank
Aug 7	City Software	106	4446		99.50	
Aug 9	Cassar Homes	107	4434		1,057.75	(note amount) Royal Bank
Aug 10	Vancouver Books	108	4440		42.73	
			4447		65.35	
					108.08	(note amount) Total to Royal Bank
Aug 11	McMillan Mills Inc.	109	4433		825.50	
			4442		1,725.79	
			4439		302.12	
			4551	1.45	76.20	
					2929.61	Deposit to Bank of Montreal
Aug 12	Cassar Homes	110	4448		429.79	Deposit to Royal Bank
Aug 15	Modern Computer Services	111	4553		2955.38	Royal Bank
Aug 15	Ricco Logistics	112	4561		1000.00	note amount
Aug 15	TFM International	113	4562		50.00	note amount

Figure 6.42   Overnight Delivery Company - Cash Receipts Journal

CASH SALES

Simply Accounting for Windows has the ability to generate a Cash invoice. This is accomplished through the Sales journal and the entry process is only slightly different from the regular Accounts Receivable invoices. You will enter a Cash invoice now.

At the Simply Accounting - ODC window (Figure 6.2) continue by

Opening the Sales journal.

Figure 6.43
Sales Journal
window

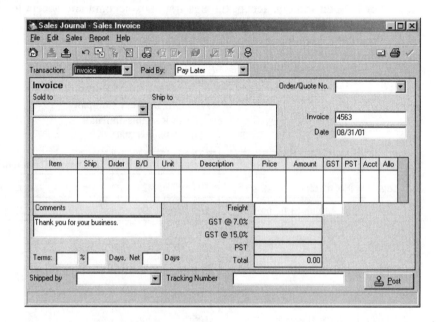

In the Sales Journal window (Figure 6.43) you will have to first select the method of payment that your customer chose for the cash sale, for example, sale with payment. In this case, continue by

Selecting *MasterCard* as the **Paid By** option.

Since you are not expecting the customer to return in the future, you do not create a new customer record. Instead use the one-time customer option. Continue by

Selecting *One-Time Customer* as the **Sold to** customer.

Within the Sold to section, continue by entering

RB Anderson
150-50th Street
Cape Breton, Nova Scotia
N5K 1L5

Continue by entering the following:

Air Freight as the **Description**
50.00 as the **Amount**.

HANDLING HST IN YOUR BUSINESS

If you are registered for GST/HST and are selling to customers in provinces that collect HST, be sure to charge HST on your invoice if applicable.

In order to charge HST on this invoice, continue by entering

5 (GST @ 15% - not included) as the **GST Code**.

As with regular service sales (non-inventory), you will have to enter the appropriate revenue account. Continue by entering

4260 (Air Freight) as the **Account**.

Figure 6.44

Sales Journal window (cash sale entered)

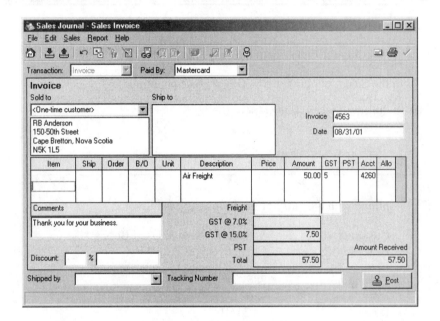

If your entry matches the one shown in Figure 6.44, continue by

Clicking the **Report** menu within the Sales Journal window (Figure 6.44).

Select the **Display Sales Journal Entry** menu option.

Figure 6.45

Sales Journal Entry window

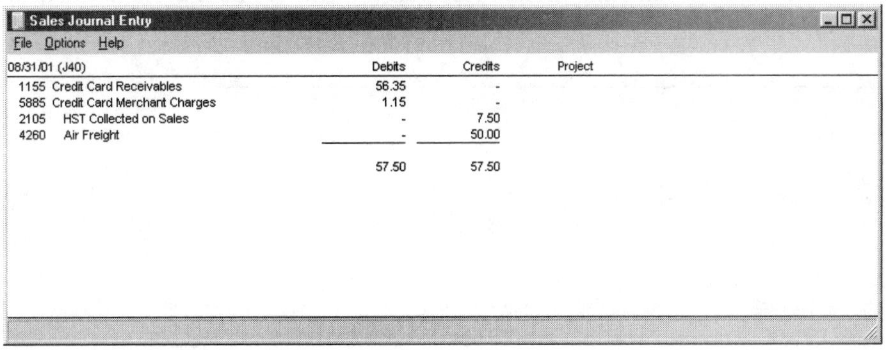

As shown in Figure 6.45, the journal entry shows that the debit for this entry is allocated to the credit card receivables as is the calculation for the merchant credit card charge, instead of the regular Accounts Receivable account. This entry represents a Cash invoice with payment received at the time of sale.

HINT: *POINT OF SALE FOR CREDIT CARDS*

If your business uses a point-of-sale system that directly deposits your credit card receipts into your company's bank account, you would replace the credit card receivable account with the appropriate bank account, (through the Setup menu, Credit Cards option).

Continue from within the Sales Journal Entry window (Figure 6.45) by

> Closing the Sales Journal Entry window.

Within the Sales Journal window (Figure 6.45) continue by

> Posting the Cash Sale invoice.

Practice Exercise 6.10

Continue with the entry of the following cash invoice.

Customer:	Vancouver New & Used Books
Paid by:	Cheque (Royal Bank)
Cheque no.:	288
Invoice no.:	4564
Date:	08/31/01
Services:	Air Freight for $500.00
GST code:	3
GST:	$35.00
Total Invoice:	$535.00
Discount:	$10.00
Total Received:	$525.00

You will notice that the amount received will be net of the 2.0% discount which is available for Vancouver New & Used Books (see Figure 6.46).

Figure 6.46
Sales Journal
(Cash Sale for
Vancouver New
& Used Books)

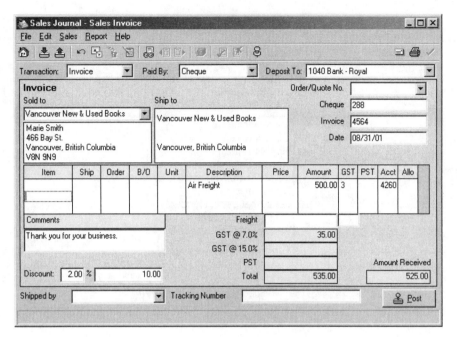

ENTERING SALES ORDERS

Sales Orders are normally handled in conjunction with the sale of inventory, thus this feature will be demonstrated in Chapter 8, Inventory.

ENTERING AND HANDLING QUOTES

Periodically, your company will be asked to provide a quote for services rendered. Simply Accounting allows you to handle this process as well as the process of excepting or modifying the quote to a final invoice for products or services sold.

This feature will be demonstrated in Chapter 8, Inventory.

RECONCILING THE ACCOUNTS RECEIVABLES LEDGER WITH THE GENERAL LEDGER

Now that you have entered all of the invoices and payments for the month of August, let us check to ensure that everything has been recorded properly.

If you have just finished the above Cash invoice entry, you should be in the Sales Journal window. Continue by

Closing the Sales Journal window.

Within the Simply Accounting - ODC window (Figure 6.2) continue by

Selecting the **Report** menu option.

Selecting the **Receivables** menu option.

Select **Customer Aged** submenu option.

Figure 6.47
Customer Aged
Report Options
window

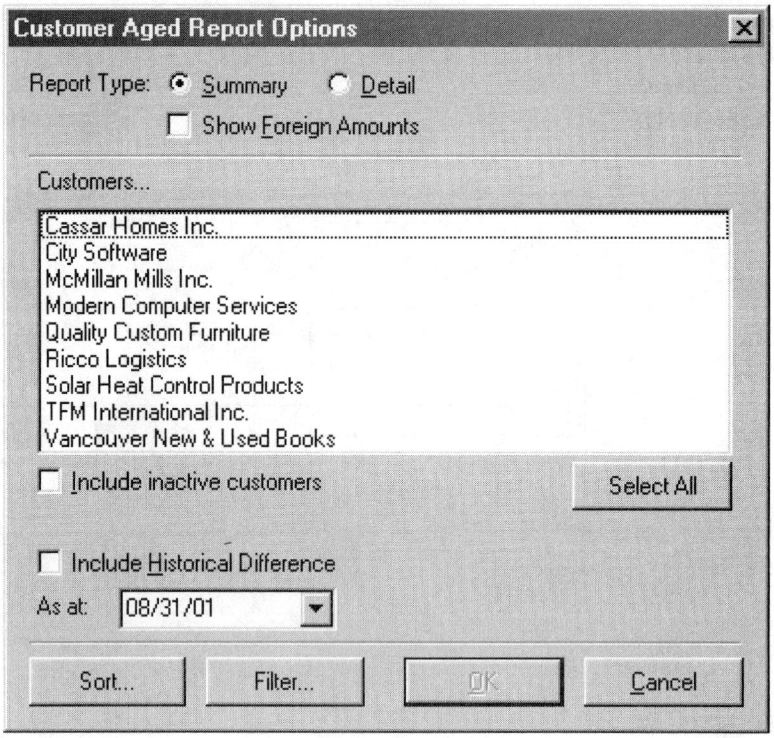

Within the Customer Aged Report Options window (Figure 6.47) continue by

> Selecting the **Detail** option.

> Select the **Select All** button.

> Click the **OK** button.

Figure 6.48
Customer Aged
Detail window

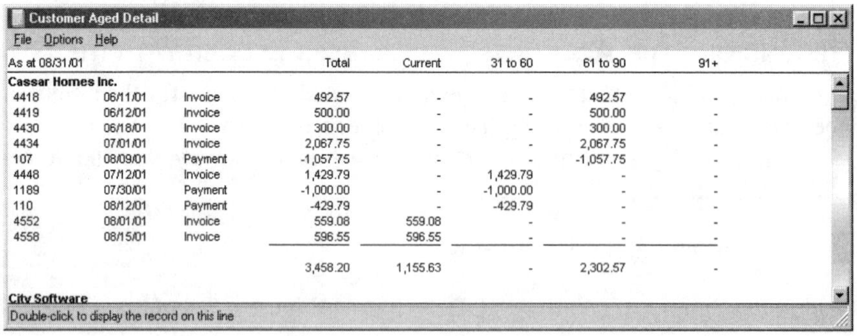

The window titled Customer Aged Detail will be displayed as shown in Figure 6.48.
In order to print the Customer Aged Detail report (Figure 6.48), continue by

> Selecting the **File** menu within the Customer Aged report window (Figure 6.48).

> Select the **Print** menu command within the **File** menu.

Figure 6.49   Printed Customer Aged Report

Overnight Delivery Company
Customer Aged Detail As at 8/31/01

			Total	Current	31 to 60	61 to 90	91+
Cassar Homes Inc.							
4418	2001-06-11	Invoice	492.57	0.00	0.00	492.57	0.00
4419	2001-06-12	Invoice	500.00	0.00	0.00	500.00	0.00
4430	2001-06-18	Invoice	300.00	0.00	0.00	300.00	0.00
4434	2001-07-01	Invoice	2067.75	0.00	0.00	2067.75	0.00
107	2001-08-09	Payment	-1057.75	0.00	0.00	-1057.75	0.00
4448	2001-07-12	Invoice	1429.79	0.00	1429.79	0.00	0.00
1189	2001-07-30	Payment	-1000.00	0.00	-1000.00	0.00	0.00
110	2001-08-12	Payment	-429.79	0.00	-429.79	0.00	0.00
4552	2001-08-01	Invoice	559.08	559.08	0.00	0.00	0.00
4558	2001-08-15	Invoice	596.55	596.55	0.00	0.00	0.00
			3458.20	1155.63	-0.00	2302.57	0.00
City Software							
4446	2001-07-15	Invoice	99.50	0.00	99.50	0.00	0.00
106	2001-08-07	Payment	-99.50	0.00	-99.50	0.00	0.00
4556	2001-08-07	Invoice	555.87	555.87	0.00	0.00	0.00
			555.87	555.87	0.00	0.00	0.00
McMillan Mills Inc.							
4299	2001-06-02	Invoice	326.71	0.00	0.00	326.71	0.00
105	2001-08-04	Payment	-326.71	0.00	0.00	-326.71	0.00
4433	2001-07-05	Invoice	825.50	0.00	825.50	0.00	0.00
109	2001-08-11	Payment	-825.50	0.00	-825.50	0.00	0.00
4442	2001-07-09	Invoice	1725.79	0.00	1725.79	0.00	0.00
109	2001-08-11	Payment	-1725.79	0.00	-1725.79	0.00	0.00
4439	2001-07-10	Invoice	302.12	0.00	302.12	0.00	0.00
109	2001-08-11	Payment	-302.12	0.00	-302.12	0.00	0.00
4429	2001-07-12	Invoice	825.52	0.00	825.52	0.00	0.00
289	2001-07-29	Payment	-500.00	0.00	-500.00	0.00	0.00
105	2001-08-04	Payment	-325.52	0.00	-325.52	0.00	0.00
4438	2001-07-21	Invoice	215.36	0.00	215.36	0.00	0.00
105	2001-08-04	Payment	-215.36	0.00	-215.36	0.00	0.00
4551	2001-08-01	Invoice	83.00	83.00	0.00	0.00	0.00
109	2001-08-11	Discount	-1.45	-1.45	0.00	0.00	0.00
109	2001-08-11	Payment	-76.20	-76.20	0.00	0.00	0.00
			5.35	5.35	0.00	0.00	0.00
Modern Computer Services							
4431	2001-07-12	Invoice	57.50	0.00	57.50	0.00	0.00
4450	2001-07-15	Invoice	29.92	0.00	29.92	0.00	0.00
816	2001-07-31	Payment	-10.00	0.00	-10.00	0.00	0.00
4553	2001-08-04	Invoice	2955.38	2955.38	0.00	0.00	0.00
111	2001-08-15	Payment	-2955.38	-2955.38	0.00	0.00	0.00
4559	2001-08-15	Invoice	1405.15	1405.15	0.00	0.00	0.00
			1482.57	1405.15	77.42	0.00	0.00
Quality Custom Furniture							
4437	2001-07-19	Invoice	674.33	0.00	674.33	0.00	0.00
4449	2001-07-29	Invoice	133.45	0.00	133.45	0.00	0.00
4554	2001-08-05	Invoice	1246.30	1246.30	0.00	0.00	0.00
			2054.08	1246.30	807.78	0.00	0.00

Ricco Logistics

4561	2001-08-15	Invoice	2495.63	2495.63	0.00	0.00	0.00
112	2001-08-15	Payment	-1512.50	-1512.50	0.00	0.00	0.00
			983.13	983.13	0.00	0.00	0.00

Solar Heat Control Products

4428	2001-07-12	Invoice	1658.17	0.00	1658.17	0.00	0.00
104	2001-08-03	Payment	-1658.17	0.00	-1658.17	0.00	0.00
4555	2001-08-07	Invoice	294.88	294.88	0.00	0.00	0.00
4557	2001-08-12	Invoice	1067.16	1067.16	0.00	0.00	0.00
4560	2001-08-15	Invoice	4133.41	4133.41	0.00	0.00	0.00
			5495.45	5495.45	0.00	0.00	0.00

TFM International Inc.

4562	2001-08-15	Invoice	378.13	378.13	0.00	0.00	0.00
113	2001-08-15	Payment	-75.63	-75.63	0.00	0.00	0.00
			302.50	302.50	0.00	0.00	0.00

Vancouver New & Used Books

4440	2001-07-12	Invoice	92.73	0.00	92.73	0.00	0.00
367	2001-07-29	Payment	-50.00	0.00	-50.00	0.00	0.00
108	2001-08-10	Payment	-42.73	0.00	-42.73	0.00	0.00
4447	2001-07-21	Invoice	165.35	0.00	165.35	0.00	0.00
369	2001-07-30	Payment	-50.00	0.00	-50.00	0.00	0.00
108	2001-08-10	Payment	-65.35	0.00	-65.35	0.00	0.00
4564	2001-08-31	Invoice	535.00	535.00	0.00	0.00	0.00
288	2001-08-31	Discount	-10.00	-10.00	0.00	0.00	0.00
288	2001-08-31	Payment	-525.00	-525.00	0.00	0.00	0.00
			50.00	0.00	50.00	0.00	0.00
			14387.15	11149.38	935.20	2302.57	0.00

Once the Customer Aged report has been printed, continue by

Closing the Customer Aged Detail report.

Now, we will have to print the General Ledger Trial Balance. To do this, continue by

Selecting the **Report** menu (from within the Simply Accounting - ODC window).

Select the **Financials** menu option.

Select the **Trial Balance** submenu option.

Figure 6.50
Trial Balance
Options

The window titled Trial Balance Options will now appear, requesting an **As At** date. This is the date for which you wish to generate the Trial Balance. This window is shown in Figure 6.50. You can also select to generate a comparative trial balance. Continue by

> Clicking the **OK** button, located inside the Trial Balance Options window, shown in Figure 6.50. This will tell Simply Accounting that you wish to generate the Trial Balance as at the default date which happens to be 08/31/01. Simply Accounting gets this date from the using date that you entered when you first opened the ODC practice case.

Figure 6.51 Trial Balance window

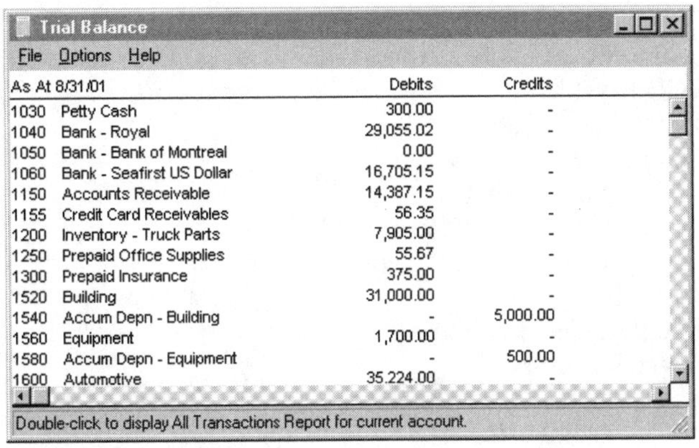

As At 8/31/01		Debits	Credits
1030	Petty Cash	300.00	-
1040	Bank - Royal	29,055.02	-
1050	Bank - Bank of Montreal	0.00	-
1060	Bank - Seafirst US Dollar	16,705.15	-
1150	Accounts Receivable	14,387.15	-
1155	Credit Card Receivables	56.35	-
1200	Inventory - Truck Parts	7,905.00	-
1250	Prepaid Office Supplies	55.67	-
1300	Prepaid Insurance	375.00	-
1520	Building	31,000.00	-
1540	Accum Depn - Building	-	5,000.00
1560	Equipment	1,700.00	-
1580	Accum Depn - Equipment	-	500.00
1600	Automotive	35,224.00	-

From the Trial Balance window (Figure 6.51)

> Click on the **File** menu option. This will invoke the **File** menu.
>
> Click on the **Print** submenu option. This will inform Simply Accounting that you wish to Print the Trial Balance as at 08/31/01. This will generate a Trial Balance report, as shown in Figure 6.52.

Figure 6.52 Printed Trial Balance Report

Overnight Delivery Company
Trial Balance As At 8/31/01

		Debits	Credits
1030	Petty Cash	300.00	-
1040	Bank - Royal	29055.02	-
1050	Bank - Bank of Montreal	0.00	-
1060	Bank - Seafirst US Dollar	16705.15	-
1150	Accounts Receivable	14387.15	-
1155	Credit Card Receivables	56.35	-
1200	Inventory - Truck Parts	7905.00	-
1250	Prepaid Office Supplies	55.67	-
1300	Prepaid Insurance	375.00	-
1520	Building	31000.00	-
1540	Accum Depn - Building	-	5000.00
1560	Equipment	1700.00	-
1580	Accum Depn - Equipment	-	500.00
1600	Automotive	35224.00	-
1620	Accum Amort - Automotive	-	5500.00
1640	Leasehold Improvements	12150.00	-
1660	Accum Amort - Leaseholds	-	3400.00

1800	Land	18000.00	-
2050	Accounts Payable	-	20730.21
2100	GST Charged on Sales	-	955.72
2105	HST Collected on Sales	-	7.50
2110	GST Paid on Purchase	18.20	-
2115	HST Paid on Purchases	-	0.00
2150	PST Payable	-	0.00
2200	Interest Payable	-	0.00
2300	Wages Payable	-	0.00
2320	CPP Payable	-	0.00
2340	EI Payable	-	0.00
2360	Income Tax Payable	-	0.00
2380	WCB Payable	-	0.00
2400	Dental Plan Payable	-	0.00
2420	CSB Plan Payable	-	0.00
2440	Medical Plan Payable	-	0.00
2460	Employee Donation Plan Payable	-	0.00
2470	Employee Stock Plan Payable	-	0.00
2750	Mortgage Payable	-	42946.50
2770	Note Payable - L. Cronkin	-	2000.00
3550	Capital - J. Demers	-	39399.87
4020	Other Freight	-	0.00
4050	Sales - Truck Parts	-	16666.55
4220	Regular Freight	-	63776.18
4240	Overnight Freight	-	27867.05
4260	Air Freight	-	16682.59
4320	Regular Freight - US	-	0.00
4340	Overnight Freight - US	-	0.00
4360	Air Freight - US	-	0.00
4410	Bank Interest	-	0.00
4430	Purchase Discounts	-	0.00
5050	Cost of Sales - Truck Parts	10358.00	-
5220	Supplies	985.00	-
5240	Fuel & Oil	14519.00	-
5260	Repairs and Maintenance	3615.00	-
5280	Insurance	1415.00	-
5300	Sales Discounts	11.45	-
5350	Import Duties	0.00	-
5520	Rent	4900.00	-
5540	Telephone and Long Distance	2503.85	-
5560	Utilities	1765.87	-
5580	Office Stationery	456.78	-
5600	Coffee Supplies	376.55	-
5620	Janitorial	1457.22	-
5640	Salaries and Benefits	23659.55	-
5660	CPP Expense	864.35	-
5680	EI Expense	1246.05	-
5700	WCB Expense	757.10	-
5800	Accounting and Legal	2209.95	-
5820	Advertising and Promotion	834.55	-
5840	Licenses and Permits	1555.00	-
5860	Insurance and Taxes	182.00	-
5880	Bank Charges and Interest	2515.21	-
5885	Credit Card Merchant Charges	1.15	-
5900	Other Freight	12.00	-

5920	Depreciation	2300.00	-
5950	Foreign Exchange	0.00	-
		245432.17	245432.17

Generated On: 2/25/01

Click on the **Control** box located in the upper-left corner of the Trial Balance window. This will in turn close the window. You can also press [Alt]+[F4] to close this window.

Now we must compare the totals from the Customer Aged Report (Figure 6.49) to the Accounts Receivable control account that appears on the Trial Balance report (Figure 6.52). As Simply Accounting prevents any postings, except postings from the Receivables Ledger and the associated Sales and Receipts journals, it is virtually impossible to have these totals out of balance.

MAINTAINING AN AUDIT TRAIL

It is extremely important that you maintain a correct audit trail. This means that you should print a sufficient amount of paper reports to provide you with a paper copy of the flow of transactions that have occurred. Not only will this provide you with information that you can use in your day-to-day operations, such as customer aging and General Ledger account balances, but a correct audit trail will provide the user with sufficient information should your Simply Accounting data set become corrupted and you have not followed the proper backup procedure. In this case, you would be able to create the data set using the audit trail report. However, it should be noted that in order to save yourself from frustration, backup your data set regularly.

Reports that should be included in your audit trail binder as listed below. The first five reports are shown in the solutions section in Appendix A.

General Ledger journal listing.
Trial Balance
Balance Sheet
Income Statement
Customer Aging in detail
Vendor Aging in detail
GST Report (to be discussed in a later chapter)
Employee Listings (to be discussed in a later chapter)
Inventory Listings (to be discussed in a later chapter)

The correct format for this audit trail binder would be a section for each type of report, followed by the reports in order of printing date. The frequency (daily, weekly or monthly) is up to the user; however, we recommend printing reports at least monthly.

BACKING UP YOUR DATA FILES

At this point, return to the Simply Accounting - ODC window and back up your data. Backup the data as follows:

Backup filename: A:\odc6d\odc
Comment: Receivables Part d

FURTHER PRACTICE

To get further practice with the concepts you have learned in this chapter, go to Chapter 14 and work through Section 6 of the National Supply Company.

CHAPTER 7

ACCOUNTS PAYABLE

CHAPTER 7

ACCOUNTS PAYABLE

OBJECTIVES

After completing this chapter you will be able to

1. Explain what the Accounts Payable module does and how it can help in transaction processing.

2. Explain what has to be done before you can convert a manual accounts payable system to a computerized one.

3. Enter vendor accounts and historical balances.

4. Add or delete a vendor account and modify vendor account information.

5. Display information about vendor accounts entered into the system and prepare various printouts.

6. Enter journal transactions — purchases and payments — into the purchase and payment journals.

THE ACCOUNTS PAYABLE SUBLEDGER

Accounts payable is the second subledger in the Simply Accounting system that we will look at. This subledger is used in conjunction with both the Purchases and Payments journals. In the Purchases journal you record all credit purchases made by the company — the amount of the purchase, the date of the purchase, the name of the supplier, and the account to which the purchase should be charged. Once you have entered the purchase through the Purchases journal, use the Payments journal to record cash disbursements made as payments to the various suppliers. In this way, the payables listing will provide you with a record of whom the company owes money to and the length of time the money has been owing. This information can then be used to determine what the cash requirements of the company will be over the next few months. This cash requirement is also known as the "cash flow" of the business.

DISCOUNTS

The information available from the Accounts Payable ledger can also be used to take advantage of cash payment discounts. Some creditors allow a discount if the invoice is paid within a certain period of time. While the Simply Accounting system does not keep track of the companies allowing discounts or the amount of the discount, it will keep track of the time since the purchase. However, a manager usually knows which companies will give the discount. By reviewing the aged listing — the list that indicates the number of days since the purchase was made— payment can be made to take advantage of discounts offered.

Discounts are usually stated in the following fashion:

2/10/N/30 (to be read "two, ten, Net, thirty").

This means that if the bill is paid within 10 days, the purchaser may reduce the amount owing by 2.0 percent (i.e. 2/10). This is intended to entice the buyer to make payment quickly so the supplier can get the cash. If the bill is not paid within the 10 days, the net amount of the purchase is due in 30 days (i.e. N/30).

CASH FLOW

Having control over your accounts payable invoices will provide you with the vital information that is required in order to determine the cash flow that your business will require in the next week, 10 days or whatever period you desire. This is one of the most important issues that a business must face, as you may have a surplus of cash this week but after you pay those unexpected bills, you may not have any cash remaining or, even worse, you may not even have enough cash to pay the outstanding bills. This problem can be managed by utilizing the Accounts Payable ledger and associated journals.

CREDIT RATING

Good control over accounts payable will also ensure that the company maintains a good credit rating. A company using a manual accounting system may forget to pay a bill or misplace it after it is recorded. The Accounts Payable module will not allow this to happen because outstanding bills are listed each time payments are made.

A good credit standing is important. It may allow you to negotiate a discount with the creditor. It may also mean that you can get a product that is in short supply, instead of a competitor who uses trade credit to finance his business. Suppliers avoid such firms because they often have difficulty collecting monies owed, on time.

OPEN ITEM ACCOUNTING

As mentioned in the previous chapter, the Simply Accounting system uses the open item method of accounting for Accounts Payable and Accounts Receivable as opposed to the balance forward method. The open item method keeps track of all individual invoices together with any payments made on behalf of that invoice. This tells you how much is owed to a specific vendor and the invoices that are still unpaid. Eventually when the invoices are fully paid, you can either retain this information or clear it out of the system, which is known as purging. If you purge it, the information is lost forever except for the printouts that you made along the way. In most cases, this is all that is necessary.

The ability to identify specific invoices is the key to good internal control. This is why the open item method is superior to the balance forward method, which only accounts for the total owing and not for specific invoices. The open item method would be difficult to implement under a manual accounting system because of the many transactions that are required. However, with a computerized accounting system such as Simply Accounting, this task is relatively easy.

The open item method of accounting for invoices payable provides the following two benefits:

LATE PAYMENTS CHARGES

The open item method provides enough detail to allow you to identify which of your invoices have been paid and which have not. By promptly paying your invoices when due you can avoid paying interest charges.

If you are charged with interest, you would enter it into the system as an invoice and pay it along with the regular payment. In this case, you would record the charge with a debit to interest expense.

DISCOUNTS

The open item method also provides sufficient detail to allow you to take advantage of discounts vendors offer for early payment. Simply Accounting for Windows now integrates the use of discounts within your purchases.

GOODS AND SERVICES TAX

All versions of Simply Accounting for Windows calculate and compile the GST automatically. The regular method of accounting for GST is to collect the GST for all services performed and goods sold. Deducted from the remittance of GST to the Receiver General, is the amount of GST paid to suppliers when purchasing goods and services. Simply Accounting will calculate the proper amount of GST paid and prepare a report useful for calculating the amount of GST owing to the government.

We discussed how these accounts should be set up in Chapter 6.

COMPUTERIZING ACCOUNTS PAYABLE

As with the Accounts Receivable module, you must organize your existing data before you can begin to convert your manual accounts payable system to the Simply Accounting system.

ORGANIZING VENDOR RECORDS

There are three steps to organizing your vendor records:

1. Prepare a listing of current vendors.

2. List the outstanding invoices to be paid.

3. Reconcile the total outstanding invoices to the control account, Accounts Payable, in the General Ledger to ensure that the accounts balance.

PREPARING A VENDOR LISTING

Prepare a complete listing of vendors from whom you can purchase goods on credit (see Figure 7.1). You need their name, street address, city, province, postal code, and telephone and fax numbers. Simply Accounting will then sort the vendors into an alphabetical listing for easy access.

Name	**Address**
Vancouver Times (entered)	Contact: Desiree Lee
	5252 Lincoln Court
	Vancouver, B.C. V2S 4N8
	Phone: 604-456-8111
	Fax: 604-456-8112
	Terms: 2.0% within 10 days, Net 30 days.
	Calculate Discount before tax
Choquette & Co. Accounting Grp. (entered)	Contact: Andre Choquette
	11850 – 236th Street
	Maple Ridge, B.C. V4R 2E1
	Phone: 604-463-8202
	Fax: 604-463-8210
	Terms: Net 30 days.
	Calculate Discount before tax

Name	**Address**
King Stationery (entered)	Contact: Lynn Cashcare #14 – 4332 South Centre Vancouver, B.C. V2S 4N9 Phone: 604-593-4444 Fax: 604-593-4443 Terms: 3.0% within 10 days, Net 15 days. Calculate Discount before tax
Exxon (entered)	Contact: Christine Barker 568 54th Ave. Toronto, Ont. M8C 3N4 Phone: 416-545-7777 Fax: 416-545-7778 Terms: Net 25 days. Calculate Discount before tax
J. & J. Rental Holdings (entered)	Contact: Colin Zackery 459 Childon Road Vancouver, B.C. V9N 3N2 Phone: 604-545-8655 Fax: 604-545-8656 Terms: Net 30 days. Calculate Discount before tax
Safesure Parcel Delivery Ltd. (entered)	Contact: Pierre J. Creek 45865 Stewardson Way Surrey, B.C. V6C 9N9 Phone: 604-545-0025 Fax: 604-545-4432 Terms: 2.0% within 10 days, Net 30 days. Calculate Discount before tax
Telus (entered)	Contact: Jan Bluewater 6565 Courtside Plaza Vancouver, B.C. V6C 3N3 Phone: 604-544-4577 Fax: 604-544-4576 Terms: Net 30 days. Calculate Discount before tax

Name	**Address**
TWK Internet Inc. (entered)	Contact: Nancy Affair 272 Upton Street Graton, MA 50849 Phone: 708-554-0382 Fax: 708-554-0385 Terms: Net 30 days Calculate Discount before tax Currency USD
Valley Office Supplies	Contact: Accounts Receivable Box 1010 Station J New York, NY 58473 Phone: 800-443-2323 Fax: 800-443-0021 Terms: Net 30 days Currency: USD
Golden Wings Freight Lines	Contact: R. Innes 45 Lansing Road Calgary, Alta. T0C 4N0 Phone: 403-593-7878 Fax: 403-593-7877 Terms: 2.0% within 10 days, Net 30 days. Calculate Discount before tax
Ronoco Truck Parts Ltd.	Contact: Sherri Barker 8455 Surrey Rd. Maple Ridge, B.C. V8N 3N9 Phone: 604-336-9393 Fax: 604-336-4346 Terms: 3.0% within 5 days, Net 30 days. Calculate Discount before tax

Figure 7.1   Vendor listing for Overnight Delivery Company

LISTING OUTSTANDING INVOICES

Make a list of all unpaid invoices for each vendor up to the time of conversion. The listing should include the date of the invoice, the invoice number, and the amount owing. Any partial payments made by vendors against these invoices must also be listed. For example, you may have the situation shown in Figure 7.2.

Overnight Delivery Company Listing of Accounts Payable July 31, 2001					
Company	**Invoice #**	**Date**	**Pre-Tax**	**Tax**	**Total**
Vancouver Times	13856	July 12, 2001	834.00	58.38	892.38
Telus	468593	July 15, 2001	336.87	23.58	360.45
Choquette & Co Accounting Group	125	July 29, 2001	2,065.37	144.58	2,209.95
King Stationery	4658	July 17, 2001	785.87	55.01	840.88
	4669	July 19, 2001	517.22	36.21	553.43
	4799	July 24, 2001	86.92	6.08	93.00
Exxon	45698	July 29, 2001	1,801.45	126.10	1,927.55
J. & J. Rental Holdings	569	July 12, 2001	1,500.00	0.00	1,500.00
Ronoco Truck Parts Ltd.	4610	July 10, 2001	6,939.89	485.79	7,425.68
	4614	July 15, 2001	3,572.62	250.08	3,822.70
	4616	July 18, 2001	2,433.82	170.37	2,604.19
Partial Payments					
Vancouver Times	Cheque 524	July 28, 2001	13856		500.00
Exxon	Cheque 526	July 30, 2001	45698		1,000.00
			Total		**20,730.01**

Figure 7.2   Listing of accounts payable Overnight Delivery Company

AGREEING TO CONTROL ACCOUNT

Total all outstanding invoices and agree this amount to the amount showing in the Accounts Payable account in the existing General Ledger or your trial balance. You must start with the listing equal to your control account or the program will not allow you to switch the Payable ledger to READY mode.

BEGINNING THE ACCOUNTS PAYABLE CONVERSION

You are now ready to begin the Accounts Payable conversion.

To speed up the data entry time, we have entered several of the customers that appear in Figure 7.1.

Before you continue, copy the starter files from the included CD-ROM. The source directory should be X:\sw0807. We would suggest that you use the enclosed installation program (X:\Setup) to install these files.

Once you have copied the above data files, continue by

Starting Simply Accounting for Windows.

Selecting the ODC (Overnight Delivery Company) data file.

Confirming the Session Date as 08/31/01.

Close the To-Do Lists window.

Close the Checklists window.

Figure 7.3
Simply
Accounting –
ODC window

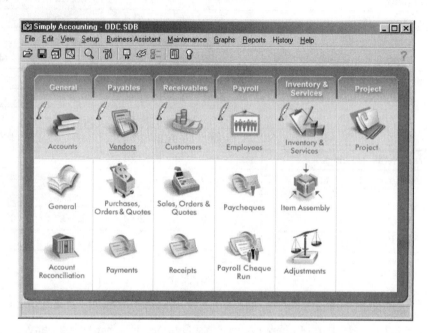

Continue from the Simply Accounting - ODC window (Figure 7.3) by

Double-clicking your mouse on the Vendors icon.

Figure 7.4
Vendors window

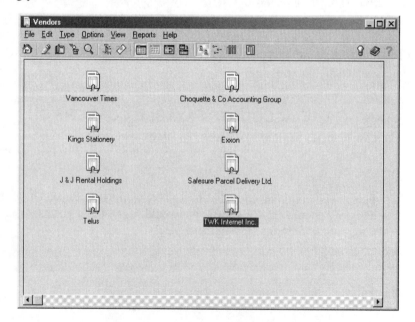

The Vendors window will now appear as shown in Figure 7.4. As with the Customers window in Accounts Receivable, the Vendors window displays each of your vendors as an icon once the vendors are entered.

Continue from within the Vendors window (Figure 7.4) by

Clicking the **Create** icon. Alternatively, you can press ⌨Alt + ⌨F to select the **File** menu, followed by pressing the ⌨c to select the **Create** command.

Figure 7.5
Payables Ledger
(Address) window

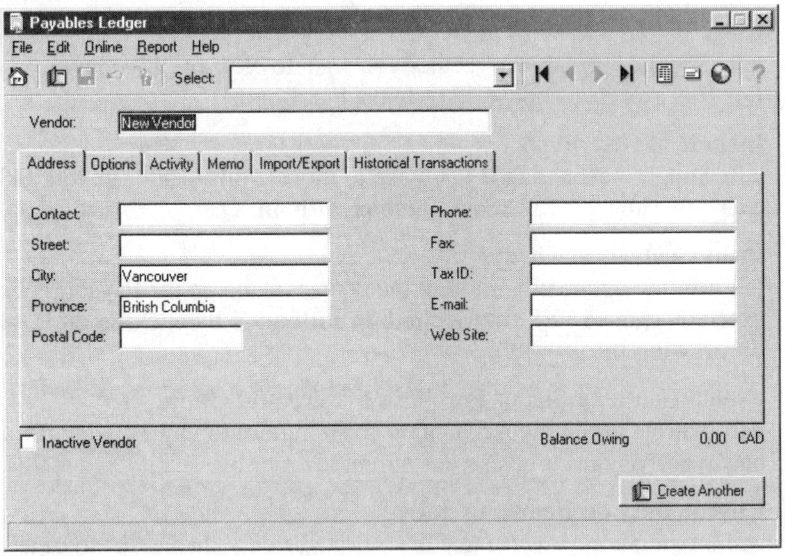

The Payables Ledger window will appear as shown in Figure 7.5. This window is similar to the Receivables Ledger window when entering customers with regard to the address and Internet. This window is also a tabbed window that will require you to enter information into all of the tabbed windows prior to selecting the **Create** button.

Entering the Internet information will allow you to send e-mail and browse your vendors' web site without having to leave Simply Accounting, providing suitable Internet software is installed on your machine along with an Internet connection.

Figure 7.6
Payables Ledger
(Options) window

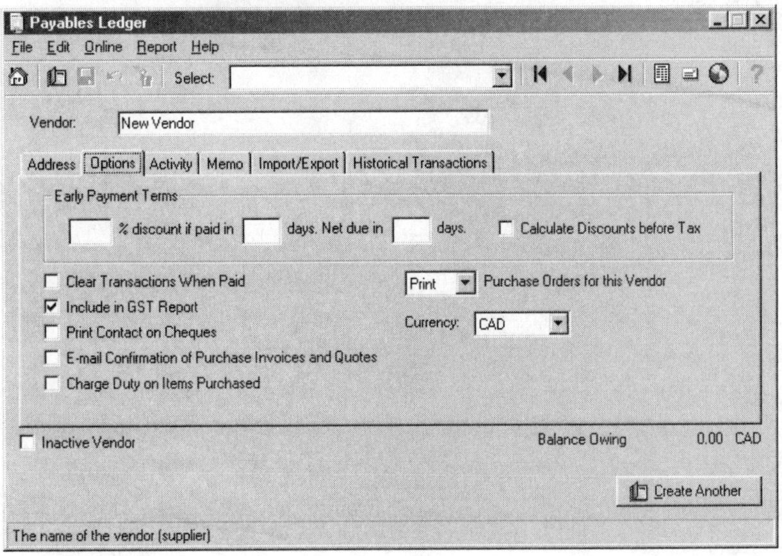

Within the Options tabbed area, you can select from the following options:

Early Payment Terms

allows you to enter custom payment terms, including a discount for prompt payment. An example would be the terms of 2.0% 10, Net 30 which would be entered as 2.0% discount if paid within 10 days. Net amount due within 30 days.

Calculate Discounts before Tax

indicates to Simply Accounting for Windows to calculate the vendors discount prior to calculating the applicable taxes so that a discount is not given to any taxes charged.

Clear Invoices When Paid

tells Simply Accounting whether you wish to clear or purge invoices once they are paid. **For this exercise, choose NO, (leave box blank).**

Include in GST Report

tells Simply Accounting if you wish to include this vendor in your GST report. **For this exercise, choose YES (mark the box with an X).**

Print Contact on Cheque

tells Simply Accounting to print the contact name on the Payables cheques. **For this exercise, choose YES (mark the box with an X by clicking on it with your mouse or by pressing the** space bar**.**

E-mail Confirmation of Purchase Invoice and Quote

will indicate to Simply Accounting for Windows to request a confirmation to be sent, once your Vendor receives your purchase order by e-mail.

Charge Duty on Items Purchased

will inform Simply Accounting that selectable duty charges are to be added when inventory items are purchased.

Print/E-mail Purchase Orders for this Vendor

allows you to select to either print or electronically transmit purchase orders to your vendor.

Currency

allows you to select the currency for this vendor. This allows you to mix both Canadian and U.S. clients for the purpose of this book.

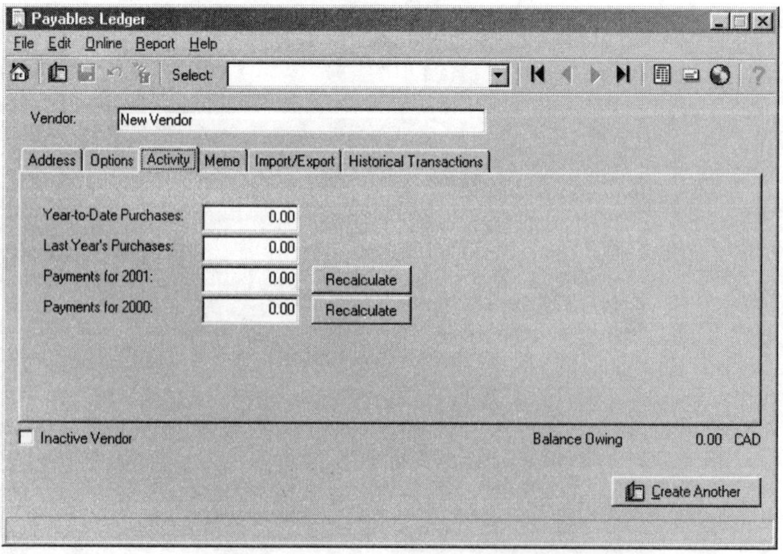

Figure 7.7
Payables
Ledger
(Activity)
window

Within the Payables Ledger (Activity) window (Figure 7.7) you can continue with the entry of both the **Year-to-Date Purchases** and **Last Year's Purchases** figures as well as payments for both last year and the current year. These figures will be helpful in tracking your purchases and payments for statistical purposes.

Figure 7.8
Payables
Ledger (Memo)
window

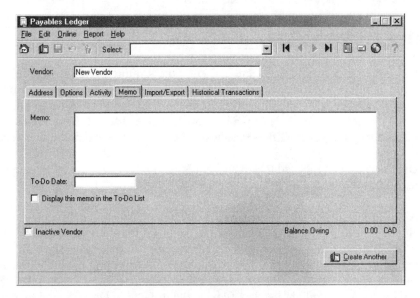

The Payables Ledger (Memo) window allows you to enter reminders that can appear within the To-Do List. For example, you may want to be reminded to send a payment to a particular vendor at a certain time in order to get the discount.

Figure 7.9
Payables
Ledger
(Import/Export)
window

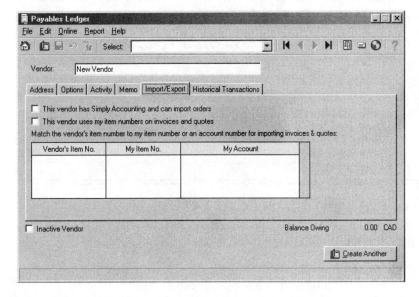

The Import/Export feature (Figure 7.9) allows Simply Accounting for Windows to communicate with your vendors' Simply Accounting for Windows program. For example, you can enter your vendor's inventory number as well as your own inventory number so that the programs adjust both inventory amounts automatically. Again, you cannot access the History tabbed window to make modifications to information about vendors until you have entered your vendors.

ENTERING VENDORS INTO THE ACCOUNTS PAYABLE LEDGER

Entering Vendors into the Payables ledger is similar to entering customers into the Receivable ledger. If you are unsure about how to enter these vendors, return to the Accounts Receivable chapter and review how you entered the customer listing.

Practice Exercise 7.1

Using the vendor listing in Figure 7.1, enter the last three vendors into the Simply Accounting Payables ledger, (all others have been entered for you). Assume the defaults for all undisplayed fields. These will include the **Clear invoices when paid** box which is not checked, but **Include in GST** report option is checked. Be sure to select USD as the currency for Valley Office Supplies and CAD for the remaining two vendors.

Once you have completed this exercise, remain in the Payable Ledger window for the next section.

Note: The data files with the vendors entered is available on disk. If you do not want to enter the vendors yourself, then copy the data files from the subdirectory on the CD-ROM in the back of the book to the **C:\Program Files\WinSim\Data** directory on your hard drive. Before you do so, you should delete any existing files to eliminate any conflicts with the new files. The data files are in the subdirectory called **ODC8MOD**. Use the Explorer to highlight the data files on the diskette in Drive A, and then drag them into the C:\Programs Files\Winsim\Data directory.

HINT: CALCULATE DISCOUNTS BEFORE TAX OPTION

If your vendor has a policy that all discounts are calculated before tax, you should select this option even if your current payment terms are Net 30 (no discount). This will prevent a potential discount calculation error in the feature, (once your vendor begins with an early payment discount). This method of discount calculation is the standard process within Canadian companies.

BACKING UP YOUR DATA FILES

At this point, return to the Simply Accounting - ODC window (Figure 7.3) and continue with the backup function.

Call this backup:

> **Backup Filename:** A:\odc\odc7a
> **Comment:**   Payables Part a

If you are unsure of how to complete the backup procedure, please refer to Chapter 3 for complete instructions.

Once you have completed the above backup, return to the Vendors window (Figure 7.4).

ENTERING THE OPENING BALANCES

After you have entered all the vendors into the Payables ledger, you are ready to enter the outstanding invoices and any partial payments made at the time of conversion. This is done through the Payables ledger and is similar to entering opening balances for the Receivables ledger. You can now enter current invoices, even though you have not entered historical transactions. However, doing so could create a potential problems if you enter a payment for a non-existent historical invoice.

Once you have entered the historical balances, and made sure that this balance compares to the balance in the General Ledger, you can change the module to the current entry mode. Keep in mind that once you change to the Current/Ready mode, you will not be able to change the historical or opening balances.

Practice Exercise 7.2

Enter all opening balances shown in Figure 7.2 for the vendors in Figure 7.1. You should still be in the Payables Ledger window.

You must first locate the appropriate vendor. You can scroll through the vendor list by clicking on the ⬆ or ⬇ buttons that are located on the vertical scroll bar located on the bottom of the Payables Ledger window. Or you can press [Alt] + [E] followed by [F] to activate the **Find** menu option, located in the **Edit** menu. When the appropriate vendor is displayed on the screen, click on the **Invoices** box to open the Historical Invoices window. Enter the invoice number, the date followed by the pre-tax, and the tax amount. Click on the **Record** button or press the [space bar] when that button is highlighted. When you have entered all of the invoices for that vendor, click on the **Close** button to close the Historical Invoices window for that vendor.

Once you have entered the historical invoices for your vendors, continue with the entry of the historical partial payments (Figure 7.2).

Accept the default terms for each invoice.

When you have completed Exercise 7.2, press [Alt] + [F4] to close the Payables Ledger window, followed by pressing [Alt] + [F4] to close the Vendors window. Alternately you can choose to click on the **Control** box for each of these windows to close them. You will then return to the Simply Accounting - ODC window, shown in Figure 7.3

BACKING UP YOUR DATA FILES

At this point, return to the Simply Accounting - ODC window (Figure 7.3) and continue with the backup function.

Call this backup:

Backup Filename: A:\odc\odc7b
Comment: Payables Part b

DEFINING THE LINKED ACCOUNTS FOR ACCOUNTS PAYABLE

Before you have finished with the process of entering historical data, you must define the integration accounts. This in turn will tell Simply Accounting which General Ledger control accounts are used by the Payables ledger.

Continue from within the Simply Accounting - ODC window (Figure 8.2) by

Selecting the **Setup** menu.

Clicking the Linked Accounts menu option.

Clicking the **Payables** submenu option.

Figure 7.10
Payable
Integration
window

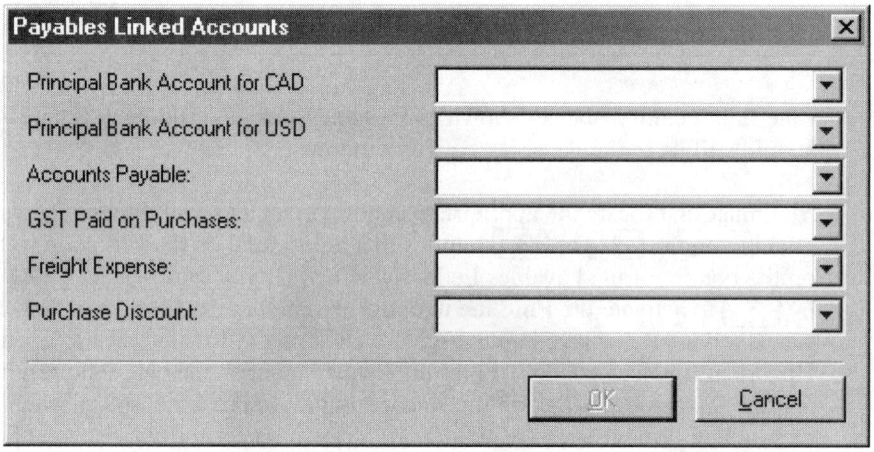

Simply Accounting has now opened the Payables Linked Accounts window (Figure 7.10).

Practice Exercise 7.3

Continue with the selection of the appropriate General Ledger accounts, (Royal Bank for Bank 1 and Seafirst for the USD Bank).

Once you have completed this exercise, your Payables Linked Accounts window should resemble Figure 7.11.

Figure 7.11
Payable Linked
Accounts
window
(completed)

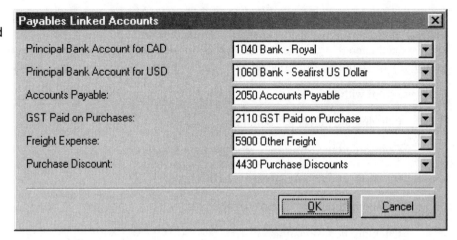

Once you have completed these steps, press

> Enter   to close the Payables Linked Accounts window. You will then return to the Simply Accounts - ODC window (Figure 7.2).

DISPLAYING REPORTS

Once you have entered the historical data into the Payables ledger, you should look at a summary display of the opening balance to ensure that it agrees with the opening balance in your manual accounts payable system. In this case this balance should agree with the total balance in Figure 7.2.

Continue from within the Simply Accounting - ODC window (Figure 7.3) by

> Selecting the **Reports** menu.

> Clicking the **Payables** menu option.

> Clicking the **Vendor Aged** submenu option.

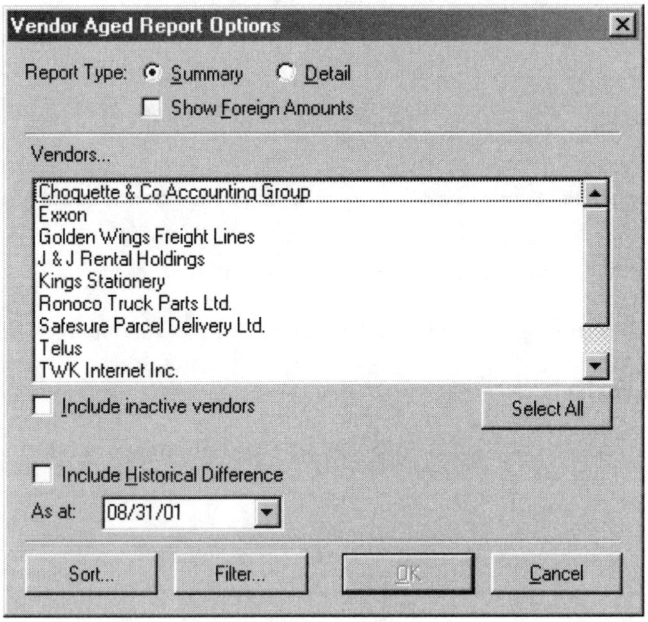

Figure 7.12
Vendor Aged
Report Options
window

Simply Accounting now displays the Vendor Aged Report Options window (see Figure 7.12). You will notice that this window is almost identical to the Customer Aged Report Options window that we encountered in Chapter 6. This option allows you to choose between printing a **Summary** or **Detail** report. You can also select which vendors you want to include in the report.

Continue from within the Vendor Aged Report Options window (Figure 7.12) by

> Clicking the **Select All** button.
>
> Confirming the **Summary** report option is selected.
>
> Clicking the **Include Historical Difference**.
>
> Changing the **As at** date to 07/31/01.
>
> Clicking the **OK** button.

Figure 7.13
Vendor Aged
Summary
window

Vendor Aged Summary					
File Options Help					
As at 07/31/01	Total	Current	31 to 60	61 to 90	91+
Choquette & Co Accounting Group	2,209.95	2,209.95	-	-	-
Exxon	927.55	927.55	-	-	-
J & J Rental Holdings	1,500.00	1,500.00	-	-	-
Kings Stationery	1,487.31	1,487.31	-	-	-
Ronoco Truck Parts Ltd.	13,852.57	13,852.57	-	-	-
Telus	360.45	360.45	-	-	-
Vancouver Times	392.38	392.38	-	-	-
	20,730.21	20,730.21	-	-	-
Vendors history is balanced.					

Simply Accounting will execute your request and display Figure 7.13, which is the window titled Vendor Aged Summary. Note that all of the invoices are in the 31 to 60 days column because of the invoice entry dates.

HINT: *USE THE REPORT DRILL DOWN FEATURE*

Remember that within any report, you can view the detail associated with a summary line by double-clicking on the specific detail line. This will display the detail associated with the selected summary line.

Once you are done viewing this window, use your mouse and

> Click on the **Control** box located in the left corner of the Vendor Aged Summary window.

Or using your keyboard

> Press ⎡Alt⎤ + ⎡F4⎤ to close the Vendor Aged Summary window.

Printing Reports

Displaying reports on the monitor is fine for quick viewing of the data. In most cases, however, you will want a printed report for a permanent record. Printing reports is similar to displaying them.

Follow the above commands to display the Vendor Aged Summary window. Once you have this window displayed, press

Alt + F4	to invoke the **File** menu option, located in the Vendor Aged Summary window.
P	to **Print** the Vendor Aged Summary report.

> *Note: Make sure your printer is turned on, and that it is on-line allowing data to flow from the computer to the printer. Make sure that there is paper in the tray if you are using a laser printer and that the print head is at the top of the paper if you are using a dot-matrix printer. This should be checked each time you wish to print something.*

Alt + F4	to close the Vendor Aged Summary window.

You can Print any report that can be displayed by Simply Accounting. This is done by selecting the **File** menu located in the window that you wish to print, followed by selecting the **Print** menu option.

You can also **Export** any report to popular program formats.

What if I do not balance?

Refer back to Chapter 6 for an explanation on how to rectify an out-of-balance issue. This will involve paying the invoice in error, clearing this invoice, and re-entering the invoice or partial payment correctly.

BACKING UP YOUR DATA FILES

At this point, return to the Simply Accounting - ODC window (Figure 7.3) and continue with the backup function.

Call this backup:

      Backup Filename: A:\odc\odc7c
      Comment: Payables Part c

If you are unsure of how to complete the backup procedure, please refer to Chapter 3 for complete instructions.

COMPLETING THE CONVERSION PROCESS

You have now entered your opening balances, so the conversion process is almost complete. You will now need to continue with the establishment of the required integration accounts.

HANDLING CREDIT CARD PAYMENTS

Simply Accounting for Windows Version 8.0 supports the use of credit cards for payments of Accounts Payable Cash invoices and Accounts Payable Payments. Since it is a common practice today to use a credit card to make a company purchase, we will continue with the setup of this function.

Practice Exercise 7.4

ENTERING GENERAL LEDGER ACCOUNTS

Continue with the entry (creation) of the following General Ledger Accounts (review Chapter 4 for instructions):

For all fields not mentioned, accept the defaulted values.

Account Number:	2060
Description:	VISA Payable
Type:	Subgroup Account
Account Class:	Credit Card
Account Number:	2065
Description:	MASTERCARD Payable
Type:	Subgroup Account
Account Class:	Credit Card
Account Number:	2069
Description:	Total Credit Card Payable
Type:	Subgroup Total

Once you have completed this exercise, return to the Simply Accounting - ODC window.

Continue from the Simply Accounting - ODC window (Figure 7.3) by

Selecting the **Setup** menu.

Selecting the **Credit Cards** menu option.

Within the Credit Card Information window, continue by

Selecting the **Credit cards used** tabbed button.

Figure 7.14
Credit Card –
used window

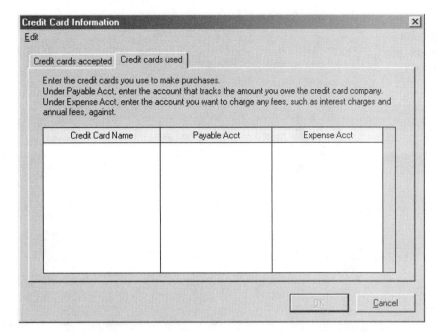

As shown in Figure 7.14, Simply Accounting allows you to establish several credit cards that you plan to use within your business. You will need to provide the following information:

Credit Card Name is the name that you will use to identify your credit card.

Payable Acct is the General Ledger account to which credit card purchases will be posted.

Expense Acct is the General Ledger account that is used to record interest or annual fee charges.

Practice Exercise 7.5

Continue with the entry of the following credit cards that will be used within your business:

Credit Card Name: VISA
Payable Acct: 2060
Expense Acct: 5880

Credit Card Name: MASTERCARD
Payable Acct: 2065
Expense Acct: 5880

Once you have completed this exercise, continue by checking your entry against Figure 7.15.

Figure 7.15
Credit Card -
used window
(entered)

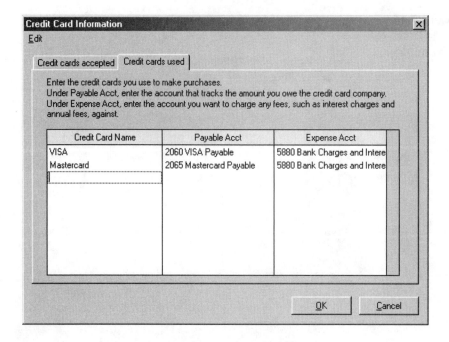

If your Credit card used window resembles Figure 7.15, continue by

Clicking the **OK** button or pressing ⌈Enter⌉.

ENTERING ACCOUNTS PAYABLE JOURNAL ENTRIES

All Accounts Payable transactions are entered through a series of journal entries similar to the journal entries for Accounts Receivable. You will use both the **Purchases** and **Payments** journals to enter this information:

1.	Purchase	Dr. Expense, Asset or Liability Account
		Dr. GST Paid on Purchases ✓
		Cr. Accounts Payable
2.	Payments	Dr. Accounts Payable
		Cr. Cash

Remember that subledgers have common accounts in their journal entries. For example, in Accounts Payable, each purchase entry will have a common credit entry to Accounts Payable. This helps to speed up the transaction entry process since you only have to enter the debit side of the entry. The program will add up the debits that you entered and automatically credit accounts payable.

ENTERING PURCHASES

Overnight Delivery Company had the following purchase transactions during the month of August 2001.

Inv. #	Date	Customer	Account	Amount	Notes
		Overnight Delivery Company **Purchases (on Account) Journal** **August 2001**			
15326	Aug 2	Vancouver Times	Advertising	497.50	Entered
		2/10 Net 30 days	GST	34.83	Entered
				532.33	Total
		The above invoice represents a recurring monthly charge			
315	Aug 4	Choquette & Co. Accounting	Accounting	450.00	
		Net 30 days	GST	31.50	
				481.50	Total
		The above invoice represents a recurring monthly charge			
116535	Aug 5	Exxon	Fuel	1,205.58	
		Net 25 days	GST	Included	
				1,205.58	Total
4263	Aug 7	J. & J. Rental	Rent	750.00	
		Net 10 days	GST	52.50	
				802.50	Total
		The above invoice represents a recurring monthly charge			
2256	Aug 7	Golden Wings	Other Freight	852.36	
		2/10 Net 30 days	GST	59.67	
				912.03	Total
189658	Aug 12	Safesure Parcel	Other Freight	998.00	
		2/10 Net 30 days	GST	69.86	
				1067.86	Total
32525	Aug 15	Telus	Telephone	325.00	
		Net 30 days	GST	22.75	
				347.75	Total
15986	Aug 15	Vancouver Times	Advertising	126.93	
		2/10 Net 30 days	GST	8.89	
				135.82	Total
456	Aug 15	Golden Wings	Other Freight	1,122.00	
		2/10 Net 30 days	GST	78.54	
				1,200.54	Total
843	Aug 15	TWK Internet	Telephone	100.00	USD
			GST	n/a	not applicable
				100.00	USD Total
		The above invoice represents a recurring monthly charge			
		Total for all invoices		$ 6,785.91	

Figure 7.16 Purchases Journal

To enter the purchase transactions, make sure that you are at the Simply Accounting - ODC window. Then continue by

Clicking on the **Purchases** icon or use your keyboard.

> **HINT:** *If you post an invoice before you store it as a recurring charge, then use the recall entry feature in the Purchases journal. When you click on the icon "Look up a posted invoice" you will get the Invoice Lookup window. Click on* **browse** *and the invoices that you have entered are displayed. Click on the one you want to store. It will be highlighted. Then click on* **Select** *and the invoice is recalled. You can then store it as a recurring charge. You will not be able to post it again.*

Figure 7.17
Purchases
Journal window

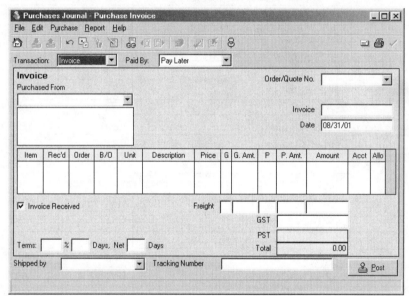

Simply Accounting will then display a window titled Purchases Journal – Purchase Invoice, as shown in Figure 7.17.

Continue by entering

(Tab) (2 times)   to move to the **Purchased From** field.

To enter the first vendor's invoice, Vancouver Times, you must first locate that vendor. Continue by entering

Van (Tab)   to enter the first part of the Vendors name, (Vancouver Times).

> **HINT: HOW TO FIND VENDORS**
>
> *You can locate a vendor by either entering the first part of the vendor's name or by selecting the vendor from the pull down list.*

Tab	to leave the **PO Number** field blank and move to the **Invoice** field. We will address the **PO Number** field and **Purchase Order** module within the Inventory chapter.
15326 Tab	to enter the **Invoice** number
08/02/01 Tab	to enter the **Date** of this purchase
Tab (several times)	to move to the **G** (GST Code) field
Enter	to display the GST code selection window (Figure 7.18)

Figure 7.18
GST Code
Selection
window

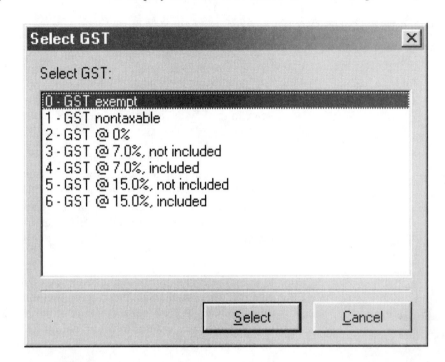

The GST Selection window (Figure 7.18) allows you to select from the following GST options:

0 – GST exempt	As a purchaser, you are exempt from GST on this purchase detail line.
1 – GST nontaxable	As a purchaser, you are not taxable under the GST/Excise Act for this purchase detail line.
2 – GST @ 0%	The item/service purchased is taxable at a zero rating with respect to GST.
3 – GST @ 7.0% not included	The item/service purchased is subject to GST at the specified rate (within the program settings). The GST is not however included within the purchase amount and is instead taxable separately from the price, (Example $100.00 plus 7.0% GST would equal $107.00).
4 – GST @ 7.0% included	The item/service purchased is subject to GST at the specified rate and is included within the purchase amount, (Example: $100.00 which includes GST).

5 – GST @ 15.0% not included   The item/service purchased is subject to GST at the secondary specified rate (within the program settings). The GST is not however included within the purchase amount and is instead taxable separately from the price, (Example $100.00 plus 15.0% HST would equal $115.00).

6 – GST @ 15.0% included   The item/service purchased is subject to GST at the secondary specified rate and is included within the purchase amount, (Example: $100.00 which includes HST).

Continue from the Select GST window (Figure 7.18) by pressing

3 [Enter]   to accept 3 – GST @ 7.0% not included as the GST code.

[Tab]   to leave the **GST Amount** blank. This field is available so that you can modify the actual invoice's GST, if required.

[Tab]   to leave the **PST Percentage** field blank. If you enter a PST percentage, the program will automatically calculate the PST amount which will be added to the appropriate account. At the present time the Provincial Sales Tax is treated as a cost and cannot be offset against PST collected as is the case with the GST.

[Tab]   to leave the **PST Amount** field blank. You could however enter the amount of PST displayed on the purchase invoice, thus allowing you to enter the details of the invoice without having to use a calculator to figure out the amount of the purchase including PST.

497.50 [Tab]   to enter the amount for this invoice.

[Enter]   to display the Select Account window.

Figure 7.19
Select Account
window

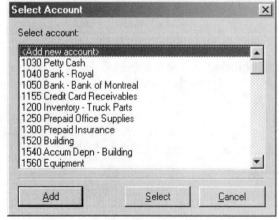

From within the Select Account window (Figure 7.19), you can easily select the appropriate General Ledger account in order to assign to this purchase detail line. You can also easily move to the appropriate accounts sections by pressing the first number for each group, ⌐1⌐ for Assets (1000 accounts), ⌐2⌐ for Liabilities (2000 accounts), ⌐3⌐ for Equity (3000 accounts), ⌐4⌐ for Revenue (4000 accounts) or ⌐5⌐ for Expense (5000 accounts).

Continue from the Select Account window (Figure 7.19) by pressing

⌐ 5 ⌐	to jump to the 5000 –5999 Expense account range.
⌐ ↓ ⌐ (several times)	to find the account titled 5680 Advertising and Promotion.
⌐ Enter ⌐	to tell Simply Accounting that you wish to allocate $497.50 to account 5680 – Advertising and Promotion.

At this point in the invoice entry, you could continue with the following:

Edit the applicable tax amounts for each detail line. This is accomplished by changing the tax amount within either the **G. Amt** and **P. Amt** fields.

Edit the total GST/HST on this invoice by changing the value within the **GST** field.

Store the entry as a recurring entry under the default name using a monthly frequency.

Practice Exercise 7.6

If you are unsure of how to store this purchase as a recurring entry, please refer to the Accounts Receivable chapter, (Chapter 6) for explanation of this feature.

Once you have completed this exercise, return to the Purchase Journal window (as displayed in Figure 7.20).

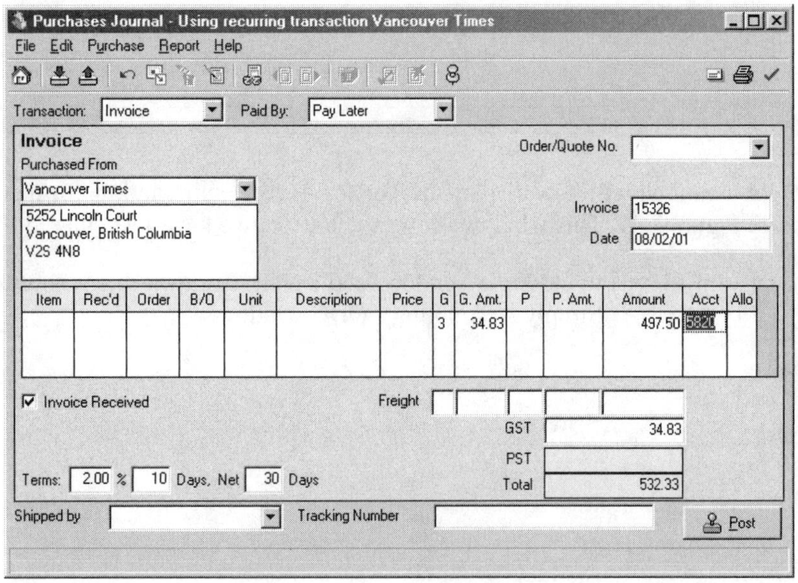

Figure 7.20
Purchases
Journal window
(entered)

Your Purchases Journal window should resemble Figure 7.20. Continue by pressing

[Alt] + [P] to **Post** the above invoice. This will allow Simply Accounting to update both the vendor's information and the General Ledger's control accounts.

Once the posting process is complete, Simply Accounting will return you to a blank Purchases Journal window, as shown in Figure 7.15. Press

[Alt] + [F4] to close this window. You will now return to the Simply Accounting - ODC window.

Now let's display the **Vendor Aged** for *Vancouver Times*. Use either your mouse or your keyboard.

Select the **Report** menu option, located in the Simply Accounting - ODC window.

Select the **Payables** submenu option.

Select the **Vendor Aged** submenu option. This will display the Vendor Aged Report Options window.

Select the **Detail** button.

Select *Vancouver Times* as the vendor.

Select the OK button.

Figure 7.21
Vendor Aged
Detail window

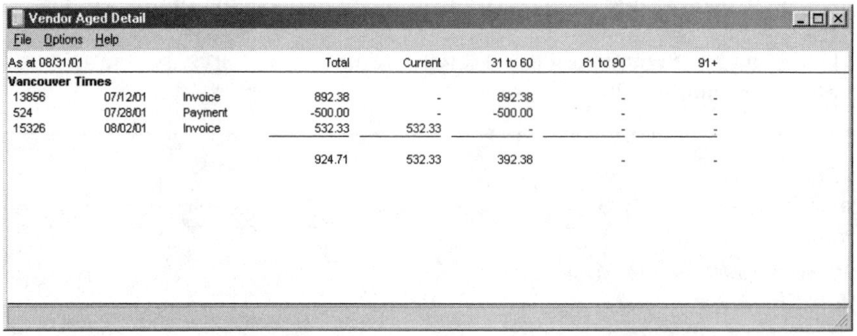 Vendor Aged Detail							
File Options Help							
As at 08/31/01			Total	Current	31 to 60	61 to 90	91+
Vancouver Times							
13856	07/12/01	Invoice	892.38	-	892.38	-	-
524	07/28/01	Payment	-500.00	-	-500.00	-	-
15326	08/02/01	Invoice	532.33	532.33	-	-	-
			924.71	532.33	392.38	-	-

Simply Accounting will now display the Vendor Aged Detail window for the *Vancouver Times*, shown in Figure 7.21. This window shows the invoice we have just entered. Press

[Alt] + [F4] to close the Vendor Aged Detail window. This will return you to the Simply Accounting - ODC window.

Practice Exercise 7.7

Enter the remaining purchase transactions for the month of August listed in the Purchases journal (Figure 7.16). Remember that you have already entered the first transaction. Watch the Exxon entry as the GST code should be code 4 which will include the GST component within the purchase amount (GST included).

Be sure to also store the noted recurring invoice entries.

Be sure to check and ensure that each invoice has the correct payment terms.

Once you have completed this exercise, close the Purchase Journal. You will then return to the Simply Accounting- ODC window.

BACKING UP YOUR DATA FILES

At this point, return to the Simply Accounting - ODC window (Figure 7.3) and backup your data files.

Call this backup:

Backup Filename: A:\odc\odc7d
Comment: Payables Part d

CASH PURCHASES

Overnight Delivery Company
Purchases (Cash/Credit Card) Journal
August 2001

Inv. No.	Date	Customer	Account	Amount	Notes
805	Aug 3	Office Depot	Office Supplies (Prepaid)	50.00	Entered
		10% Discount	GST	3.50	Entered
		Paid by MasterCard	Total	48.15	
3021	Aug 5	Java Beans	Coffee Supplies	35.00	
		5% Discount	GST	2.45	
		Paid by Visa	Total	37.45	
55847	Aug 5	Esso	Fuel	10.00	
			GST (included)		
		Paid by Visa	Total	10.00	
101-345	Aug 15	Clearnet	Telephone	69.54	
			GST	4.87	
		Paid by MasterCard	Total	74.41	
564	Aug 18	Kings Stationery	Janitorial Supplies	125.00	
		3% Discount	GST	8.75	
		Paid by Cheque #531 (Royal Bank)			
		(update cheque no.)	Total	133.75	
810-19	Aug 20	City of Vancouver	License and Permits	30.00	
			GST	0.00	
		Paid by Cheque #56 (Bank of Montreal)	Total	30.00	
345010	Aug 25	ICBC	Insurance	15.00	
			GST	0.00	
		Paid by Cash (Royal Bank)	Total	15.00	

Figure 7.22 Cash/Credit Purchase Journal

If you make frequent purchases with cash, credit card, or cheque, then you can use the **Cash Purchases** feature in Simply Accounting for Windows. This type of entry is very similar to entering purchases on credit, except that instead of the Accounts Payable control account being credited, the Cash control account is credited.

Dr. Expenses/Asset/Liability (User defined)
Cr. Bank Account

A credit card purchase is very similar to a cash purchase except that you would credit the credit card liability account instead of the bank account.

The **Cash Purchase** entry allows you to enter a purchase through the Payables ledger and enter the payment for that purchase at the same time.

Figure 7.23
Purchase
Journal window

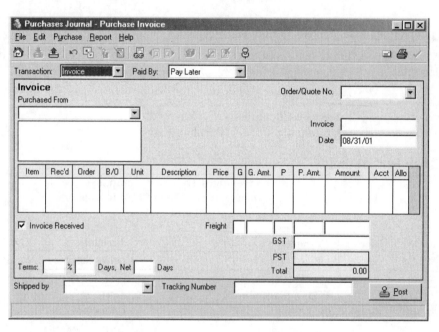

Continue by the Purchase Journal window (Figure 7.23) by

Figure 7.24
Paid by pull
down option

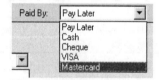

Selecting *MasterCard* as the **Paid By** option from the pull down menu (Figure 7.24).

Selecting <One-time vendor> as the **Purchased From** option.

HINT: USING ONE-TIME VENDORS

*Within your business you will make purchases from vendors and suppliers that will represent one-time cash or credit card purchases. In this case, you will not have to add these vendors, but instead select the **One-time vendor** option.*

The One-time vendor option can only be used for cash, cheque, or credit card purchases. All purchases on account must be made to a predetermined vendor.

Continue by

Entering *Office Depot* within the **Purchased From** address section. This will provide a later reference to the one-time vendor.

Enter *805* as the **Invoice** number.

Change the date to *08/03/01*.

Enter *50.00* as the **Amount**.

Select the appropriate *Prepaid Office Supplies* account from the Asset section.

Enter *3.50* as the total **GST** for this invoice.

Enter *10.00%* as the **Discount** for this invoice.

HINT: QUICK ENTRY TIPS

As described above, you can bypass the appropriate GST code and instead enter the total GST within the total GST field.

Figure 7.25
Purchase
Journal window
(entered)

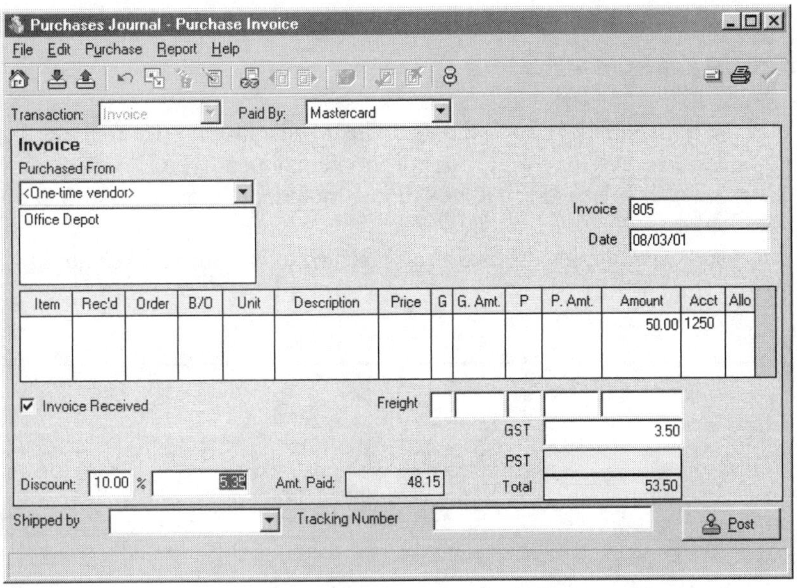

If your Purchase Journal window resembled Figure 7.25, then continue by

Selecting the **Report** menu.

Selecting the **Display Purchase Journal Entry** option.

Figure 7.26
Purchase
Journal Entry
window

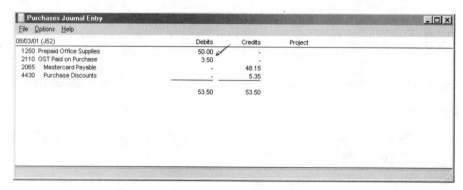

Within the Purchase Journal Entry window (Figure 7.26) you will notice that your MasterCard Payable account will be the credited account (instead of the standard Accounts Payable account).
If you had instead selected either the Cash or Cheque **Paid By** option, the credit account would be the selected bank account (Figure 7.27).

Figure 7.27
Payment by
Cheque
example

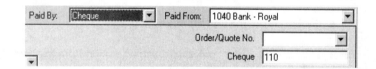

Continue from within the Purchase Journal Entry window (Figure 7.26) by

Closing the Purchase Journal Entry window.

Posting the Credit Card Purchase.

Practice Exercise 7.8

Enter the remaining **Credit Card and Cash Purchase** entries that are displayed in Figure 7.22. Be sure to select the appropriate payment type and discount (if required). Also remember to use GST Code 4 (7% – Included) for your Esso fuel purchase.

Once you have completed this exercise, return to the Simply Accounting - ODC window (Figure 7.3).

BACKING UP YOUR DATA FILES

At this point, return to the Simply Accounting - ODC window (Figure 7.3) and backup your data files.

Call this backup:

Backup Filename: A:\odc\odc7e
Comment: Payables Part e

ENTERING PAYMENTS

Unfortunately, you will eventually be required to remit payments to your vendors for purchases on account. This is done through the Payments journal.

Record the payment of invoices made during August, 2001. The listing is as follows:

\multicolumn{6}{c}{**Overnight Delivery Company**}						

\multicolumn{6}{c}{**Overnight Delivery Company** \ **Cash Disbursements Journal** \ **August 2001**}						
Date	Vendor	Cheque No.	Inv. No.	Amount	Notes
Aug 15	Golden Wings	532 (Bank - Royal)	2256	17.05	discount
				894.98	
			Total	894.98	entered
Aug 15	King Stationery	533 (Bank - Royal)	4658	840.88	
			4669	553.43	
				1394.31	Total
Aug 15	Choquette & Company Accounting Grp.	534 (Bank - Royal)	125	1,000.00	watch amount
Aug 15	Exxon	57 (Bank of Montreal)	45698	927.55	
Aug 15	Vancouver Times	VISA	113856	392.38	
Aug 15	Ronoco Truck Parts Ltd.	535 (Bank - Royal)	4610	5,000.00	watch amount
Aug 15	Telus	58 (Bank of Montreal)	468593	360.45	
Aug 15	King Stationery	536 (Bank - Royal)	4799	93.00	

Figure 7.28   Cash Disbursements Journal

To enter the vendor payments, start from the Simply Accounting - ODC window (Figure 7.2).

Click on the **Payments** icon.

Figure 7.29
Payments
Journal window

```
┌─────────────────────────────────────────────────────────────────────┐
│ ⯈ Payments Journal                                        _ □ X       │
│ File  Edit  Payment  Report  Help                                     │
│ ⌂  ⎙  ⎙  ↶ ⧉ ⧉ ▤ ▤ 🖩                                    🖨  ✓        │
│                                                                       │
│ Pay Vendor Invoices ▼   By Cheque ▼   From 1040 Bank - Royal       ▼  │
│                                                                       │
│ ┌───────────────────────────────────────────────────────────────┐   │
│ │ Overnight Delivery Company              No. 533                │   │
│ │ Pay ──────────────────────────────────────────────────00/100   │   │
│ │ To the ┌──────────────────────────▼┐  Date        Amount       │   │
│ │ Order  │                            │  ┌─────────┐              │   │
│ │ of     │                            │  │08/31/01 │    $0.00     │   │
│ │        └────────────────────────────┘                          │   │
│ └───────────────────────────────────────────────────────────────┘   │
│ ┌──────────────┬───────────┬──────────┬──────────────┬──────────┬───────────┐ │
│ │Invoice/Pre-pmt.│Original Amt.│Amt. Owing│Disc. Available│Disc. Taken│Payment Amt.│ │
│ │              │           │          │              │          │           │ │
│ │              │           │          │              │          │           │ │
│ └──────────────┴───────────┴──────────┴──────────────┴──────────┴───────────┘ │
│                                        Total ┌──────────────┐          │
│                                              │        0.00  │          │
│ Comment  ┌──────────────────────────────────┐        🖳 Post        │
│          └──────────────────────────────────┘                        │
└─────────────────────────────────────────────────────────────────────┘
```

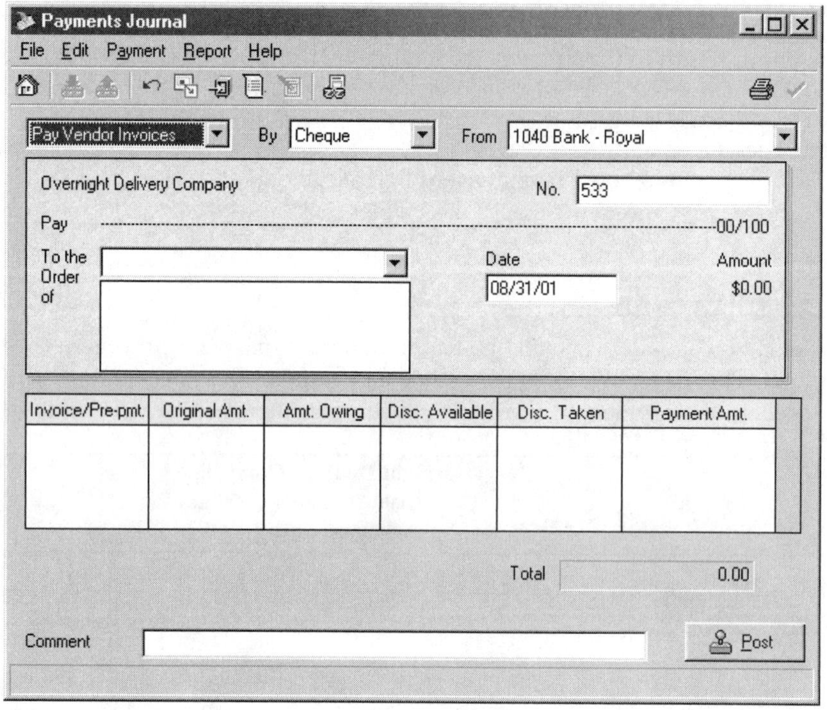

This will display the Payments Journal window shown in Figure 7.29.

Continue by pressing

| Tab | to accept **Pay Vendor Invoices**. Alternately you could select to either pay a credit card or other payments, (handled later in this chapter). |

| Tab | to accept the form of payment as cheque. You could alternately select either cash or either of the established credit cards (Visa or MasterCard). |

| Tab | to accept *1040 Bank - Royal* as the bank in which the cheque will be written. |

Now we will enter the payment for *Golden Wings Freight Lines Inc.* Continue by entering

| **Gold** Tab | to selecting *Golden Wings Freight* as the company name field. |

| Tab (4 times) | to accept the default address. |

| Tab | to accept **cheque number 532.** |

| **08/15/01** Tab | to enter the **Date** on which the payment was made. The date must fall in the range between the date of the conversion and the date that you identified as the using date. |

Figure 7.30
Payments
Journal for the
Golden Wings
entry

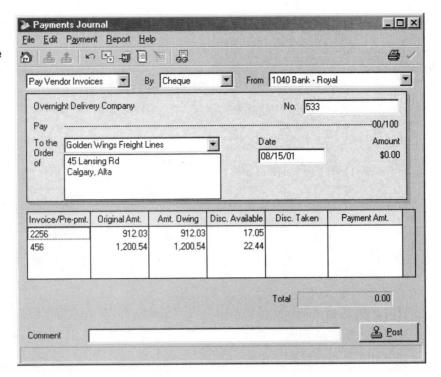

Your Payments Journal window should now resemble Figure 7.30. You must now select the appropriate invoice that you wish to pay. Continue by pressing

> Tab   to inform Simply Accounting that you wish to make a payment against **invoice number 2256.**

As a discount is available for this invoice, Simply Accounting for Windows will default to prompt you for this discount.

Continue by pressing

> Tab   to accept *17.05* as the **Discount Taken.**

> Tab   to accept the **Payment Amount** of *894.98*.

Simply Accounting for Windows will then continue with the selection of the discount for the next invoice (456). However, we will not want to pay this invoice, thus we will have to delete the highlighted discount (or payment) amount to prevent addition to the existing payment.

Continue by pressing

> Del   to delete the existing discount for invoice *456*.

Figure 7.31
Payment
Journal (Golden
Wings) Payment
entered

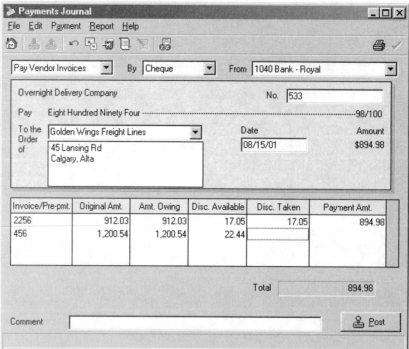

PRINTING PAYABLES CHEQUES

Simply Accounting allows you to issue cheques on preprinted forms in either continuous sheets for dot-matrix printers or in single sheets for ink-jet and laser printers.

    If you decide to use manually written cheques, you can have the Simply Accounting's Payables Cheque printing feature print a payment stub on a blank page. You then have a payment stub that includes your company name and address along with your vendor remittance information and the invoices that are to be paid with the enclosed manual cheque.

    If your Payments Journal resembles Figure 7.31, continue by pressing

   to **P**ost this payment.

Practice Exercise 7.9

Enter the remaining invoice payments listed in the Cash Disbursements Journal (Figure 7.28).

Be sure to select the appropriate bank account and payment option.

Once you have complete the exercise, remain within the Payment Journal window (Figure 7.29).

PAYMENT TO YOUR CREDIT CARDS

Just as with your vendors, you will eventually have to remit payments to your applicable credit card companies, (for credit card purchases).

Continue from within the Payments Journal window (Figure 7.29), by

> Changing the **Pay** pull down menu to *Pay Credit Card Bill*.
>
> Select *VISA* as the **Pay to the Order of.**
>
> The cheque number for Bank - Royal is *538*.
>
> Change the **Date** to *08/30/01*.

Figure 7.32
Payments
Journal (Credit
Card Payment)
window

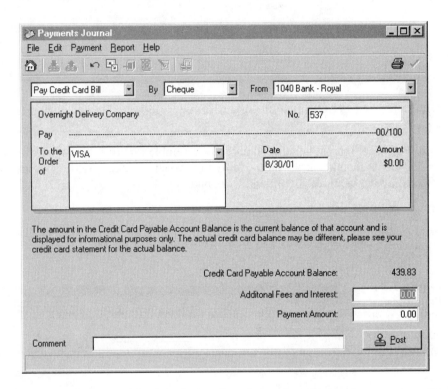

Within the Payments Journal (Figure 7.32), the window has changed to display the current credit card balance for our *VISA* credit card.

Simply Accounting will also let you enter the applicable interest charges that may have been charged on the card.

In this case, continue by

> Entering 5.00 as the **Additional fees and interest**, (this fee was a telephone balance charge levied by the credit card company).
>
> Entering 100.00 as the **Payment Amount**.

Figure 7.33
Payments
(Credit Card)
Journal window

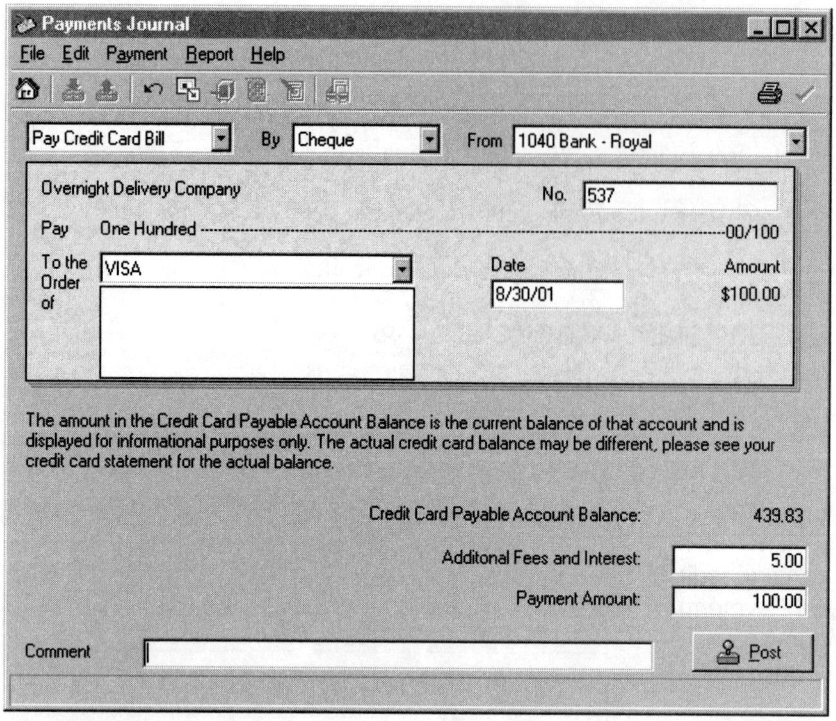

Your Payments Journal window should now resemble Figure 7.33. Let's now continue to view the Payments Journal entry window for details about what General Ledger accounts will be affected by our credit card payment. Continue by

Selecting the **Report** menu.

Selecting the **Display Payments Journal Entry** option.

Figure 7.34
Payments
(Credit Card)
Journal Entry
window

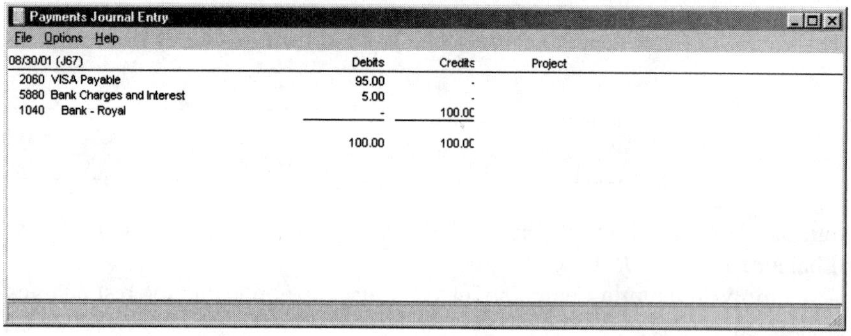

In the Payments Journal Entry window (Figure 7.34) you will notice that Simply Accounting will automatically apply the entered **Additional Fees and Interest** to the predefined expense account.

Continue from within the Payments Journal Entry window (Figure 7.34) by

Closing the Payment Journal Entry window.

Posting the Payment.

Practice Exercise 7.10

Continue with the entry of the following credit card payment:

Pay to the Order of:	MasterCard
Cheque No.:	59 (Bank of Montreal)
Date:	08/31/01
Additional fees/interest	0.00
Payment amount:	100.00

Once you have completed this exercise, remain within the Payments Journal window.

MAKING OTHER PAYMENTS

The last function within the Payments Journal is the entry for Making Other Payments.

Continue from within the Payments Journal window by

Selecting the pull down menu for the Make Other Payment option.

Figure 7.35
Payment
Journal (Other
Payment)
window

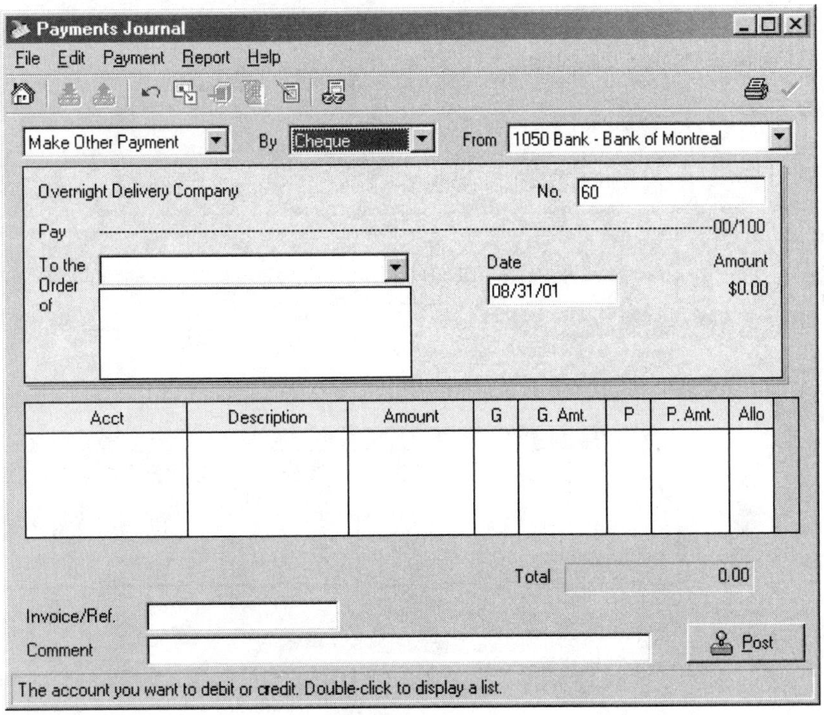

You will notice that the Other Payment will require you to define the following:

Payment Method (Cash, Cheque, VISA, or MasterCard)
Bank Account if applicable
Cheque number is applicable
To the Order of
Payment date
Account number
Description
Amount
GST code and amount
PST code and amount
Projection Allocation
Invoice reference
Comment

Continue with the entry for the following transaction:

Entry for the purchase (Invoice 504) for the additional telephone/Internet services purchased from TWK Internet Inc. in the amount of $25.00 USD drawn from the Seafirst US bank account (cheque 23) dated August 31, 2001. No GST/PST and the default exchange rate.

Once you make the following entry, your Payment Journal (Other Payment) should resemble Figure 7.36.

Figure 7.36
Payment
Journal (Other
Payment)
window

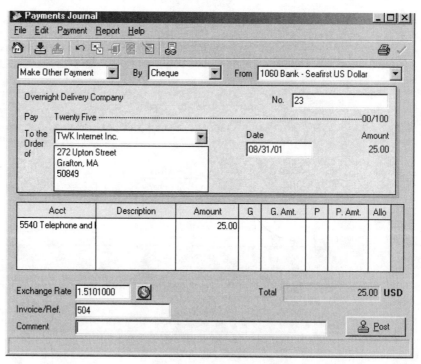

Continue by Posting the above Other Payment transaction. Once posted, close the Payments journal window. You will then return to the Simply Accounting - ODC window.

BACKING UP YOUR DATA FILES

At this point, return to the Simply Accounting - ODC window (Figure 8.3) and backup your data files.

Call this backup:

Backup Filename: A:\odc\odc7f
Comment: Payables Part f

ADJUSTING AND CORRECTING INVOICES

From time to time you will either have to adjust or correct a previously posted purchase invoice. Simply Accounting for Windows allows you to easily adjust a previously posted purchase invoice.

Continue from Simply Accounting - ODC window (Figure 7.2) by

Clicking on the **Purchases** icon.

Figure 7.37
Purchase
Journal window

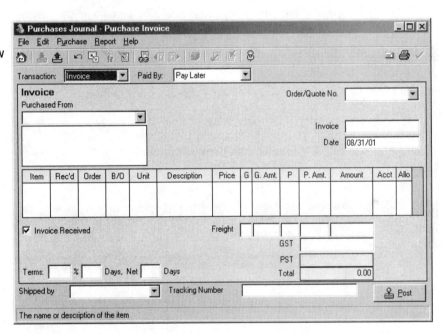

From within the **Purchase Journal window** (Figure 7.37) continue by pressing

[Ctrl] + [A]   to select the **A**djustment icon.

Figure 7.38
Adjust an
Invoice window

Adjust an invoice	☒
Start:	07/31/01 ▼
Finish:	08/31/01 ▼
Vendor Name:	‹Search All Vendors› ▼
Invoice Number:	
	OK Cancel Browse...

You will have to first look up and locate the appropriate invoice (Figure 7.38).

HINT: *LOCATING A PURCHASE INVOICE FOR ADJUSTMENT*

You can also select the Lookup icon or press ⌃Ctrl + L *to locate and display the required invoice to adjust. At this point you would then select the Adjustment icon* ⌃Ctrl + A *. This will then allow you to edit the invoice (note the following example).*

Continue from the Adjust an Invoice window (Figure 7.36) by pressing

T   to jump to *Telus*.

Alt + B   to select the **Browse** button.

Figure 7.39
Select an
Invoice window

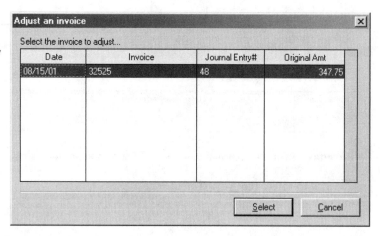

Continue from the Select an Invoice window (Figure 7.39) by pressing

Enter   to select invoice 32525.

Figure 7.40
Purchase
Journal -
Adjusting
Invoice window

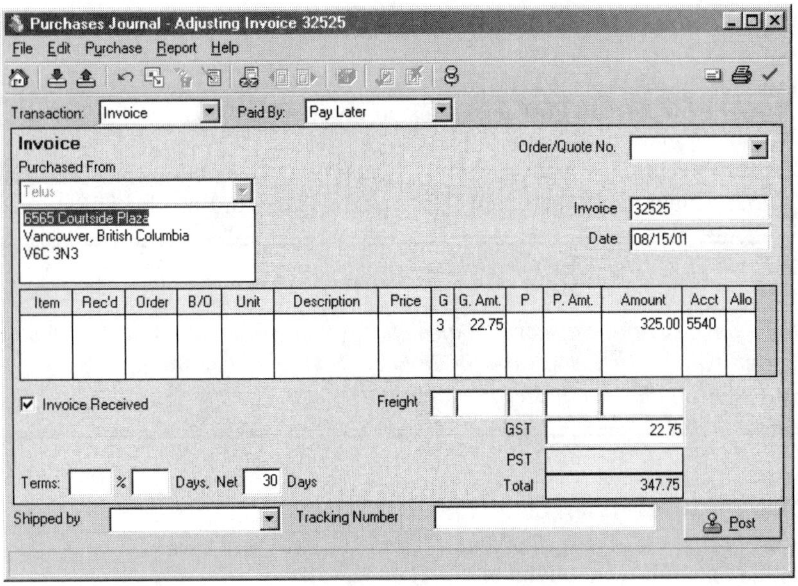

Simply Accounting for Windows will now allow you to adjust Telus invoice 32525, (note Figure 7.40).

For this adjustment, Telus invoice should be changed to display *300.00* plus *21.00* GST.

Practice Exercise 7.11

ADJUSTING AN INVOICE

Change the existing purchase amount of 325.00 to 300.00 for the BC Tel invoice number 32525.

Once you have completed this invoice, remain within the Purchase Journal—Adjusting Invoice (Figure 7.39).

Figure 7.41
Purchases Journal
- Adjusting Invoice
(Adjusted) window

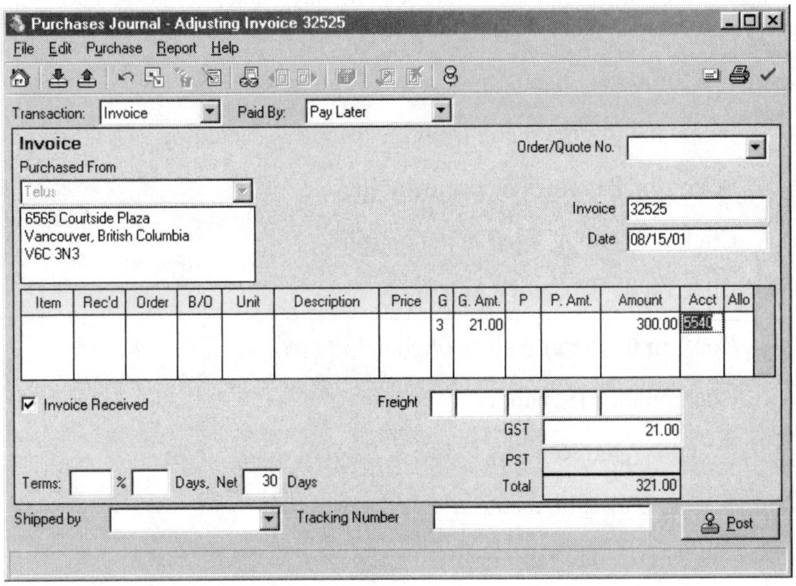

Ensure your Purchase Journal - Adjusting Invoice window resembles Figure 7.41. Continue by pressing

[Alt] + [P]   to **P**ost this adjusted invoice for *Telus*.

When you selected the **P**ost option, Simply Accounting for Windows will first remove the original invoice 32525 (Figure 7.40) and then create a new entry for the adjusted invoice (Figure 7.41).

HINT: *REVERSING AN INVOICE*

*If you want to completely reverse an invoice, you would zero out the figures in the existing invoice. Once you **Post** the invoice, Simply Accounting for Windows will ask you to confirm that you wish to reverse the selected invoice.*

Practice Exercise 7.12

Adjust the following invoice:

Vendor: Choquette & Company Accounting Group
Invoice: 315

Original Amount before taxes: 450.00
Revised Amount before taxes: 475.00

Original Total Invoice including taxes: 481.50
Revised Total Invoice including taxes: 508.25

Once you have completed the above exercise, return to the Simply Accounting - ODC window (Figure 7.2).

RECONCILING THE ACCOUNTS PAYABLE LEDGER WITH THE GENERAL LEDGER

Now that you have entered the purchases and payments, prepare a listing and compare the Accounts Payable ledger with the General Ledger.

To display a **Summary** listing, proceed as follows:

Select the **R**eport menu from the Simply Accounting - ODC window.

Select the **P**ayables report menu item.

Click on **V**endor Aged menu option.

Click on the **Select All** button.

Confirm the **As at** date as *08/31/01*.

Click on the **OK** button.

Once the Vendor Aged Report window is display, continue by

Selecting the **F**ile menu.

Clicking on the **P**rint option.

Once the Vendor Aged Report has been printed, continue by

> Closing the Vendor Aged Report window. You will then return to the Simply Accounting - ODC window.

Practice Exercise 7.13

Display the trial balance report as at **08/31/01**, and compare the Accounts Payable account total to the total shown in the Vendor Aged Summary report. Both should equal $17,487.65

MAINTAINING AN AUDIT TRAIL

If you have entered all of the transactions in this chapter in one session, you should print out the Accounts Payable journal entries for both purchases and payments for August 2001. (Review previous chapters for an example.)

Mark the printout **PURCHASES AND DISBURSEMENTS** and store them along with the previous journal entry printouts. You can review this printed listing of the Accounts Payable journal entries at any time. This listing is particularly helpful if the computer data files or the disk containing them are accidentally destroyed.

EXPORTING THE DATA FILES

As with the Accounts Receivable Ledger, all Accounts Payable reports can be exported to a spreadsheet such as Lotus or Excel or to a text file that can be used by a word processing program for generating a report. The export function is located in the **Print** menu.

BACKING UP YOUR DATA FILES

At this point, return to the Simply Accounting - ODC window and back up your data files.

Call this back up:

        Backup Filename: A:\odc\odc7g
        Comment: Payables Part g

Further Practice

To get further practice with the concepts you have learned in this chapter, go to Chapter 14. In Section 7 you can work through the National Supply Company's Accounts Payable.

CHAPTER 8

INVENTORY

CHAPTER 8

INVENTORY

OBJECTIVES

After reading this chapter you will be able to

1. Explain how inventory is acquired.

2. Explain the various types of inventory and how to control it.

3. Make purchase adjustments.

4. Record sales and sales returns.

5. Understand how the goods and services and provincial sales taxes are recorded.

6. Understand how the cost of goods is determined.

7. Understand how the two types of inventory methods operate.

8. Understand how inventory can be costed.

9. Convert a manual inventory system to a computerized inventory system.

10. Insert, modify, and delete inventory items through the inventory ledger.

11. Enter opening balances.

12. Display and print inventory reports.

13. Define inventory integration accounts.

14. Enter and track purchase orders and receive inventory.

15. Purchase inventory directly using invoices.

16. Understand how inventory levels are increased and decreased by entering purchases and sales into the appropriate ledgers.

17. Know the types of transactions that are entered into the inventory module and how to enter them.

ACCOUNTING FOR SERVICE AND MANUFACTURING COMPANIES

Up until now we have worked with Overnight Delivery Company, a service company that provides a delivery service. Service companies dominate business firms in Canada today and include gas stations, airlines, railways, hotels, theatres, real estate brokerage firms, ski resorts, and so on. These companies get their revenue by providing services; their profit is the excess of their service revenue over the cost of providing these services.

However, there are also many manufacturing and merchandising firms. The former manufacture goods and then sell them to either wholesalers, retailers, or merchandisers. A merchandising firm purchases goods — or inventory — and resells it to its customers. For a retailer, profit depends upon two factors:

1. The excess of sales over the cost of the goods that were sold (the gross margin).

2. The excess of gross margin over the operating expenses necessary to earn the revenue.

General Sales Company
Income Statement
Jan 1, 2001 - Jan 31, 2001

Revenue		Expenses	
Product Sales		Cost of Goods Sold	
Product Line A	12,000	Product Line A	7,200
Product Line B	40,000	Product Line B	24,000
Product Line C	7,000	Product Line C	3,800
Total Product Sales	59,000	Total Cost of Goods Sold	35,000
Miscellaneous Sales			
Administration Expenses			
Interest	500	Commissions	4,000
PST Commissions	1,500	Wages	2,000
Interest - Bank Loan	700	Telephone	300
		Accounting	500
Total Misc Sales	2,700	Utilities	1,500
Total Revenue	$ 61,700	Total Admin Expenses	8,300
		Total Expenses	43,300
	Income		$ 18,400

Figure 8.1   Typical income statement for a merchandising firm

Figure 8.1 shows a typical income statement for a merchandising firm. This type of firm is different from a service business because it carries inventory. This inventory is purchased periodically throughout the year and reduced as sales are made. Thus, sales revenue and cost of goods sold are two major factors on this income statement.

From the above statement, the company can calculate gross margin which is total product sales minus cost of goods sold:

Total Product Sales	59,000
Total Cost of Goods Sold	35,000
Gross Margin	$24,000

ACQUIRING INVENTORY

Inventory may be acquired in one of three ways:

1. Purchased from other manufacturers or suppliers.

2. Manufactured.

3. A combination of the above where the firm purchases raw materials and parts that are used to manufacture a finished product to particular specifications.

INVENTORY PURCHASED FROM SUPPLIERS

The most common means of acquiring inventory is to buy it from manufacturers or wholesalers. To the basic cost of the inventory, the firm adds an amount to cover its expenses and provide a profit — the *markup* . Legally, the buyer is deemed to have acquired the goods when the responsibility for the goods is transferred from the seller to the purchaser. This actual transferring of responsibility for the goods from seller to purchaser is specified when the goods are ordered, in the following way:

FOB (free on board)	signifies that the shipper transfers the responsibility for the goods when it reaches a certain point. In other words, the shipper is free from responsibility when the goods are on board at the location designated. For example, **FOB WAREHOUSE** means that the goods are the responsibility of the purchaser as soon as they leave the warehouse. **FOB DESTINATION** means that the goods are the responsibility of the purchaser when they reach their destination — the purchaser's receiving point.
FAS (free along ship)	is similar to FOB with the restriction that goods must be delivered to the ship for destination to some other point. Ship in this case need not literally mean via a ship but simply by some method of shipment.
CIF (cost, insurance, and freight prepaid)	indicates that the goods will transfer when the cost of the goods, the insurance for the transportation, and the freight have been paid for.

Once the goods have been transferred to the purchaser, the following accounting entry is made:

Dr. Inventory	xxx	
Dr. GST Paid on Purchases	xxx	
Cr. Accounts Payable or Cash		xxx

The inventory is always recorded on the books at cost. This includes the actual cost of the goods plus insurance, if required, and the cost of freight to bring the inventory to the site of sale.

Once the goods have been received, a *receiving report* should be filled out and passed on to the accounting department. The receiving report signifies to the accounting department that the goods have actually been received and should be paid for.

MANUFACTURED GOODS

Goods in inventory are often manufactured from raw materials. In this case, the purchase of the raw material would be entered into the accounting system at cost:

         Dr. Inventory – Raw Materials   xxx
         Dr. GST paid on Purchases   xxx
                 Cr. Accounts Payable or Cash   xxx

The raw materials will be transferred to new inventory items as they are processed. A *manufacturing* report would be prepared showing the accounting department the amount or number of inventory items that were used in the manufacturing process. The new product cost will consist of the cost of raw materials used, plus the labour and overhead costs incurred in the production process. The accounting entry needed to record the new item would be

         Dr. Inventory – Finished Goods   xxx
                 Cr. Inventory – Raw Materials   xxx
                 Cr. Labour Expenses   xxx
                 Cr. Overhead Expenses   xxx

COMBINATION

It is quite possible that a firm incurs a combination of the above two costs for purchasing and manufacturing. A firm might purchase a variety of parts and various raw materials and make a new product worth more in the final form than the original components. This is also known as value added. The accounting entries would be virtually identical to the previous examples, making the finished goods material partly for resale and partly for transfer.

In entering the above items for inventory, the Inventory module of a computerized accounting system keeps track of both the cost of the items as well as the number of items purchased. As you will see later in the chapter, it is important to be able to allocate a cost per item to the purchased or manufactured inventory items.

INVENTORY ADJUSTMENTS

Adjustments to inventory are necessary when the value of the inventory changes, when goods are returned, and when firms must add Goods and Services tax (GST). Let's look at each more closely.

VALUE ADJUSTMENTS

Sometimes the number of items purchased remains the same, but the value of these items either increases or decreases. You would want to reflect these changes in the cost of inventory. For example, a supplier may give a discount for purchasing a large quantity of product. The supplier might specify that if purchases of a particular item total $10,000.00 or more, the purchaser will get a 2.0% volume discount. Once you reach that level, our accounts payable to the supplier will be reduced by $200.00 ($10,000.00 x 2.0%). This adjustment would be reflected in the accounts as follows:

         Dr. Accounts Payable   xxx
                 Cr. Inventory   xxx

The recording of this entry will not affect the number of items purchased, but will reduce the total cost of the items and therefore the unit cost.

On the other hand, inventory costs might have to be increased. For example, you might order some inventory items FOB manufacturer, but at the time the order is placed you do not know the freight cost. This cost will have to be added to the inventory at a later time. You would make the following entry when the inventory was received:

    Dr. Inventory   xxx
          Cr. Accounts Payable   xxx

When you have determined the cost of the freight, you would make an adjusting entry to the inventory item:

    Dr. Inventory   xxx
          Cr. Freight Payable   xxx

As in the previous example, the number of items is not adjusted, only the cost associated with the items received.

PURCHASE RETURNS

On occasion, you, the purchaser, may return goods because they are the wrong type or are defective. When returned, the goods must be taken out of inventory at the cost that they were recorded at. In addition, the number of items returned must also be recorded. The entry made in the books would be

    Dr. Accounts payable   xxx
          Cr. Inventory   xxx
          Cr. GST Paid on Purchases   xxx

RECORDING SALES

For a retailer, total sales revenue equals the gross amount of the sale minus any returns or discounts. A sale of inventory for cash would be recorded in the books as follows:

    Dr. Cash   xxx
          Cr. Sales   xxx
          Cr. GST Charged on Sales   xxx
          Cr. PST Payable   xxx

If the merchandise is bought on credit, the journal entry is

    Dr. Account Receivable   xxx
          Cr. Sales   xxx
          Cr. GST Charged on Sales   xxx
          Cr. PST Payable   xxx

As mentioned earlier, the buyer legally becomes the owner of goods when responsibility for them is transferred from the seller to the buyer — FOB, FAS, or CIF. Conversely, a good is deemed to have been sold when the responsibility for the item is transferred to the new owner. This means that a sale is often made without the cash being received immediately. Consequently, total sales in any given period are not likely to equal the amount of cash generated in that same period.

SALES RETURNS

Most merchandising firms allow their customers to return goods purchased if the merchandise is found to be unsatisfactory. In these cases, the entry that was originally made when the sale occurred must be reversed. The reversing entry is

Dr. Sales Returns	xxx	
Dr. GST Charged on Sales	xxx	
Dr. PST Payable	xxx	
Cr. Accounts Receivable		xxx

The account, Sales Returns, is normally used instead of simply a debit to sales because management is interested in knowing the percentage of returned items. A high level of sales returns and allowances in a given time period may indicate a high level of customer dissatisfaction with the product.

GST AND PST

You will notice that the examples included GST and PST. This is on the assumption that your province requires you to collect PST from customers when you sell inventory.

You will notice that we have only recorded PST when we sell inventory and not when we acquire inventory/raw materials. This is because the PST that we will be charged by the supplier will be passed on to the customer, thus it either becomes a cost of the inventory or, if you supply your supplier with your provincial sales tax number, this tax will not be charged to you. This is because you will collect PST when you sell the product to the customer.

INVOICE
May 15, 2001
Customer:

FS Organics Inc.
556 Selma Cresc.
Burnaby, B.C.

Item Number	Description of Units	Number per unit	Cost	Total
1234	Gaskets	12	3.50	42.00
5678	Rings	14	6.10	85.40
	Total sales			$ 127.40
	Provincial Sales Tax (6.0%)			7.64
	Goods and Services Tax (7.0%)			8.92
	Total amount owing			$ 143.96

Figure 8.2   A typical invoice with GST added to a sale

We have included a complete example showing how a sale of inventory with applicable taxes would be entered (note Figure 8.2). If you instead collect HST, then this 15.0% tax amount would replace both the GST and PST.

The required journal entry for this sale would be:

Dr. Accounts Receivable	143.96	
Cr. Sales		127.40
Cr. GST Payable		8.92
Cr. Provincial sales tax payable		7.64

COST OF GOODS SOLD

One of the major differences between a service company and a merchandising company is the entries that are made on a sale. A service firm would proceed as follows:

Dr. Accounts Receivable   xxx
        Cr. Revenue   xxx
        Cr. GST Charged on Sales   xxx
        Cr. PST Payable   xxx

This is the only entry required at the time of the sale. For a merchandising company, however, a second entry is required, which takes into account the reduction in the level of inventory.

Dr. Cost of Goods Sold   xxx
        Cr. Inventory   xxx

This entry takes the item out of inventory and puts it into the Cost of Goods Sold expense account.

INVENTORY CONTROL METHODS

There are two methods of determining inventory and cost of goods sold for any given period — the periodic inventory system and the perpetual inventory system.

PERIODIC INVENTORY SYSTEM

A business that sells a variety of merchandise at relatively low prices most often uses a manual accounting method called the *periodic inventory system*. Sales are recorded on a daily basis as described above, and all purchases are recorded when received and debited to a *Purchases account*. No entry is made to record *Cost of Goods Sold* until the reporting date. At the reporting date, the ending inventory is physically counted to determine the level of inventory still on hand. Once the value of the remaining inventory is known, it is subtracted from the total amount, consisting of the opening inventory plus any purchases during the period. This amount is the value of the goods sold.

For example, assume that a company had the purchase records shown in Figure 8.3 for the month of January:

	Units	Per unit	Total Cost
Opening inventory	20	5.00	100.00
Purchases			
January 10	30	5.10	153.00
January 15	50	5.20	260.00
January 25	100	5.15	515.00
Cost of Goods Available for sale	200		$1,028.00

Figure 8.3   Purchase records for January (excluding GST)

If, at the end of January, we determine that the level of inventory is $318.00 by actually counting and valuing the inventory, then the cost of goods sold would amount to $710.00 ($1,028.00 - $318.00). We would then adjust the purchases account and the opening inventory account to record cost of goods sold to be $710.00.

> Dr. Cost of Goods Sold   710.00
>   Dr. Ending Inventory   928.00
> Cr. Purchases   218.00

Ending inventory will now be $318.00 ($100.00 from the opening entry and an increase of $218.00 in the above entry).

PERPETUAL INVENTORY SYSTEM

At one time the *perpetual inventory system* was used almost exclusively by firms selling large items with a high unit value. These firms usually had only a few sales but each sale amounted to a substantial sum. When a sale was made, these firms could make an immediate manual entry to credit Inventory and debit Cost of Goods Sold. Hence the inventory is perpetually updated.

With computerized accounting systems, however, even small firms with large numbers of transactions can use the perpetual inventory system. Computers can make the necessary entries automatically when a sale is made.

When using a perpetual inventory system, you have to make two entries each time there is a sale. First we record the sale:

> Dr. Accounts Receivable   xxx
>   Cr. Sales   xxx

Then we record the cost of that sale:

> Dr. Cost of Goods Sold   xxx
>   Cr. Inventory   xxx

PERIODIC OR PERPETUAL?

In today's competitive business market, the more up-to-date your financial information is, the more effectively you can operate. This is why Simply Accounting for Windows has chosen **perpetual** inventory as its method for accounting for inventory. As well, the **perpetual** inventory method is easier for the user to understand as no ending inventory count is required by the accounting system. However, it is recommended that an inventory count be performed at least once a year to determine spoilage and/or shrinkage. With Simply Accounting for Windows, as soon as you save your entry, (purchase, sale, or adjustment), Simply Accounting automatically updates your inventory control accounts. This allows the user to generate inventory and/or financial statements that reflect the latest changes in inventory.

It should be noted that **periodic** inventory is still used regularly by companies that operate a manual accounting system. This is because of the amount of work that would be required to maintain a manual **perpetual** inventory system.

INVENTORY COSTING METHODS

The cost of the inventory sold depends on which items are sold. In some cases it is difficult to determine the actual cost of the item sold. As shown in the example above, (Figure 8.3), some inventory items were purchased at $5.10 per unit, some at $5.15, and some at $5.20. There were also some on hand that were purchased at $5.00. How do we know which of these was actually sold so that we can correctly reduce the amount from Inventory and debit the Cost of Goods Sold account?

Four methods can be used for valuing inventory sold. They are:

1. FIFO (first-in, first-out)
2. LIFO (last-in, first-out)
3. Specific item
4. Average cost.

FIFO

The *FIFO inventory valuation method* states that the first items purchased are the first items sold. For example, when a grocery store receives a new shipment of bread, the bread from the previous shipment not yet sold is placed on top of the newer bread so that it will sell first. In this case, the FIFO method of valuing inventory is appropriate as it stands to reason that the first one purchased is the first one sold, since it is on top of the new shipment.

Look back to Figure 8.3 for a moment. Let's assume that you sold three units at $10.00 apiece on January 11. No matter which inventory system you use, the sale of the units would be recorded as follows:

Dr. Accounts Receivable   30.00
     Cr. Sales   30.00

To record the cost of goods sold using the FIFO inventory system, the first three you purchased were the first three sold. The three items that were sold would be valued at $5.00 each, totalling $15.00 (3 x $5.00). The journal entry would then be

Dr. Cost of Goods Sold   15.00
     Cr. Inventory   15.00

To record a second sale of 18 units on January 18, at $10.00 apiece, the entries made would be as follows:

Dr. Accounts Receivable   180.00
     Cr. Sales   180.00
Dr. Cost of Goods Sold   90.10
     Cr. Inventory   90.10

The cost of goods sold on a FIFO basis is calculated to be $90.10.

17 units @ $5.00	85.00
1 unit @ $5.10	5.10
total cost of goods sold	$90.10

LIFO

The *LIFO inventory valuation method* is opposite to FIFO. In using this method we assume that the last items that we purchased are the first items sold. For example, a lumber yard will put new boards on top of the existing boards because the old boards do not spoil within a reasonable time. In this case, LIFO is appropriate because the first ones sold are the last ones purchased.

Let's use the items shown in Figure 8.3, to see what the LIFO inventory valuation method will do to our cost of goods sold.

In the first sale, you sold three units at $10.00 apiece on January 11. The sale of the units would be recorded as before:

```
Dr. Accounts Receivable      30.00
        Cr. Sales                         30.00
```

Using the LIFO inventory valuation method, the three items that were sold would then be valued at $5.10 each, totalling $15.30 (3 x $5.10). You use $5.10 as the cost per item as the last purchase was on January 10. The journal entry would then be

```
Dr. Cost of Goods Sold       15.30
        Cr. Inventory                     15.30
```

To record a second sale of 18 units on January 18, at $10.00 apiece, the entries made would be as follows:

```
Dr. Accounts Receivable     180.00
        Cr. Sales                        180.00
Dr. Cost of Goods Sold       93.60
        Cr. Inventory                     93.60
```

The cost of goods sold is calculated to be $93.60 on a LIFO basis:

```
18 units @ $5.20         93.60
```

Here you use $5.20 because the last items purchased were 50 units on January 25 at $5.20 apiece. In LIFO, the timing of the sale is important as the cost of goods sold will depend on the last purchase.

SPECIFIC ITEM

The *specific item inventory valuation method* is generally used when the number of items sold is relatively low but each item represents a significant part of the inventory in cost terms. The automotive industry is a good example. Each vehicle is identified by a number and by specific options. When that vehicle is sold it is easy to identify its cost and to charge it out to cost of goods sold.

It would not be appropriate to use the specific item inventory method for the items shown in Figure 8.3, since we cannot identify one unit from the next.

AVERAGE COST

The *average cost inventory valuation method* is based on the premise that for identical items we cannot or do not care which item was purchased before another one and, therefore, cannot identify it specifically for cost of goods sold. Therefore we value each item at its average cost.

A good example is a bin of nails in a hardware store. When we replenish the stock of nails with a new purchase, we cannot tell which nails were purchased or sold first. Since they are all mixed together, it is appropriate to use the average cost inventory method — the cost of goods sold is based on the weighted average cost of the nails in the bin.

We have added sales dates to the inventory items in Figure 8.3 as shown in Figure 8.4. Notice that we have arranged sales and purchases in date order.

	Units	Per unit	Total Cost
Opening inventory	20	5.00	100.00
Purchases & Sales			
Jan. 10	30	5.10	153.00
Jan. 11	3		
Jan. 15	50	5.20	260.00
Jan. 18	18		
Jan. 25	100	5.15	515.00
Cost of Goods Available	200		$1,028.00

Figure 8.4   Purchases and sales of inventory items

For the first sale, the cost of goods sold would be calculated as three units times $5.06, which equals $15.18.

Opening inventory	20	5.00	100.00
January 10 purchase	30	5.10	153.00
Total	50		$253.00

Average Cost per unit $\dfrac{\$253}{50} = \$5.06$

The journal entry is then

Dr. Cost of Goods Sold	15.18	
Cr. Inventory		15.18

The second sale entry for 18 units would be valued at the new average cost including the purchase on January 15. The cost of goods sold would then be 18 units times $5.13, which equals $92.34.

Units available	50		253.00
Units sold	3		15.18
Units remaining	47		237.82
January 15 purchase	50	$5.20	260.00
Total available	97		$497.82

Average cost per unit $\dfrac{497.82}{97} = \$5.13$

The entry to record cost of goods sold is then

Dr. Cost of Goods Sold	92.34	
Cr. Inventory		92.34

All four of the above methods of valuing inventory are accepted by various accounting bodies; nevertheless, the retailer must choose one method and apply it consistently. The inventory valuing method that applies to the greatest number of firms is the **average cost method**. For this reason, the Simply Accounting system uses this method in its calculation of inventory.

Although the average cost method would be virtually impossible to use with a manual accounting system, it presents no problems for a computerized system. The Simply Accounting system only requires that you enter the sale. The program will automatically calculate the cost of goods sold and make the necessary entry to record the cost of goods sold and reduce the inventory based on the average cost. It will then produce the necessary reports so that you can order, transfer or value the remaining inventory.

COMPUTERIZING INVENTORY

Converting your manual inventory system to a computerized system can be done at any time during the year. It is not necessary to wait for year-end or for some time in the year when inventory is at its lowest point.

ORGANIZING INVENTORY RECORDS

As was the case with each of the other modules, some manual preparation is required to convert the system before actually using the inventory module of the Simply Accounting system. The following tasks must be completed beforehand:

1. Prepare a complete list of all inventory items that you stock on the date of conversion to the Simply Accounting system by taking a manual count.

2. Associate each inventory item with an inventory asset account, an inventory revenue account and an inventory expense account in the General Ledger.

3. Ensure that the balance of all inventory items for each General Ledger account agrees with the balances in those accounts.

PREPARING A LIST OF INVENTORY ITEMS

When computerizing Inventory for Accounts Receivable and Accounts Payable, you have to make a list of all the inventory items currently on hand. You may also want to include all items that you normally carry but are temporarily out of stock. The more complete the list, the less work will be required when that stock is replenished.

For each of the inventory items in the list, we need the following data. This information is required by the Simply Accounting system to calculate inventory levels for each item.

1. Item name

2. Unit description

3. Selling price per unit. If the units are normally sold individually, this would be the unit price. If they are normally sold in pairs, it would mean the price per pair; if sold in dozens, it would mean the price for 12 items, etc.

4. Last sale date (for inventory turnover reporting).

5. Quantity. Total quantity in units (as described in 3) on hand at the time of the conversion.

6. Amount. Represents the total cost for all of the inventory items on hand. There is no need to determine the cost per unit since the Simply Accounting system will take the total you enter and divide it by the quantity to determine the cost per unit.

7. Minimum stock level. This number is used to indicate the point at which you would like to order more stock. For example, you may sell five units of a particular item per week. If it takes three weeks to get a new shipment, you would want to reorder the item when your inventory was down to 15 units — selling five units per week times three weeks to order. The reorder point should be carefully calculated because the Simply Accounting system will tell you to reorder an item when the reorder point is reached.

8. Year-to-date values for number of transactions, total units sold, sales dollar amount, and cost of goods sold.

9. Last year values for number of transactions, total units sold, sales dollar amount, and cost of goods sold.

Maintaining a minimum stock level is an important objective of good inventory management. A key principle is to *reduce inventory carrying costs by keeping your inventory at the lowest level possible. At the same time, inventory should not be so low that you run out of stock and lose substantial sales.* If you would like to know more about calculating the optimum level of inventory to reduce various costs to their lowest point, you should consult a book on inventory management.

In addition to its delivery service, Overnight Delivery Company also sells truck parts. The result of counting inventory on hand at July 31, 2001, is the list shown in Figure 8.5.

Overnight Delivery Inc.
Schedule of Inventory
July 31, 2001

Unit Number	Unit Description	Unit	Min Qty	Selling Price	Last Sale Date
101	Sending Unit	Each	2	1,200.00	07/20/01 entered
102	Radio	Each	3	625.00	07/19/01
103	Tire	Each	6	150.00	07/25/01
104	Security Unit	Each	3	375.00	07/15/01
105	Starter	Each	1	1,150.00	07/25/01
106	Light	Each	12	75.00	06/30/01
107	Seal	Each	50	17.00	

Unit Number	Description	Trans	Year-to-Date Units	Sales	COGS
101	Sending Unit	1	2	2,400	1,060 entered
102	Radio	5	5	3,125	1,875
103	Tire	12	43	5,067	3,763
104	Security Unit	1	1	350	275
105	Starter	1	1	1,150	740
106	Light	30	61	4,575	2,645
107	Seal	0	0	0	0

Unit Number	Description	Trans	Last Year Units	Sales	COGS
101	Sending Uni	2	4	4,750	2,100 entered
102	Radio	5	5	3,100	1,875
103	Tire	5	15	2,250	1,350
104	Security Unit	0	0	0	0
105	Starter	0	0	0	0
106	Light	0	0	0	0
107	Seal	0	0		0

Unit Number	Unit Description	Qty on hand	Total Amount
101	Sending Unit	2	1,100.00 entered
102	Radio	4	1,500.00
103	Tire	12	1,080.00
104	Security Unit	4	1,100.00
105	Starter	2	1,500.00
106	Light	24	1,032.00
107	Seal	100	593.00
	Total:		7,905.00

Figure 8.5   Schedule of inventory for Overnight Delivery Company

Associating Inventory Items to the General Ledger

Unlike the other modules, the **Inventory** module does not have preset accounts in the General Ledger to record purchases and sales. It is up to you to determine the asset account, revenue account, and expense account to be associated with each inventory item. This means assigning one account between 1000 – 1999 (asset), one between 4000 – 4999 (revenue) and one between 5000 – 5999 (expense) for each item.

If a company only has one type of inventory, such as grocery items, you would only need one set of the three above-mentioned accounts. However, if you wish to break the inventory items into categories — produce, canned goods, and pop — you would have three groups of items and therefore require three groups of asset, revenue, and expense accounts.

Once the accounts have been assigned, it is necessary to set them up in the General Ledger module before proceeding.

Agree to Control Account

The final step before conversion is to ensure that the total amount of each inventory category agrees to the control account for that category in the General Ledger. You must be sure that the information entered is accurate. The Simply Accounting system will not allow you to make the Inventory module Ready until the sum of all inventory items agrees with the control account (Inventory) in the General Ledger.

BEGINNING THE INVENTORY CONVERSION TO SIMPLY ACCOUNTING

After performing the steps listed above, you are ready to enter the inventory data into the Simply Accounting for Windows system.

Practice Exercise 8.1

Start Simply Accounting for Windows. When prompted, select the odc data set.

When prompted, confirm that the Using date is 08/31/01.

Simply Accounting for Windows 8.0 will now display the To-Do List. Continue by closing this window.

Figure 8.6
Simply
Accounting -
ODC window

The Simply Accounting - ODC window will now appear as shown in Figure 8.6.

Practice Exercise 8.2

Add the following General Ledger accounts:

Account#	Account Name	Type
5810	Inventory Transfer Expense	Subgroup Acct
	Account Class: Cost of Sales	
5812	Inventory Adjustment Expense	Subgroup Acct
	Account Class: Cost of Sales	
5814	Inventory Variance Expense	Subgroup Acct
	Account Class: Cost of Sales	
5815	Total Inventory Costs	Subgroup Total

Leave **Suppress Printing** and **Budget this Account** unchecked. Once you have completed this exercise return to the Simply Accounting - ODC window (Figure 8.6).

The inventory listing in Figure 8.5 shows two sending units on hand at the conversion date for a total cost of $1,100.00. We will assign the item to the following accounts:

Asset account – (1200 – Inventory Truck Parts)
Sales account – (4050 – Sales Truck Parts)
Cost of Sales account – (5050 – Cost of Sales Truck Parts)
Variance account – (5814 – Inventory Variance Expense)

You entered these accounts into the General Ledger in Chapter 4. Review your chart of accounts to ensure that they are there.

ENTERING INVENTORY ITEMS

To enter inventory items, proceed from the Simply Accounting - ODC window (Figure 8.6) by

> Clicking on the **Inventory** icon to open it.

Figure 8.7
Inventory
window

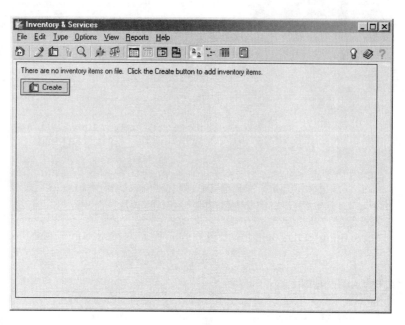

As shown in Figure 8.7, the Inventory & Services window will now be displayed. Once you have entered the inventory items, this window will display an icon for each inventory item. With this icon, each inventory item can be selected for modification or deletion. This window is similar to the window for the Customers and Vendors windows in the Receivables and Payables modules respectively.

Continue from the Inventory window by

> Clicking the **Create** icon with your mouse.

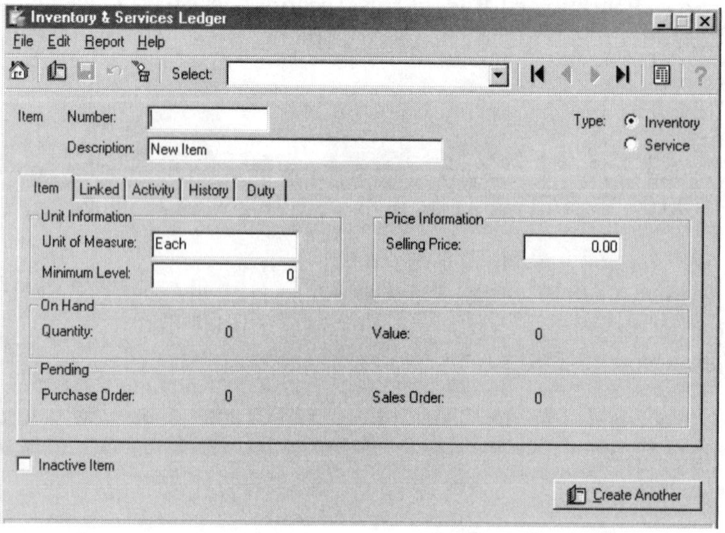

Figure 8.8
Inventory &
Services Ledger
(Item) window

The Inventory & Ledger (Item) window as shown in Figure 8.8 will now appear. As with both the Receivables and Payables module, this window contains several tabbed button (**Item, Linked, Activity, History**). Remember to enter information in all applicable tabbed areas before you either click the **Create** button or press Enter to Create the Inventory Ledger record.

Continue by typing

101 Tab	to enter the **Item Number** for the Sending Unit.
Sending Unit Tab	to enter the **Description** for the Sending Unit.
Tab	to accept Inventory as the **Type**.

HINT: *INVENTORY FOR SERVICE?*

Simply Accounting for Windows also supports the use of service descriptions within the Inventory module. This feature will also be demonstrated within this chapter.

Tab	to accept *Each* as the **Unit** of **Measure** you wish to use.
2 Tab	to enter the **Minimum Level** of stock you should have for this item. This will allow Simply Accounting to monitor your inventory items.
1200.00 Tab	to enter the **Unit Price** (suggested selling).

You will now want to move to the **Linked** tabbed button. This can be accomplished by either

Clicking on the Linked tabbed button.

Figure 8.9
Inventory &
Services Ledger
(Linked) window

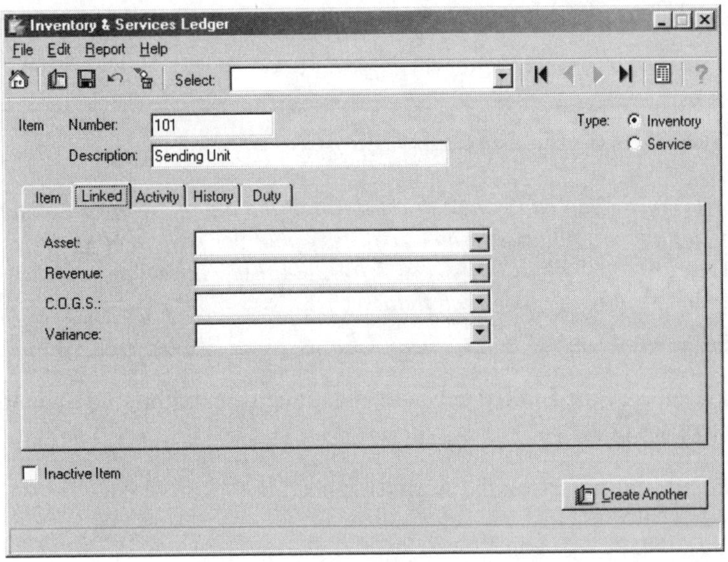

Within the Inventory & Services Ledger (Linked) window (Figure 8.9), you are prompted to select the following General Ledger accounts:

Asset	is the account that will be used to post the inventory purchases as well as the account in which the inventory cost will be deducted when the item is sold.
Revenue	is the account used to credit (increase) by the selling price of this inventory item, when sold.
C.O.G.S.	is the Cost of Goods Sold account and is the account against which the cost of the item is charged when it is sold.

HINT: GROSS PROFIT CALCULATION

*To determine the Gross Profit for an item sold. This would be the total **Revenue** less the total **C.O.G.S (Cost of Goods Sold)**.*

Variance	is the default account for any adjustment variances such as inventory shrinkage.

Continue within the Inventory & Services (Linked) window (Figure 8.9) by

Selecting 1200 – Inventory Truck Parts as the **Asset** account.

Selecting 4050 – Sales Truck Parts as the **Revenue** account.

Selecting 5050 – Cost of Sales Truck Parts as the **C.O.G.S. (Cost of Goods Sold) account**.

Selecting 5814 - Inventory Variance Expense as the **Variance** account.

HINT: SELECTING GENERAL LEDGER ACCOUNTS

*To select accounts you can either scroll through the list of General Ledger accounts using the pull down button, or you can press a number representing the appropriate account range (e.g. **1** for 1000 Assets, **2** for 2000 Liabilities), or you can enter the account number directly into each field.*

Once you have entered the **Linked** accounts, continue from within the Inventory & Services Ledger (Linked) window by

Clicking your mouse on the **Activity** tabbed button.

Figure 8.10
Inventory &
Services Ledger
(Activity)
window

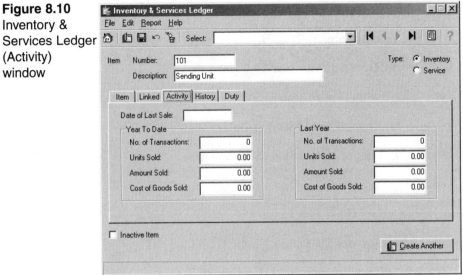

Within the Inventory & Services Ledger (Activity) window, you are prompted to enter the following:

Date of Last Sale   is the last date on which you sold this inventory item.

Year to Date/Last Year   all represent the historical sale information for both the year-
No of Transactions   to-date and last year. This data will enable Simply Accounting
Units Sold   to track the inventory turnover for each item.
Amount Sold
Cost of Goods Sold

HINT: INVENTORY TURNOVER

Any business that carries a large amount of inventory must pay particular attention to the turnover of inventory. Inventory turnover is based on how quickly inventory is sold once the business has purchased it. The quicker inventory is turned over, the more profit a firm makes.

Simply Accounting provides for inventory turnover reporting which allows you to keep track of this important function.

Continue from within the Inventory & Services Ledger (Activity) window, (Figure 8.10) by

> Entering the **Date of Last Sale** as 07/20/01.
>
> Enter 1 as the **No. of Transactions (Year-to-Date)**.
>
> Enter 2 as the **Units Sold (Year-to-Date)**.
>
> Enter 2400.00 as the **Amount Sold (Year-to-Date)**.
>
> Enter 1060.00 as the **Cost of Goods Sold (Year-to-Date)**.
>
> Enter 2 as the **No. of Transactions (Last Year)**.
>
> Enter 4 as the **Units Sold (Last Year)**.
>
> Enter 4750.00 as the **Amount Sold (Last Year)**.
>
> Enter 2100.00 as the **Cost of Goods Sold (Last Year)**.

The last step in the creation of the inventory is the entry of the Historical information which includes the Opening Quantity and Opening Value. Continue by

> Clicking on the **History** tabbed button.

Figure 8.11
Inventory &
Services
(History)
window

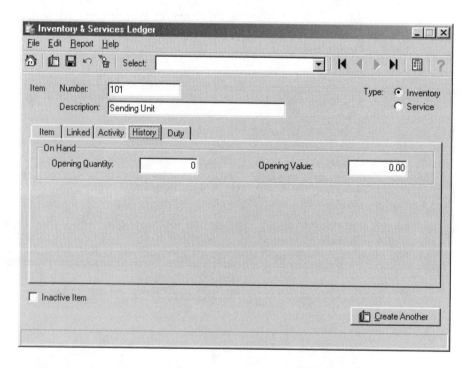

Continue within the Inventory & Services Ledger (History) window (Figure 8.11) by

> Entering 2 as the **Opening Quantity**.
>
> Entering 1100.00 as the **Opening Value**. This amount is the total cost value of the opening inventory for this item.

Continue from within the Inventory & Services Ledger (History) window (Figure 8.11) by

Clicking on the Duty tabbed button.

Figure 8.12
Inventory &
Services Ledger
(Duty) window

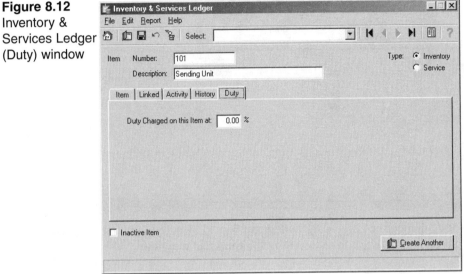

Simply Accounting for Windows now supports the application of duty percentage that can levied on sales to customers outside of your country, (Figure 8.12). For the purpose of this book, this feature will not be used.

As you have not entered all of the required information for the Sending Unit, continue by

Clicking the **Create Another** button to **Create** the inventory record.

Practice Exercise 8.3

Enter the remaining inventory items from the list provided in Figure 8.5. Remember that you have already entered the first item. Use the same asset, revenue, and expense account as you used for item no. 1 Sending Units. All items are sold in single units, shown as **Each** in the Inventory Ledger window.

For your reference, the applicable General Ledger control accounts are included:

1200 to assign the **Asset** control account
4050 to assign the **Revenue** control account
5050 to assign the **Expense** control account
5814 to assign the **Variance** control account

Note: The data files with all inventory items entered is available on disk. If you do not want to enter the inventory items yourself, then copy the data files from the subdirectory on the diskette in the back of the book to the **C:\Program Files\WINSIM\ DATA** directory on your hard drive. The data files are in the subdirectory called **sw0808**.

MODIFYING AND DELETING INVENTORY ITEM INFORMATION

It may become necessary for you to change the name, minimum quantity, and price of an item. If so, select the Inventory Ledger. Once the Inventory Ledger window is shown, use your mouse or your keyboard to scroll through the inventory list using the forward and reverse play buttons.

Figure 8.13
Inventory &
Services Edit
window

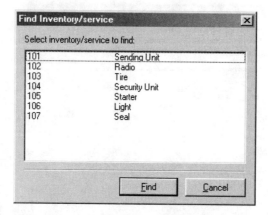

You can also locate the required Inventory & Services record by accessing the Find window, (Figure 8.13) through the **Edit** menu followed by the **Find** menu option.

MOVING AROUND THE INVENTORY LEDGER WINDOW

You will notice that within the Inventory Ledger window (modify), that this window does not have a Save or Accept Changes window. Instead, you must change this window by either moving to another inventory item or by closing the **Inventory** Ledger window.

Practice Exercise 8.4

Add the following General Ledger accounts:

Account#	Account Name	Type
5100	Regular Freight expense	Group Acct
	Account Class: Expense	
5105	Overnight Freight expense	Group Acct
	Account Class: Expense	
5110	Air Freight expense	Group Acct
	Account Class: Expense	

Leave Suppress Printing. and Budget this Account unchecked. Once you have completed this exercise return to the Simply Accounting - ODC window (Figure 8.6).

ENTERING INVENTORY SERVICE ITEMS

Simply Accounting for Windows also supports the entry and use of service items within the Inventory & Services module. Service items are shown in Figure 8.14 and once defined, allow you to easily access them.

Figure 8.14   Service Item listing

Number	Description	Unit/Measure	Selling Price	Revenue	Expense
REGFR	Regular Freight	Each	25.00	4220	5100 entered
OVNFR	Overnight Freight	Each	40.00	4240	5105
AIRFR	Air Freight	Each	50.00	4240	5110

Continue from within the Inventory & Services Ledger window (Figure 8.8) by entering

REGFR ⟨Tab⟩   as the service Number.
Regular Freight ⟨Tab⟩   as the Description.
⟨↓⟩ ⟨Tab⟩   to select Service as the Type.

Figure 8.15
Inventory
Services (Item)
window

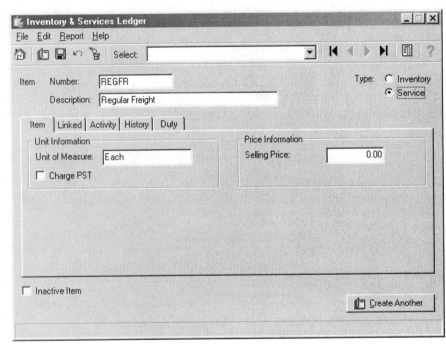

Within the Inventory Services (Item) window (Figure 8.15), you are prompted for the following:

Unit of Measure   is used to display the unit of measure. Examples of unit of measure for service items could be *each, hourly,* or *per diem.*

Selling Price   is used for the suggested selling price for each unit of service.

Charge PST   allows you to define whether Provincial Sales Tax will be charged on the sales invoice.

Continue from within the Inventory Service (item) window (Figure 8.14) by pressing

⟨Tab⟩   to accept Each as the **Unit of Measure**.

25.00 ⟨Tab⟩   to enter the default **Selling Price**.

HINT: USING THE SELLING PRICE

As with inventory products, the inventory service selling price is only the default selling price and can be modified at the time of invoice entry.

As we will not be charging PST on service items, continue from within the Inventory Service (item) window by

Clicking on the **Linked** tabbed button.

Figure 8.16
Inventory
Service (Linked)
window

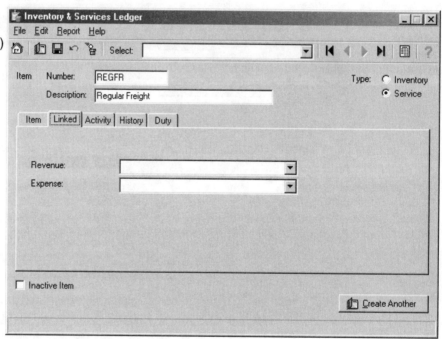

Within the Inventory Service Ledger (Linked) window, you are prompted for two accounts:

Revenue   is for the selection of the appropriate account for the posting of revenue invoices.

Expense   is for the selection of the appropriate account for the posting of purchase invoices.

Continue from within the Inventory Service (Linked) window (Figure 8.16) by

Selecting 4220 (Regular Freight) as the **Revenue** account.

Selecting 5100 (Regular Freight expense) as the **Expense** account.

Continue from within the Inventory Service (Linked) window (Figure 8.16) by

Clicking on the **Activity** tabbed button.

Figure 8.17
Inventory
Service
(Activity)
window

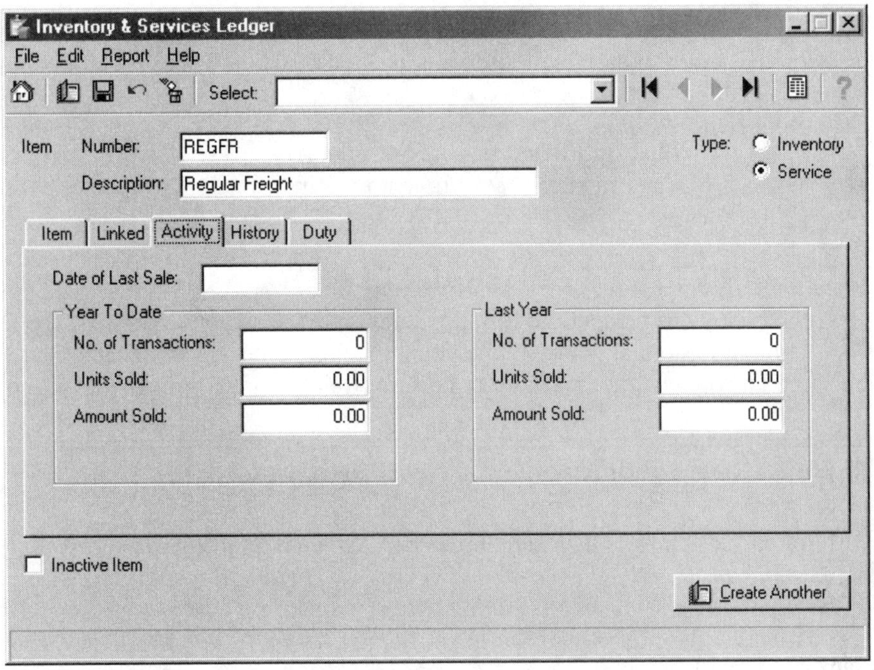

Within the Inventory Service (Activity) window (Figure 8.17), we could continue with the entry of the statistical sales information for the Regular Freight service record.

However, instead continue by

Clicking the **Create Another** button.

HINT: *ENTERING HISTORY FOR SERVICE RECORDS*

*Because the use of a service record is for the recording and management of services bought or sold, you will not have an opening inventory of services on hand. Therefore you cannot make entries when you click on the **History** tab in the Inventory and Services Ledger window.*

Practice Exercise 8.5

Continue with the entry of the remaining service items within Figure 8.14.

Once you have completed this exercise, return to the Simply Accounting - ODC window (Figure 8.6).

BACKING UP YOUR DATA FILES

At this point, return to the Simply Accounting - ODC window and backup your data files.

Call this backup:

> **Backup Filename**: A:\odc\odc8A
> **Comment**:   Inventory Part a

BALANCING TO THE GENERAL LEDGER

As with the previous General Ledger, Payables, and Receivables modules, the Inventory module is operating in Historical mode. While you are able to enter inventory transactions at this point, you should always set the Inventory to current (Ready) mode prior to making journal entries.

> **HINT:** *HISTORICAL MODE VERSUS CURRENT MODE*
>
> *With the exception of the General journal, we have entered historical amounts, for example, outstanding invoices or payments, in Historical mode. Once these items balanced to our manual accounting ledger, we then set the Simply Accounting modules, Payables, Receivables, and Inventory, to the Current (Ready) mode prior to entering new transactions. This ensures that there are no errors in the opening balances that would cause problems later.*

Continue from the Simply Accounting - ODC window (Figure 8.6) by

PRINTING THE INVENTORY REPORTS

Printing inventory reports is similar to printing reports in other ledgers. Make sure that you are still in the Inventory Ledger window.

First print the inventory list, and continue by

> Selecting the **Report** menu.
>
> Within the **Report** menu, continue by selecting the **Inventory & Services** menu option.
>
> Selecting the **Inventory** menu item.

Figure 8.18
Inventory
Report Options
window

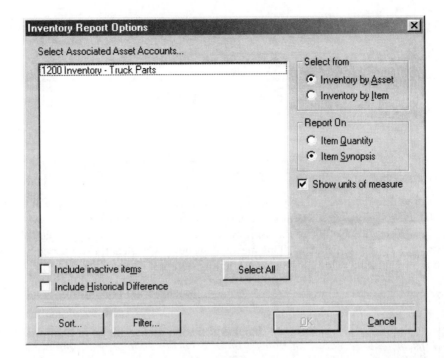

Within the Inventory Report Options window (Figure 8.18) you can select from the following options:

> **Select from**   allows you to select applicable inventory data by either asset accounts or inventory items.
>
> **Report On**   provides the option of either reporting on the inventory quantity, or item synopsis.
>
> **Include Historical Difference**   provides details pertaining to balancing to General Ledger.

Continue from within the Inventory Report Options window (Figure 8.17) by

Selecting to **Report On/Item Synopsis**.

Clicking on the **Select All** button.

Selecting **Include Historical Difference**.

Click **OK**.

Figure 8.19
Inventory
Synopsis
window

Inventory Synopsis							
File Options Help							
08/31/01			Price	Quantity	Cost	Value	Margin (%)
101	Sending Unit	Each	1,200.00	2	550.0	1,100.00	54.17
102	Radio	Each	625.00	4	375.0	1,500.00	40.00
103	Tire	Each	150.00	12	90.0	1,080.00	40.00
104	Security Unit	Each	375.00	4	275.0	1,100.00	26.67
105	Starter	Each	1,150.00	2	750.0	1,500.00	34.78
106	Light	Each	75.00	24	43.0	1,032.00	42.67
107	Seal	Each	17.00	100	5.93	593.00	65.12
						7,905.00	

Inventory & Services history is balanced.

From within the Inventory Synopsis window (Figure 8.19), you should balance to the $7,905 total as well as to each inventory item quantity, cost, and value.

You will also notice that Simply Accounting has informed you that the Inventory and Services history is balanced. This means that the total for each inventory asset account balances to the sum of the value for the corresponding inventory items.

HINT: *PRINTING REPORTS*

*Remember that you can either print or export and Simply Accounting report by selecting the **File** menu from within that specific report window.*

If you do not balance to the contents of the Inventory Synopsis (Figure 8.18), return to the Inventory Ledger and correct the in error in quantity, costs or values.

If your Inventory Synopsis balances to Figure 8.19, continue by

Closing the Inventory Synopsis window. You will then return to the Simply Accounting - ODC window (Figure 8.6).

BACKING UP YOUR DATA FILES

At this point, return to the Simply Accounting - ODC window and back up your data files.

Call this backup:

Backup Filename: A:\odc\odc8b
Comment: Chaspter 8 – Part b

DEFINING INTEGRATION ACCOUNTS

Since the Inventory module in Simply Accounting for Windows is integrated on an item-by-item basis, integration for the inventory aspect of the General Ledger is not required. However, Simply Accounting for Windows offers two additional inventory features:

Transfers allow you to transfer inventory items from one item to another. An example would be if Overnight Delivery Company replaced a seal within a light. In this case, a seal would be transferred to the light inventory item.

Adjustments   allow you to journalize an inventory transaction where one or more inventory items are consumed within the company. An example would be the use of a inventory headlight for one of Overnight Delivery Company's vehicles.

Continue from the Simply Accounting - ODC window (Figure 8.6) by

Selecting the **Setup** menu.

Selecting the **Linked Accounts** menu option.

Select the **Inventory Items** submenu item.

Figure 8.20
Inventory
Integration
Accounts
window

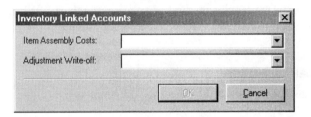

Continue with the entry of the inventory transfer and adjustment accounts (Figure 8.20) as follows

5810 [Tab]   to enter the **Transfer Costs** or Item Assembly Costs account.

5812 [Tab]   to enter the **Adjustment Write-off** account.

[Enter]   to close the Inventory Integration Accounts window. You will then return to the Simply Accounting - ODC window (Figure 8.6).

COMPLETING THE CONVERSION PROCESS

You have entered your opening balances, so the conversion process is almost complete. You will now need to continue with the establishment of the required integration accounts.

BACKING UP YOUR DATA FILES

At this point, return to the Simply Accounting - ODC window and back up your data files.

Call this backup:

Backup Filename: A:\odc\odc8c
Comment: Inventory – Part c

ENTERING INVENTORY TRANSACTIONS

You are now ready to enter current transactions into the Simply Accounting for Windows program. Unlike the other ledgers that you have looked at so far, all transactions that affect the Inventory module are entered through the **Purchase, Sales, Transfer,** and **Adjustment** journals, and not through the Inventory Ledger.

Ordering of Inventory	Purchase Journal
Receipt of Inventory	Purchase Journal
Purchase of Inventory	Purchase Journal
Sale of Inventory	Sales Journal
Transfers of Inventory	Transfers Journal
Adjustments of Inventory	Adjustments Journal

Simply Accounting for Windows offers the support for purchase order and order tracking. This allows your business to order inventory, track the status of the inventory, as well as record the receipt of the inventory, when your company receives the actual stock.

If you prefer, you can use the regular method of entering purchases: When the purchase is entered, the inventory is assumed to have been received by your company.

ENTER PURCHASE ORDERS

In most businesses, a purchase of inventory includes the following steps:

1. **Purchase Order**
   You company make a request to purchase certain inventory items from a supplier.

2. **Receipt of Invoice/Inventory**
   Your company will then receive the inventory and accompanied invoice.

The entry of purchase orders allows you to track the inventory on hand and the inventory on order from your suppliers.

Continue from the Simply Accounting ODC window (Figure 8.6) by

Clicking on the **Purchases** icon.

Figure 8.21
Purchases
Journal

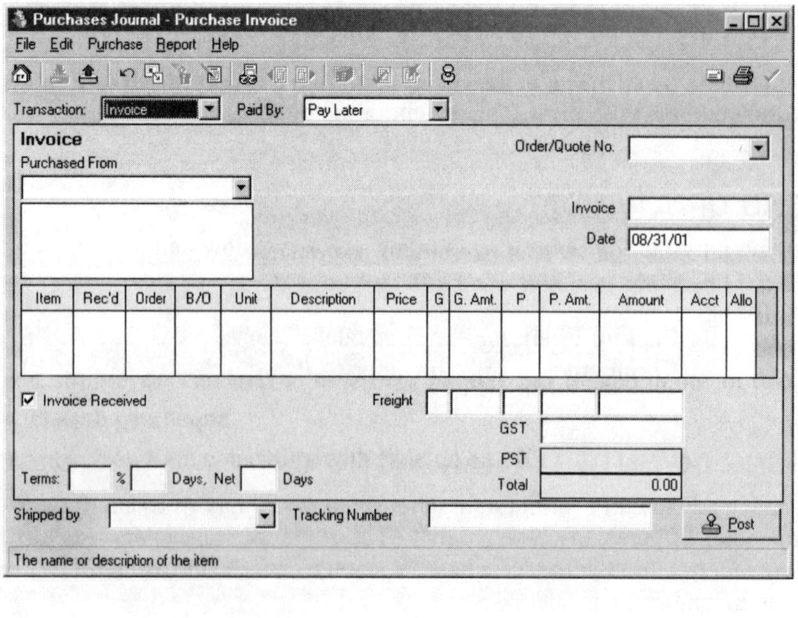

From within the **Purchases** Journal (Figure 8.21) a **Transaction** titled **Purchase Order** is available for selection.

Continue from within the **Purchase** Journal (Figure 8.21) by

>   Selecting the **Purchase Order** *Transaction* type.

Figure 8.22
Purchase
Journal –
Purchase
Order window

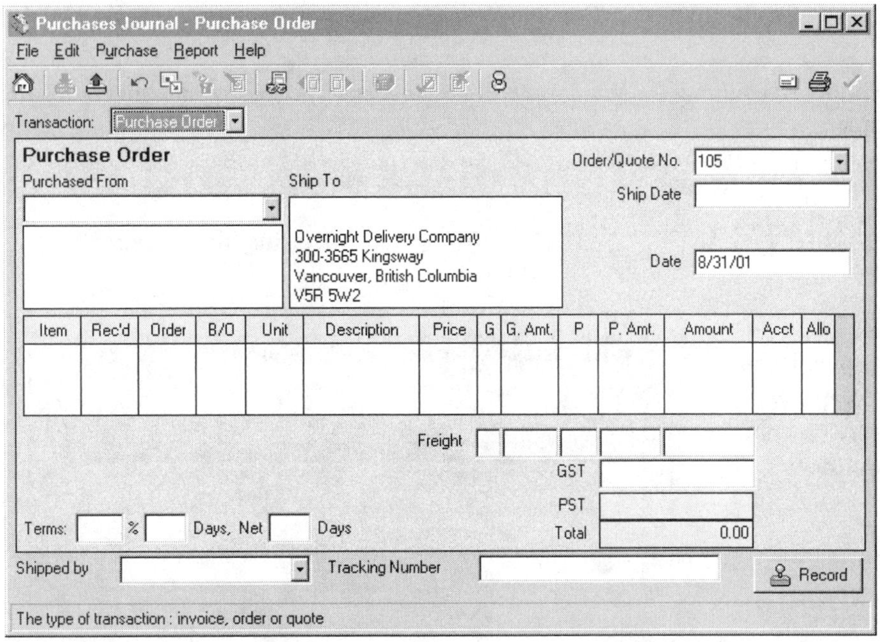

Simply Accounting for Window's Purchase Journal will change to display the Purchase Journal – Purchase Order window (Figure 8.22). This window allows you to enter the purchase order. Once in the system, it can be tracked to ensure that you did in fact receive it.

Continue by pressing

>   [Tab]   to move to the **Purchase From** field.

>   *R* [Tab]   to select *Ronoco Truck Parts* as your supplier (**Purchased From**).

>   [Tab] (several times)   to move to the **Order/Quote No.**

HINT: SELECTING A PURCHASE ORDER NUMBER

In Simply Accounting for Windows, you can select your Purchase Order number by entering the next available purchase order (PO) number within the Forms section of the Settings window, (located off the __Setup__ menu within the Simply Accounting - ODC window). Refer to Chapter 3 for detailed setup instructions.

Continue by pressing

105 (Tab)   to enter the **PO Number** (Purchase Order).

08/08/01 (Tab)   to enter the requested **Ship Date**. The Ship Date will provide
                                           you with a reminder when your inventory shipment is expected
                                           to be shipped to your company.

08/01/01 (Tab)   to enter the order **Date**. This is the date on which the order
                                           was placed.

Simply Accounting for Windows will now prompt you to enter the inventory **Item** that you have
ordered.

Continue by pressing

(Enter)   to display the **Select Inventory item** window, (note
                                           Figure 8.23).

Figure 8.23
Select
Inventory/
service item
window

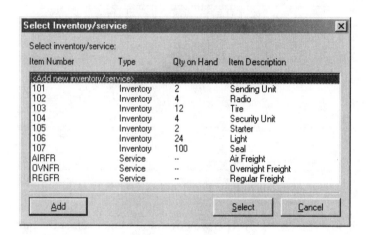

From within the Select Inventory item window (Figure 8.23) you can select from the list of
available inventory items.

HINT: *NAVIGATING THE SELECT INVENTORY WINDOW*

*As with the Select Account window, you can also jump to an associated area of
inventory items by pressing the first letter or digit that is associated to the inventory
item. For example, if you wanted to jump to the 9000 section within your inventory item
list, you would press (9). You can also add new inventory items from within the Select
Inventory/service window.*

The Select Inventory items window (Figure 8.23) also provides you with on-hand inventory
details so you can quickly determine how much inventory you currently have on hand.

Continue form the Select Inventory items window (Figure 8.30) by pressing

(↓) (Enter)   to select 101 – Sending Units as the Item.

Figure 8.24
Purchases
Journal –
Purchase Order
window

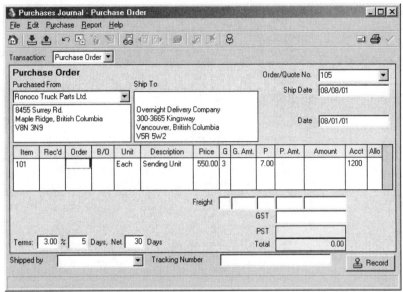

Simply Accounting for Windows will now display the retrieved details from the inventory record for 101 – Sending Units (Figure 8.24).

Continue by entering

2 [Tab]	to enter the quantity **Order**ed.
[Tab]	to accept 2 as the quantity on **B/O** (Back Order).
[Tab]	to accept the default **Unit** of measure.
[Tab]	to accept the default **Description**.
575.00 [Tab]	to enter the new **Price** for each sending unit. The previous price of 550.00 per unit was the weighted average price based on the total dollar value for sending units divided by the total quantity of on hand sending units.
[Tab]	to accept 3 as the **GST** code. This will inform Simply Accounting that the purchase amount will be subject to an additional 7.0% Goods and Services Tax that is not included within the price of each unit.
[Tab]	to accept 80.50 as the amount of **Goods and Services Tax**.
0 [Tab]	To enter the **PST** (Provincial Sales Tax) percentage. As you are purchasing this inventory for resell, you have already provided your supplier with your Provincial Sales Tax number, thus no Provincial Sales Tax will be levied at the time of order/purchase. If you should have paid Provincial Sales Tax, this amount would be added to the total cost of the items purchased.
[Tab]	to accept no **PST** amount.
[Tab]	to accept the default **Amount** $1,150.00.

Figure 8.25
Purchases
Journal –
Purchase Order
window

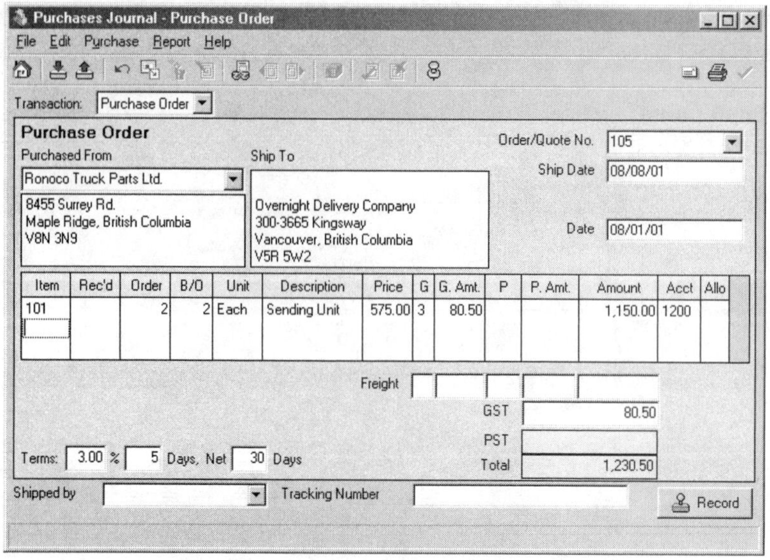

Your Purchase Journal – Purchase Order window should now resemble Figure 8.25. Continue with the following exercise.

Practice Exercise 8.6

ENTERING PURCHASE ORDERS

Continue with the entry of the following detail lines for Ronoco's Purchase Order (10S) as noted above. Once you have completed this exercise, DO NOT POST THIS ENTRY BUT REMAIN WITHIN THE PURCHASE JOURNAL – PURCHASE ORDER WINDOW.

Note that the GST code should be 3 while the PST percentage should be 0%.

Description	Order	Price	Amount
Security Units	1	280.00	280.00
Starter	1	750.00	750.00

Remember not to post this entry, but remain within the Purchase Journal – Purchase Order window when you have completed this exercise.

Figure 8.26
Purchase
Journal –
Purchase Order
window

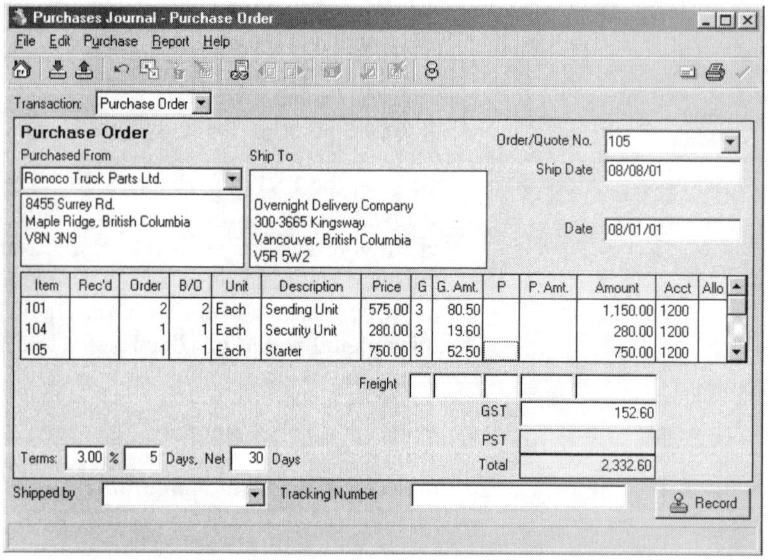

Your Purchase Journal – Purchase Order window should resemble Figure 8.26. Once you **Post** this invoice, Simply Accounting for Windows will update the inventory reports to reflect this purchase order, but no entries will be made within the General journal as this transaction is only a purchase order and not an actual purchase invoice. If this purchase had been a regular purchase invoice, the **Transaction** type would be either a Purchase or Purchase with Payment instead of the Purchase Order option.

If your Purchase Journal – Purchase Order window resembles Figure 8.26, continue by pressing

| Alt | + | P | | to **Post** this entry. |

| Y | | to select **Yes** to select the next purchase order to continue with this new numbering, (105). |

Practice Exercise 8.7

ENTERING PURCHASE ORDERS

Continue entering the following purchase orders:

Overnight Delivery Company
Purchase Orders
August 2001

Vendor: Ronoco Truck Parts

Ship Date	Order Date	Description	No. Order	Unit	Total
Order #106					
Aug 15	Aug 03	Radios	2	380.00	760.00
		Tires	6	90.00	540.00
		GST			91.00
				Total	1391.00
Order #107					
Aug 20	Aug 05	Lights	12	40.00	480.00
		Seals	25	6.00	150.00
		GST			44.10
				Total	674.10
Order #108					
Aug 25	Aug 08	Sending Units	1	560.00	560.00
		Starter	1	750.00	750.00
		Tires	6	91.00	546.00
		GST			128.92
				Total	1985.92

The GST code will be **3** while the PST percentage will be 0%.

Once you have completed the above exercise, return to the Simply Accounting - ODC window (Figure 8.6).

BACKING UP YOUR DATA FILES

At this point, return to the Simply Accounting – ODC window and back up your data files.

Call this backup:

> **Backup Filename:** A:\odc8d\odc
> **Comment:** Inventory - Part d

PURCHASE ORDER REPORTING

By entering purchase orders you can track your inventory ordered, the expected ship date, and the value of the orders. The expected quantities can also assist your company with planning appropriate inventory levels for customer requirements.

Continue from the Simply Accounting – ODC window (Figure 8.6) by pressing

> [Alt] + [R]   to select the **Report** menu.

From within the **Report** menu, continue by pressing

> [I]   to select the **Inventory** menu option.

From within the Inventory Report menu, continue by pressing

> [N]   to select the **Inventory** report option

Figure 8.27
Inventory
Report Options
window

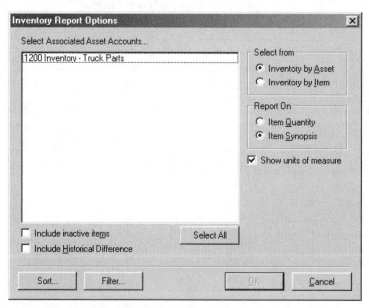

Continue from the Inventory Report Options window (Figure 8.27) by

> Clicking on the **Select All** button.
>
> Clicking on the **Item Quantity** option.
>
> Clicking on the **OK** button.

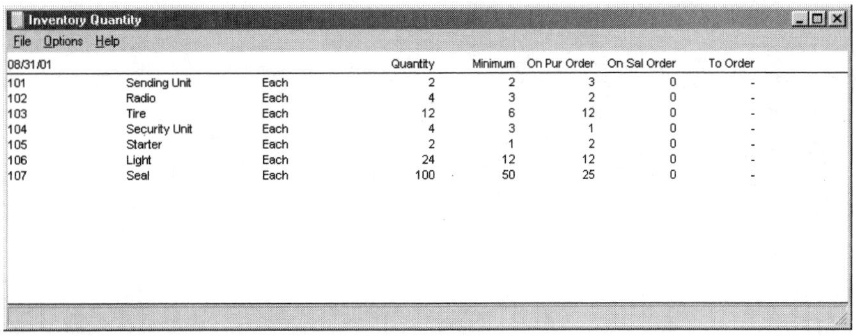

08/31/01			Quantity	Minimum	On Pur Order	On Sal Order	To Order
101	Sending Unit	Each	2	2	3	0	-
102	Radio	Each	4	3	2	0	-
103	Tire	Each	12	6	12	0	-
104	Security Unit	Each	4	3	1	0	-
105	Starter	Each	2	1	2	0	-
106	Light	Each	24	12	12	0	-
107	Seal	Each	100	50	25	0	-

Figure 8.28
Inventory Quantity report window

As shown in Figure 8.28, the Inventory Quantity Report now includes the On Order amounts. This will allow your company to plan for the arrival of inventory based on the information contained within this report.

Continue by pressing

Alt + F4 to close the Inventory Quantity Report window.

TRACKING OUTSTANDING PURCHASE ORDERS

To be able to quickly view the outstanding purchase orders, continue from the Simply Accounting – ODC window, (Figure 8.6) by

Clicking on the **Report** menu.

Clicking on the **Payables** menu option within the **Report** menu.

Clicking on the **Pending Purchase Orders** menu option.

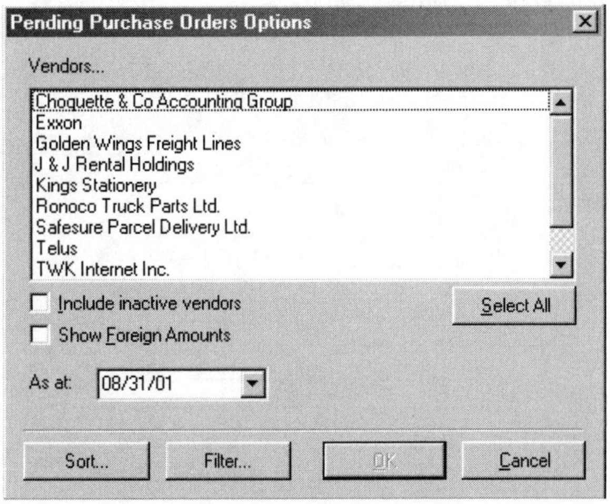

Figure 8.29
Pending Purchase Orders Options window

From within the Pending Purchase Orders Options window (Figure 8.29) continue by

Clicking on the **Select All** button.

Clicking on the **OK** button.

Figure 8.30
Pending
Purchase
Orders report
window

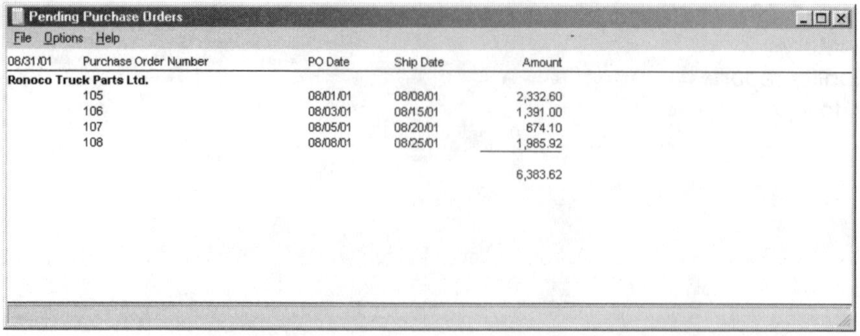

Simply Accounting for Windows will now display the Pending Purchase Orders report window (Figure 8.30). This report details the purchase order outstanding along with the purchase order date, ship date, and value of the purchase order. This report will provide you with a quick way to display all pending purchase orders.

Continue from the Pending Purchase Orders report (Figure 8.30) by pressing

⟨ Alt ⟩ + ⟨ F4 ⟩   to close the Pending Purchase Orders window.

RECEIVING INVENTORY

In the previous exercise, you entered the purchase orders for Ronoco Truck Parts. While Simply Accounting has updated the inventory reports to represent the quantity that has been ordered, no entries have been made in the General journal as the actual invoice has not been issued by Ronoco Truck Parts. Normally, the invoice is issued only when the product has been shipped, indicating that the actual purchase of the product has taken place.

We will now continue with the entry of the receipt of inventory and the associated purchase invoice.

Continue from the Simply Accounting - ODC window (Figure 8.6) by

Clicking on the **Purchases** icon.

Figure 8.31
Purchase
Journal –
Purchase
Invoice window

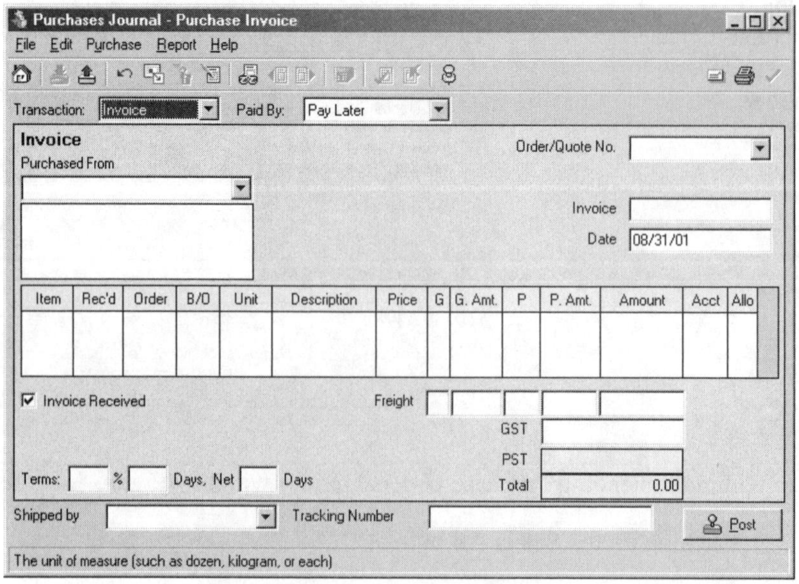

Continue from the Purchase Journal window (Figure 8.31) by pressing

> [Tab] to bypass **Purchased From** field.
>
> [↓] to display **PO Number** *105*.
>
> [Tab] to select **PO Number** *105*.

Figure 8.32
Purchase
Journal –
Purchase
Invoice
retrieved
window

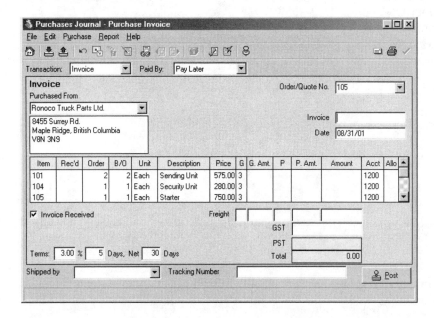

Simply Accounting for Windows has now retrieved the purchase order detail for purchase order number 105 (Figure 8.32). At this stage you are receiving both the invoice and the inventory for this purchase order.

> Continue by entering
>
> **4622** [Tab] as the **Invoice** number.
>
> **08/08/01** [Tab] to enter the **Date**.

As all of the inventory items have been received in this shipment, you could manually enter the **Received** quantity for each item.

Figure 8.33
Purchase
Journal
icon bar

To expedite the receipt of all of the ordered items, you can select all ordered items as received

or clear the back ordered item

You can choose the appropriate icon from the menu bar shown in Figure 8.33.

Continue by

> Clicking on the **Fill back-order** icon.

Figure 8.34
Purchase
Journal (Back-
orders filled)
window

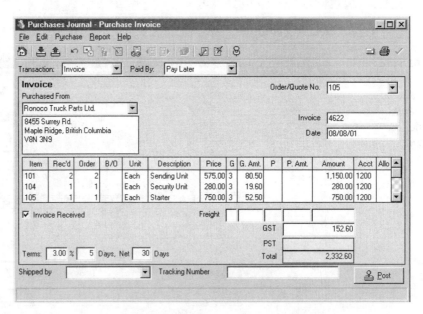

Simply Accounting has very quickly filled the back-ordered items (Figure 8.34). Continue by

> Clicking your mouse cursor within the GST code for **Freight**.

Continue by entering

3 [Tab]	to enter the GST Code for **Freight**.
[Tab] (three times)	to move to the **Freight Amount** field.
160.00 [Tab]	to enter the **Freight Amount**.

Figure 8.35   Purchase Journal – Purchases Invoices window (completed)

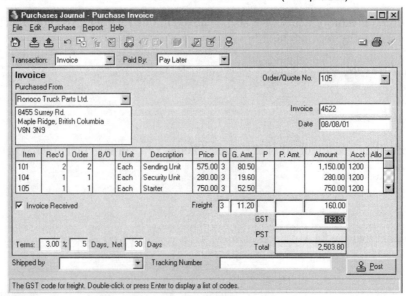

If your window resembles Figure 8.35, continue by pressing

[Alt] + [P]   to **Post** this purchase entry.

Figure 8.36
Filled &
Removed
Message
window

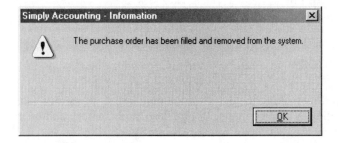

Simply Accounting for Windows will now inform you that the purchase order has been filled and will be removed from the system (Figure 8.36). Continue by pressing

[Enter]   to confirm this message.

Practice Exercise 8.8

ENTERING RECEIPT OF INVENTORY INVOICES

Continue with the following receipt of inventory invoices:
Overnight Delivery Company
Purchase Orders
August 2001

Vendor: Ronoco Truck Parts

Invoice/Order #	Date	Description	No. Order	Unit	Total
4691/106	Aug 15	Radios	2	380.00	760.00
	Tires	Backorder			
	Freight				50.00
	GST				56.70
				Total	866.70
4751/107	Aug 20	Lights	12	40.00	480.00
	Seals		25	6.00	150.00
	GST				44.10
Complete order received				Total	674.10
4813/108	Aug 25	Sending Units	1	560.00	560.00
	Starter		1	750.00	750.00
	Tires		6	91.00	546.00
	GST				128.92
Complete order received				Total	1,985.92

Once you have completed this exercise, return to the Simply Accounting - ODC window (Figure 8.6).

BACKING UP YOUR DATA FILES

At this point, return to the Simply Accounting – ODC window and backup your data files.

Call this backup:

> **Backup Filename:** A:\odc8e\odc
> **Comment:** Inventory Part e

PURCHASE OF INVENTORY

In the above example, the process of purchasing inventory involved making the entry of the purchase order followed by making the entry for the purchase of inventory. However, in your business you may combine both procedures — purchase the inventory and be invoiced for this purchase during the same transaction. In this case, you would make one entry as an inventory purchase.

Purchases of inventory are made through the Purchases journal. Be sure you are at the Simply Accounting – ODC window (Figure 8.6)

> Open the Purchases journal by
>
> Clicking on the **Purchases** icon.

or

> use your ⬆, ⬇, ⬅ or ➡ keys to position the cursor on the **Purchases** icon followed by pressing Enter to open the journal. This procedure was covered in detail in previous chapters.

The information we have for purchases in August 2001 is shown in Figure 8.37.

Overnight Delivery Company
Schedule of Purchase Invoices
August 2001

Inv #	Date	Description	From	No. Recd	Unit	Total
4816	Aug 26	Sending Units	Ronoco Truck Parts	2	565.00	1,130.00
		Security Units		1	280.00	280.00
		Freight				60.00
		GST				102.90
				Total		1,572.90
4820	Aug 28	Radios	Ronoco Truck Parts	1	380.00	380.00
		Freight				50.00
		GST				30.10
				Total		460.10
4823	Aug 30	Lights	Ronoco Truck Parts	4	42.50	170.00
		Freight				50.00
		GST				15.40
				Total		235.40

Figure 8.37   Schedule of purchases for Overnight Delivery Company

Continue from the Simply Accounting – ODC window (Figure 8.6) by

> Clicking on the **Purchases** icon.

Figure 8.38
Purchase –
Journal window

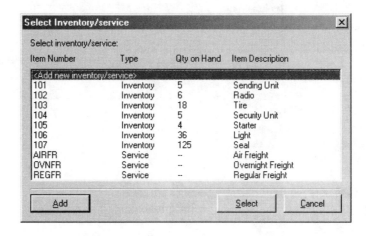

Continue from the Purchases Journal window (Figure 8.38) by pressing

Tab twice	to move to the **Purchase From** field.
Ron Tab	to select Ronoco Truck Parts as the **Purchase From** vendor.
Tab	to bypass the **PO (Purchase Order) Number**.
4816 Tab	to enter the **Invoice** number.
08/26/01 Tab	to enter the **Date**.
Enter	to display the **Select Inventory item** window (note Figure 8.39).

Figure 8.39
Select Inventory
item window

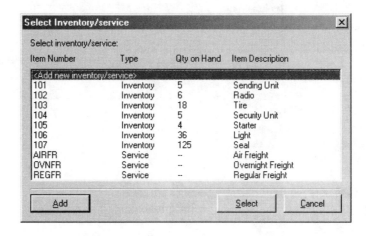

From within the Select Inventory item window (Figure 8.39), continue by pressing

[↓] [Enter]	to select 101-Sending Unit as the applicable **Item** code.
2 [Tab]	to enter the **Received** amount of inventory.
[Tab]	to confirm the **Unit** description, (Each).
[Tab]	to confirm the **Description**, (Sending Unit).
565.00 [Tab]	to override the **Price**.
[Tab]	to confirm **GST** code 3.
[Tab]	to confirm the **GST** amount.
0 [Tab]	to override the **PST** figure.
[Tab]	to bypass the **PST** amount field.
[Tab]	to confirm the **Amount**.

Figure 8.40
Purchase
Journal –
Invoice 4816

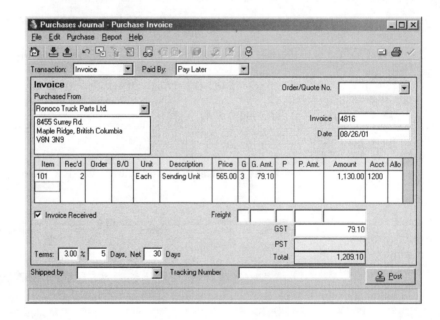

Practice Exercise 8.9

Continue with the entry of the remaining details for invoice 4816 (Figure 8.37) followed by the entry of the two remaining invoices. The GST code for all three invoices will be code 3 while the PST percentage shall be zero. Be sure to include Freight where noted and to select GST code 3 to charge GST on the freight amount as well.

Note: Some unit prices in Figure 8.37 are different from the ones displayed by the Simply Accounting program. Use the prices shown in Figure 8.37. If you are not sure of the inventory number associated with the items purchased, press [Enter] at the **Item** field. This will invoke a window titled Select Inventory Item (see Figure 8.39). To review the Purchase journal procedures, refer to the Accounts Payable Chapter.

Once you have completed this exercise, return to the Simply Accounting - ODC window (Figure 8.6).

MAINTAINING AN AUDIT TRAIL

Print out the journal entries that you have made so far to maintain an audit trail. Exit to the Simply Accounting - ODC window and select the **Report** menu ([Alt] + [R]), followed by executing Financials, followed by selecting the **General Ledger** menu option ([G] then press [Enter]). Then continue by selecting **08/01/01** to **08/31/01** for the **Start** and **Finish** dates. As this general ledger listing is only for inventory, select account 1200 Inventory – Truck Parts. Once you have printed this report, place it in your audit trail binder.

BACKING UP YOUR DATA FILES

At this point, return to the Simply Accounting – ODC window and backup your data files.

Call this backup:

> **Backup Filename:** A:\odc\odc8f
> **Comment:** Chapter 8 – Part f

SALE OF INVENTORY ITEMS

The sale of an inventory item is entered through the **Sales** journal. Overnight Delivery Company had the sales shown in Figure 8.41 during the month of August 2001.

Overnight Delivery Company
Schedule of Sales
August 2001

Inv #	Date	Description	To:	# Sold	Price/Unit	Other Costs
4565	Aug 5	Sending Units	Quality Custom	1	1,200	1,200.00
		Security Units	Furniture	1	375	375.00
		Starter		2	1,125	2,250.00
		Air Freight (Service)		2	50	100.00
		GST				274.75
		PST				267.75
		Total				4,467.50
4566	Aug 12	Overnight Freight				
		(Service)	Cassar Homes Inc.	1	55	55.00
		Radios		1	625	625.00
		Tire		6	150	900.00
		GST				110.60
		PST				106.75
		Total				1,797.35
4567	Aug 20	Lights	McMillan Mills Inc	18	75	1,350.00
		Seals		20	17	340.00
		GST				118.30
		PST				118.30
		Total				1926.60
4568	Aug 21	Sending Units	Quality Custom	1	1,200	1,200.00
		Starter	Furnitur	1	1,150	1,150.00
		Tire		6	145	870.00
		GST				225.40
		PST				225.40
		Total				3670.80
4569	Aug 25	Regular Freight				
		(Service)	City Software	3	22	66.00
		GST				4.62
		PST				0.00
		Total				70.62

Figure 8.41 Schedule of sales for Overnight Delivery Company

Now let us record the sale to Quality Custom Furniture. From the Simply Accounting – ODC window (Figure 8.6), continue by

Selecting and opening the Sales Journal by clicking on the **Sales** icon or by using your →, ←, ↑ or ↓ keys to highlight the **Sales** icon. Then press Enter to open the Sales Journal.

Figure 8.42
Sales Journal
window

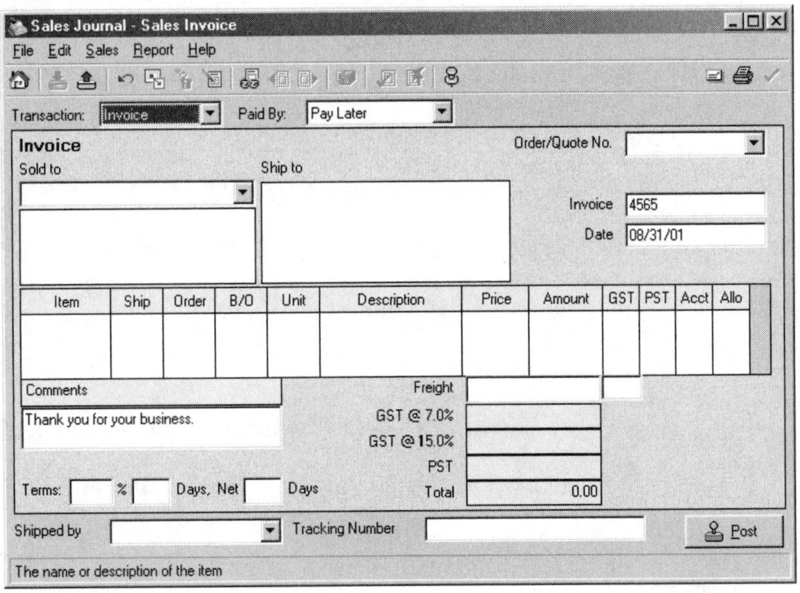

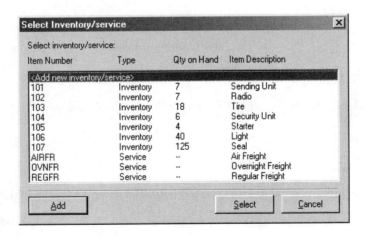

From within the Sales Journal window (Figure 8.42), continue by selecting Quality Custom Furniture as the customer. Press

Tab (twice)	to move to the **Sold to** field
Q Tab	to select Quality Customer Furniture and to move to the next field.
Tab (6 times)	to move cursor to the **Invoice** field.
Tab	to accept **4565** as the correct **Invoice Number**.
08/05/01 Tab	to enter the invoice **Date**.
Enter	to invoke the Select Inventory Item window (see Figure 8.43).

Figure 8.43
Select Inventory
Item window

From within the Select Inventory item window (Figure 8.43) continue by pressing

[↓] [Enter]	to select inventory item 101 – Sending Units.
1 [Tab]	to enter the quantity ordered.
[Tab] (2 times)	to move cursor to the **Price** field.
[Tab]	to accept the unit selling price of 1,200.00.
[Tab]	to accept the **Amount** as 1,200.00.
[Tab]	to accept **3** as the **GST** code.
[Tab]	to skip the PST field. The default value should be **7.0**.
[Tab]	to move to the next inventory **Item Number** field.

Continue with the entry of the Security Unit:

104 [Tab]	to entry the **Item** code.
1 [Tab]	to enter the quantity ordered.
[Tab] (2 times)	to move cursor to the **Price** field.
[Tab]	to accept the unit selling price of 375.00.
[Tab]	to accept the **Amount** as 375.00.
[Tab]	to accept **3** as the **GST** code.
[Tab]	to skip the **PST** field. The default value should be **7.0**.
[Tab]	to move to the next inventory **Item Number** field.

Continue with the entry of the Starter:

105 [Tab]	to entry the **Item** code.
2 [Tab]	to enter the quantity ordered.
[Tab] (2 times)	to move cursor to the **Price** field.
1,125.00 [Tab]	to enter the unit selling price of 1,125.00.
[Tab]	to accept the **Amount** as 2,250.00.
[Tab]	to accept **3** as the GST code.
[Tab]	to skip the **PST** field. The default value should be **7.0**.
[Tab]	to move to the next inventory **Item Number** field.

As you have also entered service items within your inventory list, (note Figure 8.43) continue with the entry of the Air Freight service item as follows:

AIRFR [Tab]   to select the **Item** code.

2 [Tab]   to enter the quantity ordered.

[Tab] (2 times)   to move cursor to the **Price** field.

[Tab]   to accept 50.00 as the unit selling price.

[Tab]   to accept the **Amount** as 100.00.

[Tab]   to accept **3** as the **GST** code.

[Tab]   to skip the **PST** field. The default value should be blank.

Figure 8.44
Sales Journal –
Invoice 4565

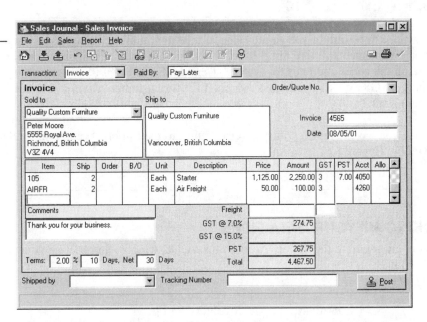

Your Sales Journal window should resemble Figure 8.44. Notice that **GST** and **PST** amounts have been calculated and are included in the total amount. Press

[Alt] + [P]   to **Post** the entry. *Note: You should receive a Credit Limit Exceeded message.* Press **Y** to continue.

[Y]   to select **Yes** to accept the sale for this customer who has exceeded their credit limit.

Simply Accounting will then clear the Sales Journal window, ready for the next invoice.

CORRECTING MISTAKES

If you make a mistake during the entry process by, for example, entering the incorrect unit selling price for one of the items sold, you can correct this error by either using your mouse or keyboard.

Using your mouse:

Position your mouse cursor over the field that is to be corrected and click your mouse button. The cursor will then appear in that field. Then enter the new amount.

Using your keyboard:

You can scroll back through the fields, by pressing [Shift] + [Tab]. Once you locate the field to be corrected, enter the correct information and press [Tab] to scroll forward to your current field.

If you have already Posted your entry and you realize that this entry contains an error, you will have to adjust the invoice. Please refer to Chapter 6 or Chapter 7 for a complete example of this feature.

Practice Exercise 8.10

Continue to record the remaining sales of inventory and service items in Figure 8.41. Note that some items, are not sold for the suggested retail selling price. Accept the default tax codes and rates for both GST and PST (GST and PST on inventory items and only GST on service items). Accept **YES** for customers who have exceeded their credit limit.

Once you have completed this exercise, return to the Simply Accounting - ODC window (Figure 8.6).

BACKING UP YOUR DATA FILES

At this point, return to the Simply Accounting – ODC window and backup your data files.

Call this backup:

Backup Filename: A:\odc\odc8g
Comment: Inventory Part g

ENTERING INVOICES FOR PRINTING

You did not print invoices for the sales that you have just entered. With the Simply Accounting system you can print the invoices at the same time as sales information is entered. This eliminates writing out an invoice by hand and entering the information again later.
To print the invoice:

1. Enter the invoice information as usual, *but do not **Post** the invoice.*
2. While in the Sales Journal window, press [Alt] + [F] to invoke the **File** menu. From this menu, press [P] to **Print** the invoice. Be sure that you have the correct type of paper in your default printer and that the default printer is on-line.

Once Simply Accounting has printed the invoice, the Sales Journal window will return so you can **Post** the invoice by pressing [Alt] + [P].

USING SIMPLY ACCOUNTING WITHIN A MAIL ORDER — PURCHASE-ON-DEMAND BUSINESS

For many small businesses, it is common to order inventory once the order has been placed by the customer. This method of sales is referred to as the "on-demand" or "just in time" inventory method. With Simply Accounting you can handle this type of inventory by allowing your inventory levels to drop below zero. This would occur, for example, if you issued an invoice prior to the entering the purchase of the required inventory for that particular invoice.

To allow Simply Accounting to process inventory sales with negative inventory levels, you must select this options in the **Inventory & Services** (Figure 8.45). This window is available through the **Setup**, **Settings** menu, located within the Simply Accounting - ODC window.

Figure 8.45
Inventory
Settings window

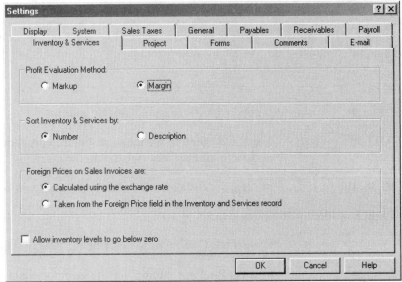

MAKING ADJUSTING ENTRIES TO ENDING INVENTORY

Even with the perpetual inventory system, it is still necessary to count ending inventory to ensure that a loss of inventory has not occurred during the month.

> During the month-end you discover that a new light was installed on your own truck. The cost must be charged to repair and maintenance. The light was to be transferred at its cost of $42.00.

To complete this entry, you must use the **Adjustments** journal. Select this journal by either using your mouse or keyboard. (Hint: You must be back at the Simply Accounting - ODC window, note Figure 8.6)

Figure 8.46
Adjustments
Journal window

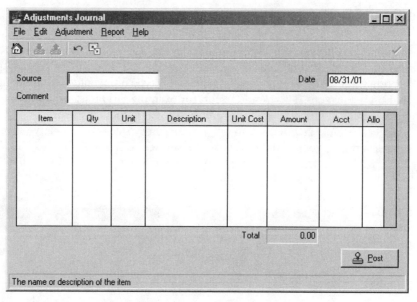

Continue from the Adjustment Journal window (Figure 8.46) by entering

ADJ109 [Tab]   to enter the **Source** for this adjustment. This should be the document number associated with the entry.

08/28/01 [Tab]   to enter the **Date** on which this adjustment was recorded.

Light installed in company truck [Tab]

        to enter the **Comment** to describe the type of adjustment.

106 [Tab]   to select the **Item** number for the inventory item (light).

-1 [Tab]   to enter the **Quantity** that is being adjusted.

[Tab]   to except the Unit as **Each**.

[Tab]   to accept the total amount associated with this light adjustment.

5260 [Tab]   to override the default expense account to replace it with the account for Repairs and Maintenance. *Note: The default adjustment write-off account was defined during the integration process.*

Figure 8.47
Adjustments
Journal entered

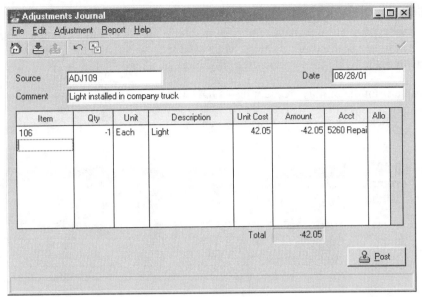

If your Adjustment Journal resembles Figure 8.47, press

⌈ Alt ⌋ + ⌈ P ⌋   to **Post** the adjustment entry.

HINT: RECURRING ENTRIES AND ADJUSTMENTS

You can also use the store and recall entries functions within the Adjustments journal, for any recurring sales, purchases, or adjustments that you make. We have discussed how this works in the previous two chapters.

You would also use the Adjustment journals for entry of any inventory adjustment caused by inventory spoilage or shrinkage.

Practice Exercise 8.11

Enter the following inventory adjustment:

A routine inventory on August 30, 2001, determined that three lights were damaged and thus destroyed. The source number will be **ADJ110**, while the adjustment write-off account is the default 5812.

Once you have completed the above exercise, press

⌈ Alt ⌋ + ⌈ F4 ⌋   to close the Adjustment Journal window.

ASSEMBLY OF INVENTORY ITEMS

The other type of entry is the assembly of inventory items. For this example, you will be use both a light and seal out of inventory, as the seal will be fitted to the light. Once the seal has been fitted, the light will be returned to inventory as a modified light.

Continue from the Simply Accounting – ODC window (Figure 8.6) by

        Clicking on the **Item Assembly** icon.

Figure 8.48
Item Assembly
Journal window

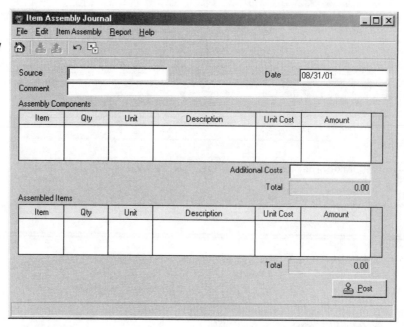

As shown in Figure 8.48, the Transfer Journal comprises two areas: items transferred out of inventory and items to transfer into inventory. Continue from the Transfer Journal window by entering

ADJ111 ⬚Tab⬚   as the **Source** for this item assembly.

⬚Tab⬚   to accept *08/31/01* as the **Date**.

Fitting of seal to light ⬚Tab⬚

      to enter the **Description**.

106 ⬚Tab⬚   to enter the *light* **Item** number.

1 ⬚Tab⬚   to select the **Quantity** to transfer out of inventory.

⬚Tab⬚   to accept the default **Unit Cost**.

⬚Tab⬚   to accept the default **Amount**.

Practice Exercise 8.12

Continue with the transfer out of inventory of **1 seal at the default unit cost and amount**.

Once you have completed this exercise, ensure your cursor is in the **Additional Costs** field (Figure 8.48).

The **Additional Costs** field allows you to expense (or contra-expense) the costs of transfer. An example would be the cost of additional labour to install the inventory item. The General Ledger account that this field is posted in is the Transfer account specified during the inventory integration process. The **Additional Costs** field allows either a negative or positive amount.

Practice Exercise 8.13

Since no additional costs are incurred with this inventory transfer, continue with the completion of this transfer. The remaining step is to transfer into inventory **1 light at the same cost as the combined transfer out costs**.

Before posting, please refer to Figure 8.49 to ensure that you transfer entry is correct.

Figure 8.49
Item Assembly
Journal window
(entered)

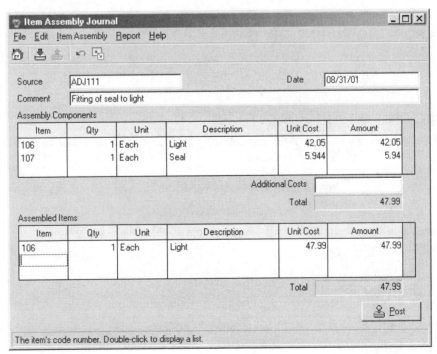

> *HINT: RECURRING/RECALLING INVENTORY TRANSFER ENTRIES*
>
> *You can store and recall inventory transfer entries made on a regular basis as mentioned previously.*

If your Transfer Journal window resembles Figure 8.49, continue by pressing

Alt + P   to **P**ost this transfer.

Although the above item assembly is completed, no financial journal entry was generated because the amount (in dollars) transferred out of inventory was transferred back in. The only time a journal entry would be generated would be if you specify a negative or positive **Additional Costs** amount.

Continue by pressing

Alt + F4   to close the Transfer Journal window and return to the Simply Accounting – ODC window.

MAINTAINING AN AUDIT TRAIL

As in other modules, it is important to establish an audit trail to have a record of all accounting entries made. To do so, generate a General Ledger listing for the inventory account.

You can use these printouts to review any of the entries made or re-enter journal entries if your data files on disk are destroyed.

EXPORTING INVENTORY DATA

As mentioned in previous chapters, all Simply Accounting reports can be exported to popular file formats. Please review previous chapters for complete instructions.

BACKING UP YOUR DATA FILES

At this point, return to the Simply Accounting - ODC window and backup your data files.

Call this backup:

Backup Filename: A:\odc\odc8h
Comment: Inventory Part H

Unless you want to continue with the next chapter, close the Simply Accounting odc window and exit the program.

Further Practice

To get further practice with the concepts you have learned in this chapter go to Chapter 15 and work through Section 9 of the National Supply Company.

CHAPTER 9

PAYROLL

CHAPTER 9

PAYROLL

OBJECTIVES

After working through this chapter you will be able to

1. Explain what the Payroll accounting ledger does.

2. Get ready to convert from a manual payroll system to the Simply Accounting Payroll Ledger.

3. Know what basic employee information must be entered into the Payroll Ledger prior to conversion.

4. Modify employee information once entered.

5. Enter historical employee data.

6. Display the information on the screen once it is entered.

7. Print a variety of reports.

8. Enter employee pay data after making the system READY.

9. Display and print detailed and summary reports of data entered into the Payroll Ledger.

10. Correct payroll data that was entered incorrectly.

THE PURPOSE OF THE PAYROLL LEDGER

In a computerized accounting system, the Payroll Ledger is one of the most important ledgers for two reasons. First, all employers are required to adhere to the Federal Income Tax Act and to the particular income tax act of the province in which the employee works regardless of where the head office of the company is located. Second, an employer must maintain accurate payroll records. Provinces have different sets of rules regarding employees and different rates for various withholding taxes. Withholding taxes are tax payments that the employee is required to make that are deducted by the employer. They include Federal Income Tax, Provincial Income Tax (in Quebec), Employment Insurance Contributions (EI), Canada Pension Plan (CPP), and Quebec Pension Plan (QPP in Quebec). The employer must then remit these payments to the Receiver General for Canada on behalf of the employee. For employers with employees in more than one province, it is difficult to keep up to date on regulations regarding employment and the rates for the various employee deductions and taxes.

The Payroll Ledger of Simply Accounting for Windows performs many functions, including:

1. Keeping track of each employee with regard to all aspects of payroll.

2. Calculating payroll and withholding taxes.

3. Reporting net pay calculations to the employee.

4. Reporting to the employee the amount of the remittance to be paid to the government regulatory agencies.

5. Preparing year-end reports such as T4s and payroll summaries.

The Payroll Ledger does NOT tell you:

1. Which benefits are taxable and which are not taxable.
2. How to complete government forms (with the exception of T4 slips).
3. When to remit funds to Revenue Canada.

Before actually preparing a payroll using the Simply Accounting system Payroll Ledger, you must become familiar with the regulations and tax rates of the federal government and the province where the business is located or has employees working. You can do this by reading:

1. Revenue Canada Payroll Deductions Tables.
2. Revenue Canada Employers' Guide to Payroll Deductions.
3. Source Deductions and Employers' Contributions Guide for the Province of Quebec.

PAYROLL ACCOUNTING

Payroll accounting is done at the end of each pay period. Pay periods are determined by how often employees are paid during the year as follows:

Times per year	Pay period
1	annual
2	bi-annual
10	monthly (sometimes used for teachers)
12	monthly
13	every four weeks
24	semi-monthly
26	bi-weekly
52	weekly

best choice

Each time the company prepares a payroll, the person in charge must go through a number of steps. These include:

1. Determining an employee's gross earnings for the pay period.
2. Determining an employee's deductions.
3. Calculating the employer's portion of payroll expenses for each employee.
4. Updating the employee's payroll records.
5. Creating the journal entries.
6. Preparing the cheques for each employee.
7. Remitting the funds withheld from the employee and the employer's portion of payroll expense to the appropriate government or benefit agency.

It is important to note that the employer is required by law to keep two sets of records for payroll; the employer's own and one for each employee. The record of each employee is then disclosed at the end of each calendar year to Revenue Canada and to the employee through the filing of a form called a "T4." These T4s are used to prepare the employee's personal income tax return.

DETERMINING EMPLOYEE GROSS EARNINGS PER PAY PERIOD

Note: The figures provided for the various calculations that follow do not necessarily reflect current rates and should only be considered as examples. For current amounts and percentages, consult the appropriate provincial or federal guides and/or an accountant.

The gross earnings of an employee for the pay period represents the total amount of compensation that is received before deductions. This can be a single amount as in the case of a salaried person or the sum total of a number of amounts such as hourly, overtime, and commission.

The most common components of gross earnings are as follows:

Regular Pay	xxx
Overtime Pay	xxx
Salary	xxx
Commission	xxx
Taxable Benefits — Cut	xxx
Vacation Pay Paid = Retain	xxx
Total Gross Earnings	xxx

REGULAR PAY

Regular pay is the amount paid per hour to an employee. For example, an employee may earn $12.00 per hour and work eight hours a day, five days a week. At the end of a two-week period, this person has worked 80 hours (10 working days, eight hours per day). To find the total regular pay you multiply the number of hours worked by the hourly rate:

80 hours x $12.00 per hour = $960.00 (regular pay)

Private- and public- sector employees may work only a certain number of regular hours in a pay period. This is set out in the labour code for the province or territory or for the federal government. A phone call to the Department of Labour or to the Employment Insurance Commission office will give you this information. Any hours in excess of regular hours are considered overtime hours.

OVERTIME PAY

An employee working in excess of the regular hours allowed will be entitled to overtime pay. Overtime pay rates are set up in the employee record and are usually the regular pay multiplied by 1.5 or "time and a half." For our employee with a $12.00 per hour regular pay rate, the overtime rate would be $18.00 ($12.00 x 1.5). This amount is set up in each individual's employee record (see defaults for payroll).

Once the number of hours have been determined for the employee, overtime pay is calculated on the same basis that regular pay is calculated — multiplying the overtime hours by the overtime rate.

4 overtime hours x $18.00 = $72.00

SALARY

Some employees are not paid by the hour, but instead get the same pay each month regardless of the total hours or days worked. These employees are paid a fixed amount called a salary. The amount of salary is most often stated as an annual amount, such as $18,000.00 per annum. To enter this employee's monthly salary you must first determine the pay period and then divide the annual amount by the number of pay periods. For example, if our employee is paid on a monthly basis or 12 times per year, the amount we would enter under the salary portion is

$18,000.00/12 = $1,500.00 per month.

It is possible for an employee to receive a salary and also receive an amount of overtime pay. In this case, you would have to keep track of each pay category and record it separately into the program.

COMMISSION

A commission is usually based on the amount sold by an employee or based on some other performance criteria. It is calculated by applying a rate of commission to a dollar value of performance (such as sales) or an amount of performance (such as piece-work). Commission amounts change each month and therefore must be calculated each time a payroll is prepared. The Simply Accounting system requires that the commission amount be entered as a total amount. For example, if a salesperson sold $20,000.00 worth of advertising during the month and has a commission rate of 20.0%, the amount that would be entered under commission would be

$20,000.00 x 20.0% = $4,000.00

TAXABLE BENEFITS

Some taxable benefits are non-cash items that the employee receives from the employer. These benefits become part of income from employment and therefore form part of taxable income. When calculating the amount of income tax to withhold from the employee, these benefits must be considered as part of the income. They will not be included as part of the paycheque that the employee will receive.

These taxable benefits must be calculated by the employer and entered as one lump sum into the Simply Accounting system. An example of a taxable benefit would be an automobile supplied by the employer or the employer's portion of payments to a provincial medical plan.

VACATION PAY

Every employee is entitled to a minimum number of days off per year for vacation. During this time the employee continues to receive regular pay. Employees who do not work regularly receive a percentage of their total pay as vacation pay. The basic rate is established by the Canada Labour Code and the various provincial labour codes. In unionized firms the minimum is set down in the collective agreement, but it must be at least as high as specified by federal and provincial legislation. Employees can elect to have their holiday pay treated in one of two ways:

1. Paid out with each paycheque.
2. Paid out at some later time coinciding with time taken off for a vacation.

The treatment of each method requires different accounting entries.

1. Vacation pay paid out with each paycheque.

    If the employee elects to have it paid out, you would calculate the gross earnings for the period and multiply that amount by the vacation pay rate applicable to that employee. If the salaried individual was entitled to two weeks holiday per year or its equivalent 4.0% per year, the holiday pay would equal:

    $18,000.00/12 = $1,500.00 per month x 4.0% = $60.00 (holiday pay)

    This amount would then form part of the gross earnings each month.

2. Vacation pay retained and paid out at some later date.

    If the employee elects to have holiday pay retained for some later date, then you must make an entry into the General Ledger to recognize that an expense was incurred when the employee was paid. The amount of the holiday pay will be the same as calculated above ($60.00) but the entry will be as follows:

    > Dr. Holiday Expense $60.00
    >
    >   Cr. Holiday Pay Payable $60.00

    This amount will then accumulate until the employee takes vacation or has it paid out for some other reason. When it is paid out, the total amount will be included in the gross pay for that particular period. The associated journal entry when it is paid out is not to debit expense but to debit holiday pay payable to clear out the amount expensed each month.

DETERMINING EMPLOYEE DEDUCTIONS

Once you have calculated the gross amount of pay for each employee, you must then determine deductions that must be withheld from employee pay. There are two types of deductions: statutory deductions, those that the employer is required by law to deduct; and other deductions, those determined by the employee or by some labour agreement between the employer and the employees.

The discussion that follows uses some 1992 federal rates for all statutory deductions. The version of Simply Accounting for Windows that you are using may have different rates. The three statutory deductions in Canada are: Canada Pension Plan contributions, Employment Insurance premiums, and income tax. These amounts must be withheld from each employee who qualifies for the deductions and remitted, along with the employer's portion, to Revenue Canada within a given time period. Late payments will result in fines and penalties as these amounts are not the property of the employer but of the employee in the trust of the employer.

CANADA PENSION PLAN

The Canada Pension Plan is a non-voluntary pension plan. An employer must deduct CPP premiums from an employee if the employee

1. is 18 years of age but not yet 70.
2. has not yet reached the maximum annual contribution limit (found in the Canada Pension Plan guide).
3. is taxed in any province or territory except the Province of Quebec, which administers its own pension plan separately.

An individual's required contribution is based on contributory earnings. These are determined by subtracting from the gross earnings for the pay period the corresponding basic exemption for that pay period. The basic exemption is based on an annual amount below which the employee is not entitled to contribute or qualify for the Canada Pension Plan. This amount is then divided by the number of pay periods being used to determine the basic amount for that period.

The basic exemption for 1992 is $3,200 and the rate is 2.4%. Assuming an individual had a salary of $18,000 per annum and the current pay period is monthly, the amount that must be deducted from this employee's pay (provided the employee has not reached the maximum payment for the year) would be

Gross pay	$18,000.00 / 12 periods =	$1,500.00
Minus basic amount $3,200.00 / 12		266.66
Contributory earnings		$1,233.34
Canada Pension Plan Rate 2.40%		
CPP contribution for the period		$29.60 ✓

The CPP Contribution is then added to the employee's year-to-date CPP contribution. If this year-to-date total exceeds the yearly maximum ($696.00 in 1992), the CPP contribution is reduced so that the total contribution from that employee does not exceed the yearly maximum.

For example, the following amounts would be deducted from the employee's gross amount based on the 1992 annual limit of $696.00 with a CPP contribution calculated to be $29.60 for the current pay period

Amount deducted to date:	$375.00 ✓	$681.00	$696.00
Withholding equals lesser of:			
Current amount	29.60	29.60	29.60
and amount necessary to			
bring total to	696.00	696.00	696.00
Current withholding	29.60	15.00	0.00

The amount withheld for Canada Pension Plan is kept by the employer and will be remitted to Revenue Canada as required. The employer's portion will also be included in the remittance. (See Remitting Withholding Taxes.)

EMPLOYMENT INSURANCE PREMIUMS

As with the Canada Pension Plan, the federal government requires an employee to contribute to the Employment Insurance Plan. This plan is supported by contributions of the employer and employee, and is specifically for the benefit of a worker who becomes unemployed and cannot find another job immediately. While looking for another job, the employee can draw from this fund based on earnings and contributions.

A person is eligible for Employment Insurance if

1. The person is employed in insurable employment.
2. The employee's gross hours worked for a pay period equal or exceed the minimum insurable hours for the corresponding pay period.
3. The employee's gross earnings from employment equal or exceed the minimum insurable earnings for the pay period.

In addition to the minimum limit, there is a maximum limit for which an employee can qualify. This maximum limit again depends on the payroll period in question.

INCOME TAXES

Each taxpayer in Canada is required to make installments on the estimated income taxes payable in the current year. The employer is required to withhold an estimated amount each pay period and remit the amount to Revenue Canada on behalf of the employee. The amount withheld covers both federal and provincial government assessments.

At the beginning of the payroll year, each employee is required to file a TD1 claim form with the employer. This claim form sets out the rate class applicable to the employee. Each employee may be in a different class, such as married or single, over age 65, or disabled depending on applicable deductions. The employer can obtain TD1 forms from Revenue Canada. Each employee on payroll must have a TD1 form filed with the employer if they wish to have the employer deduct income tax at a rate lower than the maximum.

Income tax is calculated on the amount subject to tax which is the amount remaining after registered pension plan contributions are subtracted from the gross amount. This amount is then compared to the Income Tax Withholding Table published by Revenue Canada. Once the amount is determined, it is deducted from the gross amount owing to the employee. This amount is then remitted to Revenue Canada along with the deductions for Canada Pension Plan and Employment Insurance Premiums.

Once the amounts that have to be withheld are determined, the journal for employee payroll will look like this:

Dr. Salaries expense	1,500.00	
Cr. Canada Pension Plan Premiums payable		29.60
Cr. Employment Insurance Premiums payable		45.00
Cr. Employee Income Tax payable — No employer contribution		235.00
Cr. Net payable to employee		1,190.40

In the above example, the employee would receive a check for $1,190.40 representing the net amount of pay after withholding the mandatory amounts.

REMITTING WITHHOLDING TAXES

An employer is required to remit employee tax deductions along with the premiums for Canada Pension Plan and Employment Insurance at regular intervals to Revenue Canada. For firms with fewer than 50 employees, it is monthly on the 15th of the following month. For larger firms, it is twice a month.

The employer must match the employee's contribution to the Canada Pension Plan. In the above journal entry, we see that the employee must pay $29.60 in premiums. This means that the amount that the employer must remit in total is $59.20; $29.60 withheld from the employee and $29.60 on behalf of the company.

The employer pays 1.4 times the amount deducted for each employee for Employment Insurance. Some large corporations, with a wage-loss replacement plan of their own, can pay less. Since only large corporations usually have such plans, it is not likely to apply to companies that use the Simply Accounting system. For the above employee, the employer would have to pay $45.00 x 1.4 = $63.00.

There is no additional contribution by the employer for the employee's income taxes.

The amount that the employer would remit is therefore:

Canada Pension Plan (employee portion)	29.60
Canada Pension Plan (employer portion)	29.60
Employment Insurance (employee portion)	45.00
Employment Insurance (employer portion)	63.00
Income tax	235.00
Total payable	402.20

So far we have recorded only the employee's portion of income tax withheld. We must make another entry to record the employer's portions for EI and CPP.

Dr. Canada Pension Plan expense	29.60	*Company Expense*
Dr. Employment Insurance expense	63.00	*Company*
Cr. Canada Pension		29.60
Cr. Employment Insurance payable		63.00

However, there is no need to make two separate entries. We could combine the two entries into one as follows:

Dr. Salaries expense	1,500.00	
Dr. Canada Pension Plan expense	29.60	
Dr. Employment Insurance	45.00	
Cr. Canada Pension Plan premiums payable		59.20
Cr. Employment Insurance premiums payable		108.00
Cr. Employee income tax payable		235.00
Cr. Net payable to employee		1,190.40

(handwritten: federal tax; 29.60 + 29.6; 45 + 63)

OTHER EMPLOYEE DEDUCTIONS

The employer may take other deductions on behalf of the union or the employee. Some common deductions are:

1. Registered pension plan contributions

2. Union dues

3. Medical plans

Some of these deductions may be partially paid by the employer. For example, many employees have part or all of their medical premium paid by the employer. The amount that the employee is responsible for would be withheld and remitted by the employer to the company providing the medical coverage. The employee usually pays the entire amount of union dues and registered pension plans.

Assume that the employee has a medical plan that costs $42.00 per month, with the employer paying half of the cost. In addition, the employee contributes $100.00 per month to a registered pension plan and another $27.00 per month to union dues. The net pay calculation for the employee would now resemble the following:

Salary		1,500.00
less: Canada Pension Plan premiums payable	29.60	
Employment Insurance premiums payable	45.00	
Employee income tax payable	235.00	
Employee medical premiums (_ x $42.00)	21.00	
Registered pension plan premiums	100.00	
Union dues	27.00	
		457.60
Net payable to employee		1,042.40

Now you must also change our journal entry to reflect the withholding of these amounts and the payable associated. To do this, add the lines in boldface to the journal entry. Notice that the amount of "net payable to employee" changed to reflect the amount withheld for the employee portions of medical and registered pension plan and union dues. Also note that a line for medical expense is added to reflect the employer's portion of the medical costs.

Dr. Salaries Expense	1,500.00	
Dr. Canada Pension Plan Expense	29.60	
Dr. Employment Insurance Expense	45.00	
Dr. Medical Expense	21.00	
Cr. Canada Pension Plan Premiums Payable		59.20
Cr. Employment Insurance Premiums Payable		108.00
Cr. Employee Income Tax Payable		235.00
Cr. Due to Medical Plan		42.00
Cr. Due to Registered Pension Plan		100.00
Cr. Union Dues Payable		27.00
Cr. Net Payable to Employee		1,042.40

GST PAYROLL DEDUCTIONS

If employees receive benefits that are subject to the GST the company must set up an account in the General Ledger called GST Payroll Deduction. A company car would be an example of a taxable benefit. If this is worth $100.00 per period, the GST charged on this amount would be $7.00. The employee's paycheque would show a deduction for this amount which would also be recorded in the GST Payroll Deduction account. GST for benefits provided to employees can be charged annually or per pay period.

OTHER COSTS TO EMPLOYERS

Some of the costs associated with payroll do not affect the employee at all. One example of this is Workers' Compensation payments. Most employers are required to contribute to the Workers' Compensation Plan on behalf of the employee. This is a provincial plan that covers workers who may get injured on the job.

Premiums for Workers' Compensation payments are calculated by multiplying the gross amount the employee earns times a rate that is assessed by the Workers' Compensation Board. In some provinces, the rate will also apply to taxable benefits. This rate is set by the Board based on the industry in which the person is employed and the past record of claims the company made against the plan. Each year, the rate is reviewed and may be revised up or down.

If you assume that for our company the rate is 3.2% of gross, then the amount of premium for Workers' Compensation will be

$1,500.00 x 3.2% = $48.00

(assuming that taxable benefits are not included). We must make the following entry in the books:

Dr. Workers' Compensation expense	$48.00	
Cr. Workers' Compensation payable		$48.00

Again we can incorporate this payment into the one large payroll entry.

Dr. Salaries expense	1,500.00	
Dr. Canada Pension Plan expense	29.60	
Dr. Employment Insurance expense	45.00	
Dr. Medical expense	21.00	
Dr. Workers' Compensation expense	48.00	
Cr. Canada Pension Plan payable		59.20
Cr. Employment Insurance premiums payable		108.00
Cr. Income Tax payable		235.00
Cr. Medical Payable		42.00
Cr. Pension Payable		100.00
Cr. Union Payable		27.00
Cr. Workers' Compensation payable		48.00
Cr. Bank (net payable to employee)		1,042.40

MAINTAINING EMPLOYEE RECORDS

As mentioned earlier in the chapter, not only must you keep track of the payroll transactions for the company, but the employer must also keep a record of all transactions by employee. This is called the "Employee Payroll Record." This information is necessary to allow the employer to prepare two reports for two different governmental bodies.

The first report is called a T4. A T4 is a form that is filed for each employee at the end of the calendar year. It reports to the government the amount of earnings that the employee had in the year and the amount withheld for the various deductions that were remitted on behalf of that employee. A typical T4 is shown in Figure 9.1.

Figure 9.1
T4 statement
form
(catch)

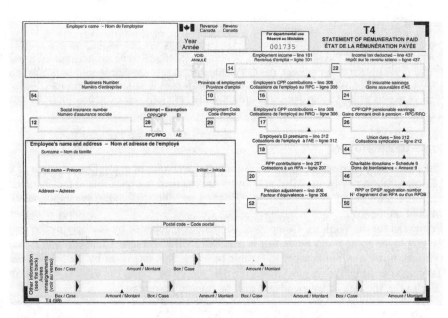

This report also indicates the amount of contributory earnings that the employee had during the year for the Canada Pension Plan and the amount of insurable earnings applicable to EI.

The second report is a "Record of Employment." The record of employment is filed when the employee terminates employment with the employer and is used to assess the level of employment insurance to which the employee is entitled. A record of employment must be filed within two weeks of the termination of employment.

EHT. *Employ health tax*

In addition to the above, the employee record also keeps track of the amount of holiday pay owing to the employee at any given time and the amount of advances paid to the employee. These amounts were discussed earlier in the chapter.

PAYROLL IN THE PROVINCE OF QUEBEC

Payroll accounting is somewhat different for employers in the province of Quebec. The Quebec government collects Quebec Pension Plan payments, provincial income tax, and payments for the regular provincial plans for Workers' Compensation (Commission de la Santé et de la Securité du Travail (CSST)) and health plan (QHIP).

The accounting entries for an employer in Quebec, therefore, add other expense and payable items to the Payroll journal entries. A typical journal entry for a Quebec employer may resemble the following:

Dr. Salaries Expense	1,500.00	
Dr. Quebec Pension Plan Expense	29.60	
Dr. Employment Insurance Expense	45.00	
Dr. Quebec Health Insurance Expense	21.00	
Dr. CSST Expense	48.00	
Cr. Quebec Pension Plan Premiums Payable		59.20
Cr. EI Payable		108.00
Cr. Employee Income Tax Payable - Federal		135.00
Cr. Employee Income Tax Payable - Quebec		100.00
Cr. Due to Quebec Health Insurance Plan		42.00
Cr. Due to Registered Pension Plan		100.00
Cr. Union Dues Payable		27.00
Cr. CSST Payable		48.00
Cr. Net Payable to Employee		1,042.40

COMPUTERIZING PAYROLL

At the beginning of August 2001, Overnight Delivery Company decided to computerize their payroll using the Simply Accounting system Payroll Ledger. ODC has two employees: both are full-time, but one receives a monthly salary, while the other is paid for the number of hours worked.

Practice Exercise 9.1

Enter the Simply Accounting for Windows program. Once prompted, select the ODC data set.

When prompted, accept 08/31/01 as the Using date. When prompted with the To-Do List window, please close this window.

ADDITIONS TO THE CHART OF ACCOUNTS

The first step is to decide which additional accounts are required in the chart of accounts and then add these to the General Ledger. The additional accounts and the account numbers for our tutorial case are listed in Figure 9.2.

Accounts to be added:

    1170 – Advances Receivable   Type = Group Account
                                          Account Class = Receivable

    2310 – Vacation Payable   Type = SubGroup Account
                                          Account Class = Payable

---

Figure 9.2   Accounts that must be added to the General Ledger or changed for payroll accounting

---

Note: For the tutorial in this book we will use only the accounts shown in Figure 9.2 because we are operating in British Columbia.

If you are using this tutorial in Ontario, you may want to add the following additional accounts to the ones listed in Figure 9.2. However, in Chapter 9 we will not make any entries to these other accounts.

Employer Health Tax   2462 - EHT Payable
                                        Type = SubGroup Account
                                        Accounts Class = Payable

Employer Health Expense   5710 - EHT Expense
                                            Type = SubGroup Account
                                        Account Class = Payroll Expense

If a company is operating in Quebec, as well as in other parts of Canada, the following accounts will have to be added to the ones shown in Figure 9.1:

Quebec Pension Plan Payable   2464 - QPP Payable
                                          Type = SubGroup Account
                                        Accounts Class = Payable

Quebec Income Tax Payable   2466 - QTAX Payable
                                            Type = SubGroup Account
                                        Accounts Class = Payable

CSST Payable   2468 - CSST Payable
                                          Type = SubGroup Account
                                        Accounts Class = Payable

Quebec Health Insurance Plan Payable   2470 - QHIP Payable
                                          Type = SubGroup Account
                                        Accounts Class = Payable

Quebec Health Insurance Plan Expense

5715 - QHIP Expense
Type = SubGroup Account
Accounts Class = Payroll Expense

Quebec Pension Plan Expense

5720 - QPP Expense
Type = SubGroup Account
Accounts Class = Payroll Expense

CSST Expense

5725 - CSST Expense
Type = SubGroup Account
Accounts Class = Payroll Expense

Practice Exercise 9.2

Add the accounts shown in Figure 9.2 to the chart of accounts. Use the type of account indicated. Once you have added the necessary accounts, continue with modifying the required accounts. Do NOT check the box for Suppress account.

Once you have added the required accounts, print out an updated chart of accounts. Then return to the Simply Accounting - ODC window (Figure 9.3).

INTEGRATING PAYROLL

Before you can go ahead and use the Payroll module, you must first integrate this module with the rest of Simply Accounting, (mainly with the General Ledger). You will also want to customize Simply Accounting for your particular types of payroll income and expenses.

Figure 9.3
Simply
Accounting –
ODC window

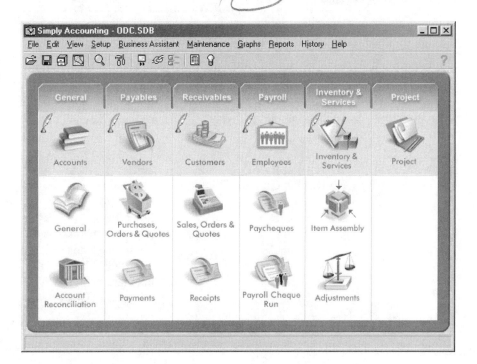

From within the Simply Accounting - ODC window (Figure 9.3), continue by

> Selecting the **Setup** menu.

From within the **Setup** menu, continue by

> Selecting the **Names** menu command.

Before continuing, we must first change the default deduction names to reflect the types of deduction that we will use with Overnight Delivery Company.

Figure 9.4
Payroll Names
window

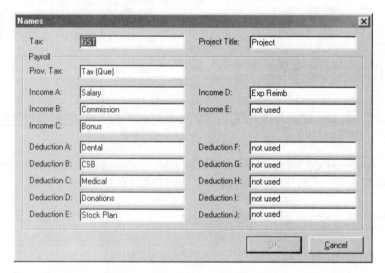

Continue from the Names window (Figure 9.4) by completing Practice Exercise 9.3.

Practice Exercise 9.3

Ensure that the payroll description names are as follows, (change any that do not match):

Tax:	GST
Project Tile:	Project
Income A:	Salary
Income B:	Commission
Income C:	Bonus
Deduction A:	Dental
Deduction B:	CSB
Deduction C:	Medical
Deduction D:	Donations
Deduction E:	Stock Plan
Deduction F:	not used <blank>
Deduction G:	not used <blank>
Deduction H:	not used <blank>
Deduction I:	not used <blank>
Deduction J:	not used <blank>

Once you have completed this exercise, close the Names window (Figure 9.4). You will then return to the Simply Accounting - ODC window (Figure 9.3).

The next step is to provide Simply Accounting with the applicable integration account information. Continue from the Simply Accounting - ODC window (Figure 9.3) by

Selecting the **Setup** menu.

Clicking on the **Linked Accounts** menu command.

Clicking on the **Payroll** menu command.

Figure 9.5
Payroll Linked
Accounts
window

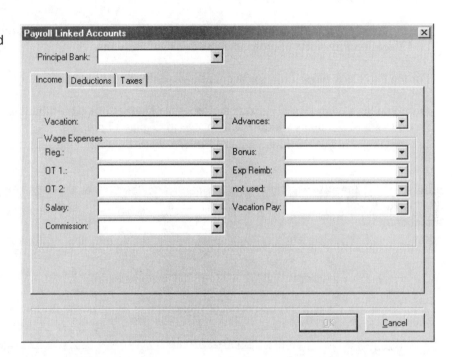

Within the Payroll Integration Accounts window, you can select from three different tabbed items. The **Income** item includes the following integration account prompts:

Bank	is used for the bank account against which payroll cheques are issued.
Vacation	is used as the liability account to record vacation payable to employees.
Advances	is used to record any payroll advances that have been issued to employees (owed back to the company).
Reg	is the payroll expense account for regular hours worked.
OT1 / OT2	is the expense account for overtime hours worked.
Salary	is the account for recording salary expense.
Commission	is used to record any commission expense.
Bonus	is used to record payroll bonuses.
Vacation Pay	is used to record vacation pay that has been paid out to employees.

Practice Exercise 9.4

Continue with the selection of the applicable General Ledger accounts for each prompt.

For the Bank account select account 1040 - Royal Bank.

For Vacation Pay Payable select account 2310-Vacation Payable. For Advances select account 1170-Advances Receivable.

For the **Reg / OT1 / OT2 / Salary / Commission / Bonus / Expense Reimbursement and Vacation Pay** select account 5640 Salaries and Benefits.

For the two blank payroll income accounts, leave these fields blank.

Once you have completed this exercise, select the **Deductions** tabbed button. Your Payroll Linked Accounts window will change to display Figure 9.6.

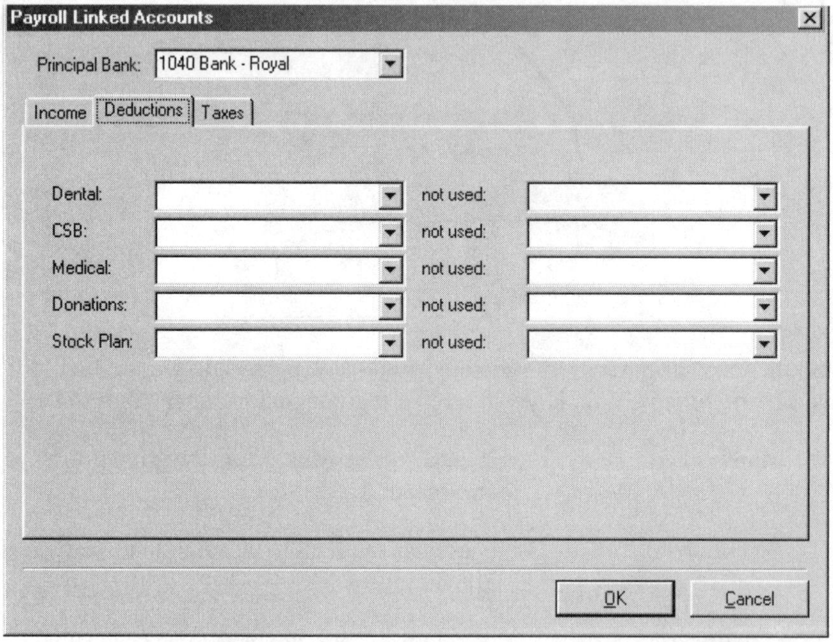

Figure 9.6
Payroll Linked
(Deductions)
window

Within the Payroll Linked (Deductions) window (Figure 9.6) you can now enter the integration accounts for the various payroll deductions. These accounts will be those that will be used to record the payable for each deduction.

Practice Exercise 9.5

Continue with the selection of the applicable payroll deduction accounts. For those unused deduction accounts, leave the relevant fields blank.

Once you have completed this exercise, continue by selecting the **Taxes** tabbed button.

The last part of the payroll integration is the selection of the applicable government tax payable and expense accounts as shown in Figure 9.7 and include the following:

Figure 9.7
Payroll Linked
Accounts
(Taxes) window

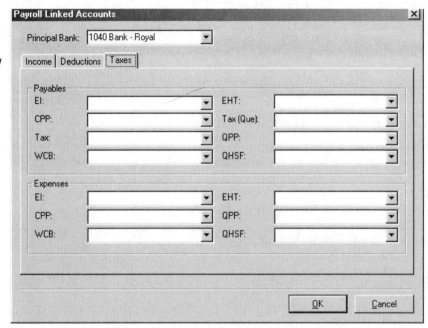

EI	is used for both the Employment Insurance payable and the employer's expense portion of the Employment Insurance premiums.
CPP	is used for both the Canada Pension Plan payable as well as the employer's portion of CPP.
Tax	is used to record the employee's income tax that will be payable to the Receiver General of Canada.
WCB	is used record both the Workers' Compensation Board payable and employer's expense.
EHT	is used for both the Ontario/Newfoundland Health Tax payable and employer's expense portion.
Tax (Que)	is used to record the Quebec provincial income tax that will be payable.
QPP	is to record both the Quebec Pension Plan payable and employer's expense portion.
QHSF	is used to record both the Quebec Health Services Fund payable and employer's expense portion.

Practice Exercise 9.6

Continue with the selection of the applicable payroll taxes integration accounts. These will include the **EI / CPP / Tax and WCB**. Leave all others blank.

Once you have completed this exercise, continue by either pressing ⌨Enter or clicking the **OK** button.

LISTING EMPLOYEE INFORMATION

To add employees to the system you must list your employees along with the required information about each. The list must include the items shown in Figure 9.8 and 9.9.

Figure 9.8   Personal Employee Information

Personal Information—Permanent
1.   Employee Name
2.   Street Address
3.   City
4.   Province
5.   Postal Code
6.   Phone Number
7.   Social Insurance Number
8.   Birth Date
9.   Province of Taxation
10. Number of Pay Periods per Year
11. Amount of Federal Claim (TD 1)
12. Amount of Quebec Claim
13. Rate of Workers' Compensation on Employee
14. Whether the employee is insurable
15. Employment Factor on employee
16. Whether vacation pay is retained and paid at a later date or paid each month
17. Rate of Vacation Pay
18. Regular Wage Rate
19. Overtime Wage Rate
20. Rate of Salary
21. Additional Federal Tax
22. Hire Date
23. Default Dental Plan Contribution (specific to company)
24. Default CSB (Canada Savings Bond)
25. Default Medical Plan Premiums (specific to company)
26. Default Employee donation (specific to company)
27. Default Employee stock plan amount (specific to company)
28. Extra Income Tax

Figure 9.9   Items that must be entered as historical data

Year-to-Date Information (if conversion not made on January 1)
1.   Regular Pay paid to date
2.   Overtime Pay paid to date
3.   Salary paid to date
4.   Commission paid to date
5.   Taxable Benefits to date
6.   Vacation Pay paid to date
7.   EI
8.   CPP
9.   QPP
10.   Federal Tax
11.   Quebec Tax
12.   Dental Plan
13.   CSB
14.   Medical Plan
15.   Stock Plan
16.   Advance owed
17.   Vacation Pay owed

Before you can actually use the Payroll journal to maintain your payroll the above information must be entered into the Simply Accounting Employee/Payroll Ledger. Since this information is required to calculate each employee's pay, it is important that the data entered is accurate.

BEGINNING THE PAYROLL CONVERSION

With the above information on hand, you are ready to begin the Payroll conversion.

Continue from the Simply Accounting - ODC window (Figure 9.3) by clicking on the Employee icon.

Figure 9.10
Employees
window

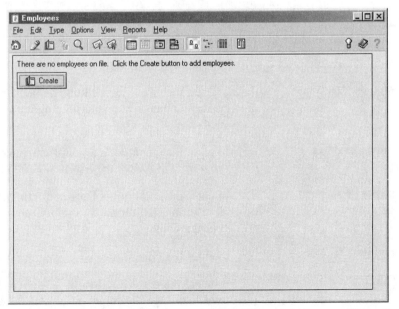

You will be greeted with a blank window. After you add employees, each one will be displayed by an icon.

To add employees,

Click on the **Create** icon.

Figure 9.11
Payroll Ledger
(Personal)
window

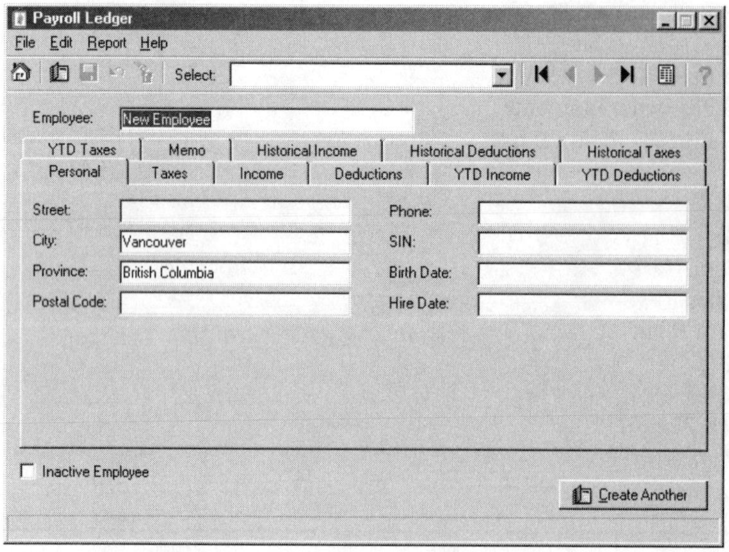

ENTERING HISTORICAL EMPLOYEE INFORMATION INTO THE PAYROLL LEDGER

Within the Payroll Ledger window (Figure 9.11) you will notice that this window has several tabbed buttons. We will start by entering the following employee information.

Jones, Graham ⌊Tab⌋	as the **Employee's** name.
123 Ogden Street ⌊Tab⌋	as the **Street** address.
Burnaby ⌊Tab⌋	as the **City**.
⌊Tab⌋	to accept the default **Province** (British Columbia).
v4n5n6 ⌊Tab⌋	as the **Postal Code**. Simply Accounting will automatically format this entry.
6046694568 ⌊Tab⌋	to enter the employee's **Phone** number. You can enter the phone number as shown. The program will format it as (604) 669-4568.
000000000 ⌊Tab⌋	to enter the employee's **Social Insurance Number**. The program will format the SIN as 000 000 000.
062051 ⌊Tab⌋	to enter the employee's **Date of Birth**. Simply Accounting will format your entry (providing you enter a six-digit date).
072399 ⌊Tab⌋	to enter the **Hire Date**.
⌊Tab⌋	to leave the employee **Status** as *Active*. This field is used to change the employee's payroll status for *Inactive* employee's.

Continue from within the Payroll Ledger (Personal) window by

Selecting the **Income** tabbed button.

Figure 9.12
Payroll Ledger
(Income)
window

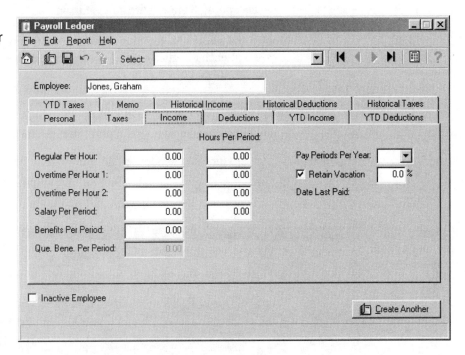

Continue from within the Payroll Ledger (Income) window (Figure 9.12) by pressing

Tab (several times)	to move to the **Regular Per Hour** dollar amount.
Tab	to skip past the **Regular Per Hour** (dollar amount).
Tab	to skip the **Regular Per Hour** (Hours per period). This is required in accordance with eligibility of employment insurance.
Tab	to skip the **Overtime Per Hour 1** (dollar amount).
Tab	to skip the **Overtime Per Hour 1** (Hours Per Period).
Tab	to skip the **Overtime Per Hour 2** (dollar amount).
Tab	to skip the **Overtime Per Hour 2** (Hours Per Period).
1800.00 Tab	to enter the **Salary Per Period**.
160.00 Tab	to enter the **Salary Per Period** (Hours per period).
30.50 Tab	to enter the **Benefits Per Period**. This amount is the taxable portion of benefits provided to the employee. Please refer to your benefit administrator for your employee's portion.

12 [Tab] to enter the number of **Pay Periods Per Year**. This means that this employee will receive a paycheque (with deductions) 12 times each year.

[Tab] to accept the **Retain Vacation**. This will allow Simply Accounting to accrue the vacation payable for this employee. If you were to unselect this option, the vacation pay would be paid on each cheque, instead of being accrued and paid when the employee goes on vacation.

4.0 [Tab] to enter the vacation rate. This will calculate 4.0% of each cheque as a vacation accrual. This will in turn allow the employee to take two weeks paid vacation each year.

Continue from within the Payroll Ledger (Income) window by

Selecting the **Deductions** tabbed button.

Figure 9.13
Payroll Ledger
(Deductions)
window

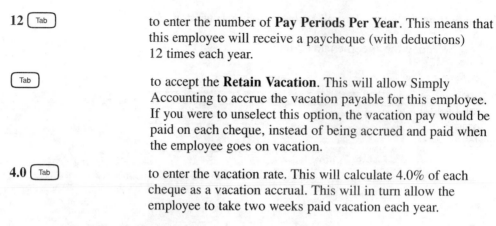
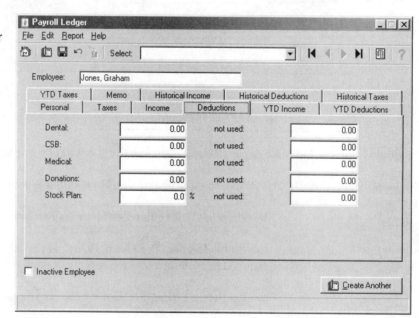

Continue from within the Payroll Ledger (Deductions) window by pressing

[Tab] (several times) to move to the default **Dental** deduction.

45.00 [Tab] to enter the default **Dental** deduction that will be taken off each paycheque.

25.00 [Tab] to enter the default **CSB** (Canada Savings Bond) deduction.

35.50 [Tab] to enter the default **Medical** deduction.

10.00 [Tab] to enter the default **Donations** deduction.

2.50 [Tab] to enter the default **Stock Plan** percentage. This percentage (can be changed to amount within the Settings screen) is a percentage of gross payroll.

Continue from within the Payroll Ledger (Deductions) window by

Selecting the **Taxes** tabbed button.

Figure 9.14
Payroll Ledger
(Taxes) window

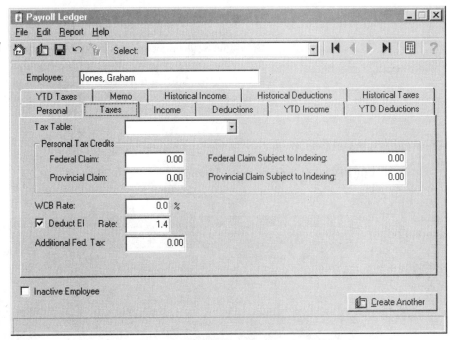

Continue from within the Payroll Ledger (Taxes) window (Figure 9.14) by pressing

Tab (two times)	to move to the **Tax Table** field.
B Tab	to select *British Columbia* as the **Tax Table**. This lets Simply Accounting know which provincial tax table to use for payroll tax calculations.

> **HINT: SELECTING THE APPROPRIATE PROVINCE OF EMPLOYMENT**
>
> *The province of employment is normally the province in which the employee is based even though he or she may work in another province for a period of time.*

6960.00 Tab	to enter the **Federal Claim.** This is the figure that has been calculated from the TD1 form that has been completed by each employee.
6960.00 Tab	to enter the Federal Claim subject to indexing.
8000.00 Tab	to enter the Provincial Claim.
8000.000 Tab	to enter the Provincial Claim subject to indexing.
Provincial indexing	8000.00 8000.00
3.2 Tab	to enter the **WCB Rate**. This is the percentage of gross payroll that the employer will have to remit for WCB (Workers' Compensation Board) premiums.

Tab   to accept the deduction of **EI**. This is the normal practice for most employee's with the exception of majority shareholder operators (more than 40.0%).

Tab   to accept the default **EI** rate (1.4). This is the EI factor for every employee-deducted dollar of EI. One dollar of employee EI equals $1.40 employer portion.

Tab   to accept the **Additional Federal Tax** amount (0.00). This field can be used if your employee requests additional income tax to be deducted from each paycheque.

Continue from within the Payroll Ledger (Taxes) window by

      Selecting the **YTD Income** tabbed button.

Figure 9.15
Payroll Ledger
(YTD Income)
window

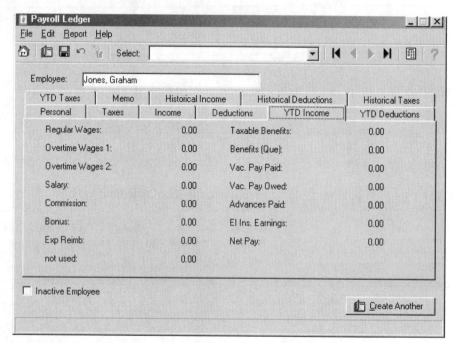

Within the Payroll Ledger (YTD Income) window (Figure 9.15) you can view the current year-to-date payroll income, along with year-to-date deductions within the YTD deduction tabbed window and year-to-date taxes within the YTD Taxes tabbed window.

All of these three tabbed windows will currently display zero balances as we have not processed any current payroll.

Continue within the Payroll Ledger (YTD Income) by

      Selecting the **Memo** tabbed button.

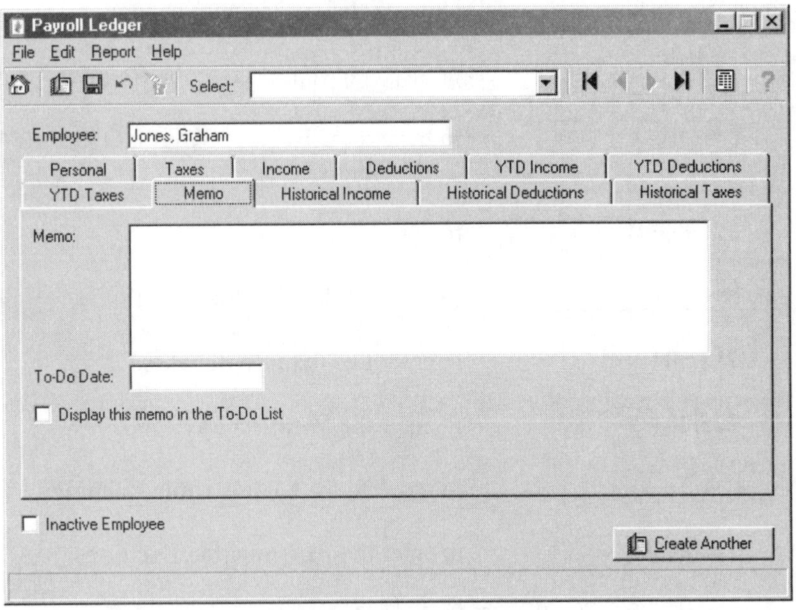

Figure 9.16
Payroll Ledger
(Memo) window

Within the Payroll Ledger (Memo) window (Figure 9.16) you can enter a **Memo** note along with the **To-Do Date** and option to display within the To-Do List.

Continue from within the Payroll Ledger (Memo) window by

Selecting the **Historical Income** tabbed button.

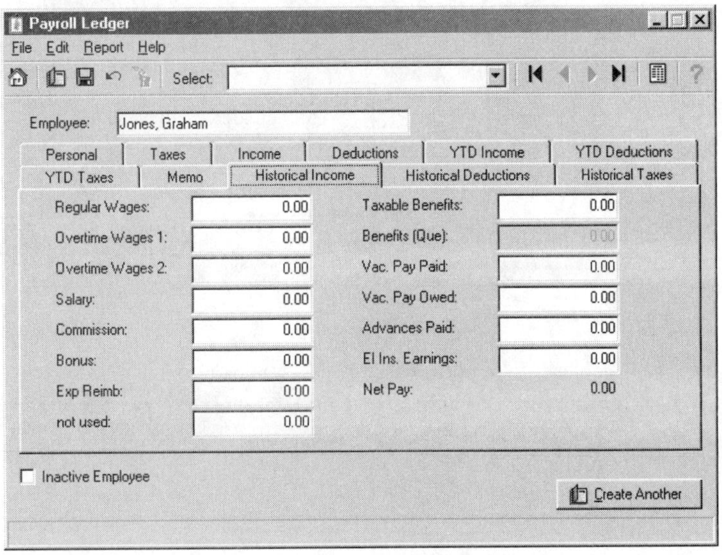

Figure 9.17
Payroll Ledger
(History
Income) window

Within the Payroll Ledger (History) window (Figure 9.17), continue entering the payroll history which represents the year-to-date figures up to the conversion date to Simply Accounting.

Continue from within the Payroll Ledger (History Income) window by pressing

[Tab]	until you have moved to the **Regular Wages** field.
[Tab] [Tab] [Tab]	to bypass the **Regular Wages**, **Overtime Wages** 1/2 and move to the **Salary**.
12600.00 [Tab]	to enter the **Salary**.
[Tab] [Tab] [Tab] [Tab]	to move to the **Taxable Benefits**.
213.50 [Tab]	to enter the **Taxable Benefits**.
225.00 [Tab]	to enter the **Vacation Pay Paid**.
[Tab] [Tab]	to move to the **EI Insurable Earnings**.
12600.00 [Tab]	to enter the **EI Insurable Earnings**.

Continue from within the Payroll Ledger (History Income) window by

Selecting the **History Deductions** tabbed button.

Figure 9.18
Payroll Ledger
(History
Deductions)
window

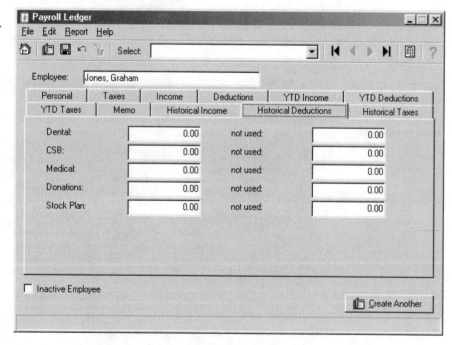

Continue from within the Payroll Ledger (History Deductions) window (Figure 9.18) by pressing

[Tab]	until you have moved to the **Dental** field.
315.00 [Tab]	to enter the dental deduction history.
175.00 [Tab]	to enter the **CSB** amount.

248.50 (Tab)   to enter the **Medical** amount.

70.00 (Tab)   to enter the **Donations** amount.

315.00 (Tab)   to enter the **Stock Plan** amount.

Continue from within the Payroll Ledger (History Deductions) window by

Selecting the **Historical Taxes** tabbed button.

Continue from within the Payroll Ledger (History Taxes) window by pressing

(Tab)   until you move to the **Income Tax** field.

1050.00 (Tab)   to enter the **Income Tax** deduction amount.

378.00 (Tab)   to enter the **EI** premiums.

257.00 (Tab)   to enter the **CPP** premiums.

You have now completed the entry of the relevant payroll information for Graham Jones, continue by

Clicking the **Create Another** button.

Practice Exercise 9.7

Continue with the entry of the following employees as shown in Figure 9.19. Once you have completed this exercise, close the Payroll ledger, selecting **No** to complete the entry of Payroll History. You will then return to the Employee window (Figure 9.10).

Figure 9.19   Employee Information

	Firguson, Adam	Bea, Desi
Employee Name	Firguson, Adam	Bea, Desi
Street Address	4558 Lange St.	1785 Columbia Valley
City	Vancouver	Cultus Lake
Province	British Columbia	British Columbia
Postal Code	v8n4n3	v7c3m4
Phone Number	6047721234	6047924435
Social Insurance #	000000000	000000000
Birth Date	01/15/61	09/16/1968
Hired Date	08/01/01	08/01/01
Status	Active	Active
Regular per Hour	7.50	9.00
Regular Hours	80.00	80.00
Overtime 1 (Rate)	11.25	13.50
Overtime 1 (Hours)	0.00	0.00
Overtime 2 (Rate)	15.00	18.00
Overtime 2 (Hours)	0.00	0.00
Salary per period	0.00	0.00
Salary Hours	0.00	0.00
Benefits per Period	35.50	22.40
Periods per year	12	12
Retain Vacation	Yes (Checked)	Yes (Checked)
Vacation rate	4.0	4.0
Dental deduction	35.50	35.50
CSB deduction	25.00	30.00
Medical deduction	32.50	32.50
Donations deduction	10.00	15.00
Stock plan	2.5	2.5
Tax Table	British Columbia	British Columbia
Federal Claim	6960.00	6960.00
Federal Claim Indexing	6960.00	6960.00
Provincial Claim	8000.00	8000.00
Provincial Indexing	8000.00	8000.00
WCB	3.2	3.2
EI Insure?	Yes (Checked)	Yes (Checked)
EI Rate	1.4	1.4
Extra Federal Tax	20.00	0.00

MODIFYING EMPLOYEE INFORMATION

If, after entering the payroll record, you wish to change some of the information, such as the address, phone number or additional federal tax, for example, you can do this by first locating the particular employee's record and then modifying it.

Change the phone number of employee Adam Firguson, to 604-772-1244. Continue by

Selecting either the **Find** icon or the **Edit** menu followed by the **Find** menu command.

Continue from within the **Find** Employee window by

Clicking on **Firguson, Adam** followed by selecting the **Find** button.

or

Double-clicking on **Firguson, Adam**.

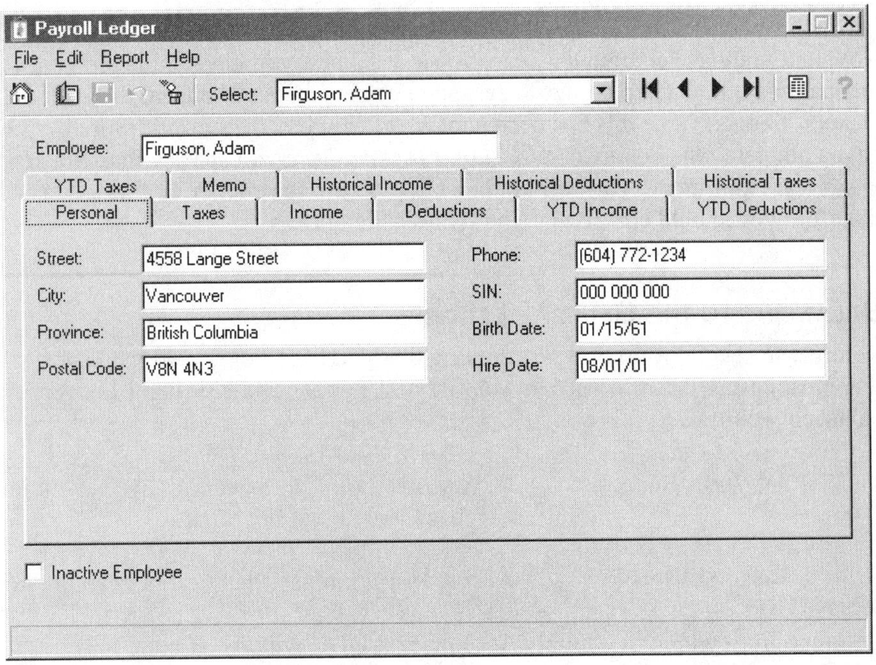

Figure 9.20
Payroll Ledger
(edit) window

In the Payroll Ledger (edit) window (Figure 9.20) you will notice that there is no **Save** or **Create** button. However, you can save any changes in any of the following ways:

Close the current window.

Select a new employee's record from either the pull down list, forward or reverse buttons or the **Edit**, **Find** menu commands.

Practice Exercise 9.8

Continue with the editing of the phone number of employee Adam Firguson, to 604-772-1244. Once you have completed this exercise, save this change by closing the Payroll Ledger window. You can also close the Employee window, (Figure 9.10) to return to the Simply Accounting - ODC window (Figure 9.3).

Simply Accounting will prompt you to confirm if you have completed the historical entry of employee data. Select **No** to this option.

BACKING UP YOUR DATA FILES

At this point, return to the Simply Accounting - ODC window and continue with the backup function.

Call this backup:

Backup Filename: A:\odc\ODC9A
Comment: Payroll Part a

CHANGING FROM HISTORICAL TO CURRENT/READY MODE

Now that you have entered the year-to-date balances, you have completed the conversion from a manual to a computerized payroll system. The next step will ensure that you will balance to the General Ledger. Once this has been confirmed, you can then inform Simply Accounting that you have completed the historical data entry process. Once you specify that you are finished in the Historical entry mode, you will not be able to return to re-enter or correct the historical figures, therefore you should ensure that your entries are correct.

BALANCING TO THE GENERAL LEDGER.

Before you specify to Simply Accounting that you have completed the historical entry process, you must ensure that you balance your Payroll Ledger to the General Ledger. The accounts to be balanced would be as follows:

Advances Receivable	Money owed from by your employees with relation to payroll advances issued, but not repaid.
Vacation Payable	Accrued vacation pay that has not been previously paid out.

Continue from within the Simply Accounting - ODC window (Figure 9.3) by

> Selecting the **Reports** menu.
>
> Selecting the **Payroll** menu command.
>
> Selecting the **Employee** submenu command.

Figure 9.21
Employee
Report Options
window

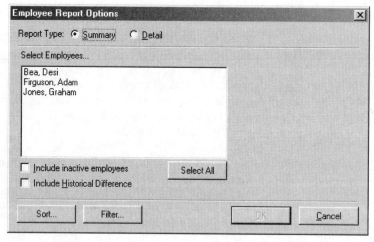

Continue from within the Employee Report Options window (Figure 9.21) by

> Clicking the **Select All** button.
>
> Select the **Summary** report option (default).
>
> Select to **Include Historical Difference** option.
>
> Clicking the **OK** button.

Figure 9.22
Employee
Summary report
window

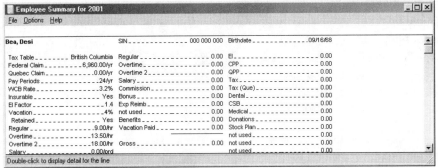

If you scroll down the Employee Summary window (using either your mouse or keyboard) you will notice that Simply Accounting will confirm that the Employee history is balanced (Figure 9.22).

Continue from within the Employee Summary report window (Figure 9.22) by

> Closing the Employee Summary report window.

CHANGING FROM HISTORICAL TO CURRENT/READY MODE

As you have entered and balanced all historical data (for all modules) you can continue with changing out of historical mode (to current mode).

Continue from within the Simply Accounting - ODC window (Figure 9.3) by

> Selecting the **History** menu.

> Selecting the **Finish Entering History** option.

Figure 9.23
Changing from
Historical -
Confirmation
window

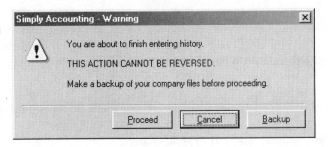

Simply Accounting will now ask you to confirm this action (Figure 9.23). Continue from within this window by

> Clicking on the **Proceed** button.

Figure 9.24
Simply
Accounting –
ODC window

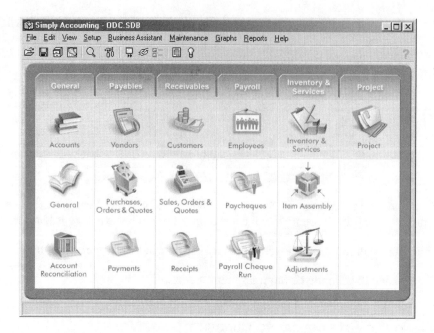

You will then return to the Simply Accounting - ODC window (Figure 9.24). You will notice that the historical symbol has been removed from the payroll module.

ENTERING PAYROLL JOURNAL ENTRIES

We will now continue entering current payroll transactions into the Payroll journal. Simply Accounting allows two different methods for entering/generating your payroll run:

Manual Entry

        will allow you to enter your payroll run by entering each employee's pay-cheque. This option will allow you to change the default deductions (if applicable). You will also be able to handle employee advances through the manual entry module.

Automatic Payroll

        will allow a quick spreadsheet style of payroll entry. This provides a simply way of entering a payroll run (range of employee's payroll).

USING THE MANUAL ENTRY (PAYCHEQUES) MODULE

For the greatest flexibility, you will use the manual entry (Paycheques module). This will allow you to change default deductions as well as handle advances.

Continue from the Simply Accounting - ODC window (Figure 9.24) by

        Clicking on the Paycheques icon.

Figure 9.25
Payroll Journal
window with no
entries

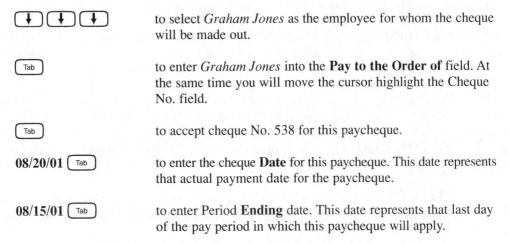

Press

↓ ↓ ↓	to select *Graham Jones* as the employee for whom the cheque will be made out.
Tab	to enter *Graham Jones* into the **Pay to the Order of** field. At the same time you will move the cursor highlight the Cheque No. field.
Tab	to accept cheque No. 538 for this paycheque.
08/20/01 Tab	to enter the cheque **Date** for this paycheque. This date represents that actual payment date for the paycheque.
08/15/01 Tab	to enter Period **Ending** date. This date represents that last day of the pay period in which this paycheque will apply.

The period ending date can be different from the cheque date, as the period ending date is the last day of the pay period. Your business may have a "cut-off" period which means that the pay period ends on a particular date and several days later the actual paycheques are generated. This allows time for the payroll staff to prepare the paycheques. For example, you might be disbursing payroll cheques for the payroll period from August 01, 2001 to August 15, 2001, therefore the period ending date would be August 15, 2001. However, you may not issue the paycheque until the 20th of August, 2001, (which would be the cheque date).

Figure 9.26
Payroll Journal
Income (default)
window

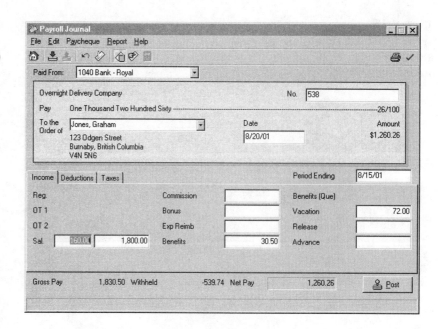

As shown in Figure 9.26, Simply Accounting has retrieved the default paycheque data for Graham Jones. This includes the number of salary hours, salary payment, benefits, and vacation pay accrual. Simply Accounting also allows the follow fields to be entered (if applicable):

Reg (Hours)
the number of regular payroll hours that have been worked, (does not display for Graham Jones as a regular hourly rate of pay was not entered within the Payroll ledger).

Reg (Payment)
is calculated by the number of regular hours times the rate of pay entered within the Payroll Ledger, (Figure 9.12).

OT1 / OT2 (Hours)
represents that number of overtime hours for both overtime 1 and overtime 2 pay scales.

OT1 / OT2 (Payment)
are calculated by the number of OT1 / OT2 hours times the OT1 / OT2 rate of pay as entered within the Payroll Ledger, (Figure 9.12).

Commission
allows you to enter or accept (if defaulted) an appropriate commission.

Bonus
allows you to enter or accept (if defaulted) an appropriate bonus.

Benefits
allows you to enter or accept (if defaulted) an appropriate benefits amounts. Benefits will not increase the amount of pay that the employee will receive, but will instead increase the taxable gross pay. This amount is then used to determine the appropriate Income Tax, EI, and CPP as well as other payroll taxes.

Vacation   will calculate the appropriate vacation pay based on the vacation
                           percentage that was entered within the Payroll Ledger,
                           (Figure 9.12).

Release   allows you to specify a release of holiday pay. This is completed
                           when an employee goes on holidays (and you have selected to
                           retain vacation pay). In this case, you would not issue a regular
                           paycheque (salary or hours worked), but instead release an
                           equivalent holiday pay amount. This field will also display a
                           figure (equivalent to the above vacation amount) if you have
                           selected not to retain vacation pay, (thus pay it to the employee
                           on each paycheque).

Advance   allows you to enter an appropriate payroll advance. This
                           advance may be a mid-month payroll advance (such as
                           Graham Jones who is paid monthly) or an emergency payroll
                           advance that your employee has asked for. Either way, Simply
                           Accounting will prompt you to recover this payroll advance
                           the next time you issue a paycheque, by displaying the total
                           advanced as a negative figure (as to recover).

Continue from within the Payroll Journal (Income) window (Figure 9.24) by

Selecting the **Deductions** tabbed button.

Figure 9.27
Payroll Journal
(Deductions)
window

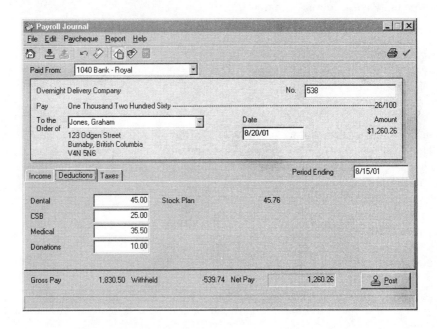

Within the Payroll Journal (Deductions) window (Figure 9.27) you are able to modify the default
deductions as specified within the Payroll Ledger (note Figure 9.13).

Continue from within the Payroll Journal (Deductions) window (Figure 9.26) by

Selecting the **Taxes** tabbed button.

Figure 9.28
Payroll Journal
(Taxes) window

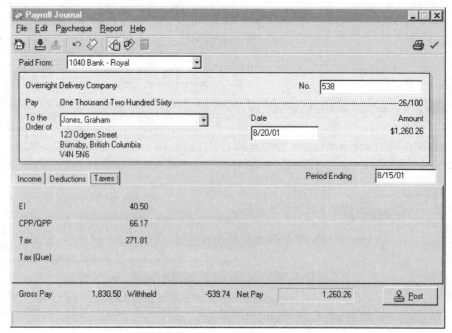

You will notice that within the Payroll Journal (Taxes) window (Figure 9.28) you are not able to modify the individual payroll tax amounts. This is because the paycheque is currently in the automatic payroll calculation module. This can be changed by selecting the following icon's within the Payroll Journal window:

Figure 9.29
Manual
Calculation icon

Once you have selected the **Manual Calculation** icon (Figure 9.29), you can override the default calculated payroll tax figures. Alternatively, you can select the **Recalculate Taxes** icon (Figure 9.30). This will allow Simply Accounting to insert the calculated EI, CPP/QPP, and income taxes amounts.

Figure 9.30
Recalculate
Taxes icon

If you want to return to the Automatic calculation mode, select the **Automatic Calculation** icon (Figure 9.31).

Figure 9.31
Automatic
Calculation icon

ISSUING A PAYROLL ADVANCE

From time to time your employee may request a payroll advance, or you may pay your employees monthly with a mid-month payroll advance. In either case, Simply Accounting allows for the entry of payroll advances. To demonstrate this feature, continue from within the Payroll Journal (Taxes) window (Figure 9.28) by

> Selecting the **Income** tabbed button.

You will then return the Payroll Journal (Income) window (Figure 9.26).

A payroll advance is not a regular paycheque but an advance that will not be subject to deductions or payroll taxes. Basically, you have extended a loan or advance to your employee who will repay this advance through a future deduction from pay. For a monthly-paid employee who receives a mid-month advance, you will first issue an advance (with no deductions and taxes) and at the end of the month, the employee will receive their monthly paycheque (less deduction and taxes) along with a deduction for the previous issued payroll advance.

Continue from within the Payroll Journal (Income) window (Figure 9.26) by

> Removing the **Salary** hours, **Salary Payment**, **Benefits,** and **Vacation** amounts. Your **Gross Pay** should now display *0.00*.

> Within the **Advance** field, insert an amount of *625.00*.

> Continue by switching to the **Deductions** tabbed area and removing all deduction amounts.

Your net payroll summary should display **Gross Pay** as *0.00*, **Deductions** as *0.00* and **Net Pay** as *625.00*. Continue by

> Selecting the **Report** menu.

> Selecting the **Display Payroll Journal Entry** menu option.

Figure 9.32
Payroll Journal
Entry (Advance)

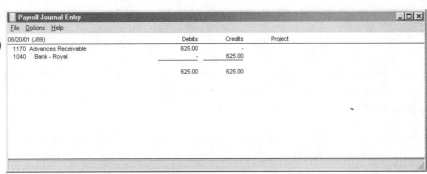

Within the Payroll Journal Entry (Advance) window (Figure 9.32) you will notice that Simply Accounting has made an entry for a payroll advance in the amount of $625.00. Continue from within this window by

> Closing the Payroll Journal Entry window.

STORING RECURRING PAYROLL ENTRIES

For salaried employees it is recommended that you use the recurring entry feature which will prevent you from having to re-enter the advance paycheque entry each mid-month. You will instead, retrieve the recurring entry and post the latest copy.

Continue from within the Payroll Journal window (Figure 9.26) by

Clicking the **Store Recurring Entry** icon.

Figure 9.33
Store Recurring
Transactions
window

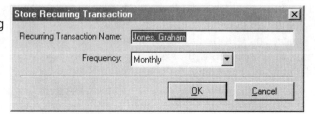

Continue from within the Store Recurring Transaction window by entering

Jones, Graham (Advance) [Tab]   to enter the **Recurring Transaction Name**.

[Tab]   to confirm a *Monthly* **Frequency**.

[Tab]   to accept the recurring entry.

You will then return to the Payroll Journal window. Continue by
Posting the payroll advance for Graham Jones ([Alt] + [P] or clicking on the **Post** icon).

IMPORTANT NOTE: *PAYROLL FORMULA ERROR MESSAGE*

*Simply Accounting may display a warning message about the payroll formulas not being correct. This message will be displayed because the payroll formulas used by your Simply Accounting program are out of date based on the current dates you are using while working through this book. Continue by selecting the **Yes** button.*

Keep in mind that if your Simply Accounting program uses an updated version of the payroll formula then the figures shown in the screen shots in this book may or may not match the figures you get on your screen. Continue keeping in mind that all future reports will be slightly different from the reports shown in this book.

However if you receive this message when preparing the payroll for your company's employees you should immediately contact ACCPAC International for a payroll update.

Practice Exercise 9.9

Continue with the entry (and posting) of the following paycheques with a cheque date of 08/20/01 and a pay period ending 08/15/01:

Bea, Desi   Regular Hours: 80
                      Overtime 1: 2.50
                      Overtime 2: 1.50

Firguson, Adam   Regular Hours: 80

Once you have completed this exercise, remain within the Payroll Journal window.

MAINTAINING ADVANCES

In the previous section, we issued a payroll advance to Graham Jones. We are now at the end of August 2001, and we will continue with the monthly paycheque issue for Graham Jones. We will also want to re-coup that previously issued advance.

Continue from within the Payroll Journal window by

Selecting *Jones, Graham* as the **Pay to the Order of**.

Accept the default cheque **Number**.

Enter **08/31/01** as the paycheque **Date**.

Enter **08/31/01** as the **Period Ending Date**.

Continue within the Payroll Journal by

[Tab] until you reach the **Advance** field.

Figure 9.34
Payroll Journal
(Advance
re-coup)
window

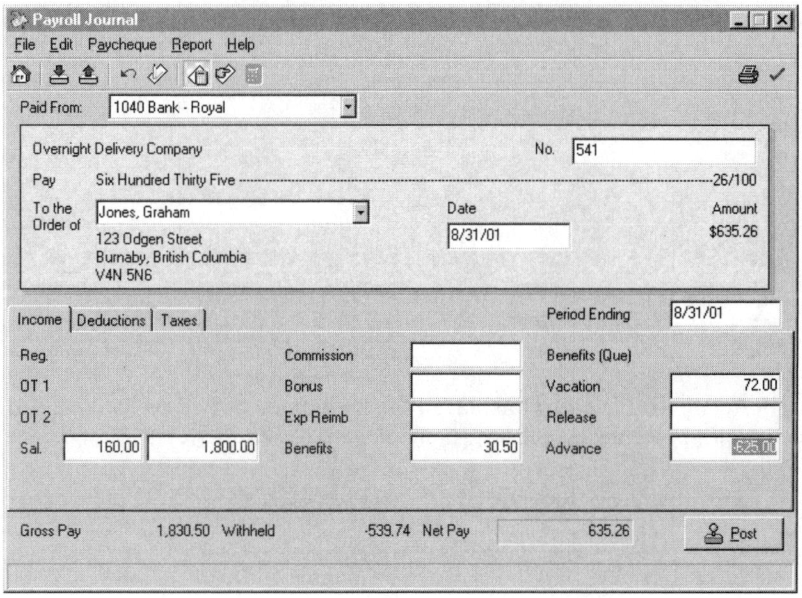

You will notice that Simply Accounting for Windows has displayed a negative 625.00 as the suggested advance to be recovered (Figure 9.34). This will prevent you from accidentally forgetting a previously issued advance amount.

Continue by pressing

> Tab   to accept the default 625.00 advance amount.
>
> Alt + P   to **Post** the month-end entry.

CORRECTING PAYROLL MISTAKES

Within the Simply Accounting for Windows Payroll Journal window, you have the option of retrieving a previously posted paycheque and modifying that paycheque. Simply Accounting will then make two entries:

> First entry to remove the previous (incorrect) paycheque.
>
> Second entry to post the correct paycheque (modified).

To the end user, it simply looks like you have been able to modify the paycheque however Simply Accounting for Windows ensures that a proper audit trail of the modified entry is maintained.

In order to demonstrate the modification of a paycheque, we have been notified that Graham Jones' paycheque should have included a bonus of $150.

Continue from within the Payroll Journal window by

> Selecting the ⬗ icon.

Figure 9.35
Select Entry to
Adjust window

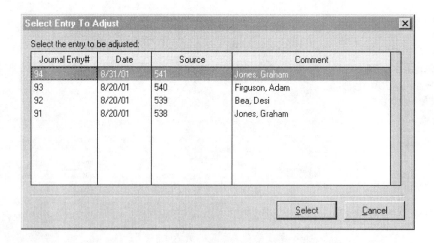

Simply Accounting has now displayed the previously posted paycheque, (to allow you to select the appropriate invoice to adjust) (Figure 9.35). Continue by

> Clicking the **Select** button to select the August 31, 2001 paycheque for *Jones, Graham.*

Figure 9.36
Advisor window

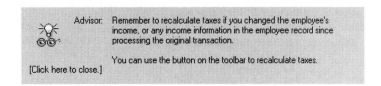

Continue from within the Advisor window (Figure 9.36) by

Clicking the **Click Here to Close** area within this window.

Figure 9.37
Adjust Pay-
cheque window

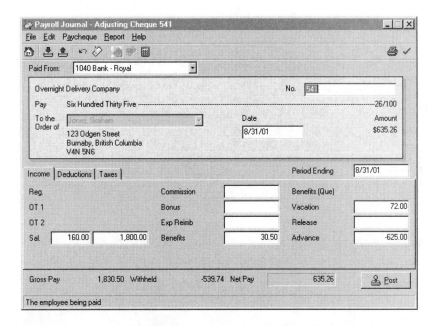

Simply Accounting will allow you to adjust any part of the Graham Jones' paycheque (Figure 9.37) with the exception of the employee name.

Continue by

Entering a bonus of *$150.00*.

You will now have to inform Simply Accounting to recalculate your paycheque due to the change in the gross pay. This function is only required during the modification mode.

Continue by clicking on the [icon] icon.

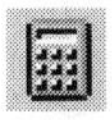

Simply Accounting will then recalculate the paycheque.

Once you have recalculated the paycheque, continue by

Posting the revised paycheque.

Simply Accounting will then continue with the entry of the reversing and new payroll journal entry. We will review these journal entries later in this chapter.

Simply Accounting will ask you confirm the posting of a duplicate cheque. Continue by

Clicking the **Yes** button to accept the posting of the duplicate cheque number.

Once the revised paycheque has been posted, continue by

Closing the Payroll Journal. You will return to the Simply Accounting - ODC window.

USING THE AUTOMATIC PAYROLL RUN

Simply Accounting for Windows also allows the issuance of a batch of paycheques such as a period-end payroll run.

Continue from within the Simply Accounting - ODC window, by

Selecting the **Payroll Cheque Run** icon.

Figure 9.38
Payroll Run
Journal window

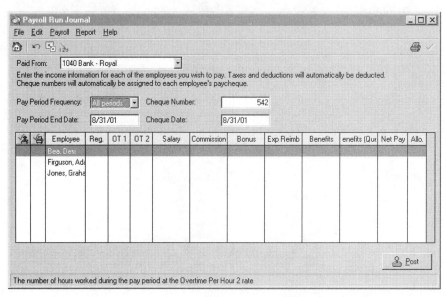

Within the Payroll Run window (Figure 9.38) you can select from the following fields:

Pay Period Frequency	allows you to specify which range of employees to include in this payroll run.
Pay Period/Cheque Date	allows you to specify the applicable period and cheque dates for this payroll run.
	Post icon to display which employees are to be included in this payroll run.
	Print icon to display which paycheques are to be printed.
Employee	Employee name.
Reg	Regular hours for each employee.
OT	Overtime rate 1 hours for each employee.
OT 2	Overtime rate 2 hours for each employee.

Salary	Salary amount for each employee.
Commission	Commission earnings for each employee.
Bonus	Bonus earnings for each employee.
Benefits	Taxable benefits for each employee.
Benefits (Quebec)	Taxable (Quebec) benefits for each employee.
Net Pay	Calculated net pay for each employee.
Allo.	Project distribution for each employee (note Chapter 10).

You will notice that the payroll run function does not allow for modification of default deductions or advances, however Simply Accounting will incorporate this information within each employee's paycheque (based on the defaults).

Continue with the entry of the following:

Bea, Desi Click the column.

80 Regular hours
3.5 Overtime (OT) hours.
2.0 Overtime (OT 2) hours.

Firguson, Adam Click the column.

80 Regular hours
1.5 Overtime (OT) hours.

Figure 9.39
Payroll Run
Journal window
(entered)

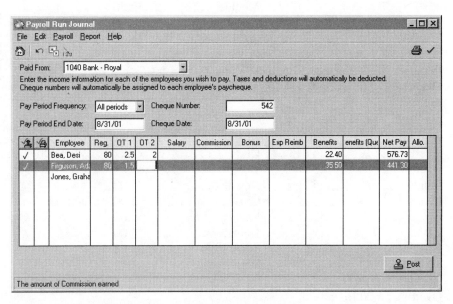

Your Payroll Run Journal window should now resemble Figure 9.39. You will notice that Simply Accounting has entered the default information for each employee, as well as the calculation of the net pay for each employee.

Continue from within the Payroll Run Journal window (Figure 9.39) by

Selecting the **Report** menu within the Payroll Run Journal window.

Selecting the **Payroll Cheque Run Summary** menu option.

Figure 9.40   Payroll Cheque Run Summary window

Payroll Cheque Run Summary

Pay Period Frequency: All periods For Pay Period: 08/31/01   Cheque Date: 08/31/01

Bea, Desi   Cheque #543

Regular 720.00	EI . . . . xx.xx	Gross. 825.65
Overtime 47.25	CPP. . . . . xx.xx	Withheld . . . . xxx.xx
Overtime 2 . . . . 36.00	Tax . . . . xxx.xx	Benefits . . . . -22.40
Benefits. 22.40	Dental 35.50	
	CSB 30.00	Net . . . . xxx.xx
Gross. 825.65	Medical 32.50	
	Donations 15.00	
	Stock Plan 20.64	
	Withheld 303.93	

Regular: 80.00 Hours @ $9.00 per Hour
Overtime: 3.50 Hours @ $13.50 per Hour
Overtime 2: 2.00 Hours @ $18.00 per Hour

Firguson, Adam   Cheque #544

Regular 600.00	EI . . . . .xx.xx	Gross 652.38
Overtime 16.88	CPP . . . . .xx.xx	Withheld . . . . .xx.xx
Benefits 35.50	Tax . . . . .xxx.xx	Benefits . . . .-35.50
	Dental 35.50	
Gross 652.38	CSB 25.00	Net . . . . .xx.xx
	Medical 32.50	
	Donations 10.00	
	Stock Plan 16.31	
	Withheld 257.19	

Regular: 80.00 Hours @ $7.50 per Hour
Overtime: 1.50 Hours @ $11.25 per Hour

Totals for this report:

Regular 1,320.00	EI . . . . .xx.xx	Gross 1,478.03
Overtime 64.13	CPP . . . . .xx.xx	Withheld . . . . .xx.xx
Overtime 2 . . . . . . .36.00	Tax . . . . .xx.xx	Benefits . . . .-57.90
Benefits 57.90	Dental 71.00	
	CSB 55.00	Net . . . . .xx.xx
Gross 1,478.03	Medical 65.00	
	Donations 25.00	
	Stock Plan 36.95	
	Withheld 561.12	

Regular: 160.00 Hours
Overtime: 5.00 Hours
Overtime 2: 2.00 Hours
Number of employees printed: 2

As shown in Figure 9.40, Payroll Cheque Run Summary window, Simply Accounting for Windows will generate two paycheques based on the information entered within the spreadsheet data entry section of the Payroll Run Journal window (Figure 9.39).

Continue from within the Payroll Cheque Run Summary window (Figure 9.40) by

Closing the Payroll Cheque Run Summary window.

The last step in the Payroll Run is the posting of the payroll run. This is accomplished in the same way (Alt + P) as a singular paycheque.

Continue from within the Payroll Run Journal window by

Posting the payroll run.

Closing the Payroll Run Journal window. You will then return to the Simply Accounting – ODC window.

DISPLAYING AND PRINTING REPORTS

Once you have entered the payroll information, you may want to display and/or print a report.

Make sure that you have returned to the Simply Accounting ODC window. (If you are still in the Payroll Journal window, press Alt + F4 to close the Payroll Journal window.

Continue from within the Simply Accounting - ODC window by

Selecting the **Reports** menu.

Continue from the Reports menu by

Selecting the **Payroll** menu option.

Continue from the Payroll Reports Menu by pressing

Selecting the **Employee** menu command.

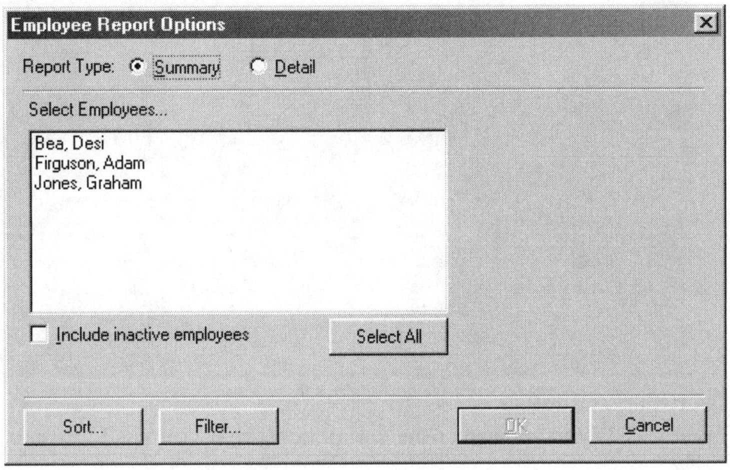

Figure 9.41
Employee
Report Options
window

The **Select All** button is used to select all of the employees instead of selecting only certain employees (Figure 9.41).

Summary Option   Displays the selected employee's payroll information such as social insurance number, date of birth, number of pay periods, and year-to-date figures (Figure 9.40).

Figure 9.42
Employee
Summary
report window

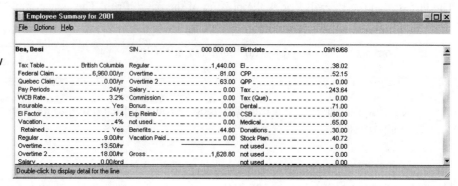

Continue by returning to the Employee Report Options window (see Figure 9.41). Once you are at this window, continue by

Clicking on the **Select All** button.

Clicking on the **Detail** option.

Figure 9.43
Employee
Report Options
window (with
details shown)

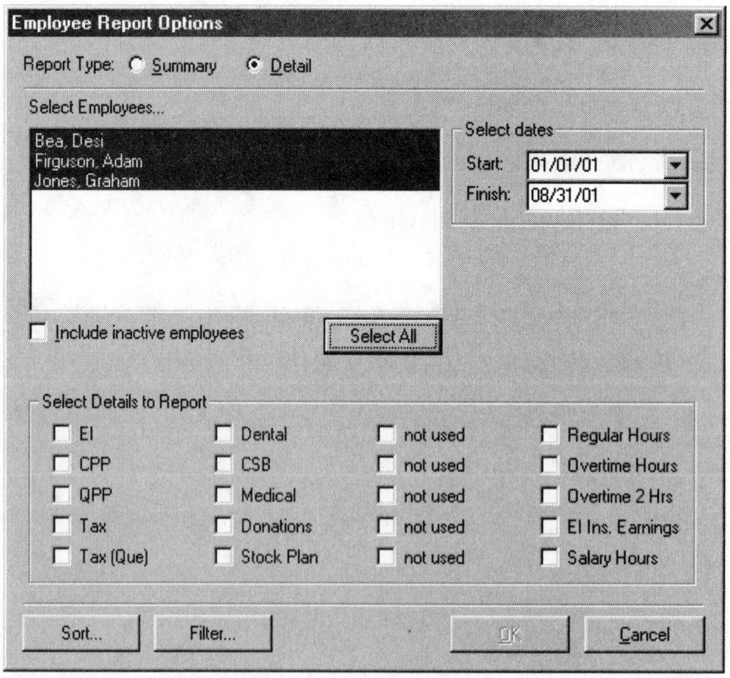

As shown in Figure 9.41, you can select the components that you wish to select to be included in your report.

Practice Exercise 9.10

Continue with selecting the following Detail options:

Employee to include	Select All
Start Date:	01/01/01
Finish Date:	08/31/01

Components to include:

EI
CPP
Tax

Once you have displayed this report, as shown in Figure 9.44, continue by printing this report.

Once you have completed this exercise, return to the Simply Accounting - ODC window.

Figure 9.44
Payroll Detail
window

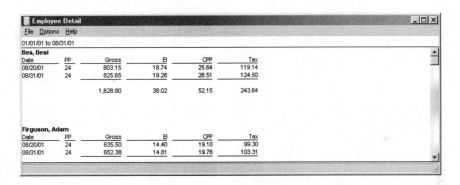

When you return to the **Reports/Payroll** menu, you will notice that there are two other employee report options:

Print T4 Slips — will print the T4 slips for all selected employees (all Canadian employees). When you select this option, please ensure that your printer is on-line with the correct T4 slips or summary form inserted.

Print Relevé 1 Slips — will print the Relevé 1 slips for all selected employees (Quebec employees). Make sure that you have the printer on-line with the correct slips or form inserted.

MAINTAINING AN AUDIT TRAIL

As discussed in previous chapters it is very important that you maintain an appropriate audit trail. We suggest that you save the reports that you have printed and place them into a binder marked Payroll.

BACKING UP YOUR DATA FILES

At this point, return to the Simply Accounting - ODC window and continue with the back up function.

Call this backup:

Backup Filename: A:\odc\odc9b
Comment: Payroll Part b

Further Practice

To get further practice with the concepts you have learned in this chapter go to Chapter 14 and work through Section 10 of the National Supply Company.

CHAPTER 10

PROJECT COSTING

CHAPTER 10

PROJECT COSTING

OBJECTIVES

After working through this chapter, you will be able to

1. Explain the function of the Project Ledger of the Simply Accounting System.
2. Prepare for using the Project Ledger — adding and deleting cost centres, as well as modifying information about them.
3. Make entries into the various Project centres that have been set up.
4. Display information in report form and print the various reports.
5. Export Project data for use in a spreadsheet or text file.

In working through the preceding chapters, you learned how the General Ledger provides overall control of business transactions and accounting data and ties the various subledgers of Accounts Payable, Accounts Receivable, Payroll, and Inventory together. With an accounting system, we can measure the state of the company's financial health through the balance sheet. The success of the firm's operation is shown by the income statement. But these statements may not be enough for purposes of decision making.

Overnight Delivery Company, the company that we have been using as an example, has three sources of service revenue:

1. Freight delivery
2. Goods storage
3. Truck rental

The accounting system will tell us whether a firm is profitable overall, but management might also want to know which divisions are making money and which ones are losing money. Are all divisions contributing to the profitability of the firm? Is one division supporting another?

WHAT IS COST ACCOUNTING?

Cost accounting is the development of cost information pertaining to a division, department, project, or manufactured product within the framework of the General Ledger. The cost information is provided by the transactions that the company completes during a particular cycle. We can compare these costs to the revenue produced by a particular activity to determine if costs and revenues are within budget.

Thus, in cost accounting, also known as project costing, we allocate the various revenues and costs to departments, divisions, or profit centres, rather than just record the costs as part of the total entity of Overnight Delivery Company.

For example, an employee of Overnight Delivery Company works in all three of the areas mentioned above. She is paid $2,500.00 per month. Our accounting entry to record this wage at the end of each month (not considering withholding taxes) would be as follows:

Dr. Wage Expense $2,500.00
     Cr. Cash $2,500.00

This entry will adequately record the payment of the monthly salary as an expense to the company. However, if we wanted to treat each department as a separate profit centre, or project cost centre, we would have to distribute that employee's salary according to some percentage of time spent in each department. If she worked 50 percent of her time in the delivery division, 30 percent of her time in the storage division, and 20 percent of her time in the truck rental division, we would show this distribution by splitting the wage cost and allocating it to each centre:

	Dept 1 Delivery	Dept 2 Storage	Dept 3 Rental
Wage expense	1,250.00	750.00	500.00

Similarly, other costs and revenues would be assigned to these departments, either in total or in part. At the end of each period, we can prepare a report by project centre, as shown in Figure 10.1, that will tell us whether or not that particular function of the business was profitable. We could also compare the department's results against the budget to determine the success of that part of the firm in meeting its plans and objectives.

	Dept 1 Delivery	Dept 2 Storage	Dept 3 Rental
Revenue	13,480.00	6,500.00	4,300.00
Expenses			
Fuel	4,350.00	1,250.00	250.00
Rent	2,100.00	2,100.00	2,100.00
Wage expense	1,250.00	750.00	500.00
Total	7,700.00	4,100.00	2,850.00
Profit	5,780.00	2,400.00	1,450.00

Figure 10.1   Report by project centre for Overnight Delivery Company

ALLOCATING OVERHEAD

Not all costs can be broken down easily among departments. Overhead costs, for example, (telephone, utilities, janitorial, accounting services, etc.) are allocated according to a formula devised by management. The formula may be based on the amount of revenue produced by the department or on the amount of direct labour used in relation to the total labour for the firm. Whatever the method used, it must be applied consistently so the results can be compared to other periods.

PREPARING TO USE THE PROJECT LEDGER

The Project Ledger is unlike any of the other ledgers, (Payables, Receivables etc.). Its function is to allocate expenses and revenues to various projects or departments. To do so, the Simply Accounting for Windows program uses information entered with journal entries made through other journals. Therefore this ledger cannot be used unless all applicable ledgers are in READY mode. This also means that the Project Ledger is always in the READY mode.

IDENTIFYING COST AND REVENUE CENTRES

Before you can begin to convert your Project Ledger to the Simply Accounting system, you must organize existing data and have it ready for entry to the system. While in other ledgers this includes making a listing of existing amounts, for the Project Ledger you only have to identify the projects or departments among which you want the costs allocated.

Identifying cost or profit centres is not a difficult task but requires some thought. The centres that you identify should be meaningful and should be measurable. If the centres are composed of too many different activities, for example, there is little benefit in identifying them separately.

As an example, use the three centres we identified earlier for Overnight Delivery Company.

	Name of Cost Centre	Date Started
1.	Freight movement	01/01/97
2.	Storage	04/01/97
3.	Rental	08/01/97

Now that you have established the cost centres and the dates at which the cost centres began, you should also determine the amount of revenue and expenses that have been accumulated since the cost centres were created. This will allow your cost centre to record the appropriate costs.

SETTING UP SIMPLY ACCOUNTING FOR USING THE PROJECT LEDGER

Once you have decided on meaningful cost or profit centres, you are ready to enter them into the Simply Accounting system.

Figure 10.2
Simply
Accounting -
ODC window

From the Simply Accounting - ODC window (Figure 10.2) continue by

Clicking on the **Project** icon.

Figure 10.3
Project window

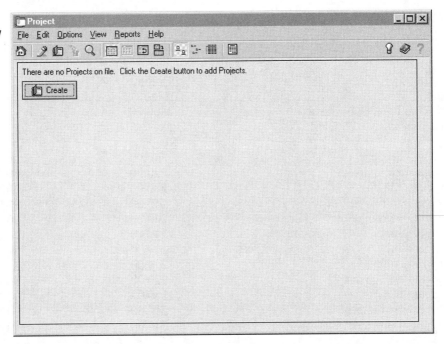

Simply Accounting for Windows will now display the Project window (Figure 10.3). Once you have set up your projects, each of these projects will appear in this window along with a small icon, (as with the Customers window for the Receivable Ledger and the Vendors window for the Payables Ledger).

Continue from the Project window by

Clicking on the **Create** button.

Figure 10.4
Project Ledger
window (blank)

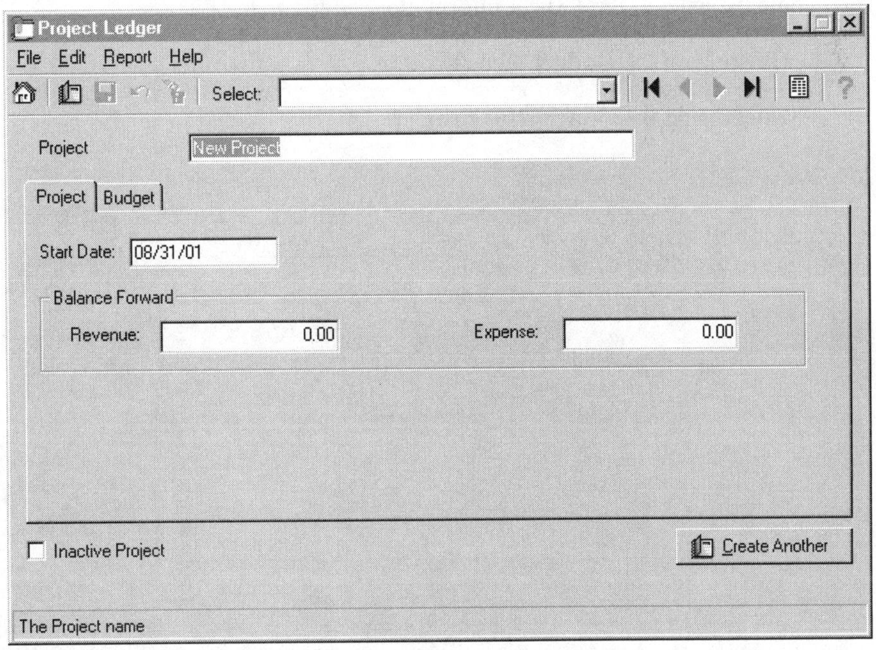

ADDING PROJECT CENTRES

Using the listing made earlier, you can now add the cost centres to the Project Ledger in the Simply Accounting system. Start by entering the following centre:

Name	Freight	
Date	01/01/01	
Revenue Balance Forward	2400.00	
Expense Balance Forward	1847.35	
	Revenue	Expense
Budget - January	240.00	200.00
Budget - February	220.00	180.00
Budget - March	230.00	185.00
Budget - April	240.00	190.00
Budget - May	240.00	190.00
Budget - June	240.00	190.00
Budget - July	220.00	180.00
Budget - August	230.00	185.00
Budget - September	220.00	180.00
Budget - October	240.00	190.00
Budget - November	240.00	190.00
Budget - December	240.00	190.00

At the Project Ledger window, type

Freight ⌞ Tab ⌟   to enter the **Name** of this project (cost centre).

01/01/01 ⌞ Tab ⌟   to enter the **Start Date** for this project.

2400.00 ⌞ Tab ⌟   to enter the **Revenue Balance Forward**.

1847.35 ⌞ Tab ⌟   to enter the **Expense Balance Forward**.

Once you have entered the Project information, continue by

Clicking on the **Budget** tabbed button.

Clicking on the **Budget this project**.

Figure 10.5
Project Budget
Ledger window

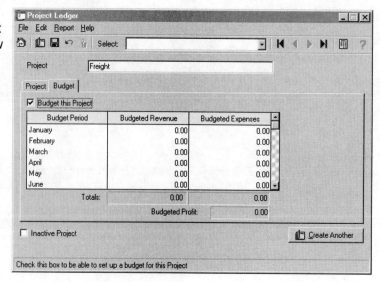

You can now enter the project budget (Figure 10.5). This will allow you to compare your actual project figures to a previously established project budget.

Practice Exercise 10.1

Continue with the entry of the budget revenue and budgeted expenses for the **Freight** project. Note that the Budgeted Profit should equal $550.00. Continue by clicking the **Create Another** button.

Repeat the above steps to enter the following three cost centres (no budgeting):

Name	**Warehouse**
Start Date	**08/01/01**
Revenue Balance Forward	**0.00**
Expense Balance Forward	**0.00**

Name	**Rental**
Start Date	**08/01/01**
Revenue Balance Forward	**0.00**
Expense Balance Forward	**0.00**

Name	**Other**
Start Date	**08/01/01**
Revenue Balance Forward	**0.00**
Expense Balance Forward	**0.00**

Once you have completed this exercise, remain in the Project Ledger window once you have created the last project.

MODIFYING PROJECT CENTRES

You may wish to change the information entered to make the name more meaningful. To do so, continue as follows:

Click on the **Select** pull down menu.

Continue by Selecting the *Warehouse* project.

Simply Accounting for Windows will now retrieve the Warehouse project. We will now continue with editing the name for this project. Continue by entering

Storage ⌞ Tab ⌟ to change the **Project** name.

As with the previous modules, in order to save your changes to an edited record you must either close the module window (Project Ledger for this example) or bring up another project record.

Practice Exercise 10.2

Select and retrieve the *Other* project. Once you have completed this exercise, remain within the Project Ledger with the *Other* project retrieved.

DELETING PROJECT CENTRES

If you no longer need a particular project or department, for example, if a project is completed, you can delete it. You should be at the Project window with the *Other* project retrieved, (note above). To complete the deletion process, continue by either

Clicking on the icon.

or by pressing

Alt + F   to invoke the **File** menu.

R   to select the **Remove** menu option.

You will now be asked to confirm the removal of this project. Continue with

Clicking the **Yes** button.

or by pressing

Y   to confirm the removal of the *Other* project record.

You have now deleted the *Other* project. Continue from within the Project Ledger window by

Closing the Project Ledger window.

Closing the Project window.

Deleting a project will not free up much space since it only records an allocation of an existing journal entry and does not store new data. Therefore you may as well keep it on the system until you are certain that you will not need it again.

GENERAL LEDGER ACCOUNTS AND PROJECTS

Prior to continuing, you will have to select the **Allow Project Allocation**, (note Figure 10.6). This is suggested for the Revenue and Expense accounts, but could also include the Balance Sheet accounts if your business wanted to project cost both income/expense and Balance Sheet accounts.

Figure 10.6
General Ledger
window

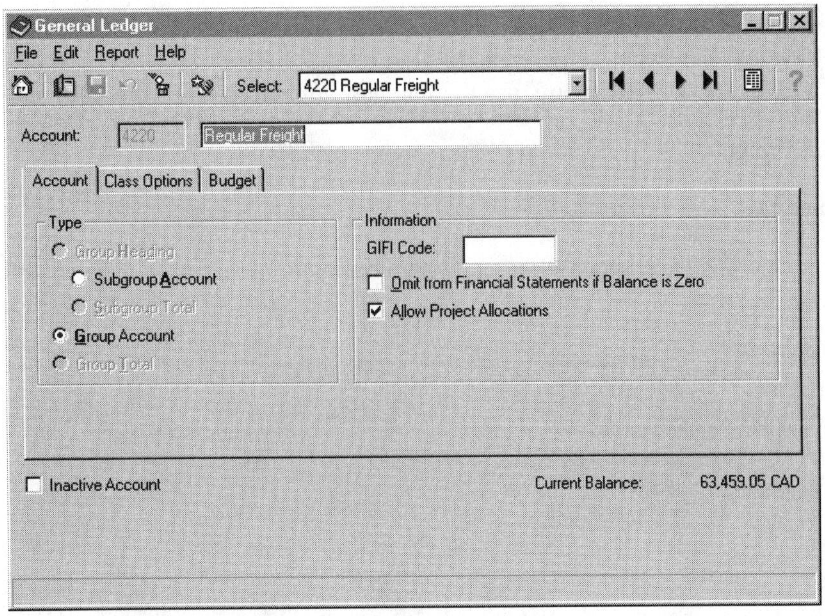

Practice Exercise 10.3

Continue with the selection of the **Allow Project Allocation** option for all Revenue and Expense accounts. This is accomplished by selecting the appropriate Revenue (4000 range) and Expense (5000 range) accounts and selecting the **Allow Project Allocation** option, (note Figure 10.6). We suggest that you scroll through the income and expense account range, selecting the **Allow Project Allocation** option for each account. Refer back to the General Ledger chapter for more information about modifying general ledger accounts.

Once you have completed this exercise, return to the Simply Accounting - ODC window.

BACKING UP YOUR DATA FILES

From the Simply Accounting - ODC window backup your data files.

Call this backup:

>**Backup Filename:** A:\odc\ODC10A
>**Comment:** Project Part a

CHANGING TO CURRENT MODE

As the Project module is only a reporting module, you will not need to change this module from Historical to Current mode, (as with other modules). You can immediately enter current data and assign it to these project centres.

ALLOCATING REVENUES OR EXPENSES TO PROJECTS

Only Revenue and Expense items can be allocated to the Project centres. To understand how to allocate costs to a Project centre, use the Purchase journal to make the following entry:

      Freight $150.00   *Vancouver Times*

Continue by

    Opening the **Purchase** journal with either your mouse or your keyboard.

Figure 10.7
Purchases
Journal window

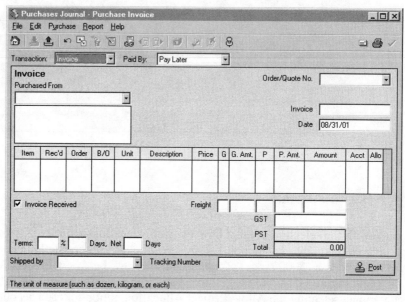

The Purchase Journal window (Figure 10.7) will now appear. You should remember this window from Chapter 7. The next entry is very similar to a regular Purchase entry. The only difference is that you are going to allocate the expense to a project. Press

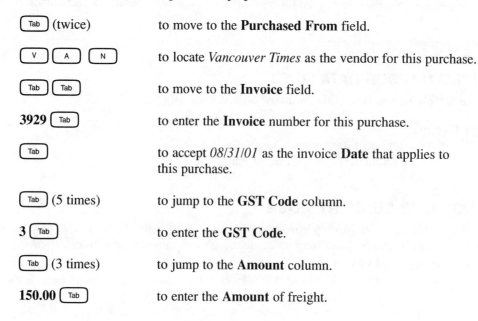

Tab (twice)	to move to the **Purchased From** field.
V A N	to locate *Vancouver Times* as the vendor for this purchase.
Tab Tab	to move to the **Invoice** field.
3929 Tab	to enter the **Invoice** number for this purchase.
Tab	to accept *08/31/01* as the invoice **Date** that applies to this purchase.
Tab (5 times)	to jump to the **GST Code** column.
3 Tab	to enter the **GST Code**.
Tab (3 times)	to jump to the **Amount** column.
150.00 Tab	to enter the **Amount** of freight.

5820   to enter the **Account** number. *Note that you do not press* [Tab] *after the account number. If you accidentally pressed* [Tab] *and moved the cursor to the next invoice line, then press* [Shift]+[Tab] *to move the cursor back to the previous field,* **Acct**.

We will now allocate this line to a certain project(s):

[Ctrl] + [D]   to select the **<u>D</u>istribute** button. You can also select the **<u>D</u>istribute** icon.

Figure 10.8
Project
Distribution
window

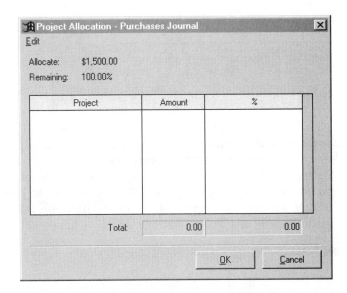

The Project Distribution window will now appear. This window is shown in Figure 10.8.

[Enter]   to display the Select Project window (Figure 10.9).

Figure 10.9
Select Project
window

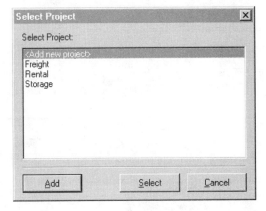

[↓]   to highlight the *Freight* project.

[Enter]   to select the *Freight* project.

[Tab]   to accept *100%* as the percentage of expense that we wish to allocate to the *Freight* project.

Figure 10.10
Project
Distribution
window
(completed)

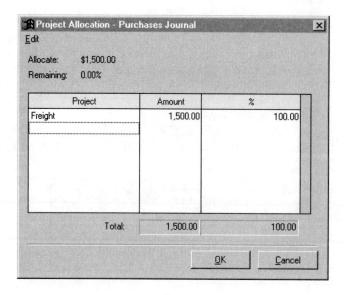

Even though you allocated 100.0% of the cost to the *Freight* project (Figure 10.10) this does not have to be the case with the selection of the percentage or amount — selected through the settings. You can instead select the appropriate percentage or amount to allocate to the particular project or projects. However, you do not have to allocate 100.0% of the amount to the project.

Your Project Allocation window should resemble Figure 10.10. If this is the case, continue by

Clicking the **OK** button.

Figure 10.11
Purchases
Journal
completed

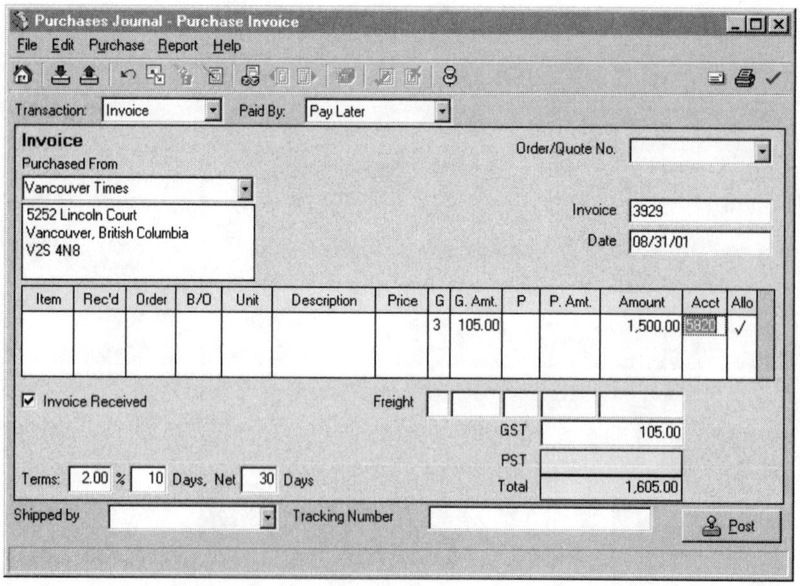

Your Purchases Journal should resemble Figure 10.11. Note the check mark in the distribution field. This means that you have allocated the expense, using the Project Distribution window.

To display the journal entries associated with this purchase, continue by

Selecting the **Reports** menu located in the Purchases Journal window.

Select the **Display Purchase Journal Entry** menu option.

Figure 10.12
Purchases
Journal Entry
window

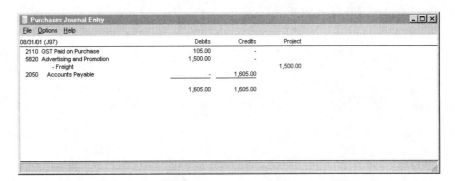

As shown in Figure 10.12, the Purchases Journal Entry window not only displays the accounts and the associated amounts, but also the project information.

We will now continue by pressing

Alt + F4   to close the Purchases Journal Entry window. This should return you to the Purchases Journal window.

Alt + P   to **Post** the above purchase with the default GST of *10.50*.

HINT: *ALLOCATION TO PROJECTS*

Simply Accounting for Windows also supports the allocation of asset, liability, and equity amounts to applicable projects. This is referred to as the allocation of resources to particular projects.

Practice Exercise 10.4

Enter two more items into the **Purchases** journal and allocate them as follows:

For the following purchases, select **GST Code** 3 on the amounts. You will notice that the program has no provision for distributing the GST among the projects because GST is either payable or refundable by the recipient.

Vendor	Invoice #	Date	Account	Amount	Project Distribution Information
Golden Wings	956	Aug 31, 01	5900	175.05	Freight 100%
Ronoco Truck	4624	Aug 31, 01	5900	230.00	Freight 43%
					Rental 14%
					Storage 18%

You will notice that the Ronoco Truck Parts entry does not fully distribute the expense. This is correct as the remaining 25% of the expense was deemed to be unallocated to an applicable project.

Enter the following invoice for regular freight into the **Sales** journal and allocate it as follows:

Customer	Invoice #	Date	Acct/Item	Ship/Price/Amount	Project Dist. Information
Cassar Homes	4570	Aug 31, 01	4220	80.00	Freight 100%
City Software	4571	Aug 31, 01	AIRFR	2/50.00/100.00	Freight 100%
Modern Computer	4572	Aug 31, 01	4220	200.00	Freight 15%
					Storage 85%

The allocation procedure is the same as for a purchase. The sales are on account. Use GST Code 3 and do not apply PST. It is also **OK** that Cassar Homes exceeds the credit limit.

Once you have completed this exercise, return to the Simply Accounting - ODC window.

DISPLAYING PROJECT ENTRIES

To see how the items were allocated to the project centres you can display the entries on your screen or print them out.

Start from the Simply Accounting - ODC window (Figure 10.2). Continue by using your mouse by

Selecting the **Reports** menu.

Selecting the **Project** menu option.

Within the project menu, you can select from three menu choices:

Income Report   displays the project revenue, project expense, and the net balance for each (project profit). This report can be printed in either a summary or detail (transactional detail) format.

Allocation Report   displays the asset, liability, and equity account amounts that have been allocated to applicable projects. This report can include current or cumulative amounts as well as balance forward amounts for transactions occurring before the start date of the report.

Budget Report   displays a report showing the actual project revenue and expenses compared to the entered project budget amounts, (note previous example in this chapter). You have the option of showing the dollar or percentage difference as well as cumulative project information.

Continue from within the Project menu by

Selecting the **Income Report** menu item.

Figure 10.13
Project Reports
Options window

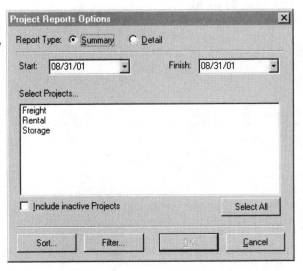

A new window titled Project Reports Options will now appear (Figure 10.13). The options available are described as follows:

Start Date   tells Simply Accounting the date it should start displaying all applicable project entries.

End Date   tells Simply Accounting the date it should stop displaying all applicable project entries.

Summary report   displays a report that shows the total allocated to each applicable account, in summary.

Detail report   displays a report that shows the transactions that have been allocated to each applicable account.

Include Inactive Projects
                                allows projects that are marked inactive in the Project Ledger window to be displayed in the report.

Select All   tells Simply Accounting that you wish the report to include all projects. If you only wish to include certain projects, you can highlight only the ones you wish to be included.

OK   tells Simply Accounting to proceed.

Cancel   returns you to the Simply Accounting - ODC window.

Practice Exercise 10.5

Select the following options while in the Project Report Options window:

Report Format	**Detail**
Start Date	**08/01/01**
End Date	**08/31/01**
Projects to include	**Freight only**

Figure 10.14
Project Reports
Options window

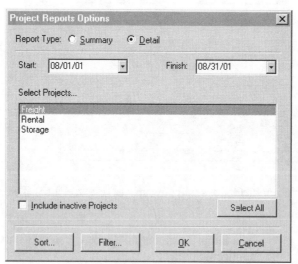

Continue with selecting the **OK** button within the Project Report Options window (Figure 10.14).

Figure 10.15
Project Reports
Options #2
window

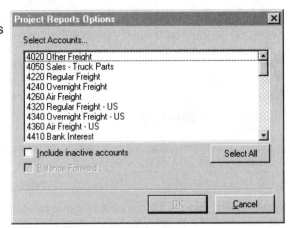

Once you have selected the **OK** button, a new window titled Project Report Options (Figure 10.15) will be displayed. In this window, you must tell Simply Accounting which General Ledger accounts you wish to include in the report. You will notice that you can only select income statement accounts, <u>not</u> balance sheet accounts. You will also notice that there is an option for choosing **Balance Forward**. This option will show both the balance forward for the project from the date that the project started until the date chosen.

Continue by

> Clicking on **Select All** to include all accounts in this project report.

> Clicking on **OK** to proceed with the display.

The report that you should have generated should resemble the report window displayed in Figure 10.16.

Figure 10.16
Sample Project
Detail report
window

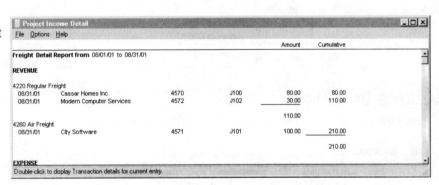

PRINTING PROJECT REPORTS

Printing reports is similar to displaying reports. While in the Project Detail window press

> Alt + F   to invoke the **File** menu.

> P   to **Print** the report window.

EXPORTING PROJECT REPORTS

The Simply Accounting System also lets you export Project reports. To do so, make sure that you are in the Project Detail window and press

| Alt | + | F | to invoke the **File** menu.

| E | to select the **Export** option.

The Export Selection window will now appear. In this window, select the filename and file format that you wish to **Export** to. If you are not sure how to do this, please refer back to Chapter 7 on how to complete the procedure.

Practice Exercise 10.6

Continue with the displaying and printing of the project report in summary form (from 08/01/01 to 08/31/01) which includes all projects, all Revenue/Expense accounts. Also select to carry forward the balances. Your report should resemble Figure 10.17.

Once you have complete this exercise, return to the Simply Accounting - ODC window.

Figure 10.17
Project Summary
(with Carry
Forward) window

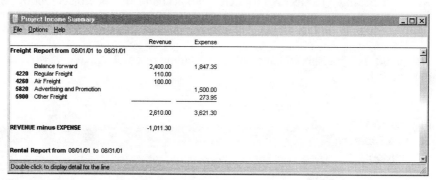

BACKING UP YOUR DATA FILES

At this point, return to the Simply Accounting - ODC window and back up your data files.

Call this backup:

Backup Filename: A:\odc\ODC10B
Comment: Project Part b

Further Practice

To get further practice with the concepts you have learned in this chapter go to Chapter 14 and work through Section 10 of the National Supply Company.

CHAPTER 11

REPORTING AND GRAPHING

CHAPTER 11

REPORTING & GRAPHING

OBJECTIVES

After reading Chapter 11, you will be able to

1. Prepare graphs using data from the various modules.

2. Customize graphs so as to enhance the information provided for the viewer.

3. Add titles and change fonts.

4. Understand the types of reports that Simply Accounting can prepare.

5. Know how to use the various forms and how to print cheques.

To this point you have learned many of the features of Simply Accounting for Windows. One of the most important features of an accounting package is the ability to report on the financial information that you have entered into the program.

Practice Exercise 11.1

Start the Simply Accounting for Windows program, select the **odc** data set and accept the default using date as **08/31/01.** When the To-Do List window is displayed, continue by closing this window.

Figure 11.1
Simply Accounting -
ODC window

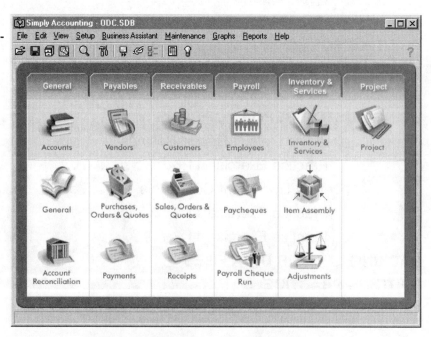

The Simply Accounting - ODC window shown in Figure 11.1 has two menu choices titled:

Graphs	allows you to generate, view, and print various graphs depicting the financial condition of your business.
Reports	provides you with a menu containing various reporting options.

USING THE GRAPHING FEATURES

Although a financial report provides you with a numerical financial picture, it is often easier to understand numerical relationships if they are shown in graphical format.

Continue from the Simply Accounting - ODC window by

Selecting the **Graph** menu option.

Figure 11.2
Graph menu

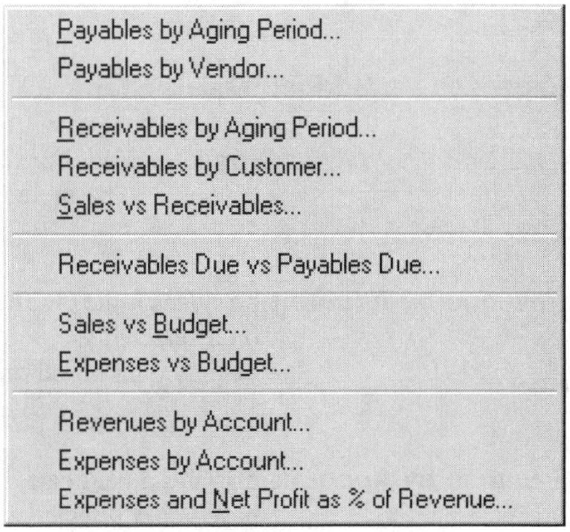

Payables by Aging Period...
Payables by Vendor...

Receivables by Aging Period...
Receivables by Customer...
Sales vs Receivables...

Receivables Due vs Payables Due...

Sales vs Budget...
Expenses vs Budget...

Revenues by Account...
Expenses by Account...
Expenses and Net Profit as % of Revenue...

The **Graph** menu (Figure 11.2) provides you with the following options:

Payables by Aging Period	provides a pie chart of the payables in categories according to aging periods. This graph will include all payables up to and including the Using date.
Payables by Vendor	provides a pie chart of the payables in categories according to vendors. This graph will include all payables up to and including the Using date.
Receivables by Aging Period	provides a pie chart of the receivables in categories according to aging periods. This graph will include all receivables up to and including the Using date.

Receivables by Customer	provides a pie chart of the receivables in categories according to customers. This graph will include all receivable transactions up to and including the Using date.
Sales vs. Receivables	provides a bar graph displaying a comparison of the current and previous months' sales versus the receivables balance. This graph will include all sales and receivables transactions up to and including the Using date.
Receivables Due vs. Payables Due	provides a bar graph displaying the receivables versus the payables due within a defined period of time.
Sales vs. Budget	produces a bar graph comparing the sales to budget for both the fiscal start to previous month as well as the current period. For this graph you can select the Revenue (sales) accounts to be included.
Expenses vs. Budget	displays a bar graph comparing the expenses to budget for both the fiscal start to previous month as well as the current period. For this graph you can select the Expense accounts to be included.
Revenue by Account	produces a pie chart displaying the revenue earned based on a selected range of Revenue accounts. This graph will display data based on a defined period of time.
Expense by Account	displays a pie chart displaying the expenses incurred based on a selected range of Expense accounts. This graph will display data based on a defined period of time.
Expenses and Net Profit as Percent of Revenue	produces a pie chart displaying the expenses and net profits as a percentage of total revenue. This graph will display data based on a defined date range.

PREPARING A GRAPH

Let's prepare a graph using Accounts Payable data. Continue from the graph menu (Figure 11.2) by

selecting **Payables by Aging Period** menu option.

Simply Accounting will now prompt you for the **As at** date. Continue by pressing

[Enter]   to accept *08/31/01* as the **As at** date.

Figure 11.3
Payables by
Aging Period
graph

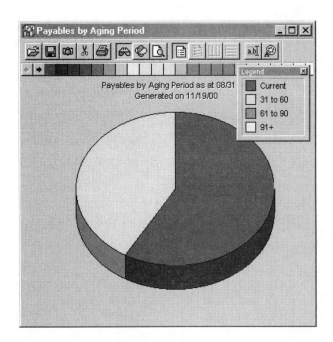

As shown in Figure 11.3, Simply Accounting for Windows generates a 3D pie chart representing the payables categorized by aging periods.

In the Payables by Aging Period graph (Figure 11.3) as well as all other graphs that you can generate, there is an icon bar.

Figure 11.4
Graph Icon Bar

This icon bar (Figure 11.4) includes the following icons (from left to right):

Import chart	will allow you to import a chart file (.chf).
Export chart	allows you to export this chart to a standard chart file (.chf) for use in other programs.
Copy to clipboard as bitmap	allows you to copy this chart to the Windows clipboard as a bitmap. You can then paste this bitmap into another Windows application.
Copy data to clipboard as text	allows you to copy the figures that comprise this chart as text to the Windows clipboard. You can then paste this information to another Windows application.

Print the chart	allows you to print a copy of this chart. If your printer supports colour printing, the colours shown on your screen will be printed. If your printer can only print in black and white, then Simply Accounting for Windows will substitute a shade of gray for each colour.
Switch between 2D and 3D views	allows you the flexibility of selecting to view the graph either in two dimensions or in a three-dimensional (default) format.
Rotate the graph	allows you to customize the position and visual focal point for the graph.
Z-Clustered series (only available for bar graphs)	allows you to convert a bar graph from an x-axis to a z-cluster format.
Zoom	gives you the option of zooming in to view the graph.
Show or hide legend	allows you the option of displaying or not displaying the legend.
Show or hide series legend (applies to bar graphs only)	allows you the option of displaying or not displaying the series legend.
Vertical grid display (bar graphs only)	displays a vertical grid.
Horizontal grid display (bar graph only)	displays a horizontal grid.
Edit titles	allows you the flexibility of adding or editing the titles for the top, bottom, left, and right sides of the graph.

CUSTOMIZING A GRAPH

Let's customize the current Payables by Aging Period graph.

Click on the 3D icon.

Figure 11.5
Payables by
Aging Period
graph (in 2D format)

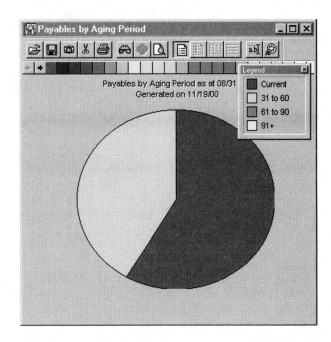

Your Payables by Aging Period graph will now resemble Figure 11.5, without the three-dimensional view. Continue by

> Closing the Payable by Aging Period window.

You will now return to the Simply Accounting - ODC window.

> Click on the **Graph** menu option.

In the **Graph** menu option

> Click on the **Expenses and Net Profit as % of Revenue** menu option.

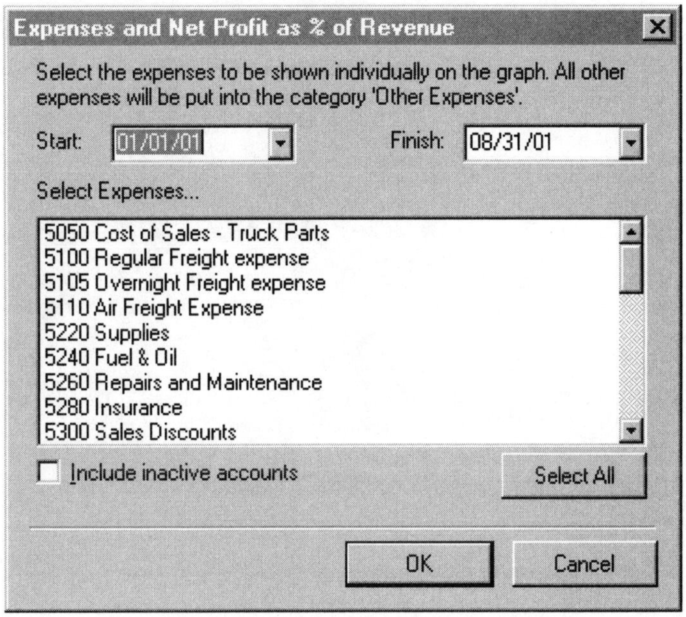

Figure 11.6
Expenses and
Net Profit as %
of Revenue options
window

Within the Expenses and Net Profit as % of Revenue options window (Figure 11.6) you must now specify the following:

Start date	The starting date as of which the Expense amounts are to be included.
Finish date	The finish date up to which the Expense amount are to be included.
Select Expenses	The range of Expense accounts that you wish to include in this graph.
Include Inactive Accounts	Allows you to include accounts that are flagged as inactive accounts within the General Ledger.
Select All	Selects all of the Expense accounts.

Continue by

Clicking on the **Select All** button.

Figure 11.7
Expenses and
Net Profit as % of
Revenue Options
window (Select All)

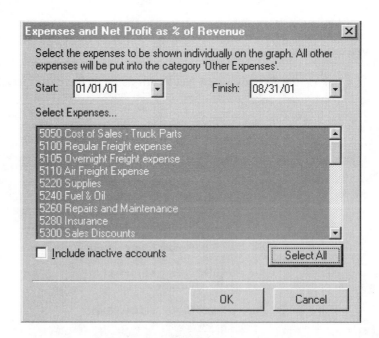

If your Expenses and Net Profit as % of Revenue Options window resembles Figure 11.7, continue by

Clicking on the **OK** button.

Figure 11.8
Expenses and
Net Profit as % of
Revenue graph
window

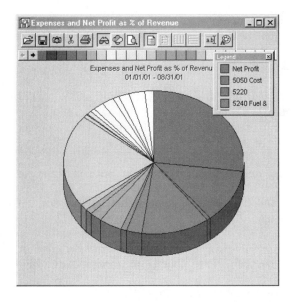

As shown in Figure 11.8, the pie chart displays the expenses and net profit in comparison to the revenue. Continue by

> Clicking on the **Zoom** icon.

HINT: *If you are unsure of the icons within the bar and their functions, position your mouse cursor over each icon and wait a couple of seconds and Simply Accounting will provide a "Clue" window to describe that particular icon.*

Position your mouse somewhere outside the graph image in the graph menu.

Press and hold your left mouse button and drag your mouse to include a portion of the graph image. You will notice that a circle is formed with the mouse cursor transformed into a magnifying glass.

Once you have selected the area, release the left mouse button.

Figure 11.9
Zoomed
graph window

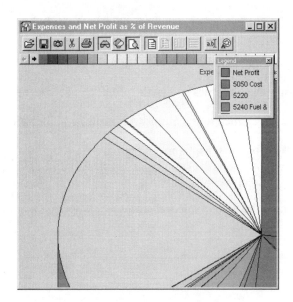

Your graph window will now have changed to display the magnified box area (Figure 11.9). Your window may be different due to the area selected to zoom. Continue by

Clicking the Zoom icon to return to the normal graph view.

Your Expenses and Net Profit as % of Revenue window will have returned to the normal graph window (Figure 11.8).

In order to emphasize an area of a graph, you would explode a piece of the graph (away from the middle of the graph). Simply Accounting for Windows supports this option. Continue by

Placing your mouse cursor into any section of the pie graph image.

Press and hold the left mouse button. Your mouse cursor will change to display the Cross icon.

Drag your mouse away from the centre of the graph, as if you wanted to expand the piece of the pie chart. Notice that the pie piece moves away from the centre of the pie chart.

Release the left mouse button.

Figure 11.10
Pie graph
expanded

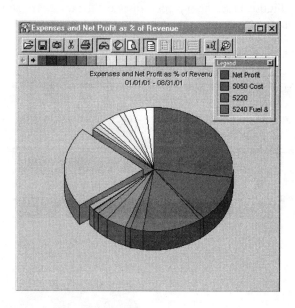

Continue from the Expenses and Net Profit as % of Revenue window by

Closing the Expenses and Net Profit as % of Revenue graph.

You will now be returned to the Simply Accounting - ODC window. Continue by

Clicking on the **Graphs** menu option.

From within the **Graphs** menu option

Click on the **Sales vs. Receivables** menu option.

Figure 11.11
Sales vs. Receivables
option window

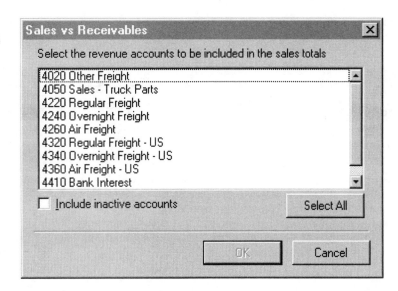

From within the Sales vs. Receivables option window (Figure 11.11) you have the option of selecting the Revenue accounts to be included within this graph. Continue by

Clicking on the **Select All** button.

Clicking on the **OK** button.

Figure 11.12
Sale vs. Receivables
graph window

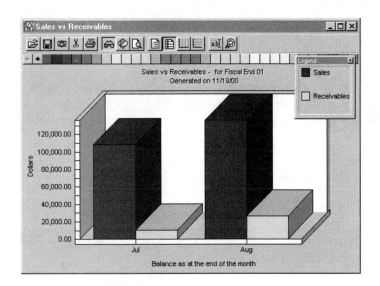

As displayed in Figure 11.12, the Sales vs. Receivables graph window is displayed. Because of the type of data, this graph is in the bar format. Continue by

Clicking on the **Rotate chart** menu icon.

HINT: *If you are unsure of the icons within the bar and their functions, position your mouse cursor over each icon and wait a couple of seconds and Simply Accounting will provide a "Clue" window to describe that particular icon.*

Figure 11.13
3D View
Properties
window

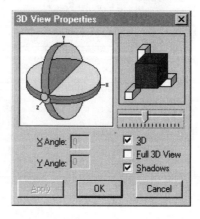

As shown in Figure 11.13, from within the 3D View Properties window you can rotate the display of the graph. You will notice that a button titled **Apply** is now displayed within this window but as yet not available for use. Once you have changed the rotation of the graph, this button becomes available for use, and allows you to change the Sales vs. Receivables window without having to exit the 3D View Properties window. You can see the change while still having the 3D Properties window open. Continue by

Positioning your mouse cursor on the slider control.

Press and hold your left mouse button.

Drag your mouse to the right to increase the 3D view of the graph. Continue dragging until the slider has moved to the furthest right position. You will notice that the above mini-window will change to display the images in increased 3D depth.

Release your left mouse button.

Click the **Ok** button.

Figure 11.14
Sales vs. Receivables
graph window
(maximum depth)

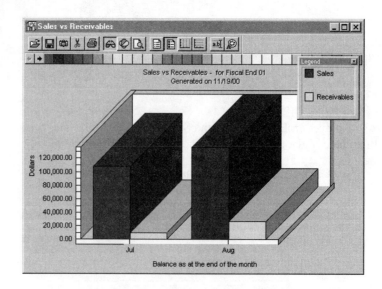

As shown in Figure 11.14, the Sales vs. Receivable window will now display the graph images with the highest depth, (thus the highest degree of 3D effect). Continue by

> Clicking on the **Horizontal grid** menu icon.

Figure 11.15
Sales vs. Receivables
grid with horizontal
grid lines

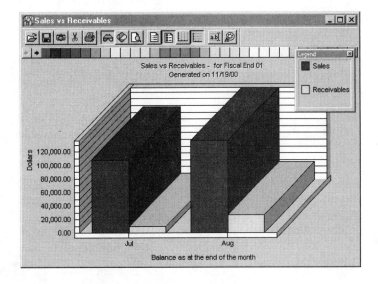

As shown in Figure 11.15, Simply Accounting will now include horizontal grid lines for each of the data groups. This helps you to get a better view of the graph and get a better idea of the relationship between the dollars amounts for each data item. Continue by

> Clicking on the Horizontal grid menu icon to return to the Sales vs. Receivables graph to the default view without horizontal grid lines.

ADDING TITLES AND USING FONTS

Of obvious importance are titles to describe what you are trying to convey with your chart. To improve the appearance of a title you can also change the font. Continue by

> Clicking on the **Edit Titles** icon.

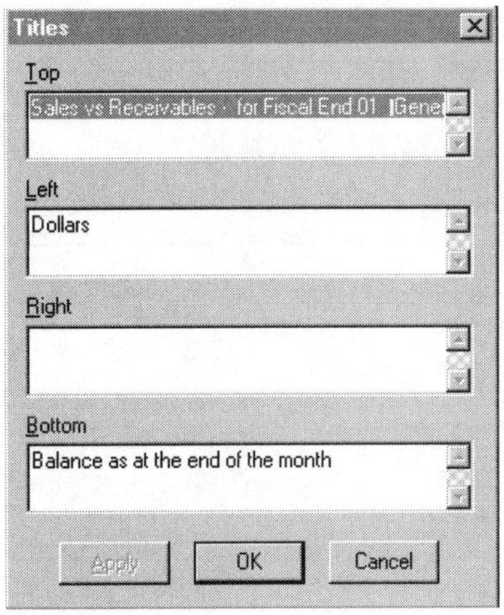

Figure 11.16
Titles window

Simply Accounting will now allow you to add or edit the titles for the graph (See Figure 11.16). Continue by pressing

Alt + B	to move to the **Bottom** title section.
End	to move to the end of the existing text.
Enter	to insert a new line.
Overnight Delivery Company	to insert the new line of text.

Continue by

Clicking the **OK** button to return to the Sales vs. Receivables graph.

Figure 11.17
Sales vs. Receivable
graph window
(bottom title changed)

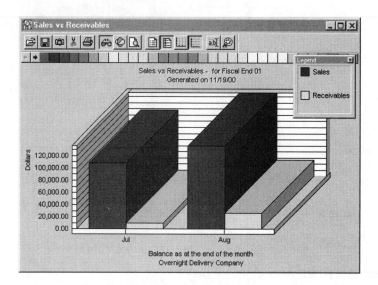

As shown in Figure 11.17, the Sales vs. Receivables graph window now displays, in addition to the previous line, the company name at the bottom of the graph. This helps to identify the company that this bar graph is for. Continue by

Clicking the **Change text fonts** menu icon.

> **HINT:** *If you are unsure of the icons within the bar and their functions, position your mouse cursor over each icon and wait a moment until Simply Accounting identifies the function of that particular icon.*

Figure 11.18
Fonts menu
(selecting title)

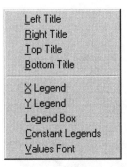

As Figure 11.18 shows, you can change the font style and size for all text areas within a graph.

Click on the **Top Title** menu option.

Figure 11.19
Font window

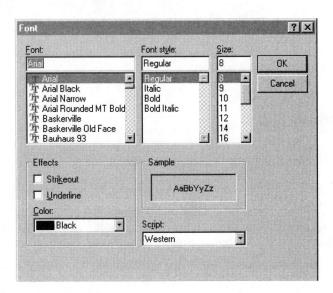

Simply Accounting for Windows will now display the standard Windows font selection window (Figure 11.19). Note that your window may display different fonts.

Practice Exercise 11.2

Select a different font for the **Top Title** of your Sales vs. Receivables graph. Once you have selected this font, click on the **OK** button to return to the Sales vs. Receivables graph window.

Figure 11.20
Sales vs.
Receivables
graph window
(Top title changed)

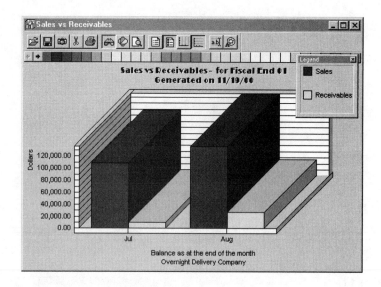

As shown in Figure 11.20, the Sales vs. Receivables graph window now displays the title in a different font which makes it stand out better.

Practice Exercise 11.3

Print a copy of the revised Sales vs. Receivables graph.

Once you have closed the Sales vs. Receivables graph window and returned to the Simply Accounting - ODC window, continue by

Displaying, customizing, and printing both the Sales vs. Budget and Expenses vs. Budget graphs. When prompted, **Select All** Sales and Expense accounts.

Once you have completed this exercise, return to the Simply Accounting - ODC window.

REPORTING FROM WITHIN SIMPLY ACCOUNTING

As mentioned earlier, the reporting function of an accounting package is of utmost importance since you must have the flexibility to extract your accounting information in a variety of ways, enabling you to make appropriate decisions.

Although graphs provide you with a visual method of identifying trends and relationships between figures, you must also have more precise financial information on which to base decisions. This is where the reporting function becomes important.

All of the major reports are available from the **Report** menu in the Simply Accounting - ODC window (Figure 11.1). Continue by

Selecting the **Report** menu.

Figure 11.21
Report menu

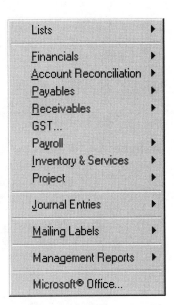

The **Report** menu (Figure 11.21) displays various report options.

FINANCIAL REPORTS

Figure 11.22
Financials menu

The **Financials** menu displays a submenu (Figure 11.22) which includes the following reports:

Figure 11.23
Balance Sheet
Options window

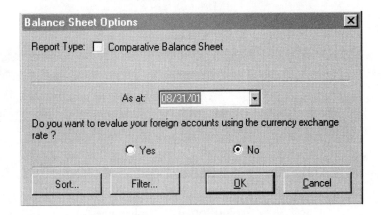

Balance Sheet displays the Assets, Liabilities, and Equity for your company. This report displays data as at a specific defined date as well as options to produce a comparative balance sheet (Figure 11.23).

Figure 11.24
Income Statement
Options window

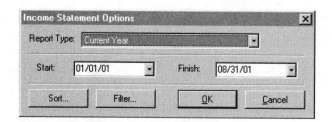

Income Statement displays the Revenue, Expenses, and Net Profit/Loss for a specific defined date range along with options to produce a comparative income statement to previous periods or in comparison to budget figures (Figure 11.24).

Figure 11.25
Trial Balance
Options window

Trial Balance displays a listing of the postable accounts with the associated debit or credit balances. This report can be printed at a specified **As at** date and can also be printed in comparison to a previous **As at** date (Figure 11.25).

Figure 11.26
Cash Flow
Projection Options
window

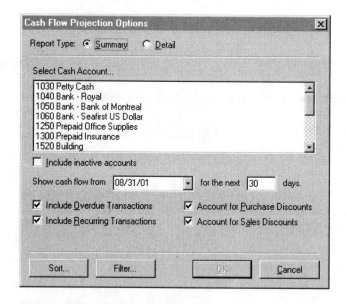

Cash Flow Projection will display a cash flow projection analysis report. This will allow your business to plan and prepare the necessary cash requirements for your business (Figure 11.26).

GENERAL LEDGER REPORTS

Figure 11.27
General Ledger
Report Options window

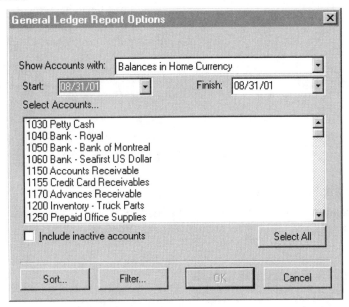

General Ledger displays the account transaction detail for a selectable range of accounts and date range (Figure 11.27).

Realized Exchange Gain/Loss

Figure 11.28
Realized Exchange
Gain/Loss Options
window

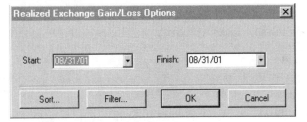

Those users who are using Simply Accounting within a multi-currency environment will be able to display and print reports for the realized foreign exchange gains and/or losses. Simply Accounting will ask you to provide a start and end date for this report (note Figure 11.28).

Unrealized Exchange Gain/Loss

Figure 11.29
Unrealized
Exchange
Gain/Loss
Options window

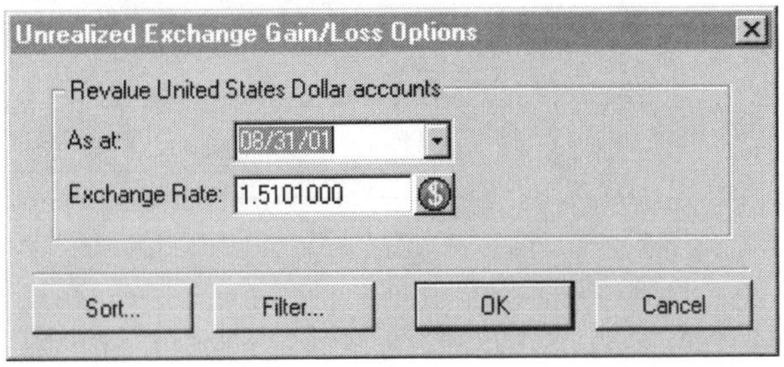

Simply Accounting will also allow you to revalue the foreign exchange accounts based on a certain date and foreign exchange rate. This will in turn report any unrealized gain/loss (Figure 11.29).

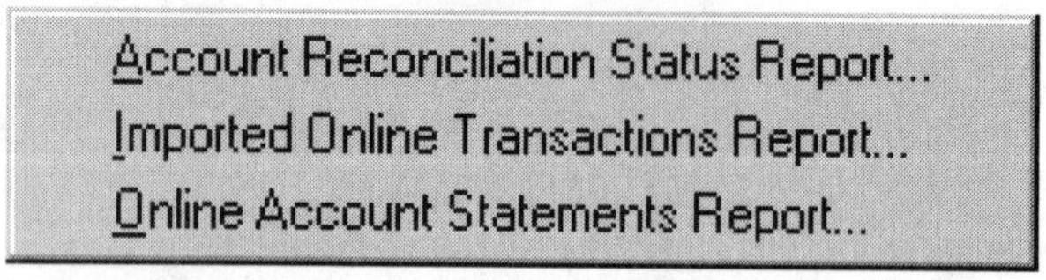

Figure 11.30
Accounts
Reconciliation
Reports submenu

Account Reconciliation Report

The **Account Reconciliation** menu (Figure 11.30) provides you with the following reports applicable to bank and account reconciliation. These options will be discussed in detail in Chapter 12.

Accounts Payable Reports

Figure 11.31
Accounts Payable
Reports
submenu

When you click on this option, a submenu is displayed (Figure 11.31) which contains the following Accounts Payable specific reports:

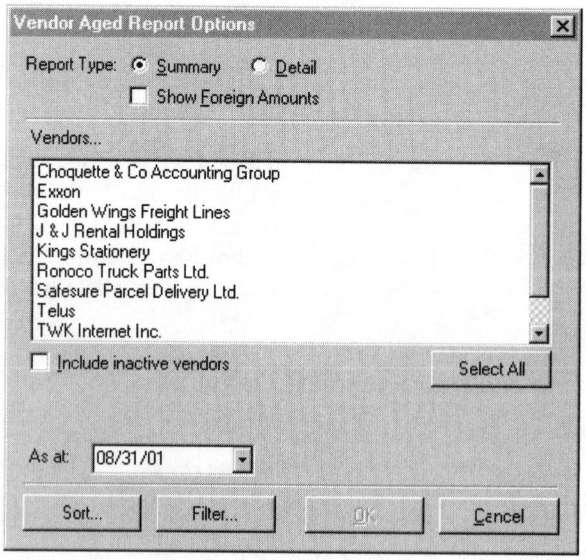

Figure 11.32
Vendor Aged
Report Options
window

Vendor Aged   displays a listing of the current vendor aged invoices. This report can be customized to include a range of vendors as well as the report date. This report can be displayed in either summary or detail mode (Figure 11.32).

Figure 11.33
Aged Overdue
Payables Option
window

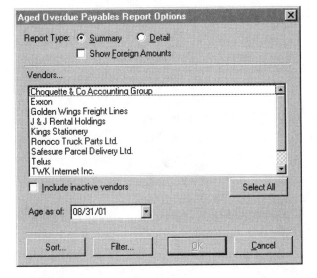

Aged Overdue Payables   displays a listing of the overdue vendor aged invoices. This report can be customized to include a range of vendors as well as the report date. This report can be displayed in either summary or detail mode (Figure 11.33).

Figure 11.34
Vendor Purchases
Option window

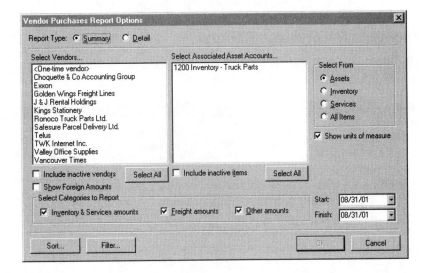

Vendor Purchases   displays a listing of the vendor purchases. This report customization includes the option to print inventory, non-inventory, or all purchases for a range of vendors and a range of inventory accounts or items. This report can be printed in either a summary or detail mode (Figure 11.34).

Figure 11.35
Pending Purchase
Orders Option window

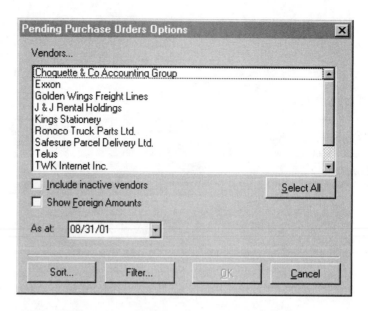

Pending Purchase Orders

displays a listing of the pending unfilled purchase orders. This report will include the purchase order date and expected ship date (Figure 11.35).

Figure 11.36
Receivables
Report submenu

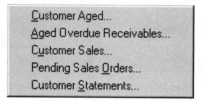

Accounts Receivables Reports

Clicking on this option displays a submenu (Figure 11.36) which contains the following Accounts Receivables specific reports:

Figure 11.37
Customer Aged
Report Options

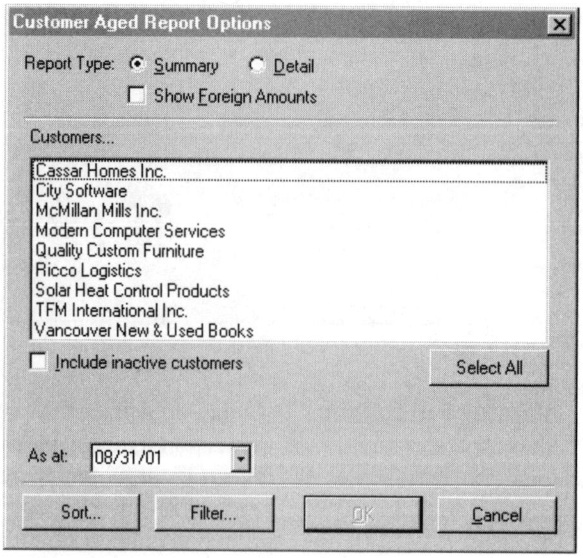

C̲ustomer Aged displays a listing of the current customer aged invoices. This report can be customized to include a range of vendors and to specify an **As at** date at which to report the data. This report can be displayed in either summary or detail mode (Figure 11.37)

Figure 11.38
Aged Overdue
Receivables Report
Options window

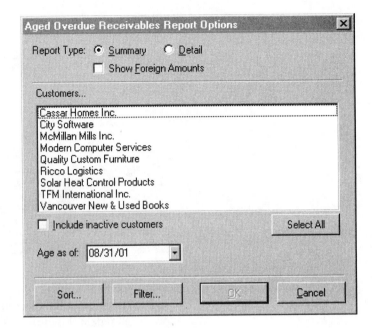

Aged Overdue Receivables displays a listing of the overdue customer aged invoices. This report can be customized to include a range of vendors as well as the report date. This report can be displayed in either summary or detail mode (Figure 11.38).

Figure 11.39
Customer Sales
Report Options
window

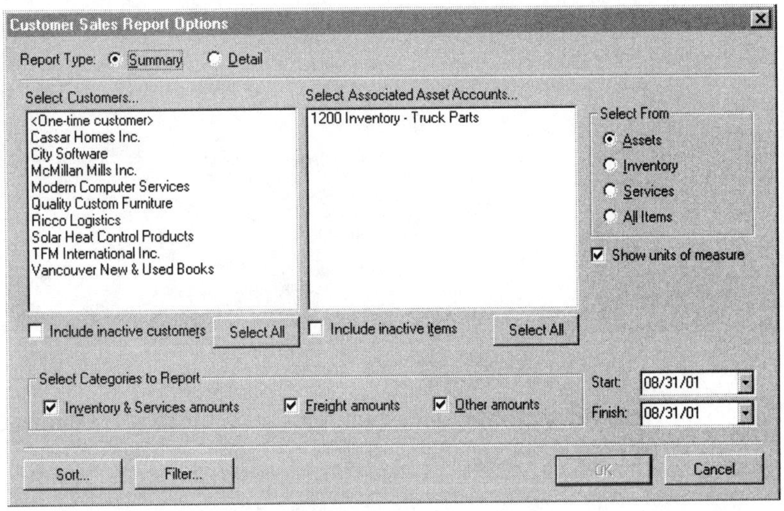

Customer Sales   displays a listing of the customer sales. This report customization includes the option to print inventory, non-inventory, or all sales for a range of customers and a range of inventory accounts or items. This report can be printed in either summary or detail mode (Figure 11.39).

Figure 11.40
Pending Sales
Order Options
window

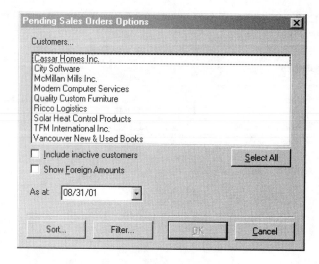

Pending Sales Orders   displays a listing of the pending unfilled customer sales orders. This report will include the sales order date and expected ship date (Figure 11.40).

Figure 11.41
Print Customer
Statements
options window

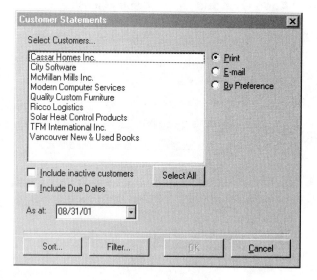

Print Customer Statements   will print your customer statements of account based on a defined selection of customers. You can also include the due dates for reference by your customers (note Figure 11.41).

Figure 11.42
GST/HST
Report Options
window

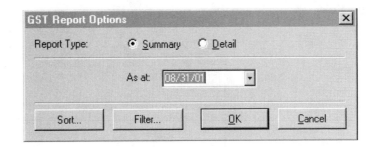

GST/HST
(Tax Report)

will produce a GST/HST report which will provide you with the details required to complete your GST/HST return (Figure 11.42). The GST/HST report option will generate a report based on entries within the Purchases and Sales journals. Entries for GST/HST made directly in the General journal will not be included in the GST/HST report.

Payroll and Employee Reports

Figure 11.43
Payroll reports
submenu

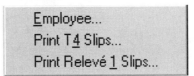

Payroll

displays a submenu (Figure 11.43) which contains the following Payroll specific reports:

Figure 11.44
Employee Report
Options window

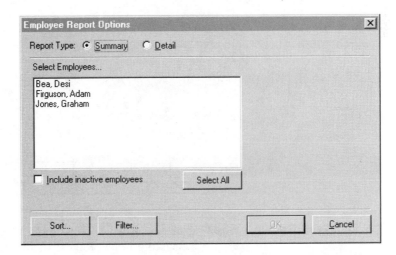

Employee

will allow you to print either a summary or a detailed employee report (Figure 11.44). This report is helpful when completing ROEs (Record of Employment) and other payroll documentation.

Figure 11.45
T4 Slips
Options window

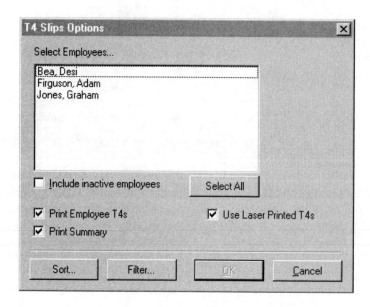

Print T4 Slips will generate T4 slips for your employees using either continuous feed (dot-matrix) or laser T4 forms. Both of these forms are available from Revenue Canada Taxation. You will also have the option of printing a T4 summary for remittance purposes (Figure 11.45)

Figure 11.46
Relevé 1 Slips
Options window

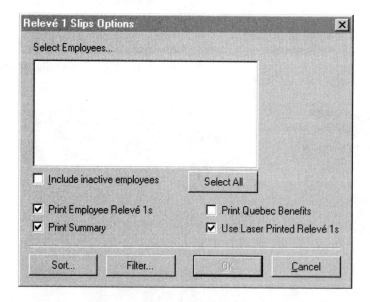

Print Relevé 1 Slips generates Relevé 1 slips for Quebec employees. You can select to print the Revelé 1 slips on either continuous or laser forms and to also print a summary and information pertaining to Quebec benefits (Figure 11.46)

INVENTORY REPORTS

Figure 11.47
Inventory Reports
submenu

The **Inventory** menu displays a submenu (Figure 11.47) which contains the following Inventory specific reports:

Figure 11.48
Inventory Report
Options window

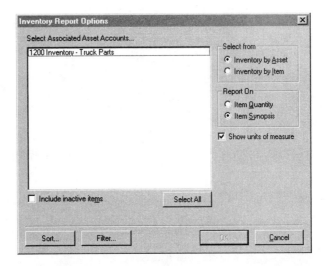

Inventory　　will generate inventory reports such as quantities on hand and below minimum inventory levels, synopsis of the cost values of the inventory, and even a detail report format which can include valuable information about your inventory turnover (Figure 11.48).

Figure 11.49
Inventory and
Services Activity
Report Options
window

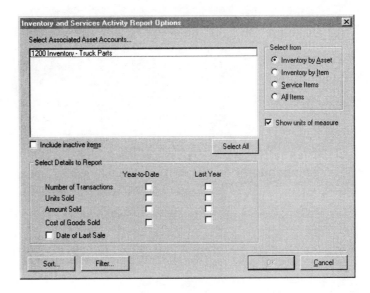

Activity　　will display either a summary or detail report containing data about your selected type of transactions (Figure 11.49).

Figure 11.50
Inventory and
Services Sales
Report Options
window

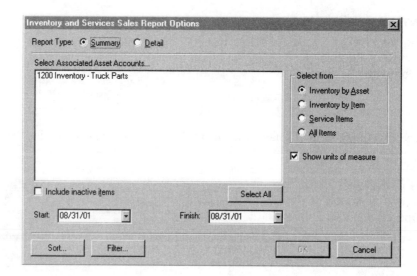

Sales will provide you with summary or detailed information pertaining to your inventory sales (Figure 11.50).

Figure 11.51
Inventory and
Service Transaction
Report Options
window

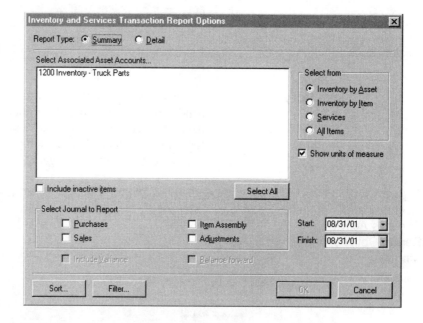

Transaction will provide you with summary or detail combined sales and purchase information (Figure 11.51).

PROJECT REPORTS

Figure 11.52
Project Reports
submenu

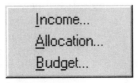

Project menu   provides several reports that allow you to display and print net earnings for each project as well as applicable project budgeting. Refer to Chapter 10 for more information on this reporting function, (note Figure 11.52).

Figure 11.53
Journal Entries
Reports submenu

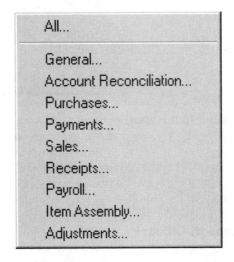

Journal Entries menu   will allow you to display and print a listing of journal entries. This provides you with a detailed listing of the entries that have been posted to Simply Accounting for Windows (note Figure 11.53).

Figure 11.54
All Journal Entries
Options window

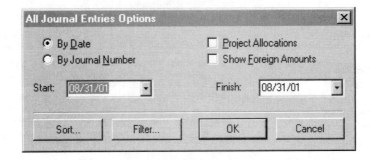

Figure 11.54 displays the options window that will be displayed for each journal entry. You can select the **Start** and **Finish** dates along with options to display by either posting date or journal entry number along with project allocations (the details pertaining to specific projects based on each entry).

Mailing Labels will allow you to print mailing labels for vendors, customers, and employees. This feature is helpful if you need to send a mass mailing to each group.

Figure 11.55
Advice (Management
Reports) window

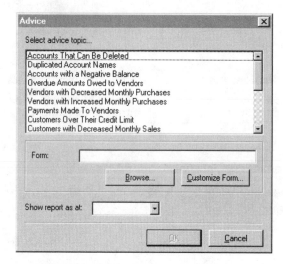

Management Reports provides you with a feature of displaying and printing customized reports (selected modules or all modules) based on your company's information (Figure 11.55). Please refer to the latter part of this chapter for information on customization of these reports as well as financial statements.

Microsoft Office will allow integration of your Simply Accounting data with the Microsoft Office group of applications. This will in turn allow you to extend the usability of your Simply Accounting data for analysis and additional reporting options (using Microsoft Office). You must, however, have the Microsoft Office applications (or compatible applications) in which to use the database, spreadsheet, and documents as noted in Figure 11.56). You can also create your own database, spreadsheets, and documents as required.

Figure 11.56
Microsoft
Compatible
Applications

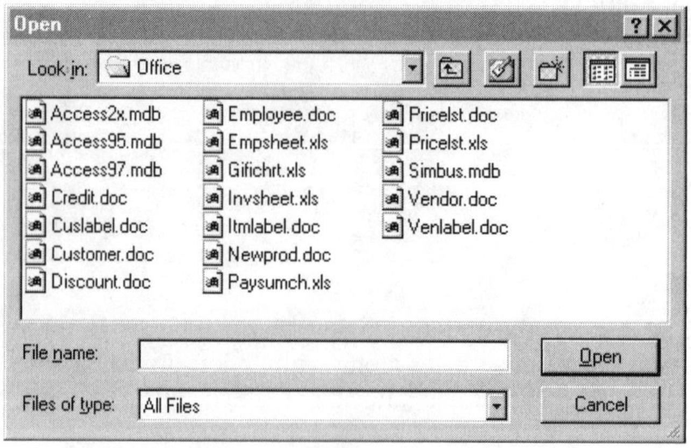

Practice Exercise 11.4

Print all applicable reports to determine the aging balance for your Payables and Receivables. Also print a Trial Balance and Balance Sheet as at August 31, 2001 and an Income Statement comparing actual figures to budget figures for the year-to-date to August 31, 2001.

PRINTING FORMS

The following section explains how to set the various options for printing cheques, invoices, statements, and labels. We will also discuss the CA-RET report writer as well as the Crystal Report Writer.

Continue from the Simply Accounting - ODC window (Figure 11.1).

You are now ready to configure the Simply Accounting system for specific printing options. Continue by

Selecting the **Setup** menu.

Figure 11.57
Setup menu

Continue from within the **Setup** menu (Figure 11.57) by

Selecting the Reports and Forms menu option.

Figure 11.58
Report & Forms
Options window

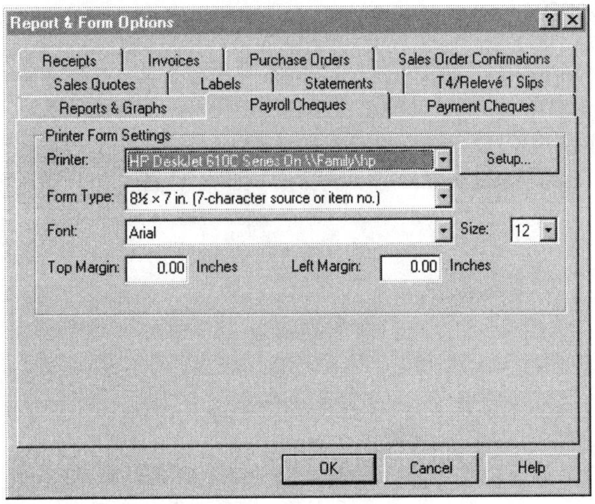

PRINTING CHEQUES

Let's first configure the printing option for Payroll cheques. Continue by

Selecting the **Payroll Cheques** tab button (Figure 11.58).

Figure 11.59
Printers Report
and Form Options
window after
Payroll Cheques
option is selected

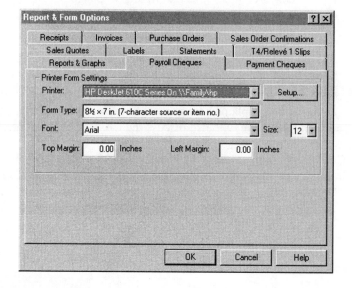

*Note: The printer options shown in Figure 11.59 are specific to the type of printer that you are using and may not be the same as the one shown in your window. If necessary, you can change these options by clicking on the pull down arrows located to the right of the **Printer** and **Font** fields.*

Now look at the **Form size** options. If you look at Figure 11.59, you will notice that the current form selected is "Regular 8 1/2 x 7 in.". If you click on the pull down button located to the right of the **Form size** button, a pull down list appears (Figure 11.60).

Figure 11.60
Printers Report
& Form Options
window showing
the various form
sizes for cheques

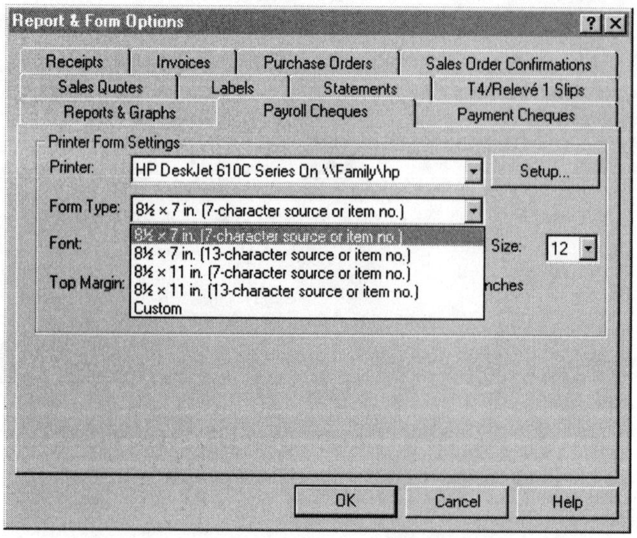

This **Form size** pull down list has three options: the "Regular 8 1/2 x 7 in.", "Letter 8 1/2 x 11 in." and "Custom". These options conform with the preprinted forms that are available for Simply Accounting for Windows, with the exception of the "Custom" option which allows you to specify or define a custom cheque specification file, (note invoice example below). Let's select the "Letter 8 1/2 x 11 in." option by either clicking on this option or by pressing [↓] key followed by [Tab].

Now select the form size for the **Payment Cheques.** Continue by pressing

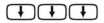 to change the **Form size** to 8 1/2 x 11 in. If this size is not desired, select the form size.

Continue from the Printers Report & Form Options window, (Figure 11.59) by

Selecting the **Labels** tabbed button.

Figure 11.61
Printers Report & Form Options window with labels selected

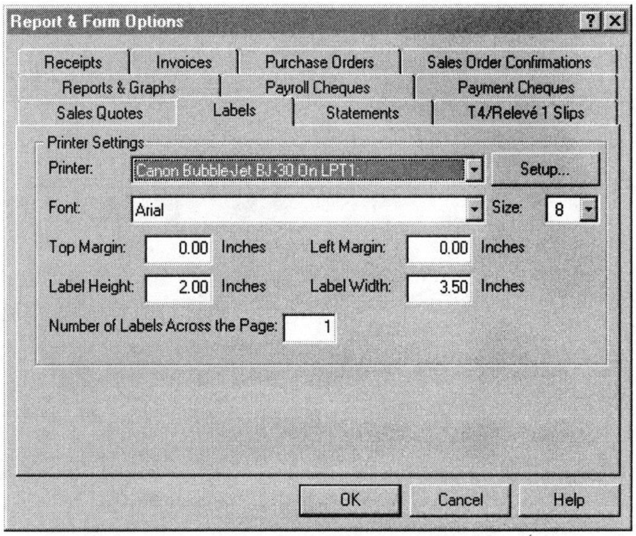

You will notice that Simply Accounting for Windows allows you to customize label printing (Figure 11.61) so that you can specify the number of labels that you want to print across the page as well as the height and width of each label. Once you have entered these parameters, Simply Accounting for Windows will use these settings until you change them again.

Practice Exercise 11.5

Select the **Statements** tabbed button. Notice that the **Form size** has defaulted to *Regular 8 1/2 x 7 in.* Change this option to Letter 8 1/2 x 11 in (13 character), as in the previous example.

Once you have completed this exercise, remain within the Report and Forms Options window (note Figure 11.61).

USING CUSTOM REPORT OPTIONS

Simply Accounting provides support for the use of both Crystal Reports and the earlier Simply Accounting for Windows report writer CA-RET.

This customization option provides you with unlimited access to the reporting and graphing capabilities within Simply Accounting for Windows.

Important Note: Installing Crystal Reports

Crystal Reports for Simply Accounting is required in order to create or modify new custom report files.

You can install Crystal Reports from the Simply Accounting CD-ROM. The installation button is located within the main installation screen.

Continue from within the Reports & Forms Options window (Figure 11.61) by

Selecting the **Invoices** tabbed button.

Figure 11.62
Report & Options
window (Invoices)

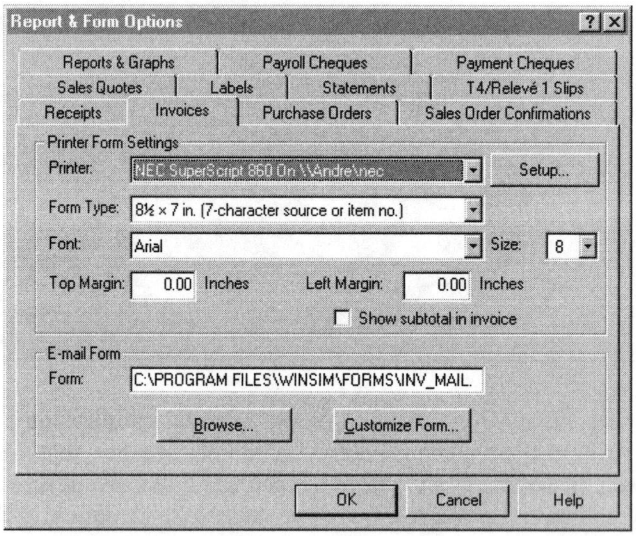

Continue from the Report & forms Options window (with **Invoices** selected, as shown in Figure 11.62) by

Clicking on the pull down arrows beside the **Form** field.

Figure 11.63
Printer Report
& Form Options
window (Invoices)
with Forms pull
down button pressed

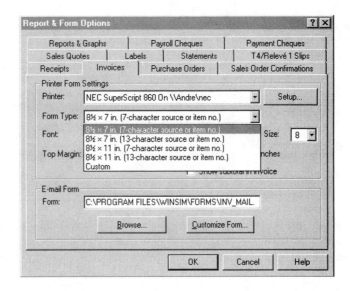

Continue from the Report & Forms Options window (Figure 11.63) by selecting the **Custom** forms option.

Figure 11.64
Printer window
(Invoices) with
Custom Forms
selected

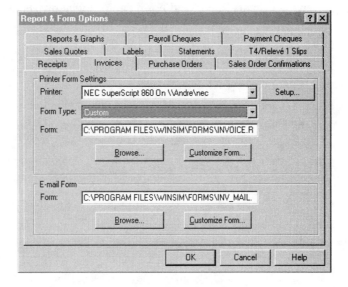

As shown in Figure 11.64, your Printers Report and Form Options window has changed to display the following:

Browse   allows you to **Browse** your hard drive for the appropriate Crystal Reports or CA-RET specification file (Figure 11.65).

Figure 11.65
Choose a Report
File window

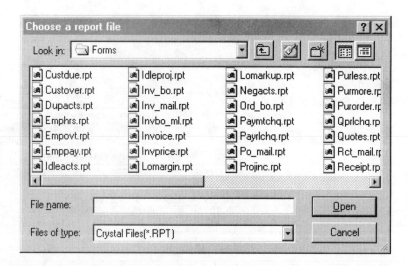

Customize Form   allows you to customize the Crystal Report or CA-RET
specification file. By selecting this option, the Crystal
Reports form editor will be opened.

Continue from the Printers Report and Form Options window (Figure 11.64) by

Clicking the **OK** button.

DEFINING DEFAULT REPORT SETTINGS

The next step is to tell Simply Accounting about the options that we wish to use when we print
invoices and cheques. From within the Simply Accounting - ODC window (Figure 11.1) continue by

Selecting the **Setup** menu (Figure 11.57).

Selecting the **Settings** menu option.

Figure 11.66
Settings window

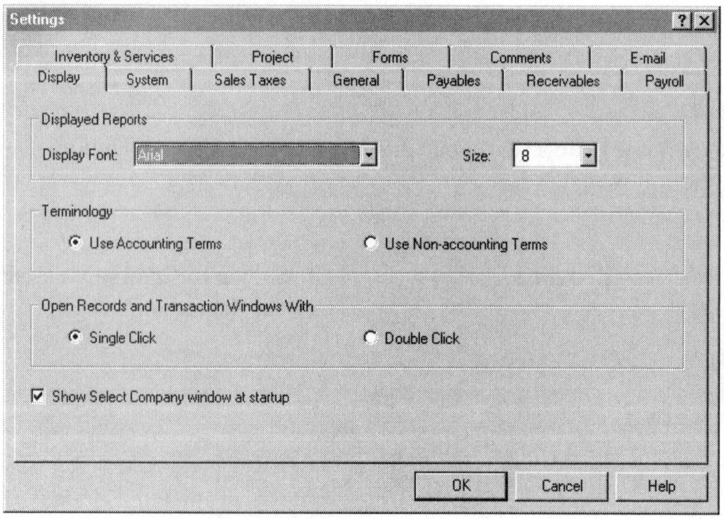

Continue from the Setting window (Figure 11.66) by

Selecting the **Forms** tabbed button.

Figure 11.67
Settings window
with the Forms
option selected

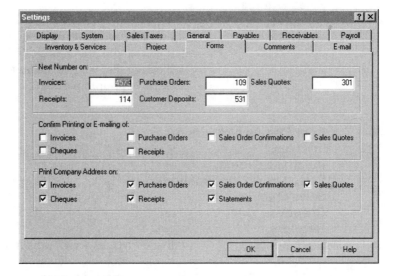

You will notice that you have many form options to choose from (Figure 11.67). Let's look at each in some detail.

Next Number on:

Invoices	This option informs Simply Accounting of your next invoice number.
Purchase Orders	The next Purchase Order is defined within this field.
Sales Quotes	The next Sales Quote number that you will issue.
Cheques	The next sequential cheque number for the main bank account. Simply Accounting will then provide a default cheque number when you print an accounts payable/cash purchase cheque (see Chapter 9), and a default cheque number when you generate a paycheque for your employee(s) (see Chapter 11). However, Simply Accounting will assume that you will use the same bank account to write cheques for either accounts payable/cash purchase or payroll.
Bank 2 Chqs:	The next cheque number for the alternate bank account.
Receipts:	The next payment receipt number (if used) for your accounts receivable payments received.

**Confirm Printing for
Invoices,
Purchase Orders,
Sales Order Confirmations,
Sales Quotes,
Cheques,
Receipts**
allows you the option of a reminder (prior to posting) that you should print a copy of the applicable form. This will ensure that you remember to print each applicable document (prior to posting).

**Print Company Address on
Invoices,
Purchase Orders,
Sales Order Confirmations,
Sales Quotes,
Cheques,
Receipts,
Statements**
will allow you to secifiy which forms are to include the company name and address information (when printing on non-customized forms).

Practice Exercise 11.6

CHANGING FORM SETTINGS

For this exercise, enter the following information:

If an option is selected, this informs Simply Accounting that "Yes" you want to complete this option.

Confirm printing for invoices:	Yes
Confirm printing for POs:	Yes
Confirm printing for cheques:	Yes
Print company address on invoices:	Yes
Print company address on POs:	Yes
Print company address on statements:	Yes
Print company address on cheques:	Yes

Once you have completed this exercise, remain within the Settings (Forms) window (Figure 11.67).

DEFAULT DOCUMENT COMMENTS

Simply Accounting also provides the flexibility of allowing you to enter default comments for invoices, sales order confirmations, and sale quotes. Continue from within the Settings (Forms) window (Figure 11.67) by

Clicking on the **Comments** tabbed button.

Figure 11.68
Settings (Comments)
window

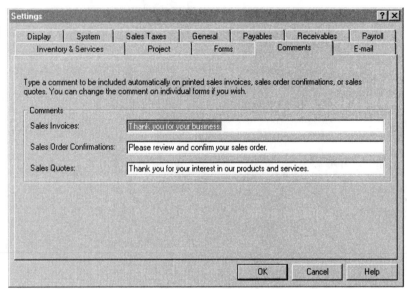

The Settings (Comments) window (Figure 11.68) provides default **Comments** fields that can be changed to reflect your company's messages for the various transactions.

Practice Exercise 11.7

Continue within the Settings (Comment) window (Figure 11.68) by changing the Sales Invoice Comment to display:

Your continued business is appreciated.

Once you have completed this exercise, continue by closing the Settings window. You will then return to the Simply Accounting - ODC window (Figure 11.1).

Practice Exercise 11.8

Now enter the following transaction and print out the corresponding invoice or cheque:

Transaction #1:   Sales invoice (Bill Later)
                   Sold to: Cassar Homes Inc.
                   Invoice: (default value which should be 4573)
                   Date: 08/31/01
                   Description: Airfreight
                   Amount: 100.00
                   GST Code: 3
                   PST: 0.0% (or blank)
                   Acct: 4260
                   Project: Freight 100.0%

Customer should exceed credit limit (which is expectable).

Transaction #2:   Purchase (Paid by Cheque - 1040 Bank - Royal)
                   Purchase from: Telus
                   Cash Purchase: Purchase with Payment selected
                   Cheque: (default which should be 544)
                   Invoice: Aug/01 (2)
                   Date: 08/31/01
                   GST Code: 3
                   GST Amount: 3.50
                   Amount: 50.00
                   Acct: 5540
                   Project: Freight 33.0%, Rental 33.0%, Storage 10.0%

Once you have completed the above practice exercise, you will notice that Simply Accounting has kept track of the invoice numbers as well as cheque numbers. Furthermore, if you print the associated invoice or cheque, you will notice that all pertinent information is contained on these documents.

You will also notice that the invoice was printed using the CA-RET customized specification file. Look to the comment section at the bottom of the invoice and you will notice that the comment is now customized to each particular customer.

BACKING UP YOUR DATA FILES

At this point, return to the Simply Accounting - ODC window and continue with the backup function.

Call this backup:

Backup Filename: A:\odc\ODC11
Comment: Reports/Graphs Part 11

Further Practice

To get further practice with the concepts you have learned in this chapter go to Chapter 14 and work through Section 11 of the National Supply Company.

CHAPTER 12

BANK RECONCILIATION AND MONTH-END ADJUSTMENT ENTRIES

CHAPTER 12

BANK RECONCILIATION AND MONTH-END ADJUSTMENT ENTRIES

OBJECTIVES

After working through this chapter you will be able to

1. Use the Bank Reconciliation feature of Simply Accounting.
2. Prepare a series of month-end adjustment entries and post them to the appropriate General Ledger accounts.

BANK RECONCILIATION

The Bank Reconciliation feature within Simply Accounting for Windows allows you to visually reconcile your General Ledger bank account entries with those printed on your bank statement.

Practice Exercise 12.1

Start Simply Accounting for Windows. When prompted for the data set, select **odc**.

When prompted for the Using Date, confirm that this date is **09/15/01**. Simply Accounting will ask you to confirm that the new using date is more than one week past the previous date. Select **OK** to confirm this action.

When the To-Do List window is displayed, remain at this window.

In previous chapters the advancement of your using date has not been completed. However this feature is extremely important and should be clearly understood as to its purpose and flexibility.

WHY DOES SIMPLY ACCOUNTING ASK FOR A USING DATE?

The purpose of the Using Date is to provide you (the user) with an entry date window in which you can make entries within Simply Accounting for Windows.

As you have advanced the Using Date to September 15, 2001 you will be able to make entries within Simply Accounting for Windows from the date of conversion (08/01/01) to the current using date of 09/15/01.

In future years, your entry date window will be from the fiscal start date (January 01 for this book) to the current using date.

When entering an optimal Using Date, remember to consider the following factors:

If you are planning to use Simply Accounting for Windows each day, entering your transactions on a daily basis, enter your Using Date as the current date on which you will be entering transactions.

If you will be entering your Simply Accounting for Windows transactions on a periodic basis, such as once per month, enter your Using Date as the last day of the period in which you will be entering transactions. For example, if you are entering transactions for the month of August, 2001, then the using date would be 08/31/01.

Simply Accounting for Windows has the following restrictions with regards to making entries and the Using Date entered:

Your transaction date can not exceed the Using Date. This prevents you from making entries outside the entry Date window.

Advancing your Using Date too far in advance will effect several of Simply Accounting for Windows reports. For example, it will effect your aging on several Simply Accounting for Windows reports, including your customer statements.

If you want to advance the Using Date past December 31, you must first change the Using Date to January 01 and then advance the Using Date to the new Using Date. This is necessary because Simply Accounting for Windows must close your payroll records for the calender year. YOU MUST HAVE A BACKUP COPY OF YOUR DATA FILES PRIOR TO ACCEPTING THE ADVANCEMENT OF YOUR USING DATE INTO THE NEW CALENDER YEAR.

If you want to advance your Using Date past your fiscal year-end date, you must first enter the first day of the new fiscal year, and then change the Using Date to the new date in the new fiscal year. This is necessary because Simply Accounting for Windows must close your fiscal year which includes the posting of the balances in your income statement accounts. YOU MUST HAVE A BACKUP PRIOR TO ACCEPTING THE ADVANCEMENT OF YOUR USING DATE INTO THE NEW CALENDER YEAR.

Continue from within the To-Do List window by

Clicking the **Recurring** tabbed button.

Figure 12.1
To-Do Lists
window

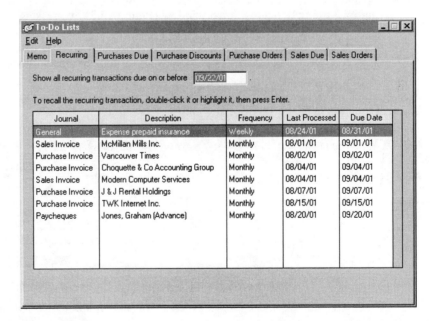

Simply Accounting for Windows will now display the To-Do Lists window as shown in Figure 12.1. The purpose of this window is to remind you of any recurring entries. As noted, you have a total of two sales, three purchases, and one General Journal entry that will be due within one week from the new Using Date of 09/15/01.

If you only wish to display a certain journal of recurring entries you could select the applicable module tabbed button as noted within the To-Do Lists window (Figure 12.1).

Continue from the To-Do Lists window (Figure 12.1) by

Double-clicking on the first recurring entry for *McMillan Mills Inc. (Sales Journal due 09/01/01).*

Figure 12.2
Sales Journal
window
(recurring entry)

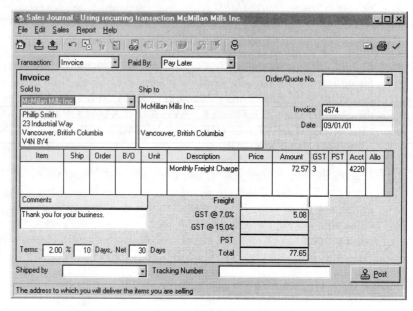

Simply Accounting for Windows will now retrieve the recurring entry for *McMillan Mills Inc.* and will display this entry in the Sales Journal window (Figure 12.2).

Continue from the Sales Journal window (Figure 12.2) by pressing

Alt + P	to **Post** this sales invoice.
Y	to select **Yes** to the posting of this invoice without printing.
Alt + F4	to close the Sales Journal window.

You will then return to the To-Do List window as noted in Figure 12.3.

Figure 12.3
To-Do Lists
window (modified)

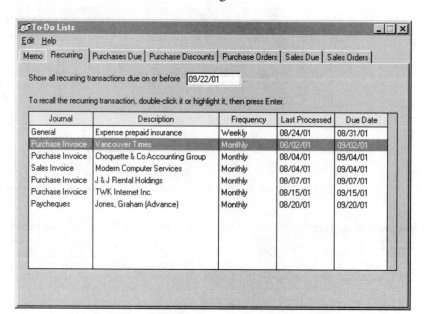

Your Simply Accounting for Windows To-Do Lists window (Figure 12.3) no longer displays the *McMillan Mills Inc.* entry because it was posted.

Practice Exercise 12.2

POSTING RECURRING ENTRIES FROM WITHIN THE TO-DO LIST WINDOW

Continue with the selection and posting of the following recurring entries (from within the To-Do Lists window - note Figure 12.3):

Re-format Journal	*Description*	*Last Posted*	*Due Date*
Purchase	Vancouver Times Invoice number #16002	8/02/01	9/02/01
Purchase	Choquette & Company Invoice number #401	8/4/01	9/04/01
Sales	Modern Computer Services	8/4/01	9/04/01
Purchase	J. & J. Rental Holdings Invoice number #4292	8/7/01	9/07/01
Purchase	TWK Internet Inc. Invoice number #910 (default exchange rate)	08/15/01	09/15/01
General	Expense prepaid insurance Source code ADJ112	8/24/01	8/31/01
General	Expense prepaid insurance Source code ADJ113	8/31/01	9/07/01
General	Expense prepaid insurance Source code ADJ119	9/07/01	9/14/01

Once you have completed this exercise, close the To-Do Lists window. You will then return to the Simply Accounting - ODC window as displayed in Figure 12.4. Also be sure to close the Checklists window.

Figure 12.4
Simply Accounting -
ODC window

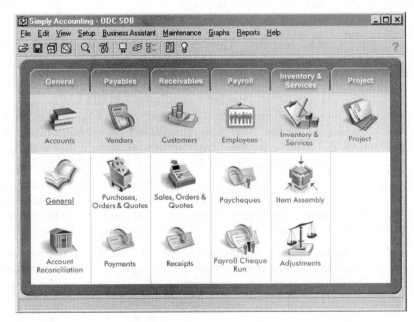

Once you have completed Practice Exercise 12.2, you should have the Simply Accounting - ODC window displayed (Figure 12.4). The next step is to locate your bank reconciliation statement. We will use the following statement:

Royal Bank of Canada

Date	Account Type	Account Number	Balance Forward
07/31/01	Current Chequing	668958	20,178.85

Overnight Delivery Company
300-3665 Kingsway
Vancouver BC V5R 5W2

Date	#/CD	Description	Withdrawal	Deposit	Balance
07/02	105	Cheque	1,200.00		18,978.85
07/15	106	Cheque	400.00		18,578.85
07/31	SC	Service Charge	12.50		18,566.35

Figure 12.5   July 31, 2001 Bank Statement

As you can see from the July 31, 2001 bank statement (Figure 12.5), two cheques have been cashed by the bank along with the withdrawal of the monthly service charge.

THE BANK RECONCILIATION PROCESS

If you have ever reconciled your bank statement for your business or personal records, you may be easily confused. Using the Simply Accounting for Windows Bank Reconciliation feature allows you to easily complete this task as follows:

1. Select the **Bank Reconciliation** icon.

2. Enter the **Ending Date.** This date is normally the Bank Statement date. Example: If you are reconciling your bank account up to July 31, 2001 the End Date would be 07/31/01.

3. Enter a Comment (if required).

4. Enter the **End Balance.** This amount will be the final bank balance from the bottom of your bank statement. This balance should be inclusive of any transactions that have been posted through the bank account. Using the above bank statements as an example, the End Balance would be 18,566.35.

5. Using either your cancelled cheques/stubs and/or your bank statement, Clear (check mark) all cleared items within the Bank Reconciliation window. A Cleared status tells Simply Accounting that this item has been posted through your bank account (thus will appear on your bank statement).

6. Clear (check mark) all reversed transaction (including both the original entry and the associated reversal entry). The net effect of each reversed transaction should be zero and the reversal entry will void the original entry amounts.

7. Enter your bank services charges, bank interest earned, and any other additional charges or credits that appear on your bank statement but not within your Simply Accounting Bank Reconciliation window. If you have forgotten to enter either a deposit or cheque/withdrawal you can select to **Save** your bank reconciliation, return to the Simply Accounting - ODC window, continue with the posting of the missing transaction and then return to your bank reconciliation to finish the reconciliation.

The unresolved amount within your Bank Reconciliation window should now be NIL (zero). If this is the case, you have successfully reconciled your bank account. If you have an unresolved amount that is not a NIL (zero) balance, use the following guidelines to locate the missing amounts:

1. If your unresolved amount is divisible by nine, this difference may be caused by a transposition entry within either your Simply Accounting or bank records. Confirm each entry on the bank statement to the corresponding Simply Accounting reconciliation window.

2. Make sure that you have entered the bank services charges and other bank transactions that you may not have previously entered.

Once you have reconciled your bank account, continue by **Posting** this reconciliation. You should then print a copy of this reconciliation from within Simply Accounting for Windows.

RECONCILING THE ODC BANK STATEMENT

To reconcile the July 31, 2001 bank statement against your General Ledger bank account entries, start from the Simply Accounting - ODC window (Figure 12.4).

Double-click on the **Accounts Reconciliation** icon.

Figure 12.6
Bank Reconciliation
Journal window

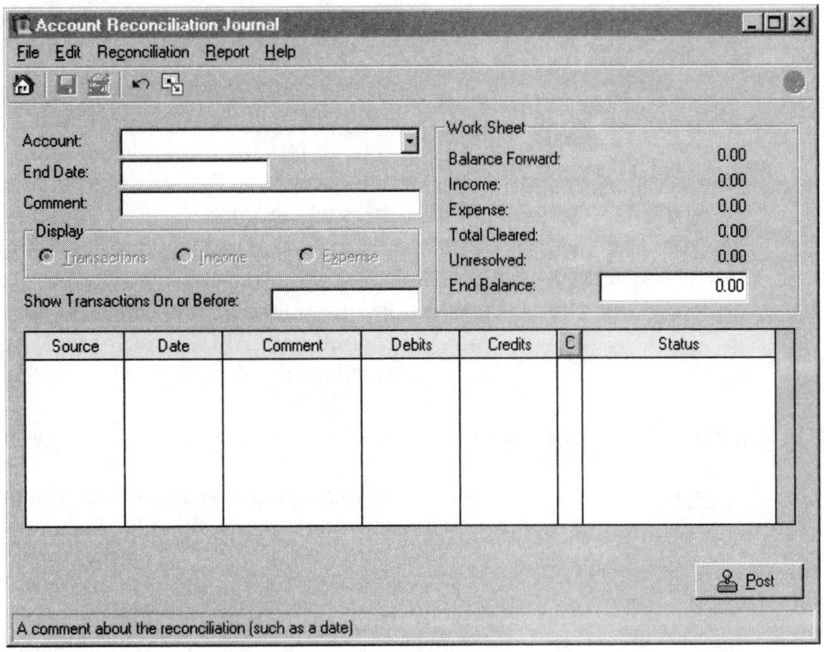

The Bank Reconciliation Journal window will now appear as shown in Figure 12.6. This window allows you to select and then enter those transactions that have been processed through the bank statement.

Press

⬇
to display *1040 Bank - Royal.*

> **HINT:** *Simply Accounting for Windows will list all accounts for which you selected the **Save transaction for Bank Reconciliation** option (see Chapter 4 for setting up General Ledger accounts).*

Continue by pressing

Tab
to move to the **End Date** field.

07/31/01 Tab
to enter the **End Date**. This date is also known as the bank statement ending date.

Prepared by DLB Tab to enter a **Comment** for this reconciliation.

Figure 12.7
Display selection area

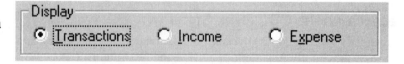

As shown in Figure 12.7, the display portion contains the following selections:

Transactions   displays the listing of transactions within the bank account as entered through applicable journals.

Income   allows you to enter transactions relating to income received on the bank statement but not previously entered into the General Journal. An example of such an entry would be the receipt of bank interest (income) on the bank account.

Expense   allows you to enter transactions relating to expenses incurred on the bank statement but not previously entered into the General Journal. An example of such an entry would be bank service charges.

You will make the service charge entry at a later point. For now, continue by pressing

Tab
to move to the **Show Transactions On or Before** field. This will filter transactions to be displayed.

073101 Tab
to enter the **Show Transaction on or Before** date. This will only display transactions that have been posted on or before July 31, 2001 (to match the period that we are reconciling).

18566.35 Tab
to enter the **End Balance** from the bank statement as shown in Figure 13.2.

Figure 12.8
Bank Reconciliation
Journal window
(header entered)

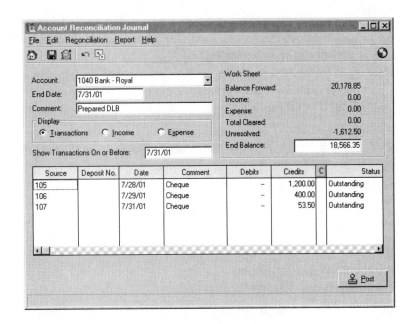

As shown in Figure 12.8, you have completed the entry portion of the header of the reconciliation. At this point, it is probably easier to use your mouse to continue.

In Figure 12.8, a listing of the entered transactions are displayed. Between the **Credits** and **Status** columns is a column titled **C**, (Cleared). This column is where you will position your mouse when instructed.

Looking back at the bank statement displayed in Figure 12.2, two cheques have been cashed on this bank statement. You must now select these cheques as being cleared within the bank reconciliation journal.

Continue as follows:

Position you mouse cursor within the **C** column for cheque 105. Once positioned, click on it with your mouse.

Figure 12.9
Bank Reconciliation
Journal window
(Cheque 105 Cleared)

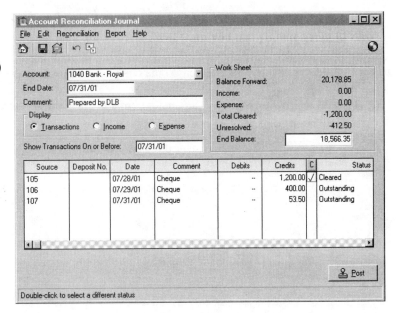

As shown in Figure 12.9, a check mark now appears in the **C** (Cleared) column. This signifies that the cheque has been cleared. You will also notice that the **unresolved balance** has been reduced by the amount of this cheque ($1,200.00).

Practice Exercise 12.3

Continue with the clearing of cheque number **#106.**

Once you have completed this exercise, remain within the Bank Reconciliation window (Figure 12.10).

Figure 12.10
Bank Reconciliation
Journal window
(Cheques cleared)

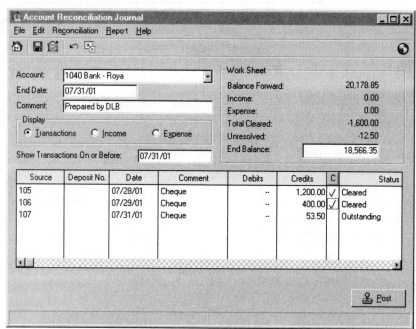

Once you have completed the above exercise, your Bank Reconciliation window will resemble Figure 12.10. At this point you have cleared the cheques as shown on the bank statement in Figure 12.5.

The next step within this bank reconciliation is to enter the service charge as recorded on the bank statement, (Figure 12.5). Continue by pressing

         Alt + X   to select the **Expense** option.

Figure 12.11
Bank Reconciliation
Journal window
(Expense display)

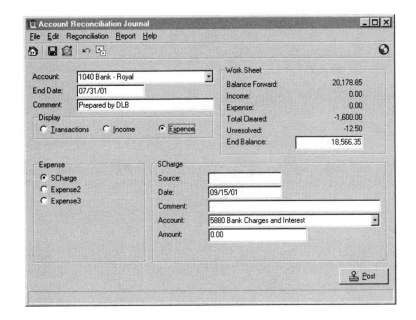

The Bank Reconciliation Journal display will change to display an entry form for recording the bank service charge (Figure 12.11).

Continue by pressing

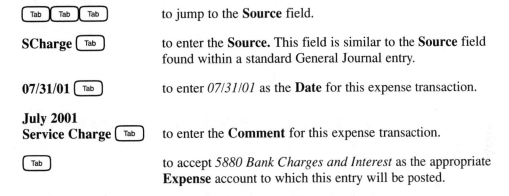

`Tab` `Tab` `Tab`	to jump to the **Source** field.
SCharge `Tab`	to enter the **Source**. This field is similar to the **Source** field found within a standard General Journal entry.
07/31/01 `Tab`	to enter *07/31/01* as the **Date** for this expense transaction.
July 2001 Service Charge `Tab`	to enter the **Comment** for this expense transaction.
`Tab`	to accept *5880 Bank Charges and Interest* as the appropriate **Expense** account to which this entry will be posted.

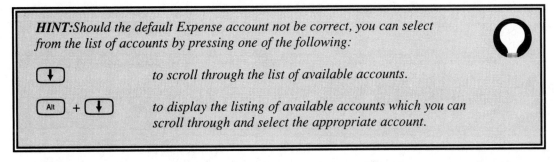

HINT: Should the default Expense account not be correct, you can select from the list of accounts by pressing one of the following:

`↓`	*to scroll through the list of available accounts.*
`Alt` + `↓`	*to display the listing of available accounts which you can scroll through and select the appropriate account.*

12.50 `Tab`   to enter the **Amount** of the expense.

Figure 12.12
Bank Reconciliation
Journal window
(Expense transaction
entered)

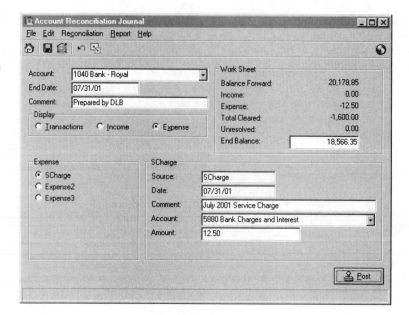

Your Bank Reconciliation Journal window should now resemble Figure 12.12. Note that the **Unresolved balance** is now zero. You have reconciled the bank account to the bank statement for July 2001.

Before posting this bank reconciliation, continue with the displaying of the bank reconciliation journal entry. Continue from the Bank Reconciliation Journal window by pressing

| Alt | + | R | | to select the **Report** menu. |

| D | | to select **Display Bank Rec. Journal Entry.** |

Figure 12.13
Bank Reconciliation
Journal Entry window

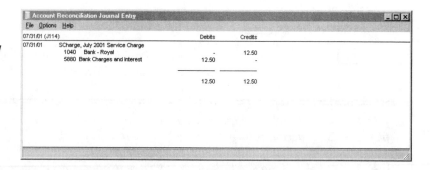

The Bank Reconciliation Journal Entry window displays the journal entry for the bank service charge (Figure 12.13).

> *HINT: The Bank Reconciliation Journal Entry window will not display any entries associated with the clearing of cheques or deposits, as this action does not affect the accounting within the General Ledger. Instead, the clearing of the cheques and deposits are used to confirm your General Ledger bank account balance to the ending bank balance contained within the bank statement (Figure 12.5).*

Continue by pressing

Alt + F4   to close the Bank Rec. Journal Entry window. You will then return to the Bank Reconciliation Journal window.

Continue by pressing

Alt + P   to **P**ost the bank reconciliation.

Y   to accept that the journal date for the bank service charge transaction precedes the Using Date. Keep in mind that normally the Bank Reconciliation is done after the end of the month.

As you have completed the bank reconciliation for July 2001, continue by pressing

Alt + F4   to close the Bank Reconciliation Journal window. You will then return to the Simply Accounting - ODC window.

DISPLAYING AND PRINTING THE BANK RECONCILIATION REPORT

Once you have reconciled your bank account, it is important that you print a copy of the reconciliation. You should store this reconciliation report with the original bank statement.

To print the bank reconciliation report, continue from the Simply Accounting - ODC window (Figure 12.4) by

Selecting the **Report** menu.

Continue from within the **Reports** menu, by

Selecting the **Accounts Reconciliation** menu option.

Figure 12.14
Account
Reconciliation
menu

Within the **A**ccount **R**econciliation menu (Figure 12.14), you can select from the following choices:

Account
Reconciliation
Status Report
will generate either a detailed or summary bank reconciliation report for display and printing.

Bank
Transactions List
will generate a report of the bank transaction that have been posted.

Download Bank
Statements
allow you to select the bank statement file that you have downloaded from your applicable on-line bank.

Continue from within the **A**ccount **R**econciliation menu (Figure 12.14) by

Selecting the **A**ccount **R**econciliation **S**tatus **R**eport menu option.

Figure 12.15
Bank Reconciliation
Report Options window
(Summary format)

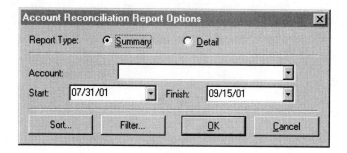

As displayed in Figure 12.15, the Bank Reconciliation Report Options window allows you to select from the following options:

Detail
allows you to display the bank reconciliation report including all of the transactions based on the report status selections.

Summary
allows the bank reconciliation to be displayed in report format (not including individual transactions).

Continue by pressing

⌨ Alt + ⌨ D
to select the **D**etail option.

Figure 12.16
Bank Reconciliation
Report Options (Detail)

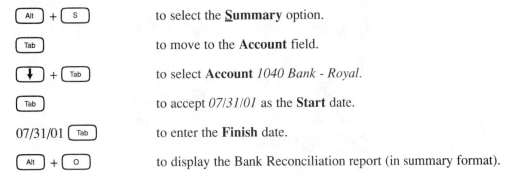

Your Bank Reconciliation Report Options window will change to display the detail format (Figure 12.16).

Continue by pressing

[Alt] + [S]	to select the **Summary** option.
[Tab]	to move to the **Account** field.
[↓] + [Tab]	to select **Account** *1040 Bank - Royal.*
[Tab]	to accept *07/31/01* as the **Start** date.
07/31/01 [Tab]	to enter the **Finish** date.
[Alt] + [O]	to display the Bank Reconciliation report (in summary format).

Figure 12.17
Bank Reconciliation
Summary Report

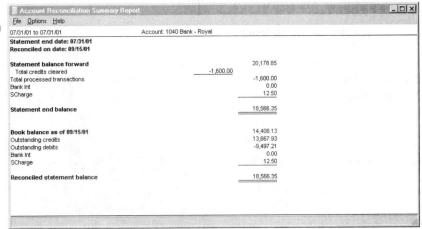

Continue from the Bank Reconciliation Summary Report window (Figure 12.17) by pressing

[Alt] + [F]   to select the **File** menu.

[P]   to **Print** the Bank Reconciliation Summary Report.

Once the bank reconciliation report has been printed, press

[Alt] + [F4]   to close the Bank Reconciliation Summary Report.

ADVANCING YOUR USING DATE

Simply Accounting for Windows provides you with an easy way to advance your using date without having to exit and re-enter Simply Accounting for Windows.

Figure 12.18
Simply Accounting -
ODC window

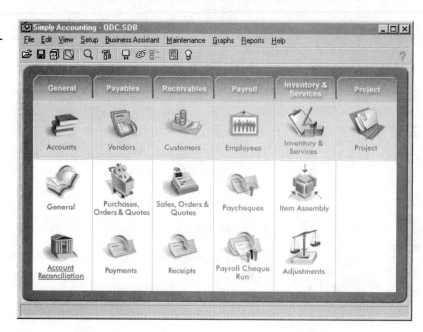

Continue from the Simply Accounting - ODC window (Figure 12.18) by

Selecting the **Maintenance** menu.

Figure 12.19
Maintenance Menu

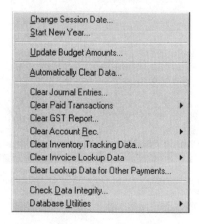

From within the **Maintenance Menu** (Figure 12.19) continue by

Selecting the **Change Session Date** menu option.

Simply Accounting may prompt you to backup your files (with an option window). If this occurs, continue by selecting the **No** button.

Figure 12.20
Advance Using
Date window

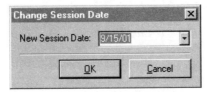

Continue from the Advance Using Date window (Figure 12.20) by entering

09/30/01 ⟨Enter⟩   to enter the new Using Date.

⟨ o ⟩   to select **OK** confirming that the new using date is more than one week past the previous using date.

Simply Accounting will now continue with the display of both the Checklists and To-Do Lists windows. Continue by

Closing the Checklists window.

Within the To-Do Lists window, continue by

Selecting the **Recurring** tabbed button.

MONTH-END ADJUSTMENT ENTRIES

At month-end, the following entries are necessary for Overnight Delivery Company.

Figure 12.21
To-Do List
(Recurring) window

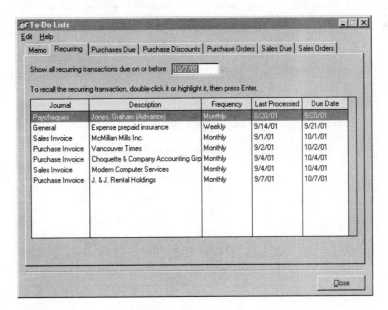

Simply Accounting for Windows will now display an updated To-Do List (Recurring) window (Figure 12.21).

Practice Exercise 12.4

POSTING RECURRING ENTRIES
FROM WITHIN THE TO-DO LIST WINDOW

Continue with the selection and posting of the following recurring entries (from within the To-Do Lists window - note Figure 12.21):

Journal Description	Last Posted	Due Date
General Expensing of prepaid ins	*9/14/01*	*9/21/01*
Source code ADJ115		
General Expensing of prepaid ins	*9/21/01*	*9/28/01*
Source code ADJ116		

Once you have completed this exercise, close the To-Do Lists window. You will then return to the Simply Accounting - ODC window as shown in Figure 12.18. Continue with the entry of the following loan payment within the General Journal. Accept that the entry will be posted to the preceding period. Once you have completed this entry close the General Journal (you will then return to the Simply Accounting - ODC window (see Figure 12.18).

LOAN PAYMENT

On August 31, 2001, an automatic debit of $870.00 (Royal Bank) for an installment on the Note Payable. This entry should have $247.95 allocated to interest expense and $622.05 allocated to principal reduction of the Note Payable.

Description:					
Source	Date	Account Name	Account	Debit	Credit
ADJ117			5880	247.95	
			1040		870.00

Practice Exercise 12.5

After preparing the journal entries on paper, enter them into the **General** Journal for Overnight Delivery Company.

Then continue with the completion of the August 2001 Bank Reconciliation.

Once the adjusting journal entries along with the bank reconciliation have been completed for August, the books can be closed for the month. Print the bank reconciliation report for August 2001 along with an updated trial balance and financial statements—the balance sheet and the income statement—which reflect the adjusting entries shown.

REVIEW OF BANK RECONCILIATION FEATURES

1. Select the **Bank Reconciliation** icon.
2. Select the *1040 Bank - Royal* as the bank account to reconcile.
3. Enter the **Ending Date.** For the above exercise this date will be *August 31, 2001*.
4. Enter a **Comment.**
5. Enter the **Ending Balance.** This amount will be the final bank balance from the bottom of your bank statement. For this exercise, the ending balance will be *$12,400.65*.
6. Using either your cancelled cheques/stubs and/or your bank statement, clear all cleared items within the Bank Reconciliation window. This is accomplished by clicking your mouse cursor within the "C" column. This will in turn place a *check mark* within this column. You will notice that both the **Total Cleared** and **Unresolved** will change based on the dollar amount of the item cleared. A cleared status tells Simply Accounting that this item has been posted through your bank account (thus will appear on your bank statement).
7. Clear (check mark) all reversed transaction (including both the original entry and the associated reversal entry). The net effect of each reversed transaction should be zero and the reversal entry will void the original entry amounts.
8. Enter your bank services charges, bank interest earned, and any other additional charges or credits that appear on your bank statement but not within your Simply Accounting bank reconciliation window. If you have forgotten to enter either a deposit or cheque/withdrawal you can select to **Save** your bank reconciliation. Return to the Simply Accounting - ODC window, continue with the posting of the missing transaction and return to your Bank Reconciliation window to finish the reconciliation.
9. Continue with **Post**ing your bank reconciliation if the unresolved amount has reached zero and you have completed the reconciliation. If you have a difference, refer to the section earlier in this chapter about locating and correcting the difference.

BANK RECONCILIATION (AUGUST 31, 2001)

Royal Bank of Canada

Date	Account Type	Account Number	Balance Forward
08/31/01	Current Chequing	668958	18,566.35

Overnight Delivery Company
300-3665 Kingsway
Vancouver BC V5R 5W2

Date	#/CD	Desc.	Withdrawal	Deposit	Balance
					18,566.35
08/01/01	107	Cheque	53.50		18,512.85
08/05/01		Deposit		1658.17	20,171.02
08/05/01		Deposit		867.59	21,038.61
08/10/01		Deposit		99.50	21,138.11
08/10/01		Deposit		1057.75	22,195.86
08/15/01		Deposit		642.00	22,837.86
08/15/01		Deposit		108.08	22,945.94
08/15/01		Deposit		429.79	23,375.73
08/15/01		Deposit		2955.38	26,331.11
08/15/01	108	Cheque	1000.00		25,331.11
08/15/01	109	Cheque	53.50		25,277.61
08/16/01	531	Cheque	130.00		25,147.61
08/16/01	532	Cheque	894.98		24,252.63
08/16/01	533	Cheque	1394.31		22,858.32
08/16/01	534	Cheque	1000.00		21,858.32
08/17/01	535	Cheque	5000.00		16,858.32
08/17/01	536	Cheque	93.00		16,765.32
08/17/01	537	Cheque	100.00		16,665.32
08/25/01		Cash	15.00		16,650.32
08/31/01	DM	LoanPymt	870.00		15,780.32
08/31/01	SC	SCharge	12.50		15,767.82

MAINTAINING AN AUDIT TRAIL

Now that we are closing the month, make sure that you print a **General Ledger** listing for all accounts for 08/01/01 to 08/31/01 as well as a trial balance (08/31/01), balance sheet (08/31/01), and income statement for the period (08/01/01 to 08/31/01).

Place these printouts in a binder and mark it as **GENERAL JOURNAL ENTRIES.** This binder should also include all other journal entry listings that you have previously printed. You can use this audit trail to review any of the entries made or, in the event that your data files on disk are destroyed, to re-enter journal entries.

BACKING UP YOUR DATA FILES

You should now backup your data files.

Backup Filename: A:\ODC\ODC12

Comment: Using Simply - Bank Rec.

You now have the data backed up.

Further Practice

To get further practice with the concepts you have learned in this chapter go to Chapter 14 and work through Section 12 of the National Supply Company.

CHAPTER 13

CLOSING THE BOOKS AND OTHER MATTERS

CHAPTER 13

CLOSING THE BOOKS AND OTHER MATTERS

OBJECTIVES

After reading this chapter you will

1. Be able to make period-end payments of applicable taxes to government authorities.
2. Know what tasks have to be done at various stages of the yearly accounting cycle—at the end of a session, month, quarter, calendar year, and fiscal year.
3. Know about the storage limits of Simply Accounting and why purging data is necessary.
4. Understand some major auditing considerations.
5. Be able to set passwords for various ledgers and journals.

While the preceding chapters described the day-to-day use of the Simply Accounting system, there are other features and functions that are used less commonly, but are nevertheless important to know. Some of these functions are required only once a year while others are required periodically throughout the year. This chapter will explain these features and functions. Before using the Simply Accounting for Windows system for an actual company, you should read this chapter.

Practice Exercise 13.1

Enter Simply Accounting for Windows - Overnight Delivery Company (ODC). When prompted for the Using Date, accept **09/30/01**. Simply Accounting will display the Checklist and To-Do List windows. Continue by closing these windows. You will then return to the Simply Accounting - ODC window as shown in Figure 13.1.

Figure 13.1
Simply Accounting - ODC window

TAXATION REMITTANCES

Within most businesses you will be required to remit payments to various government authorities. These payments can include Provincial Sales Tax, payroll withholding taxes and GST (Goods & Services Tax) or HST (Harmonized Sales Tax).

The next section will demonstrate how to remit these payments to the applicable government authorities.

GST/HST REMITTANCE

In Canada, businesses with GST taxable sales in excess of $30,000.00 per annum are required to collect and remit either GST (Goods and Services Tax) or HST (Harmonized Sales Tax). The latter includes both the federal sales tax as well as the provincial sales tax, while the GST only includes the federal sales tax component. Check with your local Revenue Canada branch for more information about the collection of the GST/HST.

For the purpose of this chapter, we will show a remittance of GST and a separate remittance for PST (Provincial Sales Tax).

From the Simply Accounting - ODC window (Figure 13.1) continue by

Selecting the **Reports** menu.

Figure 13.2
Reports Menu

Notice that your **Reports** menu does not match the one shown in Figure 13.2 because it shows GST. Continue from the **Reports** menu by

Selecting the **GST/HST** menu option.

Figure 13.3
GST Report
Options window

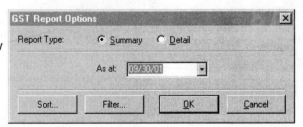

Simply Accounting will then continue with the generation of the GST/HST Report Options window (Figure 13.3).

In this window you can select from the following:

As at (Date)   The date to report the GST/HST as at. For example, you may want to report your GST/HST for the month of August, so your report would show information up to August 31, 2001, which is the date that would be entered in this field.

Summary/Detail   You have the option to either generate the GST/HST in summary or detail format depending on your requirements. The summary form will only display the applicable totals for Revenue, GST/HST Collected, Expenses and GST/HST Paid during the reporting period whereas the detail form will also include details pertaining to each applicable GST/HST transaction that makes up the reporting balances.

Continue from the GST/HST Report Options window (Figure 13.3) by entering

08/31/01 [Tab]   as the **As at** reporting date.

[Tab]   to accept the **Summary** report format.

[Enter]   to generate the GST/HST report in summary format for information as at 08/31/01.

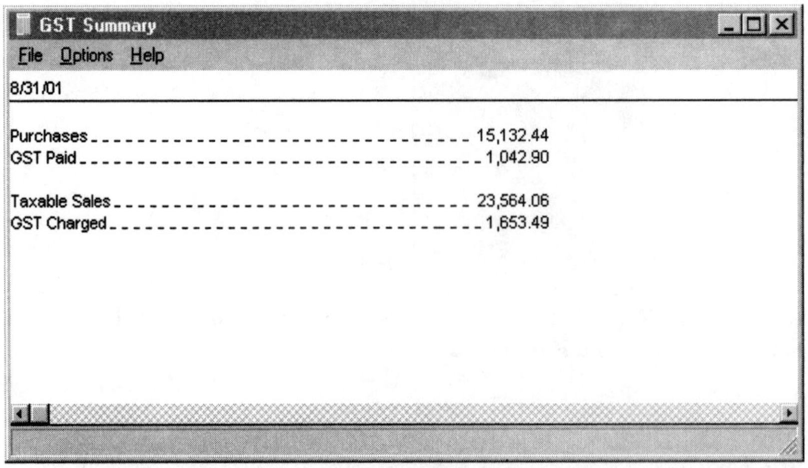

Figure 13.4
GST/HST
Summary report
window

Simply Accounting for Windows will now continue with the display of the GST/HST Summary report window (Figure 13.4). Continue by pressing

[Alt] + [F]   to select the **File** menu.

[P]   to select the **Print** option.

Once the GST/HST report has been printed, continue by pressing

[Alt] + [F4]   to close the GST/HST Summary report.

Practice Exercise 13.2

Continue with the display and printing of the GST/HST report in **Detail** format as at 08/31/01 (Figure 13.5).

Once you have completed this exercise, return to the Simply Accounting - ODC window.

Figure 13.5
GST Detail
report window

File Options Help				
08/31/01				
Vendor	Invoice	Date	Purchases	GST Paid
Vancouver Times	15326	08/02/01	497.50	34.83
Choquette & Co Accounting Group	315	08/04/01	450.00	31.50
Exxon	116535	08/05/01	1,126.71	78.87
J & J Rental Holdings	4263	08/07/01	750.00	52.50
Golden Wings Freight Lines	2256	08/07/01	852.36	59.67
Safesure Parcel Delivery Ltd.	189658	08/12/01	998.00	69.86
Telus	32525	08/15/01	325.00	22.75
Vancouver Times	15986	08/15/01	126.93	8.89
Golden Wings Freight Lines	456	08/15/01	1,122.00	78.54
TWK Internet Inc.	843	08/15/01	151.25	0.00
Office Depot	805	08/03/01	50.00	3.50
Java Beans	3021	08/05/01	35.00	2.45
Esso	55847	08/05/01	9.35	0.65

BALANCING THE GST REPORT

As noted previously, the compilation of the data in the GST report is based on transactions entered into the Purchase and Sales Journals only. Those GST applicable transaction that you may have entered through the General Journal as well as the opening balances for the GST Collected and Paid will not be included in this report.

To ensure that your GST/HST report contains all relevant data, it is important to compare the GST/HST balances to the actual account balances for both the GST Collected and GST Paid accounts.

Continue from the Simply Accounting - ODC window (Figure 13.1) by

Selecting the **Report** menu.

Select the **Financials** report option.

Figure 13.6
Financial
Report menu

Balance Sheet...
Income Statement...
Trial Balance...
Cash Flow Projection...
General Ledger...
Realized Exchange Gain/Loss...
Unrealized Exchange Gain/Loss...

Continue from the Financials Report menu (Figure 13.6) by

Selecting the **General Ledger** report option.

Figure 13.7
General Ledger
Report Options
window

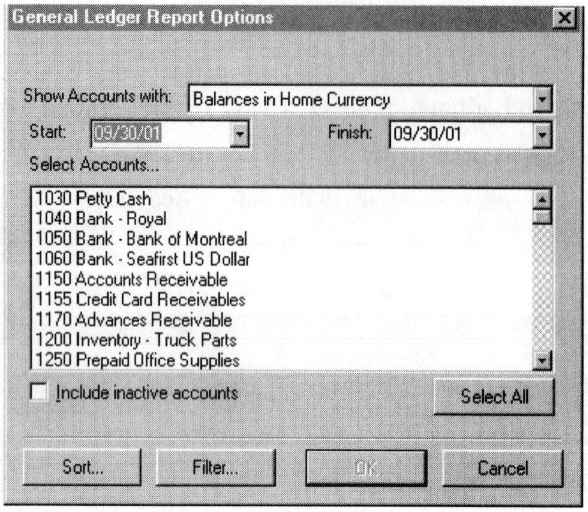

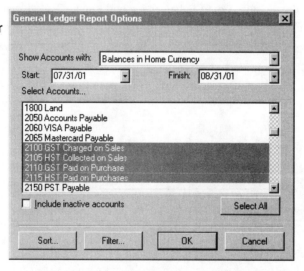

Continue from within the General Ledger Report Options window (Figure 13.7) by entering

07/31/01 [Tab]   as the **Start** date.

08/31/01 [Tab]   as the **Finish** date.

[2]   to jump to the *2000* (Liabilities) range of accounts

[↓] (repeated)   to move to display *2100 GST Charged on Sales* account.

[Shift] + [↓] (4 times)   to highlight the accounts *2100/2105/2110/2115*.

Figure 13.8
General Ledger
Report Options
window
(entered)

If your General Ledger Report Options window resembles Figure 13.8, continue by pressing

[Enter]   to display the General Ledger report for the GST/
                             HST accounts.

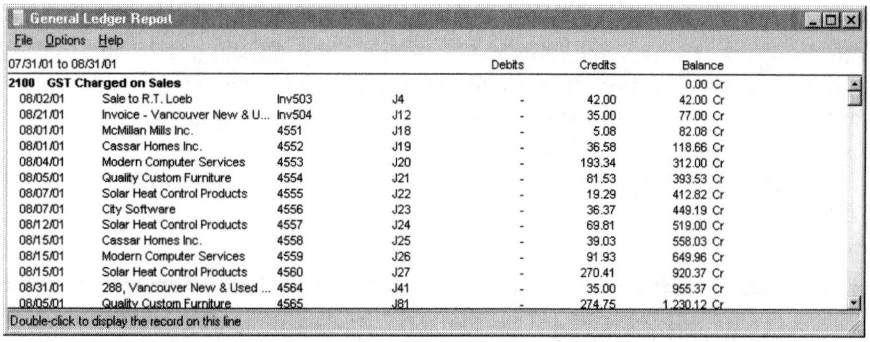

07/31/01 to 08/31/01				Debits	Credits	Balance
2100 GST Charged on Sales						0.00 Cr
08/02/01	Sale to R.T. Loeb	Inv503	J4	-	42.00	42.00 Cr
08/21/01	Invoice - Vancouver New & U...	Inv504	J12	-	35.00	77.00 Cr
08/01/01	McMillan Mills Inc.	4551	J18	-	5.08	82.08 Cr
08/01/01	Cassar Homes Inc.	4552	J19	-	36.58	118.66 Cr
08/04/01	Modern Computer Services	4553	J20	-	193.34	312.00 Cr
08/05/01	Quality Custom Furniture	4554	J21	-	81.53	393.53 Cr
08/07/01	Solar Heat Control Products	4555	J22	-	19.29	412.82 Cr
08/07/01	City Software	4556	J23	-	36.37	449.19 Cr
08/12/01	Solar Heat Control Products	4557	J24	-	69.81	519.00 Cr
08/15/01	Cassar Homes Inc.	4558	J25	-	39.03	558.03 Cr
08/15/01	Modern Computer Services	4559	J26	-	91.93	649.96 Cr
08/15/01	Solar Heat Control Products	4560	J27	-	270.41	920.37 Cr
08/31/01	288, Vancouver New & Used ...	4564	J41	-	35.00	955.37 Cr
08/05/01	Quality Custom Furniture	4565	J81	-	274.75	1,230.12 Cr

Figure 13.9
General Ledger Report (GST/HST Accounts) window

Simply Accounting for Windows will now display the General Ledger Report window (Figure 13.9). Continue by pressing

Alt + F — to select the **File** menu.

P — to select the **Print** menu option.

Once the General Ledger Report has printed, continue by pressing

Alt + F4 — to close the General Ledger Window. You will then return to the Simply Accounting - ODC window.

Both your GST and General Ledger Reports should balance with the total figures as follows:

	GST/HST Report Figures	General Ledger Figures
GST Collected on Sales	1653.49	1722.99
HST Collected on Sales	0.00	7.50
Net GST/HST Collected	1653.49	1730.49
GST/HST Paid on Purchases	1042.90	1061.10
Adjustments Required	0.00	0.00
Net GST/HST Paid	1042.90	1061.10
Net GST/HST Payable	610.59	669.39

Figure 13.10
GST Summarized

If we compare the GST figures in the GST/HST Reports with the General Ledger (Figure 13.10), we notice that they do not match. This was caused by the entries that we made within the General Journal. As mentioned within the General Ledger and Accounts Payable chapters, Simply Accounting will track the GST collected and paid from within the Sales and Purchase journals. However, entries made within the General Journal are not tracked and reported within the GST Report.

In is recommended that you generate both the GST and General Ledger reports to ensure that you have not missed GST transactions that were entered in the General Journal (as shown in Figure 13.10).

As shown in Figure 13.10, the GST summarized balances in accordance to the figures from both your GST/HST and General Ledger reports.

You will also notice that one extra row titled Adjustments Required has also been included (Figure 13.10). This row is used to enter any adjustments from the actual amount of GST/HST collected and paid according to the amounts permitted by Revenue Canada Taxation.

An example of such an adjustment is the deduction of 50.0% of the GST paid on meals and entertainment expenses and only 50.0% of those expenses are permitted for deduction under the Income Tax Act. For more information on other possible reductions and adjustments when filing your GST/HST return, you should contact a qualified accounting professional or Revenue Canada Taxation.

For this exercise, there are no adjustments to be made from the actual GST/GST Collected and Paid.

IMPORTANT NOTE: It is important to note that if your General Ledger GST/HST report details do not equal the totals within the GST/HST report details, you will also have to print a General Ledger report for all of your revenue accounts for the same period. This will allow you to adjust the taxes payable, and also the revenue reported (which is required on the GST/HST return).

REMITTING GST/HST TO REVENUE CANADA

The remittance to Revenue Canada Taxation for your GST/HST depends on whether you are making a payment or are receiving a refund from Revenue Canada.

The difference between the Liability or Receivable of GST/HST tax is based on where you will make your entry. For a liability of GST/HST tax, you will make your entry in the Purchases journal (thus establishing an accounts payable invoice to Revenue Canada). On the other hand, if you are claiming a refund of GST/HST, you would make this entry in the Sales journal (thus creating an accounts receivable invoice to Revenue Canada).

For this exercise, you are expected to remit net GST/HST to Revenue Canada Taxation. Before you continue you will have to create a vendor for the Receiver General of Canada (GST).

Practice Exercise 13.3

Create a vendor record for the following:

Vendor:	Receiver General of Canada GST/HST
Contact:	GST/HST Remittance
Address:	Summerside Tax Centre
City:	Summerside
Province:	Prince Edward Island
Postal:	C1N 6A2
Phone:	604-689-5411
Fax:	604-684-4411
Terms:	Net 30 days
Clear Invoices:	No
Print Contact:	Yes
Include GST Report:	No

Once you have created the above vendor, return to the Simply Accounting - ODC window (Figure 13.1).

The next step is to create an invoice within the Purchases journal for the GST/HST remittance.

Figure 13.11
Purchase
Journal
(GST/HST
entry)

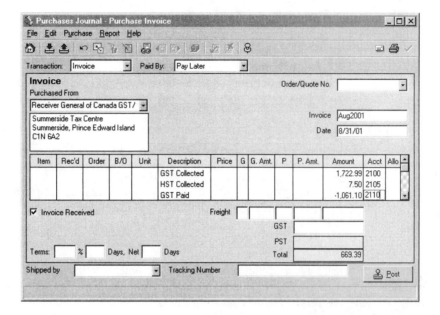

Figure 13.11 contains a completed purchase invoice for the remittance of GST/HST for the period up to 08/31/01. You will notice that this purchase invoice has been selected as a regular Purchase (without payment). This entry format is suggested as the date of the entry is August 31, 2001 (the date in which the liability was incurred). This will also place the entry within the August reporting area of the General Ledger, thus not confusing the reporting of GST/HST for later periods.

Practice Exercise 13.4

Continue with the entry of the purchase invoice for the GST/HST remittance. This invoice is a regular purchase invoice (bill later) and should resemble Figure 13.11 prior to posting.

Once you have confirmed that your Purchase journal for the GST/HST remittance is correct, print the cheque and then post this invoice. Simply Accounting will inform you that this entry precedes the current period and may effect previous reports. Select Yes to confirm the posting of this invoice.

Remitting Your GST/HST Return When A Refund Is Due

The above example was for the remittance of GST/HST payable. However if you are expecting a refund instead, then the process is as follows:

1. Create a Customer record for the Receiver General of Canada GST/HST. This record should be created with terms of Net 30 days. Do not print statements and do not include them within the GST report.

2. Enter the GST invoice within the Sales journal as shown in Figure 13.12.

3. When the refund is received, enter this refund through the Receipts journal.

Figure 13.12
Sample Sales
Journal
(GST/HST
Refund) window

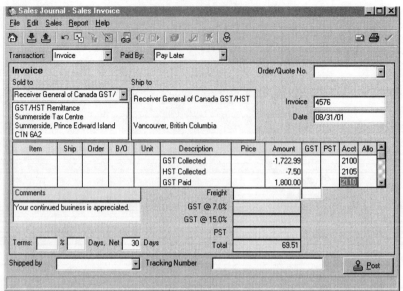

As shown in Figure 13.12, the Sales journal is used to enter a refund remittance for GST/HST. Please note that the above figure is only an example. The negative figures represent the GST/HST *Collected* and the positive figure is the GST *Paid*.

REMITTING PST (PROVINCIAL SALES TAX)

In most of Canada, the GST is collected separately from the PST, thus a separate remittance must occur for the remittance of PST (Provincial Sales Tax).

The steps required to make a remittance to your provincial government authority is as follows:

1. Create a Vendor record for the government authority.

2. Create a General Ledger account for the vendor's commission if entitled within your Province.

3. Enter the PST remittance information with the Purchases Journal.

4. Generate and print a payment for this purchase invoice.

Practice Exercise 13.5

Create a vendor record for the following:

Vendor:	Minister of Finance, PST
Contact:	PST Remittance
Address:	Parliament Buildings
City:	Victoria
Province:	British Columbia
Postal:	V8V 2M1
Phone:	604-660-4524
Fax:	604-660-1104
Terms:	Net 15 days
Clear Invoices:	No
Print Contact:	Yes
Include GST Report:	No

Once you have created the above vendor, return to the Simply Accounting - ODC window.

Continue with the creation of the following General Ledger account:

Account:	4440
Description:	Sales Tax Commissions
Account Type:	Group Account
Account Class:	Other Revenue

Once you have added the above General Ledger account, return to the Simply Accounting - ODC window (Figure 13.1).

PRINTING THE GENERAL LEDGER FOR PST INFORMATION

Continue from the Simply Accounting - ODC window (Figure 13.1) by

Selecting the **Reports** menu.

Selecting the **Financial** report option.

Selecting the **General Ledger** report option.

Figure 13.13
General Ledger
Report Options
window

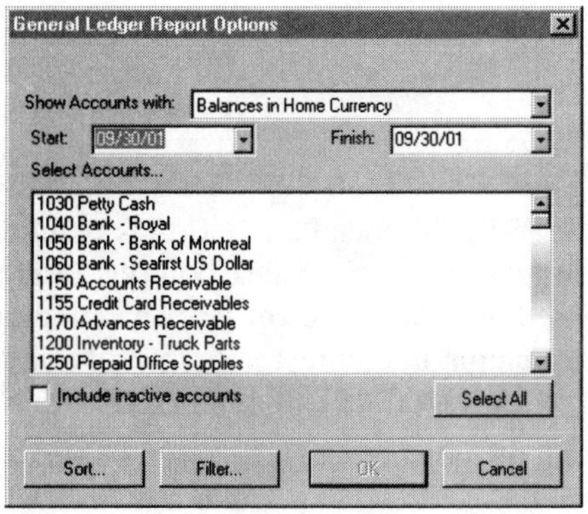

Continue from the General Ledger Report Options window (Figure 13.13) by entering

07/31/01 (Tab) to enter the **Start** date.

08/31/01 (Tab) to enter the **Finish** date.

(2) to jump to the 2000 - Liabilities range of accounts.

(↓) (several times) to highlight **2150 - PST Payable.**

Figure 13.14
General Ledger
Report Options
(PST Account)
window

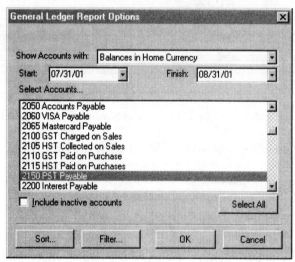

If your General Ledger Report Options window resembles Figure 13.14, continue by pressing

(Enter) to generate the General Ledger report for the 2150 - PST Payable account.

Figure 13.15
General Ledger
Report window

				Debits	Credits	Balance
07/31/01 to 08/31/01						
2150 PST Payable						0.00 Cr
08/05/01	Quality Custom Furniture	4565	J81	-	267.75	267.75 Cr
08/12/01	Cassar Homes Inc.	4566	J82	-	106.75	374.50 Cr
08/20/01	McMillan Mills Inc.	4567	J83	-	118.30	492.80 Cr
08/21/01	Quality Custom Furniture	4568	J84	-	225.40	718.20 Cr
				0.00	718.20	

As shown in Figure 4.15, the remittance of PST (Provincial Sales Tax) is required. The next step is to review the filing guidelines when remitting Provincial Sales Tax to your provincial agency. As the Overnight Delivery company is based in the province of British Columbia, a vendor commission is available. Based on the information in Figure 13.15, this discount is calculated to be $23.70. This commission is deducted from the total PST payable as shown in Figure 13.16.

Figure 13.16
Purchase
Journal (PST
Payable entry)
window

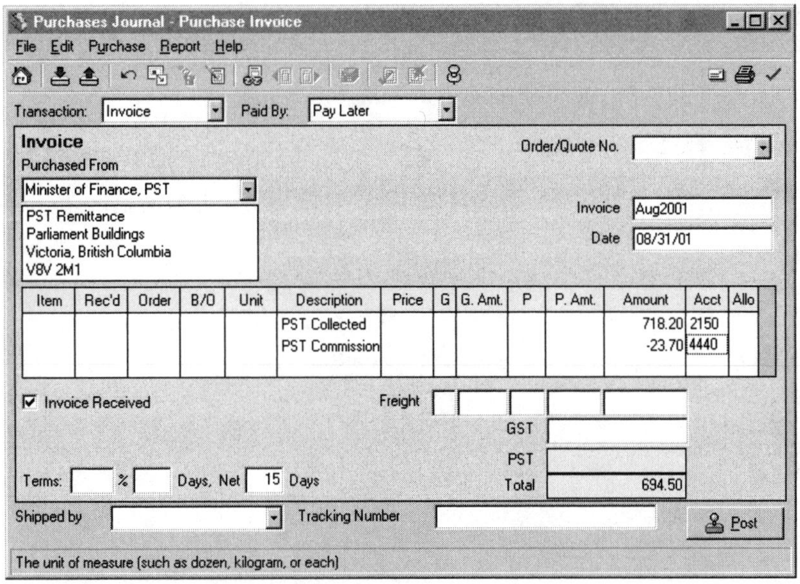

As shown in Figure 13.16, the gross amount of PST Payable is entered against account *2150 - PST Payable* along with the vendors commission available to Overnight Delivery Company of $23.70. It is entered as a negative amount against account *4440 - Sales Tax Commissions*. The net amount of this purchase invoice is the net amount of PST Payable that must be remitted to the Minister of Finance.

Practice Exercise 13.6

Make a purchase invoice entry for the PST remittance. This invoice is a regular purchase (without payment) and your Purchases journal should resemble Figure 13.16 prior to posting.

Once you have confirmed that your Purchase journal (for the PST remittance) is correct, print the cheque and then post the invoice. Simply Accounting will inform you that this entry precedes the current period and may effect previous reports. Select **Yes** to confirm the posting of this invoice. Upon completion, return to the Simply Accounting - ODC window.

REMITTING PAYROLL WITHHOLDING TAXES

If your company has employees you are normally required to remit your payroll withholding taxes (CPP, EI, Employee Income Tax, and possibly additional taxes) to Revenue Canada on a monthly basis.

The steps required to complete this remittance are as follows:

1. Create a new Vendor for the Receiver General of Canada (Payroll).

2. Print the General Ledger report including the Payroll Withholding Tax accounts.

3. Create a purchase invoice for the withholding taxes payable.

4. When required, generate and print an Accounts Payable payment for remittance to Revenue Canada.

Practice Exercise 13.7

Create the following vendor records for the following:

Vendor:	Receiver General of Canada PAYROLL
Contact:	Payroll Withholding Taxes remit
Address:	9755 King George Hwy
City:	Surrey
Province:	British Columbia
Postal:	V3T 5E5
Phone:	604-689-5411
Fax:	604-585-5769
Terms:	Net 15 days
Clear Invoices:	No
Print Contact:	Yes
Include GST Report:	No

Vendor:	Workers' Compensation Board
Contact:	Employers premium remittance
Address:	Box 9600 Stn Terminal
City:	Vancouver
Province:	British Columbia
Postal:	V6B 5J5
Phone:	604-244-6100
Fax:	604-244-6392
Terms:	Net 20 days
Clear Invoices:	No
Print Contact:	Yes
Include GST Report:	No

Once you have created the above vendor, return to the Simply Accounting - ODC window, (Figure 13.1).

Upon completion of the above exercise, continue from the Simply Accounting - ODC window (Figure 15.1) by

Selecting the **Report** menu.

Selecting the **Financial** report option.

Selecting the **General Ledger** report option.

Continue from the General Ledger Report Options window (Figure 13.13) by entering

07/31/01	to enter the **Start** date.
08/31/01	to enter the **End** date.
2	to jump to the *2000 - Liabilities* account range.
↓ (seven times)	to highlight *2320 - CPP Payable*.

Continue by holding down the ⌨Ctrl key and clicking on the following accounts:

2320 - CPP Payable

2340 - EI Payable

2360 - Income Tax Payable

2380 - WCB Payable

Figure 13.17
General Ledger
Report Options
(Payroll
remittance)
window

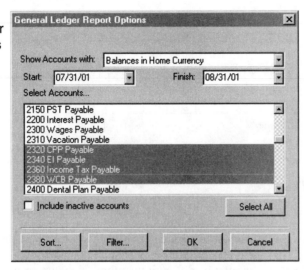

If your General Ledger Report Options window resembles Figure 13.17 continue by pressing

⌨Enter   to display the General Ledger Report window (Figure 13.18)

Figure 13.18
General Ledger
Report (Payroll)
window

				Debits	Credits	Balance
2320 CPP Payable						0.00 Cr
8/20/01	Bea, Desi	539	J92	-	43.98	43.98 Cr
8/20/01	Firguson, Adam	540	J93	-	29.56	73.54 Cr
8/31/01	Jones, Graham	541	J94	-	132.34	205.88 Cr
8/31/01	Reversing J94. Correction is J... ADJ541		J95	132.34	-	73.54 Cr
8/31/01	Jones, Graham	541	J96	-	145.24	218.78 Cr
8/31/01	Bea, Desi	542	J97	-	44.76	263.54 Cr
8/31/01	Firguson, Adam	543	J98	-	31.02	294.56 Cr
				132.34	426.90	
2340 EI Payable						0.00 Cr
8/20/01	Bea, Desi	539	J92	-	42.17	42.17 Cr
8/20/01	Firguson, Adam	540	J93	-	32.40	74.57 Cr
8/31/01	Jones, Graham	541	J94	-	97.20	171.77 Cr

Continue from the General Ledger Report window (Figure 13.18) by pressing

⌨Alt + ⌨F   to select the **File** menu.

⌨P   to **Print** the General Ledger Report.

Once the General Ledger Report has been printed, continue by pressing

⌨Alt + ⌨F4   to close the General Ledger Report window.

The next step is to create two different Purchases journal invoices for the remittances to the Receiver General of Canada (CPP, EI, & Income Tax) and a remittance to the Workers' Compensation Board (WCB Premiums).

Figure 13.19
Purchases
Journal
(Receiver
General -
Payroll) window

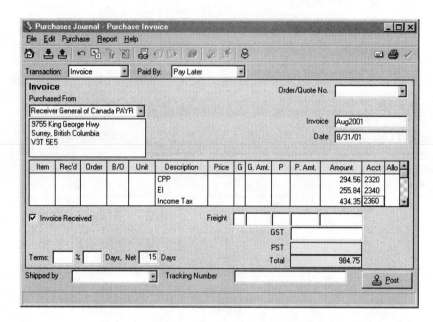

As shown in Figure 13.19, the Purchases journal includes amounts for each of the applicable payroll withholding taxes: *2320 - CPP Payable, 2340 - EI Payable*, and *2360 - Income Tax Payable*. The amounts that are shown may be different than those that appear on your General Ledger report. This may be caused by the version of Simply Accounting for Windows (with updated Payroll tables).

Practice Exercise 13.8

Make a purchase invoice entry for the Receiver General Payroll remittance. This invoice is a regular purchase (without payment) and your Purchases journal should resemble Figure 13.19 with the exception of the amounts for each withholding tax. If the amounts differ from those on your copy of the General Ledger report, enter the amounts that appear on the General Ledger report instead of those that appear in Figure 13.19. This difference is most likely due to different tax rates between the version used in writing this book and your current version.

Once you have confirmed that your Purchase journal for the Receiver General Payroll remittance is correct, print the cheque and then post the invoice. Simply Accounting will inform you that this entry precedes the current period and may effect previous reports. Select **Yes** to confirm the posting of this invoice. Upon completion, remain within the Purchase journal window.

You will be required periodically to remit Workers' Compensation premiums. This liability is again entered through the Purchases journal as noted in Figure 13.20.

Figure 13.20
Purchase
Journal (WCB
Premiums)
window

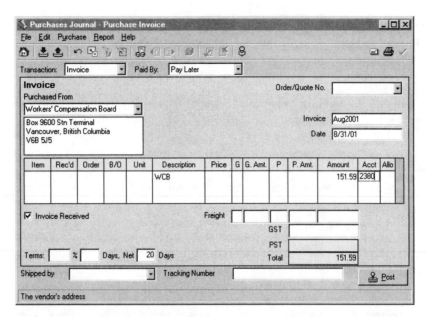

As shown in Figure 13.20, the Purchases journal is used to enter the Workers' Compensation Board (WCB) remittance invoice. The account *2380 - WCB Payable* is used to record the WCB premiums payable based on your previously printed General Ledger Report.

Practice Exercise 13.9

Make a purchase invoice entry for the Workers' Compensation Board remittance. This invoice is a regular purchase (without payment) and your Purchases journal should resemble Figure 13.20 prior to posting.

Once you have confirmed that your Purchases journal (for the Workers' Compensation Board remittance) is correct, print the cheque and then post the invoice. Simply Accounting will inform you that this entry precedes the current period and may effect previous reports. Select **Yes** to confirm the posting of this invoice. Upon completion, return to the Simply Accounting - ODC window (note Figure 13.1).

Practice Exercise 13.10

Continue with the issuance of the following remittance cheques from account 1040 Bank - Royal (using the Payment journal):

Receiver General GST/HST

Minister of Finance PST

Receiver General PAYROLL

Workers' Compensation Board

The date for each cheque should be 09/15/01.

Prior to posting, print each cheque.

Once you have completed this exercise, return to the Simply Accounting - ODC window (Figure 13.1).

BACKING UP YOUR DATA FILES

At this point, return to the Simply Accounting - ODC window and continue with the backup function.

Call this backup:

>**Backup Filename:** A:\ODC\ODC13A
>**Comment:** Closing Books Part a

PERIOD-END PROCESSING

The accounting cycle contains a number of significant periods. These are as follows:

1. End of a Session
2. End of a Month
3. End of a Quarter
4. Calendar Year-end
5. Fiscal Year-end

It is important to record these periods accurately and to follow proper procedures to maintain the integrity of the data. It is particularly important to maintain an audit trail that can be easily followed.

END OF A SESSION

After you end each session, you should print a **General Ledger** listing of journal entries made during the session. These entries should be checked at that time to ensure that no errors were made. You will not likely review these entries again except under unusual circumstances.

Once you have finished with a session, make a backup copy of your data files. Put the date of the backup on the diskette. You should keep five diskettes, one for each day of the week. This ensures that any data corruption that goes undetected for a few days will not cause undue trouble.

END OF A MONTH

Before changing the **Using** date to a new month, you should make sure that all entries for the present month are complete. Although it is possible to enter journal entries for a previous month, it is more convenient to finish completely with one month before going on to the next.

The monthly reports should be printed. You should ensure that you have hard copies for the following for each month:

a. **Journal entries.** *Instructions:* First make sure that you are at the Simply Accounting - ODC window. The next step is to highlight the **General Journal** icon. In order to access the **Report** menu, press [Alt] + [R]. You will notice that the first option on this menu is **Display General Journal**. Select this option by pressing [D] or [Enter] (if you have the option highlighted). Then select the appropriate print options.

b. **General Ledger listing for all accounts for the month.** *Instructions:* select the **Reports** menu [Alt] + [R]. Once this menu has been selected, continue by selecting the **Financial** [F] menu option. Once the **Financial** menu has been displayed, continue by selecting the **General Ledger** report option [G].

c. **Income statement.** *Instructions:* At the Simply Accounting- ODC window, select the **Reports** menu [Alt] + [R]. Once this menu is selected, press [F] for the **Financial** menu followed by pressing [I] to access the **Income**

Statement menu option. Then continue by selecting the **Start** and **Finish** dates (for example, if you wish to print the **Income Statement** for the month of August 2001, you would select 08/01/01 as the **Start** date and 08/31/01 as the **End** date).

d. **Balance sheet**. *Instructions:* At the Simply Accounting - ODC window, select the **Reports** menu ⌨ Alt + ⌨ R . Once this menu is selected, press ⌨ F for the **Financial** menu followed by pressing ⌨ B to access the **Balance Sheet** menu option. Then continue by selecting the **As at** date. For example, if you wish to display or print the **Balance Sheet** for August 31, 2001, you would select 08/31/01 as the **As at** date.

e. **Costing reports**. *Instructions:* At the Simply Accounting - ODC window, select the **Reports** menu ⌨ Alt + ⌨ R . Continue by pressing ⌨ P to select the **Project** menu option.

f. **Listings of all subledgers, Inventory, Payables, Receivables, and Payroll.** *Instructions:* These are accessed through the **Reports** menu option, found in the Simply Accounting - ODC window.

You should backup all of the data files again. Mark this copy as the archive file for the month that is being backed up. Keep this backup copy until the end of the fiscal year in case the data files are lost or destroyed during the year.

END OF A QUARTER

When the **Using** date is changed to a new quarter, the Simply Accounting system resets **quarter-to-date** amounts. You should make sure that all entries for the quarter have been made before changing the **Using** date.

END OF THE CALENDAR YEAR

When a **Using** date is entered that falls into a new year, the Simply Accounting system will zero out **calendar-to-date** totals. This is especially important to remember if you are using the **Payroll** ledger and journal. The payroll section keeps year-to-date totals for each employee. These amounts are needed to make up the T4 slips for each employee and to calculate the T4 summary. The T4s should therefore be printed before you enter a date in the new year.

When you do change that date, the program will warn you that you are about to zero these amounts. If you select the **OK** button, the program will go ahead and zero out the existing calendar year's cumulative payroll information so that you can start accumulating for the new year.

END OF A FISCAL YEAR

A fiscal year may or may not coincide with the calendar year. The fiscal year can be any 12-month period that is convenient for your business. When you start a new fiscal year, you must change the **Using** date to a new fiscal year. The Simply Accounting system resets all temporary accounts and balances to zero. Before changing to a new fiscal year, it is important to do the following:

1. Ensure that all adjusting entries for the year ended have been made.
2. Print out the current month's income statements.
3. Print out the yearly income statement and balance sheet.

4. Make an archive disk of the data. An archive disk is simply a backup of the files for the year which you will keep as an archived record of the transactions for the year. Unlike other backup copies, this one will be permanent. As you do not want to overwrite these files, place a write-protect tab over the square cutout at the side of the disk to ensure that you cannot inadvertently delete any of the files or accidentally override them.

5. Make a backup disk for the month.

6. Print out a General Ledger summary of transactions for the entire year.

To proceed with a year-end, start the Simply Accounting for Windows system and enter a **Using** date which is in a new fiscal or accounting year. The program will inform you that you have selected a new fiscal period. You will have to select the **OK** button to continue.

If you select the **OK** button, Simply Accounting will make a closing journal entry and then the program will set itself up for a new fiscal year. The balances in the income statement will also be reset to zero for the new year. The **Start** date and **Finish** dates will be advanced by 12 months.

BACKING UP DATA FILES

Since we are talking about year-end, this is the time to discuss backing up your data files. In some way we have done this throughout the book. However, in a regular business your data files are much more important. If you have backups of all transaction data you can restore the data if you lose it, or you can look at the accounting data from a previous period in the future.

There should be three backups—daily backups, monthly backups, and yearly backups.

Daily backups should be made after each session. You should keep five diskettes, one for each day of the week. This ensures that any data corruption that goes undetected for a few days will not cause undue problems.

Monthly backups should be made using the so-called grandfather-father-son system. You need three disks, alternating their use for backups at the end of each month. If you have limited memory in your computer and have to purge the data on a monthly basis, you will want to keep each monthly backup to retain the detail data.

Yearly backups, as indicated earlier in the chapter, should be made and archived for each year. These backups will not be used for restoring data but to allow you to retrieve the detail for any fiscal year.

STORAGE LIMITS OF THE SIMPLY ACCOUNTING SYSTEM

Simply Accounting for Windows is an excellent program for smaller businesses, but as a business grows to a large size, it will have to switch to a more powerful program. Therefore the limits imposed by the program are not likely to cause problems for a business using this program.

The limits are

1. no more than 5,000 General Ledger accounts, or

2. no more than 32,000 records into all of the five ledgers.

It is always wise to remove any accounts that are not needed to keep your accounting system manageable, even if you never get close to the limit of 5,000 ledger accounts. Use the **Remove** command in the **Edit** menu to remove these accounts.

Should you ever reach the second limit, it is necessary to decrease the size of the company files. The obvious answer is to clear the journal entries from the files to make room for others. Before doing this, you should back the files up. When you clear the entries, the detail will be removed and replaced by a single amount. By backing the files up, you will retain the detail information for audit purposes.

CLEARING ENTRIES

To make more room on the disk you must remove (clear) journal entries from existing files. Before you do, make a backup of the disk.

To **Clear Journal Entries** first make sure that you are in the Simply Accounting - ODC window (Figure 13.1). Then continue by

Selecting the **Maintenance** menu.

Figure 13.21
Maintenance
menu

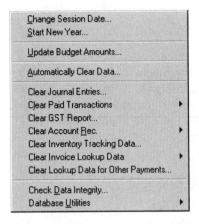

Continue from the **Maintenance** menu (Figure 13.21) by

Selecting the **Clear Journal Entries** menu option.

Figure 13.22
Clear Journal
Entries window

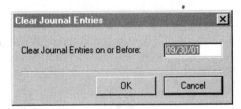

At the Clear Journal Entries window (Figure 13.22), type

08/31/01 ⌷Enter⌷   to enter the date up to which you wish to clear journal entries

Simply Accounting for Windows will then prompt you to confirm this action. Continue by

Clicking the **Yes** button to confirm the clearing of the journal entries.

Simply Accounting for Windows, will then carry out your request.

CLEARING VENDOR AND CUSTOMER INVOICES

In order to clear vendor and customer invoice, proceed by selecting the **Maintenance** menu option, followed by selecting **Clear Paid Invoices** followed by selecting either the **Clear Vendor Paid Invoices** or **Clear Customer Paid Invoices**. For this option you will also have to select the date up to which you wish to clear the entries. You will also have to tell Simply Accounting which vendors or customers to include.

Other type of entries that can be cleared include the GST report as well as the bank reconciliation report. Care should be taken when clearing both of these reports and you should only clear the data associated with these reports, once you have either filed the associated GST return or completed the bank reconciliation. Both of these functions can also be accessed through the **Maintenance** menu.

AUDITING CONSIDERATIONS

Journal entries that are recorded in any of the program's journals are stored in the program's General Journal. Each journal entry recorded is automatically assigned a sequential number for referencing. Journal entry numbers are assigned from 00001 to 50,000; the counter resets itself when it reaches 50,000. Journal entries are recorded with the date assigned, usually the **Using** date.

All journal entries are stored with the comments that were entered as well as how the revenues or expenses were distributed to various projects.

Cheque numbers are either generated and assigned by the program at the time the cheques are printed or, if you are not using computer generated cheques, are assigned sequentially between 00001 and 50,000 at which point the counter resets itself to 0.

The journal entry reference numbers, the associated comments, and the invoice and cheque numbers mean that your auditor has a complete audit trail. However, the reports must be printed and saved.

The following reports are generally required by your auditor.

Report	Calendar Month-end	Accounting Year-end	Year-end
Income Statement			
month-to-date	*		*
year-to-date	*		*
Balance Sheet	*		*
General Journal			
past month	*		*
Accounts Payable			
Purchases Journal-past month	*		*
Payments Journal-past month	*		*
detailed listing of Accounts Payable			*
Accounts Receivable			
Sale Journal past-month	*		*
Payment Journal past-month			*
detailed listing of Accounts Receivable			*
Payroll Journal			
past month	*		*
summary listing of employees	*		*
Inventory			
Transfer Journal past-month	*		*
Adjustment Journal past-month	*		*
Ledger Reports (all accounts)			
past month	*		
past yea			*
Chart of Accounts			
Payroll Report for			
each employee		*	
T4's		*	

These reports should be printed as the data is entered and not generated from backups. If you lose the reports, it may be possible to re-create them using a monthly or yearly backup, but this should only be done in an emergency situation since the backups might have been altered, thereby making an audit trail useless. These reports should be kept in a safe place along with the backups.

BACKING UP YOUR DATA FILES

At this point, return to the Simply Accounting - ODC window and continue with the backup function.

Call this backup:

Backup Filename:	A:\ODC\ODC13B
Comment:	Closing Books Part b

SETTING UP PASSWORDS

So that the system can be used by various employees and yet allow some protection of confidential information, the Simply Accounting system allows you to put a password on each of the ledgers. In this way, only those people with the right password can open particular ledgers. As well as completely restricting access, you can also set the passwords up so that a person can only view ledgers or edit only particular ledgers.

For example, you may have an employee who is responsible for Accounts Receivable and who records the **Sales** and **Receipts**. You may not want this person to have access to financial data or to payroll information, which may be the responsibility of another person. As well, you may wish this employee to only be able to view the **General** Ledger.

Figure 13.23
Simply
Accounting -
ODC window

To set the password, you must first make sure that you are at the Simply Accounting - ODC window (Figure 13.23). Continue by

Selecting the **Setup** menu.

Selecting the **Set Security** menu option.

Figure 13.24
Security - User
Maintenance
window

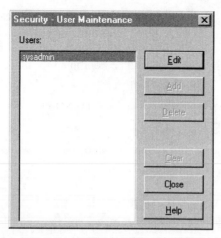

Figure 13.24 shows the User Maintenance menu where you can add users. Before you do, however, you first have to establish the sysadmin password.

From the Security - User Maintenance window (Figure 13.24) continue by

Selecting the **Edit** button.

Figure 13.25
Set Security
(sysadmin)
window

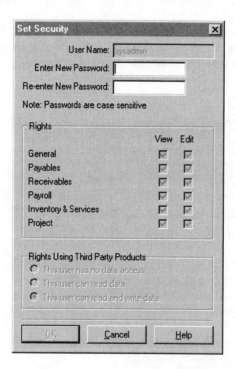

In the Set Security window, you can change the rights of access for each user; however for the sysadmin, you can only change the password (Figure 13.25).

Continue from within the Set Security window (Figure 13.25) by entering:

System ⌨Tab	to enter the New Password.
System ⌨Tab	to re-enter the New Password.
⌨Alt + ⌨o	to select the **OK**.

You will notice that in the Security - User Maintenance window (Figure 13.24) you can now **Add** a new user.

Continue from within the Security - User Maintenance window by:

Selecting the **Add** button.

Continue from within the Set Security window (Figure 13.25) by entering:

User1 Tab	to enter the **User Name**.
Pass1 Tab	to enter the **New Password**.
Pass1 Tab	to re-enter the **New Password**.

Simply Accounting will now allow you to select which modules and third-party products this user will have both View and Edit rights.

Continue by

Selecting (clicking on) the following modules:
Payroll - View
Payroll - Edit
Inventory & Services - Edit

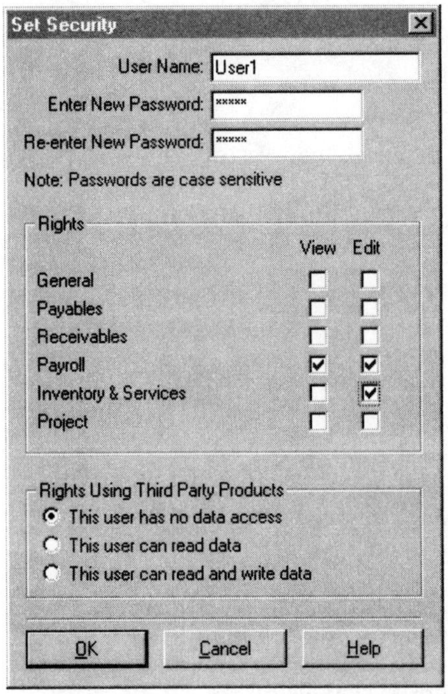

Figure 13.26
Set Security
(User1) window

Once you have made the appropriate rights for User1, your Set Security window will resemble Figure 13.26.

Continue from within the Set Security window (Figure 13.26) by:

Selecting the **OK** button.

Figure 13.27
Security - User
Maintenance
window

As shown in Figure 13.27, the Security - User Maintenance window now contains **User1** along with the **sysadmin**.

Practice Exercise 13.11

Continue with the creation of the following users:

	View	Edit
User2:		
Password = Pass2		
General	Yes	Yes
Payables	Yes	No
Receivables	Yes	No
Payroll	No	No
Inventory	No	Yes
Project	Yes	No
User3:		
Password = Pass3		
General	Yes	No
Payables	No	No
Receivables	No	No
Payroll	No	No
Inventory	No	No
Project	No	No

Once you have completed the above exercise, continue by

Closing the Set Security window.

Closing the Security - User Maintenance window.

Continue from the Simply Accounting - ODC window by pressing

[Alt] + [F4]   to close Simply Accounting for Windows.

From the Windows Program Manager, continue by

> Clicking on the Simply Accounting program icon to start Simply Accounting for Windows.

When prompted to select or open the desired data files, continue by

> Clicking on the **OK** button to select the default **odc** data set files.

Figure 13.28
Simply
Accounting -
Password
window

A new window titled Simply Accounting - Password now appears as shown in (Figure 13.28). Continue by entering

User2 ⎡ Alt ⎤	to enter the User Name.
Pass2 ⎡ Enter ⎤	to enter the Password.
⎡ Enter ⎤	to select the default **Using** date (09/30/01).
⎡ Alt ⎤ + ⎡ F4 ⎤	to close the To-Do List window.

Figure 13.29
Simply
Accounting -
ODC (pass-
worded)

You will notice that the Simply Accounting - ODC window has now changed (Figure 13.29).

1. You will notice that the **Payroll** icons for both the ledger and journal are no longer displayed in the ODC window. The person with the Password **Pass2** does not have viewing or editing access, thus can not use this ledger and associated journal.

2.

   With both **View** and **Edit** boxes checked, the person has complete access to the General Ledger which is indicated by the lack of any restriction symbols in the ledger icons.

3.

   The person has view access to Payables, Receivables and Project ledgers which prevents them from adding, changing, or deleting information, while still allowing them to display and print reports. This is indicated by the pencil symbol with the x above it.

4. With the **Edit** box checked the person cannot display or print reports or use the DDE function to send information from the ledger to other windows programs, but the person can add, change, or delete entries. The person also has access to **Clear Paid Invoices** and **Advance Using Date** commands.

TO CHANGE PASSWORDS

If you wish to change the passwords or change the access levels you can only do this if you enter the password associated with the <u>**System**</u> access level. In our tutorial the password was **System**.

BUDGETING

The purpose of budgeting in your business is to allow you to measure your business' actual progress against predefined budgeted figures. These budgeted figures are only a guideline and do not effect the posted entries in Simply Accounting for Windows.

In Chapter 4 you set up the chart of accounts which involved the entry of budget figures for numerous accounts within the income statement.

Practice Exercise 13.12

Exit and re-enter Simply Accounting for Windows. When prompted enter **sysadmin** as the User and **System** as the password. You will need to have complete password access to both the Project and General Ledger modules when you update the budget figures.

Continue and print an Income Statement for the period starting **01/01/01** and finishing **08/31/01**. Be sure to include the comparison of Actual to Budget using the **Actual vs. Budget** format.

When you view the income statement that you printed in the above Practice Exercise, you can see that your business has been profitable for the year and that you have far exceeded the budgeted figures for the year. When this happens you would normally want to update your budget figures so that they more closely resemble what you actually want to achieve.

Instead of manually changing each of the budget figures, with Simply Accounting you can use the **Budget Update** feature, located in the **Maintenance** menu.

Continue from the Simply Accounting - ODC window by

Selecting the **Maintenance** menu.

Selecting **Update Budget Amounts** from the **Maintenance** menu (Figure 13.21).

Figure 13.30
Update Budget
window

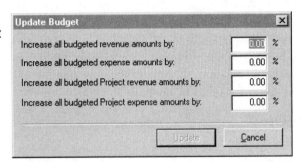

As shown in Figure 13.30, the **Update Budget** window allows you to globally update the budget for both the income statement and the Project module by entering a percentage increase for income, expenses, or both.

Continue by entering

15.0 ⌐Tab⌐   to enter the percentage by which to **Increase all budgeted revenue amounts.**

12.5 ⌐Tab⌐   to enter the percentage by which to **Increase all budgeted expense amounts.**

15.0 ⌐Tab⌐   to enter the percentage by which to **Increase all budgeted Project revenue amounts.**

12.5 ⌐Tab⌐   to enter the percentage by which to **Increase all budgeted Project expense amounts.**

⌐Enter⌐   to **Update** the budget by these figures.

Figure 13.31
Budget update
confirmation
window

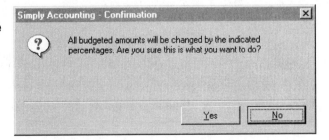

As shown in Figure 13.31, Simply Accounting will then ask you to confirm this action. Continue by pressing

☐ Y   to confirm **Yes** for this action.

Simply Accounting will then update the revenue budget amounts by 15.0% and the expense budget amounts by 12.50% for both the Income Statement and Project module.

Practice Exercise 13.13

> Print an income statement for the period starting **01/01/01** and finishing **08/31/01**. Be sure to include the comparison of Actual to Budget using the **Actual vs. Budget** format.

Once you have completed the above exercise, compare this income statement with the one printed previously in exercise 13.12. You will notice that the budget figures have been increased by 15.0% for revenue and 12.50% for expenses.

ENSURING DATA INTEGRITY

Even though you are now well aware of the importance of ensuring that your accounting files are backed up, it is also important that you ensure that the data you are backing up is free of possible errors. While Simply Accounting for Windows will ensure that your entries always balance, you may have experienced data loss due to computer failure due to power surges, outages, and even failure due to incorrect exiting procedures or various other problems that arise when you use the operating system.

> **HINT:** *You should always exit Simply Accounting for Windows by closing all of the associated windows, including the Simply Accounting - ODC (Main) window. Never close Simply Accounting by ending the task, (through the windows task manager). This method of closing Simply Accounting can result in the loss of data.*

Simply Accounting provides a self-checking function that ensures that your data is free of errors. Continue from the Simply Accounting - ODC window (Figure 13.29) by

Selecting the **Maintenance** menu.

Selecting the **Check Data Integrity** option.

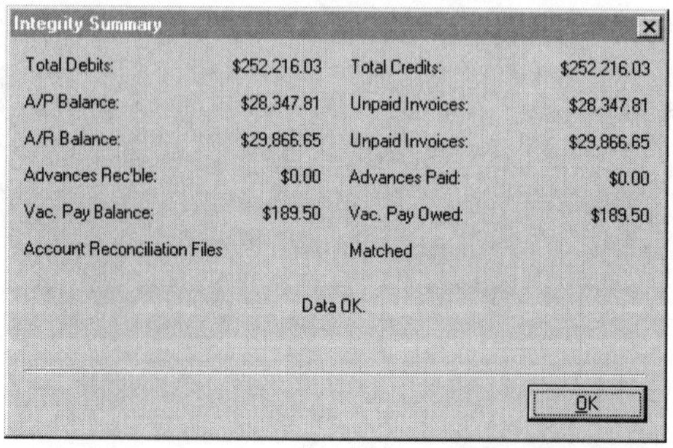

Figure 13.32
Integrity
Summary
window

Integrity Summary			
Total Debits:	$252,216.03	Total Credits:	$252,216.03
A/P Balance:	$28,347.81	Unpaid Invoices:	$28,347.81
A/R Balance:	$29,866.65	Unpaid Invoices:	$29,866.65
Advances Rec'ble:	$0.00	Advances Paid:	$0.00
Vac. Pay Balance:	$189.50	Vac. Pay Owed:	$189.50
Account Reconciliation Files		Matched	
		Data OK.	

Simply Accounting will then access your data to check for their integrity. Once this has been completed, the **Integrity Summary** window (Figure 13.32) will be displayed.

> ***HINT:** You Integrity Summary window may not resemble the same financial figures as those displayed in Figure 13.32. This may be caused by the payroll tax tables used within your version of Simply Accounting for Windows.*

At the bottom of the **Integrity Summary** window you will see a message saying *Data OK* or, another message informing you of the error in the integrity of your accounting data.

Continue by pressing

 to close the Integrity Summary window and return to the Simply Accounting - ODC window.

BACKING UP YOUR DATA FILES

At this point, return to the Simply Accounting - ODC window and continue with the backup function.

Call this backup:

Backup Filename:	A:\ODC13C\ODC
Comment:	Closing Books Part c

You have now completed Chapter 13 and with it the Overnight Delivery Company case study which demonstrated most of the major features of Simply Accounting for Windows. You can now exit the Simply Accounting program in the usual manner.

Further Practice

To get further practice with the concepts you have learned in this chapter go to Chapter 14 and work through Section 13 of the National Supply Company.

PART III

COMPREHENSIVE PRACTICE CASE

NATIONAL SUPPLY COMPANY

In Chapter 14 you are given instructions for a practice case, the National Supply Company. Each section in Chapter 14 corresponds to one of the Overnight Delivery Company chapters from 3 to 13. You can complete each section in this chapter as you work through the ODC chapters or work through the entire Chapter 14 after completing the ODC exercises to the end of Chapter 13.

CHAPTER 14

COMPREHENSIVE PRACTICE CASE— NATIONAL SUPPLY COMPANY

CHAPTER 14

NATIONAL SUPPLY COMPANY

SECTION 14.3 — CREATING THE DATA FILES

We suggest that you create a new directory within the C:\PROGRAM FILES\WINSIM directory titled NATIONAL. The suggested name for the Simply Accounting for Windows data files is suggested as NATIONAL.

You should also create the NATIONAL data files from scratch instead of using one of the templates supplied by Simply Accounting for Windows.

National Supply Company is an office supply retailer located in Toronto, Ontario. The address of the head office is as follows:

National Supply Company
Unit 150-1250 Eglinton Ave.
Toronto, Ontario
M5K 3L4
Telephone: 416-785-9483
Facsimile: 416-785-0009

After reviewing the accounting records for National Supply Company, you have found the following information:

Fiscal Start:	02/01/2001
Fiscal End:	01/31/2002
Conversion:	03/01/2001

Functions that you will want to use within Simply Accounting for Windows:

1. Keeping track of vendors
2. Keeping track of customers
3. Paying employees
4. Keeping track of goods and services you sell
5. Allocation revenue and expenses to projects
6. Use Accounting Terms
7. Revenue Canada Business Number: 44995341
8. Use Quebec Sales Tax: No (not checked)

After reviewing the payroll files, you have determined the following:

Two types of payroll are incurred.

1. Salary
2. Bonuses
   Remaining income labels should read "not used."

Employee deductions include the following:

1. Medical Premiums (Med Premiums)
2. Canada Savings Bonds (CSB)
3. Union Dues (Union)
4. Charitable Donations (Donations)

Remaining income labels should read "not used."

Other miscellaneous matters are as follows:

Prov. Tax Header:	Tax (Que)
Fed. Tax:	G.S.T.
Project Title:	Project
Printer Settings:	Default, no modification required.
Store Invoice Lookup Details:	Yes (checked)
Use Cash-Basis Accounting:	No (not checked)
Budget Accounts:	Yes (checked)
Budget Period Frequency:	Annual
Budget Project Accounts:	Yes (checked)
Budget Period Frequency:	Annual
Use Cheque No as Source Code:	Yes (checked)

G.S.T. rate 1 is 7.0%, G.S.T. rate 2 is 15.0% while the P.S.T. rate is 8.0%.

P.S.T. will not be applied against freight charges, and P.S.T. will not be applied to GST.

All payroll income types will be taxable (checked).

Select to use Automatic Payroll Deductions and all deductions will be deducted after tax (checked).

All payroll deductions will be calculated as an amount versus a percentage of gross pay.

The EI factor is 1.4% while the extended Health Tax is set at .85% and the QHSF will be 0.00 for National Supply Company.

The next receipts number will be 855 while the invoice number will be 1874, next sales quote will be 1, next purchase order will be 306, while the next customer deposit will be 1.

Once you have access the Simply Accounting main window, continue with changing the additional program settings:

Vendor aging normally is typically 30, 60, and 90 days.

Customer aging is typically 30, 60, and 90 days.

Calculate both purchase and sales discounts before tax for one-time vendors and customers.

Early payment discounts for customers are 2.0% within 10 days, net 30 days.

Management has decided that interest charges will not be charged at this time.

Management is very interested in the flexibility of using Projects and wanted to be able to distribute Payroll information to the Projects by percentage while other journals are to be distributed by amount.

Once you have completed this section, be sure to backup your files under backup point **NSC3** with a comment entitled **National Setup**.

SECTION 14.4 — SETTING UP THE GENERAL LEDGER

Now that you have created the data files for National Supply Company, the next step is to create and convert the chart of accounts and opening balances as at 03/01/2001. You should first create the new accounts and then enter the opening balances. At that time backup your data files. Then continue by entering the monthly budget information.

You have been able to obtain the interim financial statements for the one month ending 02/28/01. These statements are displayed as follows:

National Supply Company
Balance Sheet As At February 28, 2001

ASSETS

CURRENT ASSETS

Petty Cash	50.00	
Bank — Royal (next cheque #457)	2,561.25	
Bank USD — Seafirst (USD curency next cheque #101)	0.00	
Cash		2,611.25
Accounts Receivable	16,350.00	
Doubtful Accounts	-250.00	
Net Accounts Receivable		16,100.00
Advances Receivable		0.00
Inventory — Office Supplies		45,630.00
Prepaid Insurance		1,100.00
TOTAL CURRENT ASSETS		65,441.25

FIXED ASSETS

Equipment	5,450.00	
Accum Depn — Equipment	-1,200.00	
Net Equipment		4,250.00
Automotive	65,450.00	
Accum Depn — Automotive	-12,500.00	
Net Automotive		52,950.00
Leasehold Improvements	7,800.00	
Accum Amort — Leaseholds	-3,200.00	
Net Leasehold Improvements		4,600.00
TOTAL FIXED ASSETS		61,800.00

TOTAL ASSETS		127,241.25

LIABILITIES

CURRENT LIABILITIES

Accounts Payable		36,500.00
G.S.T. Charged on Sales	4,350.00	
G.S.T. Paid on Purchases	-850.25	
G.S.T. Owing (Refund)		3,499.75
HST Charged on Sales	0.00	
HST Paid on Purchases	0.00	

HST Owing (Refund)		0.00
P.S.T. Payable		950.00
Interest Payable		411.56
Wages Payable	0.00	
Income Tax Payable	0.00	
Vacation Pay Payable	0.00	
CPP Payable	0.00	
EI Payable	0.00	
WCB Payable	0.00	
EHT Payable	0.00	
Medical Plan Premiums Payable	0.00	
Canada Savings Bonds Payable	0.00	
Union Dues Payable	0.00	
Charitable Donations Payable	0.00	
Total Payroll Liability		0.00
TOTAL CURRENT LIABILITIES		41,361.31
LONG-TERM DEBT		
Note Payable		58,000.00
TOTAL LONG-TERM DEBT		58,000.00
TOTAL LIABILITIES		99,361.31
EQUITY		
CAPITAL		
Capital — P. Joseph		22,912.01
Current Earnings *(already created #3600)*		4,967.93
TOTAL CAPITAL		27,879.94
TOTAL EQUITY		27,879.94
LIABILITIES AND EQUITY		127,241.25

National Supply Company
Income Statement for 1 month ending February 28, 2001

REVENUE	Actual	Budget (Annual)
SALES		
Office Supply Sales	33,582.50	360,000.00
TOTAL SALES REVENUE	33,582.50	360,000.00
SERVICE		
Equipment Maintenance	2,430.00	33,600.00
TOTAL SERVICE REVENUE	2,430.00	33,600.00
MISC REVENUE		
Bank Interest earned	0.00	0.00
Foreign exchange gain/loss	0.00	0.00
TOTAL MISC REVENUE	0.00	0.00
TOTAL REVENUE	36,012.50	393,600.00
EXPENSE		
COST OF SALES		
Cost of Sales — Office Supplies	16,850.00	192,000.00
TOTAL COST OF SALES	16,850.00	192,000.00

OPERATING EXPENSES

Supplies		352.00	1,800.00
Fuel and Oil		4,250.00	21,600.00
Repairs and Maintenance		250.00	9,600.00
Insurance		100.00	1,200.00
TOTAL OPERATING EXPENSES		4,952.00	34,200.00

ADMINISTRATIVE EXPENSES

Rent		650.00	7,800.00
Telephone and Pager		265.24	2,160.00
Utilities		80.50	960.00
Office Stationery		52.35	300.00
Coffee Supplies		42.50	510.00
Wage and Salary Expense	5,950.25		72,000.00
CPP Expense	470.60		5,520.00
EI Expense	780.30		9,360.00
EHT Expense	50.58		600.00
WCB Expense	89.25		1,080.00
Total Payroll Expense		7,340.98	88,560.00
Accounting and Legal		120.00	1,440.00
Advertising and Promotion		0.00	1,200.00
Licences		0.00	300.00
Insurance and Taxes		0.00	1,200.00
Bank Charges and Interest		441.00	5,400.00
Bad Debt Expense		0.00	600.00
Other Freight		0.00	0.00
Depreciation		250.00	3,000.00
Inventory Assembly Expense	0.00		0.00
Inventory Adjustment Expense	0.00		0.00
Total Inventory Costs		0.00	0.00
TOTAL ADMIN EXPENSES		9,242.57	113,430.00
TOTAL EXPENSE		31044.57	339,630.00
NET INCOME		4967.93	53,970.00

Note: *At this point, only create the chart of accounts. You will enter the opening balances and budget balances after backing up your data. (See NSC4 below).*

Management has given you the task of creating the chart of accounts with the following account range guidelines:

Current Assets	1000 to 1499
Fixed Assets	1500 to 1599
Current Liabilities	2000 to 2499
Long-Term Liabilities	2500 to 2599
Capital/Equity	3000 to 3999
Sales Revenue	4000 to 4099
Service Revenue	4100 to 4199
Miscellaneous Revenue	4900 to 4999
Cost of Sales	5000 to 5099
Operating Expenses	5100 to 5199
Administrative Expense	5200 to 5999

Be sure that you assign the appropriate Account Class for each account.

Note: *If you have problems in setting up the account numbers, then view the sample chart of accounts located on the disk in the back of the book. Put the disk in Drive A and type README.*

Continue with the following:

Allow transactions in a Foreign Currency.

Track exchange and rounding differences to the Foreign exchange gain/loss account.

Foreign currency: United States Dollar

Foreign exchange rate information:

Date	Exchange Rate
03/01/01	1.5350

Remember to close the currency on the Seafirst account.

The details for the Royal bank account's last reconciliation are as follows. Remember that you will not be selecting from previous journal entries as you are setting up the General Ledger at this point:

Setup the integration with one income type for the bank interest earned and one expense type for the bank service charges.

Last Reconciled Balance:	4651.18
Less Cheque 454 Dated 02/27/01	(350.20) Credit
Less Cheque 455 Dated 02/28/01	(1,200.40) Credit
Less Cheque 456 Dated 02/28/01	(539.33) Credit
General Ledger Balance:	2,561.25

The details for the Seafirst bank account's last reconciliation are as follows. Remember that you will not be selecting from previous journal entries as you are setting up the General Ledger at this point:

Setup the integration with one income type for the bank interest earned and one expense type for the bank service charges.

Last Reconciled Balance:	0.00
General Ledger Balance:	0.00

Management has requested that you first enter the accounts. Once this has been completed, back-up your data using backup **NSC4** with a comment **National Chart of Accts.**

SECTION 14.5 — ENTERING OPENING BALANCES

Enter the opening balances as well as the budget information for the financial statements as shown in Section 14.4.

Backup your data using backup **NSC5A (National GL Opening Balances).**

Define the retained earnings account from the above financial statements, (3010 Capital — P. Joseph).

Print the financial statements (balance sheet and income statement) and compare them to those displayed in Section 14.4. You should also print out the trial balance for your records.

Backup your data using backup **NSC05B (National GL Ready)**.

SECTION 14.6 — MAKING JOURNAL ENTRIES

The following journal entries are for March 2001. You should advance the using date to March 31, 2001.

The following transactions occurred during March 2001. When recording these entries, start with source code **ADJ01** and continue in sequence.

1. An insurance policy for one automobile was purchased on March 2, 2001 by automatic debit from the Royal bank account. The amount paid for this policy was $3,900.00 for a 12-month period. Hint: *This purchase should be debited to the applicable prepaid account within the asset section of the chart of accounts.*

2. Operating expense insurance (for the automobiles) was expensed (incurred) for March 2001 (March 31, 2001 entry date) at $416.67. It is suggested that you set up a recurring entry for the monthly expensing for this transaction.

3. The following three entries can be combined into one journal entry with an entry date of March 31, 2001:

   a. Depreciation must be entered for the equipment which has been determined at $200.00 for March 2001.

   b. The depreciation for the automobiles has been determined at $620.00 based on the annual mileage driven.

   c. Leasehold improvements amortization has been determined at $50.00 for March 2001.

As the above monthly depreciation entries are all based on a straight line basis for depreciation, we suggest that you create a recurring entry for future periods.

4. Bank interest on the note payable has been determined on March 31, 2001 to be $458.89. Management has requested that you continue entering the interest payable in a separate account to the principal portion of the loan due to the repayment arrangement with the lender (interest only payable for the current year). The accounts effected by this entry will be Interest Payable and the Interest Expense accounts.

   On March 31, 2001, the Royal Bank withdrew the previous month's interest payable for your loan in the amount of $411.56. The accounts effected by entry include the Interest Payable and Bank Account.

Continue with the entry of the following foreign exchange rate information:

Date	Foreign Exchange rate
03/15/01	1.5240
03/31/01	1.5390

Continue with the following entry:

5. On March 31, 2001, $2,500.00 USD was transferred from the Seafirst Bank account to the Royal Bank account. Accept the default exchange rate of 1.5390.

Once you have entered the above journal entries, be sure to print out the General Journal for the period. Management has also requested that you print out a General Ledger listing for the Depreciation Expense account for March 2001.

Backup your data using backup **NSC06 (National General Entries)**.

SECTION 14.7 — ACCOUNTS RECEIVABLE

Now that you have mastered the use of the General Ledger, management has suggested that you now convert the manual accounts receivable modules to Simply Accounting for Windows.

The customer list is as follows:

Johnston Distribution Ltd.
Beverly Card   Telephone: 416-443-0392
6055 Don Valley Parkway   Facsimile: 416-443-0393
Don Mills, Ontario
M7L 4L4

YTD Sales:	$ 2,450.47
Last Year Sales:	$ 21,350.00
Credit Limit:	$ 5,000.00
Terms:	2/10, Net 30
Clear Transactions when paid	No (not checked)
Print Statements for Customer	Yes (checked)
Include in G.S.T. Report	Yes (checked)
Currency:	CAD

VanHaven Management Group   Telephone: 416-792-2033
Sharon Bridges   Facsimile: 416-792-5093
420-5066 Bay Street
Toronto, Ontario
M6M 4L1

YTD Sales:	$ 5,289.82
Last Year Sales:	$ 23,300.00
Credit Limit:	$ 4,000.00
Terms:	2/10, Net 30
Clear Transactions when paid	No (not checked)
Print Statements for Customer	Yes (checked)
Include in G.S.T. Report	Yes (checked)
Currency:	CAD

Hanover Development Corp.   Telephone: 416-791-4393
Jeffery Black   Facsimile: 416-791-4394
1105-1205 Younge Street
Toronto, Ontario
M6L 4K1

YTD Sales:	$ 0.00
Last Year Sales:	$ 0.00
Credit Limit:	$2,500.00
Terms:	Net 30
Clear Transactions when paid	No (not checked)
Print Statements for Customer	Yes (checked)
Include in G.S.T. Report	Yes (checked)
Currency:	CAD

City Broadcasting Group Inc.   Telephone: 416-888-4052
Tessa Hollyhock   Facsimile: 416-888-4065
1020-4393 Richmond Street
Toronto, Ontario
M5K 3L4

YTD Sales:	$ 14,267.05
Last Year Sales:	$ 42,800.00

Credit Limit:	$ 5,000.00
Terms:	2/10, Net 30
Clear Transactions when paid	No (not checked)
Print Statements for Customer	Yes (checked)
Include in G.S.T. Report	Yes (checked)
Currency:	CAD

Ruda Office Management	Telephone: 905-933-6601
Rollande Ruda	Facsimile: 905-933-6601
1040 North York Ave.	
New York, New York	
900925	
YTD Sales:	$ 159.82 USD
Last Year Sales:	$ 1,250.00 USD
Credit Limit:	$ 5,000.00 USD
Terms:	2/10, Net 30
Clear Transactions when paid	No (not checked)
Print Statements for Customer	Yes (checked)
Include in G.S.T. Report	No (not checked)
Currency:	USD

Russell Development Corp.	Telephone: 905-442-2931
Randy Russell	Facsimile: 905-442-2932
250-1000 West 1st Ave.	
New York, New York	
900847	
YTD Sales:	0.00
Last Year Sales:	0.00
Credit Limit:	$ 4,000.00 USD
Terms:	2/10, Net 30
Clear Transactions when paid	No (not checked)
Print Statements for Customer	Yes (checked)
Include in G.S.T. Report	No (not checked)
Currency:	USD

Be sure to backup your data using backup **NSC07A (National AR Customers)** after entering the customers (but before entering the outstanding invoices).

The outstanding invoices and partial payments as of February 28, 2001 are as follows:

OUTSTANDING INVOICES

Customer	Inv#	Date	Amount
Johnston Distribution	1868	Feb 04, 01	2,622.00
Terms: 2/10 Net 30			
VanHaven Management Group	1866	Feb 02, 01	5,660.10
Terms: 2/10 Net 30			
City Broadcasting	1869	Feb 06, 01	3,055.20
Terms: 2/10 Net 30			
	1871	Feb 11, 01	7,239.00
	1872	Feb 20, 01	171.00
	1873	Feb 27, 01	4,971.54

PARTIAL PAYMENTS

Customer	Chq#	Payment Date	Inv#	Amount
VanHaven Management Group	5604	Feb 27, 01	1866	4,500.00
City Broadcasting	304	Feb 28, 01	1869	2,868.84

Once the outstanding invoices and partial payment have been entered, you should backup using backup **NSC07B (National AR Outstanding Invoices)**.

Continue with the entry of the linked accounts for the Accounts Receivable module. G.S.T. rate 1 should be used for the G.S.T. charged on sales while G.S.T. rate 2 should be used for HST charged on sales.

Once linked, continue with the display of the Receivables Customer Aged (including Historical Differences) for all customers in a detail form. The outcome of this report should be a total of $16,350.00.

Continue by backing up your data using **NSC07C (National AR Balanced)**.

The following invoices were issued during March 2001 (keep the Using Date as 03/31/01).

On March 1, 2001, an invoice on account was generated for VanHaven Management Group for $2,500.00 plus G.S.T. for equipment maintenance. This invoice was billed in accordance with a monthly contract which states that $2,500.00 per month plus G.S.T. will be billed once per month. It is suggested that you create a recurring sales invoice for this transaction. Accept the default terms.

On March 3, 2001, City Broadcasting made a payment of $4,000.00 (cheque 312), which is to be applied as follows:

Invoice #1869	186.36
Invoice #1871	3,813.64

Based on this payment, management has agreed that City Broadcasting should be entitled to a credit limit of $15,000.00.

On the same day, City Broadcasting also agreed to provide payment (cheque 314), for a new equipment maintenance (sales invoice with payment by cheque) in the amount of $1,000.00 plus G.S.T. which was completed on this day. A net payment in the amount of $1,048.60 was made at the time the invoice was generated.

On March 4, 2001, Ruda Office Management received equipment maintenance service (on account) in the amount of $500.00 (USD). Accept default terms.

On March 5, 2001, City Broadcasting received equipment maintenance service (on account) in the amount of $3,100.00 plus G.S.T..

On March 6, 2001, Johnston Distribution Ltd. paid its account in full with cheque #3065.

On March 6, 2001, Russell Development Corp. received equipment maintenance service (on account) in the amount of $2,200.00 (USD). Default terms.

Once you have entered the above entries, be sure to backup your data using backup **NSC07D (National AR Entries)**.

SECTION 14.8 — ACCOUNTS PAYABLE

You have now been asked by management to convert and use the Accounts Payable ledger.

A vendor list is as follows:

Bell Canada   Telephone: 416-280-8880
Customer Accounts   Facsimile: 416-280-8881
P.O. Box 1304
Don Mills, Ontario
M7L 3K2
Terms: Net 30
Clear Invoices When Paid: No (not checked)
Print Contact on Cheques: Yes (checked)
Include in G.S.T. Report: Yes (checked)
Currency: CAD
YTD Purchases: $ 265.24
Last Year Purchases: $ 2,640.50

Peterson & Co.   Telephone: 800-667-9254
Client Services   Facsimile: 416-258-2761
300-3665 Kingsway
Toronto, Ontario
M5K 4L3
Terms: Net 30
Clear Invoices When Paid: No (not checked)
Print Contact on Cheques: Yes (checked)
Include in G.S.T. Report: Yes (checked)
Currency: CAD
YTD Purchases: $ 120.00
Last Year Purchases: $ 2,200.00

Saturn Office Wholesalers   Telephone: 604-564-8925
Accounts Receivable Dept.   Facsimile: 604-564-8934
102-540 West 14th Ave
Vancouver, B.C.
V4J 5L2
Terms: 2/10 Net 30
Calculate Discounts before Tax   Yes (checked)
Clear Invoices When Paid: No (not checked)
Print Contact on Cheques: Yes (checked)
Include in G.S.T. Report: Yes (checked)
Currency: CAD
YTD Purchases: $ 34,990.00
Last Year Purchases: $ 54,650.00

Twin Flags Property Management   Telephone: 416-365-5674
Don Lambert   Facsimile: 416-365-5004
1106-4596 King Street
Toronto, Ontario
M6L 6L3
Terms: Net   30
Clear Invoices When Paid: No   (not checked)
Print Contact on Cheques: Yes (checked)
Include in G.S.T. Report: Yes (checked)
Currency: CAD
YTD Purchases: $650.00
Last Year Purchases: $7,800.00

Revenue Canada Taxation   Telephone: 416-333-3332
Payroll Source Deductions   Facsimile: 416-333-3333

P.O. Box 607
Toronto, Ontario
M5L 1K3

Terms:	Net 30
Clear Invoices When Paid:	No (not checked)
Print Contact on Cheques:	Yes (checked)
Include in G.S.T. Report:	No (not checked)
Currency:	CAD
YTD Purchases:	$2,942.04
Last Year Purchases:	$33,304.23

Alp Service Corp.   Telephone: 905-343-3231
Maddy Alp   Facsimile: 905-343-3231
4923 Woodstock Ave.
New York, New York
93437

Terms:	Net 30
Clear Invoices When Paid:	No (not checked)
Print Contact on Cheques:	Yes (checked)
Include in G.S.T. Report:	No (not checked)
Currency:	USD
YTD Purchases:	0.00
Last Year Purchases:	0.00

Once you have entered the above vendors, be sure to backup your data using backup **NSC08A (National AP Vendors)**.

The outstanding invoices and partial payments as of February 28, 2001 are as follows:

Vendor	Inv#	Date	Amount	Tax
Bell Canada				
Terms: Net 30	Feb 01	Feb 02, 01	283.81	
Peterson & Co.				
Terms: Net 30	504	Jan 15, 01	1,678.46	
Terms: Net 30	508	Feb 15, 01	128.40	
Saturn Office Wholesaler				
Terms: 2/10 Net 30	5994	Feb 05, 01	15,750.00	1,110.00
Terms: 2/10 Net 30	5999	Feb 08, 01	6383.18	446.82
Terms: 2/10 Net 30	6008	Feb 22, 01	4,532.71	317.29
Terms: 2/10 Net 30	6020	Feb 27, 01	6,028.04	421.96

Partial Payments

Vendor	Chq#	Payment Date	Inv#	Amount
Saturn Office Wholesaler	453	Feb 20, 01	5994	430.67
Bell Canada	456	Feb 28, 01	Feb 99	150.00

Once the outstanding invoices and partial payments have been entered, be sure to backup your data using backup **NSC08B (National AP Outstanding Invoices)**.

Continue with the entry of the applicable integration accounts. Then make sure that your historical Accounts Payable entries match those listed above.

Backup your data using NSC08C (**National AP History Entered**).

During March 2001 (thus the Using Date remains 03/31/01), the following Accounts Payable transactions occurred:

On March 2, 2001, a bill was received from Bell Canada for March telephone services. No invoice number was visible (thus use Mar01) on the telephone bill and the amount was $752.00 plus 45.12 G.S.T.

On March 3, 2001 you issued a payment to Saturn Office Wholesaler for $1,000.00 for a payment against invoice 5994.

On March 11, 2001, you received a bill (invoice 515) from Peterson & Co. for account-ing services. The amount of the bill was $120.00 for accounting services plus $8.40 G.S.T. This bill is for monthly accounting services and will be billed once per month. It is suggested that you create a recurring purchase invoice for future periods.

On March 15, 2001, you issued a cheque to Saturn Office Wholesalers for $4,500.00, which was applied with $3,000.00 to invoice 5994 and the remainder to invoice 5999.

On March 16, 2001, you established an account with the following new vendor:

Toronto Times Newspaper	Telephone: 416-995-6641
Accounts Receivable Dept	Facsimile: 416-995-6642
1200 Eglinton Ave.	
North York, Ontario	
M5L 3L2	
Terms:	Net 30
Last Year Purchases:	$ 0.00
YTD Purchases:	$ 0.00
Clear Invoices when paid:	No (not checked)
Print Contact on Cheques:	Yes (checked)
Include in G.S.T. Report:	Yes (checked)

On March 17, 2001, you received an invoice for advertising services from Toronto Times Newspaper. The invoice number was 44954 and the amount was $1,500.00 plus $105.00 G.S.T.

On March 17, 2001 an invoice was received from Alp Service Corp. for sub-contract labour (a new General Ledger account will be required within the payroll expense sec-tion). The invoice number is 1015 with an amount of $850.00 USD. Accept default exchange rate.

On March 17, 2001 you issued a cheque for immediate payment for the purchase of cof-fee supplies from Sally's Lunch Truck Co. This purchase will not require the setup of a permanent vendor records for this vendor as it is only a one-time transaction. The invoice was number 52 for $12.50 plus $0.88 G.S.T.

Once you have entered the above payable transactions, be sure to backup your data using backup **NSC08D (National AP Entries)**.

SECTION 14.9 — INVENTORY

With the Accounts Receivable and Accounts Payable now converted and in full operation, the next step is to convert the Inventory module.

Management has provided you with a listing of the inventory items as well as inventory on hand on February 28, 2001.

Item Number:	101
Item Description:	20kg Paper 8.5 x 11
Unit:	Ream
Minimum Level:	10
Selling Price:	6.99
Asset Account:	Inventory — Office Supplies
Revenue Account:	Office Supply Sales
Expense Account:	Cost of Sales — Office Supplies
Variance Account:	Cost of Sales — Office Supplies
Date of Last Sale:	02/15/01
Year to Date:	
No. Transactions:	2
Units Sold:	895
Amount Sold:	6,256.05
C.O.G.S.:	2,237.50
Last Year:	
No. Transactions:	12
Units Sold:	1,450
Amount Sold:	10,048.50
C.O.G.S.:	3,523.50
Opening Quantity:	110
Opening Value:	275.00

Item Number:	102
Item Description:	20kg Paper 8.5 x 14
Unit:	Ream
Minimum Level:	10
Selling Price:	7.99
Asset Account:	Inventory — Office Supplies
Revenue Account:	Office Supply Sales
Expense Account:	Cost of Sales — Office Supplies
Variance Account:	Cost of Sales — Office Supplies
Date of Last Sale:	02/12/01
Year to Date:	
No. Transactions:	3
Units Sold:	1,200
Amount Sold:	9,540.00
C.O.G.S.:	3,480.00
Last Year:	
No. Transactions:	28
Units Sold:	6,900
Amount Sold:	54,579.00
C.O.G.S.:	19,872.00
Opening Quantity:	690
Opening Value:	2,001.00

Item Number:	103
Item Description:	30kg Paper 8.5 x 11
Unit:	Ream
Minimum Level:	10
Selling Price:	8.50
Asset Account:	Inventory — Office Supplies
Revenue Account:	Office Supply Sales

Expense Account:	Cost of Sales — Office Supplies
Variance Account:	Cost of Sales — Office Supplies
Date of Last Sale:	02/01/01
Year to Date:	
No. Transactions:	5
Units Sold:	2,093
Amount Sold:	17,786.45
C.O.G.S.:	11,132.50
Last Year:	
No. Transactions:	52
Units Sold:	12,450
Amount Sold:	104,580.00
C.O.G.S.:	64,863.00
Opening Quantity:	1,250
Opening Value:	3,812.50
Item Number:	104
Item Description:	30kg Paper 8.5 x 14
Unit:	Ream
Minimum Level:	10
Selling Price:	8.90
Asset Account:	Inventory — Office Supplies
Revenue Account:	Office Supply Sales
Expense Account:	Cost of Sales — Office Supplies
Variance Account:	Cost of Sales — Office Supplies
Date of Last Sale:	(blank)
Year to Date:	
No. Transactions:	0
Units Sold:	0
Amount Sold:	0.00
C.O.G.S.:	0.00
Last Year:	
No. Transactions:	0
Units Sold:	0
Amount Sold:	0.00
C.O.G.S.:	0.00
Opening Quantity:	200
Opening Value:	620.00
Item Number:	201
Item Description:	Ballpoint Pens
Unit:	10 Pack
Minimum Level:	10
Selling Price:	6.00
Asset Account:	Inventory — Office Supplies
Revenue Account:	Office Supply Sales
Expense Account:	Cost of Sales — Office Supplies
Variance Account:	Cost of Sales — Office Supplies
Date of Last Sale:	(blank)
Year to Date:	
No. Transactions:	0
Units Sold:	0
Amount Sold:	0.00
C.O.G.S.:	0.00

Last Year:

No. Transactions:	0
Units Sold:	0
Amount Sold:	0.00
C.O.G.S.:	0.00
Opening Quantity:	9,650
Opening Value:	35,512.00

Item Number:	202
Item Description:	3B Pencils
Unit:	10 Pack
Minimum Level:	10
Selling Price:	3.05
Asset Account:	Inventory — Office Supplies
Revenue Account:	Office Supply Sales
Expense Account:	Cost of Sales — Office Supplies
Variance Account:	Cost of Sales — Office Supplies
Date of Last Sale:	(blank)

Year to Date:

No. Transactions:	0
Units Sold:	0
Amount Sold:	0.00
C.O.G.S.:	0.00

Last Year:

No. Transactions:	0
Units Sold:	0
Amount Sold:	0.00
C.O.G.S.:	0.00
Opening Quantity:	1,895
Opening Value:	3409.50

Once you have entered the inventory items and opening inventory, back up your data using backup **NSC09A (National Inventory Items)**.

Continue with the selection of the appropriate linked accounts for the Inventory module. Backup your data using **NSC09B (National Inventory Ready)**.

The following inventory transactions occurred during March 2001 (thus the Using Date should remain as 03/31/01):

On March 2, 2001, under invoice 6045 a purchase on credit from Saturn Office Wholesaler was for

10 reams of 20kg 8.5 x 11 of paper for $2.60 each pack.

5 reams of 30kg 8.5 x 14 of paper for $3.12 each pack.

The freight on this order was $5.00 while the G.S.T. was $3.26. *No P.S.T. on this invoice.*

On March 4, 2001, management decided to use another supplier for some of the office supply stock. This supplier is as follows:

Office Direct Distribution Group
Denise Jones
Unit 506-3460 Pacific Blvd
Barrie, Ontario
M6L 3O2

Telephone: 416-598-4931
Facsimile: 416-698-4431
Terms: 2/10 Net 30
Calculate Discounts before Tax   Yes (Checked)
Clear Invoices when Paid   No (not checked)
Print Contact on Cheque   Yes (checked)
Include in G.S.T. Report   Yes (checked)

The above vendor will provide the following inventory items:

Item Number: 301
Item Description: #10 Envelopes
Unit: 10 Pack
Selling Price: 4.50
Minimum Level: 10
Asset Account: Inventory — Office Supplies
Revenue Account: Office Supply Sales
Expense Account: Cost of Sales — Office Supplies
Variance Account: Cost of Sales — Office Supplies

Item Number: 401
Item Description: Steno chair
Unit: Each
Unit Price: 120.30
Minimum Level: 3
Asset Account: Inventory — Office Supplies
Revenue Account: Office Supply Sales
Expense Account: Cost of Sales — Office Supplies
Variance Account: Cost of Sales — Office Supplies

On March 5, 2001, a sale on account (customer to pay later) was made to Hanover Development Corp. which included

5 reams of 20kg 8 x 14 paper at $7.89 each, plus G.S.T. and 8.0% P.S.T.

2 packs of ballpoint pens at $6.00 each, plus G.S.T. and 8.0% P.S.T.

$25.00 Freight, plus G.S.T.

Total for this invoice is $85.92.

On March 10, 2001, a purchase order was issued (Ship Date March 15, 2001) to Office Direct Distribution Group Inc. for 250 packs of #10 envelopes for $2.00 each (no P.S.T.) and 5 steno chairs for $62.80 each (no P.S.T.). The total freight on this purchase was $25.00 while the G.S.T. was $58.73. Total amount of purchase order was $897.73.

Management reported that as of March 10, 2001 they had used 2 packs of ballpoint pens for use within the office. The source code will be ADJ06. Be sure to confirm that you are decreasing the inventory and increasing the Office Stationery Expense account (debit).

On March 15, 2001 the outstanding purchase order from Office Direct Distribution Group Inc. was received as invoice 6102, in its entirety.

On March 15, 2001, a sale (on account) to Ruda Office Management for the following:

2 steno chairs at $120.00 each plus G.S.T. and 8.0% P.S.T.

15 reams of 20kg 8.5 x 11 paper at $6.99 each plus G.S.T. and 8.0% P.S.T.

$15.00 Freight, plus G.S.T.

Total invoice amount $412.63.

On March 15, 2001, a sale (on account, default exchange rate) to Russell Development for the following:

2 reams of 20kg 8.5 x 11 paper at $3.99 (USD), no taxes.

$3.00 (USD) Freight

Total invoice amount $10.98 (USD)

Once you have completed the above entries, be sure to backup your data using backup **NSC09C (National Inventory Entries)**.

SECTION 14.10 — PAYROLL

Management has now suggested that you continue with the conversion of the manual payroll records to computerized records.

The employees that have recently been hired include the following:

Harrison, Steven
1243-400 King Street
Toronto, Ontario
M6L 3K2

Telephone:	416-785-4403
Social Insurance Number:	000-000-000
Birth Date:	07/21/62
Hire Date:	03/01/01
Tax Table:	Ontario
Federal Claim:	6560.00
WCB Rate:	2.5%
EI:	Yes with a factor of 1.4.
Regular per Hour:	14.60 for 80 hours
Overtime per Hour:	21.90 for 15 hours
Pay Periods per year:	26
Vacation:	Retain at 4.0%

Deductions:	Medical:	25.25 per pay period
	CSB:	10.00 per pay period
	Union Dues:	12.50 per pay period
	Donations:	5.00 per pay period

Penner, Christine
431 Light Street
Oshawa, Ontario
M7L 3K3

Telephone:	416-654-5551
Social Insurance Number:	000-000-000
Birth Date:	09/01/55
Hire Date:	02/14/94

Tax Table:		Ontario
Federal Claim:		6560.00
WCB Rate:		2.5%
EI:		Yes with a factor of 1.4.
Regular per Hour:		15.06 for 80 hours
Overtime per Hour:		22.59 for 15 hours
Pay Periods per year:		26
Vacation:		Retain at 4.0%
Deductions:	Medical:	25.25 per pay period
	CSB:	10.00 per pay period
	Union Dues:	12.50 per pay period
	Donations:	5.00 per pay period

Jones, Clare
101-1040 Blanshard Ave.
North York, Ontario
M4J 4L6

Telephone:		416-859-6600
Social Insurance Number:		000-000-000
Birth Date:		10/15/57
Hire Date:		01/01/92
Tax Table:		Ontario
Federal Claim:		6560.00
WCB Rate:		2.5%
UIC:		Yes with a factor of 1.4.
Additional Income Tax:		50.00 per pay period
Salary per period:		1250.00 for 80 hours
Dalary hours per period:		80.00
Pay Periods per year:		26
Vacation:		Retain at 4.0%
Deductions:	Medical:	25.25 per pay period
	CSB:	10.00 per pay period
	Union Dues:	none
	Donations:	5.00 per pay period

Once you have added these employees, backup your data using backup **NSC10A (National Payroll Employees)**.

The following payroll history is present for the current year:

Penner, Christine

Regular Wages		666.90
	Less CPP contributions	55.38
	Less EI contributions	61.30
	Less Income Tax	60.05
	Less Medical deductions	25.25
	Less CSB deductions	10.00
	Less Union Dues	5.00
Net Pay		449.92
EI Insurable Earnings		666.90

Jones, Clare

Gross Salary		5,000.00
	Less CPP contributions	415.22
	Less EI contributions	496.05

Less Income Tax	1,060.50
Less Medical deductions	101.00
Less CSB deductions	40.00
Less Donations	20.00
Net Pay	2,867.23
EI Insurable Earnings	5,000.00

Backup your data using **NSC10B (National Payroll Historical)**.

Once you have entered the above historical payroll information, select the appropriate payroll integration accounts, (no accounts to be integrated for Tax (Que), QPP, QHIP payables of QPP or QHIP expenses). For payroll expense accounts use account 5300 Wages and Salary Expense.

Backup your data using **NSC10C (National Payroll Linked)**.

As you have now entered all of the historical data for each of the modules (General, Payables, Receivables, Payroll and Inventory), you can now continue with informing Simply Accounting that you have finished the historical entry of this information.

Continue with this option selection (through the **History** menu — Simply Accounting Main window).

Backup your data using **NSC10D (National History completed)**.

Continue with the entry of the following current payroll:

On March 16, 2001 a cheque is issued for March 15, 2001 payroll for Steven Harrison, who worked 80 regular hours and 3.5 overtime hours.

On March 16, 2001 a cheque is issued for March 15, 2001 payroll for Christine Penner, who worked 80 regular hours.

On March 16, 2001 a cheque is issued for March 15, 2001 payroll for Clare Jones, who received a gross salary of $1,250 (80 hours worked) plus a bonus of $250.00.

Once you have completed the above entries, backup your data using backup **NSC10E (National Payroll Entries)**.

SECTION 14.11 — PROJECT COSTING

With the conversion of all the major ledgers complete, management has decided to include Project Costing within the accounting system.

The following projects have been established:

Wholesale — Phone Order
Started: 03/01/01

Wholesale — Walk-In
Started: 03/01/01

Retail — Phone Order
Started: 03/01/01

Retail — Walk-In
Started: 03/01/01

Continue with the editing of all of the accounts within the 4000 and 5000 ranges (Revenue and Expenses) to allow for project allocation.

Continue with the changing of the project setting to allocate Payroll and other journals by percentage.

Backup your data using **NSC11A (National Projects Setup)**.

Continue with the following March 2001 transactions.

On March 16, 2001, an invoice on account was issued to Russell Development Corp. for the following:

50 packs of 30lb Paper 8.5 x 11 at $4.25 (USD) no taxes.

5 packs of 30lb Paper 8.5 x 14 at $4.40 (USD) no taxes.

This order should be distributed to Retail — Phone Order.

Total invoice $234.50 (USD).

A cash sale (CAD) to S. Smith on March 17, 2001 was for the following:

1 steno chair for $120.50 plus G.S.T. and 8.0% P.S.T..

As this sale is retail — Walk-in no freight is applicable (don't forget to distribute to Retail — Walk-in).

Total invoice $138.58

On March 24, 2001, an invoice is received from Toronto Times Newspaper. This invoice is for advertising and amounts to $1,250 plus 87.50 G.S.T. This invoice should be distributed as follows:

Wholesale — Phone Order	12.0% of the total
Wholesale — Walk-In	13.0% of the total
Retail — Phone Order	35.0% of the total
Retail — Walk-In	40.0% of the total

Total amount of this invoice is $1,337.50.

On March 30, 2001 management stated that the retail division has consumed 10 packs of ballpoint pens (inventory) at the default cost. Be sure to distribute this amount to 60.0% phone order and 40.0% walk-in and to expense this use to the appropriate Office Stationery Expense account. The source for this entry can be **ADJ07.** Be sure that the Inventory is being decreased while the Expense is increased (debit) for this transaction.

On March 31, 2001 a cheque is issued for March 31, 2001 payroll for Steven Harrison who worked 80 regular hours and 6.5 overtime hours. During this pay period he worked 65.0% percent on Wholesale — Walk — in order and 30.0% on Retail — Walk-in. The remaining 5.0% was non-allocated time.

On March 31, 2001, a cheque is issued for March 31, 2001, payroll for Christine Penner who worked 80 regular hours and 12.5 overtime hours. During this pay period, she worked an even 50.0% in Retail — Phone Order and the remaining 50.0% of the time in Wholesale — Phone Order.

On March 31, 2001, a cheque is issued for March 31, 2001 payroll for Clare Jones, who received a salary of $1,300.00 (permanently increased — update payroll ledger record) for 80 salaried hours worked, plus a bonus of $450.00. Eighty percent of her time was evenly divided among all four project centres, 20.0% was non-allocated).

Once you have completed the above entries, be sure to backup your data using backup **NSC11B (National Projects Entries)**.

SECTION 14.12 — REPORTING AND GRAPHING

If you would like to prepare some special reports and graphs, review Chapter 12.

SECTION 14.13 — BANK RECONCILIATION AND MONTH-END ADJUSTMENT ENTRIES

As it is now April 01, 2001 (advance Using Date). You have just received the Royal Bank statement for March, 2001. The bank statement contains the following:

Statement End Date:	03/31/01
Ending Balance:	942.05
Cheques cleared:	
454	350.20
455	1,200.40
456	539.33
457	1,000.00
458	4,500.00
459	13.38
Deposits Received:	
03/01/01	1,048.60
03/03/01	4,000.00
03/06/01	2,622.00
03/17/01	138.58
Other Items:	
3/2/01 Insurance withdrawal	3,900.00
3/31/01 Bank Service Charge(*)	15.00

(*) For the Bank Service Charge use Source **SCharge**.

P. Joseph has deposited $10,000.00 (to the Canadian bank account) on April 1, 2001, as an additional investment. The source code for this entry can be **ADJ08**. *Credit 3010 Capital-P. Joseph* for this account.

You have been instructed to pay and remit the balances within the employee withholdings (Income Tax, EI and CPP to Revenue Canada Taxation) accounts for the period ending March 31, 2001. This entry should be a purchase with cheque payment dated April 01, 2001, Invoice number: Mar01. Print the trial balance as at 03/31/01 to receive this information.

Continue with the recalling and posting of the recurring entries within the General Journal, Sales Journal and Purchase Journal. For the accounting purchase invoice, the invoice number will be Apr01. Be sure to use the default sales invoice number and the next sequential ADJ number for the General Journal entry. This function can be easily accomplished by selecting the To-Do List function from within the **Business Assistant** menu.

Once you have completed the above entries, be sure to backup your data using backup **NSC13 (National Bank Rec/Other)**. Once completed, continue with the following:

1. Trial Balance as at March 31, 2001.

2. Balance Sheet as of March 31, 2001.

3. Income Statement for the year-to-date period from February 01, 2001 through March 31, 2001. This Income Statement should be comparable with the budget information.

4. Print the Customer Aging Report in summary.

5. Print the Vendor Aging Report in detail.

6. Print a graph displaying the aging of the Accounts Receivable.

7. Print a graph comparing the actual Sales to budgeted revenue.

8. Print a graph comparing the actual Expenses to budgeted Expenses.

You have now completed the exercise for National Supply Company. You can now go to Chapter 15, Canadiana Decorating Sales and Service Inc.

PART IV

COMPREHENSIVE PRACTICE CASE

CANADIANA DECORATING SALES & SERVICE INC.

Part IV allows you to put to use the knowledge you have gained from working through the previous chapters. Start with some basic accounting data and follow the instructions given to work through the General Ledger, Accounts Payable, Accounts Receivable, Payroll and Inventory modules. As you work through each section, you will appreciate how using the various modules can speed up your data entry. Some hints are provided to guide you through unusual entries. If you need additional help you can review the appropriate sections in Chapters 3 to 12.

CHAPTER 15

COMPREHENSIVE PRACTICE CASE — CANADIANA DECORATING SALES & SERVICE INC.

CHAPTER 15

CANADIANA DECORATING SALES & SERVICE INC.

Canadiana Decorating Sales & Service Inc. is a practice case covering the six major modules of the Simply Accounting system: General Ledger, Accounts Payable, Accounts Receivable, Payroll, Inventory, and Projects.

You will keep Canadiana's books for the six-month period July to December. By the end of December, you should have a full understanding of how the six major modules apply in a practical business situation. Also, you will add one of the modules each month.

THE COMPANY

Canadiana Decorating Sales & Service Inc. is a custom home decorating and sales business. It is a non-public company incorporated in the province of British Columbia. The store has five departments:

> Sales - Paint
> Sales - Wallpaper
> Sales - Fabric
> Decorating Service
> Delivery Service

All sales and purchases are on credit with discounts available for early payment. All sales of merchandise and freight are subject to 7.0% G.S.T. In addition, there is a provincial sales tax of 7.0% but P.S.T. is not charged on labour.

The fiscal year for the business is January 1 to December 31. The date on which the manual accounting system was converted (Conversion Date) to the Simply Accounting system was June 30. Each month an estimate is made of the cost of goods sold. A balance sheet is generated monthly to show year-to-date financial position. An income statement is generated for each month's activity and for the year-to-date.

MODULE ONE — GENERAL LEDGER

OBJECTIVE

After you have worked through this practice set, you will be able to complete the following tasks:
1. Create new company files.
2. Enter necessary defaults and integration accounts.
3. Create a General Ledger chart of accounts.
4. Enter historical data to General Ledger accounts.
5. Set the General Ledger to READY mode.
6. Enter transactions into the General Ledger module.
7. Print journals, ledgers, trial balances, income statements, and balance sheets.

INSTRUCTION #1

Create a new directory and/or disk for Canadiana. This practice case will refer to this directory as **C:\CANADEC**.

INSTRUCTION #2

Create company files using the following information:

Create the chart of accounts from scratch.

Store the files as **C:\CANADEC\CANADEC.ASC**

Fiscal Start Date:	01-01-01
Fiscal End Date:	12-31-01
Conversion Date:	06-30-01

Keeping track of vendors:	Yes (Checked)
Keeping track of customers:	Yes (Checked)
Paying employees:	Yes (Checked)
Keeping track of goods and services you sell:	Yes (Checked)
Allocating revenue and expenses to projects:	Yes (Checked)

Company Information:

Canadiana Decorating Sales & Service Inc.
19696 Bidwell Street
Vancouver
British Columbia
V6Y 1Y8
Phone: 604-683-5514
Fax: 604-683-5515

Accounting Terminology: Use Accounting Terms

Business Number   13887327

Use Quebec Sales Tax: No (unchecked)

Payroll Income names:
	Income A:	Salary
	Income B:	Bonuses

Payroll Deduction names:
	Deduction A:	Pension
	Deduction B:	Union
	Deduction C:	Medical

Prov. Tax name:	Tax (Que)
Fed. Tax:	G.S.T.
Project title:	Project

Store Invoice Lookup Details: Yes (checked)

Cash Based Accounting: No (unchecked)

Budget Revenue and Expense Accts:	Yes (checked)
Budget Period frequency:	Annual

Budget Project:	Yes (checked)	
Budget Period frequency:	Annual	
Use Cheque No as the Source Code for Cash Purchases and Sales:	No (unchecked)	
G.S.T. Rate 1:	7.0	
G.S.T. Rate 2:	0.00	
P.S.T. Rate:	7.0	
Apply P.S.T. to Freight:	No (unchecked)	
Apply P.S.T. to G.S.T.:	No (unchecked)	
Taxable Income (Yes = Checked):	Salary	Yes
	Bonuses	Yes
Automatic Payroll Deductions:	Yes	
Deduct Pension after tax:	Yes	
Deduct Union Dues after tax:	Yes	
Deduction Medical after tax:	Yes	
Deduction style:	Pension	Amount
	Union Dues	Amount
	Medical	Amount
EI factor:	1.4	
EHT factor:	0.0	
QHSF factor:	0.0	
Next document numbers:	Receipts:	1
	Invoices:	405
	Sales Quotes:	1
	Purchase Orders:	234

INSTRUCTION #3

BACKING UP YOUR DATA FILES

Create a backup disk for your data. Insert a formatted diskette into your Drive A. Label it **Canadiana Backup**.

Use the backup function within Simply Accounting for Windows.

Call this backup **GL1 (Canadiana Account Entry)**.

INSTRUCTION #4

Your next step is to enter the current chart of accounts with historical balances into Simply Accounting. Check to ensure that each account is entered as the appropriate **Type**.

	Canadiana Decorating Sales & Service Inc. Chart of Accounts/Historical Balances - 06/30/01			
Account	**Description**	**Type**	**Debit**	**Credit**
1000	CURRENT ASSETS	D		
1040	Petty Cash (Cash)	A	100.00	
1080	Royal Bank (Bank-Cheq 346)	A	15,234.67	
1090	Seafirst Bank (Bank-Cheq 1)	A	0.00	
1120	CASH: TOTAL	S		
1160	Advances Receivable (Receivable)	G	0.00	
1200	Accounts Receivable (Acct Receivable)	G	21,675.43	
1240	Inventory-Paint (Inventory)	A	24,536.75	
1280	Inventory-Wallpaper (Inventory)	A	18,700.76	
1320	Inventory-Fabric (Inventory)	A	42,389.75	
1360	TOTAL INVENTORY	S		
1400	Office Supplies (Current Asset)	G	675.34	
1440	Prepaid Insurance (Current Asset)	G	2,400.00	
1480	TOTAL CURRENT ASSETS	T		
1520	FIXED ASSETS	D		
1560	Buildings (Capital Assets)	A	210,000.00	
1600	Deprec-Building (Capital Assets)	A		10,500.00
1620	Building - Net	S		
1640	Automobile (Capital Asset)	A	13,320.00	
1680	Deprec-Auto (Capital Asset)	A		1,110.00
1720	Automobile - Net	S		
1760	Land (Capital Asset)	G	105,500.00	
1800	TOTAL FIXED ASSETS	T		
2000	CURRENT LIABILITIES	D		
2040	Accounts Payable (Accounts Payable)	G		5,768.90
2080	EI Payable (Current Liability)	A		345.25
2120	CPP Payable (Current Liability)	A		471.30
2160	Tax Payable (Current Liability)	A		3,447.78
2200	TOTAL WITHHOLDING TAX PAYABLE	S		
2240	Pension Payable (Current Liab)	R		616.23
2280	Medical Payable (Current Liab)	R		270.00
2290	WCB Payable (Current Liability)	R		0.00
2320	Short-Term Loan (Debt)	R		6,000.00
2360	P.S.T. Payable (Current Liability)	A		2,216.35
2400	G.S.T. Collected (Current Liab)	A		222.50

2440	G.S.T. Paid (Current Liability)	A	42.37	
2480	G.S.T. Owing/(Refund)	S		
2520	TOTAL CURRENT LIABILITIES	T		
2560	LONG-TERM DEBT	D		
2600	Mortgage Payable (Debt)	G		79,670.56
2640	TOTAL LONG-TERM DEBT	T		
3000	SHARES	D		
3040	Class A Shares (Share Capital)	G		5,000.00
3080	Class B Shares (Share Capital)	G		9,000.00
3120	TOTAL SHARES	T		
3160	EARNINGS	D		
3560	Retained Earnings (R/E)	G		229,238.53
3600	Current Earnings (Entered)	X		0.00
3640	TOTAL EARNINGS	T		
	Canadiana Decorating Sales & Service Inc.			
	Chart of Accounts/Historical Balances - 06/30/01			
4000	SALES REVENUE	D		
4040	Sales-Paint (Revenue)	A		61,987.65
4080	Sales-Wallpaper (Revenue)	A		43,098.75
4120	Sales-Fabric (Revenue)	A		101,574.89
4160	TOTAL SALES REVENUE	S		
4200	Returns-Paint (Revenue)	A	3,457.89	
4240	Returns-Wallpaper (Revenue)	A	4,653.23	
4280	Returns-Fabric (Revenue)	A	5,234.87	
4320	TOTAL RETURNS	S		
4360	TOTAL NET SALES REVENUE	T		
4400	SERVICE REVENUE	D		
4440	Decorating (Revenue)	G		85,679.67
4480	Delivery (Revenue)	G		23,876.05
4520	TOTAL SERVICE REVENUE	T		
4560	OTHER REVENUE	D		
4600	Interest (Other Revenue)	G		1,436.86
4610	Purchase Disc (Other Rev)	G		0.00
4620	Foreign Exchange (Other Rev)	G		
4640	TOTAL OTHER REVENUE	T		
5000	COST OF GOODS SOLD	D		
5020	COGS-Paint (Cost of Sales)	G	30,045.37	

5040	COGS-Wallpaper Cost of Sales	G	18,937.37	
5060	COGS-Fabric (Cost of Sales)	G	39,802.32	
5080	Freight Exp (Cost of Sales)	G	4,765.92	
5090	Sales Disc (Cost of Sales)	G	0.00	
5100	TOTAL COST OF GOODS SOLD	T		
5120	OPERATING EXPENSES	D		
5140	Salary Exp (Payroll expense)	A	73,948.02	
5160	EI Expense (Payroll expense)	A	1,208.40	
5180	CPP Expense (Payroll exp)	A	1,413.90	
5190	WCB Expense (Payroll exp)	A	1,848.70	
5200	TOTAL PAYROLL EXPENSE	S		
5240	Fuel Expense (Expense)	A	4,694.28	
5280	Insurance Exp (Expense)	A	2,400.00	
5320	Repair Exp (Expense)	A	1,232.59	
5360	Permits Exp (Expense)	A	555.65	
5400	TOTAL AUTOMOTIVE EXPENSE	S		
5440	TOTAL OPERATING EXPENSES	T		
5480	OVERHEAD	D		
5520	Office exp (G&A expense)	G	980.75	
5560	Telephone exp (G&A expense)	G	1,324.67	
5600	Advertising exp (G&A exp)	G	1,765.87	
5640	Utilities exp (G&A exp)	G	2,135.67	
5680	Amortization-Building (exp)	G	10,500.00	
5720	Amortization-Auto (exp)	G	1,110.00	
5760	TOTAL OVERHEAD	T		
5800	OTHER EXPENSES	D		
5840	Interest Exp (Expense)	G	4,685.84	
5880	Bank Charges (Expense)	G	254.89	
5920	TOTAL OTHER EXPENSES	T		
	Total		671,531.27	671,531.27

Continue with the entry/activation of the budgeting amounts (for the applicable accounts):

Note that the budget amounts are stated as annual amounts.

Acct	Description	Budget Amt
4040	Sales-Paint	126,000.00
4080	Sales-Wallpaper	78,000.00
4120	Sales-Fabric	198,000.00
4200	Returns-Paint	6,000.00
4240	Returns-Wallpaper	-9,000.00
4280	Returns-Fabric	-9,000.00
4440	Decorating	144,000.00
4480	Delivery	48,000.00
4600	Interest	2,760.00
5020	COGS-Paint	60,000.00
5040	COGS-Wallpaper	36,000.00
5060	COGS-Fabric	78,000.00
5080	Freight Expense	9,420.00
5140	Salary Expense	150,000.00
5160	EI Expense	2,400.00
5180	CPP Expense	2,880.00
5240	Fuel Expense	13,200.00
5260	Permits expense	1,200.00
5280	Insurance Expense	4,800.00
5320	Repair Expense	2,400.00
5520	Office Expense	3,000.00
5560	Telephone Expense	3,000.00
5600	Advertising Expense	3,600.00
5640	Utilities Expense	4,200.00
5680	Amortization Exp.-Building	21,000.00
5720	Amortization Exp.-Automotive	2,220.00
5840	Interest Expense	7,200.00
5880	Bank Charges	480.00

Management has reminded you that both bank accounts will need to be set up. The details are as follows:

1080 (Royal Bank) will have to be reconciled. The suggestion is that you set up an income code named **INT** which will be for bank interest earned as well as an Expense code titled **SCharge** for the bank service charges incurred. The uncleared transactions for this account are as follows (Select **No** to selecting outstanding amounts from previous journal entries):

Last Reconciled Balance   12,430.15

#	Description	Date	Debit	Credit
343	Cheque	6/27/01		1,240.30
344	Cheque	6/27/01		50.00
345	Cheque	6/30/01		125.00
DEP	Deposit	6/30/01	4,219.82	

Continue with setting the Bank Reconciliation to Ready.

1090 (Seafirst) will have to be reconciled. The suggestion is that you set up an income code named **INT** which will be for bank interest earned as well as an expense code titled **SCharge** for the bank service charges incurred. The uncleared transactions for this account are as follows (Select **No** to selecting outstanding amounts from previous journal entries). As this is a new account, the last reconciled balance will be zero.

As the company will be transacting U.S. dollar entries, set up the foreign currency as follows:

Track exchange differances in 4620 Foreign Exchange
Foreign currency United States Dollar
Currency Code, Symbol, Symbol Position, Thousands Separator, Decimal Separator, and Decimal places as default.

Exchange rate information:

Date	Exchange Rate
07/31/01	1.535
08/31/01	1.546
09/30/01	1.5501
10/31/01	1.5432
11/30/01	1.5698
12/31/01	1.5801

INSTRUCTION #5
BACKING UP YOUR DATA FILES

Backup your data to **GL2 (Canadian GL Ready)**.

INSTRUCTION #6

Important Note:
Continue with selecting the appropriate General Ledger integration accounts.

Advance the Using Date of July 31, 2001, or you can select **Advance Using date** from the **Maintenance** Menu.

INSTRUCTION #7

Now you are ready to begin entering July 2001 transactions. As you have only set up the General Ledger at this point, **enter the following transaction into the General and Bank Reconciliation journals only. Do not set up the Payable, Receivable, Payroll, or Inventory journals until instructed**. If you are unsure of a particular entry, then prepare it on paper first. After you make the journal entry, check it through the **Report** menu before you save it. For the first part of this exercise enter all transactions into the General Ledger module only.

Canadiana Decorating Sales & Service Inc.	**Royal Bank cheque 346**
	07/01/01 $149.80 (CAD)
Pay to Westcoast Publications	
	per:_____
57684 557463	

Reference
Advertising $140.00   G.S.T. $9.80

HINT: ENTER G.S.T. AS A DEBIT AMOUNT.

The following sale is on account. Do not make an entry for the inventory used and expended. Instead only complete the sales portion of this entry. The company will instead complete a month-end inventory and expense the difference at that point.

Canadiana Decorating Sales & Service Inc. Payment Received			
From **George Sprint**	to Royal Bank acct.	Date	**07/06/01**
Chq. **964**		Invoice Total	**3,458.56 (CAD)**

Canadiana Decorating Sales & Service Inc.
Sales Invoice
(Cash Sale - Seafirst Bank)

Bill To:	**Barb Alp Enterprises**			
Date:	**07/06/01**		Invoice No.	**404**

USD currency (07/31/01 rate)

Qty	Desc	Unit		Total
	Decorating revenue			6,500.00
		Subtotal		6,500.00
		P.S.T.		0.00
		G.S.T.		0.00
		Total		6,500.00

Canadiana Decorating Sales & Service Inc.
Sales Invoice
(on Account)

Bill To:	**Caroline Clare**			
Date:	**07/06/01**		Invoice No.	**405**

CAD currency

Qty	Desc	Price		Total
50	Ceiling Flat Paint	16.00		800.00
103	Jack/Jill Wallpaper	12.00		1,236.00
568	Sq/yd Sheer Fabric	10.00		5,680.00
		Subtotal		7,716.00
		P.S.T.		540.12
		G.S.T.		540.12
		Total		8,796.24

Hollybush Interior Supply
Purchase Invoice
(on Account)

Sold To:	**Canadiana Decorating Sales & Service Inc.**			
Date:	**07/08/01**		Invoice No.	**1096**

CAD currency

Qty	Desc	Price	Total Acct	Acct
415	Eggshell Latex Paint	11.00	4,565.00	1240
367	Jack and Jill Wallpaper	6.00	2,202.00	1280
192	Select Wallpaper	7.00	1,344.00	1280
468	Sheer Fabric	5.00	2,340.00	1320
		Subtotal	10,451.00	
		Freight	272.00	
		G.S.T.	750.61	
		Total	11,473.61	

HINT:

You can only enter one amount for each account.

Canadiana Decorating Sales & Service Inc.   **Royal Bank cheque 347**

07/11/01 $1,435.68 (CAD)

Pay to Lutzman Paint & Supply Ltd.

per:_____

57684 557463

Reference

Payment on Account (Debit Accounts Payable)

Canadiana Decorating Sales & Service Inc.   **Royal Bank cheque 348**

07/11/01 $4,333.22 (CAD)

Pay to Rainbow World Inc.

per:_____

57684 557463

Reference

Payment on Account (Debit Accounts Payable)

Canadiana Decorating Sales & Service Inc.
Sales Invoice
(on Account)

Bill To:	**Bernie Stanton**		
Date:	**07/12/01**	Invoice No.	**406**

CAD currency Net 30 Days

Qty	Desc	Price		Total
36	Eggshell Latex Paint	22.00		792.00
102	Select Wallpaper	14.00		1,428.00
91	Velveet Fabric	50.00		4,550.00
		Subtotal		7,716.00
		P.S.T.		540.12
		G.S.T.		540.12
		Total		8,796.24

HINT: *There is no P.S.T. on labour*

Canadiana Decorating Sales & Service Inc.   **Royal Bank cheque 349**

07/15/01 $4,264.33 (CAD)

Pay to the Receiver General of Canada

per:_____

57684 557463

Reference

EI withheld	$345.25
CPP withheld	$471.30
Income Tax withheld	$3,447.78

Canadiana Decorating Sales & Service Inc.   **Royal Bank cheque 350**

07/15/01 $145.24 (CAD)

Pay to Motor Vehicle Branch

per:_____

57684 557463

Reference

| Vehicle Permit | $145.24 |

HINT:

Use office supplies asset instead of expense account.

Canadiana Decorating Sales & Service Inc.   **Royal Bank cheque 351**

07/15/01 $64.84 (CAD)

Pay to Office Supplies Inc.

per:_____

57684 557463

███████   ███████   ███████   ███████   ███████   ███████   ███████   ███████

Reference

Office Supplies (Asset) $60.60
G.S.T. $4.24
No P.S.T due; out of Province purchase

The cheques numbered 352 to 356 shown below represent payroll advance payments.
Enter the total amount of $3,698.40. *Prior to posting, create a recurring entry (monthly).*

Canadiana Decorating Sales & Service Inc.   **Royal Bank cheque 352**

Canadiana Decorating Sales & Service Inc.   **Royal Bank cheque 353**

Canadiana Decorating Sales & Service Inc.   **Royal Bank cheque 354**

Canadiana Decorating Sales & Service Inc.   **Royal Bank cheque 355**

Canadiana Decorating Sales & Service Inc.   **Royal Bank cheque 356**

07/15/01 $878.40

Pay to Gillian Barker

per:_____

57684 557463

███████   ███████   ███████   ███████   ███████   ███████   ███████   ███████

Reference
Payroll advance

(Total Payroll Advance 07/15/01 = $3,698.40)

	Canadiana Decorating Sales & Service Inc.				
	Sales Invoice				
	(on Account)				
Bill To:	**Carolyn Campbell**				
Date:	**07/18/01**			Invoice No.	**407**
CAD currency					
Qty	Desc		Price		Total
60	Eggshell Latex Paint		22.00		1,320.00
78	Waldec Wall paper		16.00		1,248.00
268	Cotton Fabric		20.00		5,360.00
	Subtotal				7,928.00
	P.S.T.				554.96
	G.S.T.				554.96
	Total				9,037.92

Canadiana Decorating Sales & Service Inc.   **Royal Bank cheque 357**

07/20/01 $331.70 (CAD)

Pay to AcDev Auto Parts & Repair

per:_____

57684 557463

■ ■ ■ ■ ■ ■ ■ ■

Reference

Auto Repair	$310.00
G.S.T.	21.70

Canadiana Decorating Sales & Service Inc.   **Royal Bank cheque 358**

07/20/01 $2,216.35 (CAD)

Pay to Minister of Finance

per:_____

57684 557463

■ ■ ■ ■ ■ ■ ■ ■

Reference

P.S.T. Sales Tax remittance

Canadiana Decorating Sales & Service Inc. Payment Received			
From **Susie Quon**	to Royal Bank acct.	Date	**07/21/01**
Chq.	21	Invoice Total	**5,042.91 (CAD)**

Canadiana Decorating Sales & Service Inc.
19696 Bidwell Street
Vancouver, B.C.
V6Y 1Y8
Phone: 604-683-5514
Fax: 604-683-5515

Returned merchandise received on July 24, 2001 from Caroline Clare, original invoice no. 405, Credit Memo # **CM56**:(CAD Currency)

3	Units of Ceiling Flat Latex Paint @ 16.00	=	48.00
5	Units of Jack & Jill Wallpaper @ 12.00	=	60.00
16	Units of Sheer Fabric @ 10.00	=	160.00
	Subtotal		268.00
	P.S.T.		18.76
	G.S.T.		18.76
	Total Credit		305.52

Set the following entry as a recurring entry with a monthly frequency.

Canadiana Decorating Sales & Service Inc.   **Royal Bank cheque 359**

07/29/01 $616.23 (CAD)

Pay to London Life Insurance Company

per:_____

57684 557463

████ ████ ████ ████ ████ ████ ████ ████

Reference
Pension Plan Payable

Save the following entry as a recurring (monthly) entry.

Canadiana Decorating Sales & Service Inc.   **Royal Bank cheque 360**

07/29/01 $270.00 (CAD)

Pay to B.C. Medical Services Plan

per:_____

57684 557463

████ ████ ████ ████ ████ ████ ████ ████

Reference

Medical Plan Payable $270.00

Canadiana Decorating Sales & Service Inc.   **Royal Bank cheque 361**

Canadiana Decorating Sales & Service Inc.   **Royal Bank cheque 362**

Canadiana Decorating Sales & Service Inc.   **Royal Bank cheque 363**

Canadiana Decorating Sales & Service Inc.   **Royal Bank cheque 364**

Canadiana Decorating Sales & Service Inc.   **Royal Bank cheque 365**

07/31/01 $874.17

Pay to Gillian Barker

per:_____

57684 557463

████ ████ ████ ████ ████ ████ ████ ████

Reference

Month-end Payroll

CAD Currency

Salary Expense	$12,324.67
EI Withheld	-$230.75
CPP Withheld	-$279.79
Income Tax	-$3,385.19
Pension Plan	-$616.23
Medical Plan	-$270.00
Advance Receivable	-$3,698.40
Net Bank	-$3,844.31

Create a monthly recurring entry prior to posting:

Internal Journal Entries - 07/31/01

Record employer's payroll expenses **M75** (CAD Currency). Create a monthly recurring entry prior to posting:

EI	346.13
CPP	279.79
WCB	184.87

Christine has finished the July 31, 2001 bank reconciliation **M76/M77** as follows:

Royal Bank
Bank Statement - July 31, 2001

Date	Desc	No.	Deposits	Withdrawal
06/27	Cheque	343		1,240.30
06/27	Cheque	344		50.00
06/30	Cheque	345		125.00
06/30	Deposit	DEP	4,219.82	
07/01	Cheque	346		149.80
07/06	Deposit	DEP	3,458.56	
07/11	Cheque	347		1,435.68
07/11	Cheque	348		4,333.22
07/15	Cheque	349		4,264.33
07/15	Cheque	350		145.24
07/15	Cheque	351		64.84
07/15	Cheques	352-356		3,698.40
07/20	Cheque	357		331.70
07/20	Cheque	358		2,216.35
07/21	Deposit	DEP	5,042.91	

Statement end date:	07-01-31
Statement balance fwd:	12,430.15
Bank Service Charges (M76):	53.23
Statement end balance:	7,043.35

Seafirst
Bank Statement - July 31, 2001

Date	Desc	No.	Deposits	Withdrawal
07/06	Deposit	DEP	6,500.00	

Statement end date:	07-01-31
Statement balance fwd:	0.00
Bank Service Charges (M77):	5.00
Statement end balance:	6,495.00

On 07/31/01, record adjusting entry for insurance expense incurred (credit prepaid insurance) for $400.00 **M78** (CAD Currency). This entry will be a recurring entry with a monthly frequency.

On 07/31/01, record adjusting entry for office supplies used up in July. Total amount is $145.78 **M79** (CAD Currency) (credit account 1400 - Office Supplies).

On 07/31/01, record estimated amortization expense incurred for July M80 (CAD Currency). This entry will be a recurring entry with a monthly frequency:

Building	1,750.00
Automotive	185.00

On 07/31/01, estimated cost of goods for all invoices and credit memos for the month of July is as follows **M81**:

Paint Cost of Goods	1,474.96
Wallpaper Cost of Goods	1,983.78
Fabric Cost of Goods	7,946.45

INSTRUCTION #8
BACKING UP YOUR DATA FILES
Backup your data to **GL3 (Canadian GL Entries)**.

INSTRUCTION #9
1. Print General Journal from 07/01/01 to 07/31/01.
2. Print Income Statement for July 2001 to July 2001, comparing actual to budget.
3. Print Balance Sheet as at 07/31/01.
4. Print Bank Reconciliation in summary from 06/30/01 to 07/31/01.

MODULE TWO — ACCOUNTS RECEIVABLE

OBJECTIVE
After you have worked through this practice set, you will be able to complete the following tasks:
1. Create customer files.
2. Enter historical data to customer accounts.
3. Enter necessary defaults and integration accounts.
4. Set the Accounts Receivable as READY.
5. Enter transactions for:

   -Sales on credit

   -Sales returns on credit

   -Cash receipts on account.
6. Print aging schedule for all customers in both detail and summary format.
7. Verify total customer accounts agree with the General Ledger Accounts Receivable control account.

INSTRUCTION #1

The following customer list has been provided by Christine. She has also provided a memo detailing the historical Accounts Receivable balances. Enter this data into the Accounts Receivable ledger.

Customer Name:	Address:	Phone:	Facsimile:	Terms:	Currency:	G.S.T. Report:	Statements	Credit Limit:
						Yes	Yes	
Bird, Debbie	345 Burger Rd. Whistler, BC V0L 4H9	604-987-9789	604-987-6208	2.0% 10 days, Net 30	CAD	Yes	Yes	10,000
Campbell, Carolyn	6872 Rumble St. Burnaby, BC V5J 2G5	604-434-6798	604-434-6799	Net 30	CAD	Yes	Yes	10,000
Clare, Caroline	4432 Water St. Vancouver, BC V9L 0Y7	604-683-6754	604-683-6756	Net 30	CAD	Yes	Yes	10,000
Crawford, R.	234 Southben Hwy Vancouver, BC V7T 8K9	604-684-6789	604-684-6722	2.0% 10 days Net 30	CAD	Yes	Yes	10,000
Highley, Marg	789 Wing St. Vancouver, BC V4L 9H7	604-675-3456	604-675-3456	2.0% 10 days Net 30	CAD	Yes	Yes	10,000
Marshall, Liz	3478 Snowbird St. Vancouver, BC V9L 7J9	604-687-0987	604-687-0988	2.0% 10 days Net 30	CAD	Yes	Yes	8,000
Park, Jim	1020 King Edward Vancouver, BC V3J 9L0	604-687-2365	604-687-2321	2.0% 10 days Net 30	CAD		Yes	12,000
Quon, Susie	5678 Quebec St. Vancouver, BC V8K 6H7	604-682-9087	604-682-1154	2.0% 10 days Net 30	CAD	Yes	Yes	10,000
Roach, Stella	17600 20th Ave. Surrey, BC V4K 1L0	604-531-7575	604-531-7575	2.0% 10 days Net 30	CAD	Yes	Yes	10,000
Smith, S.	5436 Sydney Coquitlam, BC V8E 1L9	604-426-8945	604-426-8948	2.0% 10 days Net 30	CAD	Yes	Yes	10,000
Sprint, George	5346 - 206th St. Langley, BC V7W 9D0	604-534-7623	604-534-7628	2.0% 10 days Net 30	CAD	Yes	Yes	10,000
Stanton, Bernie	5678 Patterson Burnaby, BC V4K 0U8	604-434-6543	604-434-8821	Net 30	CAD	Yes	Yes	11,000
Thompson, Mary	560 Agnes New Westminster,BC V3K 6T9	604-522-8888	604-522-8888	2.0% 10 days, Net 30	CAD	Yes	Yes	12,000
Ulmer, John	376 E St. North Vancouver, BC V4T 8Y9	604-980-3333	604-981-2536	2.0% 10 days Net 30	CAD	Yes	Yes	14,000

Winston, Mary	9567 Dayton Ave. Richmond, BC V3T 7K9	604-271-6655	604-271-6685	2.0% 10 days Net 30	CAD	Yes	Yes	12,000
Barb Alp Enterprises	1100 West 1st Ave Seattle, WA 90023	206-334-3219	206-334-3220	Net 30	USD	No	Yes	10,000 USD
Madison Coldicutt Inc. Contact Name: Ben Coldicutt	301-1050 Ocean Park Rd Seattle, WA 93452	206-443-6521	206-443-6528	Net 30	USD	No	Yes	10,000 USD
Lecerf, Ed & Jacqueline	Box 410-115 Park St Seattle, WA 93232	206-447-0001	206-447-0001	Net 30	USD	No	Yes	10,000 USD

BACKING UP YOUR DATA FILES

Backup your data to **AR1 (Canadian AR Customers)**.

Memo To: Gillian
From: Claudio
Date: 07/31/01
RE: Historical Accounts Receivables

Here is the list of historical Accounts Receivables that you asked for at yesterday's staff meeting:

Campbell, Carolyn (Net 30 days)
        407   06/30/01*   9,037.92   Total   9,037.92

Clare, Caroline (Net 30 days)
        405   06/30/01*   8,796.24
        Cm56   06/30/01*   -305.52**   Total   8,490.72

Stanton, Bernie (Net 30 days)
        406   06/30/01*   12,104.80   Total   12,104.80

Thompson, Mary (2/10 Net 30 Days)
        404   06/28/01   13,173.96   Total   13,173.96

                                                    Total   42,807.40

* To conform with the conversion datXe of 06/30/01, enter this date instead of the actual transaction dates. This is due to the tiered conversion (over several months).
** enter as a historical invoice.

Be sure to balance Accounts Receivable module to the General Ledger control account.

INSTRUCTION #2

Using the General Ledger chart of accounts as a reference, enter the required Accounts Receivable linked accounts. Note that only one bank account and one G.S.T. rate will be charged. Also use the deliver services revenue account for the Freight Revenue linked account.

INSTRUCTION #3

Set the default settings to the following:

Receivable settings:

Aging:	30, 60, 90
Interest:	not applicable = 0%
Include invoices paid in the last	31 days on statement
Early Payment Terms	2.0% 10 days Net 30 days.
Calculate discounts before tax:	Yes (Checked)
Update all customers terms?	No

Tax Settings:

G.S.T. Rate1	7.0 %
G.S.T. Rate2	0.0 %
P.S.T.	7.0 %
Apply P.S.T. to freight:	No
Apply P.S.T. to G.S.T.	No

Forms settings:

Next invoice number:	408
Next receipt number:	1

Confirm printing for invoices:	Yes

Comment settings:

Default invoice comment:	Thank you for your business.

Printer settings:

Invoices:	Form size 8.5 x 11 inches

INSTRUCTION #4
BACKING UP YOUR DATA FILES

Backup your data to **AR2 (Canadian AR Ready)**.

INSTRUCTION #5

Advance the **Using** Date to August 31, 2001.

INSTRUCTION #6

Make the accounting entries for August 2001. Be sure to use each applicable ledger — General Ledger, Accounts Payable, and Accounts Receivable.

Note: Some customers may exceed their credit limit. Press **Y** *for* **Yes** *and make the sale.*

Canadiana Decorating Sales & Service Inc. Payment Received				
From **Caroline Clare**		to Royal Bank acct.	Date	08/01/01
Covering Inv.	21	(6,796.24 less Cm56 for 305.52)	Total	6,490.72

Canadiana Decorating Sales & Service Inc. Payment Received			
From	to Royal Bank acct.		
Mary Thompson		Date	**08/01/01**
Covering Inv.	**404**	Total	**13,173.96 (CAD)**

Canadiana Decorating Sales & Service Inc. Sales Invoice				
Bill To:	**John Ulmer**			
Date:	**08/01/01**		Invoice No.	**408**
Terms: 2/10 Net 30				
Qty	**Unit**	**Desc**	**Price**	**Amount**
80	4 Litre	Ceiling Flat Latex Paint	16.00	1,280.00
150	Roll	Waldec Wallpaper	16.00	2,400.00
100	Sq/m	Lace Fabric	40.00	4,000.00
			Subtotal	7,680.00
			Freight	75.00
			P.S.T.	537.60
			G.S.T.	542.85
			Total	8,835.45

HINT:

Freight is G.S.T. code #3

Canadiana Decorating Sales & Service Inc. Sales Invoice				
Bill To:	**Mary Winston**			
Date:	**08/01/01**		Invoice No.	**409**
Terms: 2/10 Net 30				
Qty	**Unit**	**Desc**	**Price**	**Amount**
70	4 litre	Satin Latex Paint	18.00	1,260.00
15	Rolls	Jack & Jill Wallpaper	12.00	180.00
80	Sq/m	Velvet Fabric	50.00	4,000.00
			Subtotal	5,440.00
			Freight	80.00
			P.S.T.	380.80
			G.S.T.	380.80
			Total	6,287.20

Williams Paint
Purchase Invoice
(on Account)

Sold To:	Canadiana Decorating Sales & Service Inc.			
Date:	08/08/01		Invoice No.	155784
USD Currency				

Description	Acct	Qty	Price	Total
Ceiling Flat Latex Paint	1240	304	8.00	2,432.00
Select Wallpaper	1280	192	7.00	1,344.00
Sheer Fabric	1320	685	5.00	3,425.00
			Subtotal	7,201.00
			G.S.T.	504.07
			Total	7,705.07

Canadiana Decorating Sales & Service Inc.
Payment Received

From	to Royal Bank acct.		
Carolyn Campbell		Date	08/06/01
Covering Inv. 407		Total	9,037.92 (CAD)

Canadiana Decorating Sales & Service Inc.
Sales Invoice

Bill To:	Barb Alp Enterprises			
Date:	08/08/01		Invoice No.	410
Exchange rate: 1.535				

Qty	Unit	Desc	Price	Amount
80	4 Litre	Eggshell Latex Paint	22.00	1,760.00
70	Roll	Colorol Wallpaper	8.00	560.00
60	Sq/m	Cotton Fabric	20.00	1,200.00
			Subtotal	3,520.00
			Freight	90.00
			P.S.T.	exempt
			G.S.T.	exempt
			Total	3,610.00 USD

To identify the following transaction, enter "CUSTOMER RETURN" in the **Ship To** field. Be sure to enter the quantities as negative and check your journal entry before saving it.

Canadiana Decorating Sales & Service Inc.
Credit Memo

Bill to	**Bernie Stanton (Sales Return)**				
Date	**08/08/01**	Clerk	**Claudio**	Invoice No.	**411**

Service Summary

Qty	Unit	Description	Price	Amount
-10	4 Litre	Eggshell Latex Paint	22.00	-220.00
- 5	Roll	Select Wallpaper	14.00	-70.00
-20	Sq/m	Velvet Fabric	50.00	-1,000.00
			Subtotal	-1,290.00
			P.S.T.	-90.30
			G.S.T.	-90.30
			Total	-1,470.60

Canadiana Decorating Sales & Service Inc.   **Royal Bank cheque 366**

08/15/01 $4,521.65 (CAD)

Pay to the Receiver General of Canada

per:_____

57684 557463

Reference

EI	576.88
CPP	559.58
Income Tax	3,385.19

Canadiana Decorating Sales & Service Inc.   **Royal Bank cheque 367**

08/15/01 $134.78 (CAD)

Pay to Telus

per:_____

57684 557463

Reference

| Phone Expense | 125.96 |
| G.S.T. | 8.82 |

Canadiana Decorating Sales & Service Inc.   **Royal Bank cheque 368**

08/15/01 $87.53 (CAD)

Pay to Petro-Canada

per:_____

57684 557463

Reference

| Fuel Expense | 81.80 |
| G.S.T. | 5.73 |

Canadiana Decorating Sales & Service Inc.   **Royal Bank cheque 369**

08/15/01 $235.79 (CAD)

Pay to B.C. Hydro

per:_____

57684 557463

Reference

| Utilities Expense | 220.36 |
| G.S.T. | 15.43 |

Canadiana Decorating Sales & Service Inc.   **Royal Bank cheque 370**

Canadiana Decorating Sales & Service Inc.   **Royal Bank cheque 371**

Canadiana Decorating Sales & Service Inc.   **Royal Bank cheque 372**

Canadiana Decorating Sales & Service Inc.   **Royal Bank cheque 373**

Canadiana Decorating Sales & Service Inc.   **Royal Bank cheque 374**

08/15/01 $878.40

Pay to Gillian Barker

per:_____

57684 557463

Reference

Payroll Advance

(Total Payroll Advance 08/15/01 = $3,698.40, Cheques 370 – 374)

The cheques numbered 370 to 374 shown above represent payroll advance payments. *Retrieve the previous recurring entry within the General Journal.*

Memo To: Claudio
From: Gillian
Date: 08/15/01

Please record the following:

Royal Bank Partial short-term loan payment M82

Aug 15, 01		
Short-Term Payment	10,000.00	
Interest Expense	340.06	
Total	10,340.06	

Canadiana Decorating Sales & Service Inc.
Invoice

Bill To:	**S. Smith**			

Date:	**08/16/99**		Invoice No.	**412**

Terms: 2/10 Net 30

Qty	Unit	Desc	Price	Amount
60	4 Litre	Ceiling Flat Latex Paint	16.00	960.00
50	Roll	Dimensional Wallpaper	10.00	500.00
15	Sq/m	Lace Fabric	40.00	600.00
			Subtotal	2,060.00
			Freight	60.00
			P.S.T.	144.20
			G.S.T.	148.20
			Total	2,412.40

Canadiana Decorating Sales & Service Inc.   **Royal Bank cheque 375**

08/16/01 $616.23 (CAD)

Pay to London Life Insurance Company

per:_____

57684 557463

Reference
       Recurring entry   616.23

Canadiana Decorating Sales & Service Inc.   **Royal Bank cheque 376**

08/16/01 $270.00 (CAD)

Pay to B.C. Medical

per:_____

57684 557463

Reference
Recurring entry   270.00

Canadiana Decorating Sales & Service Inc.   **Royal Bank cheque 377**

08/16/01 $1,550.22 (CAD)

Pay to Minister of Finance

per:_____

57684 557463

Reference
P.S.T. Payable Payment   1,550.22

Canadiana Decorating Sales & Service Inc.   **Royal Bank cheque 378**

Canadiana Decorating Sales & Service Inc.   **Royal Bank cheque 379**

Canadiana Decorating Sales & Service Inc.   **Royal Bank cheque 380**

Canadiana Decorating Sales & Service Inc.   **Royal Bank cheque 381**

Canadiana Decorating Sales & Service Inc.   **Royal Bank cheque 382**

08/31/01 $874.17

Pay to Gillian Barker

per:_____

57684 557463

Reference
Month-end Payroll

The cheques numbered 378 to 382 shown above represent the payroll for the period ended August 31, 2001 (recurring entries). The total amounts for these cheques are shown below. Use the previous recurring entry.

Internal Journal Entries - August 31, 2001

Salary Expense	$12,324.67
EI Withheld	-$230.75
CPP Withheld	-$279.79
Income Tax	-$3,385.19
Pension Plan	-$616.23
Medical Plan	-$270.00
Advance Receivable	-$3,698.40
Net Bank	-$3,844.31

Record employers payroll taxes **M83**:

EI	346.13
CPP	279.79
WCB	184.87

Christine has completed the September bank reconciliation. Service charge source code for Royal Bank **M84** and Seafirst **M85**.

Royal Bank
Bank Statement - August 31, 2001

Date	Description	No.	Deposits	Withdrawal
08-01	Cheque	359	0.00	616.23
08-01	Cheque	360	0.00	270.00
08-02	Cheque Group	361-365	0.00	3,844.31
08-02	Deposit	DEP	8,490.72	0.00
08-02	Deposit	DEP	13,173.96	0.00
08-08	Deposit	DEP	9,037.92	0.00
08-15	Loan Payment	DM	0.00	10,340.06
08-17	Cheque	366	0.00	4,521.65
08-17	Cheque	367	0.00	134.78
08-18	Cheque	369	0.00	235.79
08-19	Cheque	368	0.00	87.53
08-19	Cheque Group	370-374	0.00	3,698.40
08-20	Cheque	376	0.00	270.00
08-21	Cheque	375	0.00	616.23
08-21	Cheque	377	0.00	1,550.22

Statement end date:	08-31-01
Statement balance fwd:	7,043.35
Bank Service Charge:	24.35
Statement end balance :	11,536.40

Seafirst
Bank Statement - August 31, 2001

Date	Description	No.	Deposits	Withdrawal
	Statement end date:		08-31-01	
	Statement balance forw:		6,495.00	
	Bank Service Charge:		5.00	
	Statement end balance :		6,590.00	

Record adjusting entry for Insurance Expense incurred **M86**. Recall the appropriate recurring entry for this entry.

Record adjusting entry for Office Supplies consumed **M87**, $125.78.

Record adjusting entry for the Monthly Amortization Expense incurred **M88**. Use the recurring entry option.

The estimate Cost of Goods Sold for September, **M89**:

Paint	2,562.64
Wallpaper	2,443.16
Fabric	8,648.91

INSTRUCTION #7
BACKING UP YOUR DATA FILES

Create the **AR3 (Canadiana AR Entries)** directory on your backup diskette and copy the **Canadec** data files to it.

INSTRUCTION #8

1. Print Aged Schedule of Accounts Receivable in summary and detail form for all accounts.
2. Verify that the total of all customers' account balances agree with the Accounts Receivable control account.
3. Print Aged Schedule of Accounts Payable in summary and detail form for all ccounts.
4. Verify that the total of all vendors account balances agree with the Accounts Payable control account.
5. Print General journal entries from 08/01/01 to 08/31/01.
6. Print Income Statement from January 2001 to August 2001 comparing the actual to budget.
7. Print a comparative Income Statement for July 2001 and August 2001.
8. Print Balance Sheet as at 08/31/01.

MODULE THREE — ACCOUNTS PAYABLE

OBJECTIVE

After you have worked through this practice set, you will be able to complete the following tasks:

1. Create vendor files.

2. Enter historical data to vendors' accounts.

3. Enter necessary defaults and define the integration accounts.

4. Set the Accounts Payable system to ready.

5. Enter transactions for purchases on credit, purchase returns on credit, and cheque payments.

6. Print aging schedule of the accounts payable in summary and detail formats.

7. Verify that vendors' payables agree with the Accounts Payable control account in the General Ledger module.

INSTRUCTION #1

The following vendor name and address list was located along with the historical data that follows. Last Year's and YTD purchase figures are not available and will not be required (statistical). Also be sure to select and calculate the discount before tax for those vendors that have discount terms. Be sure to set the **G.S.T. Report flags** to **YES** for each vendor with the exception of:

> B.C. Medical
> Barker, Gillian
> London Life Insurance Co.
> Marie, Christine
> Michaels, David
> Minister of Finance
> Parkins, Graham
> Receiver General of Canada
> Ricci, Claudio

Vendor Listing - Canadiana Decorating Sales & Service Inc. as of August 2001

Vendor Name	Address	City	Prov	Postal	Phone	Fax	Terms	Last Year	YTD Purch
Barker, Gillian	3456 Marine Dr.	Vancouver	BC	V4K 8P0	604-675-2349	604-675-2350	No	10,490.04	6,993.36
B.C. Hydro	457 Nelson	Vancouver	BC	V5H 6J7	604-683-7777	604-683-7785	N30	4,160.67	2,520.96
B.C. Medical	345 Wharf St.	Victoria	BC	V3L 9P8	250-436-8986	250-436-8545	N30	3,240.00	2,160.00
Hollybush Interior Supply	4256 Creekside Dr.	Oakville	ONT	L6H 4Z3	905-369-2451	905-369-2608	N30	43,947.22	28,547.22
Islander Paint & Paper	1949 - 1st Street	St. John's	NFLD	S7H 3F6	709-456-9876	709-456-9941	2/10N30	0.00	0.00
London Life Insurance Co.	345 Main St.	London	ONT	L4T 7J8	519-654-8986	519-654-5623	N30	7,394.76	4,929.84
Lutzmann Paint & Supply	2356 Main St.	London	ONT	L8H 1F0	519-387-0564	519-387-2254	N30	12,650.01	7,860.91
Marie, Christine	6547 Main St.	Vancouver	BC	V5Y 7U9	604-683-4590	604-683-4591	N0	8,202.97	5,551.92
Michaels, David	4567 Steveston	Richmond	BC	V8L 2J8	604-271-7890	604-271-5514	N0	9,076.92	6,112.4
Minister Of Finance	567 Empress St.	Victoria	BC	V4M 7K8	604-435-7865	604-435-7866	N15	27,448.45	16,322.27
Parkins, Graham	3457 - 272nd St.	Aldergrove	BC	V8T 3K8	604-572-9087	604-572-9092	N0	8,644.80	5,792.16
Petro-Canada	3452 Rupert St.	Vancouver	BC	V4L 1J9	604-678-2367	604-678-2254	N30	13,850.34	7,088.52
Rainbow World Inc.	3245 - 40th St.	Calgary	AB	T3E 2X7	403-432-9087	604-432-9087	N30	83,554.23	22,887.22
Receiver General Of Canada	345 Government St.	Ottawa	ONT	L8T 2K0	613-347-9087	613-347-9945	N15	52,944.23	35,988.64
Ricci, Claudio	7879 - 118th St.	Delta	BC	V7K 0L8	604-596-2389	604-596-2364	N0	9,374.27	6,312.64
Sunnybook Paint & Paper	2345 Green Gable	Charlottetown	PEI	J9Y 2D5	902-765-2345	902-765-2346	2/10N30	0.00	0.00
Telus	768 Seymour	Vancouver	BC	V3K 1K0	604-643-4242	604-643-8881	N30	3,652.18	1,552.18
Tremblay Inc.	4038 No. 3 Road	Richmond	BC	V7X 3W7	604-555-2222	604-555-2152	2/10N30	0.00	0.00
Williams Paint	3455 King George	Halifax	NS	J3T 6U8	902-444-8923	902-444-8945	N30	33,100.45	12,678.34
Wilson Stationery Co.	6785 Lougheed Hwy	Burnaby	BC	V6M 9U0	604-437-6789	604-437-6745	N30	0.00	0.00

INSTRUCTION #2
BACKING UP YOUR FILES

Backup your data using **AP1 (Canadian AP Vendors)**.

Memo to: Gillian Barker
From: Claudio Ricci
Date: August 31, 2001
RE: Historical accounts payable

The only historical outstanding invoice is as follows:

Hollybush Interior Supply
Invoice #1096
on 06/30/01* Net 30 $11,473.61

Williams Paint Invoice #155784
on 06/30/01* Net 30 $7,705.07
                                     19,178.68

*Even though the transactions occurred within July and August, use the conversion date. This is due to the tiered conversion date (over several months).

INSTRUCTION #3

Now advance the Using Date through the **Maintenance** menu. Use **September 30, 2001** as the Using date.

INSTRUCTION #4

Set the appropriate linked accounts for the Accounts Payable module. Only one bank account is to be used.

INSTRUCTION #5

Check and ensure that the Accounts Payable balance to the General Ledger Control account.

Settings

        Payables Aging: 30, 60, 90 months
        Calculate discounts before tax for one-time vendors: Yes

Form Settings:
        Next Cheque Number (Royal Bank): 383
        Next Cheque Number (Seafirst): 1
        Confirm printing for cheques: Yes
        Print company address on cheques: Yes

Printer Settings for Cheques:
        Form size = 8.5 x 11 inches

If you are unsure of how to enter form and printer settings, refer to Appendix E.

BACKING UP YOUR DATA FILES

Backup your data using **AP2 (Canadian AP Ready)**.

INSTRUCTION #6

You are now ready to enter the accounting entries for August 2001. Be sure to enter all applicable Accounts Payable entries through the Accounts Payable module. For all other entries, use the General Ledger module.

Note: When you print the Accounts Payable cheque, Simply Accounting will notify you that the Using date and the Journal entry date are not the same. Press the Enter key to proceed.

Canadiana Decorating Sales & Service Inc. **Royal Bank cheque 383**

09/01/01 $11,473.61 (CAD)

Pay to Hollybush Interior Supply

per:_____

57684 557463

■■ ■■ ■■ ■■ ■■ ■■ ■■ ■■

Reference

Outstanding Invoice #1096 $11,473.61

Memo to:	Gillian Barker
From:	Claudio Ricci
RE:	Short-Term Loan
Date:	September 01, 2001

Just a quick note to inform you that we have received the short-term loan proceeds from the Royal Bank today. The total amount that we received was $15,000.00 CAD. I will enter this entry (General Journal) using the source document code "DN1" with the proceeds of the loan being deposited to the Royal Bank account.

Tremblay Inc. **Purchase Invoice**				
Sold To:	**Canadiana Decorating Sales & Service Inc.**			
Date:	**09/01/01**		Invoice No.	**8643**
CAD currency, Terms 2/10 N30				
Qty	**Description**	**Price**	**Total Acct**	**Acct**
545	Ceiling Flat Latex Paint	8.48	4,621.60	1240
721	Jack & Jill Wallpaper	6.36	4,585.56	1280
189	Lace Fabric	21.20	4,006.80	1320
		Subtotal	13,213.96	
		Freight	647.89	
		G.S.T.	980.33	
		Total	14,832.18	

Canadiana Decorating Sales & Service Inc.
Sales Invoice

Bill To:	**Jim Park**			
Date:	**09/08/01**		Invoice No.	**413**

CAD currency, Terms: 2/10 Net 30 days

Qty	Unit	Desc	Price	Total
145	4 Litre	Ceiling Flat Latex Paint	16.00	2,320.00
83	Roll	Waldec Wallpaper	16.00	1,328.00
114	Sq/m	Velvet Fabric	50.00	5,700.00
			Subtotal	9,348.00
			P.S.T.	654.36
			G.S.T.	654.36
			Total	10,656.72

Sunnybrook Paint & Paper
Purchase Invoice

Sold To:	**Canadiana Decorating Sales & Service Inc.**			
Date:	**09/08/01**		Invoice No.	**208**

Terms: 2/10, N30

Qty	Description	Price	Total Acct	Acct
137	Oil Base Paint	16.96	2,323.52	1240
1069	Colorol Wallpaper	4.24	4,532.56	1280
446	Cotton/Polyester Fabric	15.90	7,091.40	1320
		Subtotal	13,947.48	
		Freight	345.35	
		G.S.T.	1,000.50	
		Total	15,293.33	

Canadiana Decorating Sales & Service Inc.
Payment Received

From	John Ulmer		Date	09/06/01
Reference	Partial payment for invoice 408 $5,000.00			
Deposit to	Royal Bank		Payment Total	5,000.00

Returned Merchandise to Tremblay Inc. on Sep 08, 2001 original purchase invoice #8643, Debit Memo # DM46:

-33 Units of Ceiling Flat Latex Paint	@ 8.48	=	279.84
-68 Units of Jack & Jill Wallpaper	@ 6.36	=	432.48
-26 Units of Lace Fabric	@ 21.220	=	551.20
	Subtotal		1,263.52
	G.S.T.		88.44
	Total		1,351.96

HINT: *Enter the previous as a negative purchase invoice with the accounts representing the appropriate inventory accounts.*

Canadiana Decorating Sales & Service Inc. Sales Invoice				
Bill To:	**S. Smith**			
Date:	**09/08/01**		Invoice No.	**414**
CAD currency, Terms: 2/10 Net 30 days				
Qty	Unit	Desc	Price	Total
111	4 Litre	Eggshell Latex Paint	16.00	1,776.00
289	Roll	Colorol Wallpaper	8.00	2,312.00
326	Sq/m	Cotton Fabric	20.00	6,520.00
		Decorating Service Fee		7,640.00
			Subtotal	18,248.00
			P.S.T.	742.56
			G.S.T.	1,277.36
			Total	20,267.92

Enter the following three entries as purchase invoices with cheque payments drawn from the Royal Bank account.

Canadiana Decorating Sales & Service Inc.   **Royal Bank cheque 384**

09/15/01 $4,498.57 (CAD)

Pay to the Receiver General of Canada

per:_____

57684 557463

Reference Aug/01
EI Payable	553.80
CPP Payable	559.58
Income Tax Payable	3,385.19
Total	4,498.57

Canadiana Decorating Sales & Service Inc.　　　**Royal Bank cheque 385**

09/15/01　　$154.78 (CAD)

Pay to Telus

per:_____

57684 557463

███ ███ ███ ███ ███ ███ ███ ███

Reference　Aug 15, 01
　　　　　　Phone Expense　　　　　　144.65
　　　　　　G.S.T.　　　　　　　　　　10.13

Canadiana Decorating Sales & Service Inc.　　　**Royal Bank cheque 386**

09/15/01　　$74.90 (CAD)

Pay to Petro Canada

per:_____

57684 557463

███ ███ ███ ███ ███ ███ ███ ███

Reference　Aug 15, 01
　　　　　　Fuel Expense　　　　　　70.00
　　　　　　G.S.T.　　　　　　　　　 4.90

For the following payroll advances, enter as a purchase invoice with cheque payment drawn from the Royal Bank. Post the advance to the Advances Receivable account. Prior to posting, create a monthly recurring entry with the description as "Payroll Advance with the *employee's name*."

Canadiana Decorating Sales & Service Inc.　　　**Royal Bank cheque 387**

09/15/01　　$660.00 (CAD)

Pay to Christine Marie

per:_____

57684 557463

███ ███ ███ ███ ███ ███ ███ ███

Reference　M90
　　　　　　Mid-month Advance　　　　660.00

Canadiana Decorating Sales & Service Inc.   **Royal Bank cheque 388**

09/15/01 $720.00 (CAD)

Pay to David Michaels

per:_____

57684 557463

Reference   M91
    Mid-month Advance   720.00

Canadiana Decorating Sales & Service Inc.   **Royal Bank cheque 389**

09/15/01 $750.00 (CAD)

Pay to Claudio Ricci

per:_____

57684 557463

Reference   M92
    Mid-month Advance   750.00

Canadiana Decorating Sales & Service Inc.   **Royal Bank cheque 390**

09/15/01 $690.00 (CAD)

Pay to Graham Parkins

per:_____

57684 557463

Reference   M93
    Mid-month Advance   690.00

Canadiana Decorating Sales & Service Inc.　　　**Royal Bank cheque 391**

09/15/01　　　$878.40 (CAD)

Pay to Gillian Barker

per:_____

57684 557463

Reference M934
　　　　Mid-month Advance　　　878.40

Canadiana Decorating Sales & Service Inc.
Sales Invoice

Bill To:	**Madison Colducitt Inc.**			
Date:	**09/16/01**		Invoice No.	**415**

USD Currency - Exchange 1.546, Terms: Net 30 days

Qty	Unit	Desc	Price	Total
40	4 Litre	Eggshell Latex Paint	15.50	620.00
104	Roll	Jack & Jill Wallpaper	8.00	832.00
479	Sq/m	Sheer Fabric	7.50	3,592.50
		Decorating Service		4,580.00
			Subtotal	9,624.50
			P.S.T.	exempt
			G.S.T.	exempt
			Total	9,624.50

Canadiana Decorating Sales & Service Inc.
Payment Received

From	**Tremblay Inc.**	Date	**09/16/01**
Reference	Payment on Account for 8643	14,832.18	
	less DM46 (no discount)	-1,351.98	
Cheque **392** - Royal Bank		Payment Total	**$13,480.20**

Rainbow World Inc.
Purchase Invoice

Sold To:	**Canadiana Decorating Sales & Service Inc.**			
Date:	**09/16/01**		Invoice No.	**1239**

Terms: Net 30

Qty	Description	Price	Acct	Total
432	Ceiling Flat Latex Paint	8.00	1240	3,456.00
293	Waldec Wallpaper	8.00	1280	2,344.00
218	Velvet Fabric	25.03	1320	5,456.54
			Subtotal	11,256.54
			G.S.T.	787.96
			Total	12,044.50

Memo To: Claudio
From: Gillian
Date: Sept 16/01
RE: Short-Term Loan

This memo is to advise you that the company has arranged to borrow an extra $20,000.00 CAD currency from the Royal Bank on a short-term basis. This will be deposited into our account today. Enter this transaction in the General journal using the source document # **DN2**.

Enter the following in the Purchases Journal as a purchase with payment drawn from the Royal Bank. Also be sure to create a monthly recurring entry for these invoices.

Canadiana Decorating Sales & Service Inc.   **Royal Bank cheque 393**

                                        09/16/01 $616.23 (CAD)

Pay to London Life Insurance Company

per:_____

57684 557463

Reference Sept/01
           Pension Plan Payable   616.23

Canadiana Decorating Sales & Service Inc.   **Royal Bank cheque 394**

                                        09/16/01 $270.00 (CAD)

Pay to B.C. Medical

per:_____

57684 557463

Reference Sept/01
           Medical Plan Payable   270.00

Enter the following in the Purchases Journal as a purchase with payment drawn from the Royal Bank.

Canadiana Decorating Sales & Service Inc.　　　　**Royal Bank cheque 395**

09/16/01　　　$972.70 (CAD)

Pay to Minister of Finance

per:_____

57684 557463

■　■　■　■　■　■　■　■

Reference　Aug/01
P.S.T. Payable　　　　　　　972.70

Canadiana Decorating Sales & Service Inc.
19696 Bidwell Street
Vancouver, B.C.
V6Y 1Y8
Phone: 604-683-5514
Fax:　 604-683-5515

Returned Merchandise Received on Sep 22, 2001 from S. Smith original invoice
no. 414, Credit Memo # **416**:

9	Units Eggshell Latex paint	@	16.00	=	144.00
27	Units Colorol Wallpaper	@	8.00	=	216.00
18	Units Cotton Fabric	@	20.00	=	360.00
		Subtotal			720.00
		P.S.T			50.40
		G.S.T			50.40
		Total			820.80

Enter a negative sale on account using the Sales Return account.

Canadiana Decorating Sales & Service Inc.　　　　**Royal Bank cheque 396**

09/22/01　　$15,293.33 (CAD)

Pay to Sunnybrook Paint & Paper

per:_____

57684 557463

■　■　■　■　■　■　■　■

Reference　Aug/01
Payment on account for 208　　15,293.33

	Canadian Decorating Sales & Service Inc. **Payment Received**			
From	**Madison Coldicutt Inc.**		Date	**09/22/01**
Reference	$9,624.50　　　　USD - Exchange 1.546			
Chq	**415**		Payment Total	**9,624.50**

Canadiana Decorating Sales & Service Inc. **Payment Received**				
From	**Barb Alp Enterprises**		Date	**09/30/01**
Reference	$3,610.00	USD - Exchange 1.5501		
Chq	**410**		Payment Total	**3,610.00**

Transfered money from Seafirst bank account to Royal Bank on September 30, 2001. Source code: **M95**. The amount transferred is $15,000.00 USD at 1.5501 exchange rate.

Make this entry within the General Journal with USD currency selected.

> **HINT:** *When entering the following payroll amounts into the Purchases journal with payment drawn from the Royal Bank, enter the salary as a positive figure. Enter all other amounts as negative figures, in other words, as deductions from salary (applied to the applicable Liability/Asset accounts). What finally remains is the net pay the person will receive and is the amount credited to Accounts Payable. All entries for Payroll are issued as a purchase with payment with a source number of Sept/01.*

These month-end payroll entries can be entered as cash purchases. Create monthly recurring entries for each (with the description as "Payroll plus the *employee's name* prior to posting").

Canadiana Decorating Sales & Service Inc.   **Royal Bank cheque 397**

09/30/01 $693.99 (CAD)

Pay to Christine Marie

per:_____

57684 557463

Reference Sept/01	
Salary	2,200.00
(less EI)	46.15
(less CPP)	49.60
(less Tax)	590.26
(less Pension)	110.00
(less Medical)	50.00
(less advance)	660.00

Canadiana Decorating Sales & Service Inc. **Royal Bank cheque 398**

09/30/01 $764.05 (CAD)

Pay to David Michaels

per:_____

57684 557463

Reference	Sept/01	
	Salary	2,400.00
	(less EI)	46.15
	(less CPP)	54.40
	(less Tax)	645.40
	(less Pension)	120.00
	(less Medical)	50.00
	(less advance)	720.00
	Net Pay	764.05

Canadiana Decorating Sales & Service Inc. **Royal Bank cheque 399**

09/30/01 $789.07 (CAD)

Pay to Claudio Ricci

per:_____

57684 557463

Reference	Sept/01	
	Salary	2,500.00
	(less EI)	46.15
	(less CPP)	56.80
	(less Tax)	672.98
	(less Pension)	125.00
	(less Medical)	60.00
	(less advance)	750.00
	Net Pay	789.07

Canadiana Decorating Sales & Service Inc.   **Royal Bank cheque 400**

09/30/01 $724.02 (CAD)

Pay to Graham Parkins

per:_____

57684 557463

Reference	Sept/01	
	Salary	2,300.00
	(less EI)	46.15
	(less CPP)	52.00
	(less Tax)	617.83
	(less Pension)	115.00
	(less Medical)	55.00
	(less advance)	690.00
	Net Pay	724.02

Canadiana Decorating Sales & Service Inc.   **Royal Bank cheque 401**

09/30/01 $874.17 (CAD)

Pay to Gillian Barker

per:_____

57684 557463

Reference	Sept/01	
	Salary	2,925.67
	(less EI)	46.15
	(less CPP)	66.99
	(less Tax)	858.73
	(less Pension)	146.23
	(less Medical)	55.00
	(less advance)	878.40
	Net Pay	874.17

Internal Journal Entries - September 30, 2001

Record employer's payroll taxes **M96**:

EI	323.05
CPP	279.79
WCB	184.87

Record adjusting entry for Insurance Expense incurred **M97**. This entry can be recalled from the recurring entries.

Christine has completed the September bank reconciliation. The bank service charge will use source **M98** for the Royal Bank and **M99** for Seafirst:

Royal Bank
Bank Statement - September 30, 2001

Date	Description	No.	Deposits	Withdrawal
09-01	Cheque Group	378-382	0.00	3,844.31
09-01	Cheque	383	0.00	11,473.61
09-01	Bank loan	CM	15,000.00	0.00
09-10	Deposit	DEP	5,000.00	0.00
09-18	Cheque	384	0.00	4,498.57
09-18	Cheque	385	0.00	154.78
09-19	Cheque	387	0.00	660.00
09-19	Cheque	388	0.00	720.00
09-20	Cheque	386	0.00	74.90
09-20	Cheque	389	0.00	750.00
09-21	Cheque	390	0.00	690.00
09-21	Cheque	391	0.00	878.40
09-16	Bank loan	CM	20,000.00	0.00
09-21	Cheque	392	0.00	13,480.20
09-21	Cheque	393	0.00	616.23
09-21	Cheque	394	0.00	270.00
09-21	Cheque	395	0.00	972.70
09-25	Cheque	396	0.00	15,293.33

Statement end date:	09-30-01
Statement balance fwd:	10,972.08
Bank Service Charge:	45.67
Statement end balance:	(3,450.64)

Seafirst Bank
Bank Statement - September 30, 2001

Date	Description	No.	Deposits	Withdrawal
09-22	Deposit	DEP	9,624.50	0.00
09-30	Deposit	DEP	3,610.00	0.00
09-30	Transfer	TSF	0.00	15,000.00

Statement end date:	09-30-01
Statement balance fwd:	6,490.00
Bank Service Charge:	5.00
Statement end balance :	4,719.50

Record adjusting entry for office supplies consumed **M100**, $115.23.

Record adjusting entry for estimated amortization expense incurred **M101**. You can use the previous recurring entry for this transaction.

Estimated Cost of Goods Sold for September, **M102**:

Paint	6,734.90
Wallpaper	7,123.68
Fabric	7,890.45

INSTRUCTION #7
BACKING UP YOUR DATA FILES
Backup to **AP3 (Canadiana AP Entries)**.

INSTRUCTION #8
1. Print Aging Schedule of Accounts Payable in summary and detail form for all accounts.
2. Verify that the total of all vendors' account balances agree with the General Ledger Accounts Payable control account.
3. Print General journal entries from 09/01/01 to 09/30/01.
4. Print Income Statement from January 2001 to September 2001 comparing actual to budget.
5. Print a comparative income statement comparing August 2001 actual to September 2001 actual.
6. Print Balance Sheet as at 09/30/01.

MODULE FOUR — INVENTORY

OBJECTIVE
After you have worked through this practice set, you will be able to complete the following tasks:
1. Create Inventory Item files.
2. Enter historical data into Inventory Item files.
3. Enter necessary defaults and integration accounts.
4. Enter transactions for inventory sales and sales returns with the system on-line for generating invoices; sales discounts with the system off-line for generating invoices; end-of-month adjustments to Inventory accounts.
5. Print detailed stock report of all inventory items.

INSTRUCTION #1
Enter the following inventory items and historical data. Use the COGS account for the variances linked account.

Canadiana Decorating Sales & Service Inc.
INVENTORY Oct 31, 2001, completed by Claudio

Item	Description	Unit	Last Sale	Selling Price	Min.	Stock	Value	Margin	Category
1	Ceiling Flat Latex	4 litre	09/08/01	$16.00	508	300	$4,425.53	50.0	Paint
2	Colorol	Roll	09/08/01	$8.00	524	400	$2,096.00	50.0	Wallpaper
3	Cotton	Sq/m	09/08/01	$20.00	967	200	$9,670.00	50.0	Fabric
4	Cotton/Polyester	Sq/m		$30.00	300	280	$4,200.00	50.0	Fabric
5	Dimensional Living	Roll	08/16/01	$10.00	200	912	$4,558.45	50.0	Wallpaper
6	Eggshell Latex	4 Litre	09/16/01	$22.00	200	400	$4,400.00	50.0	Paint
7	Jack & Jill	Roll	09/16/01	$12.00	150	876	$5,256.00	50.0	Fabric
8	Lace	Sq/m	08/16/01	$40.00	300	486	$9,720.00	50.0	Fabric
9	Oil Base	4 Litre	06/28/01	$32.00	200	500	$8,000.00	50.0	Paint
10	Satin Latex	4 Litre	08/01/01	$18.00	150	600	$5,400.00	50.0	Paint
11	Select	Roll	07/12/01	$14.00	150	834	$5,838.00	50.0	Wallpaper
12	Semi-gloss Latex	4 Litre		$24.00	200	721	$8,657.00	49.9	Paint
13	Sheer	Sq/m	09/16/01	$10.00	200	1119	$5,593.48	50.0	Fabric
14	Velvet	Sq/m	09/08/01	$50.00	150	419	$10,489.00	49.9	Fabric
15	Waldec	Roll	09/08/01	$16.00	150	665	$5,321.33	49.9	Wallpaper
					Paint		$30,522.53		
					Wallpaper		$23,069.78		
					Fabric		$39,672.48		
					Total		$93,264.79		

Canadiana Decorating Sales & Service Inc.
INVENTORY 2001 Year-to-Date figures

Item	Description	# Trans	Units Sold	Amt Sold	C.O.G.S
1	Ceiling Flat Latex	32	838	13,400.00	7,035.00
2	Colorol	2	359	2,872.00	1,436.00
3	Cotton	14	898	32,650.00	17,167.50
4	Cotton/Polyester	0	0	0.00	0.00
5	Dimensional Living	12	128	1,183.00	651.15
6	Eggshell Latex	99	1060	9,022.33	4,114.18
7	Jack & Jill	31	555	6,660.00	4,062.60
8	Lace	18	302	22,575.00	11,739.00
9	Oil Base	3	20	650.00	300.00
10	Satin Latex	10	179	3,222.45	1,611.23
11	Select	18	479	7,182.00	4,668.30
12	Semi-gloss Latex	0	0	0.00	0.00
13	Sheer	12	2749	30,232.00	15,720.71
14	Velvet	8	355	17,750.00	7,455.00
15	Waldec	9	311	4,986.00	3,150.00

Canadiana Decorating Sales & Service Inc.
INVENTORY Last Year Sales

Item	Description	# Trans	Units Sold	Amt Sold	C.O.G.S
1	Ceiling Flat Latex	26	771	12,328.00	6,472.20
2	Colorol	0	0	0.00	0.00
3	Cotton	6	943	34,283.00	17,998.31
4	Cotton/Polyester	0	0	0.00	0.00
5	Dimensional Living	5	160	1,478.75	776.34
6	Eggshell Latex	114	1219	10,361.50	4,766.29
7	Jack & Jill	0	0	0.00	0.00
8	Lace	14	320	21,220.50	11,034.66
9	Oil Base	0	0	0.00	0.00
10	Satin Latex	14	206	3,706.00	1,874.00
11	Select	11	613	9,193.00	5,239.00
12	Semi-gloss Latex	0	0	0.00	0.00
13	Sheer	6	2600	26,430.00	18,401.10
14	Velvet	10	320	15,320.00	9,460.00
15	Waldec	11	301	4,140.00	2,030.00

INSTRUCTION #2

Continue modifying the appropriate General Ledger accounts with the following information:

Account No	Description	Type	Class
5065	COGS-Decorating	Group Account	Expense
5092	Inventory Assemble costs	Group Account	
5094	Inventory Adjustment exp	Group Account	

Continue with the creation of the following Inventory Service item:

Inventory Number:	DEC
Description:	Decorating fee
Unit of Measure:	Hour
Selling Price:	90.00
Charge P.S.T.:	No
Linked accounts:	Applicable revenue and expense accts

Continue with the selection of the applicable inventory linked accounts.

Ensure that your Inventory ledger balances to the applicable General Ledger control accounts.

INSTRUCTION #3
BACKING UP YOUR DATA FILES

Backup your data to **INV1 (Canadiana INV Opening)**.

INSTRUCTION #4

Ensure the inventory settings are as follows:

Profit Evaluation Method:	Margin
Sort Inventory ledger by:	Number
Foreign Prices on Sales Invoices are:	Calculated using the exchange rate.
Allow inventory levels below zero:	No
Advance the Session date to 10/31/01.	

INSTRUCTION #5

Enter the following General Ledger, Accounts Payable, Accounts Receivable, Payroll, and Inventory transactions into the applicable ledgers.

Canadiana Decorating Sales & Service Inc. Sales Invoice					
Bill To:	**Bernie Stanton**				
Date:	**10/02/01**			Invoice No.	**417**
Terms: Net 30 days					
Item	**Qty**	**Unit**	**Desc**	**Price**	**Total**
06	120	4 Litre	Eggshell Latex Paint	22.00	2,640.00
02	150	Roll	Colorol Wallpaper	8.00	1,200.00
14	180	Sq/m	Velvet Fabric	50.00	9,000.00
DEC	54	Hour	Decorating fee	100.00	5,400.00
				Subtotal	18,240.00
				Freight	187.67
				P.S.T.	898.80
				G.S.T.	1,289.94
				Total	20,616.41

Canadiana Decorating Sales & Service Inc.
Sales Invoice

Bill To:	George Sprint				
Date:	10/02/01			Invoice No.	**418**

Terms: 2/10 Net 30 days

Item	Qty	Unit	Desc	Price	Total
09	120	4 Litre	Oil Base Paint	32.00	3,840.00
05	245	Roll	Dimensional Wallpaper	10.00	2,450.00
13	357	Sq/m	Sheer Fabric	10.00	3,570.00
DEC	67	Hour	Decorating fee	100.00	6,700.00
				Subtotal	16,560.00
				Freight	218.45
				P.S.T.	690.20
				G.S.T.	1,174.49
				Total	18,643.14

Canadiana Decorating Sales & Service Inc.
Sales Invoice

Bill To:	Ed & Jacqueline Lecerf				
Date:	10/02/01			Invoice No.	**419**

Exchange: 1.5501 (U.S. Currency)   Terms: 2/10 Net 30 days

Item	Qty	Unit	Desc	Price	Total
12	100	4 Litre	Semi Gloss Paint	15.50	1,550.00
07	90	Roll	Jack & Jill Wallpaper	7.75	697.50
08	95	Sq/m	Lace Fabric	25.80	2,451.00
DEC	57	Hour	Decorating fee	64.50	3,676.50
				Subtotal	8,375.00
				Freight	90.00
				P.S.T.	n/a
				G.S.T.	n/a
				Total	8,465.00

Canadiana Decorating Sales & Service Inc.
Payment Received

From	Bernie Stanton	Date	10/02/01
Reference	Payment for invoice 406 less 411, Invoice 406 12,104.80 Invoice 411 (1,470.60)		
Chq	**669**-Royal Bank	Payment Total	**10,634.20**

Canadiana Decorating Sales & Service Inc.
Sales Invoice (Returned Merchandise)

Bill To:	**Ed & Jacqueline Lecerf**				
Date:	**10/12/01**			Invoice No.	**420**

Terms: Net 30 days   Exchange rate: 1.5501 (U.S. Currency)

Item	Qty	Unit	Desc	Price	Total
12	-10	4 Litre	Semi Gloss Latex Paint	15.50	-155.00
07	-15	Roll	Jack & Jill Wallpaper	7.75	-116.25
08	-20	Sq/m	Lace Fabric	25.80	-516.10
				P.S.T.	n/a
				G.S.T.	n/a
				Total	-787.35

Canadiana Decorating Sales & Service Inc.
Payment Received

From	**Ed & Jacqueline Lecerf**	Date	**10/12/01**
Reference	Payment for invoice 419 Less inv. 420	$8,465.00 ($787.35)	
Deposit to	Seafirst - Foreign exchange 1.5501	Payment Total	**$7,677.65**

Canadiana Decorating Sales & Service Inc.   **Royal Bank cheque 402**

10/14/01 $12,044.50 (CAD)

Pay to Rainbow World Inc.

per:_____

57684 557463

Reference
Invoice 1249 $12,044.50

Canadiana Decorating Sales & Service Inc.
Purchase Order

Vendor:	**Williams Paint**		Ship Date	**10/20/01**
Date:	**10/14/01**		Order No.	**234**

Terms: Net 30 days

Item	Order	Description	Price	Total
02	200	Colorol	4.00	800.00
			Subtotal	800.00
			G.S.T.	56.00
			Total	856.00

Canadiana Decorating Sales & Service Inc.　　　　**Royal Bank cheque 403**

10/15/01　　$4,498.58 (CAD)

Pay to the Receiver General of Canada

per:_____

57684 557463

Reference　Sept/01
EI Payable　　　　　　553.80
CPP Payable　　　　　559.58
Income Tax Payable　3,385.20　　　$3,698.40

Canadiana Decorating Sales & Service Inc.　　　　**Royal Bank cheque 404**

10/15/01　　　　$145.89

Pay to Telus

per:_____

57684 557463

Reference　Oct/01
Phone Expense　　　　136.35
G.S.T.　　　　　　　　9.54

Canadiana Decorating Sales & Service Inc.　　　　**Royal Bank cheque 405**

10/15/01　　　　$98.78

Pay to Petro-Canada

per:_____

57684 557463

Reference　Oct/01
Fuel Expense　　　　92.32
G.S.T.　　　　　　　6.46

Canadiana Decorating Sales & Service Inc.　　　　**Royal Bank cheque 406**

10/15/01　　　　$235.40

Pay to B.C. Hydro

per:_____

57684 557463

Reference　Oct/01
Utilities Expense　　220.00
G.S.T.　　　　　　　15.40

Canadiana Decorating Sales & Service Inc.   **Royal Bank cheque 407**

10/15/01 $660.00

Pay to Christine Marie

per:_____

57684 557463

██████ ██████ ██████ ██████ ██████ ██████ ██████ ██████

Reference Oct 15/01
Mid-month Advance   660.00 (Recurring Entry)

Canadiana Decorating Sales & Service Inc.   **Royal Bank cheque 408**

10/15/01 $720.00

Pay to David Michaels

per:_____

57684 557463

██████ ██████ ██████ ██████ ██████ ██████ ██████ ██████

Reference Oct 15/01
Mid-month Advance   720.00 (Recurring Entry)

Canadiana Decorating Sales & Service Inc.   **Royal Bank cheque 409**

10/15/01 $690.00

Pay to Claudio Ricci

per:_____

57684 557463

██████ ██████ ██████ ██████ ██████ ██████ ██████ ██████

Reference Oct 15/01
Mid-month Advance   878.40 (Recurring Entry)

Canadiana Decorating Sales & Service Inc.   **Royal Bank cheque 410**

10/15/01 $690.00

Pay to Graham Parkins

per:_____

57684 557463

██████ ██████ ██████ ████████ ██████ ██████ ██████ ██████

Reference Oct 15/01
        Mid-month Advance   878.40 (Recurring Entry)

Canadiana Decorating Sales & Service Inc.   **Royal Bank cheque 412**

10/15/01 $616.23

Pay to London Life Insurance Company

per:_____

57684 557463

██████ ██████ ██████ ████████ ██████ ██████ ██████ ██████

Reference Oct/01
        Company Pension   616.23 (Recurring Entry)

Canadiana Decorating Sales & Service Inc.   **Royal Bank cheque 413**

10/15/01 $270.00

Pay to B.C. Medical

per:_____

57684 557463

██████ ██████ ██████ ████████ ██████ ██████ ██████ ██████

Reference Oct/01
        Medical Premiums   270.00 (Recurring Entry)

Canadiana Decorating Sales & Service Inc.   **Royal Bank cheque 414**

10/16/01 $1,346.12

Pay to Minister of Finance

per:_____

57684 557463

Reference Sept/01
P.S.T.   1,346.12

Memo To: Claudio
From: Gillian
Date: Oct 15, 2001
RE: Partial Bank Payment

Please record the transfer of $12,000.00 U.S. Currency that was deposited to the Royal Bank from the Seafirst bank account. The date of this transfer was October 16, 2001 with a foreign exchange rate of 1.5501. Source code for entry is M103.

Continue with debiting our Royal Bank account for a partial payment of the short-term loan. The partial payment was for $5,000.00. This payment should be debited in full to the Bank Loan Payable account. Use the General Journal with source code: **M104**.

Memo To: Claudio
From: Gillian
Date: Oct 20, 2001
RE: Receipt of Purchase Order

Just a quick note to let you know that we have received the order from Williams Paint. All items on purchase order 234 were received on William's invoice number **155801**.

Remember that the payroll cheques have been previously entered as recurring entries.

Canadiana Decorating Sales & Service Inc.　　　**Royal Bank cheque 415**

10/31/01　　　　$693.99

Pay to Christine Marie

per:_____

57684 557463

Reference	Oct/01	
	Salary	2,200.00
	(less EI)	46.15
	(less CPP)	49.60
	(less Tax)	590.26
	(less Pension)	110.00
	(less Medical)	50.00
	(less advance)	660.00
	Net Pay	693.99

Canadiana Decorating Sales & Service Inc.　　　**Royal Bank cheque 416**

10/31/01　　　　$764.05

Pay to David Michaels

per:_____

57684 557463

Reference	Oct/01	
	Salary	2,400.00
	(less EI)	46.15
	(less CPP)	54.40
	(less Tax)	645.40
	(less Pension)	120.00
	(less Medical)	50.00
	(less advance)	720.00
	Net Pay	764.05

Canadiana Decorating Sales & Service Inc.   **Royal Bank cheque 417**

10/31/01 $789.07

Pay to Claudio Ricci

per:_____

57684 557463

████ ████ ████ ████ ████ ████ ████ ████

Reference Oct/01

Salary	2,500.00
(less EI)	46.15
(less CPP)	56.80
(less Tax)	672.98
(less Pension)	125.00
(less Medical)	60.00
(less advance)	750.00
Net Pay	789.00

Canadiana Decorating Sales & Service Inc.   **Royal Bank cheque 418**

10/31/01 $724.02

Pay to Graham Parkins

per:_____

57684 557463

████ ████ ████ ████ ████ ████ ████ ████

Reference Oct/01

Salary	2,300.00
(less EI)	46.15
(less CPP)	52.00
(less Tax)	617.83
(less Pension)	115.00
(less Medical)	55.00
(less advance)	690.00
Net Pay	724.02

Canadiana Decorating Sales & Service Inc.		**Royal Bank cheque 419**
	10/31/01	$874.17
Pay to Gillian Barker		

per:_____

57684 557463

██ ██ ██ ██ ██ ██ ██ ██

Reference	Oct/01	
	Salary	2,925.67
	(less EI)	46.15
	(less CPP)	66.99
	(less Tax)	858.73
	(less Pension)	146.23
	(less Medical)	55.00
	(less advance)	878.40
	Net Pay	874.17

Internal Journal Entries - October 31, 2001

Record employer's payroll taxes **M105**:

EI	323.05
CPP	279.79
WCB	184.87

Christine has completed the October bank reconciliation. The bank service charge will use source **M106** for the Royal Bank and **M107** for the Seafirst bank.

Royal Bank
Bank Statement - October 31, 2001

Date	Desc	No.	Deposits	Withdrawal
10-01	Transfer		23,251.50	
10-01	Cheque	397	0.00	693.99
10-01	Cheque	398	0.00	764.05
10-01	Cheque	400	0.00	724.02
10-02	Cheque	399	0.00	789.07
10-02	Cheque	401	0.00	874.17
10-02	Deposit		10,634.20	0.00
10-15	Loan Payment		0.00	5,000.00
10-15	Transfer		18,601.20	
10-17	Cheque	402	0.00	12,044.50
10-18	Cheque	404	0.00	145.89
10-19	Cheque	403	0.00	4,498.58
10-19	Cheque	405	0.00	98.78
10-19	Cheque	406	0.00	235.40

10-19	Cheque	407	0.00	660.00
10-19	Cheque	408	0.00	720.00
10-21	Cheque	410	0.00	690.00
10-22	Cheque	409	0.00	750.00
10-22	Cheque	411	0.00	878.40
10-22	Cheque	412	0.00	616.23
10-22	Cheque	413	0.00	270.00
10-22	Cheque	414	0.00	1,346.12

Statement end date: 01-10-31
Statement balance fwd: (3,450.64)
Bank Service Charge: 35.98
Statement end balance: 18,547.20

Seafirst
Bank Statement - October 31, 2001

Date	Desc	No.	Deposits	Withdrawal
10-12	Deposit		7,677.65	
10-15	Transfer		12,000.00	

Statement end date: 10/31/01
Statement balance fwd: 4,719.50
Bank Service Charge: 5.00
Statement end balance: 392.15

Record adjusting entry for insurance expense incurred **M108**. Recall the recurring entry for this transaction.

Record adjusting entry for office supplies consumed **M109**, $165.89.

Record adjusting entry for estimated depreciation expense incurred **M110**. Recall the recurring entry for this transaction.

INSTRUCTION #6
BACKING UP YOUR DATA FILES

Backup your data to **INV2 (Canadiana INV Entries)**.

INSTRUCTION #7

1. Print a list of all stock by item showing price, stock, minimum, cost, value, margin. (Quantity and Synopsis).
2. Print a list of stock by account showing price, stock, minimum, cost, value, margin. (Quantity and Synopsis).
3. Verify that the total stock by department agrees with the Inventory control accounts in the General Ledger.
4. Print individual employee earnings records using Summary layout for current month and year-to-date.

5. Print Aged Schedule of Accounts Receivable in summary and detail form for all accounts.

6. Verify that the total of all customers' account balances agree with the Accounts Receivable control account.

7. Print Aged schedule of Accounts Payable in summary and detail form for all vendors.

8. Verify that the total of all vendors' account balances agree with the Accounts Payable control account.

9. Print General Journal entries from 10/01/01 to 10/31/01.

10. Print Income Statement for October 1, 2001 to October 31, 2001 comparing actual to budget.

11. Print the Income Statement from 01/01/01 to 10/31/01.

12. Print the Balance Sheet as at 10/31/01.

13. Print the Trial Balance as at 10/31/01.

MODULE FIVE — PAYROLL

OBJECTIVE

After completing this practice set for payroll, you will be able to do the following:

1. Create employee files.

2. Enter historical data to accounts.

3. Enter necessary defaults and integration accounts.

4. Set the system to READY.

5. Enter transactions for middle of month advances and end of month payroll.

6. Print individual employee earnings records.

7. Print payroll register of all employees.

8. Verify total employee accounts agrees with Payroll control accounts in the General Ledger.

INSTRUCTION #1

Enter the following employee payroll information and historical data. Be sure to also enter monthly deductions and YTD totals as shown below. Note that the Federal Claim amount is 100.0 percent subject to Indexing.

Enter the following employee payroll information and historical data. Be sure to also enter monthly deductions and YTD totals as shown below.

Barker, Gillian		
	Street . . . . .3456 Marine Street	Regular 0.00
	City . . . . .Vancouver	Overtime 0.00
	Province . . . . .British Columbia	Salary 19,933.81
	Postal V4K 8P0	Commission 0.00
	Phone 604-675-2349	Benefit 0.00
	SIN 000-000-000	Vacation Paid 0.00
	Birth 12-25-55	Gross 19,933.81
	Table . . . . .British Columbia	Hire date: 06/01/91
	FedClaim . . . . .8,500.00 /year	EI 258.93
	QClaim . . . . .0.00 /year	CPP 506.98

Periods . . . . .12 /year	QPP 0.00
WCB 1.5%	Tax 7,861.68
EI . . . . .Yes @ 1.4	QTax 0.00
Vacation . . . . .Retain @ 4.0%	Pension 1,316.07
Salary . . . .$2924.67 / 160 hours	Union 0.00
Pension . . . .$146.23 / period	Medical 495.00
Medical . . . .$55.00 / period	Withheld 10,438.65
EI Insurable Earnings 19,933.81 YTD	Net Pay 9,495.16
	Vacation Owed 0.00
	Advance Paid 0.00

Marie, Christine

Street . . . . .6547 Main St.	Regular 0.00
City . . . . .Vancouver	Overtime 0.00
Province . . . . .British Columbia	Salary 19,800.00
Postal V5Y 7U9	Commission 0.00
Phone 604-683-4590	Benefit 0.00
SIN 000-000-000	Vacation Paid 0.00
Birth 04-28-54	Gross 19,800.00
Table . . . . .British Columbia	Hire date: 09/14/93
FedClaim . . . . .6,000.00 /year	EI 258.93
QClaim . . . . .0.00 /year	CPP 376.47
Periods . . . . .12 /year	QPP 0.00
WCB 1.5%	Tax 5,415.93
EI . . . . .Yes @ 1.4	QTax 0.00
Vacation . . . . .Retain @ 4.0%	Pension 990.00
Salary . . . .$2,200.00 / 160 hours	Union 0.00
Pension . . . .$110.00 / period	Medical 450.00
Medical . . . .$50.00 / period	Withheld 7,491.33
EI Insurable Earnings 19,800.00 YTD	Net Pay 12,308.67
	Vacation Owed 0.00
	Advance Paid 0.00

Michaels, David

Street . . . . .4567 Steveston	Regular 0.00
City . . . . .Richmond	Overtime 0.00
Province . . . . .British Columbia	Salary 19,500.00
Postal V8L 2J8	Commission 0.00
Phone 604-271-7890	Benefit 0.00
SIN 000-000-000	Vacation Paid 0.00
Birth 06-23-49	Gross 19,500.00
Table . . . . .British Columbia	Hire date: 06/01/90
FedClaim . . . . .8,000.00 /year	EI 258.93
QClaim . . . . .0.00 /year	CPP 12.47
Periods . . . . .12 /year	QPP 0.00
WCB 1.5%	Tax 5,905.89
EI . . . . .Yes @ 1.4	QTax 0.00
Vacation . . . . .Retain @ 4.0%	Pension 1,080.00
Salary . . . .$2,400.00 / 160 hours	Union 0.00
Pension . . . .$120.00 / period	Medical 450.00
Medical . . . .$50.00 / period	Withheld 8,107.29
EI Insurable earnings 19,500.00 YTD	Net Pay 11,392.71
	Vacation Owed 0.00
	Advance Paid 0.00

Parkins, Graham

Street ....3457 - 272nd Street	Regular 0.00
City ....Aldergrove	Overtime 0.00
Province ....British Columbia	Salary 18,000.00
Postal V8T 3K8	Commission 0.00
Phone 604-572-9087	Benefit 0.00
SIN 000-000-000	Vacation Paid 0.00
Birth 09-23-47	Gross 18,000.00
Table ....British Columbia	Hire date: 12/05/93
FedClaim ....7,000.00 /year	EI 258.93
QClaim ....0.00 /year	CPP 394.47
Periods ....12 /year	QPP 0.00
WCB 1.5%	Tax 5,660.91
EI ....Yes @ 1.4	QTax 0.00
Vacation ....Retain @ 4.0%	Pension 1,035.00
Salary ....$2,300.00 / 160 hours	Union 0.00
Pension ....$115.00 / period	Medical 495.00
Medical ....$55.00 / period	Withheld 7,844.31
EI Insurable Earnings 18,000.00 YTD	Net Pay 10,155.69
	Vacation Owed 0.00
	Advance Paid 0.00

Ricci, Claudio

Street ....7879 - 118th Street	Regular 0.00
City ....Delta	Overtime 0.00
Province ....British Columbia	Salary 22,500.00
Postal. V7K 0L8	Commission 0.00
Phone 604-596-2389	Benefit 0.00
SIN 000-000-000	Vacation Paid 0.00
Birth 08-23-45	Gross 22,500.00
Table ....British Columbia	Hire date: 06/01/90
FedClaim ....9,000.00 /year	EI 258.93
QClaim ....0.00 /year	CPP 430.47
Periods ....12 /year	QPP 0.00
WCB 1.5%	Tax 6,185.61
EI ....Yes @ 1.4	QTax 0.00
Vacation ....Retain @ 4.0%	Pension 1,125.00
Salary ....$2,500.00 / 160 hours	Union 0.00
Pension ....$125.00 / period	Medical 540.00
Medical ....$60.00 / period	Withheld 8,540.01
EI Insurable Earnings 22,500.00 YTD	Net Pay 13,959.99
	Vacation Owed 0.00
	Advance Paid 0.00

Important Note: *Because the Payroll ledger is regularly updated with the latest EI, CPP, and tax rates, the amounts shown in this book may not always agree with the amounts shown in your particular version of the program. You will have to keep this in mind as you work through this ledger.*

INSTRUCTION #2
BACKING UP YOUR DATA FILES

Backup your data to **Pay1** (Canadian Pay Opening).

INSTRUCTION #3

Set the linked accounts for the Payroll module. Add Acct 2300 Vacation Payable (Group Account) as well as 2310 Union Dues Payable (Group Account)). Use account 5140 for all payroll income linked account fields. Continue with confirming the following settings (assume defaults for undisplayed options):

Payroll settings:

Taxable Income (Salary):	Yes
Taxable Income (Bonuses):	Yes
Deduct Pension after tax:	Yes as Amount
Deduct Union Dues after tax:	Yes as Amount
Deduct Medical after tax:	Yes as Amount
EI factor:	1.4
Keep employee data for	2 years

Forms:

Payroll cheque size:	= 8.5 x 11

Continue with balancing the Payroll module to the applicable General Ledger control accounts. Continue with the **Finish Entering History** option (**History** menu) within main window. This will set your Simply Accounting data from within the Historical mode to Current Entry mode.

BACKING UP YOUR DATA FILES

Backup your data to **Pay2** (Canadian Payroll Ready).

INSTRUCTION #4

Advance the Using Date to 11/30/01. Now you are ready to enter the November 2001 transactions. Be sure to use the General Ledger, Accounts Payable, Accounts Receivable and Payroll ledgers when entering the transactions.

Canadiana Decorating Sales & Service Inc. Payment Received				
From	**John Ulmer**		Date	**11/01/01**
Reference	Payment covering invoice 408 $3,835.45			
Chq	**153**-Royal Bank		Payment Total	**$3,835.45**

Canadiana Decorating Sales & Service Inc. Payment Received			
From	**S. Smith**	Date	**11/01/01**
Reference	Payment for all outstanding invoices and credits (412, 414, 416)		
Chq	**154 - Royal Bank**	Payment Total	**$21,859.72**

Canadiana Decorating Sales & Service Inc.
Sales Invoice

Bill To:	**Stella Roach**				
Date:	**11/01/01**			Invoice No.	**421**

Item	Qty	Unit	Desc	Price	Total
06	60	4 Litre	Eggshell Latex Paint	22.00	1,320.00
11	50	Roll	Select Wallpaper	14.00	700.00
14	70	Sq/m	Velvet Fabric	50.00	3,500.00
DEC	43	Hour	Decorating fee	100.00	4,300.00
				Subtotal	9,820.00
				Freight	78.89
				P.S.T.	386.40
				G.S.T.	692.92
				Total	10,978.21

Canadiana Decorating Sales & Service Inc.   **Royal Bank cheque 420**

11/08/01 $7,705.07

Pay to Williams Paint

per:_____

57684 557463

Reference
          Payment on Account Invoice 155784   7,705.07

Canadiana Decorating Sales & Service Inc.
Purchase Invoice

Vendor:	**Hollybush Interior Supply**		Ship Date	
Date:	**11/08/01**		Order No.	**248**
Acct	**Qty**	**Description**	**Price**	**Total**
06	295	Eggshell Latex Paint	11.00	3,245.00
07	224	Jack & Jill Wallpaper	6.00	1,344.00
13	650	Sheer Fabric	5.00	3,250.00
			Subtotal	7,839.00
			G.S.T.	548.73
			Total	8,387.73

Canadiana Decorating Sales & Service Inc. **Royal Bank cheque 421**

11/15/01 $4,521.65

Pay to the Receiver General of Canada

per:_____

57684 557463

███ ███ ███ ███ ███ ███ ███ ███

Reference Oct/01
  EI Payable   576.88
  CPP Payable   559.58
  Income Tax   3385.19

Canadiana Decorating Sales & Service Inc. **Royal Bank cheque 422**

11/15/01 $165.89

Pay to Telus

per:_____

57684 557463

███ ███ ███ ███ ███ ███ ███ ███

Reference Nov/01
  Phone Expense   155.04
  G.S.T.   10.85

Canadiana Decorating Sales & Service Inc.   **Royal Bank cheque 423**

11/15/01 $86.35

Pay to Petro-Canada

per:_____

57684 557463

▬▬ ▬▬ ▬▬ ▬▬ ▬▬ ▬▬ ▬▬ ▬▬

Reference Nov/01
Fuel Expense   80.70
G.S.T.   5.65

Hint: *Remember to use the payroll journal for the payroll cheques. If you get a message that payroll formulas are outdated press Y for Yes and continue. For the mid-month advances, be sure that you delete all other amounts shown on the payroll form. Only enter the amount of the advance. Be sure to create recurring entries for the payroll advances with each description containing the employee's name and "advance."*

Canadiana Decorating Sales & Service Inc.   **Royal Bank cheque 424**

11/15/01 $660.00 (CAD)

Pay to Christine Marie

per:_____

57684 557463

▬▬ ▬▬ ▬▬ ▬▬ ▬▬ ▬▬ ▬▬ ▬▬

Reference
Advance   660.00

Canadiana Decorating Sales & Service Inc.   **Royal Bank cheque 425**

11/15/01 $720.00 (CAD)

Pay to David Michaels

per:_____

57684 557463

▬▬ ▬▬ ▬▬ ▬▬ ▬▬ ▬▬ ▬▬ ▬▬

Reference
Advance   720.00

Canadiana Decorating Sales & Service Inc.   **Royal Bank cheque 426**

11/15/01 $750.00

Pay to Claudio Ricci

per:_____

57684 557463

Reference
       750.00

Canadiana Decorating Sales & Service Inc.   **Royal Bank cheque 427**

11/15/01 $690.00

Pay to Graham Parkins

per:_____

57684 557463

Reference
       Mid-month Advance   690.00

Canadiana Decorating Sales & Service Inc.   **Royal Bank cheque 428**

11/15/01 $877.40

Pay to Gillian Barker

per:_____

57684 557463

Reference
       Mid-month Advance   878.40

Canadiana Decorating Sales & Service Inc.　　**Royal Bank cheque 429**

11/16/01　　　　$616.23

Pay to London Life Insurance Company

per:_____

57684 557463

▆▆▆　▆▆　▆▆▆　▆▆　▆▆▆　▆▆　▆▆▆　▆▆

Reference
Recurring entry　　　　　　616.23

Canadiana Decorating Sales & Service Inc.　　**Royal Bank cheque 430**

11/16/01　　　　$270.00

Pay to B.C. Medical

per:_____

57684 557463

▆▆▆　▆▆　▆▆▆　▆▆　▆▆▆　▆▆　▆▆▆　▆▆

Reference
Recurring entry　　　　　　270.00

Canadiana Decorating Sales & Service Inc.　　**Royal Bank cheque 431**

11/16/01　　　　$2,058.00

Pay to Minister of Finance

per:_____

57684 557463

▆▆▆　▆▆　▆▆▆　▆▆　▆▆▆　▆▆　▆▆▆　▆▆

Reference Oct/01
P.S.T. Payable　　　　　　2,058.00

Note: Payroll cheques are issued via the Payroll ledger.

Important Note: *Because the program is regularly updated with the latest EI, CPP, and tax rates, the amounts shown in this book may not always agree with the amounts your program displays because of your particular version. You will have to keep this in mind as you work through this ledger. Accept the default values that your version displays. Accept the default vacation figures.*

November 30, 2001
Payroll Summary - for information only, issued through Payroll ledger
Prepared by Gillian

Name	Salary	EI	CPP	Tax	Pension	Medical	Advance	Net
Marie, Christine	2,200.00	Calc	Calc	Calc	110.00	50.00	-660.00	Calc
Michaels, David	2,400.00	Calc	Calc	Calc	120.00	50.00	-720.00	Calc
Ricci, Claudio	2,500.00	Calc	Calc	Calc	125.00	60.00	-750.00	Calc
Parkins, Graham	2,300.00	Calc	Calc	Calc	115.00	55.00	-690.00	Calc
Barker, Gillian	2,924.67	Calc	Calc	Calc	146.23	55.00	-877.40	Calc

---

Canadiana Decorating Sales & Service Inc.   **Royal Bank cheque 432**

11/30/01 $ Calculated

Pay to Christine Marie

per:_____

57684 557463

████ ████ ████ ████ ████ ████ ████ ████

Reference
Month-End Payroll   Calculated

Canadiana Decorating Sales & Service Inc.   **Royal Bank cheque 433**

11/30/01 $ Calculated

Pay to David Michaels

per:_____

57684 557463

████ ████ ████ ████ ████ ████ ████ ████

Reference
Month-End Payroll   Calculated

Canadiana Decorating Sales & Service Inc.   **Royal Bank cheque 434**

11/30/01 $ Calculated

Pay to Claudio Ricci

per:_____

57684 557463

Reference
Month-End Payroll   Calculated

Canadiana Decorating Sales & Service Inc.   **Royal Bank cheque 435**

11/30/01 $ Calculated

Pay to Graham Parkins

per:_____

57684 557463

Reference
Month-End Payroll   Calculated

Canadiana Decorating Sales & Service Inc.   **Royal Bank cheque 436**

11/30/01 $ Calculated

Pay to Gillian Barker

per:_____

57684 557463

Reference
Month-End Payroll   Calculated

Internal Journal Entries - November 30, 2001

Christine has completed the November bank reconciliation. The bank service charge can use source **M111** for the Royal Bank account and **M112** for the Seafirst account.

Royal Bank
Bank Statement - November 30, 2001

Date	Desc.	No.	Deposits	Withdrawal
11-01	Cheque	415	0.00	693.99
11-01	Cheque	416	0.00	764.05
11-01	Cheque	417	0.00	789.08
11-01	Cheque	418	0.00	724.02
11-01	Cheque	419	0.00	874.17
11-01	Deposit		3,835.45	0.00
11-01	Deposit		21,859.72	0.00
11-08	Cheque	420	0.00	7,705.07
11-15	Cheque	421	0.00	4,521.65
11-15	Cheque	422	0.00	165.89
11-15	Cheque	423	0.00	86.35

Statement end date: 11/30/01
Statement balance fwd: 18,547.20
Bank Service Charge: 14.23
Statement end balance: 27,903.88

Seafirst
Bank Statement - November 30, 2001

Date	Desc.	No.	Deposits	Withdrawal

Statement end date: 11/30/01
Statement balance fwd: 392.15
Bank Service Charge: 5.00
Statement end balance: 387.15

Record adjusting entry for Insurance Expense incurred **M113**. Recall the recurring entry for this transaction.

Record adjusting entry for Office Supplies consumed **M114**. Recall the recurring entry for this transaction.

Record adjusting entry for monthly Amortization Expense incurred **M115**. Recall the recurring entry for this transaction.

INSTRUCTION #5
BACKING UP YOUR DATA FILES

Backup your data to **Pay3** (Canadian Pay complete).

INSTRUCTION #6

1. Print individual employee earnings records using summary layout for current month and year-to-date.

2. Print Aged Schedule of Accounts Receivable in summary and detail form for all accounts.

3. Verify that the total of all customers' account balances agree with the Accounts Receivable control account.

4. Print Aged Schedule of Accounts Payable in summary and detail form for all accounts.

5. Verify that the total of all vendors' account balances agrees with the Accounts Payable control account.

6. Print General Journal entries from 11/01/01 to 11/30/01.

7. Print Income Statement for November 1, 2001 to November 30, 2001 comparing actual to budget.

8. Print Balance Sheet as at 11/30/01.

MODULE SIX — PROJECTS

OBJECTIVE

After you have worked through this practice set, you will be able to complete the following tasks

1. Create Projects.

2. Track daily transactions for Revenue and Expenses and itemize them by Project.

3. Print Project-related statements.

INSTRUCTION #1

Through the Project module, add the following projects:

Memo To: All Staff
Memo From: Gillian
Date: December 01, 2001
RE: Department Costing

Effective immediately, we will be tracking our revenue and expenses by departments. This will allow us to better determine our company's progress. I have instructed our accounting department to setup the following departments:

Department	Start Date
Paint Department	Dec 01, 2001
Wallpaper Department	Dec 01, 2001
Fabric Department	Dec 01, 2001
Decorating Department	Dec 01, 2001

As the project tracking will start on December 01, 2001, no balance forward is required.

Confirm that the distribution settings distribute the Payroll journal by percent, while the other journals are also distributed by percent.

INSTRUCTION #2

First advance the Using Date to 12/31/01. You will then have to continue with the activation of all revenue and expense accounts (General Ledger—modify each revenue and expense account) to allow for allocation to projects. Then continue with entering the following transactions into the appropriate journals. **Be sure to allocate all revenues and all expenses to the departments as required.**

Canadiana Decorating Sales & Service Inc.
Sales Invoice

Bill To:	Caroline Clare				
Date:	12/01/01			Invoice No.	**422**
Item	**Qty**	**Unit**	**Desc**	**Price**	**Total**
01	2	4 Litre	Ceiling Latex	16.00	32.00
05	1	Roll	Dimensional	10.00	10.00
14	15	Sq/m	Velvet Fabric	50.00	750.00
DEC	450	Hour	Decorating fee	100.00	4,500.00
				Subtotal	5,292.00
				Freight	222.56
				P.S.T.	55.44
				G.S.T.	386.02
				Total	5,956.02

HINT: *Distribute the above invoice to each applicable department. Freight distribution is not required.*

Canadiana Decorating Sales & Service Inc.
Sales Invoice

Bill To:	Susie Quon				
Date:	12/01/01			Invoice No.	**423**
Item	**Qty**	**Unit**	**Desc**	**Price**	**Total**
10	15	4 Litre	Satin Latex	18.00	270.00
05	2	Roll	Dimensional	10.00	20.00
04	4	Sq/m	Cotton/Poly	30.00	120.00
DEC	25	Hour	Decorating fee	100.00	250.00
				Subtotal	660.00
				Freight	46.00
				P.S.T.	28.70
				G.S.T.	49.42
				Total	784.12

HINT: *Allocate to appropriate departments.*

Canadiana Decorating Sales & Service Inc.
Sales Invoice

Bill To:	Bernie Stanton				
Date:	12/01/01			Invoice No.	424
Item	**Qty**	**Unit**	**Desc**	**Price**	**Total**
10	4	Litre	Satin Latex	18.00	72.00
15	1	Roll	Waldec Wallp	16.00	16.00
				Subtotal	88.00
				Freight	8.00
				P.S.T.	6.16
				G.S.T.	6.72
				Total	108.88

HINT: *Allocate to appropriate departments.*

Canadiana Decorating Sales & Service Inc.
Sales Invoice

Bill To:	George Sprint				
Date:	12/01/01			Invoice No.	425
Item	**Qty**	**Unit**	**Desc**	**Price**	**Total**
12	1	4 Litre	Semi-Gloss	24.00	24.00
07	18	Roll	Jack & Jill	12.00	216.00
08	14	Sq/m	Lace Fabric	40.00	560.00
DEC	22.25	Hour	Decorating fee	10000	2,225.00
				Subtotal	3,025.00
				Freight	50.00
				P.S.T.	56.00
				G.S.T.	215.25
				Total	3,346.25

Canadiana Decorating Sales & Service Inc.
Purchase Order

Vendor:	Sunnybrook Paint & Paper			
Date:	12/05/01		Invoice No.	235
Ship Date:	12/10/01			
Item	**Order**	**Description**	**Price**	**Total**
08	300	Lace Fabric	20.00	6,000.00
			Subtotal	6,000.00
			Shipping	150.00
			G.S.T.	430.50
			Total	6,580.50

You will notice that this transaction is not allocated to a department because it is the purchase of inventory, which is an asset. Only a revenue or expense can be distributed.

Canadiana Decorating Sales & Service Inc. Purchase Order					
Vendor:	**Islander Paint & Paper**				
Date:	**12/05/01**			Invoice No.	**236**
Ship Date:	**12/10/01**				
Item	**Order**	**Description**		**Price**	**Total**
14	300	Velvet Fabric		25.00	7,500.00
			Subtotal		7,500.00
			Shipping		231.00
			G.S.T.		541.17
			Total		8,272.170

Note: Be sure to adjust the price to that shown on the above purchase order, since the program will indicate a different price.

Canadiana Decorating Sales & Service Inc.   **Royal Bank cheque 437**

12/15/01 $856.00

Pay to Williams Paint

per:_____

57684 557463

██ ██ ██ ██ ██ ██ ██ ██

Reference
Payment on Account   856.00

Canadiana Decorating Sales & Service Inc.   **Royal Bank cheque 438**

12/15/01 $134.78

Pay to Telus

per:_____

57684 557463

██ ██ ██ ██ ██ ██ ██ ██

Reference Dec/01
          Phone Expense   125.96
          G.S.T.   8.82
Distribute equally to all departments

Memo To: Claudio
Memo From: Gillian
Date: December 15, 2001

Please note that both Outstanding Purchase Orders from Sunnybrook Paint & Paper (PO# 235, Invoice #986) and Islander Paint & Paper (PO# 236, Invoice # 1142) have been totally filled.

Canadiana Decorating Sales & Service Inc.   **Royal Bank cheque 439**

                                    12/15/01 $78.37

Pay to Petro-Canada

                        per:_____

57684 557463

■■■■ ■■■■ ■■■■ ■■■■ ■■■■ ■■■■ ■■■■ ■■■■

        Reference Dec/01
                Fuel Expense   73.24
                G.S.T.   5.13
        Distribute equally between all departments

For the following payroll remittance cheque, print the Trial Balance as at 11/30/01 to obtain the amounts for EI Payable, CPP Payable, and Income Tax Payable.

Canadiana Decorating Sales & Service Inc.   **Royal Bank cheque 440**

                                    12/15/01 $xxxx.xx

Pay to the Receiver General of Canada

                        per:_____

57684 557463

■■■■ ■■■■ ■■■■ ■■■■ ■■■■ ■■■■ ■■■■ ■■■■

        Reference Nov/01
                EI Payable   xxx.xx
                CPP Payable   xxx.xx
                Income Tax Payable   xxx.xx

Canadiana Decorating Sales & Service Inc.   **Royal Bank cheque 441**

                                    12/16/01 $616.23

Pay to London Life Insurance Company

                        per:_____

57684 557463

■■■■ ■■■■ ■■■■ ■■■■ ■■■■ ■■■■ ■■■■ ■■■■

        Reference Dec/01
                Recurring entry   616.23

Canadiana Decorating Sales & Service Inc.　　　　**Royal Bank cheque 442**

12/16/01　　　　　$386.40

Pay to Minister of Finance

per:_____

57684 557463

████　████　████　████　████　████　████　████

　　Reference　Nov/01
　　　　Provincial Sales Tax　　　　$386.40

Canadiana Decorating Sales & Service Inc.　　　　**Royal Bank cheque 443**

12/16/01　　　$270.00 (CAD)

Pay to B.C. Medical

per:_____

57684 557463

████　████　████　████　████　████　████　████

　　Reference　Dec/01
　　　　Recurring entry　　　　270.00

Remember to retrieve the following Payroll advance recurring cheques in the Payroll journal.

Canadiana Decorating Sales & Service Inc.　　　　**Royal Bank cheque 444**

12/15/01　　　　　$660.00

Pay to Christine Marie

per:_____

57684 557463

████　████　████　████　████　████　████　████

　　Reference
　　　　Mid-month Payroll Advance　　　660.00

Canadiana Decorating Sales & Service Inc.　　　　**Royal Bank cheque 445**

12/15/01　　　　　$720.00

Pay to David Michaels

per:_____

57684 557463

████　████　████　████　████　████　████　████

　　Reference
　　　　Mid-month Payroll Advance　　　720.00

Canadiana Decorating Sales & Service Inc.   **Royal Bank cheque 446**

12/15/01 $750.00

Pay to Claudio Ricci

per:_____

57684 557463

██████   ██████   ██████   ██████   ██████   ██████   ██████   ██████

Reference

Mid-month Payroll Advance   750.00

Canadiana Decorating Sales & Service Inc.   **Royal Bank cheque 447**

12/15/01 $690.00

Pay to Graham Parkins

per:_____

57684 557463

██████   ██████   ██████   ██████   ██████   ██████   ██████   ██████

Reference

Mid-month Payroll Advance   690.00

Canadiana Decorating Sales & Service Inc.   **Royal Bank cheque 448**

12/15/01 $878.40

Pay to Gillian Barker

per:_____

57684 557463

██████   ██████   ██████   ██████   ██████   ██████   ██████   ██████

Reference

Mid-month Payroll Advance   878.40

Memo To: Claudio
Memo From: Gillian
Date: December 31, 2001
RE: Payroll Allocation

Please note that I have listed how the employees should be allocated, (using the departments):

Christine Marie
        Paint Department   33.33%
        Wallpaper Department   33.33%
        Fabric Department   33.34%
David Michaels
        Decorating Department   100.00%
Claudio Ricci & Gillian Barker
        Paint Department   25.00%
        Wallpaper Department   25.00%
        Fabric Department   25.00%
        Decorating Department   25.00%
Graham Parkins
        Decorating Department   100.00%

Payroll Summary - for information only, issued through Payroll ledger
Prepared by Gillian

Name	Salary	EI	CPP	Tax	Pension	Medical	Advance	Net
Marie, Christine	2,200.00	Calc	Calc	Calc	110.00	50.00	660.00	Calc
Michaels, David	2,400.00	Calc	Calc	Calc	120.00	50.00	720.00	Calc
Ricci, Claudio	2,500.00	Calc	Calc	Calc	125.00	60.00	750.00	Calc
Parkins, Graham	2,300.00	Calc	Calc	Calc	115.00	55.00	690.00	Calc
Parker, Gillian	2,924.67	Calc	Calc	Calc	146.23	55.00	877.40	Calc

Note: Use the amounts calculated by your program. Retrieve and use the previously created payroll recurring entries. Be sure to update each recurring entry with the project information.

Canadiana Decorating Sales & Service Inc.   **Royal Bank cheque 449**

                                      12/31/01 $ Calculated

Pay to Christine Marie

                      per:_____

57684 557463

      Reference
            Month-End Payroll   Calculated

Canadiana Decorating Sales & Service Inc.   **Royal Bank cheque 451**

12/31/01 $ Calculated

Pay to Claudio Ricci

per:_____

57684 557463

██████   ██████   ██████   ██████   ██████   ██████   ██████   ██████

Reference
          Month-End Payroll   Calculated

Canadiana Decorating Sales & Service Inc.   **Royal Bank cheque 452**

12/31/01 $ Calculated

Pay to Graham Parkins

per:_____

57684 557463

██████   ██████   ██████   ██████   ██████   ██████   ██████   ██████

Reference
          Month-End Payroll   Calculated

Canadiana Decorating Sales & Service Inc.   **Royal Bank cheque 453**

12/31/01 $ Calculated

Pay to Gillian Barker

per:_____

57684 557463

██████   ██████   ██████   ██████   ██████   ██████   ██████   ██████

Reference
          Month-End Payroll   Calculated

Canadiana Decorating Sales & Service Inc.
Purchase Invoice

Vendor:	**Wilson Stationery Co.**				
Date:	**12/31/01**			Invoice No.	**1901**
Item	**Order**	**Description**		**Price**	**Total**
		Office supplies			250.00
				Subtotal	250.00
				G.S.T.	17.50
				Total	267.50

Post this invoice to the office supplies asset account.

Internal Journal Entries - December 31, 2001

Christine has completed the December bank reconciliation. The bank service charge will use source **M116** for the Royal Bank account and **M117** for the Seafirst bank account.

Royal Bank
Bank Statement - December 31, 2001

Date	Desc.	No.	Deposits	Withdrawal
12-01	414	Cheque	1,346.12	
12-01	347	Cheque	0.00	1,435.68
12-15	424	Cheque	0.00	660.00
12-15	425	Cheque	0.00	720.00
12-15	426	Cheque	0.00	750.00
12-15	427	Cheque	0.00	690.00
12-15	428	Cheque	0.00	877.40
12-15	429	Cheque	0.00	616.23
12-15	430	Cheque	0.00	270.00
12-15	431	Cheque	0.00	2,058.00
12-15	437	Cheque	0.00	856.00
12-15	438	Cheque	0.00	134.78
12-15	439	Cheque	0.00	78.37
12-15	441	Cheque	0.00	616.23
12-15	442	Cheque	0.00	386.40
12-15	443	Cheque	0.00	270.00
12-15	444	Cheque	0.00	660.00
12-15	445	Cheque	0.00	720.00
12-15	446	Cheque	0.00	750.00
12-15	447	Cheque	0.00	690.00
12-15	448	Cheque	0.00	877.40

Statement end date:	12/31/01
Statement balance fwd:	27,903.88
Bank Service Charge:	33.28
Statement end balance:	12,407.99

Seafirst
Bank Statement - December 31, 2001

Date	Desc.	No.	Deposits	Withdrawal
	Statement end date:		12/31/01	
	Statement balance fwd:		387.15	
	Bank Service Charge:		5.00	
	Statement end balance:		382.15	

Record adjusting entry for Insurance Expense incurred **M118**. Recall the recurring entry for this transaction. Once recalled, be sure to distribute equally between all departments.

Record adjusting entry for Office Supplies consumed **M119** using the recurring entry. Allocate the expense portion equally between all departments.

Record adjusting entry for estimated Depreciation Expense incurred **M120**. Allocate equally between all departments. Recall the recurring entry for this transaction.

INSTRUCTIONS #3
BACKING UP YOUR DATA FILES

Backup your date to **PRJ1** (Canadiana Project Complete).
   Once the backup is completed, re-start Simply Accounting.

INSTRUCTIONS #4

1. Print a summary and detailed departmental reports of Revenue minus Expense for all departments and accounts, from 12/01/01 to 12/31/01.
2. Print a list of stock by asset showing price, stock, minimum, cost, value, margin (Quantity and Synopsis).
3. Verify that the total stock by department agrees with the Inventory control accounts in the General Ledger.
4. Print individual employee earnings records using summary layout for year-to-date.
5. Print Aging Sechedule of Accounts Receivable in summary and detail form for all accounts.
6. Verify that the total of all customers' account balances agree with the Accounts Receivable control account.
7. Print Aging Schedule of Accounts payable in summary and detail form for all accounts.
8. Verify that the total of all vendors' account balances agree with the Accounts Payable control account.
9. Print General Journal entries from 12/01/01 to 12/31/01.
10. Print Income Statement for 12/01/01 to 12/31/01.
11. Print Income Statement for 01/01/01 to 12/31/01.
12. Print Balance Sheet for 12/31/01.
13. Print the G.S.T. report.

You have now completed the Canadiana Decorating Sales & Service Inc. case for Simply Accounting for Windows. You should now feel comfortable using all of the ledgers and associated journals. By now you may have realized the full potential of the Simply Accounting System and how it may be suited to your small business accounted requirements.

APPENDIX A

WHAT IS ON THE CD-ROM

The CD-ROM included in this book contains the following:

1. Backup points (as referenced throughout the text).
2. Simply Accounting Pro (Version 8.5) update, in Adobe Acrobat format.
3. Web links which include:

   - **www.pearsoned.ca/fuhrmanchoquette8**, the Pearson Education Canada course-specific Web site which supports the text. This site provides a password-protected Instructor's Resource Manual with Solutions and Test Item File for the text, and the Journal Entries for Overnight Delivery Company. It also contains backup points for Chapter 14 (National Supply Company) and Chapter 15 (Canadiana Decorating Sales and Service Inc.).
   - **www.UsingSimply.com**, the authors' own support site for this book (and past/future releases). From within this Web site you can access the following: book updates, free Simply Accounting Version 8.0 trial software, a discussion board, an additional practice case, live chat with fellow users and the authors, and more.
   - Adobe Acrobat Reader Web site. You are able to download Acrobat Reader (free) from this site.

INSTALLING THE BACKUP POINTS AND OTHER FILES

IMPORTANT: Before you place this CD-ROM in your computer, close all files and programs you are currently working in. The installation begins immediately, and will require you to restart your computer.

When you install the CD, an InstallShield Wizard will automatically run, taking you through the installation process. As it progresses, you have several options:

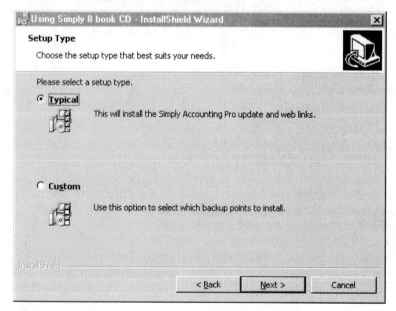

Figure CD.01

As shown in Figure CD.01, you can select from either the **Typical** or **Custom** options:

Typical   Will install the backup points, as well as the Simply Accounting Pro update, Web links, and additional material.

Custom   Will allow you to select which backup points you want to install.

If you select the **Custom** option, you will be able to select which backup points you want to install. You must complete the following screens:

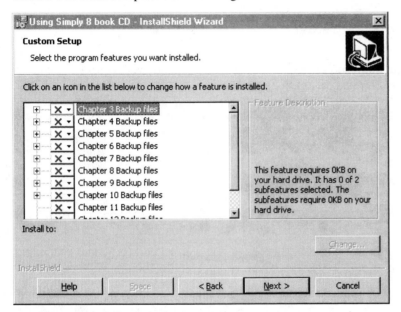

Figure CD.02

As shown in Figure CD.02, you can select from the particular chapters. Each chapter will then open up to display the available backup points.

Figure CD.03

If you want to install a particular backup point, left click on that backup point. A submenu will be displayed (note Figure CD.03). You can then select to install the backup point on your hard drive (left click first option).

Please Note: The backup points, by default, will be installed to the *C:\Program Files\Winsim\ Data* directory with each backup point in a separate subdirectory; for example, backup point odc6b would be installed (by default) to *C:\Program Files\Winsim\Data\odc6b*. You can then open this file and either use the file within the subdirectory or save it overtop the current odc file within the data directory.

INDEX

"AS IS" LICENSE AGREEMENT AND LIMITED WARRANTY

READ THIS LICENSE CAREFULLY BEFORE OPENING THIS PACKAGE. BY OPENING THIS PACKAGE, YOU ARE AGREEING TO THE TERMS AND CONDITIONS OF THIS LICENSE. IF YOU DO NOT AGREE, DO NOT OPEN THE PACKAGE. PROMPTLY RETURN THE UNOPENED PACKAGE AND ALL ACCOMPANYING ITEMS TO THE PLACE YOU OBTAINED THEM. *THESE TERMS APPLY TO ALL LICENSED SOFTWARE ON THE DISK EXCEPT THAT THE TERMS FOR USE OF ANY SHAREWARE OR FREEWARE ON THE DISKETTES ARE AS SET FORTH IN THE ELECTRONIC LICENSE LOCATED ON THE DISK:*

1. GRANT OF LICENSE and OWNERSHIP: The enclosed computer programs <<and any data>> ("Software") are licensed, not sold, to you by Pearson Education Canada Inc. ("We" or the "Company") in consideration of your adoption of the accompanying Company textbooks and/or other materials, and your agreement to these terms. You own only the disk(s) but we and/or our licensors own the Software itself. This license allows instructors and students enrolled in the course using the Company textbook that accompanies this Software (the "Course") to use and display the enclosed copy of the Software for academic use only, so long as you comply with the terms of this Agreement. You may make one copy for back up only. We reserve any rights not granted to you.

2. USE RESTRICTIONS: You may not sell or license copies of the Software or the Documentation to others. You may not transfer, distribute or make available the Software or the Documentation, except to instructors and students in your school who are users of the adopted Company textbook that accompanies this Software in connection with the course for which the textbook was adopted. You may not reverse engineer, disassemble, decompile, modify, adapt, translate or create derivative works based on the Software or the Documentation. You may be held legally responsible for any copying or copyright infringement which is caused by your failure to abide by the terms of these restrictions.

3. TERMINATION: This license is effective until terminated. This license will terminate automatically without notice from the Company if you fail to comply with any provisions or limitations of this license. Upon termination, you shall destroy the Documentation and all copies of the Software. All provisions of this Agreement as to limitation and disclaimer of warranties, limitation of liability, remedies or damages, and our ownership rights shall survive termination.

4. DISCLAIMER OF WARRANTY: THE COMPANY AND ITS LICENSORS MAKE NO WARRANTIES ABOUT THE SOFTWARE, WHICH IS PROVIDED "AS-IS." IF THE DISK IS DEFECTIVE IN MATERIALS OR WORK-MANSHIP, YOUR ONLY REMEDY IS TO RETURN IT TO THE COMPANY WITHIN 30 DAYS FOR REPLACE-MENT UNLESS THE COMPANY DETERMINES IN GOOD FAITH THAT THE DISK HAS BEEN MISUSED OR IMPROPERLY INSTALLED, REPAIRED, ALTERED OR DAMAGED. THE COMPANY DISCLAIMS ALL WAR-RANTIES, EXPRESS OR IMPLIED, INCLUDING WITHOUT LIMITATION, THE IMPLIED WARRANTIES OF MERCHANTABILITY AND FITNESS FOR A PARTICULAR PURPOSE. THE COMPANY DOES NOT WARRANT, GUARANTEE OR MAKE ANY REPRESENTATION REGARDING THE ACCURACY, RELIABILITY, CURRENT-NESS, USE, OR RESULTS OF USE, OF THE SOFTWARE.

5. LIMITATION OF REMEDIES AND DAMAGES: IN NO EVENT, SHALL THE COMPANY OR ITS EMPLOY-EES, AGENTS, LICENSORS OR CONTRACTORS BE LIABLE FOR ANY INCIDENTAL, INDIRECT, SPECIAL OR CONSEQUENTIAL DAMAGES ARISING OUT OF OR IN CONNECTION WITH THIS LICENSE OR THE SOFTWARE, INCLUDING, WITHOUT LIMITATION, LOSS OF USE, LOSS OF DATA, LOSS OF INCOME OR PROFIT, OR OTHER LOSSES SUSTAINED AS A RESULT OF INJURY TO ANY PERSON, OR LOSS OF OR DAM-AGE TO PROPERTY, OR CLAIMS OF THIRD PARTIES, EVEN IF THE COMPANY OR AN AUTHORIZED REP-RESENTATIVE OF THE COMPANY HAS BEEN ADVISED OF THE POSSIBILITY OF SUCH DAMAGES. SOME JURISDICTIONS DO NOT ALLOW THE LIMITATION OF DAMAGES IN CERTAIN CIRCUMSTANCES, SO THE ABOVE LIMITATIONS MAY NOT ALWAYS APPLY.

6. GENERAL: THIS AGREEMENT SHALL BE CONSTRUED AND INTERPRETED ACCORDING TO THE LAWS OF THE PROVINCE OF ONTARIO. This Agreement is the complete and exclusive statement of the agreement between you and the Company and supersedes all proposals, prior agreements, oral or written, and any other communications between you and the company or any of its representatives relating to the subject matter.

Should you have any questions concerning this agreement or if you wish to contact the Company for any reason, please contact in writing: Editorial Manager, Pearson Education Canada, 26 Prince Andrew Place, Don Mills, Ontario, M3C 2T8.